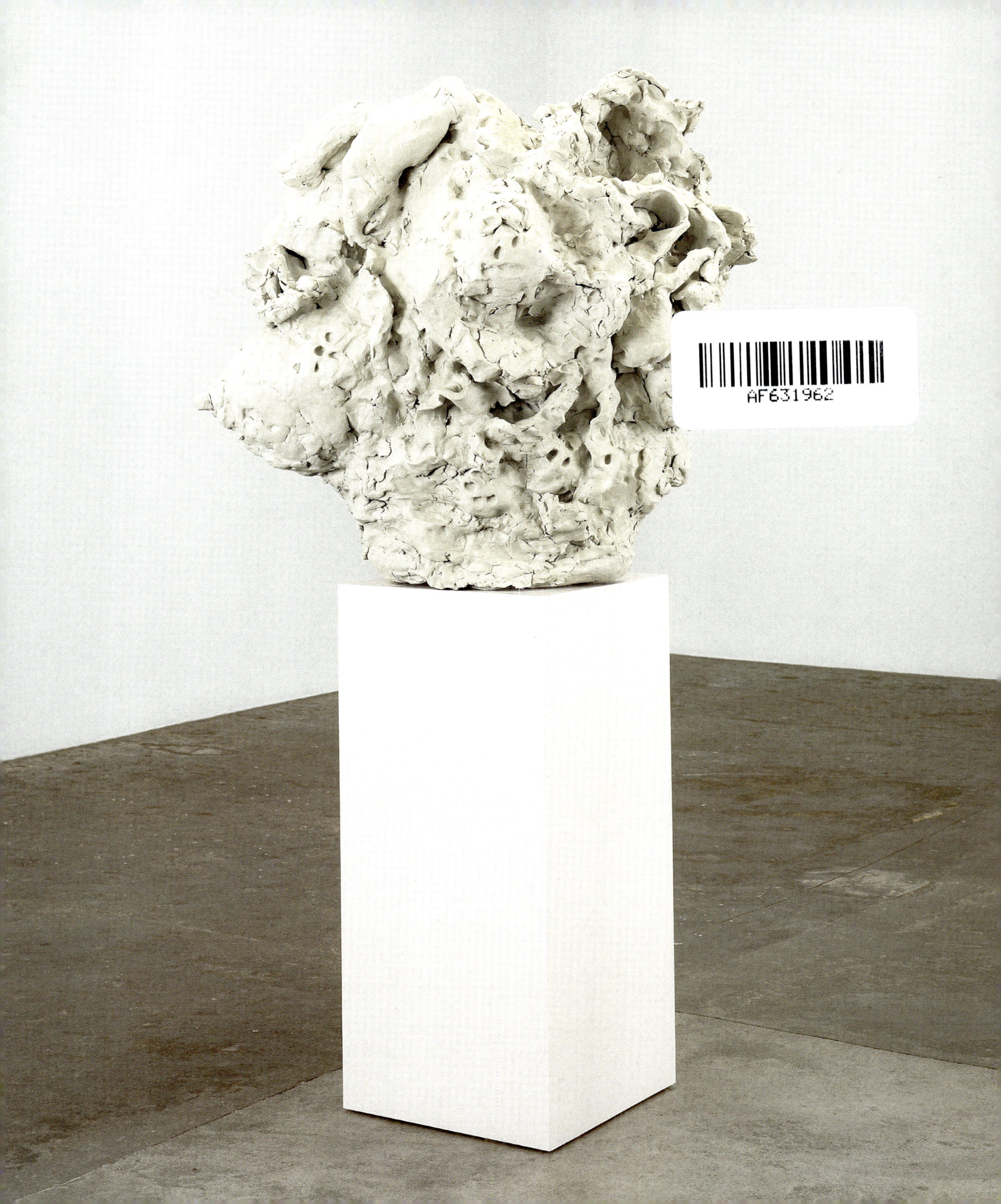

DIE PARKETT-REIHE MIT GEGENWARTSKÜNSTLERN / THE PARKETT SERIES WITH CONTEMPORARY ARTISTS

Book Series with contemporary artists in English and German, published three times a year. Each volume is created in collaboration with artists, who contribute an original work specially made for the readers of Parkett. The works are reproduced in the regular edition and available in a limited and signed Special Edition.

Buchreihe mit Gegenwartskünstlern in deutscher und englischer Sprache, erscheint dreimal im Jahr. Jeder Band entsteht mit Künstlern oder Künstlerinnen, die eigens für die Leser von Parkett einen Originalbeitrag gestalten. Diese Werke sind in der gesamten Auflage abgebildet und zusätzlich in einer limitierten und signierten Vorzugsausgabe erhältlich.

PARKETT NR. 79 ENTSTEHT IN COLLABORATION MIT • **JON KESSLER, MARILYN MINTER, ALBERT OEHLEN** • WILL BE COLLABORATING ON PARKETT NO. 79

JAHRESABONNEMENT (DREI NUMMERN) / ANNUAL SUBSCRIPTION (THREE ISSUES) SFR. 120.– (SCHWEIZ), € 85 (EUROPA), US$ 88 (USA AND CANADA ONLY)

ZWEI- UND DREIJAHRESABONNEMENTSPREISE SIEHE GELBE BESTELLKARTE IM HEFT / FOR TWO & THREE YEAR RATES, PLEASE CONSULT YELLOW ORDER FORM.

Zürichsee Druckereien AG (Stäfa) Satz, Litho, Druck / Copy, Printing, Color Separations

PARKETT-VERLAG AG ZÜRICH DECEMBER 2006 PRINTED IN SWITZERLAND ISBN 978-3-907582-38-1 ISSN 0256-0917

HEFTRÜCKEN / SPINE 76–78: KOO JEONG-A

Cover / Umschlag: ERNESTO NETO, LEVIATHAN THOT, 2006, Panthéon Paris.
Cover flap / Umschlagklappe: REBECCA WARREN, TEACHER (M.B.) / LEHRER (M.B.), 2003.
Inner cover flap: OLAF NICOLAI, CONSTANTIN, 1996, installation view / Installationsansicht Kunstraum Dornbirn (Austria).
Page / Seite 1: REBECCA WARREN, IN THE LAST DITCH I THINK OF YOU / BEIM LETZTEN ATEMZUG DENKE ICH AN DICH, 2005.
Back cover / Rückseite: OLAF NICOLAI, 30 FARBEN (30 Colors), 2001, Göteborg Kunsthall.
(All images slightly cropped / Alle Bilder leicht beschnitten.)

PARKETT Zürich New York

Bice Curiger Chefredaktorin / Editor-in-Chief; **Jacqueline Burckhardt** Redaktorin / Senior Editor; **Cay Sophie Rabinowitz** Redaktorin USA / Senior Editor US; **Mark Welzel** Textredaktion und Produktion / Editing and Production; **Hanna Koller · Simone Eggstein** Graphik / Design, **Trix Wetter** Graphisches Konzept / Founding Designer (–2001); **Catherine Schelbert** Englisches Lektorat / Editorial Assistant for English; **Claudia Meneghini Nevzadi** Korrektorat / Proof Reading

Beatrice Fässler Vorzugsausgaben, Inserate / Special Editions, Advertising; **Nicole Stotzer** Buchvertrieb, Administration / Distribution, Administration; **Mathias Arnold** Abonnemente / Subscriptions; **Jeremy Sigler** Redaktionsassistenz USA / Associate Editor US; **Monika Condrea** Vorzugsausgaben, Inserate und Abonnemente USA / Special Editions, Advertising and Subscriptions US; **Meghan DellaCrosse** Praktikantin USA / Intern US

Jacqueline Burckhardt – Bice Curiger – Dieter von Graffenried Herausgeber / Parkett Board;
Jacqueline Burckhardt – Bice Curiger – Dieter von Graffenried – Walter Keller – Peter Blum Gründer / Founders

Dieter von Graffenried Verleger / Publisher

www.parkettart.com

PARKETT-VERLAG AG, QUELLENSTRASSE 27, CH-8031 ZÜRICH, TEL. 41-44-271 81 40, FAX 41-44-272 43 01
PARKETT, NEW YORK, 145 AV. OF THE AMERICAS, N.Y. 10013, PHONE (212) 673-2660, FAX (212) 271-0704

E D I T O R I A L

VOM GESTALTEN UND FORMEN

Wie weitgreifend und andersartig als in Zeiten des «guten alten Formalismus» doch die Beschäftigung mit der Form heute sein kann! Wenn Ernesto Neto, Olaf Nicolai und Rebecca Warren sich ans Gestalten und Formen machen, sind sie sich all der Bedeutungsmyriaden bewusst, die sie als Bild-Alchemisten und -Ingenieure auslösen und die sich bei jeder Arbeit immer wieder ganz anders entfalten.

Ihre individuellen Wirkungsuniversen könnten andersartiger nicht sein – und doch beziehen sich alle drei Künstler auf den grossen «Pool» des kollektiv konditionierten Daseins, Wahrnehmens und Denkens.

Ernesto Netos Werke basieren auf dem Paradox einer mit voluminösem Aplomb vorgetragenen visuellen Leichtigkeit, einer wuchernden Präsenz, die Verstörung und Verzauberung auszulösen vermag. Die Hüllen seiner skulpturalen Gebilde überqueren vorerst in kleinen Päckchen den Ozean, um ihr ambulantes Wucherpotenzial dann irgendwo auf der Welt voll zu entfalten. Sein bisher spektakulärstes Werk, LEVIATHAN THOT (2006), hat sich in den gigantischen, geschichtsträchtigen Kontext des Pariser Panthéon eingefügt (siehe S. 126–143).

Rebecca Warrens «neugierige Aneignung künstlerischer Praktiken der Vergangenheit» (Martin Herbert, S. 55) setzt eine Atomisierung der Materie frei, ein Verfahren, das ein Staubkorn, die Wollquaste genauso wie die hehre Bronze nicht als Gegenpole, sondern als Elemente in einem psychodynamisch aufgeladenen Echoraum der Formen einsetzt. All die in ihren Skulpturen aufblitzenden kunsthistorischen Erkennungsmelodien fordern jene tief greifende «Re-perzeption» heraus, ein zweites Hinschauen, welches Charles Esche gleicherweise bei Olaf Nicolais künstlerischen Untersuchungen und Setzungen ins Feld führt (S. 92).

Wie dabei ein imaginäres Kunstwerk zustande kommen kann, gefügt aus einem «Arrangement von Sehstrahlen», beschreibt Anne von der Heiden (S. 100) am Beispiel von Nicolais Beitrag für die Biennale in Venedig (2005). Dort forderte der Künstler die Öffentlichkeit auf, nach Sternschnuppen Ausschau zu halten, den ‹Tränen des Heiligen Laurentius›.

Im Insert (S. 177) präsentiert Anne Collier eine Art popkulturelle *Homage to the Square*, indem sie sich auf das Format verblichener LP-Covers und deren Rolle als beglückende Bild-, Stimmungs- und Attitüdenstimulatoren besinnt. Dass sich die wiedergefundene Romantik so kühl seziert entfaltet, ist allein das Verdienst einer nobilitierenden photographischen Form, die auf die sicheren Reflexe der formalismusgeschulten Betrachter vertrauen kann.

E D I T O R I A L

OF SHAPING AND FORMING

What a difference between the "good old formalism" of the past and the kaleidoscopic sweep of today's treatment of form! When Ernesto Neto, Olaf Nicolai, and Rebecca Warren tackle the challenge of shaping and forming worlds of their own making, they know full well that their visual feats of alchemy and engineering will unlock an unruly array of semantic potential that changes with every work.

The personal universe that each inhabits could not be more different, and yet all three artists draw their energy and inspiration from the same vast pool of collectively conditioned being, perception, and thinking.

Ernesto Neto's works rest on the paradox between a thoroughly self-assured visual lightness and a rampant, luxuriating presence, which provokes both distress and enchantment. The shells of his sculptural inventions are often shipped across oceans in deceptively small packages, developing the full thrust of their potential only upon arrival. Neto's most spectacular work to date, LEVIATHAN THOT (2006), has taken up residence in a place fraught with history: the overwhelming vault of the Panthéon in Paris (see pp. 126–143).

In her "inquisitive inhabiting of artistic practices of the past" (Martin Herbert, p. 48), Rebecca Warren atomizes matter, such that a particle of dust, a woolen pompom and the venerable metal, bronze, do not stand as opposites but rather as elements in the psychodynamically charged echo chamber of form. Her work is alight with memory-triggering flashes of art historical allusion that demand a radical "re-perception," a prolonged second look, which is also of the essence in the study of Olaf Nicolai's artistic investigations and projects, as Charles Esche observes (p. 86). Anne von der Heiden describes the imaginary work of art that results (p. 107). It is the virtual "arrangement of visual rays" in Nicolai's contribution to the Venice Biennale (2005), where the artist called upon the public to keep an eye out for falling stars, for 'The Tears of St. Lawrence.'

In the Insert (p. 177), Anne Collier presents a kind of pop-cultural "Homage to the Square" by enlisting the services of the now defunct LP cover and its role as harbinger of happiness in stimulating images, moods, and attitudes. The artist's cool dissection of this resurrected romanticism owes its existence exclusively to the "ennobling" faculty of photography that can rely on the unfailing reflexes of viewers schooled in formalism.

BICE CURIGER

TIRDAD ZOLGHADR

Speech Bubbles

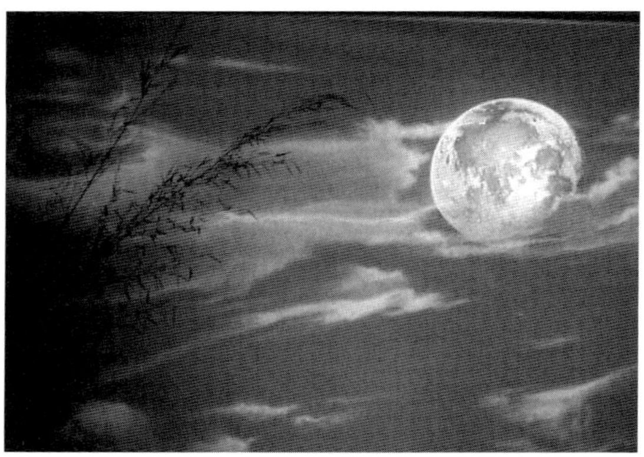

ANDRO WEKUA, NEIGHBOUR'S YARD, 2005, video still, 35 mm color film transferred to DVD, 3 min. 16 sec. / NACHBARS GARTEN, Videostill.
(ALL PHOTOS: COURTESY THE ARTIST AND GALERIE PETER KILCHMANN, ZURICH)

Marc Chagall reportedly had a habit of judging his paintings by placing them next to trees and flowers, saying that if they "clashed," they weren't art. You may laugh, but this sums up the knee jerk ontology of much recent art palaver. If, today, no one would ever admit to such picnic naturalism, it bears mentioning that Chagall's fairytale dreamscapes never strived for simple verisimilitude either. Likewise, in more contemporary venues, the idea is that the work and the real should interact gracefully either qua abstraction, thus keeping out of each other's way by transcending representation altogether, or by contextual engagement, thus explaining something within the real in some manner, be it a flower, a tree, or a political trauma. Most approaches try to combine the two and pepper them with disclaimers left and right. Either by being representational, to then quote Rancierian aesthetics ("autonomy *and* politics"), or by being post-figurative, to then coyly explain they're "allegorizing the art market." At the risk of making Andro Wekua sound like a one-man Hegelian synthesis, his approach is instructive in that it reveals the genuine Chagallism that lurks behind art discourse at large.

Wekua engages with a suspension of disbelief that is less fine arts—a place where realist impulses are broken a posteriori by aesthetic and rhetorical measures—and more theatrical in temperament. By this I'm not referring to some dramatic disposition but to the very question of referentiality, and to the fact that the stage is never indebted to the idea of naturalism in the first place, but, rather, even in its most conservative forms, persistently plays on the pleasures of a *mise-en-scène* that only eventually leads to a

TIRDAD ZOLGHADR is a freelance critic and curator based in Zurich.

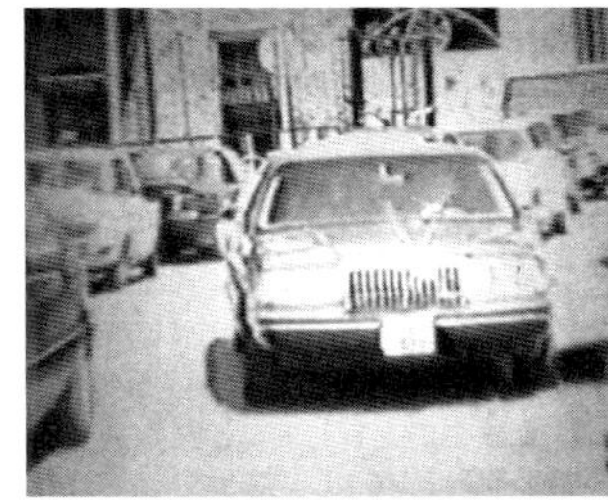

ANDRO WEKUA, SICUT LILIUM INTER SPINAS (Like a lily in the back), 2003, video still, 35 mm b/w film transferred to DVD, 7 min. / Wie eine Lilie im Rücken, Videostill.

Notes on Andro Wekua

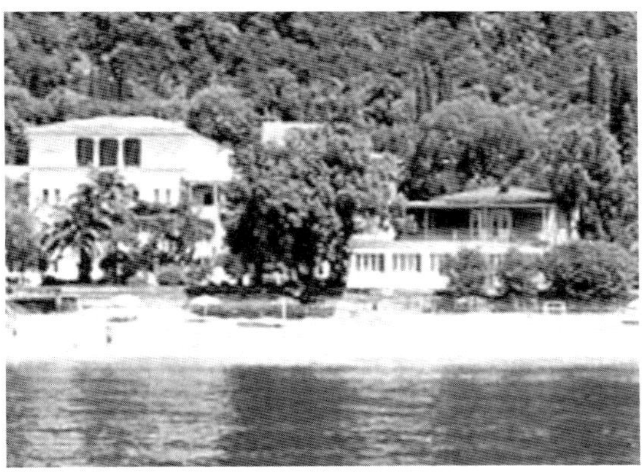

ANDRO WEKUA, NEIGHBOUR'S YARD, 2005, video still, 35 mm color film transferred to DVD, 3 min. 16 sec. / NACHBARS GARTEN, Videostill.

suspension of disbelief. Brechtian and other forms of alienation redefined the politics of on-stage reality effects that never attempted to transcend a stilted, partial notion of illusionism to begin with. And it is only if you confuse the two modes of storytelling that you begin to psychologize Wekua's work.

Therefore you could frame the discussion here as a question of referentiality in itself, pointing, say, to the human figures in his sculptural artworks that are cast rather than sculpted, adopting an eerie, life-like veneer, or to the way Wekua's landscapes and leitmotifs are embedded within a bulky system of signification that strives to be strictly his own. But to appreciate the work's reception you would also need to account for the aura of sincere narrative intention projected into the work, particularly by virtue of the trademark "darkness" that pervades and characterizes it. Rather than a deliberate effect or strategy, pure and simple, this darkness in hue, tone, and content is widely and easily perceived as a (theatrical, dramatic) signifier of authentic depth of some kind. Which is why, even when it is at its most disjunctive, the complexity of Wekua's work, rather than point to ever more ambiguous shades of possibility, inadvertently runs the risk of discreetly flipping over into the very opposite.

Generally speaking, when it comes to certain artists, what is fascinating to behold is the impact they have on people who write about them. By this I do not mean the artist's popularity, or the ability to spark the odd art-world hysteria or scandal. But whether an artist brings out the best in the writers, or whether he throws them into an art critical *horror vacui* that can only be bridged with vague affirmations that, say, the oeuvre in question is extremely "poetic," or deeply "dream-like," or really "melancholic," often coupled with the most revealing indications of clueless abandon—the artist is a place where East meets West. At times, the art critical sleight of hand is to condemn the exoticization of Andro Wekua as a "Georgian exile" before immediately delving in mushy musings on danger, memory, pain, and travel, as if we'd never heard of Freudian displacements of sign and fetish. But then again, it is of course very hard to depart from these typecasts entirely. Since Wekua's images are so obscure, grainy,

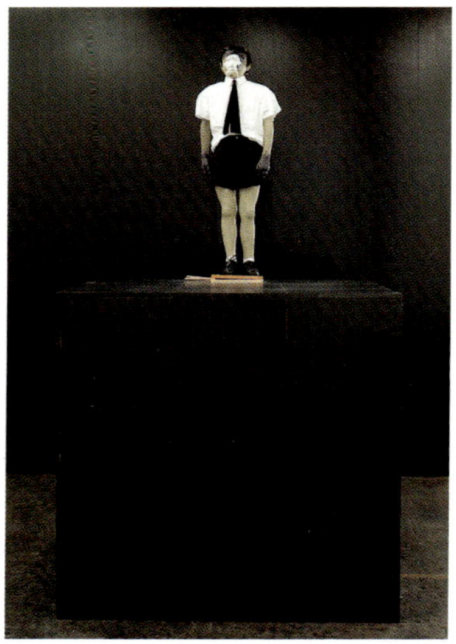

ANDRO WEKUA, WHAT'S YOUR NAME MY CHILD?, 2004, installation view, wax figure, fabric, leather and hair on ceramic base, painting (lacquer on canvas), size variable / WIE HEISST DU MEIN KIND? Installationsansicht, Wachsfigur, Textilien, Leder, Haar auf Keramikuntergrund und Gemälde (Lack auf Leinwand), Format variabel. (PHOTO: STEPHAN ROHNER)

hesitant, or partial they may be located almost anywhere, from Oaxaca to the Schwarzwald (Black Forest), and much of the ensuing geopsychological guesswork is possibly prompted, even pursued, by the artist himself, with the help of his titles (BLACK SEA DWELLER, BLACK SEA SURFER), or his fragmentary prose in the catalogues, invoking many a youthful seaside disruption and more.

But surely there must be less predictable ways to underline a persona's entanglement with his work if you were inclined to do so in the first place. You could, for instance, mention how Andro exudes the somber, winning charisma of the bad boy in class that everyone wanted to be friends with. Or you could point out that his quiet sense of despair and desperation possibly springs from nothing other than living and working in Zurich, a cutesy, well-mannered place where "strong work" is ultimately nice looking and a little bit ironic. Needless to say, at first glance, compared to the semi-self-deprecating glitter of Zurich, Wekua is about as ironic as a Swiss bank. But if you make an effort to look beyond the obvious poetics of quasi-Caspian *tristesse royale*, it's not hard to identify a stylized smirk lurking just on the edges of his drawings, rendering the obscurity rather more playful and lithe, and far less Chagall.

Take the video piece NEIGHBOR'S YARD (2005), a three-and-a-half minute motion picture that is as minimal in content as it is deliciously tortuous in questions of prop and backdrop, medium specificity, and the narrative consequences of color saturation and tastefully portioned kitsch. To the sounds of an outlandishly serrated musical soundtrack, a camera pulls back from a near-painterly panorama of a seaside sunset, into a luxuriously fitted living room, a bespectacled boy awkwardly scrunched into a sumptuous sofa, then moves slowly along, ending the indoor journey with the full moon framed by a window on the far side of the room. Both the sunset and the moon are filmed through window panes, reflecting barely discernable, ghostly movements within the room, just barely out of sight. Watching the film recently, I realized I'd forgotten the film holds a coda of two still images, one of a bedroom, one of a seaside house, imagery that is bizarrely, poignantly affecting without holding any narrative function, at least not in a manner that might accord it some mnemonic footing. Although Wekua has thus far spent most of his time cutting, casting, pasting, drawing, and installing, rather than filming and editing, the piece is a fittingly dense illustration of the Wekuan universe—not only by virtue of the leitmotifs, such as a portentous sense of the secluded and far-flung, the ominous beachhead, the adorable

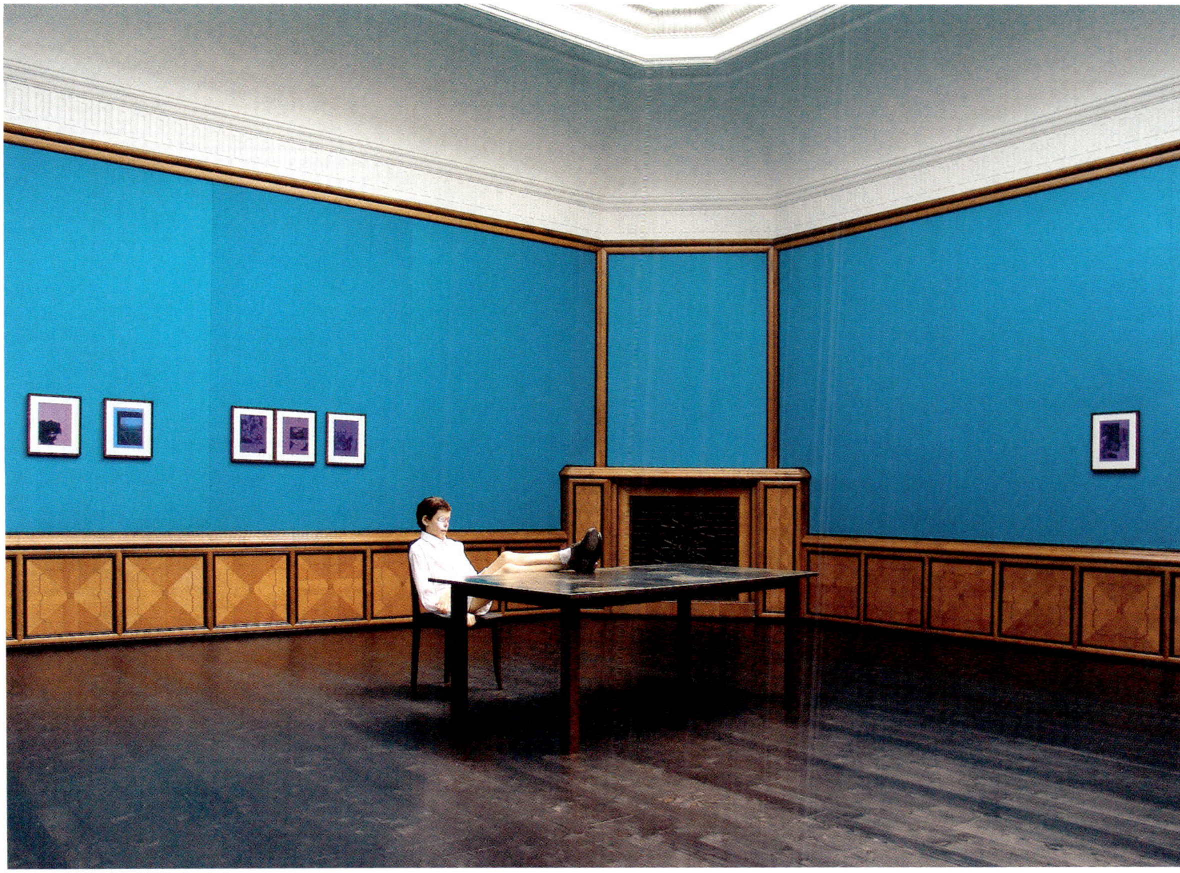

ANDRO WEKUA, GET OUT OF MY ROOM, 2006, installation view, wax figure, wooden table and wax, bronze chair painted with enamel, 8 silk screen prints, and etching / RAUS AUS MEINEM ZIMMER, Installationsansicht, Wachsfigur, Holztisch und Wachs, Bronzestuhl mit Emailbemalung, 8 Siebdrucke und Radierung. (PHOTO: A. BURGER)

schoolboy, the bourgeois setting, the thick sensation of darkness, and the plush celebration thereof; but also by virtue of a nominal, degree zero plot that still manages to trigger unwieldy narrative kinetics in the mind's eye, narratives indeed always skirting the said artist-biography-docudramatics. In other words, the film is also very Wekua in that it is an art critical booby trap.

By and large, Wekua's work in itself is flawlessly composed, even when it indulges in lovingly roughened, big-budget cut and paste, the kind of visual daring that takes buckets of hard talent to pull off. Wekua's collages, if largely resorting to the strict panoply of leitmotifs, are intensely patchy rather than cohesive in character, with the respective cohesion summoned only by delicately traced lines, scrawls and smudges criss-crossing the work. Sometimes two images are aligned horizontally, the dissimilar halves brought to feed into one another without clarifying matters of depth and surface, before and after, or any other psychoaesthetic divisions of labor. Other pieces consist of a single found photograph graphically beset with Wekua's vaguely human figurines, or jagged constellations of rectangles and circles, or

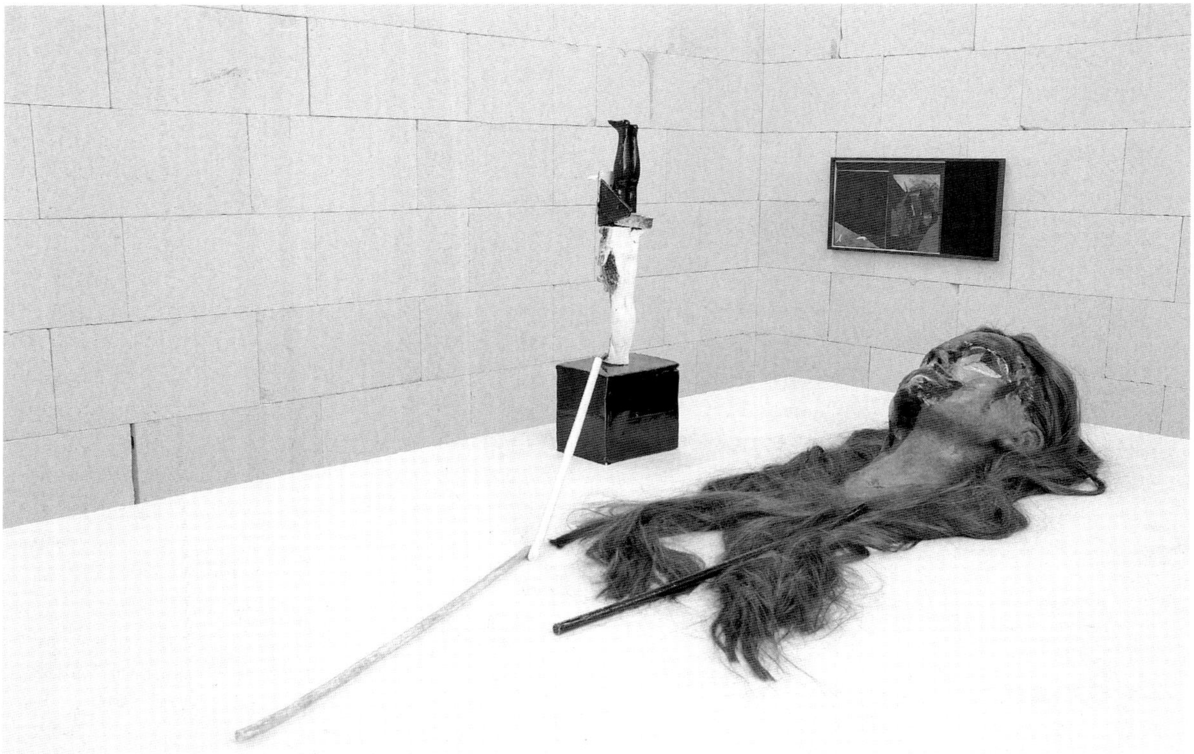

marked simply by the trace of a folded crease. Much of the sculptural work, meanwhile, offers an exultant display of human heads and mutilated mannequins, almost always combined with a concerted study of the form and function of the plinth. Sometimes the dummies rest on platforms elaborate and massive, adorned with various geometric assortments of cubes and clutter, other times they're perched on pedestals that are flat and petite, though perhaps slightly tilted, or carefully careworn. It is particularly when it comes to installations combining his drawings with such three-dimensional work that Wekua becomes, quite simply, an obvious argument that more artists should be curating themselves rather than leaving this science to others, such as critics like myself, who rarely transcend the panicky discursive pyrotechnics outlined above.

But for all the hands-on artistic proficiency that is so immediately apparent, the work is obviously not so effortless a thing to write one's way into, and one

ANDRO WEKUA, BOY OH BOY, 2006, installation view, 2 wax figures, ceramic figure, table (wood and plaster), collage, house, concrete walls, wooden ceiling, size variable / JUNGE JUNGE, 2 Wachsfiguren, Keramikfigur, Tisch (Holz und Gips), Kollage, Haus, Betonwand, Holzdecke, Format variabel. (PHOTO: UWE WALTER) reason for this lies in the—at times overlapping—strategies of slapdash coincidence, on the one hand, and fine tuning of twilight *ambiente* on the other. Not only do the two strategies form an unlikely couple, the resulting atmospherics do sometimes get ever so slightly out of hand, tilting ever so slightly towards stagy overkill rather than handsome ease, and this arguably does make the work a little more of an enjoyable gamble for everyone involved. Another factor at play here is the fact that, like a joke's punch line spelled out for you, the distinctly Wekuan shades of gloom are rather hard to describe without obliterating their very attractiveness. Suffice to say that the dusky congregations of figure and backdrop manage to steer clear of the usual prototypical effects of doom and gloom, including even the standard stylistics of "human-condition" type murk (Georgia notwithstanding), offering a blend of obscurity that is mannered without being affected, excessive without being annoying, dense without ever being maladroit.

Rather less delicately and tenuously sculpted, perhaps, is the gendered subtext running through the oeuvre, the prim women in 50s outfits and the little kids in school uniforms, a casting exercise in the pristine psychoses of house and home, thrashed and distorted into something very becoming, if blatantly and boyishly macho. This is not only prominent in the collages, but also in Wekua's texts ("she had a shothole beneath her eye"), and in the brutalized mannequins structuring the silent spleen of the installations. I have to admit, I've often stared at the beheaded women gracing the work thinking the day Wekua holds any extensive type of retrospective, it will be tricky to juggle the many mangled women in a single space, and the question of the womanly cadaver as depth or deco would need to be addressed more rigorously. However, to be fair, it is defacement in a broader sense which is at stake here, not only that of the Other sex, with Wekua's jubilant orchestrations of disfigurement offering enough material to fill several PhDs in many different disciplines, from the schoolboys happily caked in cream pie to more radical forms of facial disembowelment. Finally, to return to the drawings and collages, one decisive leitmotif among all these expressionless figures are the speechless speech bubbles, snakelike protrusions sprouting from their mouths, but left blank, as if the things they might tell us would amount to so much pain and trauma they're better left unsaid.

ANDRO WEKUA, SICUT LILIUM INTER SPINAS (Like a lily in the back), 2003, video still, 35 mm b/w film transferred to DVD, 7 min. / Wie eine Lilie im Rücken, Videostill.

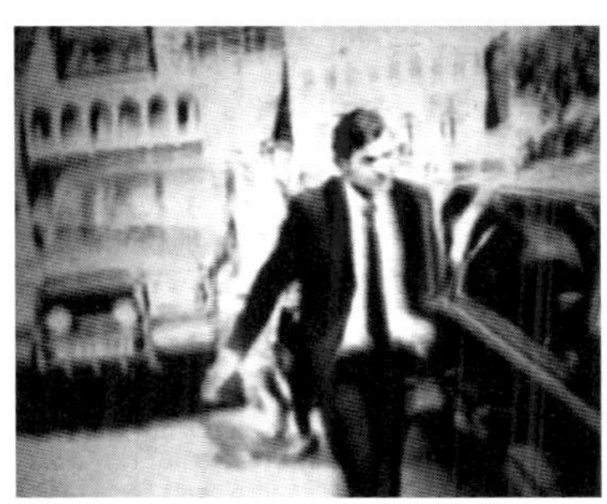

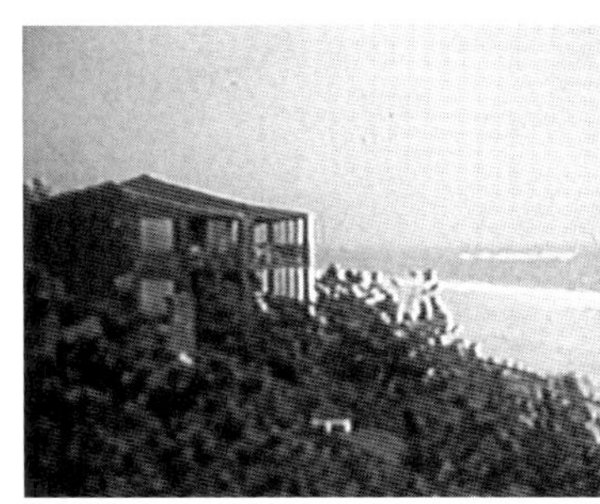

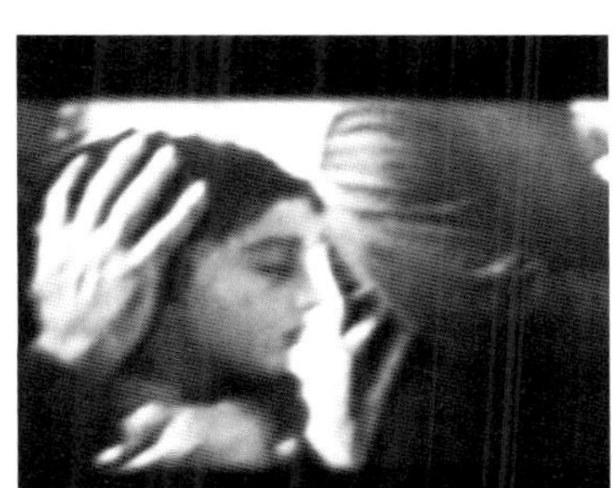

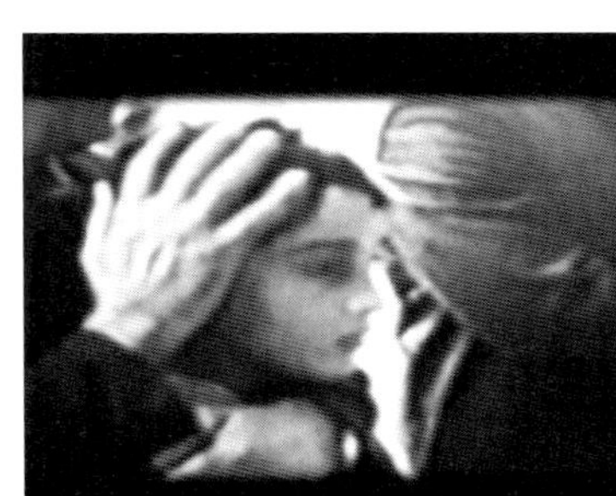

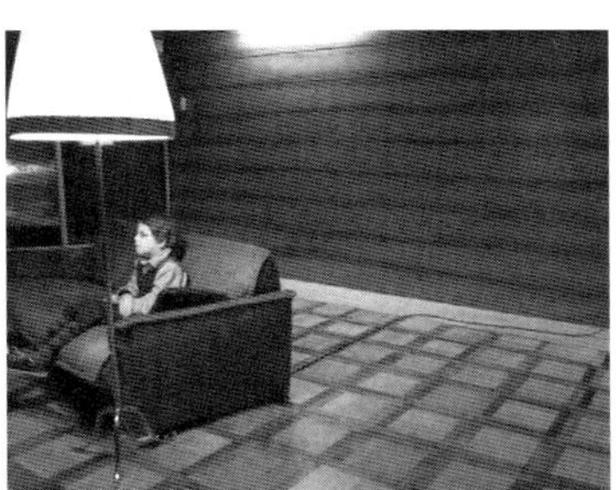

NEIGHBOUR'S YARD, 2005, video still, 35 mm color film transferred to DVD, 3 min. 16 sec. / NACHBARS GARTEN, Videostill.

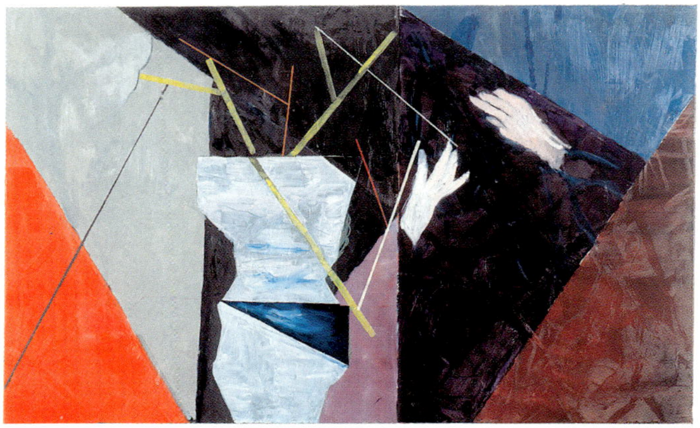

ANDRO WEKUA, THE SUN OF THE SLEEPLESS I, 2005, oil on canvas, 39 3/8 x 63" / DIE SONNE DER SCHLAFLOSEN I, Öl auf Leinwand, 100 x 160 cm. (PHOTO: A. BURGER)

TIRDAD ZOLGHADR

Sprechblasen

Es wird berichtet, dass Marc Chagall die Angewohnheit hatte, seine Bilder zu begutachten, indem er sie neben Bäume und Blumen stellte, und wenn sie dabei fehl am Platz erschienen, sagte er, handle es sich nicht um Kunst. Sie lachen vielleicht, aber das umschreibt exakt die reflexartige Ontologie eines grossen Teils des jüngsten Kunstgeschwätzes. Wenn sich heute auch niemand mehr zu einem derartigen Picknicknaturalismus bekennen würde, muss doch gesagt werden, dass Chagalls märchenhafte Traumlandschaften ebenfalls nie auf Realismus aus waren. Auch in aktuelleren Kontexten findet man die Vorstellung, dass Werk und Wirklichkeit in einem eleganten Verhältnis zueinander stehen sollten, entweder mittels Abstraktion, wobei sie einander nicht in die Quere kommen können, weil die Darstellung vollkommen transzendiert wird, oder durch Einbetten in einen Kontext, wodurch etwas innerhalb der Wirklichkeit irgendwie erklärt wird, sei es eine Blume, ein Baum oder ein politisches Trauma. Die meisten Ansätze versuchen beides zu kombinieren und links und rechts mit Dementis zu pfeffern: entweder indem man figurativ darstellend arbeitet und dazu Jacques Rancières Ästhetik zitiert («Autonomie und Politik») oder sich postfigurativ gibt, um alsbald neckisch zu erklären, man «allegorisiere den Kunstmarkt». Auf das Risiko hin, Andro Wekua zu einer wandelnden hegelschen Synthese emporzustilisieren: Sein Ansatz ist aufschlussreich, da er den ursprünglichen Chagallismus enthüllt, der hinter dem Kunstdiskurs an sich lauert.

Wekua arbeitet mit einer Aufhebung des Unglaubens, oder der Entfremdung, die im Temperament weniger der bildenden Kunst entspricht – einem Ort, wo aus der Realität stammende Impulse nachträglich durch ästhetische und rhetorische Massstäbe gebrochen werden –, sondern eher dem Theater. Damit will ich keineswegs auf irgendeine dramatische Veranlagung hinaus, sondern auf die Frage der Referenzialität selbst sowie auf die Tatsache, dass die

---

TIRDAD ZOLGHADR ist freier Kritiker und Kurator und lebt in Zürich.

Bühne nie in erster Linie der Idee des Naturalismus verpflichtet ist, sondern vielmehr – selbst in ihren konservativsten Formen – beharrlich die Freuden einer Inszenierung durchspielt, welche nur sporadisch zu einer Aufhebung des Unglaubens führt. Die Bühneneffekte, gegen die sich brechtsche und andere Verfremdungseffekte richteten, hatten nie das Ziel über einen gespreizten, bruchstückhaften Illusionismus hinauszugelangen. Nur wenn man diese beiden Arten des Geschichtenerzählens durcheinanderbringt, kann man auf die Idee kommen, psychologisierend an Wekuas Arbeit heranzugehen.

So könnte man die Diskussion als Frage der Referenzialität an sich darstellen, indem man etwa auf die menschlichen Figuren in Wekuas skulpturalen Arbeiten verwiese, die eher gegossen als modelliert sind und eine gespenstisch lebensnahe Fassade an den Tag legen, oder auf die Art und Weise, wie seine Landschaften und Leitmotive in ein sperriges Bedeutungssystem eingebettet sind, das ein strikt eigenes

Notizen zu Andro Wekua

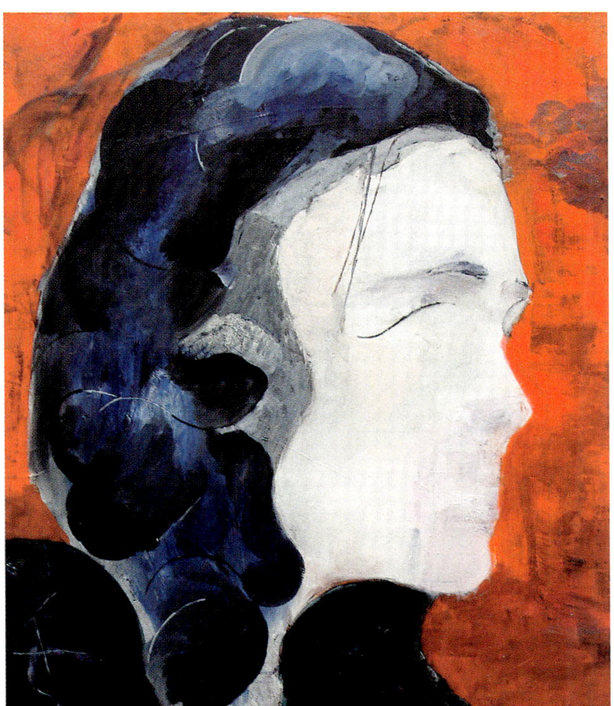

ANDRO WEKUA, STILLNESS, 2005, oil on canvas, 24 3/4 x 20 3/4" / STILLE, Öl auf Leinwand, 62,7 x 52,7 cm. (PHOTO: KERRA QUARLES)

sein will. Aber um der Rezeption des Werks gerecht zu werden, müsste man auch die Aura der aufrichtigen narrativen Intention mit in Betracht ziehen, die ins Werk hineinprojiziert wird – insbesondere dank der für Wekua typischen, alles durchdringenden und prägenden «Düsterkeit». Diese Düsterkeit der Farbwerte, Tonlagen und Inhalte wird weniger als bewusst gewollter Effekt oder Taktik, sondern meistens leicht als (theatralisches, dramatisches) Merkmal einer gewissen authentischen Tiefe wahrgenommen. Das ist auch der Grund dafür, dass die Komplexität von Wekuas Arbeit selbst in den Momenten ihrer grössten Sprengkraft nicht zwangsläufig auf immer noch zwiespältigere Schattierungen des Möglichen verweist, sondern droht, unversehens ins genaue Gegenteil zu kippen.

Allgemein ist es bei manchen Künstlern interessant zu beobachten, welche Wirkung sie auf die Leute haben, die über sie schreiben. Damit meine ich nicht die Popularität des Künstlers oder seine Fähigkeit, in der Kunstszene gelegentlich eine Hysterie oder einen Skandal vom Zaun zu reissen, sondern

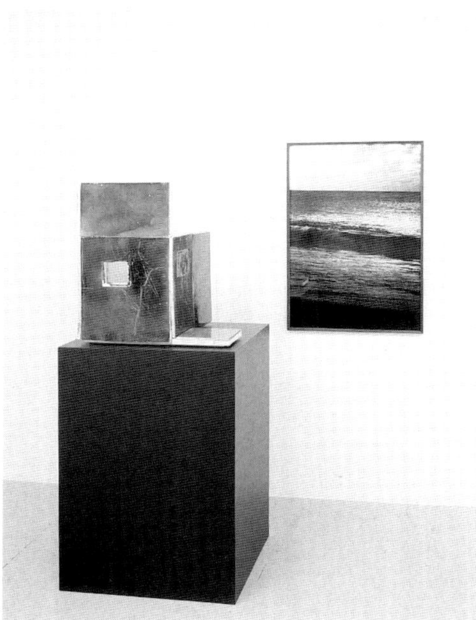

ANDRO WEKUA, THE LAST HOUSE, 2006, installation view, ceramic and wooden base, found poster, size variable / DAS LETZTE HAUS, Installationsansicht, Keramik- und Holzsockel, gefundenes Plakat, Format variabel. (PHOTO: A. BURGER)

vielmehr, ob ein Künstler die Schreibenden zur Höchstleistung anspornt oder ob er sie in einen kunstkritischen *Horror vacui* stürzt, der nur mit vagen Sterotypen verschleiert werden kann, etwa dahingehend, dass das in Frage stehende Werk ausgesprochen «poetisch» oder zutiefst «traumähnlich» oder echt «melancholisch» sei, häufig gepaart mit Anzeichen absoluter Ahnungslosigkeit: der Künstler als Schauplatz des Aufeinandertreffens von Ost und West. Manchmal besteht der kunstkritische Taschenspielertrick auch darin, die Exotisierung von Andro Wekua als «Georgischer Exilant» zu verdammen, um sich gleich darauf in zähen Grübeleien über Gefahr, Erinnerung, Schmerz und Reisen zu verlieren, als ob wir noch nie etwas von der freudschen Theorie zu Fetisch und Verdrängung gehört hätten. Andrerseits ist es natürlich schwierig, sich von solchen Stereotypen zu lösen. Wekuas Bilder können noch so dunkel, körnig, zögerlich oder unvollständig sein, dass sie sich von Oaxaca bis zum Schwarzwald fast überall ansiedeln lassen; möglicherweise wird das damit verbundene geopsychologische Rätselraten wesentlich vom Künstler selbst angeregt oder gar betrieben, etwa über die Werktitel (SCHWARZMEERBEWOHNER, SCHWARZMEERSURFER) oder Wekuas fragmentarische Katalogprosa, die manch eine jugendliche Erinnerung anführt, etwa an Strandbäder.

Aber gewiss gibt es weniger festgetretene Pfade, um die Verflechtung einer Person mit ihrem Werk hervorzuheben, falls überhaupt. Man könnte etwa davon sprechen, dass Andro über die düster anziehende Ausstrahlung des schönen Klassenflegels verfügt, mit dem jeder in der Schule befreundet sein wollte. Oder man könnte hervorheben, dass sein stilles Gespür für Verzweiflung und Hoffnungslosigkeit letztlich nur davon herrührt, dass er in Zürich lebt und arbeitet, einem adretten, gesitteten Ort, wo eine «starke Arbeit» letzten Endes hübsch, ein wenig ironisch und clever sein muss. Unnötig zu betonen, dass Wekua verglichen mit dem quasi selbstironischen Glitzern Zürichs etwa so ironisch daherkommt wie eine Schweizer Bank. Aber wenn man den Versuch unternimmt, hinter die poetische Oberfläche seiner post-kaspischen *Tristesse royale* zu blicken, ist es nicht schwer, das an den Rändern seiner Zeichnungen lauernde, stilisierte Schäkern zu sehen, das deren Inhalt geschmeidiger macht und entschieden von jeglichen Chagallismen wegrückt.

Betrachten wir etwa die Videoarbeit NEIGHBOR'S YARD (Nachbars Garten, 2005), ein dreieinhalbminütiger Film, der inhaltlich so knapp ist und gleichzeitig eigenwillig überladen, sobald es um Fragen geht zu Requisiten und Hintergrund, mediengerechter Gestaltung, narrativen Konsequenzen der Klang- und Farbsättigung und des geschmackvoll dosierten

Kitschs. Zum Klang eines absonderlich ruckelnden Soundtracks schwenkt die Kamera von einem mehr oder minder malerischen Panorama eines Sonnenunterganges am Meer zurück in ein geschmackvoll ausgestattetes Wohnzimmer, auf einen Schuljungen, der verschüchtert auf einem prächtigen Sofa kauert, bewegt sich dann langsam weiter und beendet die Reise durch Raum und Medium mit einer beinahe malerischen Ansicht des Vollmondes im Fenster am anderen Ende des Raumes. Sonnenuntergang wie Mond sind durch die Fensterscheiben gefilmt, welche knapp erkennbare, wundersam-geisterhafte Bewegungen im Raum reflektieren. Als ich den Film kürzlich wieder sah, fiel mir auf, dass ich die Koda vergessen hatte; zwei Stills – das Bild eines Schlafzimmers und das einer Strandvilla, Bilder, die unerklärlich ergreifend sind, ohne eine narrative Funktion aufzuweisen oder etwa eine damit zusammenhängende mnemonische Spur. Obwohl Wekua seine Zeit bisher eher mit Schneiden, Giessen, Kleben, Zeichnen und Installieren verbracht hat als mit Film und Montage, liefert diese Arbeit eine kompakte Illustration seines Universums. Nicht nur dank gewisser Leitmotive, wie der vernebelten Atmosphäre des Abgeschiedenen und Entlegenen, dem ominösen Strandpanorama, dem liebenswerten Schuljungen, der bürgerlichen Szenerie, der unheilschwangeren Stimmung und deren genüsslicher Zelebration, aber auch dank einer fast inexistenten Handlung, die vor unserem geistigen Auge dennoch verschachtelte narrative Abläufe in Gang setzt, Abläufe, die mitunter tatsächlich um das bereits erwähnte künstlerbiographische Dokudrama kreisen. Mit anderen Worten, der Film ist auch insofern sehr Wekua, als er eine kunstkritische Sprengfalle ist.

Insgesamt ist Wekuas Werk als solches makellos durchkomponiert, selbst dort, wo es sich in der liebevoll ruppigen Collage gefällt, einer Sorte visueller Kühnheit, zu deren Gelingen enormes Talent gehört. Wekuas Collagen bieten im Wesentlichen, auch wenn sie weitgehend dem Panoptikum seiner Leitmotive folgen, eher Splitterhaftes als behagliche Verlinkungen, diese werden im besten Fall durch fein gezogene Linien, Kritzeleien und Kleckse angedeutet, die kreuz und quer durch die jeweilige Arbeit verlaufen. Wenn beispielsweise zwei Bilder übereinander stehen, wobei sie ineinander übergehen, ohne inhaltlich zusammenzuhängen, und ohne dass Fragen um Tiefe und Oberfläche, Vorher und Nachher oder andere psychoästhetische Arbeitsteilungen geklärt würden. Andere Arbeiten bestehen aus einer einzigen Photographie, die von Wekuas Menschengestalten graphisch besetzt wird oder von zerklüfteten Formationen aus Rechtecken und Kreisen, oder sie weisen lediglich eine Faltspur auf. Bei vielen skulpturalen Arbeiten stösst man auf kunstvoll versehrte Schaufensterpuppen, fast immer in Kombination mit einer gezielten Studie zu Form und Funktion des Sockels. Manchmal lagern die Puppen auf kunstvoll ausgearbeiteten, massiven Podesten, die mit verschiedenen geometrischen Anordnungen von kubischem Gewirr und atmosphärischer Haptik verziert sind, dann wieder hocken sie auf flachen und kleinen Sockeln, leicht schief oder verschlissen. Besonders wenn es um Installationen geht, in denen

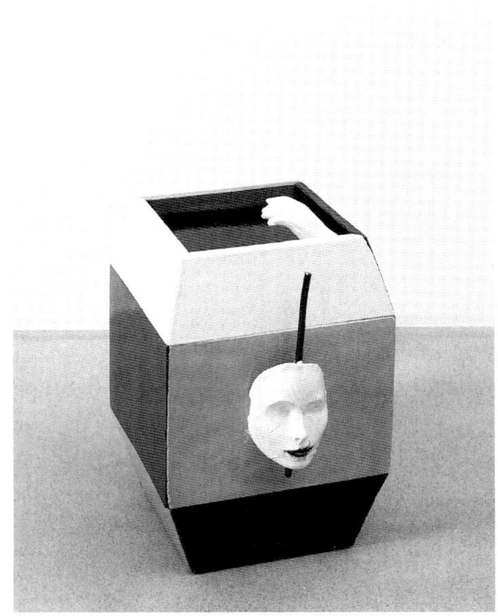

ANDRO WEKUA, THREE TIMES 3, 2006, ceramic, 22 x 14 1/2 x 14 3/4" / DREI MAL 3, Keramik, 55,8 x 37 x 37,5 cm. (PHOTO: A. BURGER)

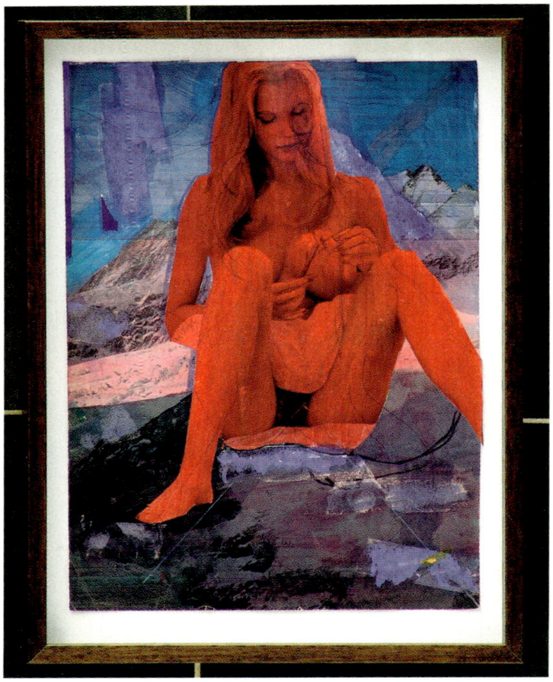

ANDRO WEKUA, *READY*, 2006, *felt pen and photocopy on photocopy*, 11 ³/₄ x 8 ³/₄" / *BEREIT*, *Filzstift und Photokopie auf Photokopie*, 29,7 x 22 cm.

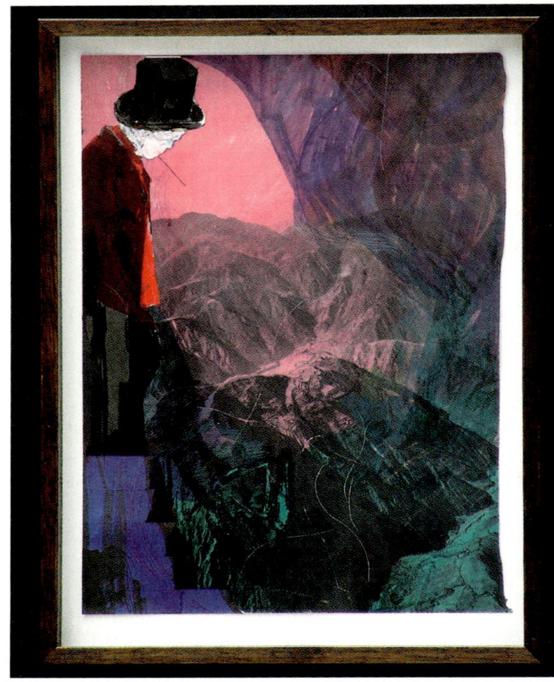

ANDRO WEKUA, *MY PLACE*, 2006, *color pencil, felt pen and Tipp-Ex on photocopy*, 14 ¹/₂ x 11 ¹/₄" / *BEI MIR*, *Farbstift, Filzstift und Tipp-Ex auf Photokopie*, 37 x 28,5 cm.

seine Zeichnungen mit solch dreidimensionalen Arbeiten kombiniert werden, wird Wekua leicht zum überzeugenden Argument dafür, dass mehr Künstler ihre eigenen Kuratoren sein sollten, statt diese Wissenschaft anderen zu überlassen, etwa Kritikern wie mir, die kaum je über die oben skizzierte, panisch diskursive Pyrotechnik hinauskommen.

Trotz all diesem ins Auge springenden, praktischen künstlerischen Können findet man schreibenderweise nicht ganz so mühelos in dieses Werk hinein, und ein Grund dafür liegt wohl in der – sich manchmal überschneidenden – Doppelstrategie von liebevoller Beliebigkeit auf der einen und sorgfältiger Feinabstimmung des zwielichtigen Ambiente auf der anderen Seite. Die Kombination dieser beiden Strategien ist nicht nur ungewöhnlich, die dadurch auftretenden atmosphärischen Kurzschlüsse geraten manchmal auch ausser Kontrolle, und damit in die Nähe der Theatralik statt des Bühnenhaften, was die Arbeit für alle Beteiligten risikoreicher und spannender macht. Ferner sind – wie beim Erklären einer Pointe – die typisch wekuanschen Schattierungen kaum zu beschreiben, ohne ihre eigentliche Attraktivität kaputtzureden. Nur so viel sei gesagt: Wekuas Kombinationen von Figur und Hintergrund schaffen es mühelos, die üblichen Effekte in Sachen Untergang und Verhängnis zu vermeiden, einschliesslich der Standardmetaphern zur rabenschwarzen *Conditio humana* (Georgien zum Trotz), und bieten stattdessen eine Melange, die manieriert ist, ohne affektiert zu wirken, überzeichnet, ohne ärgerlich zu sein und dicht, ohne je linkisch zu wirken.

Etwas weniger delikat modelliert ist vielleicht der geschlechterspezifische Subtext, der sich durch das Œuvre zieht, die prüden Frauen in 50er-Jahre-Outfits und die Kinder in ihren Schuluniformen, eine Castingstudie zu den adretten Psychosen um Heim und Herd, welche zu etwas äusserst Stattlichem zurechtgeprügelt werden, wenn auch in leicht bubenhafter Manier. Das ist nicht nur in bestimmten Collagen augenfällig, sondern auch in Wekuas Texten («sie hatte ein Einschussloch unterm Auge») und bei den malträtierten Schaufensterpuppen, die seine wortkarg-narrativen Installationen strukturieren. Ich muss zugeben, dass ich angesichts der geköpften Frauen, die sein Werk zieren, oft gedacht habe, dass anlässlich einer umfassenden Wekua-Retrospektive die weibliche Leiche als Hintergrund oder Kulisse rigoroser angegangen werden müsste. Fairerweise muss man sagen, dass es sich hier um eine umfassendere Verunglimpfung handelt als um jene des anderen Geschlechts. Wekuas fröhliche Orchestrierungen der Verstümmelung bieten dabei genug Stoff für zahlreiche Doktorarbeiten in verschiedensten Disziplinen, von den mit Crèmetorten bekleckerten Schuljungen bis zu den radikaleren Gesichtsmetzeleien. Um abschliessend noch einmal auf die Zeichnungen und Collagen zurückzukommen: Ein wichtiges Leitmotiv unter all den ausdruckslosen Figuren sind die sprachlosen Sprechblasen, schlangenähnliche unbeschriftete Wölbungen, die aus ihren Mündern quellen, als ob die Dinge, die sie uns erzählen könnten, so düster und traumatisch wären, dass sie besser ungesagt bleiben.

(Übersetzung: Suzanne Schmidt)

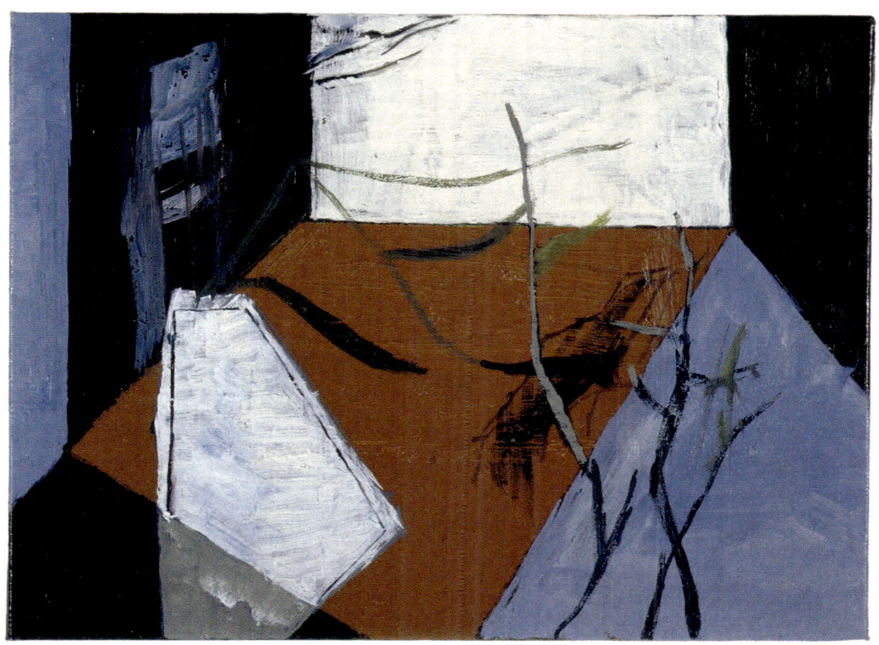

ANDRO WEKUA, LIVING ROOM 9.43 PM, 2005, oil on canvas, 11 5/8 x 15 3/4"/
WOHNZIMMER 21.43 Uhr, Öl auf Leinwand, 30 x 40 cm. (PHOTO: A. BURGER)

CINDYS URSZENE

DOLL CLOTHES

SHERMANS FRÜHER FILM

GABRIELE SCHOR

Was den Spiegel angeht, so ist er das Instrument der universellen Magie, die die Dinge in Schauspiele verwandelt, die Schauspiele in Dinge, die mich in den anderen verwandeln, und den anderen in mich.

Maurice Merleau-Ponty

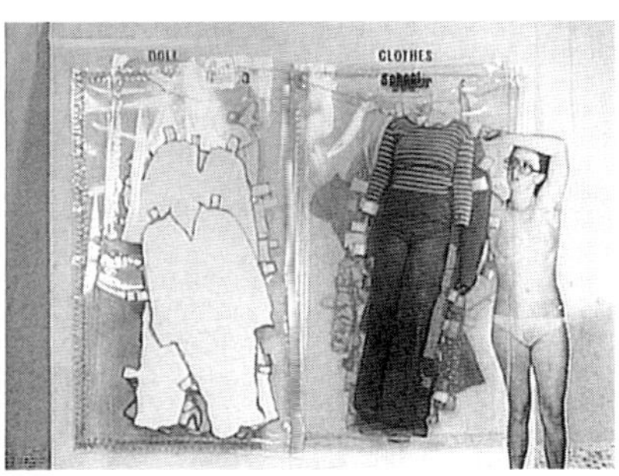

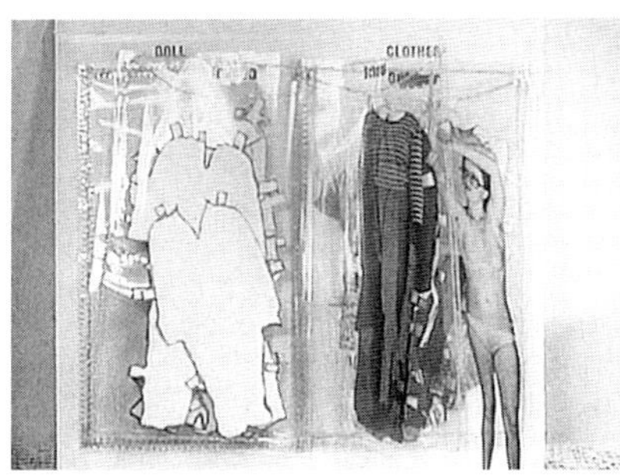

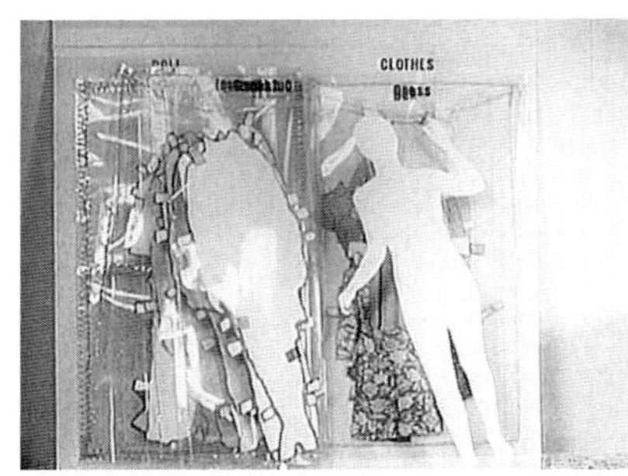

Cindy Shermans noch wenig bekanntes Frühwerk erfährt in letzter Zeit besondere Aufmerksamkeit.[1)] Dies nicht zuletzt, weil man nach einer inzwischen dreissigjährigen Schaffenszeit gern auf ihre performativen Anfänge zurückblickt, die allerdings nicht – wie allgemein angenommen – in den klassischen *Untitled Film Stills* (1977–80) zu finden sind, sondern in den Arbeiten davor, als die angehende Künstlerin in Buffalo studierte. Dort setzte sich die damals Zwanzigjährige in den Hallwalls, einem von Künstlern betriebenen Ausstellungsraum, mit konzeptuellen Kunstströmungen ihrer Zeit auseinander. Von

GABRIELE SCHOR ist Kunstkritikerin der *Neuen Zürcher Zeitung*, leitet die Sammlung Verbund und arbeitet am Catalogue raisonné von Cindy Shermans Frühwerk.

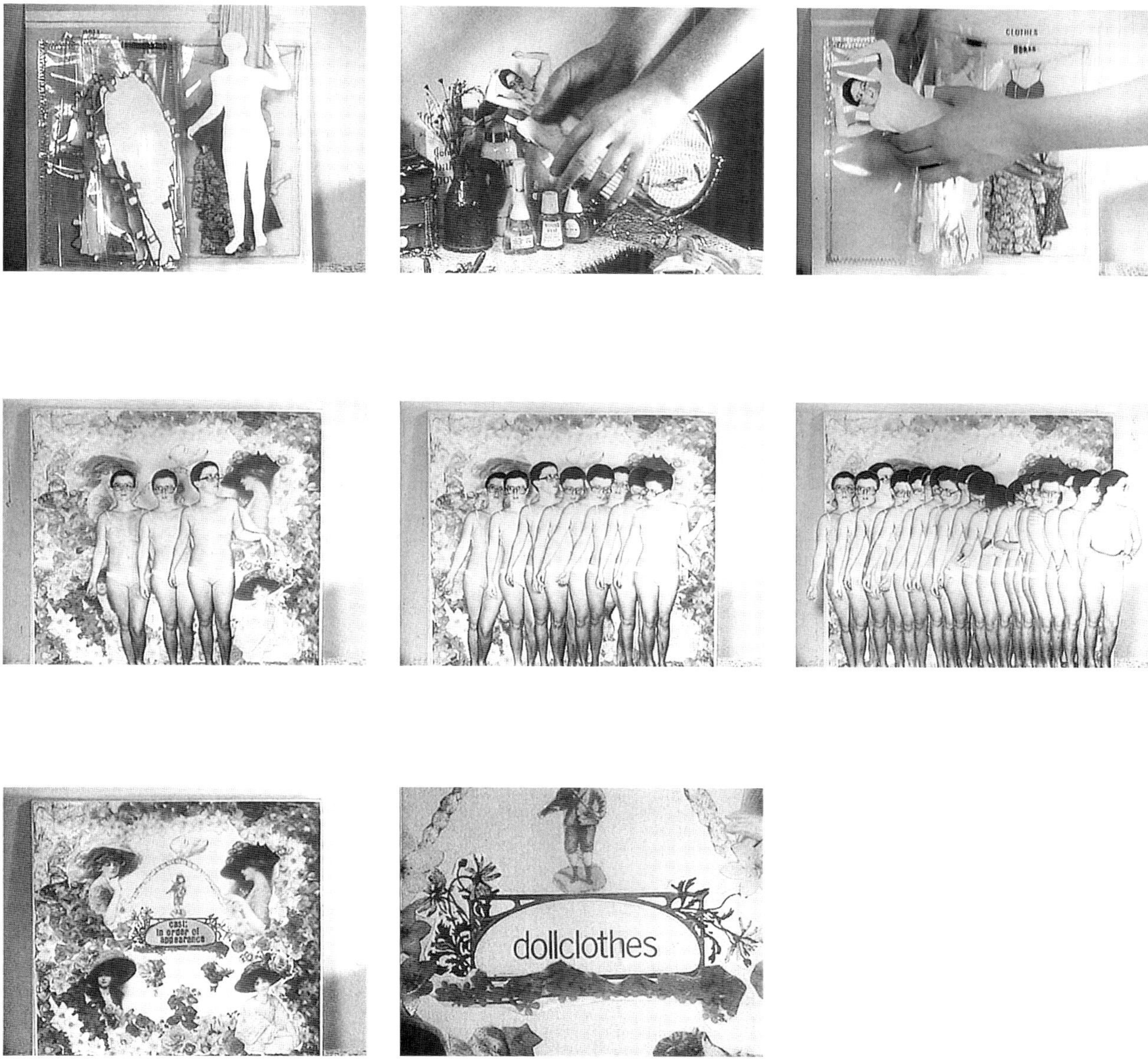

CINDY SHERMAN, DOLL CLOTHES, 1975, videostills / PUPPENKLEIDER, Video Stills.
(ALL PHOTOS: COURTESY OF THE ARTIST AND METRO PICTURES, NEW YORK)

den zahlreichen Gastkünstlern war es vor allem Vito Acconci, der sie mit seinen provokanten Performances beeindruckte, ebenso schätzte Sherman *key figures* wie Eleanor Antin, Hannah Wilke, Adrian Piper und Lynda Benglis, «weil sie sich selbst in ihre Werke einbrachten».[2] Der gewagte Vorstoss der feministischen Avantgarde sollte sie ermutigen. Denn schon in ihrer Jugend liebte es Sherman, ihr darstellerisches Talent auszuleben, oft verkleidete sie sich *just for fun,* entweder gemeinsam mit einer

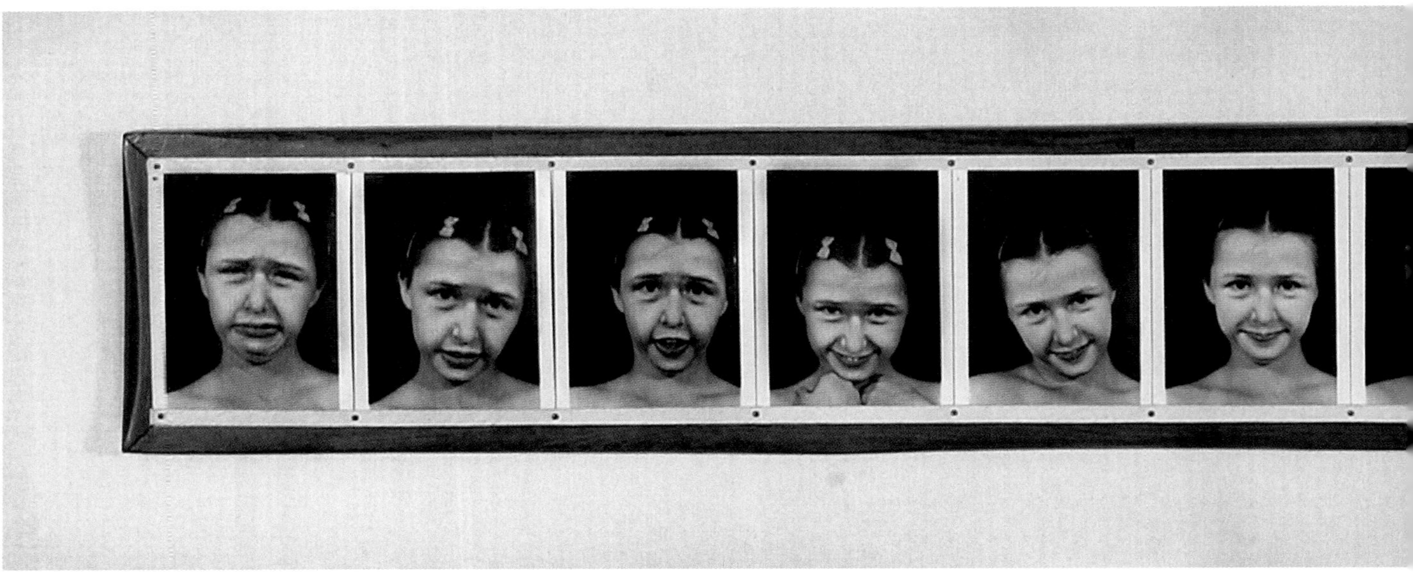

Freundin als alte Dame oder als schreckliches Monster und Hexe. Offenbar gelang es Sherman über all die Jahre hinweg, diesen spielerischen Trieb – sich in eine andere Person zu verwandeln – zu bewahren, zu verteidigen, sodass er sich bis heute in eine enorme künstlerische Ausdrucksvielfalt transformieren liess.

Einige Arbeiten aus den beiden letzten Collegejahren 1975 und 1976 thematisieren die psychischen und sozialen Existenzbedingungen einer Adoleszenz. Eine Abfolge von dreizehn kleinen Porträts zeigt, wie aus einem Schulmädchen mit Haarspange und all seinen emotionalen Stimmungen, mal weinend, verzweifelt, grinsend und offenherzig, ein schnippisches Girl mit Kopftuch wird und wie sich dieses wiederum zu einer kühl und distanziert wirkenden Frau entwickelt. Die Künstlerin meint dazu: «Bei dieser Arbeit geht es um das Erwachsenwerden – von Kind an.»[3] Erwachsen zu werden, scheint kein erstrebenswerter Zustand zu sein, wenn er in eine solche emotionslose und starre Passphoto-Ästhetik mündet. Werden uns hier die Stadien eines Entfremdungsprozesses vor Augen geführt?

Im Film DOLL CLOTHES (Puppenkleider, 1975) erkennen wir Sherman, in Gestalt einer Papierpuppe, die zum Leben erweckt wird. Zu Beginn steckt sie noch in einer engen Plastikhülle, aus der sie dann bald herausspringt. Sie bemerkt aber, dass sie bis auf ihre Brille und Unterwäsche entblösst ist, und will deshalb eine passende Kleidung finden. Eine Fülle von Gewändern – zuerst photographiert und dann ebenfalls aus Papier geschnitten – ist fein säuberlich nach Kategorien wie *Play, Casual, School, Outdoor* und *Dress* geordnet. Schliesslich wählt die Puppe ein nettes Sommerkleid, zieht es an und macht sich auf den Weg zum Schminktischchen. Doch während sie sich genüsslich im Spiegel betrachtet und Freude an ihrem neuen Kleidchen empfindet, taucht plötzlich aus dem Off eine übergrosse, bedrohliche Hand auf, schnappt die erschrockene Papierpuppe und reisst ihr das Kleid vom Leib. Wieder nackt bis auf die

Unterwäsche wird die Puppe in die Enge der Plastikhülle, in das Korsett der Konformität, zurückgesteckt. Natürlich protestiert und rebelliert das kleine Wesen vehement, doch es hilft nichts – letztlich erstarrt es wieder in seiner ursprünglichen Anonymität, aus der es doch gerade erst mit Hilfe der Bekleidung entfliehen wollte.

Wie kann aber der alltägliche Vorgang des Sich-Bekleidens überhaupt zu einem bedeutungsvollen Akt von Emanzipation werden? Die Kleidung steht dazu verführt, von dem auszugehen, was visuell (unmittelbar) erfahrbar ist. Doch schauen wir für einen kurzen Augenblick hinter die Kulissen. Wie vollzieht sich der Transformationsprozess im Atelier? Dazu heisst es: «Was ich mache, ist Schauspielerei – ich versuche das, was ich im Spiegel sehe, in etwas zu verwandeln, das für mich neu und überraschend ist.»[5] Die Erfahrung vor dem Spiegel ist für die Künstlerin schon deshalb konstitutiv, weil sie im Atelier allein arbeitet. «I was always a loner.»[6] Der Blick

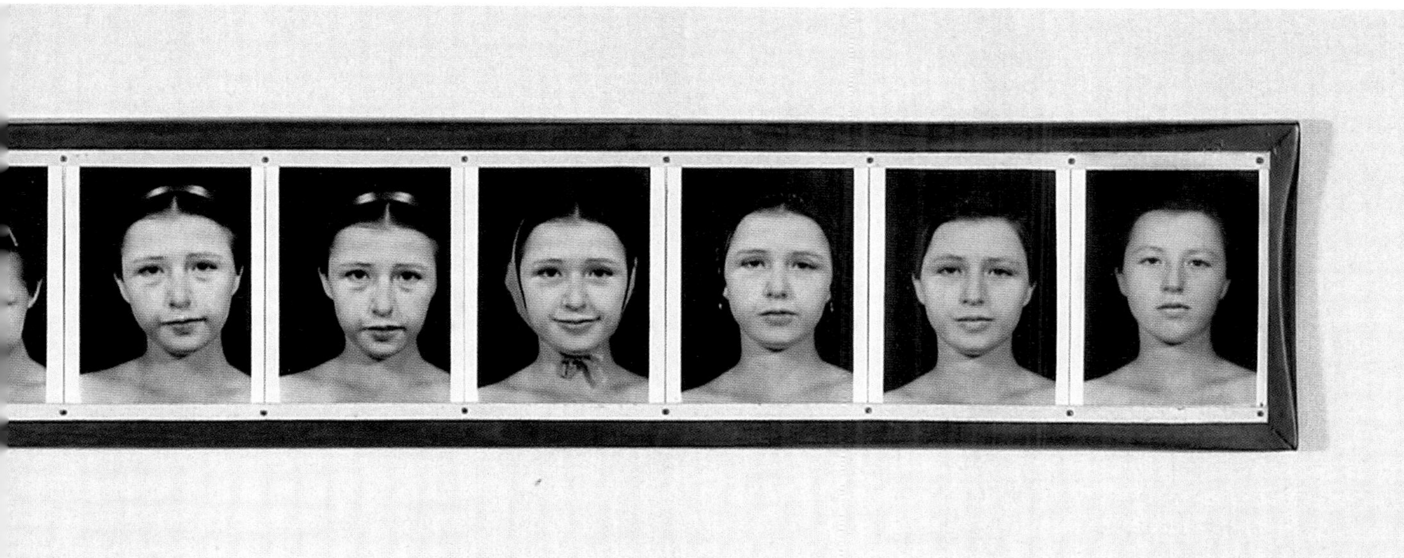

CINDY SHERMAN, UNTITLED, 1975, black-and-white photographs, 9 3/4 x 45" / OHNE TITEL, Schwarz-Weiss-Photographien, 24,8 x 114,5 cm.

für das Potenzial der Maskerade, welches Sherman schon als Teenager beherrschte. «Als Teenager machte ich kleine Zeichnungen all meiner Kleider – und immer Sonntagnacht legte ich die Schulkleidung für die kommende Woche fest.»[4] Indem sich das Schulmädchen mit einem von ihm gewählten Kleid vor dem Spiegel betrachtet, entkommt es einer trostlosen Anonymität und kann sich seiner Identität und Individualität gewahr werden. In diesen 2 Minuten und 22 Sekunden spielt sich nichts Geringeres ab als die Urszene von Shermans System multipler Persönlichkeiten.

Bisher fand die Funktion des Spiegels in Shermans Werk keine besondere Beachtung. Dies ist nachvollziehbar, weil das Medium Photographie

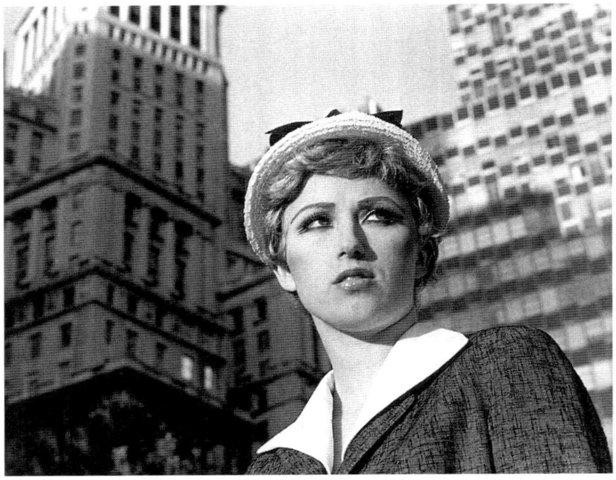

CINDY SHERMAN, UNTITLED FILM STILL # 21, 1978, black-and-white photograph, 8 x 10" / FILMSTILL OHNE TITEL, Schwarz-Weiss-Photographie, 20,3 cm x 25,4 cm.

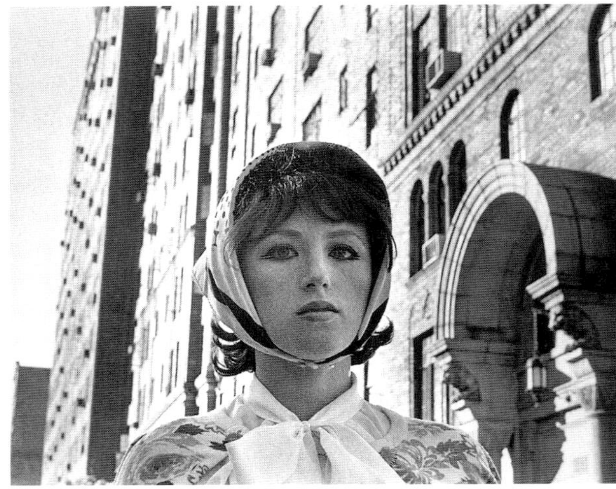

CINDY SHERMAN, UNTITLED FILM STILL # 17, 1978, black-and-white photograph, 8 x 10" / FILMSTILL OHNE TITEL, Schwarz-Weiss-Photographie, 20,3 cm x 25,4 cm.

in ihr Spiegelbild ist also die *conditio sine qua non*, es ist das Zwiegespräch, welches ihr ermöglicht, immer wieder eine andere Rolle einzunehmen. Wie sonst sollte sie den Sitz der Perücke, das aufgetragene Make-up und die angezogenen Kleider checken können? «Es war wie beim Malen: mein Gesicht im Spiegel anzuschauen und dann herauszufinden, was ich mit diesem einen Teil meines Gesichts anstellen konnte und wie ich diesen anderen schattieren konnte.»[7] Wie sonst sollte sie all die Charaktermasken ergründen, seien es die *Bus Riders*, die *Murder Mysteries*, die Frauen der *Film Stills* und der *Centerfolds*, die üppigen *History Portraits*, die verzweifelten *Hollywood Types* oder die traurigen *Clowns*, wie sonst hätte sie all diese Typologien hervorgebracht, wäre da nicht ihr treuer Talisman: der Spiegel und seine zuverlässige Gabe, das Spiegelbild.

Die Puppe in DOLL CLOTHES vollzieht also, um mit Jacques Lacan zu sprechen, das Spiegelstadium, welches den Prozess der Individuation in Gang setzt. Sie beginnt den Anderen wahrzunehmen, entweder in Form des eigenen Spiegelbildes oder in Form eines anderen Menschen. Der Spiegel hat nämlich zwei Funktionen: Wie sehe ich mich? Aber noch mehr: Wie sehen mich die anderen? «Man kann das Spiegelstadium als eine Identifikation verstehen (...), als eine beim Subjekt durch Aufnahme des Bildes ausgelöste Verwandlung.»[8] In DOLL CLOTHES geht es natürlich nicht im Sinne von Lancans *stade du miroir* um eine Subjektkonstitution innerhalb einer kindlichen Entwicklungsphase, sondern um die Bildung des künstlerischen Selbst.

In DOLL CLOTHES ereignet sich ein Riss im Subjekt, das Ich spaltet sich einmal in ein Objekt und erst danach in ein Subjekt. Wenn die Puppe in der Plastikhülle steckt – ganz regungslos und passiv –, dann verkörpert sie, im Sinne von Deleuze, das *moi* (*me*), wenn sie allerdings aus dieser ausbricht, verkörpert sie das aktive *je* (*I*). Dieser Akt (ich denke) ist es, der ihre Existenz aktiv bestimmt (ich bin).[9] Cindys Urszene kann also auch als die *mise en scène* von Cindys Cogito verstanden werden.

In dem Photoalbum A CINDY BOOK (1964–75) sehen wir sie in unterschiedlichen Situationen, als Kind am Strand, als Jugendliche mit Freunden oder als junge Frau mit einem Mann. Das Besondere an diesem privaten Album ist nun, dass sie sich beinahe auf jedem Photo mit einem Stift selbst eingeringelt hat und darunter steht immer geschrieben: «That's me,». Danach setzt sie merkwürdigerweise kein Ausrufezeichen, sondern stets ein Komma.[10] Diese Selbstvergewisserung, das Man-hat-mich-abgebildet: also-bin-Ich, dieses Axiom ihres Repräsentationssystems, ist also nicht vokativ konnotiert, sondern auf reine Progression ausgerichtet. Es markiert eine symbolische Progression, eine an sich nie zum Abschluss kommende, in ferner Zukunft nur zum Abbruch gelangende Sinnkette. Das Komma ist somit das Zeichen des Kontinuums, das strukturelle Signal der Identitätenabfolge, insofern aber die Identitätsstruktur radikal offen ist, steht das Komma auch für das Koma des Individuums, das hier zum Dividuum mutiert, ist es doch einer permanenten Diskontinuität unterworfen. Genau das macht Cindys Maskeraden zu einem abgründigen Spiel. Wie ein Mantra taucht bei jedem Photo diese ostinate Selbstvergewisserung auf. Die mit dem Stift vollzogene Einkerkerung erinnert an den passiven Zustand der Puppe in der Plastikhülle. Es verwundert nicht, dass Cindy mit diesen Einringelungsaktionen genau dann aufhört, als 1975 ihr künstlerisches *je* (*I*) einsetzt und sich zu entfalten und zu wirken beginnt. Im selben Jahr entsteht auch der Film.

DOLL CLOTHES zeigt die stumme, farblose Geschichte eines Scheiterns. Der Film erzählt von einem namenlosen Wesen, dem es letztlich nicht gelingen soll, seine selbstdefinierte Subjektivität zu erlangen. Sherman erklärt, welche Funktion die bedrohliche Hand für sie hat: «Die Hand steht für die Eltern, die das Kind tadeln und es zwingen in der Hülle zu bleiben.»[11] Wird uns hier etwa ein negativer Entwicklungsroman en miniature vorgespielt? Sollen wir DOLL CLOTHES als eine von der Negativität heimgesuchte *éducation sentimentale* verstehen? Handelt es sich um eine feministisch motivierte Warnung? Die Hand verkörpert und veranschaulicht das Dispositiv einer repressiven Kultur, die darauf abzielt, Lebendigkeit, Kreativität und Andersartigkeit einer Frau zu verhindern. Diese gesellschaftlichen Mechanismen bewirken Eindimensionalität, verhindern die Entwicklung einer künstlerischen Person, denn das Wort *persona* benennt jenes Mittel, das im Zentrum von Shermans Kunst steht, nämlich die Maske des Schauspielers und jene Rolle, die durch die Maske dargestellt wird. Die Künstlerin versteht es aber, ihre radikale Gesellschaftskritik im Kontext des Feminismus der 70er Jahre auf subtile Weise zu camouflieren. So versetzt uns der Vorspann in eine frühere, idyllisch anmutende Zeit und stimmt uns so auf ein romantisches Szenarium ein, das bald darauf ins absolute Gegenteil umschlagen wird. Der Film kombiniert heterogene Filmgenres wie Stummfilm, Trickfilm und Problemstudie. Geschickt baut Sherman Slapsticks ein, wie etwa den Augenblick, in dem die Papierpuppe ausgerechnet angesichts der *school uniform* in Ohnmacht fällt.

Die Urszene von Shermans künstlerischer Ausdrucksvielfalt, der Urknall ihres Repräsentationssystems, ist die Szene vor dem Spiegel, in der die Puppe ihre Chance ergreifen will, eine von Rimbaud abgewandelte Wahrheit zu erkennen: Ich ist eine andere. Der Spiegel sollte in der Kamera seine instrumentelle Verlängerung, seine methodische Entsprechung finden. Und eines hat Cindy Sherman immer schon gewusst: «Die Kamera lügt.»[12]

1) The Unseen Cindy Sherman: Early Transformation 1975–76, Montclair Art Museum 2004. Cindy Sherman: Working Girl, Contemporary Art Museum St. Louis 2005. Sherman-Retrospektive, Jeu de paume, Paris; Kunsthaus Bregenz; Louisiana Museum of Modern Art, Humlebaek; Martin-Gropius-Bau, Berlin, 2006/07. Besprechungen der Schau in St. Louis und Paris durch die Autorin, *Neue Zürcher Zeitung*, 9. Dezember 2005 und 15./16. Juli 2006.

2) Gail Stavitsky, *The Unseen Cindy Sherman: Early Transformation 1975/76*, Ausstellungskatalog (Santa Monica: Smart Art Press, 2004), S. 12.

3) Gail Stavitsky, op. cit., S. 14.

4) Cindy Sherman, E-Mail an die Autorin, 1. Juni 2006. Schon in dieser strukturellen Vorausplanung steckt ein Abstraktionsprozess, der ihr späteres Variationsprinzip antizipiert.

5) Cindy Sherman. *Clowns*, Interview Isabelle Graw, (Hannover: Schirmer/Mosel und Kestnergesellschaft, 2004), S. 47.

6) Gail Stavitsky, op. cit. (Anm. 2), S. 6.

7) Gerald Marzorati, «Imitation of Life», *Artnews*, September 1983, S. 84–85.

8) Jacques Lacan, «Das Spiegelstadium als Bildner der Ichfunktion» (1949), in: ders., *Schriften I*, Suhrkamp, Frankfurt a. M. 1975, S. 61–70.

9) Gilles Deleuze, *Kritik und Klinik*, Suhrkamp, Frankfurt a. M. 2000, S. 44.

10) Régis Durand (Hrsg.), *Cindy Sherman*, Ausstellungskatalog, (Paris: Flammarion, 2006), S. 232.

11) Cindy Sherman, E-Mail an die Autorin, 1. Juni 2006.

12) Gerald Marzorati, «Imitation of Life», *Artnews*, September 1983, S. 81.

CINDY'S ORIGINAL SCENE

DOLL CLOTHES

SHERMAN'S EARLY FILM

GABRIELE SCHOR

As for the mirror, it is the instrument of universal magic, which transforms things into spectacles, spectacles into things, which transforms me into another, and another into me.

Maurice Merleau-Ponty

Cindy Sherman's lesser-known early work has recently been attracting critical attention,[1] not least because it is a delight to look back at her beginnings after three decades of creative output. Contrary to received opinion, these beginnings do not lie in her now classical *Untitled Film Stills* (1977–80) but rather in earlier experiments with performance art when she was still attending school in Buffalo. There, in the artists'-run space Hallwalls, the 20-year-old student became acquainted with the then current conceptual trends. Among the many visiting artists to come through the program, Vito Acconci made the greatest impact on her with his provocative performances, but she also appreciated other key figures like Eleanor Antin, Hannah Wilke, Adrian Piper, and Lynda Benglis "because they used their own selves in their works."[2] Sherman found the bold thrust of the feminist avant-garde encouraging. As a young girl she had already delighted in dressing up, becoming an old lady, along with a girlfriend, or turning herself into a monster or a witch. She has clearly succeeded in preserving and cultivating this playful drive to transform herself into someone else, and it has yielded an extraordinarily wide-ranging and diverse oeuvre.

During her last two years in college (from 1975 to 1976), Sherman explored the mental and social circumstances of life as an adolescent. A sequence of thirteen small portrait shows how a schoolgirl with a barrette in her hair runs the gamut of emotions from desperation and tears to grinning and openhearted smiles, later turning into a pert little lady wearing a headscarf and finally becoming a cool, aloof young woman. In the words of the artist, "This work was

GABRIELE SCHOR is an art critic at the Neue Zürcher Zeitung, directs the Sammlung Verbund, and is preparing a catalogue raisonné of Cindy Sherman's early work.

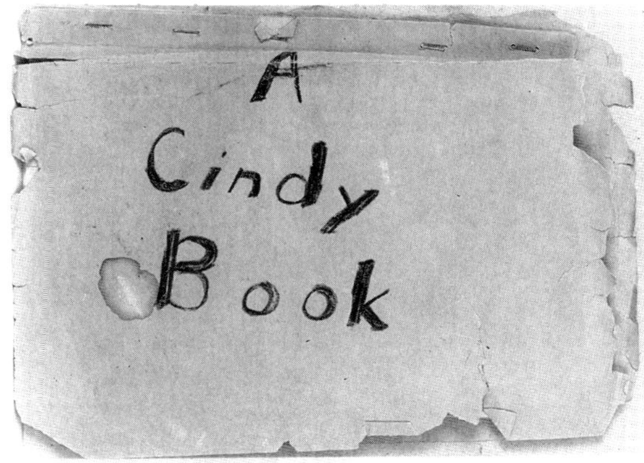

CINDY SHERMAN, A CINDY BOOK (1964–1975), photo album / Photoalbum.

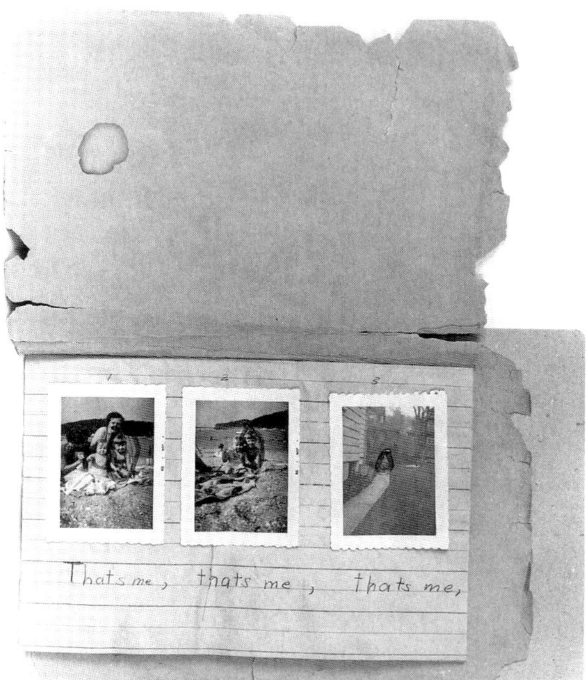

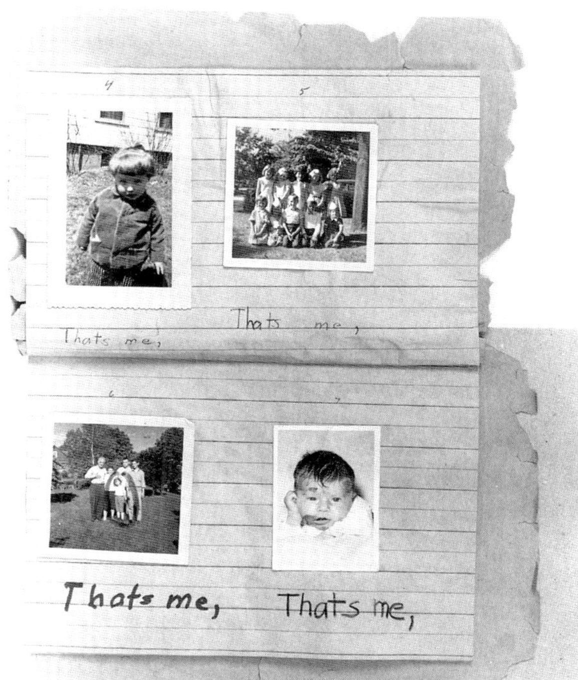

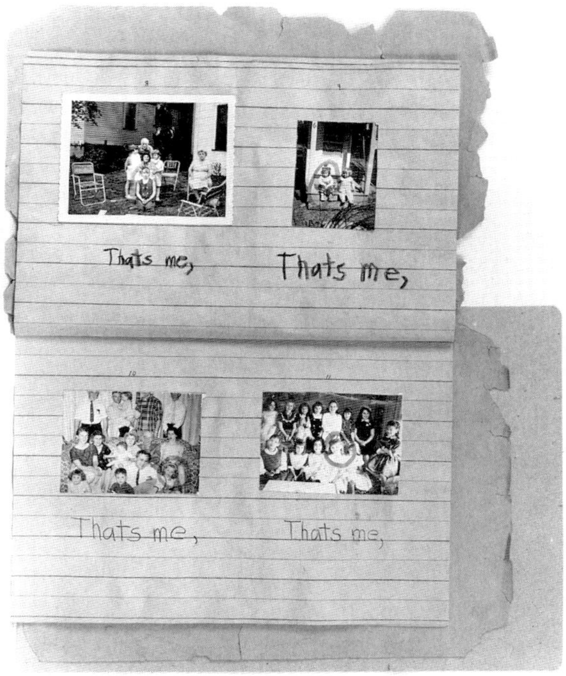

CINDY SHERMAN, A CINDY BOOK (1964–1975), photo album / Photoalbum.

about starting out as a child and growing up."[3] But growing up doesn't seem to be worth aspiring to if it ends in the apathetic and rigid passport-photo aesthetics of the later images. Are we here confronted with stages in a process of alienation?

In the film DOLL CLOTHES (1975), we see Sherman in the guise of a paper doll, initially tucked away in a plastic sleeve. When she comes to life and jumps out of the sleeve, she is dismayed to realize that she is wearing only glasses and underwear and proceeds to set out in search of suitable clothing. A wealth of apparel—first photographed and later cut out of paper—is neatly arrayed in categories: Play, Casual, School, Outdoor, and Dress. She finally chooses a pretty little summer dress, puts it on, and walks over to her dressing table where she admires herself in the mirror and delights in her new dress. Suddenly a menacing, oversized hand appears from off screen, grabs the startled paper doll, and tears off her dress. Again wearing nothing but her underwear, she is stuffed back into the plastic sleeve, back into the corset of conformity. Naturally the little being puts up a fierce battle, but in vain—she finally sinks back into the anonymity she had just tried to escape by getting dressed.

How can the ordinary business of getting dressed actually become a significant act of emancipation? Clothing stands for the potential of the masquerade, a skill that Sherman had already mastered in her teens. "When I was a young teenager – I made little drawings of all my clothes and each Sunday night I would figure out my school outfits for the week."[4] By choosing a dress, putting it on, and gazing at herself in the mirror, the schoolgirl escapes dreary anonymity and discovers an identity of her own. The entire original scene of Sherman's system of multiple personalities unfolds before our eyes in a brief 2 minutes and 22 seconds.

The function of the mirror had previously never figured prominently in Sherman's work, understandably so because the medium of photography tends to foreground immediate visual experience. But let us take a brief look behind the scenes. How does the artist implement her transformation in the studio? She says, "What I am doing is superficial acting: I attempt to change what I see in the mirror into something new and surprising for me."[5] The use of the mirror is indispensable because the artist works alone in her studio. "I was always a loner."[6] Her mirror image, therefore, is the *conditio sine qua non*; it is a partner in the dialogue that enables her to keep adopting different roles. Otherwise, how can she make sure her wig is in place, how can she put her makeup on, and how can she check the effect of her costumes? "It was like painting in a way: staring at my face in a mirror, trying to figure out how to do something to this part of my face, how to shade another part."[7] And how else could she study all the character masks in the *Bus Riders* or the *Murder Mysteries*, the women in the *Film Stills* and the *Centerfolds*, the elaborate *History Portraits*, the desperate *Hollywood Types* or the melancholy *Clowns*? How could she ever have produced all of these typologies without her faithful talisman: the mirror and its reliable gift, the mirror image.

The doll in DOLL CLOTHES is seen at the moment in our development when the process of individuation sets in; Jacques Lacan calls it the "mirror stage." She begins to take note of the other, either in the form of her own image or in the form of another person. Mirrors have two functions that make us ask: How do I see myself, and even more importantly, how do others see me? "The mirror stage can be understood as identification..., as transformation of the subject brought about by awareness of the image."[8] Of course, DOLL CLOTHES is not strictly about Lacan's *stade du miroir*, that is the stage of development in which the child recognizes itself as subject, but rather about the formation of the artistic self.

In DOLL CLOTHES, the subject is split, the ego first becomes an object and only later a subject. From a Deleuzian perspective, the doll, utterly immobile and passive in her plastic sleeve, embodies the *moi* (me), but when she escapes she embodies the active *je* (I). This act (I think) actively determines her existence (I am).[9] Hence, Cindy's original scene can also be interpreted as the *mise en scène* of Cindy's *cogito*.

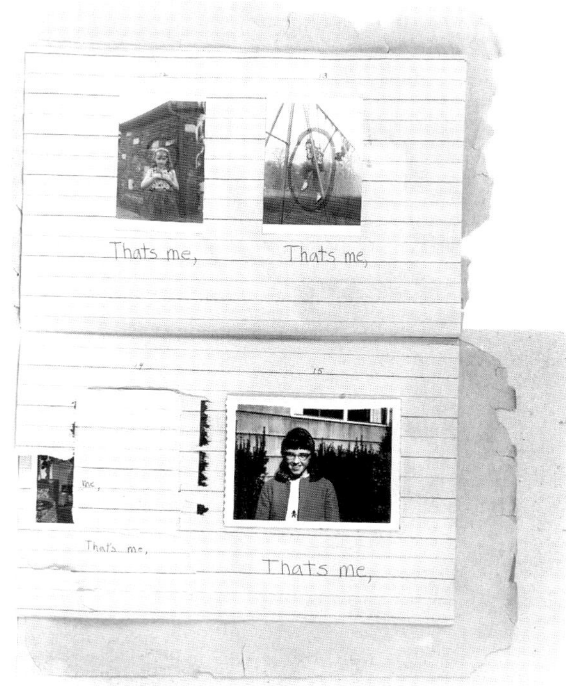

CINDY SHERMAN, A CINDY BOOK (1964–1975), photo album / Photoalbum.

In the photo album, A CINDY BOOK (1964–75), we see Sherman in several situations: as a child at the beach, as a young girl with friends, as a young woman with a man. The album might be mistaken for a perfectly ordinary personal keepsake if it weren't for the fact that the artist has drawn a circle around her own image in almost every photograph and written "That's me," underneath each one. Significantly, instead of punctuating her sentence with an exclamation point, she has used a comma.[10] This reassurance that somebody-took-a-picture-of-me-therefore-I-am is axiomatic of her system of representation and, as such, it does not function as a vocative but is rather based on pure progression. It marks a symbolic progression, a semantic chain that will never come to an end but will only break off in some distant future. The comma is indicative of a continuum, the structural signal of a sequence of identities. However, since the identity structure is radically open-ended, the comma also stands for the coma of the individual, who has mutated into a divided self, subject to permanent discontinuity. It is this that turns Sherman's masquerades into unfathomable play. The obstinate reassurance of the self crops up in every photograph, like a mantra. The line she has drawn, like a cage around herself, is related to the passive state of the doll in her plastic cover. One is therefore not surprised to learn that the act of encircling herself stopped the moment her artistic *je* entered the scene in 1975 and began to take effect. She shot the film that same year.

DOLL CLOTHES tells a mute, colorless story of failure. It stars a nameless being who tries unsuccessfully to acquire a self-defined subjectivity. Sherman explains what the threatening hand means to her,

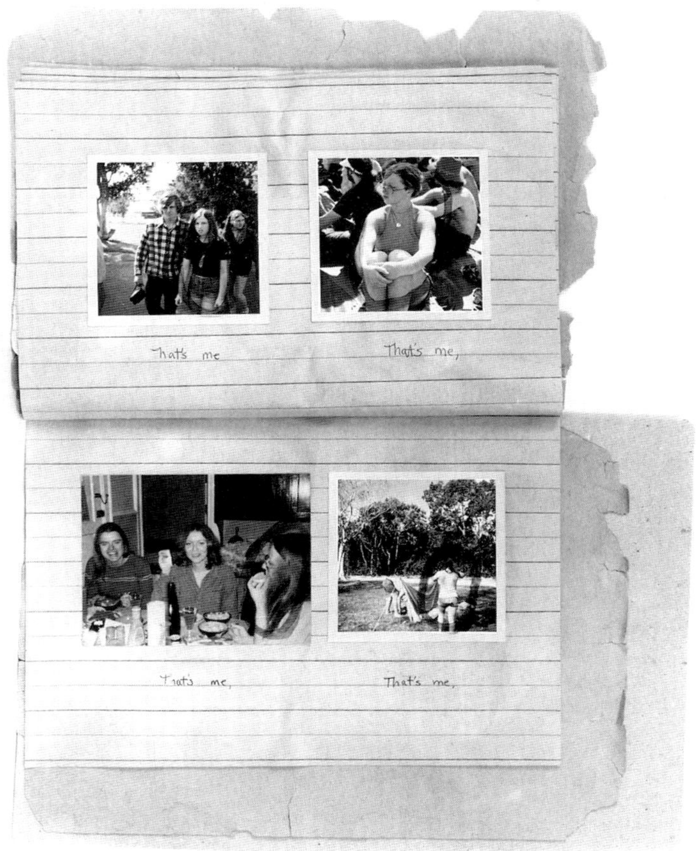

CINDY SHERMAN, A CINDY BOOK (1964–1975), photo album / Photoalbum.

"The hand is like the parent telling the child that they are misbehaving and have to stay in the booklet."[11] Has the artist created a negative *Entwicklungsroman* in miniature? Is DOLL CLOTHES the negative flip side of an *éducation sentimentale*? Is the film a feministically motivated warning? The hand is the vision incarnate of a repressive civilization that strangles the vitality, creativity, and otherness of women. It stands for social mechanisms that lead to one-dimensionality and prevent the development of an artistic persona, the persona being at the very heart of Sherman's agenda: it is the mask of the actress and the role that is embodied by that mask. However, Sherman shows great subtlety in camouflaging the 1970s feminism that informs her radical critique of society. The opening credits transport us to an earlier, idyllic age; they set the stage for a romantic scenario only to shatter, instantly, the expectations they have evoked. The film combines heterogeneous genres: silent film, cartoon, and psychodrama. Sherman even skillfully includes slapstick when, for example, the paper doll faints at the sight of the school uniform.

The original scene of Sherman's oeuvre in all its diversity—the big bang of her system of representation—is the scene in front of the mirror in which the doll wants to take advantage of her insight into a truth modified by Rimbaud, who stated in essence: I is someone else. The camera should be an instrumental extension of the mirror, its methodological correlate. And as Cindy Sherman says, she has always known that "the camera lies."[12]

(Translation: Catherine Schelbert)

1) "The Unseen Cindy Sherman: Early Transformation 1975–76," Montclair Art Museum, 2004; "Cindy Sherman: Working Girl," Contemporary Art Museum St. Louis, 2005; "Cindy Sherman Rétrospective," Jeu de Paume, Paris; Kunsthaus Bregenz; Louisiana Museum of Modern Art, Humlebaek; and Martin-Gropius-Bau, Berlin, 2006/07.
2) Gail Stavitsky, *The Unseen Cindy Sherman: Early Transformation 1975–76*, exhib. cat. (Santa Monica: Smart Art Press, 2004), p. 12.
3) Ibid., p. 14.
4) Cindy Sherman, email to the writer, June 1, 2006. Planning ahead in this way involves a process of abstraction that prefigures Sherman's later principle of variation.
5) Isabelle Graw, "No Make-Up, An Interview with Cindy Sherman," in *Cindy Sherman Clowns* (Hanover: Schirmer/Mosel and Kestnergesellschaft, 2004), p. 57.
6) Gail Stavitsky, op. cit., p. 6.
7) Gerald Marzorati, "Imitation of Life," *Artnews*, September 1983, pp. 84–85.
8) Jacques Lacan, "The Mirror Stage as Formative of the *I* Function, as Revealed in Psychoanalytic Experience," (1949) in *Ecrits: A Selection*, transl. by Bruce Fink (New York: Norton, 2002), pp. 3–10.
9) Gilles Deleuze, *Critique et Clinique* (Editions de Minuit, 1999).
10) Régis Durand, ed., *Cindy Sherman*, exhib. cat. (Paris: Flammarion, 2006), p. 232.
11) Cindy Sherman, email to the writer, June 1, 2006.
12) Gerald Marzorati, "Imitation of Life," *Artnews*, September 1983, p. 81.

Ernesto Neto
Born 1964 in Rio de Janeiro, where he lives and works.
Geboren 1964 in Rio de Janeiro, wo er lebt und arbeitet.

Olaf Nicolai
Born 1962 in Halle, Germany, lives and works in Berlin.
Geboren 1962 in Halle an der Saale, lebt und arbeitet in Berlin.

Rebecca Warren
Born 1965 in London, where she lives and works.
Geboren 1965 in London, wo sie lebt und arbeitet.

REBECCA WARREN

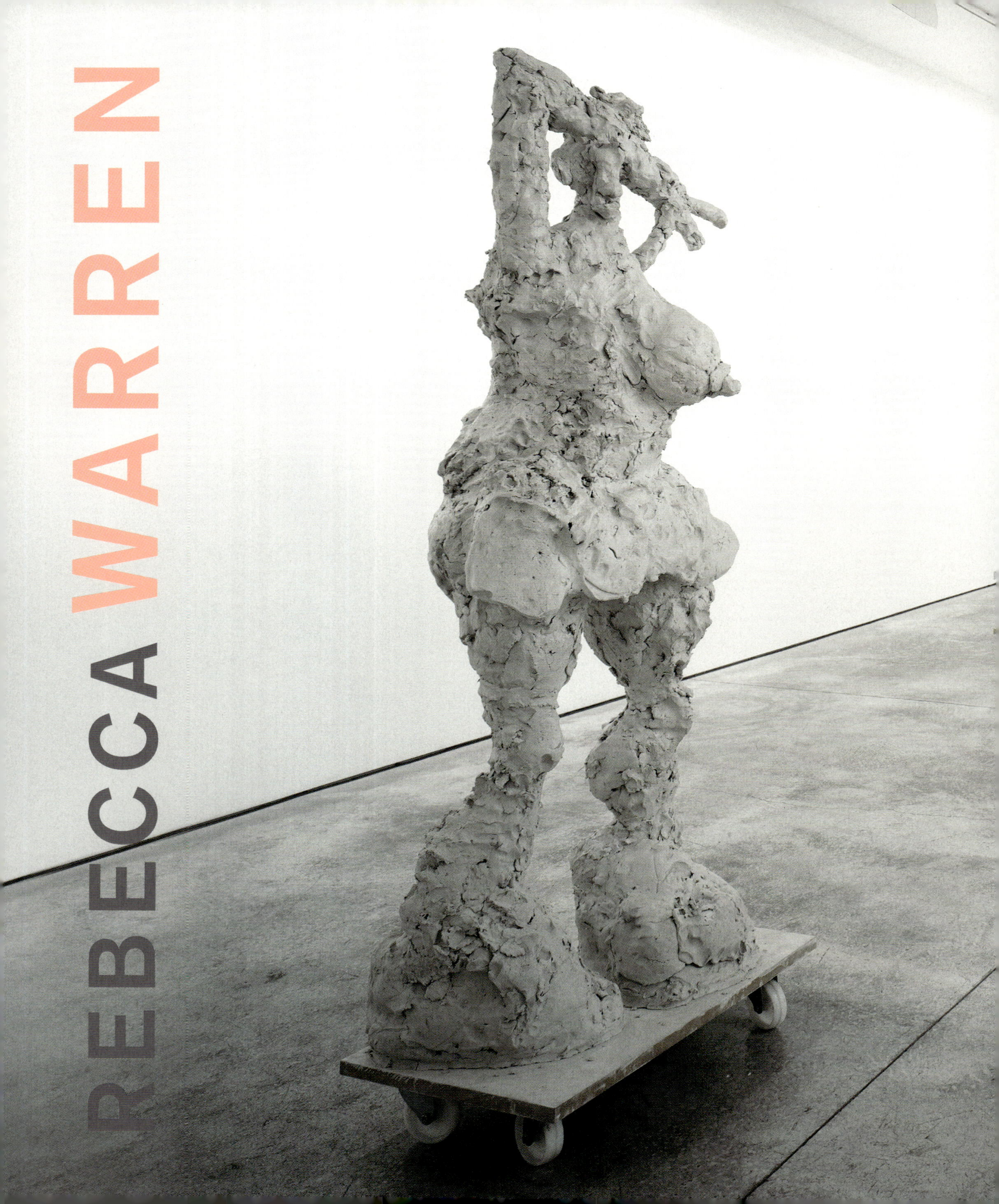

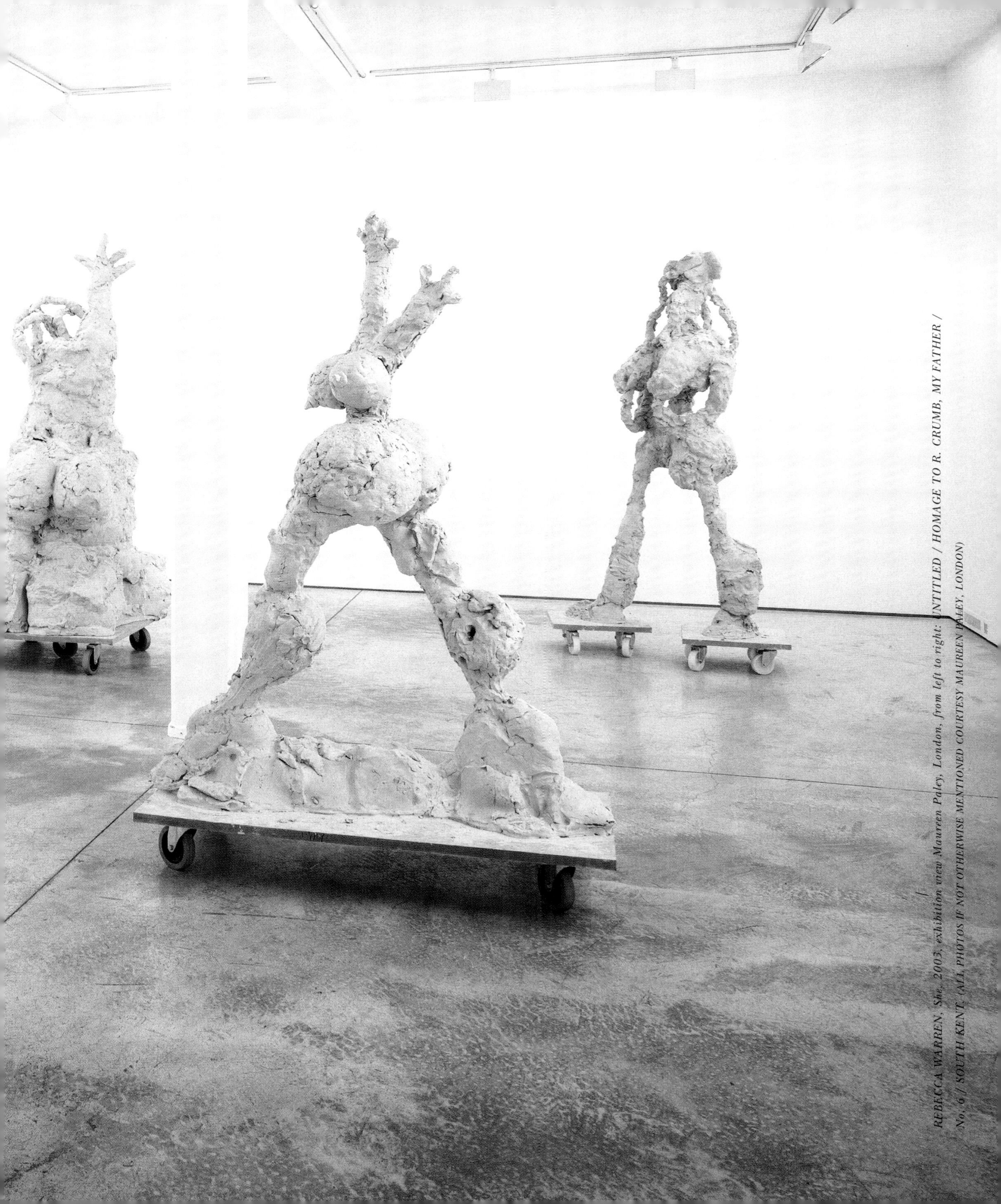

REBECCA WARREN, *She*, 2003, *exhibition view Maureen Paley, London, from left to right:* UNTITLED / HOMAGE TO R. CRUMB, MY FATHER / No. 6 / SOUTH KENT. (ALL PHOTOS IF NOT OTHERWISE MENTIONED COURTESY MAUREEN PALEY, LONDON)

Mad and Ugly

NEAL BROWN

Rebecca Warren often seems to be in character in her work and this, in combination with the wryly detached or separated quality of her intonation, facilitates her success. Abstracted from the gravity of sensible analysis, the tragicomedy of life's misshapen pleasures and problems can then float deliriously free in the outer space of the artist's brave psychology. In this way, Warren overcomes the problem of how an artist, especially a female artist, can negotiate intimate bodily images while, at the same time, resisting an autobiographical interpretation. Everyone knows that to reference Edgar Degas, Pablo Picasso, Auguste Rodin, and Robert Crumb in your work, as Warren does, is to summon hard-core males whose artistic genius includes (subject to certain interpretative qualifications) rampant sexual triumphalism. But Warren holds her esteemed giants of art in critical abeyance, which is not that of Stockholm syndrome, nor that of the attitudinal fearlessness characteristic of the UK's current aristocracy of female artists like Sarah Lucas and Tracey Emin. Warren's interest in the trademark conquests made by the male artists that she gathers together—gender outrages of unlikely breasts and bodily objectification—seems to be in their reductive physicality as much as anything else, from which she squeezes something more universal and tragic than just sexual triumphalism.

Warren's narrative includes childhood themes shaped within the white, virginal clay she uses; it is a special, self-setting kind of clay related to the earthy brown clay of the potter but which never needs be fired in a kiln, and so it retains the delicate "skin" quality of its youth. The pretty pastel colors that the artist sometimes applies to this unsullied whiteness, the effete ribbons her figures sometimes wear, and the doll, toy, or cartoon quality that pervades many of her works, all relate to (a usually female) childhood. Materially, the white clay is

NEAL BROWN is an artist and writer based in London. He is the author of *Tracey Emin* (Tate 2006) and was curator of "To the Glory of God: New Religious Art" at the second Liverpool Biennial.

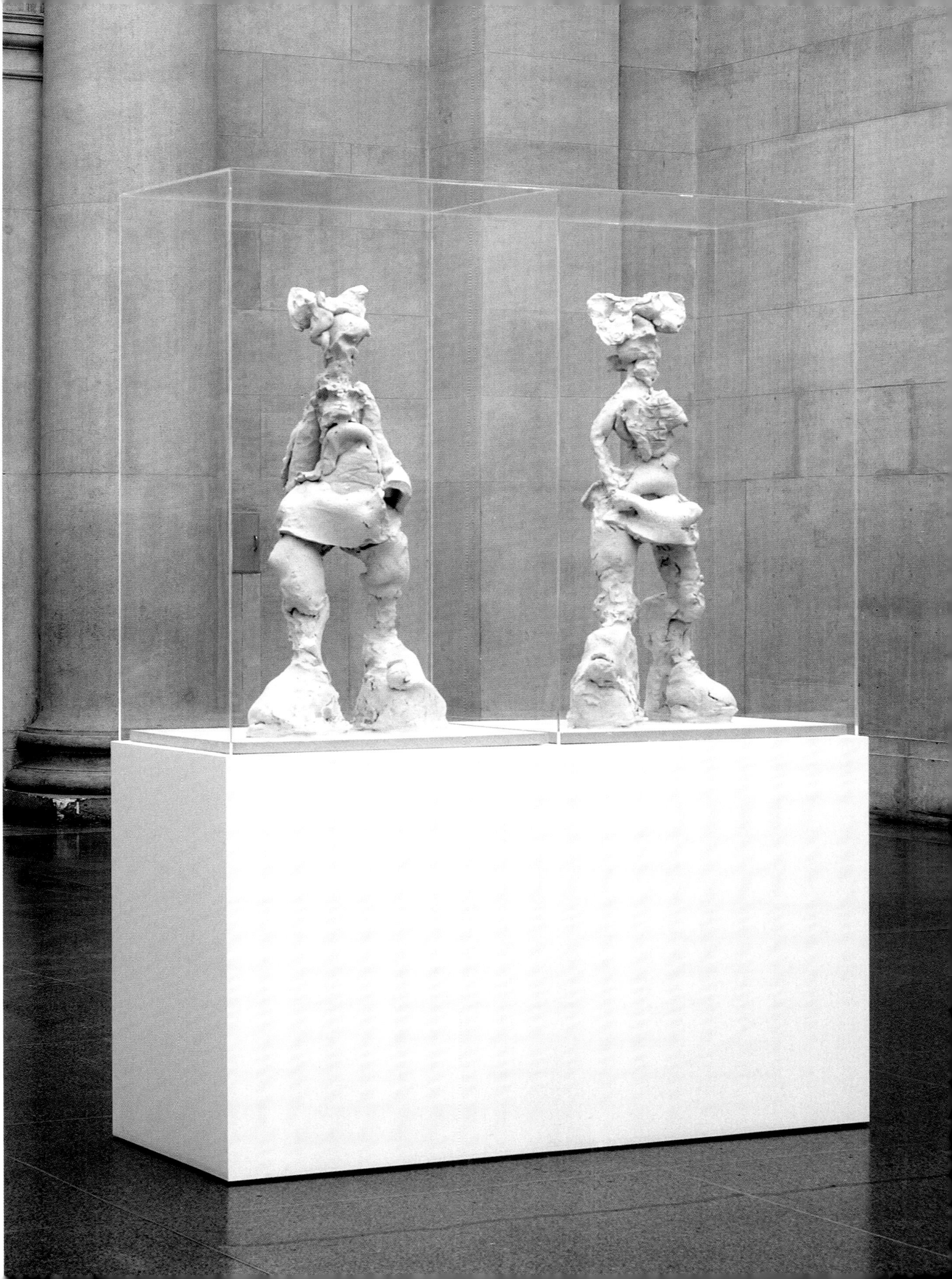

REBECCA WARREN, *COME, HELGA*, 2006, *reinforced clay, paint, plinth, perspex, 84 5/8 x 24 x 60 7/8" / KOMM, HELGA, verstärkter Ton, Farbe, Sockel, Plexiglas, 215 x 61 x 154,5 cm.*

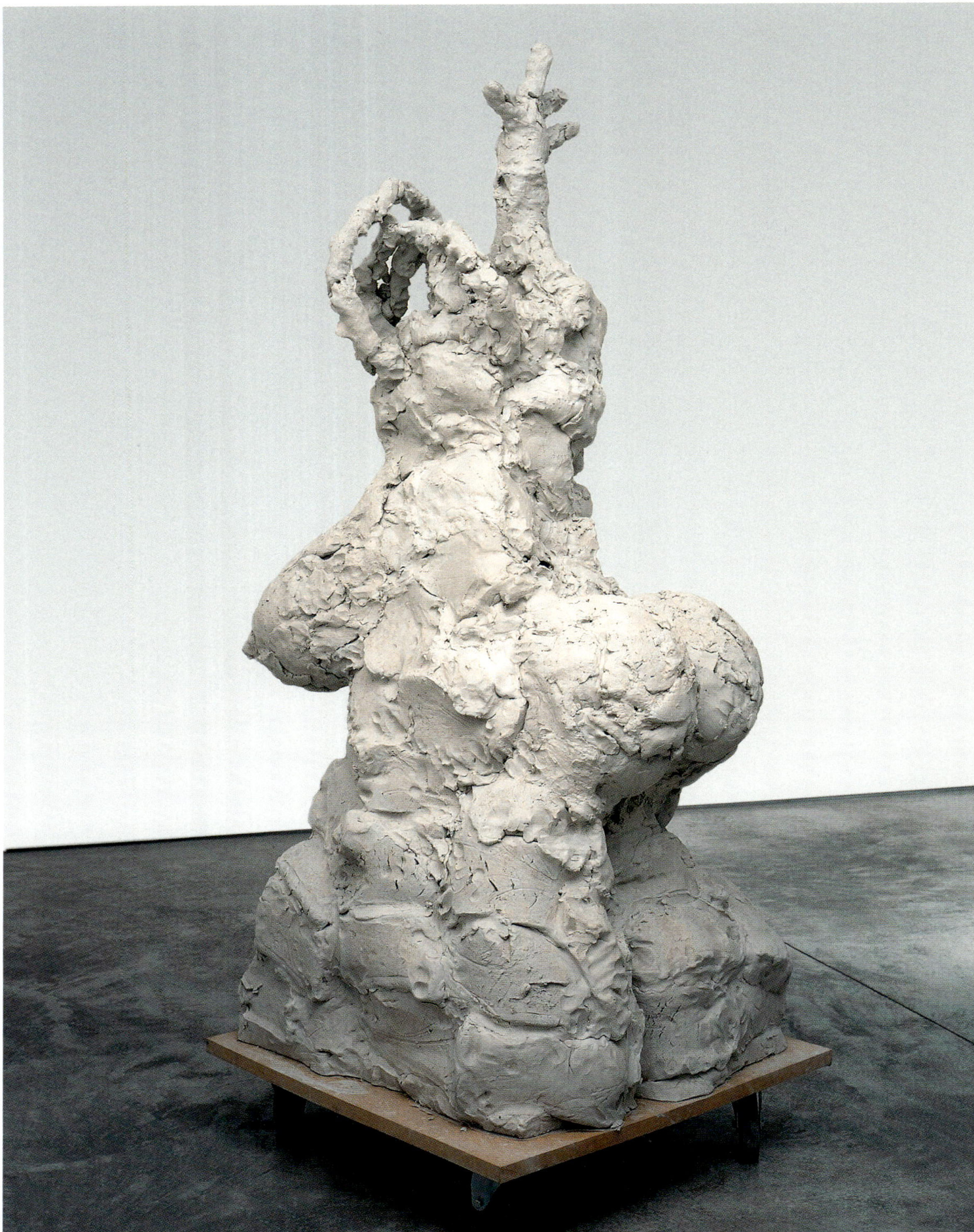

REBECCA WARREN, HOMAGE TO R. CRUMB, MY FATHER, 2003, reinforced clay, MDF, wheels, 83 7/8 x 32 1/8 x 32 1/8" /
HOMMAGE AN R. CRUMB, MEINEN VATER, verstärkter Ton, MDF, Räder, 213 x 81,5 x 81,5 cm.

related to children's modeling compounds but, stylistically, in Warren's hands, more to the anarchic little Plasticine sculptures, piles of mess, and spent chewing gum that children like to leave behind. Such discord is epitomized in Warren's appropriation of Degas' famous little ballerina (LITTLE DANCER AGED FOURTEEN, 1880–81), who she subverts in her own THE TWINS (2004) and COME, HELGA (2006) by displacing the ballerina's delicate, modest stance with a gauche, lumpy physicality, twice over.

As happens to lots of people, for lots of reasons—some biological, some socially ordained, some accidental—things go wrong when puberty signals the change from auto-acting childhood to the reacting self-consciousness of adolescence and adulthood. The consequences can include self-doubt, shame, insecurity, sadness, and fear. Although women are particularly diminished by gender expectation and fashion magazine perfectionism, there is a kind of disillusionment, if not perceptual collapse, that people have of their bodily selves that is not gender specific, and which relates to a lack of self-acceptance. This breakdown of bodily self-esteem affects men as well as women, for whom disordered equivalences between erotic or romantic sexuality, physical appearance, and identity can become overwhelming. These manifestations can be tragically comic, as well as catastrophic, and aspects of such dysphoric breakdowns can be seen in Warren's DEUTSCHE BANK (2002), PRIVATE SCHMIDT (2004), and LOG LADY (2003). Art—clay—is a very good way of interpreting or emphasizing bodily physicality, and the frenzied buttocks, vulvas, nipples, clitoral folds, and penises of Warren's work are part of a mad, discontinuous, physical hyphenism. Warren works her soft clay into something that is exultant, orgasmic, libidinous, fleshy, autoerotic, and pleasurable; her figures and plinth pieces are then fingered and improperly squeezed into something that is compulsively chaotic, masturbatory, fat, ugly, disgusted, repressed, incontinent, excretory, bestial, bulimic, collapsed, hung-over, unidentifiable, abject, debased, and self-critical. In other words, her work is a highly adjectival chaos of bodily regard: the pleasurable—less significant than the dysphoric.

Complex psychological inter-correlations between the Picasso that Warren summons in pieces like SHE (2003) and the Rembrandt that Picasso repeatedly summons in etchings from his 347 SERIES (1968) create an unlikely convergence between these three artists on the theme of failure. Picasso's 1968 etchings collectively depict wild, sexual, and other fantasies, in which he uses esteemed artists, such as Rembrandt, as avatars, casting himself as a voyeur. Rembrandt's own self-portraits equate to tragic physicality, the pain of his life's duress, deaths, and failures becoming the "gold" of his art, created from the mining of ignominious physiology—like Picasso, Rembrandt did not care for obvious beauty and can still shock people with his interest in what is considered "ugly." Picasso's depictions of Rembrandt within his etchings (he depicted Rembrandt many times during his career) were not just the honoring of an artist he revered; they were also meant to employ Rembrandt as a character player in the struggle between desire, propriety, ability, and failure. This was especially so towards the end of Picasso's life, as the artist's libido strutted and then crawled its way to the impotent death it feared so much. Rembrandt was, for Picasso, the acceptable representation of failure—the failure that Picasso so wished to avoid himself.

In HELMUT CRUMB (1998) and HOMAGE TO R. CRUMB, MY FATHER (2003), Warren references Robert Crumb, whose cartoons are another complex adjunct to this theme. Crumb's relationship with sexual failure and triumph is a horribly frank and funny one, which includes as much diminishment of women as any misogynist male (or misanthropist female) could wish for, but which also includes highly eroticized, appreciative affirmation of

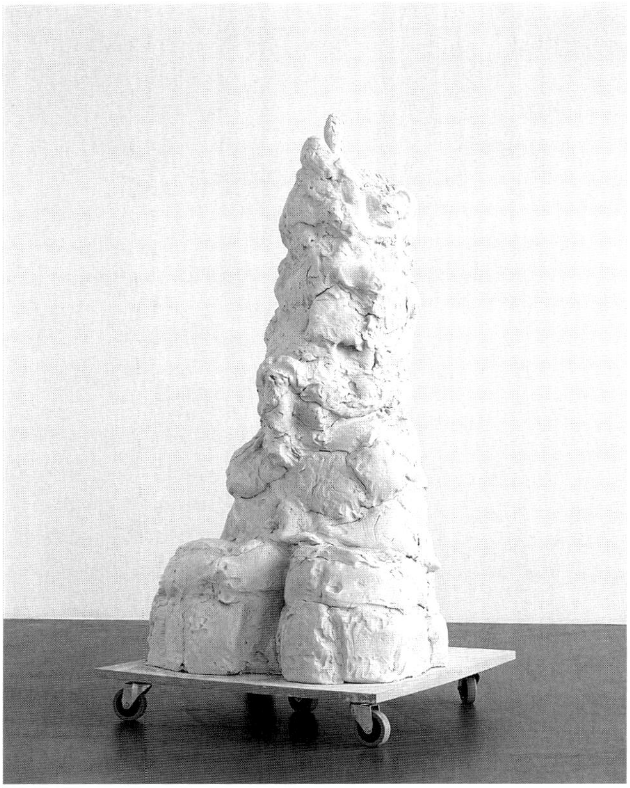

REBECCA WARREN, PRIVATE SCHMIDT, 2004, reinforced clay, MDF, wheels, 72 7/8 x 35 7/8 x 35 7/8" / SOLDAT SCHMIDT, verstärkter Ton, MDF, Räder, 185 x 91 x 91 cm.

the particular bodily types that are regarded so disfavorably in females these days: wide hips, thick goose-thighs, big bottoms, and general big-bonedness. Elements of many sexual *paraphilias* can be seen in Crumb's work, such as *Saliromania*, which is the deriving of erotic pleasure from soiling or spoiling the object of desire. (This may include tearing or damaging their clothing, covering them in mud or filth, or otherwise disheveling them—a fetish that can also involve the defacing of statues or pictures of attractive people, especially celebrities, and the forming of collections of defaced art.) Crumb, as a cartoonist, also summons ideas of *Schediaphilic* (more humorously known as *Toonophilia*), which is love or sexual arousal towards cartoon characters. Crumb's work, unlike Warren's, includes visceral hatreds, often towards conventionally beautiful women and the highly esteemed status they enjoy, and it is possible to consider Warren's appropriation of him as allusive of the need, or not, to "earn" or "deserve" love in this world—for men as well as women—much of it centered around exaggerated ideas of beauty.

Warren's work (as she has described it herself) is "mad and ugly" and conflicting feelings of the loveable and unlovable run throughout it. These feelings could include those of being unlovable but sexually desired, and of being attractive but deliberately repellent—both of these states being purposeful disruptions of the usual sense of things. A similar contrary principle can be seen in Warren's vitrines which, although usually peripheral to her work—they are always shown on the walls, never in the center of her exhibited works—display irregular aspirations. The strange contents of these containers are devoid of sense, purpose, or known value, but are accorded a condition of damaged importance. They are highly deliberated presentations, to which a hard-won neutrality of intonation is critical—a "mad neutrality," as important to her as a supposed even-handedness is to the institutional curator.

Even the wheeled plinths that support so many of Warren's larger sculptures are implicated in her sense of contrary failure. The wheels imply carefree movement (skateboarding, roller-skating or whatever) but also emphasize the heavy fatness, bodily weight, and inertia of her figures, which would need to be overcome in order for movement to be possible. Inability and, by extension, disability could be invoked by this—possibly creating a familial relationship between the wheeled plinths and wheelchairs. And themes of disability could relate to the idea that Rembrandt's SLAUGHTERED OX (1655)—a nude amputee, if ever there was one—is an art-historical antecedent for the potent category of expressive bodily limblessness in art, which would include works by Picasso, Warren, and Francis Bacon.

There are stylistic points of comparison between Warren and Bacon. These include a shared emphasis on reductive bodily physicality and truncated monstrousness, as well as similarities between Bacon's spermy, Vaseline smearings and Warren's slippery sexualizing of clay. That there could be "a female Francis Bacon" is a strangely appealing idea to consider, both in the abstract and in respect to Warren's work. But it wouldn't be correct to attempt to describe Warren as this impossible person. Unlike Bacon, her work is self-deprecating and not grandiose, and is infinitely wittier. More importantly, the idea of love—damaged and dysfunctional as this love might be—is not extinguished, and, in spite of all the debauchery and outrage, is characteristically the voice of Rebecca Warren.

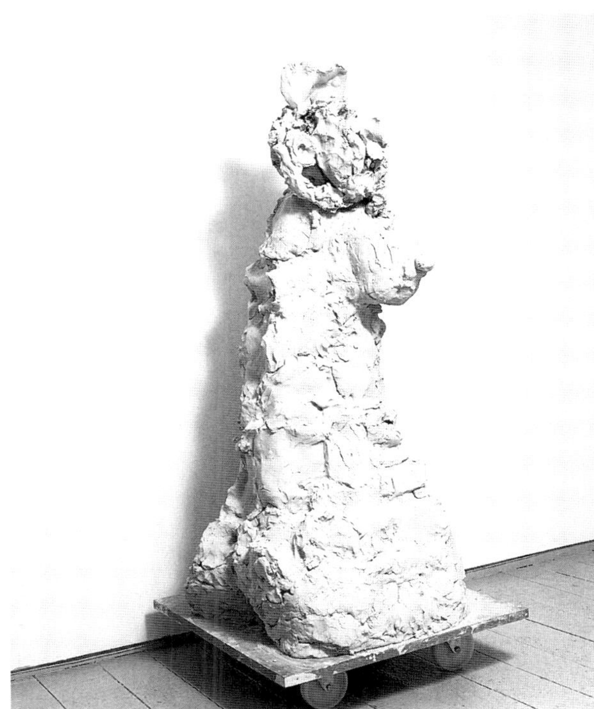

REBECCA WARREN, DEUTSCHE BANK, 2002, reinforced clay, MDF, wheels, 29 1/8 x 29 1/8 x 29 1/8" / verstärkter Ton, MDF, Räder, 166 x 74 x 74 cm.

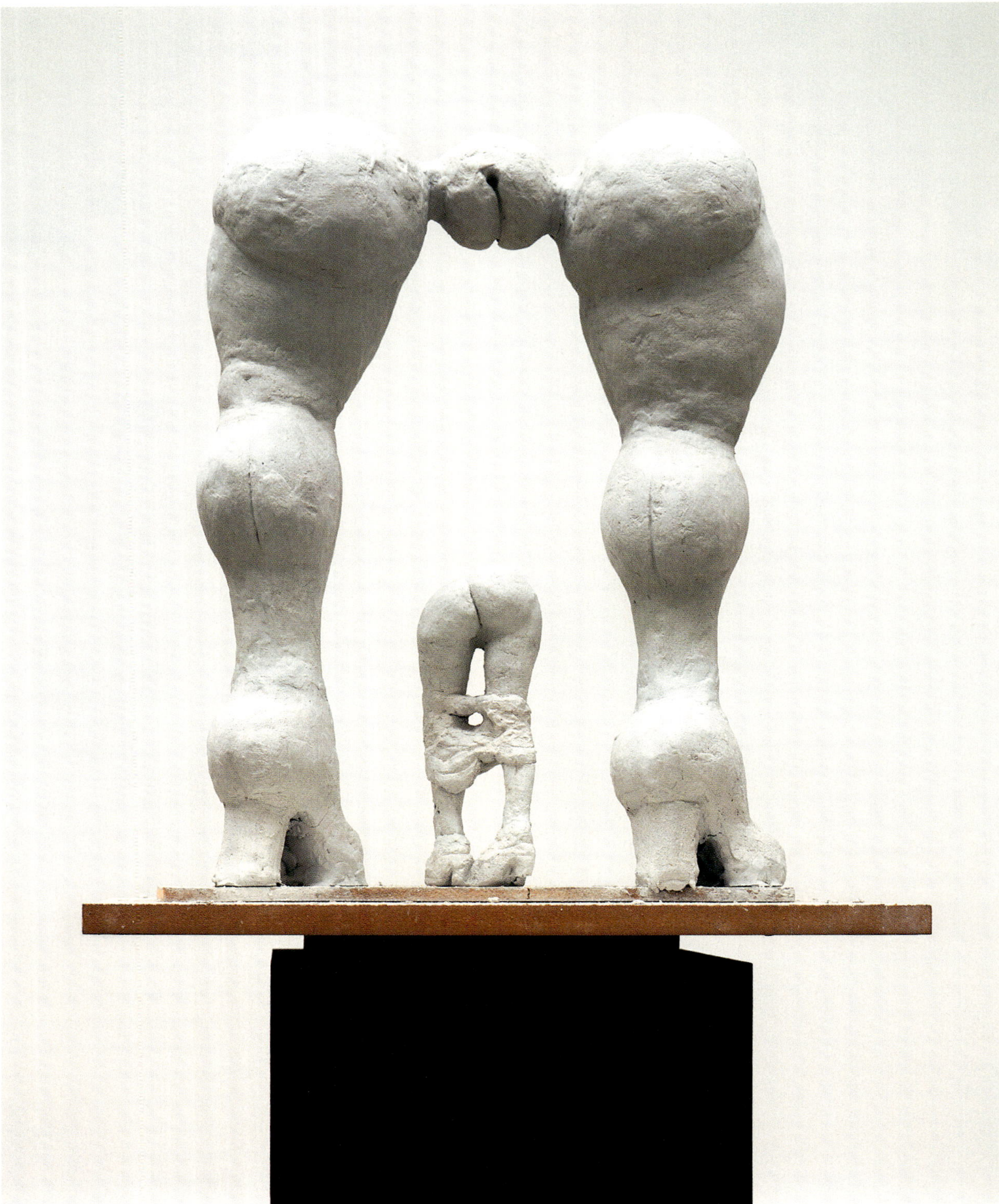

REBECCA WARREN, ROBERT CRUMB, 1998, reinforced clay, MDF, stacked plinths, 77 1/2 x 12 x 12" / verstärkter Ton, MDF, gestapelte Sockel, 196,9 x 30,5 x 30,5 cm.

Verrückt und hässlich

NEAL BROWN

Rebecca Warren bleibt mit ihren Arbeiten offenbar gern der eigenen Linie treu, und zusammen mit ihrem ironisch distanzierten oder dezidierten «Tonfall» begünstigt dies ihren Erfolg. Unbehelligt von der Ernsthaftigkeit rationaler Analyse kann sich die Tragikomödie missgestalter Lebensfreuden und -leiden im All von Warrens Unerschrockenheit in ekstatischer Schwerelosigkeit entfalten. Damit löst Warren auch das Problem, wie ein Künstler, und insbesondere eine Künstlerin, mit der Darstellung des nackten Körpers umgehen und gleichzeitig die autobiographische Deutung vermeiden kann. Es liegt auf der Hand, dass der Rückgriff auf Edgar Degas, Pablo Picasso, Auguste Rodin und Robert Crumb, den Warren in ihrer Arbeit wagt, auch bedeutet, Männer der härteren Sorte auf den Plan zu rufen, Männer, deren Künstlergenie mit einer (je nach Interpretationsweise) mehr oder weniger kruden Sexualprotzerei einhergeht. Aber Warren neutralisiert die von ihr verehrten Kunstgiganten durch eine kritische Distanz, die nichts mit dem Stockholm-Syndrom[1)] zu tun hat und auch nichts mit der furchtlosen Attitüde von Vertreterinnen der weiblichen Crème de la Crème der aktuellen britischen Kunst, wie Sarah Lucas oder Tracey Emin. Warrens Interesse für die von ihr zusammengetragenen klassischen Beuteobjekte männlicher Künstler – Übertreibungen des Geschlechtlichen in Gestalt unglaublicher Brüste und Körperobjekte – gewichtet dieses reduzierte Körperverständnis nicht stärker als alles Übrige, sodass etwas viel Universelleres und Traurigeres zum Vorschein kommt als nur sexuelle Triumphgebärden.

NEAL BROWN ist Künstler und Publizist und lebt in London. Er ist Autor des Katalogs *Tracey Emin* (Tate Modern, 2006) und kuratierte im Rahmen der Liverpool Biennial 2002 die Ausstellung «To the Glory of God: New Religious Art».

Zu Warrens Stoff gehören auch Kindheitsmotive, die sie in dem von ihr gerne verwendeten, jungfräulich weissen Ton umsetzt; es handelt sich um einen speziellen, selbsthärtenden Modellierton, der zwar mit der braunen Tonerde des Töpfers verwandt ist, aber nicht im Ofen gebrannt werden muss und daher seine feine Oberflächenbeschaffenheit beibehält. Die hübschen Pastellfarben, welche die Künstlerin manchmal auf dieses makellose Weiss aufträgt, die schlaffen Schleifen, welche ihre Figuren hin und wieder tragen, und die puppen-, spielzeug- oder trickfilmhafte Qualität zahlreicher Arbeiten, haben ihre Wurzeln in der Kindheit (einer zumeist weiblichen). Rein materiell ähnelt dieser weisse Ton gewissen Modelliermassen für Kinder, doch stilistisch gleicht er – in Warrens Händen – mehr den anarchischen kleinen Plastilinskulpturen, Krümelhaufen und Kaugummiresten, die Kinder gern zurücklassen. Ein solch Gestalt gewordener Missklang ist auch Warrens Appropriation von Degas' berühmter kleiner Ballerina, PETITE DANSEUSE DE QUATORZE ANS (Kleine vierzehnjährige Tänzerin, 1880–81), welche sie in den Arbeiten THE TWINS (Die Zwillinge, 2004) und COME, HELGA (Komm, Helga, 2006) selbst wiederum subversiv unterläuft, indem sie die sensible bescheidene Position der Ballerina gleich zweimal durch eine tölpelhafte, ungestalte körperliche Gestalt ersetzt.

Wie bei vielen Leuten und aus den verschiedensten Gründen – ob biologischen, sozialen, oder zufälligen – läuft manches schief, wenn die Pubertät den Übergang von der autonomen Aktivität des Kindes zum reaktiven Verhalten und Selbstbewusstsein des jugendlichen Erwachsenen ankündigt. Die Folgen können Selbstzweifel, Scham, Unsicherheit, Depression und Angst sein. Obwohl besonders Frauen unter geschlechtsspezifischen Erwartungen und dem Perfektionismus der Modezeitschriften zu leiden haben, gibt es eine Art von Desillusionierung und Kollaps der Selbstwahrnehmung in Bezug auf den eigenen Körper, die nicht geschlechtsspezifisch ist und auf mangelndes Selbstwertgefühl zurückgeht. Diese Krise der körperlichen Selbstachtung trifft Männer genauso wie Frauen, für welche die Störung des Gleichgewichts zwischen erotischer und romantischer Sexualität, äusserer Erscheinung und eigener Identität allerdings zu einer übermächtigen Erfahrung werden kann. Diese Vorgänge können auf tragische Weise komisch sein, aber auch katastrophale Folgen haben; Warrens DEUTSCHE BANK (2002), PRIVATE SCHMIDT (Soldat Schmidt, 2004) oder LOG LADY (Lady mit Baumstamm, 2003) weisen Aspekte solch dysphorischer Zusammenbrüche auf. Die Kunst – Lehm – ist als Medium sehr geeignet, um die physische Körperlichkeit darzustellen und zu überbieten: die rasenden Hinterbacken, Schamlippen, Brustwarzen, Klitorisfalten und Penisse in Warrens Arbeiten sind Teil einer verrückten, zusammenhanglosen, physischen Aneinanderreihung. Kaum ist der weiche Ton unter Warrens Händen zu etwas jubelnd-wollüstig-lustvoll-fleischlich-autoerotisch Genussvollem geraten, werden die Figuren und Sockelarbeiten mit den Fingern bearbeitet, misshandelt und zerquetscht, sodass etwas triebhaft-chaotisch-masturbatorisch-fett-hässlich-angewidert-unterdrückt-inkontinent-exkretorisch-bestialisch-bulimisch-zusammengebrochen-verkatert/heruntergekommen-unidentifizierbar-abscheulich Erniedrigtes und Selbstkritisches entsteht. Mit anderen Worten, ihre Kunst ist ein mit vielen Adjektiven befrachtetes Chaos zum Thema Körperlichkeit, wobei das Lustvolle weniger wichtig ist als das Freudlose.

Es gibt komplexe psychologische Entsprechungen zwischen dem Picasso, auf den Warren in Arbeiten wie SHE (Sie, 2003) Bezug nimmt, und dem Rembrandt, den Picasso in den Radierungen seiner SERIE 347 (1968) mehrmals zitiert, und sie führen zu einer unwahrscheinlichen Übereinstimmung zwischen allen drei Künstlern im Hinblick auf das Thema des Scheiterns. Picassos Radierungen aus dem Jahr 1968 zeigen allesamt wilde sexuelle und andere Phantasien, für die er von ihm geschätzte Künstler wie Rembrandt als Avatars benutzt und selbst in die Rolle des Voyeurs schlüpft. Rembrandts eigene Selbstporträts spiegeln die Tragik des Körperlichen, den Schmerz seines harten Lebens, wobei Todesfälle und Misserfolge zum Schatz seiner Kunst wurden, was er der Ausbeutung der schändlichen physiologischen Fakten verdankte; denn wie für Picasso barg das offensichtlich Schöne für Rembrandt keinen Reiz, und seine Vorliebe für das allgemein als hässlich Empfundene vermag die Leute bis heute vor den Kopf zu stossen. Die Darstellungen von Rembrandt in Picassos Radierungen (Picasso hat Rembrandt im Lauf seines Lebens mehrmals dargestellt) sind keine blosse Reverenz an den verehrten Künstler, sondern hatten auch die Funktion, Rembrandt eine tragende Rolle im Kampf zwischen Begehren, Anstand, Können und Scheitern spielen zu lassen. Das gilt insbesondere für Picassos letzten Lebensabschnitt, als die Libido des Künstlers sich nochmals aufbäumte, um dann doch dem so gefürchteten, impotenten Tod zu ergeben. Rembrandt war für Picasso ein akzeptables Bild des Scheiterns – eines Scheiterns, dem Picasso so verzweifelt zu entkommen suchte.

In HELMUT CRUMB (1998) und HOMAGE TO R. CRUMB, MY FATHER (Hommage an R. Crumb, meinen Vater, 2003) nimmt Warren Bezug auf Robert Crumb, dessen Cartoons ein weiteres komplexes Kapitel zum selben Thema darstellen. Crumbs Verhältnis zu sexuellem Versagen und Triumph ist erschreckend freimütig und lustig und so frauenfeindlich, wie ein männlicher Frauenfeind (oder eine menschenfeindliche Frau) es sich nur wünschen kann, es bringt jedoch auch eine hoch erotische Wertschätzung bestimmter Körpertypen zum Ausdruck, die heute gemeinhin nicht als vorteilhaft gelten: breite Hüften, fette Taillen, grosse Ärsche und einen derben Körperbau. In Crumbs Arbeiten finden sich zahlreiche Beispiele diverser abweichender sexueller Vorlieben, so etwa die *Saliromanie*, den erotischen Lustgewinn durch Besudeln oder Beflecken des begehrten Objektes. (Auch das Zerreissen oder Beschädigen der Kleidung kann dazu gehören, indem man sie mit Schmutz und Kot bekleckert oder sonstwie zerfleddert – eine Manie, die bis zum Schänden der Gesichter bei Statuen führen kann oder von Bildern attraktiver Leute, besonders von Berühmtheiten, oder gar zum Anlegen ganzer Sammlungen aus Kunstwerken mit zerstörten Gesichtern.) Crumb bringt in seinen Cartoons auch die Idee der *Schediaphilie* auf (von griech. *schediasma*, humoristisch auch *Toonophilie* bzw. *Cartoonophilie* genannt), die Liebe zu Comicfiguren bezie-

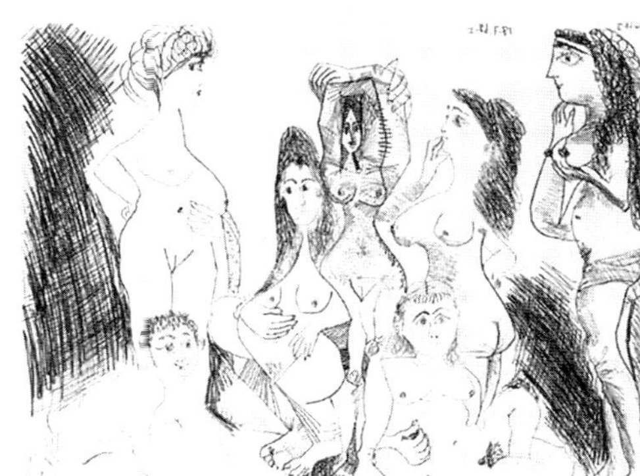

PABLO PICASSO,
from the 347 series, 1968, etching /
aus der Serie 347, Radierung

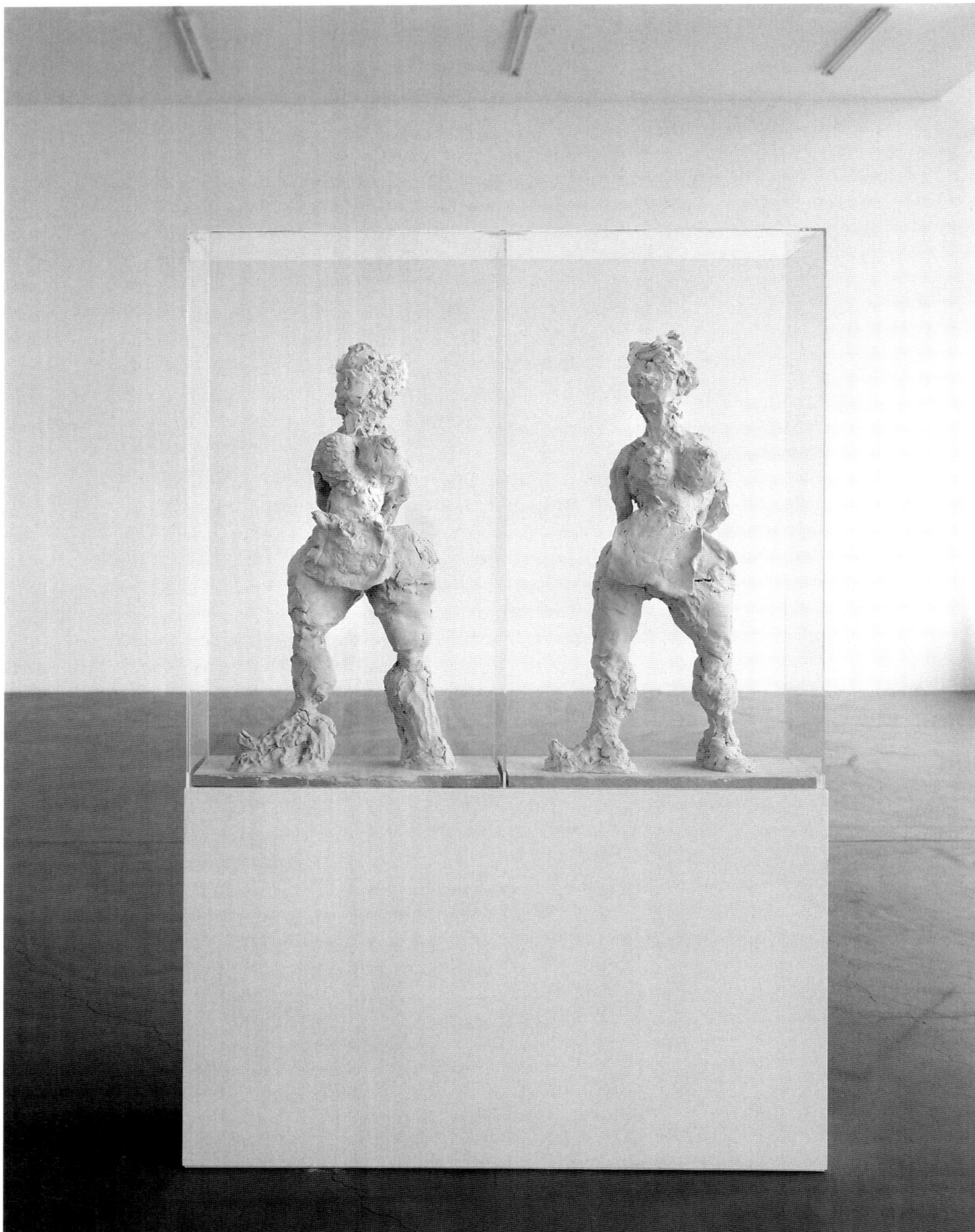

REBECCA WARREN, THE TWINS, 2004, reinforced clay, perspex vitrine, plinth, 78 3/4 x 52 x 14 1/8" / DIE ZWILLINGE, verstärkter Ton, Plexiglas-Vitrine und Sockel, 200 x 132 x 36 cm.

hungsweise die sexuelle Erregung durch dieselben. Anders als bei Warren gibt es bei Crumb abgrundtiefe Hassgefühle, die sich oft gegen konventionell schöne Frauen richten und gegen die hohe Wertschätzung, die sie geniessen; man könnte Warrens Rückgriff auf Crumb auch als Anspielung auf das Bedürfnis – von Männern wie Frauen – verstehen, schon auf dieser Welt Liebe zu «verdienen» (als verdienter Lohn oder moralisches Grundrecht), bei welchem übertriebene Schönheitsideale meist eine zentrale Rolle spielen.

Warrens Werk ist laut ihrer eigenen Beschreibung «verrückt und hässlich» und voller widerstreitender Gefühle darüber, was liebenswert ist und was nicht. Dazu könnte auch das Gefühl gehören, zwar nicht liebenswert, aber sexuell begehrenswert zu sein, oder das Gefühl, wohl attraktiv zu sein, sich aber bewusst abstossend zu verhalten: In beiden Fällen findet eine bewusste Störung des üblichen Sachverhalts statt. Ein ähnliches Widerspruchsprinzip ist in Warrens Vitrinen zu erkennen, die, obwohl sie im Gesamtwerk eine eher periphere Rolle spielen – sie werden immer entlang von Wänden gezeigt und stehen nie im Zentrum einer Ausstellung –, Bestrebungen zeigen, die aus dem Rahmen fallen. Die seltsamen Inhalte dieser Behälter sind jeglichen Sinns, Zwecks oder erkennbaren Wertes beraubt, und doch wird ihnen eine leicht verminderte Bedeutung zugebilligt. Es handelt sich um extrem ausgeklügelte Präsentationen, bei denen ein hart erarbeiteter neutraler «Tonfall» entscheidend ist – eine verrückte Neutralität, die der Künstlerin so wichtig ist, wie dem Museumskurator seine vorgebliche Unvoreingenommenheit.

Selbst die mit Rollen bestückten Sockel, auf denen viele von Warrens grösseren Skulpturen stehen, hängen mit ihrem Sinn für das widerspenstige Scheitern zusammen. Die Rollen implizieren sorglose Bewegung (Skateboardfahren, Rollschuhlaufen oder was auch immer), unterstreichen jedoch gleichzeitig die Grösse und Schwere, das Körpergewicht und die Unbeweglichkeit ihrer Figuren, die es zu überwinden gilt, wenn man sie bewegen will. Damit ist vielleicht ein an Behinderung grenzendes Unvermögen angesprochen – womit eine direkte Verwandtschaft zwischen den Rollsockeln und Rollstühlen angedeutet wird. Körperliche Behinderung als Thema bringt einen zudem auf den Gedanken, dass Rembrandts GESCHLACHTETER OCHSE (1655), ein nackter amputierter Körper par excellence, ein kunsthistorischer Vorläufer der potenten Kategorie expressiver Körperdarstellungen mit fehlenden Gliedmassen sein könnte, zu der auch Werke von Picasso, Warren und Francis Bacon gehören.

Es gibt stilistische Vergleichspunkte zwischen Warren und Bacon. Dazu gehören die gemeinsame Betonung einer aufs Physische reduzierten Körperlichkeit und einer verstümmelten Monstrosität ebenso wie die Ähnlichkeiten zwischen Bacons an Sperma erinnerndes Vaseline-Geschmiere und Warrens schlüpfriger Sexualisierung der Modelliermasse. Dass es tatsächlich einen «weiblichen Francis Bacon» geben könnte, ist eine seltsam ansprechende Idee, sowohl abstrakt betrachtet als auch mit Hinblick auf Warrens Werk. Doch es wäre nicht richtig, Warren als diese unmögliche Person beschreiben zu wollen. Im Gegensatz zu Bacons Werk ist ihres bescheiden, nicht pompös und weitaus witziger. Aber wichtiger noch: Die Idee der Liebe – wie beschädigt und gestört diese Liebe auch sein mag – wird nicht ausgelöscht und ist trotz aller Ausschweifungen und Übertreibungen kennzeichnend für die Stimme von Rebecca Warren.

(Übersetzung: Suzanne Schmidt)

1) *Stockholm-Syndrom*: das psychologische Phänomen, dass Opfer ein positives emotionales Verhältnis zum Täter aufbauen und mit ihm sympathisieren, kooperieren, ja sich vielleicht sogar in ihn verlieben.

PRESSURE ZONE

MARTIN HERBERT

BoBo came home in bad shape. Cigarettes had been stubbed out on his body, hot tea spilled down his back. His previously sharp contours had gone soft and incoherent, due to endless sluicings of water over his powdery skin. Parts of him had been snapped off and tossed in the box alongside his ravaged body when the technicians sent him back from the foundry. To be fair, it wasn't their job to take care of him—he was, after all, merely the raw clay cast for a bronze sculpture, and assumedly expendable—and, to be fairer, he'd *arrived* in bad shape, thanks to the ministrations of his maker, Rebecca Warren.

The resultant bronze, BOBO (2006), Warren's latest stab at the medium, makes that clear enough. It is, on one level, a burlesque of a commemorative statue, the subject wearing a patriarchal beard, a serious expression, and his neck angled just so: dreaming of posterity. But some inner ridiculousness or pomp (and here it is perhaps worth noting that while Warren won't say where the title came from, "BoBo" is a moderately recent neologism designating a "bourgeois bohemian") appears to be rising up and wrecking his big moment, making him appear hysterically unworthy of an everlasting memorial. His body is contorted and gnarled like ancient roots. His single foot—faint shades of Giacometti—is clodhopping, huge, its big toe pointing skyward. He seems to be wearing a skirt and a conical party hat. A final bathetic touch: His warped, outstretched arm supports a precariously balanced twig.

In Warren's art, however, what you can hold onto in iconographical terms counts for less than what you can't, and what matters most are the implications and effects of her refusals. When she got back the ruined cast of BOBO, for example, she began working back into it, piling more febrile, finger-worked masses of clay onto its already-exploited armature—generally speaking this is not done, but Warren never saw a restriction she didn't immediately want to transgress—and the result was given a title intentionally difficult to pronounce: DOU DOU CHÉ (2006). The lower half, particularly the huge foot and upraised toe, is recognizable from its predecessor. From thereon up, however, the figure has turned appreciably ladylike, notwithstanding the tartan cloth covering her chest. She wears a bow in her hair, which has been colored; this, as with the applied textile, feels like something of a formal no-no. She is a touch more graceful than BOBO, but still a wreck.

As such, she joins the parade of unlovely female figures that have emerged from Warren's studio since 1998's HELMUT CRUMB, an architectonic merger of imagery by counterculture cartoonist

MARTIN HERBERT is a writer and critic based in Tunbridge Wells, Kent.

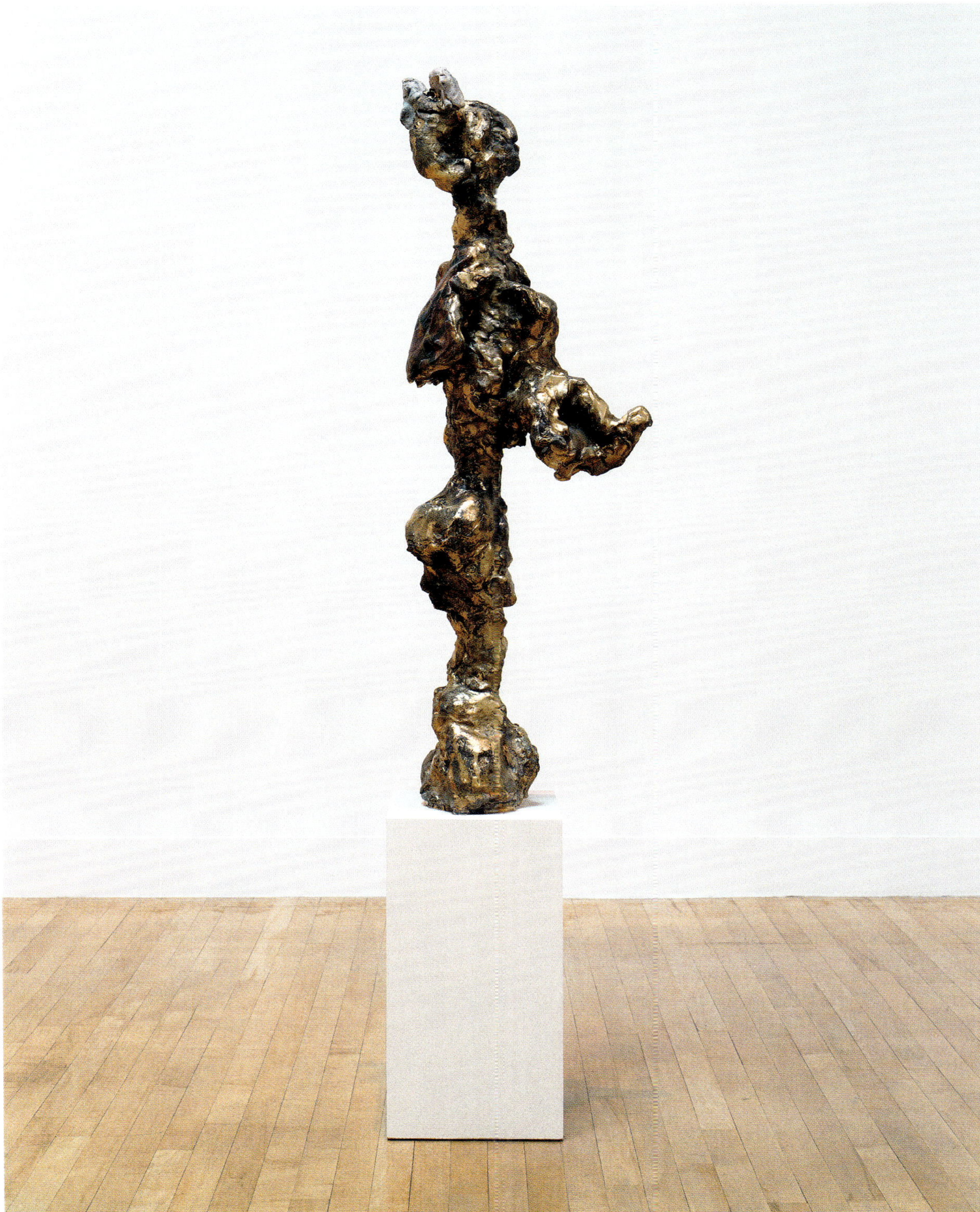

REBECCA WARREN, DOU DOU CHÉ, 2006, bronze, 47 1/4 x 15 3/4 x 17 3/4" / Bronze, 126 x 43 x 37 cm.

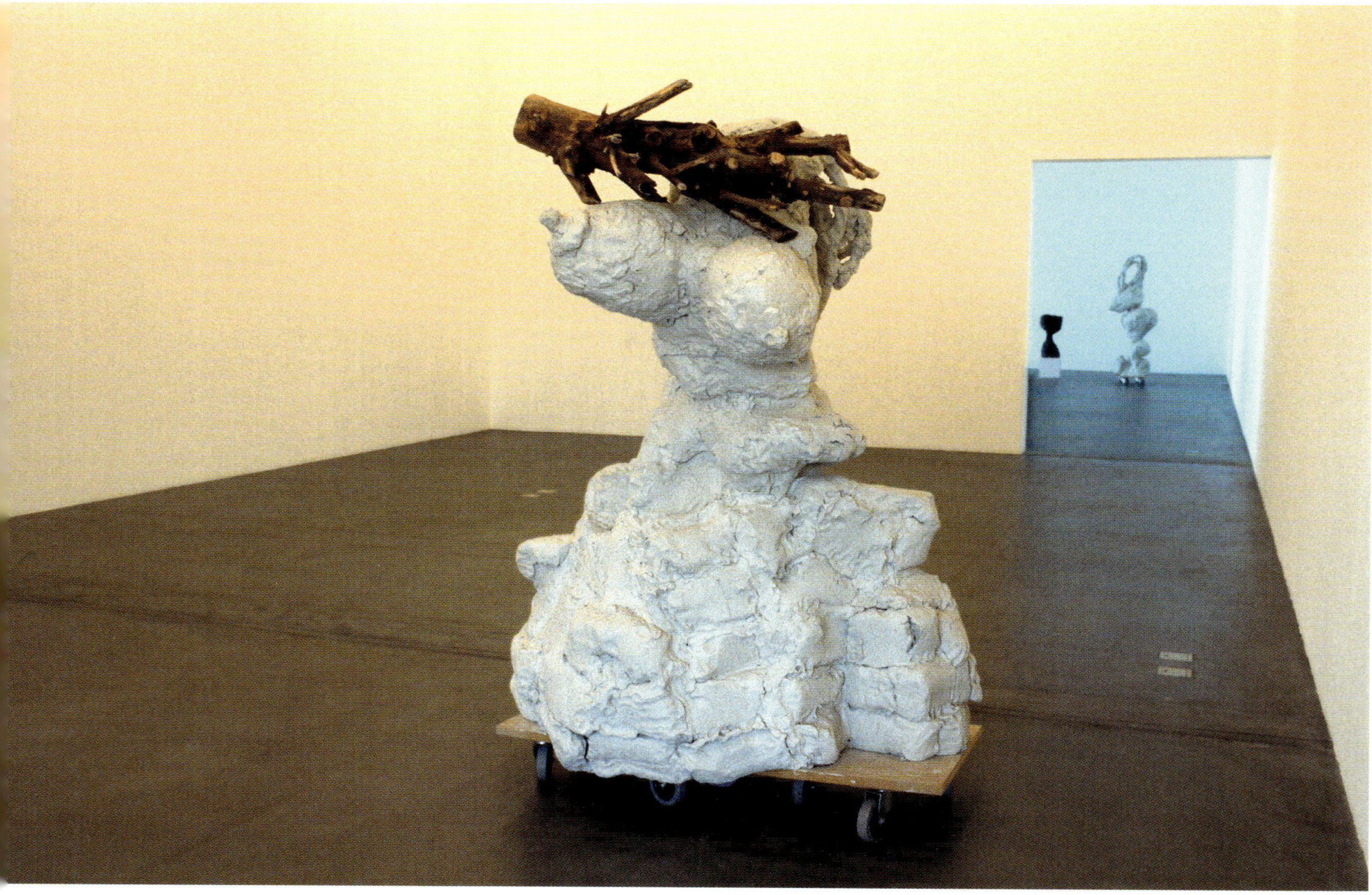

REBECCA WARREN, "Dark Passage", 2004, exhibition view Kunsthalle Zurich, from left to right: LOG LADY, THE LIGHT OF THE WORLD, TEACHER (M.B.), PRIVATE SCHMIDT / Ausstellungsansicht, von links nach rechts: BAUMSTAMM-FRAU, DAS LICHT DER WELT, LEHRER (M.B.), SOLDAT SCHMIDT.

Robert Crumb and the photographer Helmut Newton that bluntly objectifies the female form. Malignly wishful representations of women by male artists have long been in the foreground of her art (as, to an extent, have others by Hollywood cinema: see the 2003 series collectively entitled *She*, after the 1965 film starring Ursula Andress, and the gold-painted recumbent figure SAPERSTEIN, 2004, named in tribute to the Satanist doctor in *Rosemary's Baby*). One extended engagement has been with Edgar Degas' wax fetish of a pubescent ballerina, the LITTLE DANCER AGED FOURTEEN (1880–81), which was never cast by the artist during his lifetime but kept close to hand in his studio. Its phantasmal presence—proportions inflated into Crumb-like voluptuousness—haunts Warren's PONY (2003) and the double sculpture THE TWINS (2004), and is distantly echoed in DOU DOU CHÉ and several other recent bronzes. It is insufficient to say, however, that as a female artist appropriating such imagery she is simply charging these males with a predatory sexism. Her art is not *a priori* analytic in that way (and nor can those practitioners' undeniable artistry be so easily separated from their attitudes—a confliction that propels Warren's own art). Rather it is a tool for treating external forces with some kind of disguised grace under pressure, whether they be those of sexual inequality, the seductive authority of an artistic forebear who may also appear unreconstructed, or the latent conventions of art-making.

In responding to these anxieties, Warren's practice, while it seems superficially aggressive, might be more correctly read as a sophisticated, modular system of circumventions and defenses against them—and against a symbolic possession through total comprehension. Take LOG LADY (2003), a headless and armless cracked-clay female figure wearing what appears to be a billowing skirt, a densely branched log balanced on her gravity-defying breasts. Crumb, the notorious woman-decapitator (see, for example, his 1991 comic strip *A Bitchin' Bod!*, which even the cartoonist claims to find discomfiting), is once again in there. So is David Lynch's television series *Twin Peaks* (1990–91), in which the Log Lady was a character, one brimful of secrets. Beyond this, in intent the work remains something of an enigma—indeed, you could almost imagine it in a De Chirico painting—resisting positioning in a conceptual schema. Aspects of it seem on the cusp of transformation, as when one begins to discern miniaturized legs in the dress. LOG LADY seems monumental but also, due to the seemingly fragile medium, on the verge of falling apart; she sits there, a quandary. The sculpture rests on chipboard fitted with castors, as if its own lack of conceptual fixity, its mobility, were being analogized on a material level.

You don't know, as you never really know with Warren, what this work expresses about her feelings on any of its reference points, or on gender politics, but you can sense her own current not-knowing and desire for clarification, perhaps aided by making such an obtuse object. A work such as this is, on one level, a hand raised, requesting forbearance while she works it out. In the meantime, Warren places you in the midst of flux and provisionality. In 1914, Sigmund Freud (whose photograph appeared on the cover of her Kunsthalle Zurich catalogue in 2004, and who is not only one of many looming father figures in her art but also, of course, formulator of the Oedipus Complex) characterized his psychoanalytic method in terms of "remembering, repeating, and working through." This doesn't seem irrelevant to Warren's reactive, performative methodology. For a

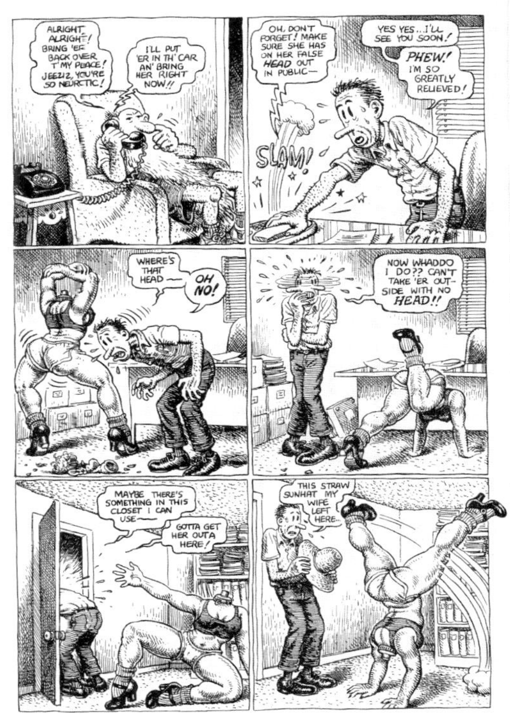

ROBERT CRUMB, *from A Bitchin' Bod! / Ein Hurenstück!*, 1992. (COPYRIGHT BY ROBERT CRUMB, 1992)

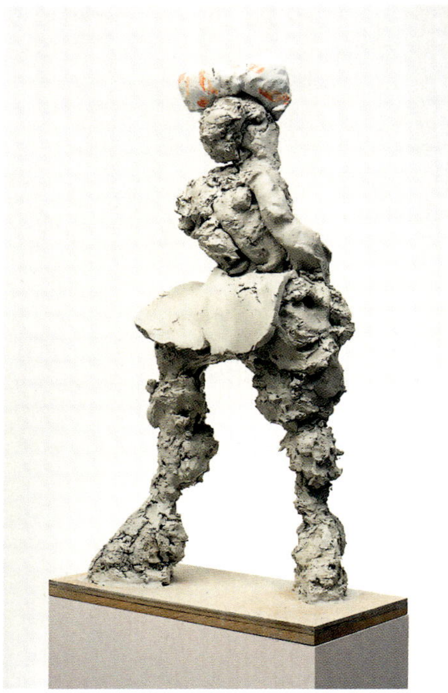

REBECCA WARREN, PONY, 2003, reinforced clay, acrylic paint, plinth, 37 x 10 5/8 x 22 1/2" / Verstärkter Ton, Acrylfarbe, Sockel, 94 x 27 x 57 cm.

long time, her work has involved something resembling an inquisitive inhabiting of artistic practices of the past—trying them on for size and often trying several on at once, as if rifling through a dress-up box found in a dusty attic.

There are signs, however, that she's starting to drop these borrowed mantles. For evidence one might note the increased prevalence in her oeuvre of the parallel stream of small-scale sculptural arrangements—mixtures of preserved studio detritus, swirls of neon, and crafted chunks of clay—that Warren inaugurated in 1996 with EVERY ASPECT OF BITCH MAGIC. A slightly later example, BITCH MAGIC: THE MUSICAL (2001–03) serves to illustrate how these fragile systems work. With its apparently painstakingly arranged, almost painterly composition of painted clay forms and a loop of rosy neon inside a glassed plinth, it at first suggests some kind of feminine voodoo or gris-gris. But it can also be interpreted as a set of narrative feints in relation to sculptural display, as a confidence trick (What are these unlovely fragments worth, after all?), and, furthermore, as a display of bloody-mindedness: Warren, as so often, coyly places one part of the grouping on t o p of the glass, rather than inside it.

But this is also a model of layering which the work consequently performs in terms of tone: Spend time with BITCH MAGIC ... and a mood of protectiveness and sympathy towards its constituents comes through; you can imagine Warren having somehow saved them from oblivion, irrelevance, lack of use,

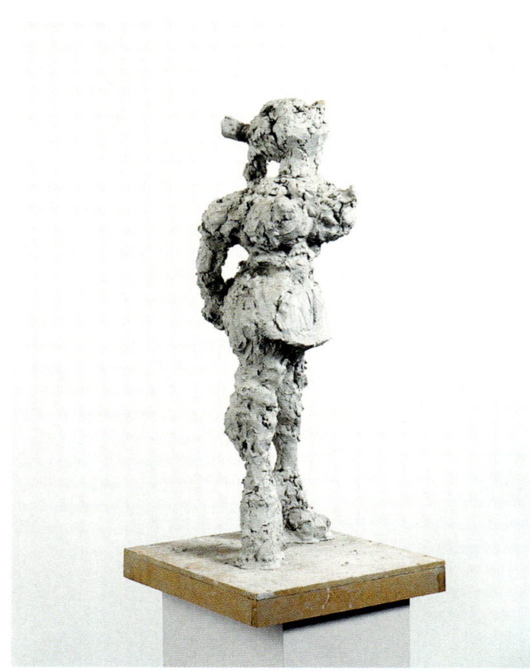

REBECCA WARREN, BUNNY, 2002, reinforcd clay, plinth, 28 7/8 x 15 x 13 5/8" / Verstärkter Ton, Sockel, 73,5 x 38 x 34,5 cm.

just as she saved BOBO's cast from the studio dustbin. These are tender emotions, and Warren clearly wants them to be a facet of her work. In order to smuggle them in, however—because, appearances to the contrary, there are powerful criteria concerning what is and isn't acceptable in a work of contemporary art, and part of Warren's renegade praxis is to expose them—she has perforce become a tactician.

This demonstrative autonomy inflects her figure sculptures too. They have become increasingly twitchy with life (compare the clean contours of HELMUT CRUMB with the raw and frantic surfaces of the fellatio scenario, THE PEARLS OF SWITZERLAND, 2004, seemingly produced from rolled and ripped up lengths of clay), their handcrafted surfaces privileging a fervent and nowadays verboten expressivity. That mortal connection, you feel, is something that Warren—who began to make art when the ruling dogma of detachment held that one had an idea first, then phoned up an artisan to realize it—loves and wanted to rescue. To accommodate it, she needed to set up an acceptable, superficial lattice of irony and abjection in relation to earlier art. Progressively, however, that armature is being dismantled, albeit without sacrificing an iota of the work's slippery ability to evade narrow categorizations. DOU DOU CHÉ et al may contain fleeting afterimages of other art (some of them impressively opaque: BOBO's balanced twig, for example, stems from similarly incongruous juxtapositions Warren saw in Rodin's studio), but they are finally answerable only to themselves.

All of which suggests that the artist has, to some extent, "worked through" her artistic crushes, shifting her focus to other pressures—what's expected of her as an artist in mid-career with a recognizable "style," for example; or what one should or shouldn't do with a particular medium; or how a female artist should represent the female form. It is in her response to this last example, and the friction she thereby sets up, that Warren's profoundest objective might, I believe, be glimpsed. Think again of Degas' LITTLE DANCER, of the advanced art of his era as a whole, its edge now blunted by familiarity and all that came after; try, so far as it is possible, to imagine that earlier era in all its bright and dangerous newness. If Warren's sculptures desire to echo anything from the past, it is that moment: the electric frisson of the modern in its nascence, transliterated here through the most irreducible aspects of the contemporary—a potent cocktail of ugly female strength, formal grotesquery, radical ambivalence of attitude, and generalized inconclusiveness—and leading to fundamental uncertainty punctuated by awkward laughter. To echo that moment and ensure that it reverberates for as long as possible remains an exhilarating problem—for her, and for us.

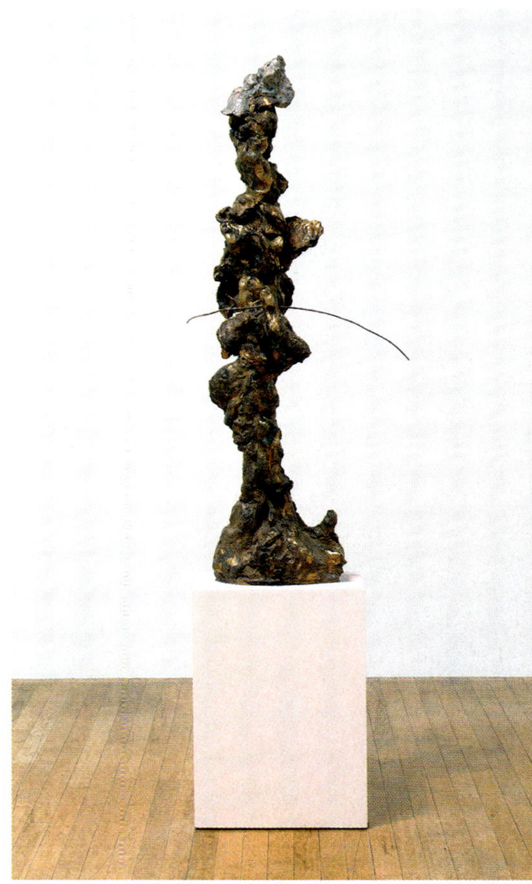

REBECCA WARREN, BOBO, 2006, bronze, acrylic paint, branch, 51 1/8 x 14 1/8 x 13"/ Bronze, Acrylfarbe, Ast, 130 x 36 x 33 cm.

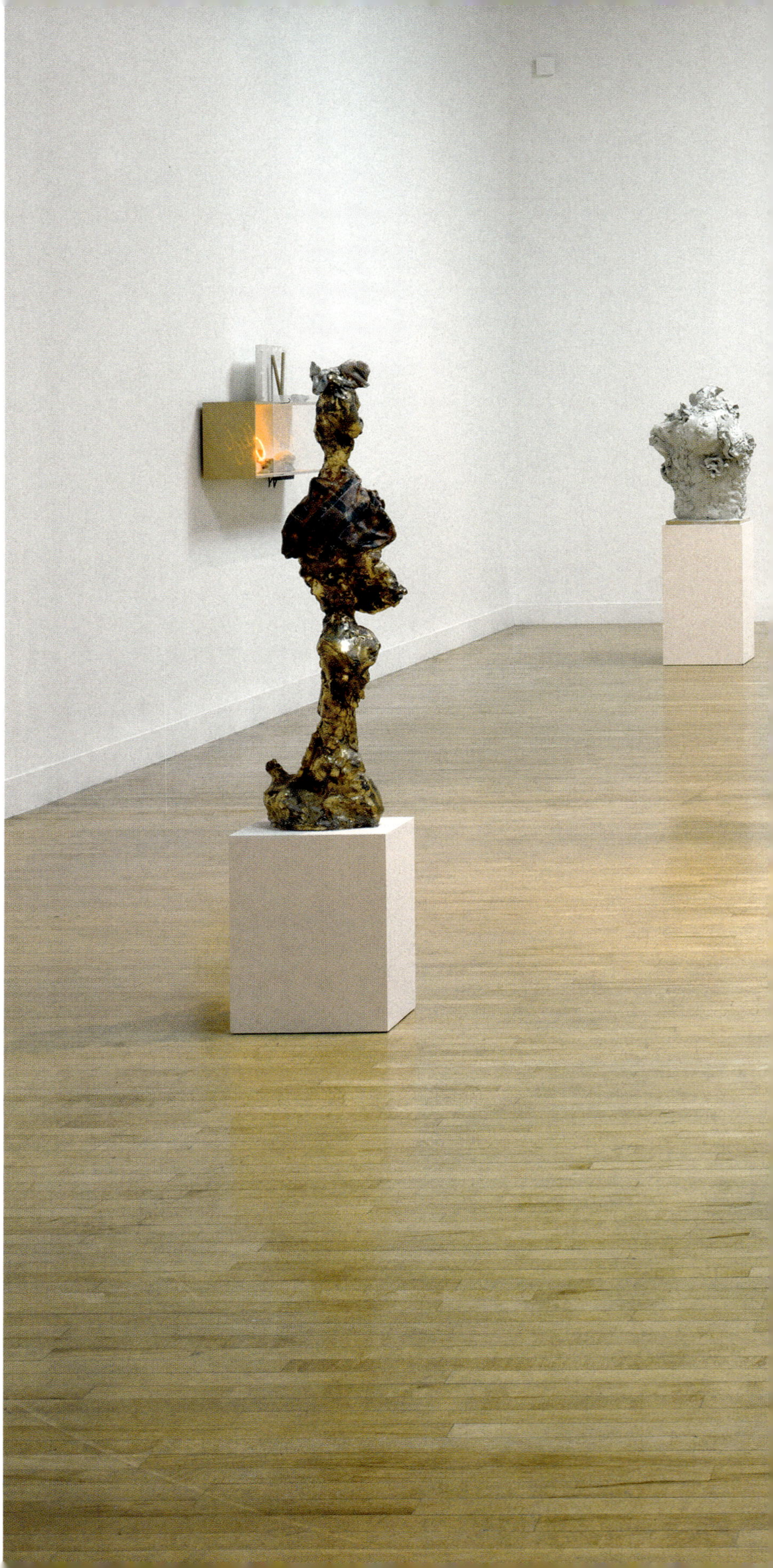

REBECCA WARREN, The Turner Prize, exhibition view, Tate Britain, 2005 / Ausstellungsansicht, Turner-Preis.

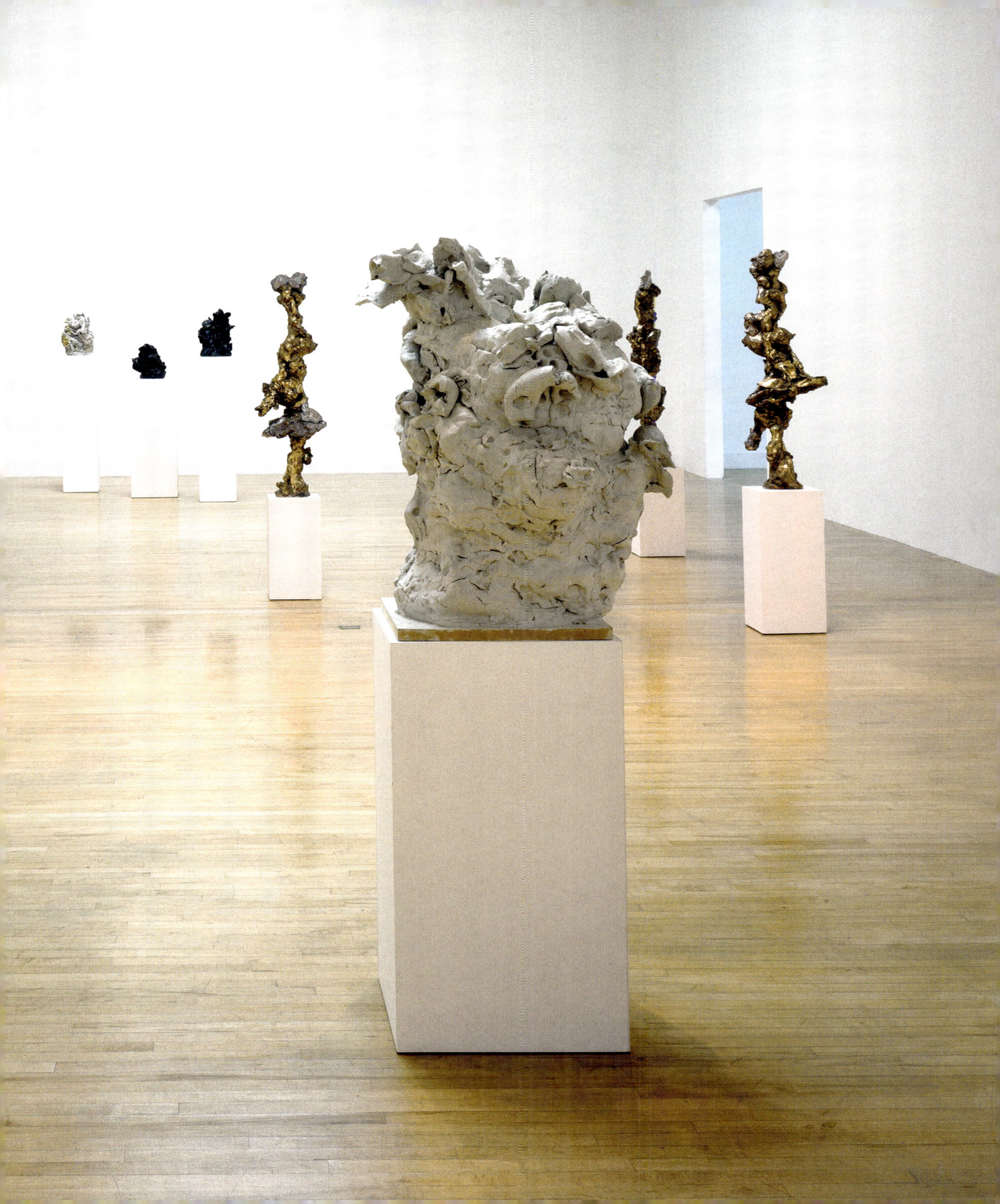

DRUCKSTELLEN

MARTIN HERBERT

BoBo kam übel zugerichtet nach Hause. Auf seinem Körper waren Zigaretten ausgedrückt und heisser Tee über seinen Rücken verschüttet worden. Seine ursprünglich klaren Konturen waren jetzt weich und aufgelöst, da die bröckelige Haut wiederholt mit Wasser abgespritzt wurde. Teile von ihm waren abgebrochen und in die Kiste neben seinen verwüsteten Körper geworfen worden, als die Arbeiter ihn aus der Giesserei zurückschickten. Um fair zu sein, muss man zugeben, dass es nicht ihre Aufgabe war, sich um ihn zu kümmern – schliesslich war er nur ein rohes Tonmodell für eine Bronzeskulptur und daher wohl Wegwerfware –, und um noch fairer zu sein, er war dort bereits in schlechtem Zustand angekommen, dafür hatte nämlich seine Schöpferin, Rebecca Warren, gesorgt.

In der daraus hervorgegangenen Bronze, BOBO (2006), Warrens erstem Versuch in diesem Medium, wird das mehr als deutlich. In gewissem Mass ist sie die Karikatur eines Denkmalstandbildes: Mit ihrem Patriarchenbart, dem ernsten Ausdruck und gestrecktem Nacken scheint sie von der Nachwelt zu träumen. Doch eine innere Lächerlichkeit oder Pompositát scheint sich gegen die Figur zu wenden, ihr grosses Moment zu zerstören und lässt sie, als eines für die Ewigkeit bestimmten Denkmals, eklatant unwürdig erscheinen (dabei dürfte es aufschlussreich sein, anzumerken, dass «BoBo» ein nicht mehr ganz neuer Neologismus für den «bourgeois bohemian», den bürgerlichen Bohemien, ist, obwohl Warren nicht verraten will, wie sie auf den Titel kam). BOBOs Körper ist krumm und knorrig wie altes Wurzelgeflecht. Sein einziger Fuss – eine vage Erinnerung an Giacometti – ist ungestalt, riesig, der grosse Zeh zeigt himmelwärts. Er scheint einen Rock zu tragen und einen Spitzhut aus Pappe. Und ein definitiv lächerlicher Zug: Sein knorriger, ausgestreckter Arm balanciert einen Zweig, der jeden Moment herunterzufallen droht.

Bei Warrens Werken kommt es jedoch weniger darauf an, worauf man sich in ikonographischer Hinsicht verlassen kann, als worauf man sich nicht verlassen kann, und am wichtigsten sind die Implikationen und Auswirkungen ihrer Verweigerungen. Als sie beispielsweise das kaputte Modell von BOBO zurückbekam, begann sie es zu bearbeiten und klatschte noch febrilere, mit den Fingern bearbeitete Tonmassen auf die schon einmal benutzte Armierung – im Allgemeinen tut man das nicht, aber Warren ist noch auf keine Einschränkung gestossen, über die sie sich nicht flugs hinweggesetzt hätte; das Resultat, das einen bewusst schwierig auszusprechenden Titel bekam, war DOU DOU CHÉ (2006). Die untere Hälfte, besonders der riesige Fuss und der aufgestellte grosse Zeh, stammt erkennbar vom Vor-

MARTIN HERBERT ist Autor und Kritiker. Er lebt in Tunbrigde Wells, Kent.

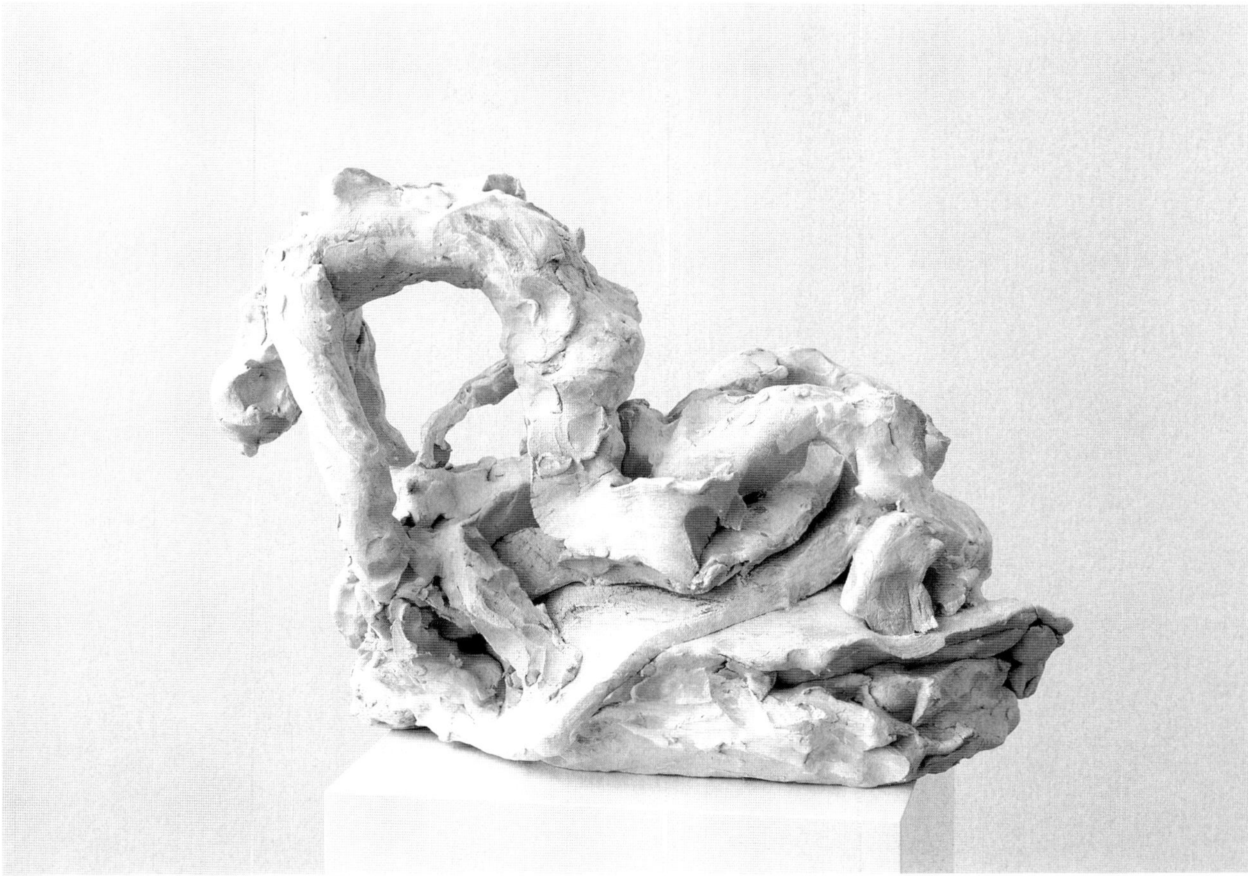

REBECCA WARREN, THE PEARLS OF SWITZERLAND, 2004 reinforced clay, acrylic paint, 14 5/8 x 15 3/4 x 9 1/2" / DIE PERLEN DER SCHWEIZ, verstärkter Ton, Acrylfarbe, 37 x 40 x 24 cm.

gänger. Doch im oberen Teil ist die Figur merklich damenhafter geworden, ungeachtet des über die Brust gelegten Tuchs aus Schottenstoff. Sie trägt eine Schleife im gefärbten Haar; das erweckt, genau wie das hinzugefügte Stoffteil, den Eindruck eines formalen Tabubruchs. Sie ist um eine Nuance graziöser als BOBO, aber noch immer ein Wrack.

Als solches fügt sie sich nahtlos ein in die Parade unattraktiver Frauenfiguren, die aus Warrens Atelier entsprungen sind, angefangen bei HELMUT CRUMB 1998, einer architektonischen Verschmelzung der Bildsprachen von Subkultur-Cartoonist Robert Crumb und Photograph Helmut Newton, beide degradierten die weibliche Gestalt in ausgesprochen kruder Weise zum Objekt. Unsägliche Frauenwunschbilder männlicher Künstler standen lange im Vordergrund von Warrens Arbeit. (Bis zu einem gewissen Grad gilt das auch für solche aus der Filmfabrik Hollywoods: etwa im Fall der Serie aus dem Jahr 2003 mit dem Titel *She* (Sie) – nach dem gleichnamigen Film von 1965 mit Ursula Andress in der Hauptrolle – oder im Fall der golden bemalten, liegenden Figur, SAPERSTEIN, 2004, benannt nach dem satanistischen Arzt in *Rosemary's Baby.*) Auch mit Edgar Degas' Wachsfetisch einer pubertierenden Ballerina hat sie sich eingehend auseinandergesetzt: Die PETITE

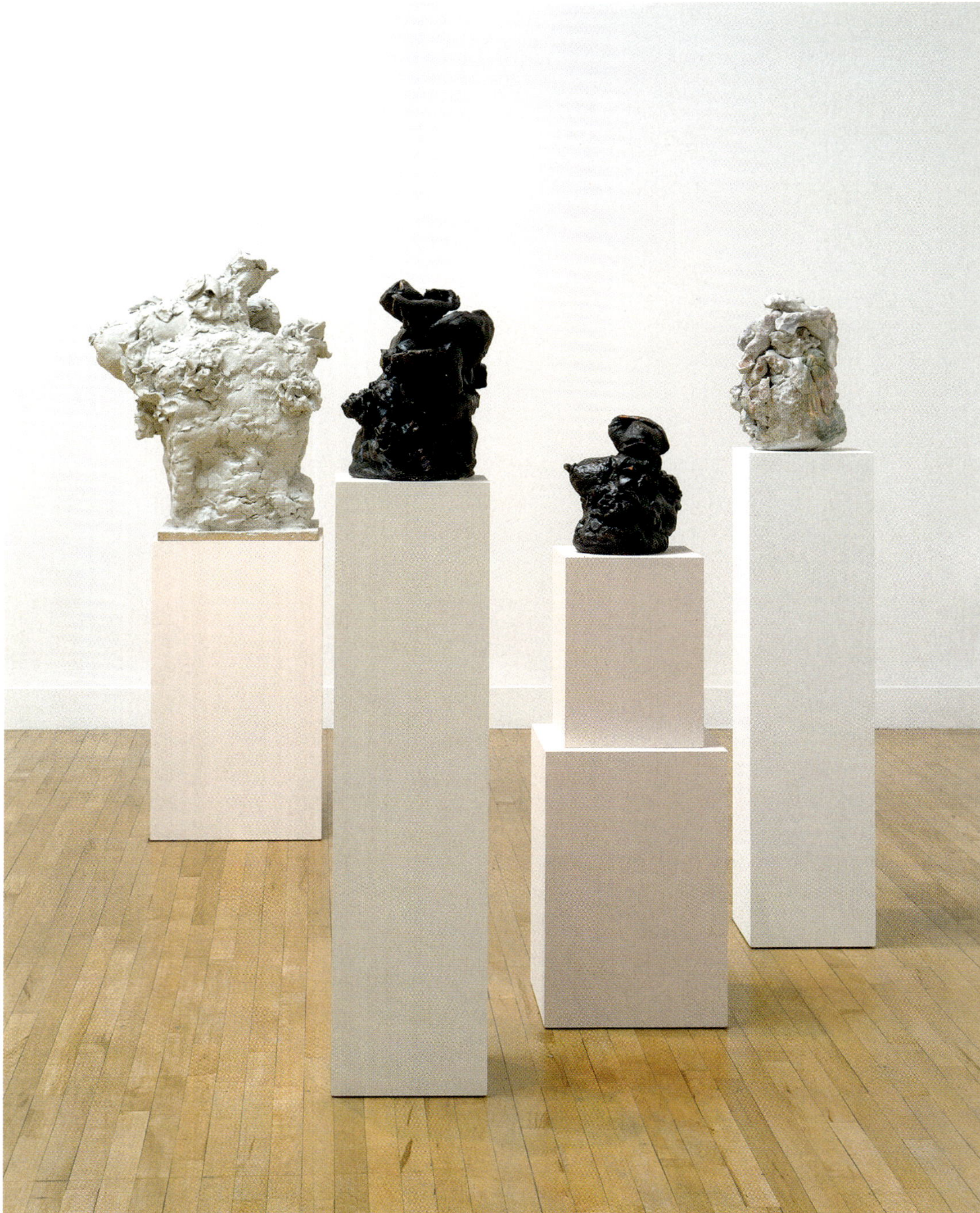

REBECCA WARREN, *The Turner Prize*, exhibition view, Tate Britain, 2005 / Ausstellungsansicht, Turner-Preis.

DANSEUSE DE QUATORZE ANS (1880–81) hat der Künstler zu Lebzeiten nie giessen lassen, sondern stets bei sich im Atelier behalten. Zu einer Üppigkeit aufgeblasen, die an Crumb gemahnt, ist sie gespenstisch präsent in Warren's PONY (2003) sowie in der Doppelskulptur THE TWINS (Die Zwillinge, 2004); von ferne klingt sie auch in DOU DOU CHÉ und weiteren neueren Bronzen an. Mit der Feststellung, dass Warren als weibliche Künstlerin diese Männer schlicht der sexuellen Ausbeutung anklagt, indem sie sich ihrer Bildsprache bemächtigt, ist es jedoch nicht getan. Ihre Kunst ist nicht in dieser Weise *a priori* analytisch (doch die unbestrittene Kunstfertigkeit dieser Männer kann nicht losgelöst von ihren Ansichten betrachtet werden, ein Konflikt, der Warrens Arbeit antreibt); sie ist vielmehr ein Instrument, um unter Druck mit einer Art maskierter Anmut gegen äussere Zwänge vorzugehen, egal, ob es sich dabei um die geschlechtliche Ungleichheit handelt oder um die verführerische Autorität eines künstlerischen Vorfahren, dessen Haltung überholt sein mag, oder aber um unterschwellige Konventionen der Produktion von Kunst an sich.

Da sie auf solche Ängste eingeht, sollte man Warrens Kunst, auch wenn sie oberflächlich betrachtet aggressiv wirkt, wohl eher als differenziertes modulares Umgehungs- und Abwehrsystem gegen diese Ängste verstehen – aber auch gegen die symbolische Besessenheit eines allumfassenden Verstehen-Wollens. Betrachten wir etwa LOG LADY (Baumstamm-Frau, 2003), eine kopf- und armlose weibliche Figur in rissigem Ton, die anscheinend einen sich bauschenden Rock trägt und auf ihren der Schwerkraft trotzenden Brüsten einen dicht mit Ästen bestückten Baumstamm balanciert. Hier begegnen wir einmal mehr dem notorischen Frauen-Enthaupter Crumb (man denke etwa an den Comic *A Bitching' Bod! / Ein Hurenstück!* aus dem Jahr 1991, bei dem es sogar dem Zeichner selbst, wie er sagt, etwas mulmig wurde), aber auch David Lynchs Fernsehserie *Twin Peaks* (1990–91), in der eine äusserst geheimnisvolle Lady mit Baumstamm vorkommt. Darüber hinaus, hinsichtlich seiner Intention, bleibt das Werk ziemlich rätselhaft – tatsächlich könnte man es sich beinah in einem Bild von De Chirico vorstellen –, und es widersteht jeglicher schematischen begrifflichen Einordnung. Einzelne Elemente scheinen unmittelbar vor einer Verwandlung zu stehen, etwa da, wo man im Kleid winzige Beine zu erahnen beginnt. LOG LADY wirkt monumental, droht aber wegen des offensichtlich fragilen Materials auch jeden Moment auseinander zu brechen; da sitzt sie – ein echtes Dilemma. Die Skulptur steht auf einer mit Rollen versehenen Spanplatte, als würde ihr Mangel an begrifflicher Beständigkeit, analog auf der materiellen Ebene zum Ausdruck gebracht.

Wie immer bei Warren, weiss man nicht, was dieses Werk über ihre Gefühle hinsichtlich seiner Bezugspunkte oder über den politischen Umgang mit Geschlechterfragen aussagt, aber man spürt ihre gegenwärtige Unsicherheit und den Wunsch nach Klärung, zu der vielleicht die Schaffung eines derart dumpf wirkenden Objektes beitragen kann. Ein derartiges Werk ist wie eine erhobene Hand, die um etwas Geduld bittet, bis die Lösung gefunden ist. Inzwischen versetzt uns Warren ins Zentrum des Fliessenden und Provisorischen. Sigmund Freud – dessen Photographie den Umschlag des Katalogs zu ihrer Ausstellung in der Kunsthalle Zürich 2004 ziert und der nicht nur eine von vielen übermächtigen Vaterfiguren in ihrer Kunst ist, sondern natürlich auch als erster den Ödipuskomplex beschrieb – charakterisiert seine psychoanalytische Methode mit den Begriffen "Erinnern, Wiederholen und Durcharbeiten"[1]. Das scheint für Warrens reaktive, performative Vorgehensweise nicht unwesentlich zu sein. Über einen langen Zeitraum war eine Art neugierige Aneignung künstlerischer Praktiken der Vergangenheit Bestandteil ihrer Arbeit – gleichsam ein Anprobieren, oft von mehreren Stilen gleichzeitig, als würde sie auf einem verstaubten Dachboden in einer Kostümtruhe stöbern.

Es gibt jedoch Anzeichen dafür, dass sie beginnt, diese geborgten Hüllen fallen zu lassen. Ein Indiz könnte die wachsende Bedeutung der parallel laufenden Produktion von kleinformatigen plastischen Arrangements sein – Kombinationen aus aufbewahrten Atelierabfällen, Neonleuchtkabeln und von Hand bearbeiteten Lehmbrocken –, welche Warren mit EVERY ASPECT OF BITCH MAGIC (Ludermagie in all ihren Aspekten, 1996) in Angriff nahm. Ein etwas späteres Beispiel, BITCH MAGIC: THE MUSICAL

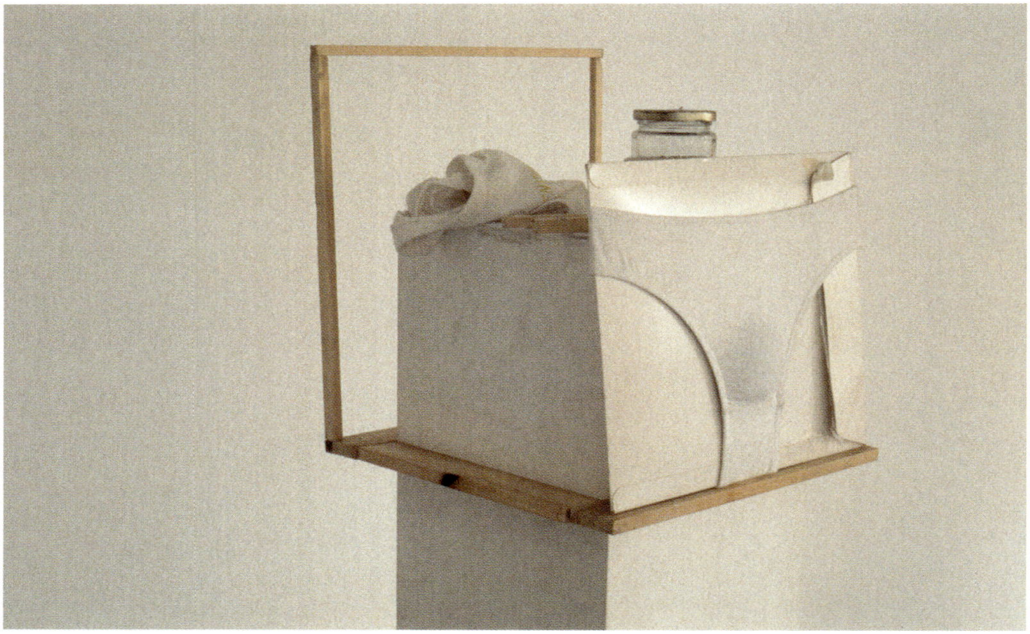

REBECCA WARREN, EVERY ASPECT OF BITCH MAGIC, 1996, mixed media, 52 x 11 3/4 x 11 3/4" / LUDERMAGIE IN ALLEN ASPEKTEN, verschiedene Materialien, 132 x 30 x 30 cm.

(Ludermagie: das Musical, 2001–2003), mag illustrieren, wie diese fragilen Systeme funktionieren. Mit ihrer offenbar sorgfältig arrangierten, fast schon malerischen Komposition aus bemalten Lehmformen und einer rosig leuchtenden Neonkabelschlaufe auf einem Sockel unter Glas erinnert die Arbeit zunächst an eine Art weiblichen Voodoo- oder Grisgris-Zauber. Doch man kann sie auch als Set narrativer Simulationen zur Präsentation plastischer Kunst verstehen, als Schwindelei (denn was sind diese unschönen Fragmente schon wert?) und zudem auch als Demonstration ihrer Widerspenstigkeit: Denn wie so oft legt Warren ein Element des Ensembles neckisch auf die Glashaube statt darunter.

Die Arbeit ist aber auch ein Beispiel für atmosphärisch konsequent umgesetzte Mehrschichtigkeit: Man muss nur ein bisschen bei BITCH MAGIC verweilen, und schon kommt Fürsorge und Sympathie für die einzelnen Elemente auf; man kann sich vorstellen, dass Warren sie irgendwie dem Vergessen, der Irrelevanz, dem Nichtgebrauch entreissen wollte, genau wie sie das Gussmodell Bobos davor bewahrt hat, in den Abfall zu wandern. Es sind zarte Empfindungen, die Warren offensichtlich als Facette in ihre Arbeit einbinden will. Um sie jedoch einschmuggeln zu können, musste sie zwangsläufig gewiefte Taktiken entwickeln. Denn – obwohl das Gegenteil der Fall zu sein scheint – es gibt strenge Regeln, was bei einem zeitgenössischen Kunstwerk aktzeptabel ist und was nicht, und diese sichtbar zu machen, ist Teil ihres rebellischen Treibens.

Dieselbe Demonstration von Autonomie beutelt auch ihre grossen Figuren. Sie zucken zunehmend vor Lebendigkeit (man vergleiche etwa die klaren Konturen von HELMUT CRUMB mit den rauen und wilden Oberflächen der Fellatioszene, THE PEARLS OF SWITZERLAND (Die Perlen der Schweiz, 2004), die offenbar aus gerollten und aufgerissenen Lehmwürsten bestehen), denn die von Hand gestalteten Oberflächen begünstigen eine heftige, heutzutage verpönte Expressivität. Man hat den Eindruck, dass Warren – die zu einer Zeit Kunst zu machen begann, als das herrschende Dogma Distanziertheit vorschrieb: also zuerst eine Idee zu entwickeln, um deren Umsetzung einem Kunsthandwerker zu überlassen – diesen Kontakt zum Sterblichen liebt und bewahren wollte. Um ihm Platz einzuräumen, musste sie als Oberfläche zunächst ein akzeptables Gitternetz aus Ironie und Abscheu gegenüber der älteren Kunst aufbauen. Dieser Schutzpanzer wird jedoch mehr und mehr abgebaut; dennoch geht dadurch kein Iota der schlüpfrigen Wendigkeit dieser Werke verloren, ihrer Geschicklichkeit sich einengenden Kategorisierungsversuchen zu entziehen. DOU DOU CHÉ mag flüchtige Reminiszenzen an andere Kunstwerke enthalten (manche davon unerhört dunkel: So geht beispielsweise der Ast, den BOBO balanciert, auf ähnlich unvereinbare Kombinationen zurück, die Warren in Rodins Atelier gesehen hat), aber letztlich erschliessen sich Warrens Werke nur durch sich selbst.

REBECCA WARREN, BITCH MAGIC: THE MUSICAL, 2001–2003, mixed media, plinth, 55 x 19 1/4 x 13 1/2" / LUDERMAGIE: DAS MUSICAL, verschiedene Materialien, Sockel, 139,7 x 48,9 x 34,3 cm

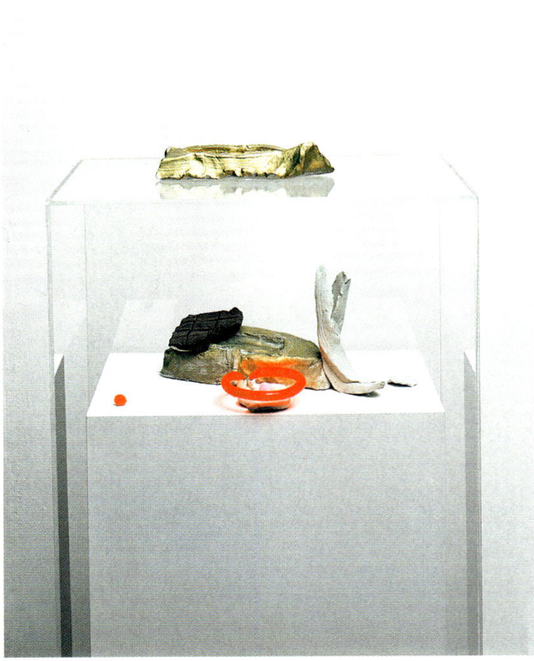

All das legt nahe, dass die Künstlerin ihre künstlerischen Vorlieben «durchgearbeitet» hat, indem sie ihre Aufmerksamkeit auf andere Dringlichkeiten verlagerte. Beispielsweise darauf, was man von ihr als Künstlerin mit erkennbarem «Stil» in der Mitte ihrer Laufbahn erwartet, oder darauf, was man mit einem bestimmten Medium tun darf oder nicht oder wie eine Künstlerin die weibliche Gestalt darstellen soll. Ich glaube, in ihrer Antwort auf diese letzte Frage und in der Reibung, die sie damit erzeugt, wird vielleicht Warrens tiefstes Anliegen erkennbar. Rufen wir uns nochmals Degas' PETITE DANSEUSE in Erinnerung und die hoch entwickelte Kunst jener Epoche insgesamt, deren Wirkung sich mittlerweile durch die Vertrautheit und alles, was danach kam, abgestumpft hat; versuchen wir uns, soweit möglich, diese vergangene Epoche in ihrer ganzen strahlenden und bedrohlichen Neuartigkeit vorzustellen. Wenn Warrens Skulpturen irgendetwas aus der Vergangenheit aufleben lassen wollen, so ist es dieser Moment: Der elektrisierende Schauder des Modernen im Augenblick seiner Geburt, hier übersetzt durch auf das Minimalste reduzierte Elemente des Zeitgenössischen – eine wirksame Mischung aus hässlicher weiblicher Stärke, formaler Groteske, einer radikal ambivalenten Haltung und der generellen Abwesenheit jeglicher Schlüssigkeit –, in eine fundamentale Unsicherheit mündend, die allein von hilflosem Lachen unterbrochen wird. Diesen Moment also gilt es noch einmal aufleben zu lassen und dafür zu sorgen, dass er als heiteres Problem so lange wie möglich nachhallt: in ihr und in uns.

(Übersetzung: Suzanne Schmidt)

1 Titel des gleichnamigen Essays in: Sigmund Freud, *Gesammelte Werke*, Bd. X, Frankfurt am Main 1981, S. 129.

TRYING IT ON I SUPPOSE

CATHERINE LAMPERT

A few years ago, when I encountered Rebecca Warren's sculptures in the venues where serious art is exhibited and debated, it was a pleasure to witness their frolicking, reckless qualities. But it was natural to be nervous; something that is hand-made and invites intimacy might prove an anachronistic confection, one that is especially upsetting if the viewer has an abiding attachment to the observation-based, figurative sculpture of Rodin, Giacometti, and others. Subsequent exposure to the tall, standing figures set in rows like chorus girls at Matthew Marks Gallery in late 2005 gave me enough reason to suggest a studio visit in connection with a film Jake Auerbach and I were planning to make—its subject: living British artists talking about Rodin (part of the exhibition I was curating for the Royal Academy).[1] When we finished recording for the film, the single common experience amongst our eight participants turned out to be that they had all responded emphatically to Rodin (and the Musée Rodin in Paris) when they were teenagers; however, as they'd developed and thought about their own options, they'd each begun to see this artist-giant as too expressive and too emotional. When Warren was a student at Goldsmiths College from 1989 to 1992, she explains that "life-drawing wasn't encouraged, it was old-fashioned... expressionism was talked about in a disparaging way."[2] Nevertheless, a few years later, she began to look seriously at Degas, Rodin, and Rosso, principally in reproductions. (I can imagine Rebecca thinking to herself, "That's not bad.")

As soon as Rodin received his first public commission in 1880—monumental doors for a planned decorative arts museum—he decided to model figures, each about forty centimeters high, that would illustrate narrative episodes from Dante's *The Divine Comedy*. In a matter of five years, he had assembled some two-hundred figures, drifting ever closer to Baudelaire's archetypal erotic, degraded lovers. Visitors to the studio on the rue de l'Université would have seen someone intoxicated with the spirit of spontaneous creation—a "countless host of damned women came into being and writhed in his fingers. Some of them lived for a few hours before being returned to the mass of reworked clay."[3] Nevertheless, in his well-organized studio, with its complement of technicians, many figures were cast in plas-

CATHERINE LAMPERT was Director of the Whitechapel Art Gallery until 2001 and is now a free-lance curator and art historian. Recent books and exhibitions include *Francis Alÿs: The Prophet and the Fly* and *Rodin* at the Royal Academy. *Euan Uglow: The Complete Paintings* will be published by Yale University Press in 2007.

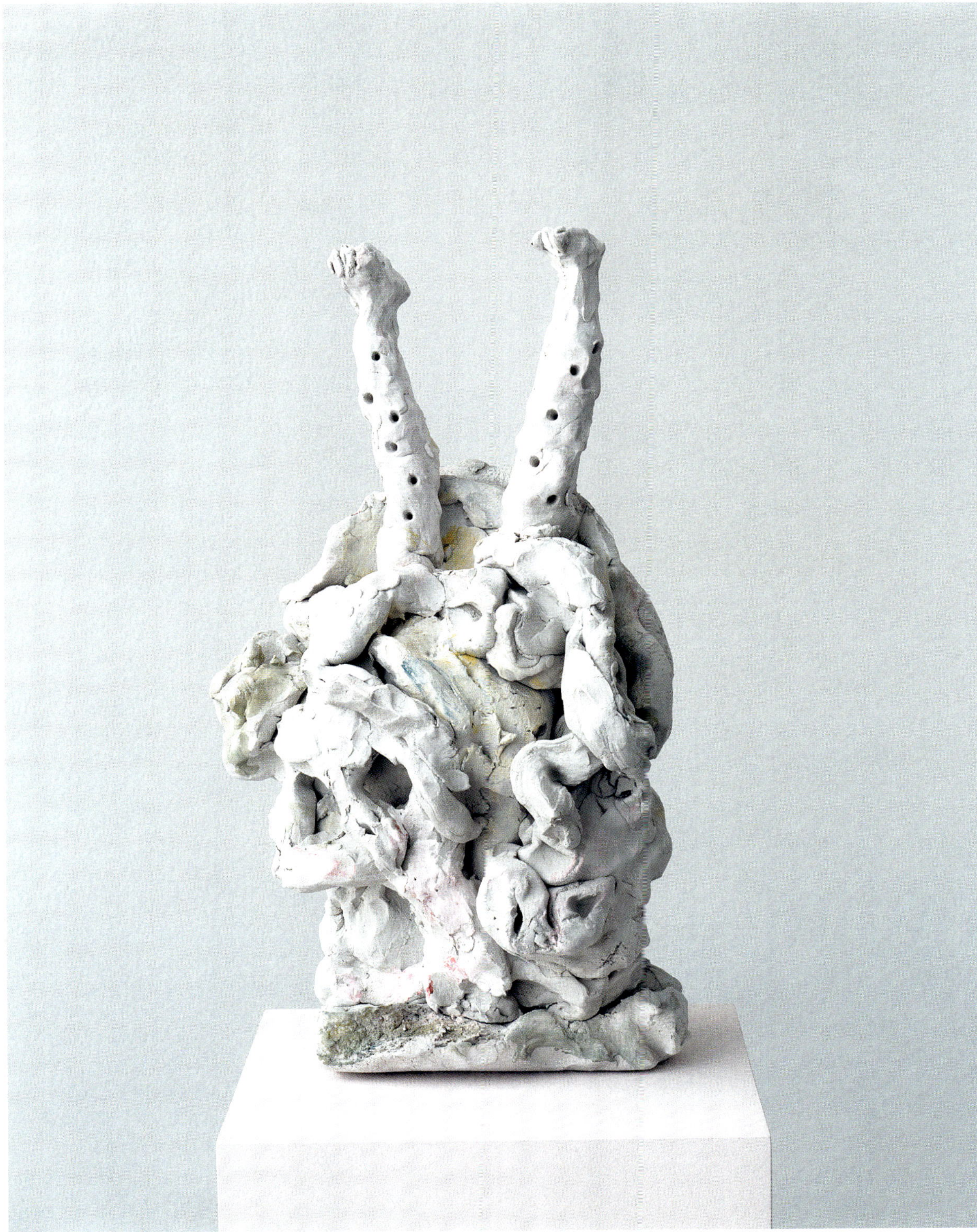

REBECCA WARREN, HUNDEMEISTER (Dog Master), 2004, reinforced clay, acrylic paint, $19\,^1/_4 \times 9 \times 8\,^1/_4$" / verstärkter Ton, Acrylfarbe, 49 x 23 x 21 cm.

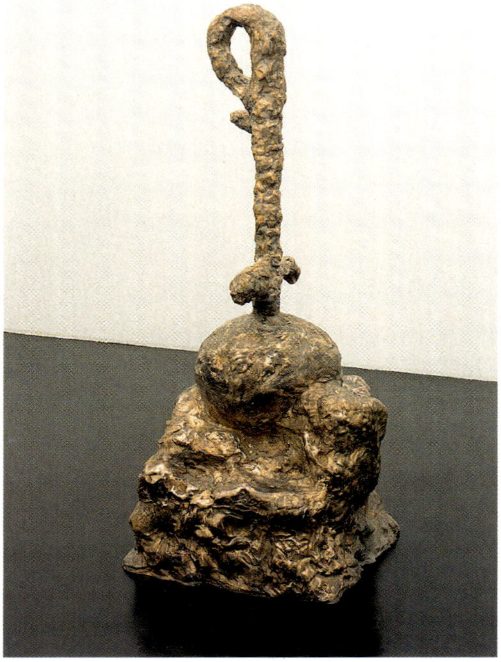

REBECCA WARREN, P.E., 2005, bronze, 62 1/4 x 26 3/8 x 24 3/4" / Bronze, 158 x 67 x 63 cm.

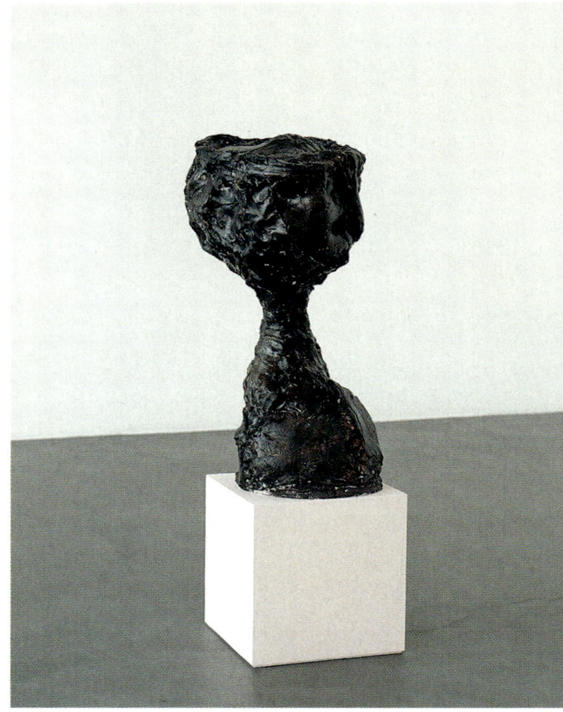

REBECCA WARREN, LIGHT OF THE WORLD, 2004, reinforced clay, acrylic paint, pom pom, 44 1/8 x 13 3/8 x 13 3/8" / LICHT DER WELT, verstärkter Ton, Acrylfarbe, Pompon, 112 x 34 x 34 cm.

ter, the piece-molds sometimes re-filled with fresh clay, the originals and the variations remaining in Rodin's possession for the rest of his life.

Retrospectively, we credit Rodin's work with both advancing and destroying the integrity of figurative sculpture. Depending on one's argument, one is apt to isolate examples of Rodin's focus on process, his exploitation of the expressive power of fragments, the simulation of movement and a kind of burgeoning cubism, his myopic eyes and the successive profiles they recorded. The liberties that Rodin took with his figures brings to mind the painted facets and *insouciant* sexual markers that Warren has been imposing on her new bronzes and her "doubles" (the first cast's twin—its adaptation). On the other hand, Rodin avoided claiming formal or gender-bound milestones; indeed, he continually and sincerely protected himself and his ambition from ridicule and censorship by repeating, like a mantra, that his core daily experience came from what was "real," or what he observed while watching models pose. They were "nature"—various, amoral, and suggestive as trees, rocks, and animals.[4)] Rodin's rapport with individual models led him to record a specific moment involving one of his favorite girls, Adèle Abruzzesi, who was encouraged to remain still while holding a most vulgar crouching pose—one hand on her breast, the other on her foot—a gesture readily understood by a French audience as a metaphor for orgasm. Stepping into the female experience of arousal was thus Rodin's goal. At the end of his life, he made another CROUCHING WOMAN (1895)—a lumpy pseudo-dancer with split legs. Our eyes and feelings travel over this work's rugged, pruned terrain, peering in through the gapping knife-cut aperture under the left arm and contemplating the brutal, but tender, contortions in the sculpture's face.

It is impossible for Warren, or perhaps for any intelligent living artist, to treat the making of figurative images as a wholesome, centered occupation.[5)] Warren uses the word "ludicrous" to describe her treatment of her subject, as did Willem de Kooning in a 1960 interview with David Sylvester. The critic questioned whether the impetus to paint the *Women* series came from a moral decision, a theoretical decision, or only desire. De Kooning skirted around such ponderous notions, protesting how "that word 'figure' becomes such a ridiculous omen." "It's really absurd to make an image, like a human image...but then all of a sudden it was even more absurd not to do it," said De Kooning. "Indeed, the ludicrous personage hijacks the creative process," he continued. "I put it [the woman] in the center of the canvas, you know, because there was no reason to put it a bit on the side—do you see what I mean? So I thought I might as well stick to the idea that it's got two eyes, a nose and mouth and neck ... I felt myself almost getting flustered. ... the idea that it really is very funny, you know, to get stuck with a woman's knees, for instance." De Kooning downgraded content—making it more "a glimpse of something"—before adding a further disclaimer: "It's very tiny, very tiny, content." The character of both De Kooning's women and Warren's is a bit brazen; when we circle her figures we understand what De Kooning meant when he fancied being in conversation with them in the studio, "like they were ladies of Gertrude Stein. Like one of them would say: how do you like me?"[6)] When Warren sees her figures return from the foundry a bit battered and coarse, she builds in the changes before they re-emerge.

With hindsight, De Kooning admitted that his images of women were somewhat "vociferous and ferocious," especially those women sporting grins achieved by collaging mouths cut from printed mass media, for he agreed that this feature made them appear more "like Mesopotamian idols ... astonished about the forces of nature." Tate curator Clarrie Wallis, writing in the Tate Triennial catalogue, found Warren's SHE (2003)—a figure with ample breasts and buttocks—reminiscent of "Mesopotamian fertility figurines."[7)] Warren accepts that she amasses "all sorts of influences from all sorts of different places...trying [them] on for size ..." One might see her approach as using some delay and refractory tactics, and this is literally the case, as a work will be positioned so that its back faces the entrance to the gallery. Being less self-conscious is, in Warren's words, simply "better."[8)]

Pots boiling

In the studio, Warren likens her activity to watching several pots boiling at the same time. In the gallery, it is a struggle for even the most aware visitor to absorb the collective identity of the series. Going from one figure to the next in the Tate's Turner Prize show (a context of general restlessness), reading names in her works' titles (WILLIAM, PAULINE, DOU DOU CHÉ), I found that, due to their quality and finesse, her works demanded even more thorough viewing than in the studio. The gawky, ostrich-like figures stood on narrow plinths—some pinkish, others white—set at heights where the heads of the tallest were visible above the crowd of museum-goers. The unpatinated bronze, rubbed with wax, looked garish, like jewelry, bumped and twisted, deliberately superfluously—until a random look brought a flash of something. It occurred to me that the armature of these upright figures—a steel pole—was analogous to the creatures on carousels, pumping up and down. One can appreciate an innate flair in Warren's sensibility—the sporty acrylic-patterned fabric she uses for capes, the passages of applied makeup.

The forms in her unfired clay pieces are more tumbling and soft, like bouquets, with poetic names. One is titled GARDEN OF MY SPOUSE (2006) but I am reluctant to elicit facts about this work. After all, it is art, so its associations can be evocative for me without merely belonging to the artist's stream-of-consciousness. Here I glean a special quality, that of Arshile Gorky's *Garden in Sochi* series—take, for example, the nostalgia of the most resolved gouache, one with a yellow ground, sharp slipper shapes, and floating objects.[9)]

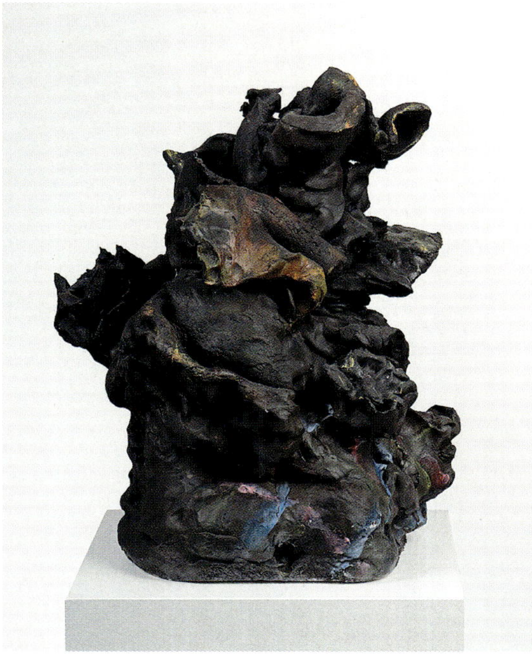

REBECCA WARREN, LOULOU, 2006, painted reinforced clay, plinth, 16 1/2 x 13 3/4 x 13" / bemalter verstärkter Ton, Sockel, 42 x 35 x 33 cm.

Critical projection

One of the few especially clichéd reviews of the Royal Academy exhibition I curated was written by Germaine Greer, entitled "Are Rodin's bronzes erotic? Hardly—but they do tell us a lot about the sculptor's womanizing." Greer asserts that "sculpture is monumental, immobile and, in our necropolitan museum system, out of reach. Its silent statement is that of a *Playboy* bunny. 'Look, fantasize, but don't touch.'" Greer imagines a squalid session, where Rodin poses the model he has chosen to represent IRIS (1890/91) on her back (which is correct), and then "models her, with head and left arm missing, in clay," intimating that the amputation was done in the presence of the model/victim, rather than what really happened—the more risky editing of a form already cast and marked by seams and plaster drips. Greer leaves readers with the advice that "intimidation is not usually associated with the raising of desire."[10] Living on one's nerves and conflicted emotions can offer rich possibilities for artists, but biographical voyeurism can cast their protagonists in trivial roles. One hears a fresh, non-feminist note in Warren's language, as she occasionally has admitted: "I'm interested in making sculpture that perhaps looks like it was made by a male artist"—using the word "pervy" as an incentive.[11]

Michael Craig-Martin taught artists of Warren's generation at Goldsmiths College (although Warren was not there during Craig-Martin's tenure) and has spoken of the outstanding 70s artists who were his contemporaries—especially Bruce Nauman—who, as he sees it, marked a significant change: "Art isn't about representing things, it is about acting things out." They acted out "the problem of being an artist in the world."[12] Occasionally such an art-historical emphasis concertinas into the critic-friendly strategy of referencing. Lately, I've detected a reluctance to be constricted by twenty-first century "referencing" disclaimers. A curator of similar age to Warren describes her as being "at odds with the position of mastery and authority assumed by her predecessors." Although Warren herself maintains that it may be pointless to aspire to be a virtuoso modeler, it seems just as disingenuous, in her case, to pretend to be indifferent to the quality of the forms.[13] I recently overheard a Tate tour guide facing the Warren vitrines intoning names as if by pedigree: "She positions herself within a tradition of artists ... Beuys, Cornell ..." Warren explains that these influences can indeed be "overwhelming, but it is pointless to try and hide them ..." Warren describes herself as a "book flickerer," but in conversation, when she mentions something that arrests her attention, you nod and see it in your mind. Take, for example, how for a magazine feature on portraits of women, she selected an image of Maria Callas being served a writ from a Diane Vreeland book—and then a clay monsteress appears.

As she becomes a better and better artist, Warren's teasing engagement with hindrances and palliatives is honed. Different zones—Perspex a size too small—time marked by titles like *2001, 2002, 2004, or*

2005—it's as if the installation scheme anticipates the mores and ethos proffered by a particular art institution. *Un condamné à mort s'est échappé* (1956), Robert Bresson's film, is amongst those to which Warren relates. A man sentenced to death by the Gestapo escapes, or goes where the wind takes him. In the cinematography, the details are exaggerated and sounds reverberate. A slow developer, Warren wants to keep her options open while trying to "get to the bottom" of what it means to make art. "I've not found it an easy thing to achieve. At first. You get some kind of love, in some sense, from the things that you're doing."

1) "Rodin at the Royal Academy," 26 September 2006–1 January 2007 and then the Kunsthaus Zurich, 9 February–13 May 2007.
2) This quote and subsequent ones not given other references are from the recording in Warren's studio on 18 May 2006 for *Rodin: The Sculptors' View,* directed by Jake Auerbach, and notes from a previous conversation in the studio on 11 April 2006.
3) Hughes le Roux, "La Vie à Paris," *Le Temps*, Paris, 20 June 1889.
4) A typical quote is "Nature offers symbols and synthesis on the breast of the strictest reality. It suffices to know how to read them," Camille Mauclair, *Auguste Rodin. The Man—His Ideas—His Works*, trans. Clementina Black (London: Duckworth and Co., 1905), p. 53.
5) "amplifying it, exaggerating the hole and the bumps so as to give them more light," Rodin, *Le Journal*, Paris, 12 May 1898.
6) David Sylvester, *Interviews with American Artists* (London: Chatto & Windus, 2001), pp. 48–53.
7) Clarrie Wallis, Tate Triennial 2006, "New British Art," Tate Britain, 1 March–14 May 2006, p. 138.
8) Rebecca Warren speaking on the film produced by the Tate for the Turner Prize 2006.
9) Arshile Gorky, GARDEN IN SOCHI, 1940–41, gouache on board, 22 x 28", purchase with bequest of C. Donald Belcher, High Museum of Art, Atlanta.
10) Germaine Greer, "Are Rodin's bronzes erotic? Hardly—but they do tell us a lot about the sculptor's womanizing," *The Guardian*, 9 October 2006, p. 24.
11) Tate Turner Prize film, 2006. One thinks of the dismal male physiques and libido in John Coplans, Paul McCarthy, etc., Nevertheless the British critics rail against her subject matter, Adrian Searle "bored," by her "big-assed and -breasted clay floozies," (*The Guardian*, 3 October 2006), several complaining about a "feminist message." Julian Keeling, in his article, "Shapes of things to come," *Harper's Bazaar*, November 2006, p. 200, explains with charm that his efforts to turn the conversation into personal territory are rebuffed "with a discourse on art" or another distraction.
12) Michael Craig-Martin, "The Power of Now," *The Guardian*, 14 October 2006, p. 11.
13) Lizzie Carey-Thomas, Brochure, *Turner Prize 2006*, Tate Britain 2006.

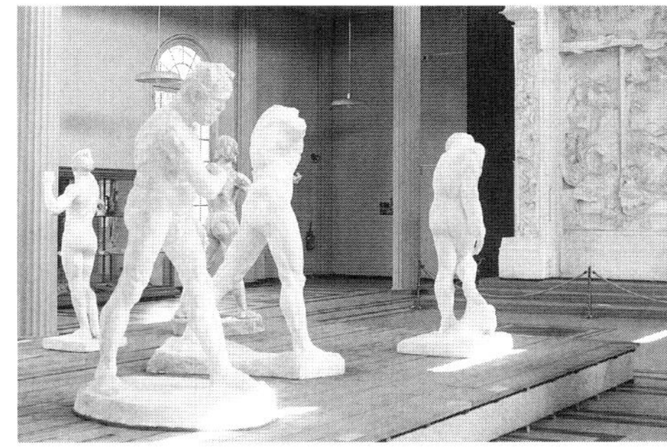

AUGUSTE RODIN, standing figures and THE GATE OF HELL, Musée Rodin, Meudon / Skulpturen und HÖLLENTOR. (PHOTO: COURTESY OF IVOR HEAL)

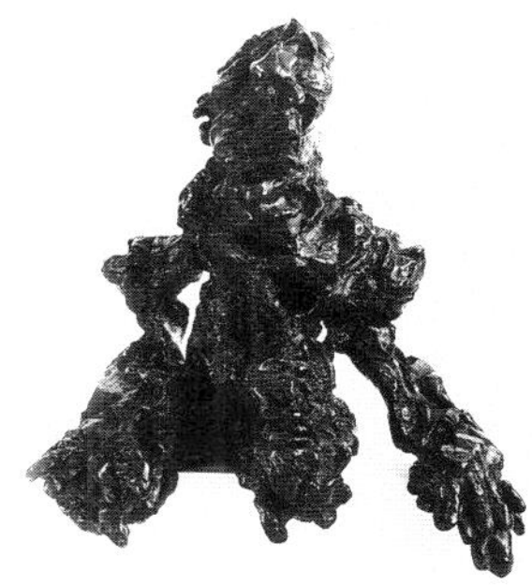

WILLEM DE KOONING, LARGE TORSO, 1974, bronze, 36 x 36 x 26 1/2" / GROSSER TORSO, Bronze, 91,5 x 91,5 x 67,3 cm.

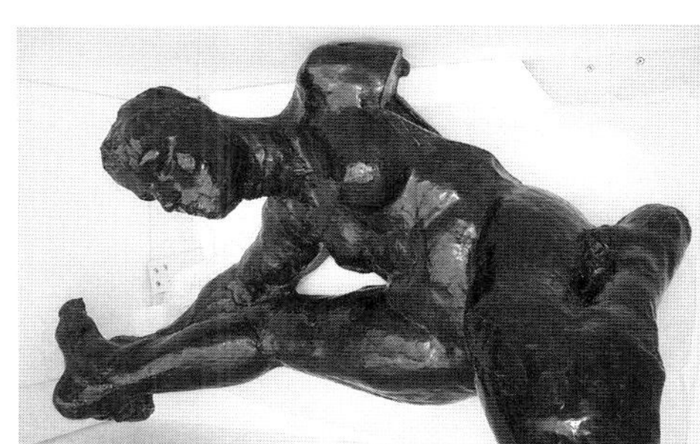

AUGUSTE RODIN, CROUCHING WOMAN, ca.1895, bronze, 20 3/4 x 13 3/8" / KAUERNDE FRAU, Bronze, 53 x 34 cm. (PHOTO: COURTESY OF IVOR HEAL)

VERMUTLICH EIN PROBEWEISES HINEINSCHLÜPFEN

CATHERINE LAMPERT

Als man vor wenigen Jahren an Orten, wo ernst zu nehmende Kunst ausgestellt und diskutiert wird, auf Rebecca Warrens Skulpturen stiess, war es eine wahre Lust, die Ausgelassenheit und Sorglosigkeit zu sehen, die in ihnen steckte. Aber es war nur natürlich, auch etwas nervös zu reagieren: Etwas Handgefertigtes, das Gefahr läuft, allzu vertraut zu wirken, und sich im Nachhinein auch als anachronistische Konserve entpuppen könnte, und zwar als eine besonders ärgerliche für jene Betrachter, die den auf Naturbeobachtung basierenden figurativen Skulpturen von Rodin, Giacometti und anderen nach wie vor einiges abgewinnen können. Die nächste Begegnung mit den wie Tänzerinnen aufgereihten, stehenden Figuren in der Matthew Marks Gallery, Ende 2005, war für mich Grund genug, einen Atelierbesuch in Erwägung zu ziehen, und zwar im Zusammenhang mit einem Film, den Jake Auerbach und ich drehen wollten. Sein Thema: lebende englische Künstler, die über Rodin sprechen (als Bestandteil der Ausstellung in der Royal Academy, die ich damals vorbereitete).[1] Als wir mit den Aufnahmen fertig waren, stellte sich heraus, dass die einzige allen acht Teilnehmenden gemeinsame Erfahrung darin bestand, dass sie als Teenager lebhaft auf Rodin (und das Musée Rodin in Paris) reagiert hatten; doch später, als sie ihre eigenen Ansichten entwickelten und reflektierten, erschien ihnen dieser Gigant allzu expressiv und emotional. Als Warren 1989–1992 am Goldsmith College studierte, sagt sie, «wurde das Zeichnen nach dem lebenden Modell nicht unterstützt, es galt als altmodisch ... alles Expressionistische wurde heruntergemacht.»[2] Dennoch hat sie sich wenige Jahre später Degas, Rodin und Rosso angeschaut, vorwiegend auf Abbildungen. (Ich kann mir vorstellen, wie Rebecca dachte: «Gar nicht mal schlecht.»)

Kaum hatte Rodin 1880 seinen ersten öffentlichen Auftrag erhalten – monumentale Türen für ein geplantes Museum der dekorativen Künste –, beschloss er Figuren zu modellieren, die, je etwa vierzig Zentimeter hoch, Szenen aus Dantes *Divina*

CATHERINE LAMPERT war bis 2001 Direktorin der Whitechapel Gallery und ist nun als freie Kuratorin und Kunsthistorikerin tätig. Zu ihren jüngsten Publikationen/Ausstellungen gehören *Francis Alÿs. The Prophet and the Fly* (2003), *Rodin* (Royal Academy, 2006) sowie *Euan Uglow: The Complete Paintings,* ein Catalogue raisonné, der 2007 erscheint (Yale University Press).

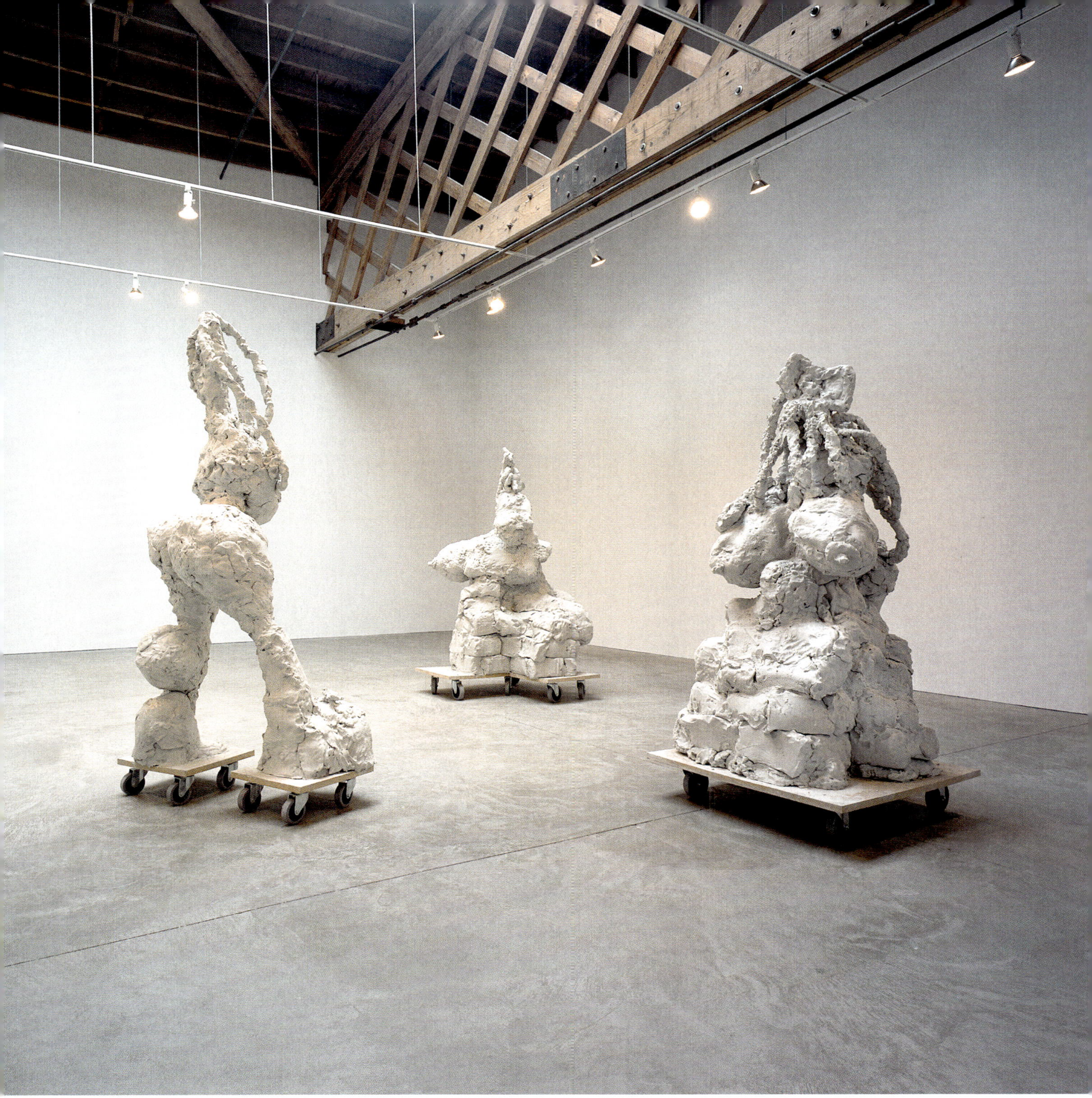

REBECCA WARREN, exhibition view, Donald Young Gallery, Chicago, 2003, from left to right: TEACHER (M.B), TEACHER (W), TEACHER (R) / Ausstellungsansicht, von links nach rechts: LEHRER (M.B.), LEHRER (W), LEHRER (R).

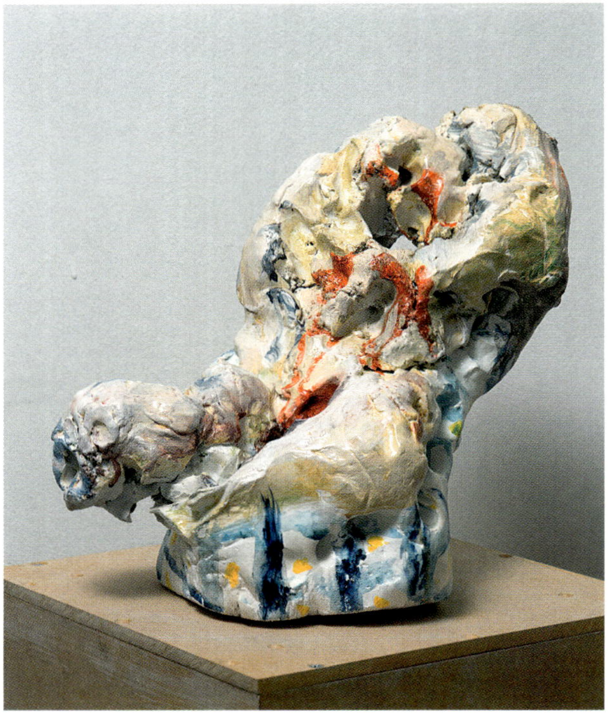

REBECCA WARREN, DER TOTSCHLÄGER (The Manslayer), 2002, self-firing, painted clay, plinth, 12 1/4 x 12 1/4 x 8 5/8" / selbsttrocknender, bemalter Ton, Sockel, 31 x 31 x 22 cm.

Commedia illustrieren sollten. In ungefähr fünf Jahren hatte er rund zweihundert Figuren beisammen, die Baudelaires erotischen, dekadenten Liebenden immer ähnlicher sahen. Ein Besucher des Ateliers an der Rue de l'Université hätte einen vom Geist der spontanen Kreation Besessenen, ja Vergifteten erblickt. Ein «unermessliches Heer todgeweihter Frauen wurde zum Leben erweckt und wand sich in seinen Händen. Einige lebten ein paar Stunden, bevor sie wieder in die Masse des stetig neu verarbeiteten Tons eingingen.»[3] Dennoch wurden in diesem gut organisierten Atelier, in dem eine Reihe technischer Spezialisten zu Gange waren, viele Figuren in Gips gegossen und Negativformen manchmal wieder mit frischem Ton gefüllt, obwohl Rodin sämtliche Originale und Variationen für den Rest seines Lebens bei sich behielt.

Im Rückblick müssen wir Rodins Werk zugutehalten, dass es die Integrität der figürlichen Bildhauerei ebenso vorangetrieben wie zerstört hat. Je nach Argumentationsbedarf greifen wir Beispiele für Rodins Prozessorientiertheit, seine Ausbeutung der expressiven Kraft des Fragmenthaften, seine Simulation von Bewegung oder eine Art aufkeimenden Kubismus heraus und stellen uns vor, wie seine kurzsichtigen Augen die wechselnden Profile registrierten. Die Freiheiten, die sich Rodin bei seinen Figuren herausnimmt, erinnern an die bemalten Details und die frech hingeklatschten Geschlechtsmerkmale von Warrens neuen Bronzen und deren Doubles (dem ersten Abguss und seinem Zwilling, dem bearbeiteten Abguss). Andrerseits hat Rodin es vermieden, formale oder geschlechtsspezifische Marksteine zu setzen; tatsächlich hat er sich selbst und sein Ansinnen unaufhörlich und offen vor Spott und Kritik geschützt, indem er wie ein Mantra unermüdlich wiederholte, dass seine zentrale, tägliche Erfahrung sich aus dem zusammensetze, was «real» sei oder was er bei der Beobachtung seiner Modelle sehe. Sie waren «Natur» – mannigfaltig, amoralisch und so anregend wie Bäume, Steine und Tiere.[4] Rodins intime Beziehung zu einzelnen Modellen brachte ihn darauf, einen besonderen Moment festzuhalten: Eines seiner Lieblingsmodelle, Adèle Abruzzesi, hielt er dazu an, reglos in einer äusserst vulgären, kauernden Pose zu verharren, eine Hand an der Brust, die andere am Fuss – eine Haltung, die ein französisches Publikum als Metapher für den Orgasmus zu verstehen wusste. Rodin will also die Erfahrung des weiblichen Orgasmus nachvollziehen. Gegen Ende seines Lebens schuf er noch einmal eine KAUERNDE FRAU (1895), eine schlaffe Pseudotänzerin mit gespreizten Beinen. Unser Blick und unsere Gefühle wandern über die raue, zerklüftete Oberfläche dieses Werks, spähen durch die klaffende, messerscharfe Öffnung unter dem linken Arm und betrachten die grausamen und dennoch zarten Verzerrungen des Gesichts.

Für Warren und vielleicht für jeden intelligenten lebenden Künstler ist es undenkbar, das Schaffen figürlicher Darstellungen als gesunde, ausgewogene Beschäftigung zu betrachten.[5)] Wie Willem de Kooning verwendet Warren das Wort «lächerlich» zur Beschreibung ihres Umgangs mit dem Thema. Wenn man David Sylvesters Interview von 1960 mit de Kooning liest, hören wir ihn fragen, ob der Impuls zur Serie *Women* aus einer moralischen oder theoretischen Entscheidung oder einfach aus einem Wunsch heraus entstanden sei. De Kooning vermied derart schwerfällige Begriffe und protestierte, dass «das Wort ‹Figur› so lächerlich ominös geworden sei». «Es ist wirklich absurd, ein Bild zu malen, etwa das Bild eines Menschen», bekennt de Kooning, «... doch dann erschien es plötzlich noch absurder, es nicht zu tun.» Tatsächlich torpediert die Lächerlichkeit des Persönlichen den kreativen Prozess. De Kooning fährt fort: «Ich setzte sie in die Mitte der Leinwand, nun ja, weil es keinen Grund gab, sie mehr seitlich zu platzieren – sehen Sie, was ich meine? Also dachte ich, ich könnte geradeso gut daran festhalten, dass sie zwei Augen, Nase, Mund und Hals hat ... Ich konnte beinah fühlen, wie ich nervös wurde ... der Gedanke, dass es wirklich sehr drollig ist, na ja, beispielsweise an den Knien einer Frau zu scheitern.» De Kooning reduzierte den Inhalt, liess ihn mehr wie «einen flüchtigen Eindruck von etwas» erscheinen, fügte dann aber einen weiteren Rückzieher hinzu: «er ist sehr winzig, sehr winzig, der Inhalt.» Der Charakter der Frauen bei de Kooning wie bei Warren ist etwas dreist; wenn wir um Warrens Figuren herumgehen, verstehen wir, was de Kooning meinte, als er sich vorstellte, im Atelier mit ihnen zu sprechen, «als wären es Frauenfiguren von Gertrude Stein. Als würde eine von ihnen sagen: Wie gefalle ich dir?»[6)] Warren sieht ihre Figuren leicht angeschlagen und lädiert aus der Giesserei zurückkommen und baut die Veränderungen ein, bevor sie sie wieder aus dem Atelier entlässt.

Im Rückblick gab de Kooning zu, dass seine Frauenbilder etwas «lautstark und wild» waren, besonders jene Frauen, die ein Grinsen im Gesicht trugen, das mittels Collage aus den Printmedien entliehen war; er gab zu, dass dieses Element sie eher aussehen liess wie «über die Naturkräfte staunende Idole mesopotamischer Gottheiten». Tate-Kuratorin Clarrie Wallis fand (im Tate Triennial-Katalog 2006), dass Warrens SHE (Sie, 2003) – eine Figur mit üppigen Brüsten und Hinterbacken – an «mesopotamische Fruchtbarkeitsidole» erinnere.[7)] Warren stimmt zu, dass sie «allerlei Einflüsse verschiedenster Herkunft» aufnimmt ... «vermutlich ein probeweises Hineinschlüpfen und Schauen ob die Grösse passt». Man könnte ihr Vorgehen auch so interpretieren, dass sie Verzögerungs- und Widerstandstaktiken anwendet; dies ganz wörtlich, denn oft ist vom Eingang des Ausstellungsraums her nur die Rückansicht ihrer Arbeiten zu sehen. Etwas weniger Befangenheit ist, um ihre Worte zu gebrauchen, «besser».[8)]

Dampfende Töpfe

Im Atelier vergleicht Warren ihre Tätigkeit mit dem Beobachten mehrerer dampfender Töpfe auf dem Herd. In der Ausstellung kämpft selbst der aufgeweckteste Besucher damit, die kollektive Identität der Serie zu verkraften. Als ich in der Ausstellung zum Turner Prize von einer Figur zur nächsten ging und die Titel der Arbeiten las – WILLIAM, PAULINE, DOU DOU CHÉ –, schien mir, dass diese Arbeiten, aufgrund ihrer Qualität und Raffinesse, im Kontext der allgemeinen Ruhelosigkeit nach einer eingehenderen Betrachtung rufen. Die ungelenken, straussenähnlichen Gestalten standen auf schmalen Sockeln, manche blassrosa, andere weiss, in einer Höhe platziert, dass die Köpfe der grössten Figuren jene der Besucher überragten. Die unpatinierte, mit Wachs eingeriebene Bronze leuchtete grell, wie Schmuck, absichtlich und völlig unnötig gebeutelt und verrenkt, bis ein zufälliger Blick etwas aufblitzen liess. Die Armatur dieser aufrechten Figuren, eine Eisenstange, hätte zu den auf und ab tanzenden Kreaturen auf einem Karussell gepasst. Ein angeborenes, sensibles Flair fällt angenehm auf, die Einführung sportlicher Acrylmuster-Stoffe für die Capes, die Stellen mit Make-up.

Die Formen der Arbeiten in ungebranntem Ton sind taumelnder und weich, wie Bouquets mit poetischen Namen. Eine trägt den Titel GARDEN OF MY SPOUCE (Garten meines/r Lebensgefährten/in, 2006), doch ich schrecke davor zurück, diesem Werk irgendwelche Fakten zu entlocken. Schliesslich ist es

Kunst, also können die damit verbundenen Assoziationen in mir etwas wecken, was nicht unbedingt mit dem Bewusstseinsstrom der Künstlerin zusammenhängt. Ich erkenne darin eine spezielle Qualität aus Arshile Gorkys Serie *Garden in Sochi* (Garten in Sochi, 1940–41) wieder. Man denke etwa an die Wehmut der am stärksten aufgelösten Gouache, eine mit gelbem Grund, scharf umrissenen Pantoffelformen und schwebenden Objekten.[9)]

Kritische Projektion

Eine der wenigen extrem klischeehaften Kritiken zu der (von mir kuratierten) Rodin-Ausstellung in der Royal Academy, stammte von Germaine Greer und trug den Titel, «Sind Rodins Bronzen erotisch? Kaum – doch sie verraten uns eine Menge über das Verhältnis dieses Bildhauers zu den Frauen.» Greer behauptet, «Skulpturen sind monumental, unbeweglich und, in unseren Nekropolen gleichenden Museen, ausser Reichweite. Ihre stumme Aussage ist die eines *Playboy*-Bunnys: ‹Schau, träume, aber rühr mich nicht an.›» Greer stellt sich eine schmuddelige Szene vor, in der Rodin das Modell für IRIS (1890/91) auf den Rücken legt (was zutrifft) und dann «ohne Kopf und linken Arm in Ton modelliert», womit sie andeutet, dass er die Amputation in Gegenwart des Modells/Opfers vornahm, statt offen zu sagen, wie sie in Wirklichkeit zustande kam – nämlich durch eine ziemlich heikle Überarbeitung einer bereits gegossenen Form, die Gussnähte und Gipsspritzer aufwies. Schliesslich gibt Greer ihren Lesern noch zu bedenken, dass «Einschüchterung in der Regel nicht mit dem Wecken von Begierde zusammengeht».[10)] Das Ausbeuten der eigenen nervösen Befindlichkeit und widerstreitenden Gefühle hat Künstlern ein weites Feld eröffnet, aber der biographische Voyeurismus schiebt den Protagonisten oft eine allzu triviale Rolle zu. Aus Warrens Sprache hört man einen frischen, nicht-feministischen Ton heraus, und gelegentlich hat sie auch zugegeben, «ich möchte eine Skulptur schaffen, die möglicherweise aussieht, als ob sie von einem Mann gemacht worden sei», und hat dabei das Wort «pervy» (pervers) in positiv anregendem Sinn verwendet.[11)]

Michael Craig-Martin hat Künstler aus Warrens Generation am Goldsmith College unterrichtet.

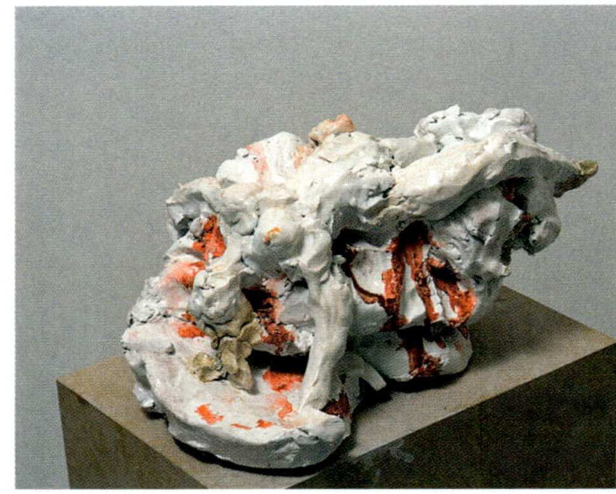

REBECCA WARREN, MORD (Murder), 2002, reinforced clay, plinth, 43 1/4 x 29 1/8 x 29 1/8" / verstärkter Ton, Sockel, 110 x 74 x 74 cm.

(Warren selbst studierte allerdings erst später dort und nicht während Craig-Martins Professur.) Von den herausragenden Künstlern der 70er Jahre – seiner eigenen Generation – und insbesondere von Bruce Nauman sagte er, sie stünden für einen Umbruch in der Kunst: «In der Kunst geht es nicht um das Darstellen von Dingen, sondern um das Ausleben von Dingen ...», um das Ausleben des Problems, «ein Künstler in der Welt zu sein».[12)] Diese kunsthistorische Akzentuierung der Optionen beim Herstellen eines unnützen Objekts geht manchmal in das kritikerfreundliche Verfahren des Verweisens über. In jüngster Zeit habe ich an mir einen Widerwillen entdeckt, mich vom «Verweisverbot» des einundzwanzigsten Jahrhunderts einschränken zu lassen. Ein Kurator, etwa im Alter von Warren, beschreibt sie als eine Künstlerin «im Konflikt mit der Position der Meisterschaft und Autorität, die ihre Vorgänger eingenommen haben». Auch wenn Warren selbst darauf besteht, dass es sinnlos sei, ein virtuoser Modelleur sein zu wollen, so erscheint es mir in ihrem Fall genauso unredlich, so zu tun, als pfeife sie auf die Qualität der Formen.[13)] Kürzlich habe ich gehört, wie ein Führer der Tate einer Besuchergruppe vor Warrens Vitrinen Namen herunterbetete, als handle es sich um einen Stammbaum: «Sie sieht sich selbst in einer Tradition von Künstlern ...

Beuys, Cornell ...» Warren erklärt, dass diese Einflüsse tatsächlich «überwältigend» sein können, «aber es ist zwecklos, sie verstecken zu wollen ... [als wolle man zu verstehen geben] ... ‹Ich habe das gerade eben erfunden.›» Warren beschreibt sich selbst als jemanden, der in Büchern stöbert. Wenn sie jedoch etwas erwähnt, das ihre Aufmerksamkeit fesselt, nickt man und sieht es im Geiste vor sich. So hat sie etwa für einen Magazinbeitrag über Frauenporträts ein Bild von Maria Callas gewählt, auf dem ihr eine Stelle aus einem Buch von Diana Vreeland präsentiert wird – und dann tritt ein weibliches Lehmmonster auf.

Je besser sie als Künstlerin wird, desto mehr verfeinert sich ihr neckischer Umgang mit Hindernissen und Beschönigungen. Unterschiedliche Zonen – Perspexhauben, die eine Nummer zu klein sind – zeitlich bezeichnet mit einem Titel wie 2001, 2002, 2004 oder 2005: Es ist, als ob die Installationsanordnung die Sitten und Bräuche der jeweiligen Institution vorweg mit einbezöge. Robert Bressons *Un condamné à mort s'est échappé (Ein zum Tode Verurteilter ist entkommen)* ist einer der Filme, auf die Warren Bezug nimmt. Ein von der Gestapo zum Tode Verurteilter flieht oder geht dahin, wo der Wind ihn hinträgt; da ist ein Fluchtseil, lang und dünn; im Film sind die Details übertrieben und die Geräusche hallen nach. Als Spätentwicklerin will Warren sich alle Optionen offenhalten und gleichwohl dem «auf den Grund gehen», was es heisst, Kunst zu machen. «Das ist mir nicht leicht gefallen. Zunächst. In gewissem Sinn erfährt man eine Art Liebe von den Dingen, die man tut.»

(Übersetzung: Suzanne Schmidt)

1) «Rodin at the Royal Academy», 26. Sept. 2006–1. Jan. 2007, danach im Kunsthaus Zürich (9. Feb.–13. Mai 2007).
2) Dieses Zitat und alle folgenden Zitate ohne anderslautende Angaben stammen aus der Aufnahme für Jake Auerbachs Film, *Rodin: The Sculptors' View,* vom 18. Mai 2006 in Warrens Atelier, oder aus schriftlichen Notizen von einer früheren Unterhaltung im Atelier der Künstlerin am 11. April 2006.
3) Hugues Le Roux, «La Vie à Paris», *Le Temps,* 20. Juni 1889. (Zitat aus dem Engl. übers.)
4) Ein klassisches Zitat lautet: «Wenn man der Natur folgt, findet man alles. (...) Es handelt sich also nicht darum, Neues zu erschaffen ... In dem, was uns umgibt, ist alles enthalten.» Camille Mauclair, *Auguste Rodin, Leben und Werk,* Simon & Wahl, Egweil, o.J., S. 66–67.
5) «es noch verstärken, indem man die Vertiefung und die Buckel übertreibt, damit mehr Licht darauf fällt», Rodin, *Le Journal,* Paris, 12. Mai 1898. (Zitat hier aus dem Engl. übers.)
6) David Sylvester, *Interviews with American Artists,* Chatto & Windus, London 2001, S. 48–53. (Zitat aus dem Engl. übers.)
7) *Tate Triennial 2006: New British Art,* hrsg. v. Clarrie Wallis und Beatrix Ruf, Tate Britain, 2006, S. 138.
8) Rebecca Warren im Gespräch über den Film, den die Tate Gallery anlässlich der Turner-Prize-Verleihung 2006 produzierte.
9) Arshile Gorky, GARDEN IN SOCHI (1940–41), Gouache auf Karton, 55,9 x 71,1 cm.
10) Germaine Greer, «Are Rodin's bronzes erotic? Hardly – but they do tell us a lot about the sculptor's womanizing», *The Guardian,* 9. Oktober 2006, S. 24. (Zitat im Text aus dem Engl. übers.)
11) Film der Tate Gallery zum Turner Prize 2006. Man denkt dabei an die trostlosen Darstellungen männlicher Physis und Sexualität bei John Coplans, Paul McCarthy etc., und dennoch laufen die Kritiker Sturm gegen Warrens Sujets: Adrian Searle erklärt sich «gelangweilt» von ihren «fettarschigen und -brüstigen Lehmnutten» (*The Guardian,* 3. Okt. 2006); mehrere beklagen eine «feministische Botschaft». Julian Keeling beschreibt in seinem Artikel, «Shapes of things to come» (Harper's Bazaar, November 2006, S. 200), charmant, wie seine Bemühungen, das Gespräch in persönlichere Bahnen zu lenken, «mit einem Vortrag über Kunst» oder einem anderen Ablenkungsmanöver pariert wurden.
12) Michael Craig-Martin, «The Power of Now», *The Guardian,* 14. Okt. 2006, S. 11.
13) Lizzie Carey-Thomas, *Turner Prize 2006,* Broschüre der Tate Britain, 2006.

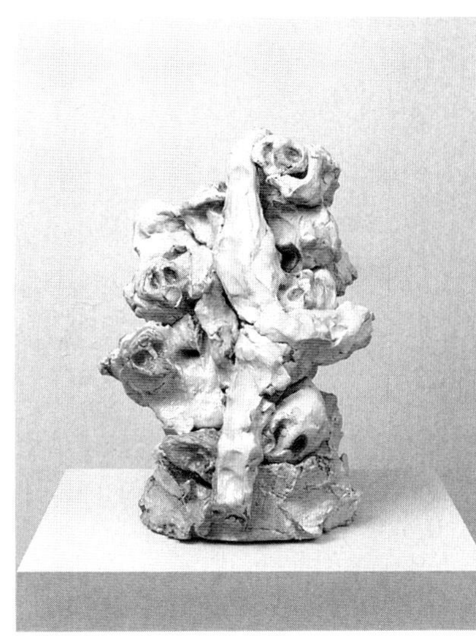

REBECCA WARREN, MADDER ROSE, 2003, self-firing, painted clay, plinth, 14 5/8 x 11 x 10 5/8" / VERRÜCKTERE ROSE, selbsttrocknender Ton, Sockel, 37 x 28 x 27 cm.

EDITION FOR PARKETT

REBECCA WARREN

Poincaré, 2006

Pompom and shoe, hand painted, mixed media,
2 3/4 x 2 3/4 x 2 3/8".
Edition of 35 / XX, signed and numbered certificate.

Pompom und Schuh, handbemalt, verschiedene Materialien
7 x 7 x 6 cm.
Auflage 35 / XX, signiertes und nummeriertes Zertifikat.

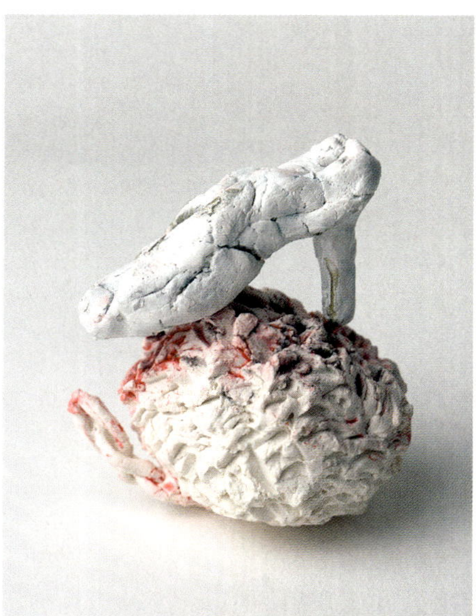

(PHOTOS: JAKE WALTERS, LONDON)

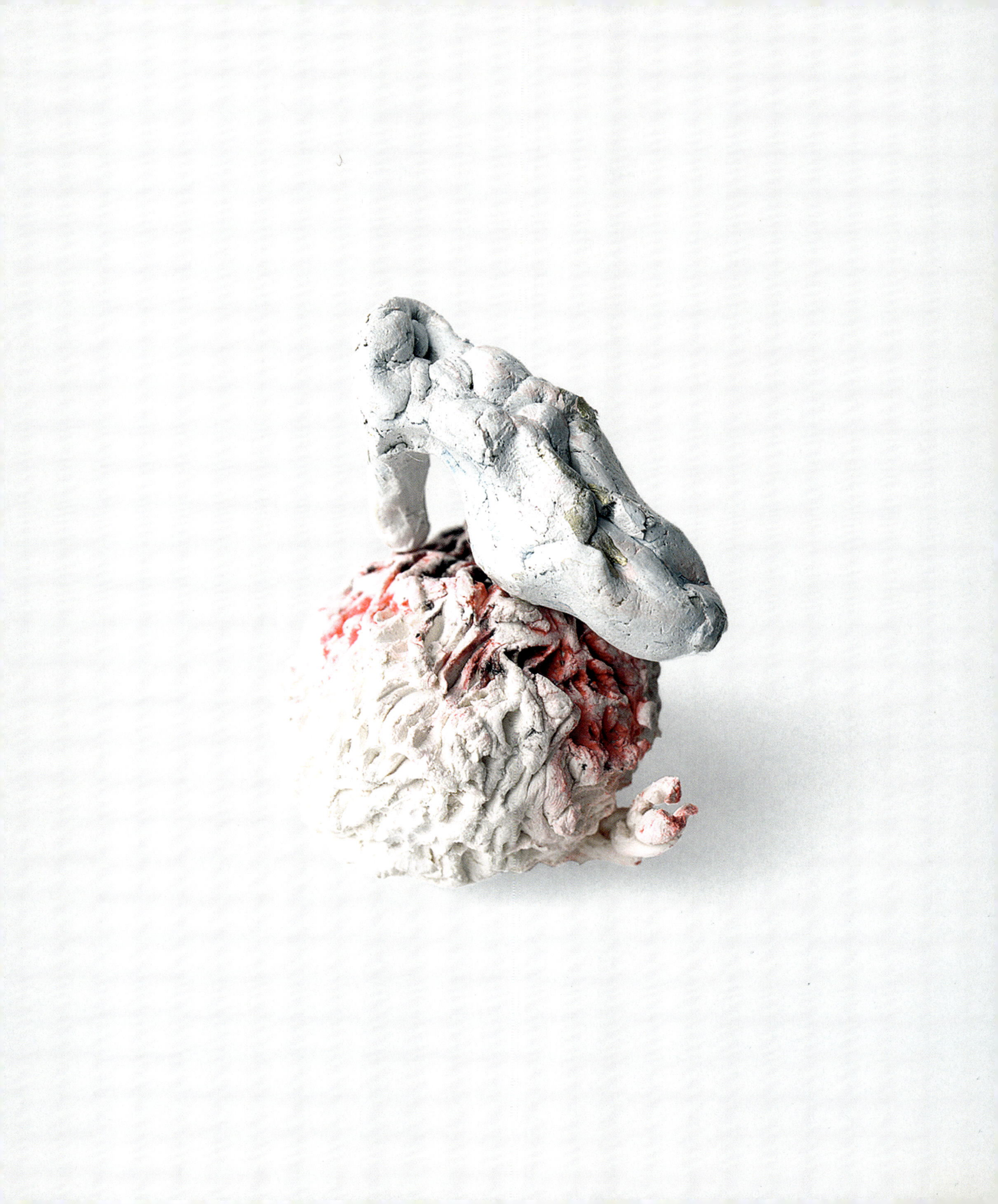

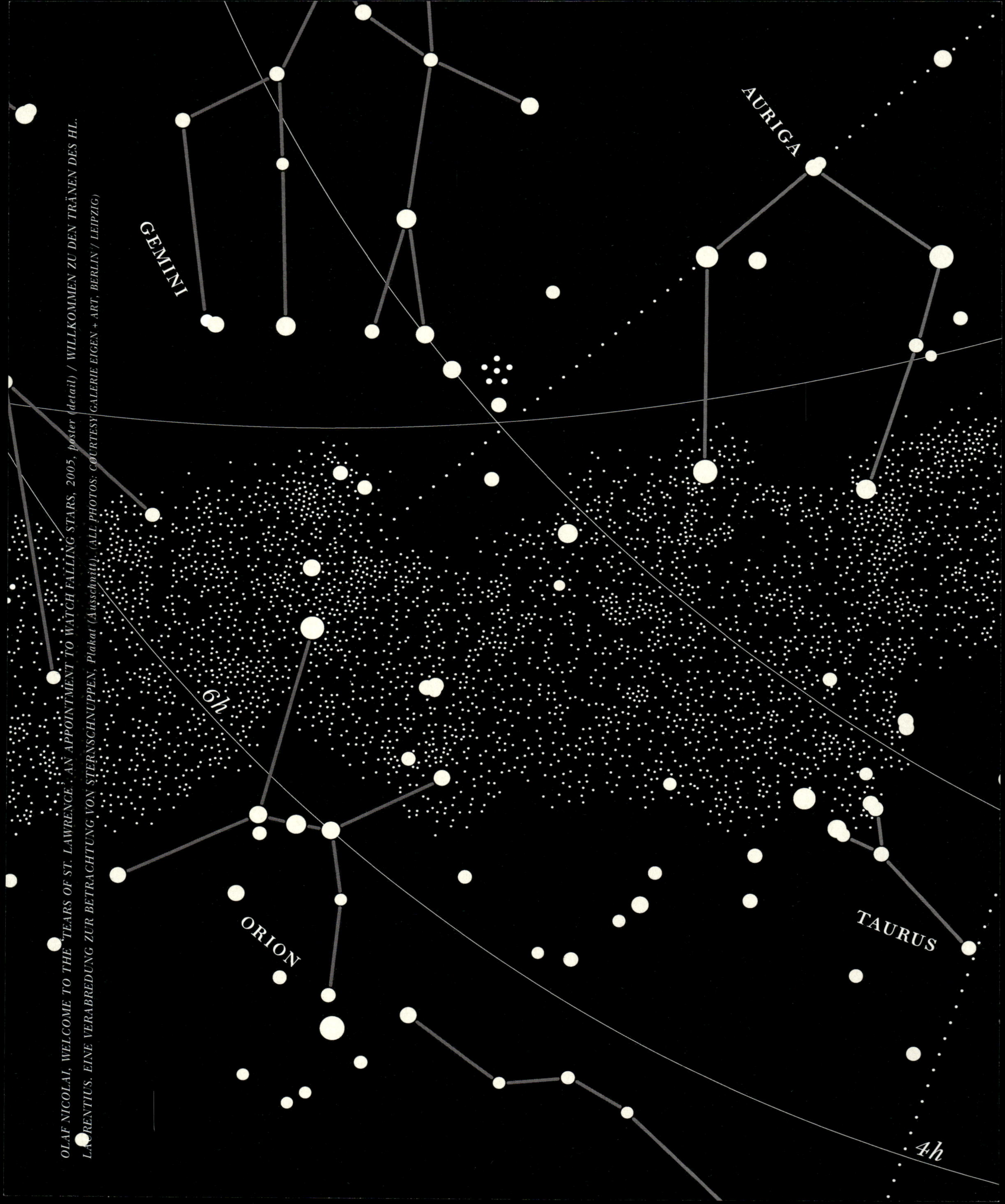

OLAF NICOLAI, WELCOME TO THE TEARS OF ST. LAWRENCE: AN APPOINTMENT TO WATCH FALLING STARS, 2005, *poster (detail)* / WILLKOMMEN ZU DEN TRÄNEN DES HL. LAURENTIUS. EINE VERABREDUNG ZUR BETRACHTUNG VON STERNSCHNUPPEN, *Plakat (Ausschnitt)*. (ALL PHOTOS: COURTESY GALERIE EIGEN + ART, BERLIN / LEIPZIG)

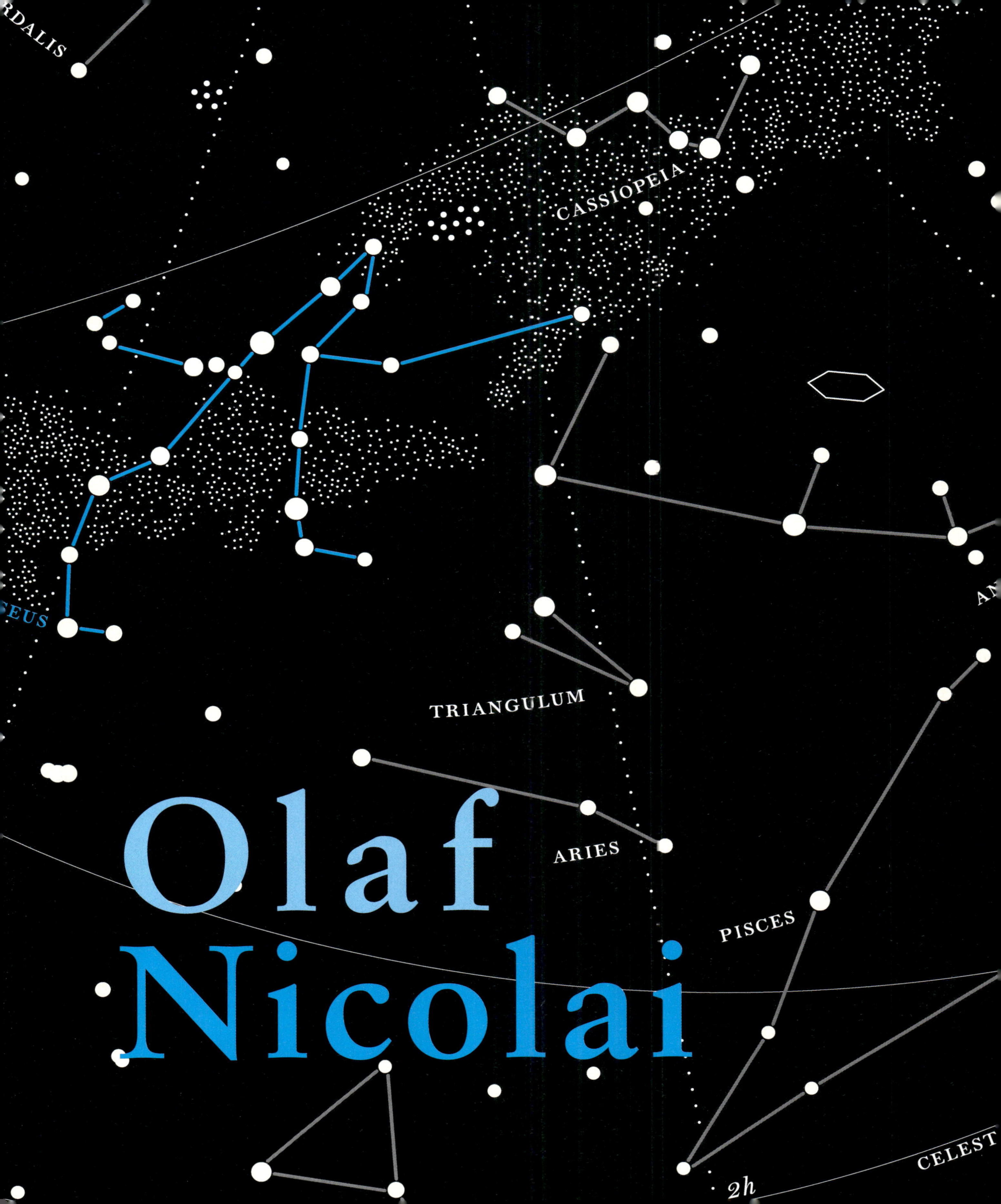
Olaf
Nicolai
CASSIOPEIA
TRIANGULUM
ARIES
PISCES
2h

Inside the Outside

VINCENT PÉCOIL

Though formalism was progressively discredited in the realm of art during the sixties and seventies, it is omnipresent today. With the advent of post-industrial capitalism and the invention of choice between competing products, "lifestyle" has become the ultimate manifestation of formalism in daily life. It is the secular brand of formalism, the form that emerges *after* the autonomy of art, in the era of value-added aesthetics, when the cultural industry has brought to completion the avant-garde project of integrating art and life. People carefully choose the color of their cars or their hair; they choose their outfits and the objects around them, according to elaborate formal criteria. Olaf Nicolai's publication of the "sampler" titled *Stilleben* (Still Life, 1999) offers to guide the reader through these choices, though ambiguously. Divided into three parts, the booklet contains the following categories: "space" (architecture), "human" (modeled after descriptions of people in fashion magazines), and "object/tool" (products like books, movies, and records, as well as designer furniture and high-tech equipment). The format of the book, with its horizontally divided page and perforations following each section, allows the reader to select one of the categories and combine it with the other two. Recalling the amalgam of objects, styles, and personalities, and one's experience of navigating them, the book alludes to the fact that, in contemporary culture, experience and life itself have become paramount market values, and the products of art have simply become an array of accessories. It seems a particular form of irony, when as a possible entrée to the work Nicolai selected a quote by filmmaker Jean-Luc Godard as an epigraph: "To me style is just the outside of content, and content the inside of style."

This kind of formalism has infiltrated every economic sector. In a market saturated by over-production, aesthetic value is of the utmost importance. Over the past few decades, the formalist aesthetic has therefore become the ultimate ambition of art's competitors, those against whom art has ceaselessly defined itself (negatively) during the last century as, for instance, interior decoration, advertising, marketing, or the entertainment industry. All of this formalism has spread outside the confines of art and has

VINCENT PÉCOIL is a writer and critic living in Dijon, France.

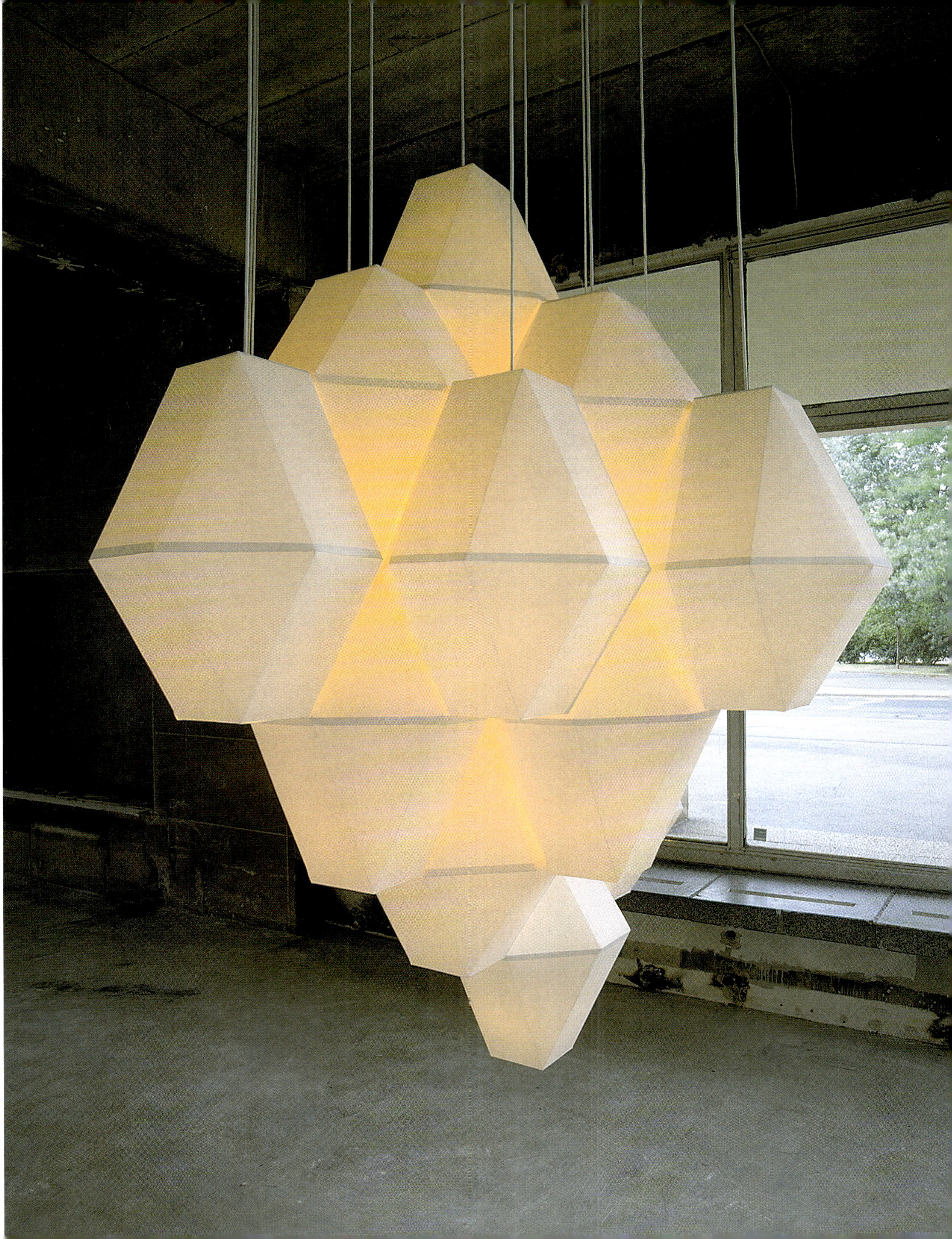

OLAF NICOLAI, DRESDEN 68, 2000, lamp made of 16 polyhedron elements, 78 ³/₄ x 78 ³/₄ x 78 ³/₄" / Lampe aus 16 Polyeder-Elementen, 200 x 200 x 200 cm.

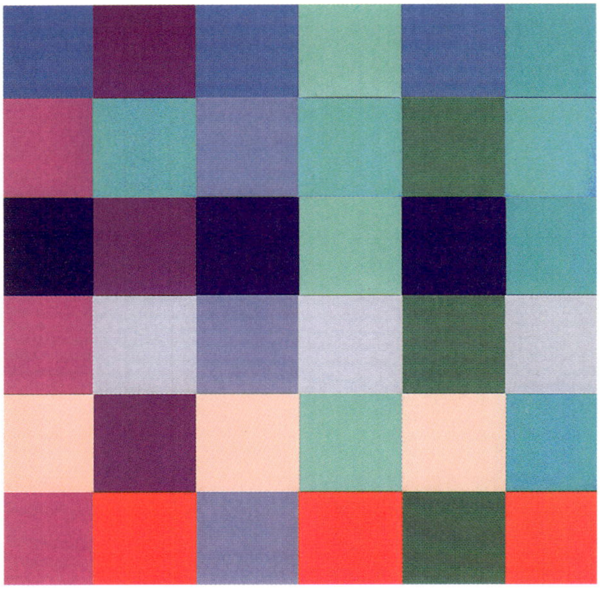

OLAF NICOLAI, KOMBINATION, since 2002, colored papers, 9 1/2 x 9 1/2" / farbige Papiere, 24 x 24 cm.

been taken over by corporate public relations, its formal principles placed at the service of communicative efficiency. One of the main problems with the issue of form today is the question of free use. Who owns forms and colors today? Those who author them, or those who use them? Artists and other members of the cultural industry all claim, as in a Socratic debate, that forms are their prerogative. Today, every simple form and every color is likely to refer to a brand. Just as we once spoke of an Ultramarine Blue, shall we soon get accustomed to speaking of a UPS Brown?

With PANTONE WALL (2000) and its companion piece, the pattern book *30 Farben* (30 Colors), Nicolai attempts a kind of symbolic and self-reflexive reappropriation of the codification of colors. PANTONE WALL consists of a wall covered with colored paper in thirty different hues chosen from the Pantone chart. The installation also includes commissioned, looped segments of ambient music, composed by the group To Rococo Rot (from which users can choose their favorites), like a historical reminder of early abstract art's analogy with musical composition, and its correlation of sound and color.

Nicolai is, in fact, fascinated by Pantone's promotion of its own licensed products as a "new language of colors." The invention of such a language was previously the domain of theorists, scientists, architects, and artists in search of an objective grammar of sensations. Today, it is the public relations experts who are turning to the color codes of modernism, parsing through the codified associations between hues and emotions as they were once formalized by the pioneers of pictorial abstraction.

Countering this codifying effort, Nicolai has continued working on the question of color with *Kombinationen* (Combinations, since 2002). Each *Kombination* piece (multicolor 36-square chessboard patterns) is created from the pre-defined set of thirty colors selected for the piece PANTONE WALL. The arrangement of the colors is determined by chance, based on the stochastic procedure of the Urn model, a production technique that allows for 2×30^{12} variations. The recourse to mathematics may recall the historical ambition (since Post-Impressionism and until the 1950s) to turn the use of color in art into an exercise endowed with scientific legitimacy. But while the goals of science are certitude, order, and invariance, here, for the artwork, the use of probability calculations ensures the continual and disorderly variation of the composition. Rather than expressing a preconceived, transcendental order, meaning and form become surface effects. They "slide down the surface of things," as in the U2 song The Real Thing, which the narrator in *Glamorama* keeps repeating as a leitmotif,[1)] or like the "facts" of Stoic philosophy that glide on the surface of profound being, as Gilles Deleuze describes it in *The Logic of Sense.*[2)]

In NOMS DE GUERRE (Pseudonyms, 2006), the words and phrases printed on the page, or mounted on the wall with neon tubes of black light, no longer simply refer to the things they designate. Beyond the poetic, free associations they trigger, they are the code names of military operations (a description of the respective military campaign is included on the back of each piece of paper); words like "evening light" or "sculpture" thus function like history erupting in the tranquil universe of art for art's sake. In this set of concrete poems, meaning could be thought of as camouflaged, or as appearing only stealthily, depending on the lighting. One might also conceive of artworks as screens over which forms merely slide, as a number of pieces by Nicolai seem to suggest. In CELIO (2004), for example, the pictorial surface becomes a screen, thus displacing the old analogy of painting as a window onto an imaginary space or a mirror of optical reality (as also suggested by Duchamp's FRESH WIDOW, 1920). The work recalls the formal vocabulary of minimal art and, ultimately, the influence of the Bauhaus, with its insistence on openness and transparency. But here this ideal of transparency is undermined by an opaque screen, whose overlaid grid-like structure evokes the bars on the windows of Italian prisons. Though the bars are turned inwards and projected within the space of art rather than being placed on the outside of a façade, the piece conjures the "cultural confinement" once denounced by Robert Smithson—referring, as it does, to the reality of imprisonment—while its scale metaphorically underscores the "privacy" of the relationship between the viewer and the work.

The building façades of contemporary society, as in Times Square, Ginza, or Piccadilly, have gradually turned into giant screens. The Bauhaus wall/glass curtain and its ideal of transparency has now given way to the building façade as a screen for the moving image, thus marking the shift of television and cinema from domestic to public space. The relationship that forms between a viewer and a screen differs from that between a viewer and a painting. To point to the meaning of the word WYSIWYG (computer software vernacular for a type of graphic interface, an abbre-

OLAF NICOLAI, 30 COLORS, 2000, installation with sound, monochrome strips of paper in 30 color combinations, dimensions variable / 30 FARBEN, Rauminstallation mit Sound, monochrome Papierstreifen, 30 Farben, Dimensionen variabel.

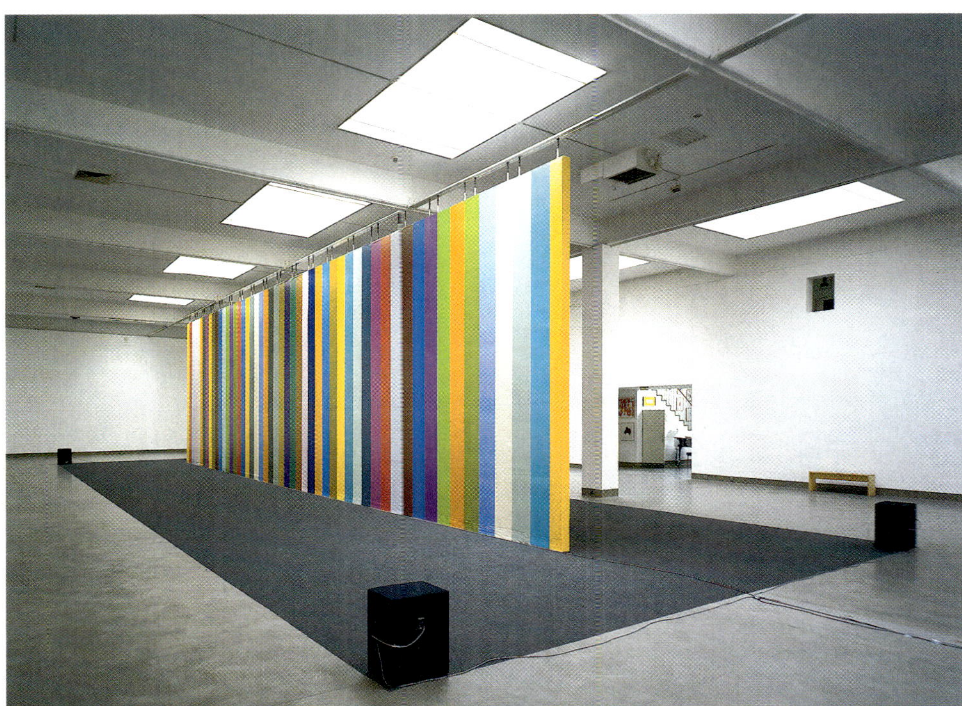

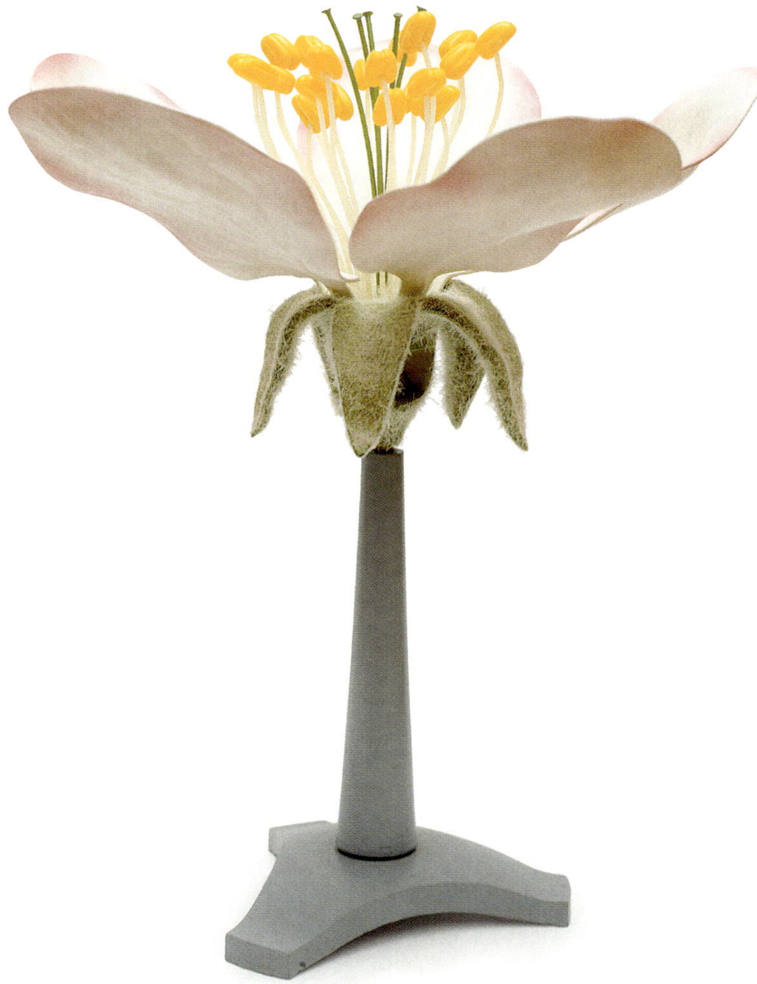

OLAF NICOLAI, APPLE BLOSSOM, 1996/1998, plastic, wood, 15 1/8 x 11 3/4 x 11 3/4" / APFELBLÜTE, Kunststoff, Holz, 38,5 x 30 x 30cm.

viation of "What you see is what you get"), as Nicolai wrote in "Even Better...WYSIWYG,"[3)] is a way of suggesting that the aesthetic has become an interface between the viewer and the world, while also alluding to Frank Stella's famous statement, "what you see is what you see," and introducing doubt about that tautology's seeming self-evidence. What you get is what you see, but it may not be all there is to get, thus pointing out one of the obvious conditions of the digital image and, in fact, of images per se, namely their dependence on a carrier, in this case a screen, which serves both to subtract something from the viewer's eyes and to support what is shown.

The wall painting YEUX DE PAON (Peacock Eye Feather, 2004) is one such screen-surface. "The bright pattern of white, blue and cream lines, and drops set against a brown background originate in a common Bulgarian pottery pattern."[4)] To promote tourism in the early 1970s, the traditional craft of patterned pottery was reintroduced and went into mass production. In Nicolai's work patterns function as seductive objects of visual pleasure, reminiscent of Op Art motifs with their hallucinatory effects or the peacock's tail with its mimetic eyes: what you see may not be what you get. ARCUS (2004), another wall painting, consists of the duplicated and symmetrically mirrored shape of a graphic tool used to draw curves. Again, the composition suggests that what we see is not what we get, but rather what we project onto the image. ARCUS is a do-it-yourself image, a tool for producing not the "right" image, but just an image. Meaning and function glide over forms, and Nicolai's work is an invitation to follow the movement through, as in the models, reduced to half their original size, of Judd's objects such as MÖBEL / SKULPTUR (NACH DONALD JUDD) I-IV (Furniture/ Sculpture, After Donald Judd, 2000), some of which were inverted to be used as benches in the exhibition space where they were shown, drawing attention to the status of industrially produced functional artworks. The poster INSTRUCTION FOR PRODUCING A WORK AFTER DONALD JUDD (2000), like a manual for IKEA furniture assembly, reinforces the fact that these "precious" objects could be made by all, and at will.

DRESDEN 68 (2000) and BASTEI (2004) draw attention to the secularization of perspective through the formal idiom of modernism. In a re-appropriating move, DRESDEN 68 uses as its basic element a shape repeated in a decorative pattern on the façade of a department store. The transformation of the pattern into a lamp sculpture functions as a reminder of the derivative usage of artworks in architectural decoration. In BASTEI, the forms re-used by Nicolai come from an ornamental stone on the wall of a 1960s shopping mall boulevard in the same city of Dresden. The smooth finish and varied, modular shape of the fiberglass cast gives it a minimal look, ultimately foregrounding the shift of meaning produced by an "applied" sculpture that can be variously presented and viewed.

Since we are condemned to live in this world (here and now), we must invent uses for the forms that populate it. This is the implicit statement of a series of works, *Die Flamme der Revolution*, in its different guises. The sculpture, titled DIE FLAMME DER REVOLUTION, LIEGEND (IN WOLFSBURG) (The Flame of the Revolution, Reclining, in Wolfsburg, 2002), is inspired by a monument to the fiftieth anniversary of the Russian Revolution by Siegbert Fliegel. Instead of being erected vertically, like the original monument, Nicolai's piece lies horizontally on the floor, alluding, as it were, to the destiny of monuments and their propensity to end up symbolically toppled. DIE FLAMME... is a paradoxical monument, a monument twice over: it commemorates the end of a commemoration. A possible monument to the end of the revolution, it becomes, when lying flat, an abstract formal gesture. Emptied of its "content," relocated from the exterior of the public space to the interior of the museum, it becomes a cultural product comparable to a slightly baroque, minimal art work. FLAMME DER REVOLUTION, FLIEGEND (Flame of the Revolution, Flying, 2004) is a series of technical drawings representing nine views of this same shape rotating in space, like three-dimensional computer renderings of a technological machine or an architectural model.

Whereas our age seems obsessed with the "contents" of different media and their correct usage, Nicolai himself is more interested in form and its uses. This is not synonymous with formalism. Nicolai proposes the idea that artistic work, far from being an innocent formal game, could be a method for engaging with forms, thereby offering a possible definition for today's art. If concepts are tools and philosophy the box that contains them (it is in this manner that Deleuze and Foucault spoke of them), art can be viewed as the practice of living in forms, and works of art as specific exercises.

(Translation from the French: Anthony Allen)

1) Quoted by Olaf Nicolai, "Even Better...WYSIWYG," in *Kritisches Lexikon der Gegenwartskunst*, vol. 75, no. 20, 3rd quarter 2006, Munich, 2006. *Glamorama* is a 1998 novel by Bret Easton Ellis.
2) Gilles Deleuze, *The Logic of Sense*, Chapter 2: "Second series of paradoxes of surface effects" (New York: Columbia University Press, 1990), pp. 4-11.
3) Olaf Nicolai (see note 1).
4) Christian Rattemeyer, "Model Modelisms" (Artist Space exhibition publication, 2005).

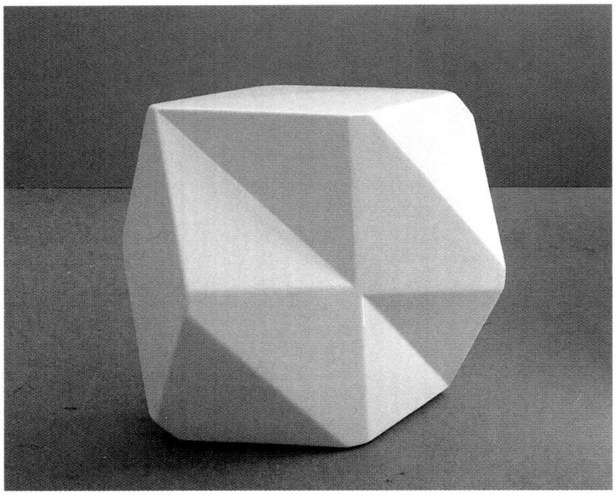

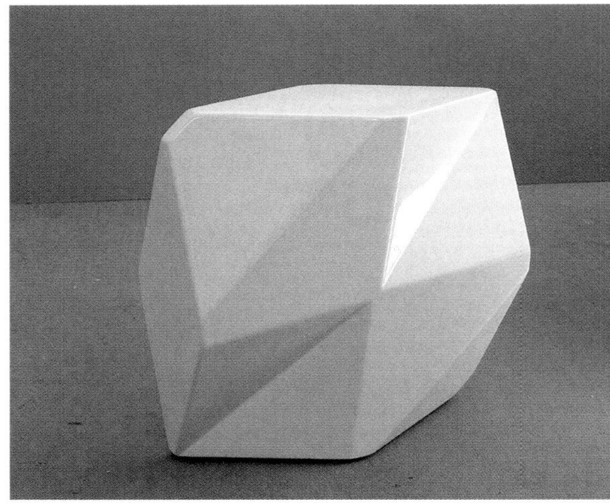

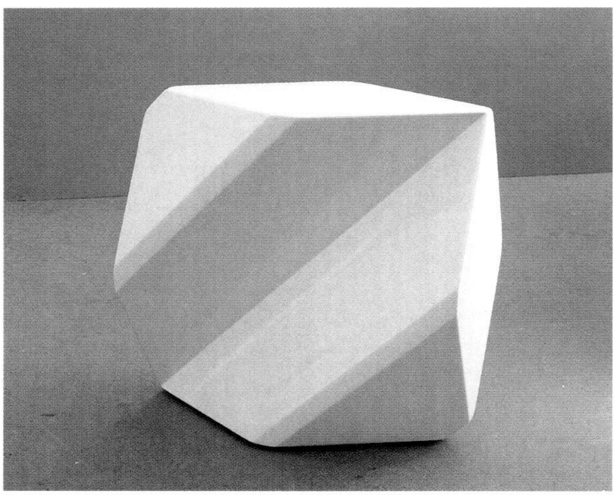

OLAF NICOLAI, BASTEI, 2004, fiberglas, acrylic lacquer, 9 x 25 1/8 x 23 3/4" / Fiberglas, Acryllack, 23 x 64 x 60 cm.

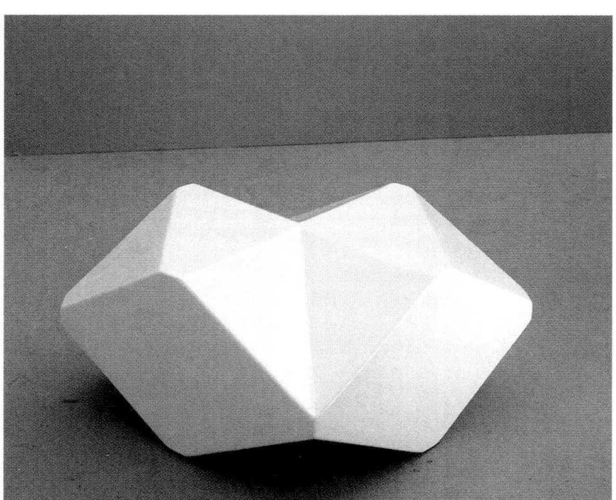

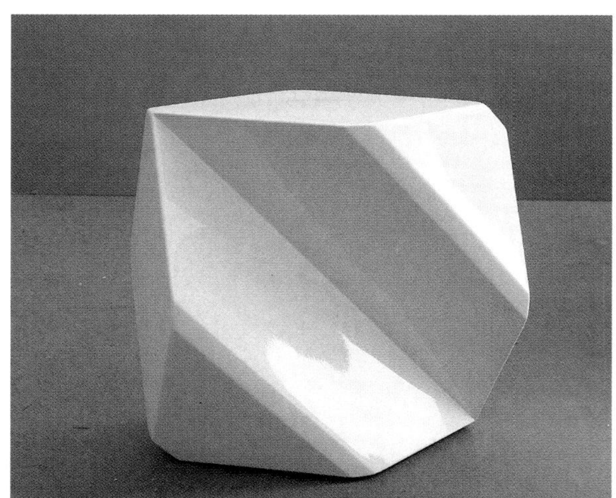

Die Innensicht der Aussensicht

VINCENT PÉCOIL

Obschon der Formalismus in der Kunst der 60er und 70er Jahre zunehmend in Misskredit geriet, ist er im heutigen Alltag wieder allgegenwärtig. Mit der Ausbildung, des postindustriellen Kapitalismus und dessen Vollendung: der freien Verfügbarkeit konkurrierender Produkte – ist der *Lifestyle* zum ultimativen Ausdruck des Formalismus im täglichen Leben geworden. Es ist dies eine säkularisierte Variante des Formalismus, die die Autonomie der Kunst ablöst, in einer Ära der Dominanz des ästhetischen Werts, in der das Projekt der Avantgarde, die Kunst in den Alltag zu integrieren, von der Kulturindustrie vollendet wird. Aufgrund elaborierter formaler Kriterien entscheiden die Leute über die Farbe ihres Autos oder ihrer Haare, sowie die Kleidung und die Gegenstände, mit denen sie sich umgeben. Nicolais Buch *Stilleben, A Sampler* (2000) bietet dem Leser eine hintersinnige Anleitung für die Wahl zwischen verschiedenen Optionen. Horizontal in drei Abschnitte unterteilt, ist die Broschüre in folgende Kategorien gegliedert: «Space» (Architektur), «Human» (Beschreibungen von Personen, wie in Modemagazinen) und «Objekt/Tool» (Produkte wie Bücher, Filme, Schallplatten, Designermöbel und Hightech-Geräte). Das System der horizontal unterteilten Seiten, die der Gliederung folgend perforiert sind und aufgetrennt werden können, erlaubt es dem Leser, eine Kategorie zu wählen und das Gewählte dann mit Dingen aus den anderen Kategorien zu samplen. Denkt man an den Mix der Objekte, Stile und Persönlichkeiten und den Umgang mit ihnen, so spielt das Buch darauf an, dass in der zeitgenössischen Kultur die Erfahrung und das Leben den höchsten Marktwert haben und dem künstlerischen Produkt nicht mehr als der Status eines Accessoires zukommt. Es scheint eine besondere Form von Ironie am Werk, wenn Nicolai ein Zitat von Jean-Luc Godard an den Anfang der Publikation stellt: *To me style is just the outside of content, and content the inside of style...* (Für mich ist Stil nur das Äussere des Inhalts und Inhalt das Innere des Stils...)

Diese Art von Formalismus hat tatsächlich alle Bereiche der Wirtschaft erfasst. In einem durch Überproduktion satuierten Markt kommt dem ästhetischen Wert erstrangige Bedeutung zu. Aufgrund dieser Tatsache hat der formalistische Ehrgeiz in den letzten Jahrzehnten auch jene mit der Kunst konkurrierenden Bereiche erfasst, durch welche sie sich im Lauf des letzten Jahrhunderts unermüdlich (negativ) definiert hat: Innenarchitektur, Werbung, Marketing, Unterhaltungsindustrie... Der Formalismus hat den engeren Bereich der Kunst verlassen, um von den Public Relations vereinnahmt zu werden, und seine ästhetischen Prinzipien stehen nun im Dienste kommunikativer Effizienz. Eine akute Frage in der gegenwärtigen Diskussion um Brands betrifft die freie Verfügbarkeit. Wem gehören Formen und

VINCENT PÉCOIL ist Publizist und Kurator und lebt in Dijon, Frankreich.

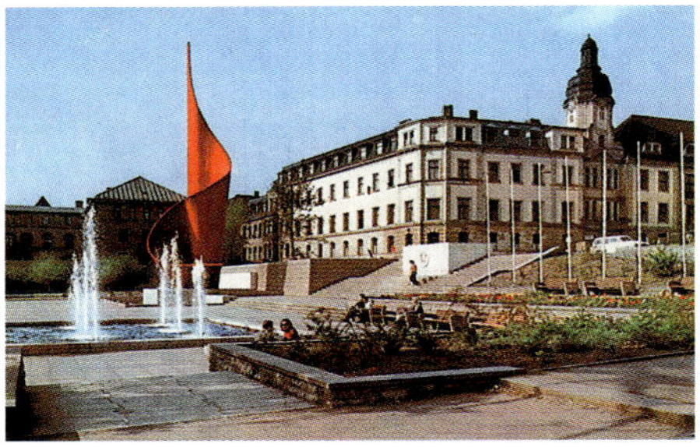

SIEGBERT FLIEGEL, THE FLAME OF THE REVOLUTION / FLAMME DER REVOLUTION, 1968, Halle (Saale).

Farben heute? Den Urhebern oder den Anwendern? Künstlerinnen und Künstler und die Vertreter der Kulturindustrie, alle behaupten, wie in einem sokratischen Dialog, dies fiele in ihr Ressort. Verweisen doch heute bestimmte Formen oder Farben bereits auf ganz konkrete Marken. Werden wir uns bald daran gewöhnen müssen, von UPS-Braun zu sprechen, so wie man früher von Ultramarin-Blau sprach?

Mit PANTONE WALL (2000) und dem begleitenden Musterbuch, *30 Farben,* unternimmt Nicolai eine Art symbolische und reflexive Wiederaneignung der Farbkodifizierung. Die Arbeit besteht aus farbigen Papierbögen, die in 30 Pantone-Farben eine Wand bedecken. Die Installation wird begleitet von verschiedenen Loops elektronischer Ambient-Musik, zwischen denen die Nutzer wählen können und die speziell für diese Arbeit bei der Band To Rococo Rot in Auftrag gegeben wurden. All das wirkt wie eine historische Reminiszenz auf die frühen Abstrakten und deren Versuche, Klangfarben und Farbtöne zu analogisieren.

Nicolai war durch die Tatsache fasziniert, dass der Farbhersteller sein lizenziertes Sortiment als «neue Farbensprache» anpries; früher war die Erfindung einer solchen Sprache den Philosophen, Naturwissenschaftlern, Architekten und Künstlern vorbehalten gewesen, im Rahmen ihrer Suche nach einer objektiven Grammatik der Sinneswahrnehmungen. Heute hingegen sind es vielmehr Kommunikations-Experten, die sich der Regeln der modernen Farbkodifizierung bemächtigen, indem sie Entsprechungen von Farbtönen und Emotionen klassifizieren, die ursprünglich von Pionieren der abstrakten Malerei formuliert und formalisiert wurden. Nicolai wirkt diesem Kodifizierungsversuch entgegen und führte seine Arbeit mit der Serie *Kombinationen* (seit 2002) fort. Sämtliche Werke der *Kombinationen* (mehrfarbige schachbrettartige Motive mit 36 Feldern) entstehen anhand der vorgegebenen 30 Pantone-Farben der Arbeit PANTONE WALL aus dem Jahr 2000. Die Anordnung der Farben bei den verschiedenen Versionen ist zufällig und die Produktionstechnik ermöglicht – nach Berechnungen mithilfe des Urnemodells, einem stochastischen Verfahren – eine extrem hohe Anzahl von Kombinationen (2x30^{12} Varianten). Dieser Rückgriff auf die Mathematik mag uns an frühere Versuche – vom Postimpressionismus bis in die 50er Jahre – erinnern, die Anwendung der Farbe in der Kunst zu einer wissenschaftlich untermauerten Methode zu machen. Wenn die wissenschaftlichen Zielsetzungen Gewissheit, das Wegfallen der Willkür, Ordnung, mit anderen Worten etwas Beständiges anstreben, sichert die Anwendung einer Produktionsrgel dem Kunstwerk die fortwährende Variation der Komposition. Statt Ausdruck einer bereits vorab ausgedachten transzendentalen Ordnung zu sein, werden Sinn und Form zu Oberflächeneffekten. «*Slide down the surface of things*» – sie gleiten an der Oberfläche der Dinge ab – wie in dem Song *The Real Thing* von U2, der dem von Nicolai zitierten Protagonisten des Romans *Glamorama* nicht mehr aus dem Kopf will,[1] oder wie die Tatsachen an der Oberfläche des «tiefen und wirklichen Seins» in der Philosophie der Stoiker, die Gilles Deleuze in *Logik des Sinns* schildert.[2]

In NOMS DE GUERRE (2006) steigert die Aneinanderreihung der – auf Papier gedruckten oder in Form von Schwarzlicht-Leuchtröhren an der Wand montierten – Wörter und Sätze die freien poetischen Assoziationen; hier wird nicht mehr nur buchstabengetreu auf die bezeichneten Dinge verwiesen, sondern auf Codenamen militärischer Operationen (eine Beschreibung der jeweiligen militärischen Kampagne findet sich auf der Rückseite jedes einzelnen Blattes). Mit «Evening Light» (Abendlicht) or «Sculpture» (Skulptur) bricht die Geschichte schlagartig in die Stille des *L'art pour l'art*-Universums ein. In diesem Ensemble experimenteller Gedichte ist der Sinn quasi «getarnt» oder wird erst im Rahmen der Aufklärung als ein geheimer sichtbar. Man kann

OLAF NICOLAI, THE FLAME OF THE REVOLUTION, RECLINING (IN WOLFSBURG), 2002, wood, steel, concrete plaster, special paint, 173 1/4 x 669 1/4 x 240" / FLAMME DER REVOLUTION, LIEGEND (IN WOLFSBURG), Holz, Stahl, Betonputz, Spezialfarbe, 440 x 1700 x 610 cm.

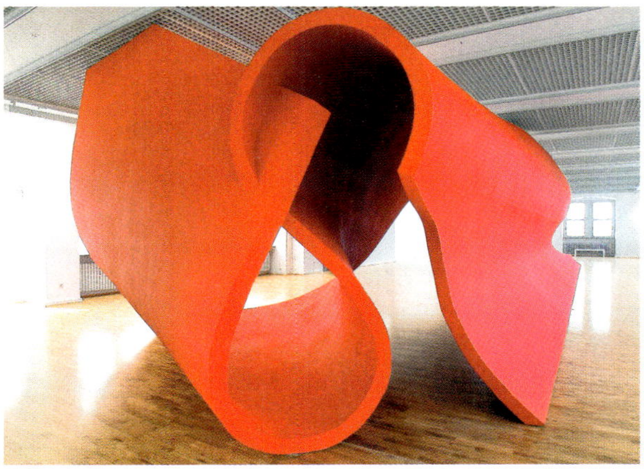

sich die Arbeiten auch als Projektionsflächen vorstellen, auf denen die Form ins Gleiten gerät: Implizit wird dies in anderen Werken von Nicolai angedeutet, etwa in CELIO (2004), wo die Malfläche zur Projektionsfläche wird und an die Stelle der alten Analogie Bild/Fenster tritt, egal, ob sie einen imaginären Raum eröffnet oder als Spiegel der optischen Realität dient (wie angedeutet in Duchamps FRESH WIDOW, 1920). Der Anblick des Werkes erinnert an die formale Sprache der Minimal Art, die letztlich auf das Bauhaus zurückgeht und auf Offenheit und Transparenz gegründet ist, nur ist das Prinzip der Transparenz hier durch eine undurchdringliche Bildschirmfläche ersetzt, die einen an die Gitter vor den Fenstern italienischer Gefängnisse erinnert. Hier allerdings, nicht an der Aussenfassade angebracht, sondern ins Innere des Kunstraumes vorspringend, sprechen die Gitter strukturell das Gefangensein in der Kultur *(cultural confinement)* an, das Robert Smithson anprangerte, auch wenn er des-

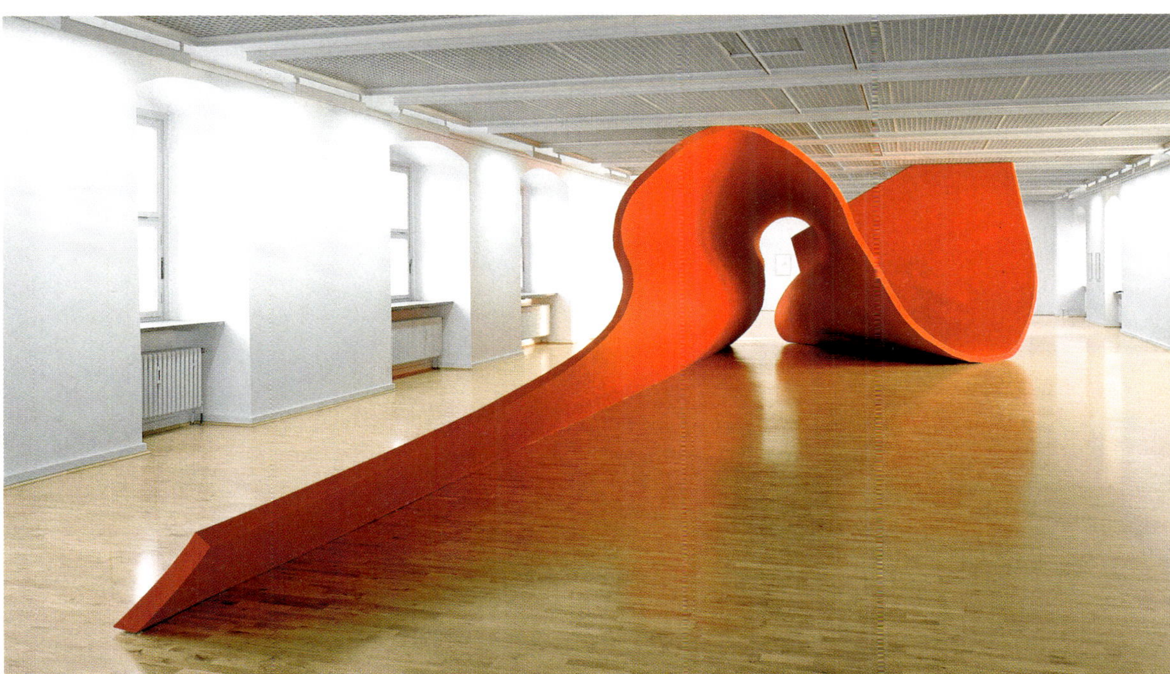

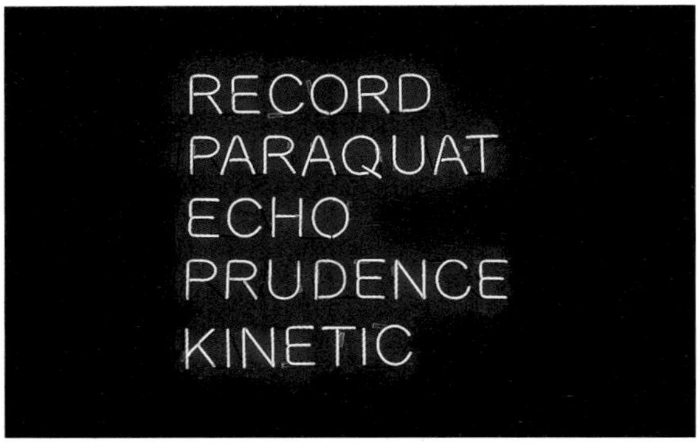

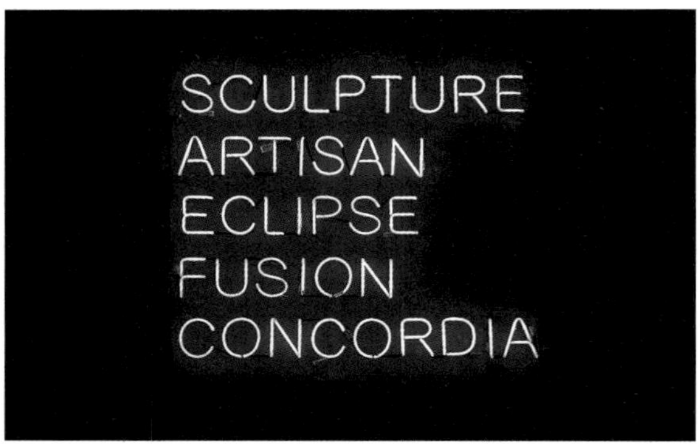

OLAF NICOLAI, NOMS DE GUERRES, 2006, argon, black light filter, height of text, 7 7/8" / Argon, Schwarzlicht-Filter, Höhe Text 20 cm.

sen Tragweite gleichzeitig relativierte, indem er auf unsere reale Gefangenschaft im Universum verwies und in seiner Metaphorik den physischen Charakter des Privaten in der Beziehung zwischen Betrachter und Werk betonte.

Im heutigen urbanen Umfeld verwandeln sich Gebäudefassaden – Times Square, Ginza oder Picadilly Circus mögen als Beispiel dienen – allmählich in gigantische Bildschirme. Auf die ideale Transparenz der Glasvorhangfassade der Bauhaus-Architektur folgte die Integration des bewegten Bildes und markiert den Vorstoss von Film und Fernsehen aus dem privaten in den öffentlichen Raum. Die Beziehung zwischen Betrachter und Bildschirm ist eine andere als beim Bild. Hier sei der Sinn des Wortes WYSIWYG in Erinnerung gerufen (eine Abkürzung von *What You See Is What You Get* – ein in der Informatik gebräuchlicher Ausdruck zur Bezeichnung des Prinzips der graphischen Benutzeroberfläche: Was man sieht, ist, was man bekommt), wie Nicolai es in seinem Text «Even Better ... WYSIWYG» (März, 2000) schreibt, um darauf hinzuweisen, dass die Ästhetik zur Schnittstelle zwischen Betrachter und Welt geworden ist.[3)] Gleichzeitig ist es aber auch ein listiges Spiel mit Frank Stellas bekanntem Ausspruch, *What you see is what you see* (Was man sieht, ist, was man sieht), indem das offensichtlich Tautologische des Satzes in Zweifel gezogen wird. Was man bekommt, ist was man sieht, aber das ist vielleicht nicht alles, was zu haben ist – ein Hinweis auf eine der offensichtlichen Bedingungen der Sichtbarkeit nicht nur des digitalen Bildes, nämlich seiner Abhängigkeit von Projektionsflächen, die als Bildträger immer auch etwas verbergen, indem sie sichtbar machen.

Nicolais Wandbild YEUX DE PAON (Pfauenaugen, 2004) ist eine solche Projektionsfläche. «Das helle Muster in weisser, blauer und beigen Linien auf braunem Grund geht zurück auf ein in der bulgarischen Keramik gebräuchliches Motiv.»[4)] In den frühen 70er Jahren, ging die gemusterte Keramik zur Förderung des Tourismus als traditionelles bulgarisches Kunsthandwerk in Massenproduktion. In Nicolais Arbeiten funktionieren die Muster als verführerische Objekte eines visuellen Vergnügens und wecken Erinnerungen an die Muster der Op-Art mit ihren Täuschungseffekten. Die Pfauenaugen sind Köder: *What you see is maybe not what you get ...* (Was man sieht, ist vielleicht nicht, was man bekommt.) ARCUS (2004), ein weiteres Wandbild, besteht aus der vielfach gespiegelten Form eines Graphikwerkzeuges, das zum Zeichnen von Kurven dient. Die Komposition erinnert ebenfalls daran, dass was man sieht, einmal mehr nicht das ist, was man bekommt, sondern eher, was man hineinprojiziert. ARCUS ist also ein *Do-it-yourself*-Bild, ein Werkzeug, das eben nicht das «richtige» Bild erzeugt, sondern einfach nur Bilder. Sinn und Funktion gleiten über die Formen, und die Arbeit von Nicolai ist eine Einladung, dieser Bewegung zu folgen; das gilt auch für die in fünfzig Prozent der Originalgrösse reproduzierten Modelle einiger Objekte von Judd (MÖBEL / SKULPTUR NACH DONALD JUDD, I–IV, 2000), die unter anderem um 180 Grad gedreht im Ausstellungsraum als Sitzbänke verwendet wurden und auf den Status von industriell hergestellten Kunstwerken verwiesen. Das Plakat INSTRUCTION FOR PRODUCING A WORK AFTER DONALD JUDD (2000) (Anleitung zur Produktion eines Kunstwerks nach Donald Judd) glich einer Montageanleitung für IKEA-Möbel und unterstrich noch einmal den Do-it-yourself-Charakter der «kostbaren» Objekte.

DRESDEN 68 (2000) und BASTEI (2004) schärfen den Blick für die Säkularisierung der Formensprache des Modernismus. In einer re-appropriativen Gebärde verwendet DRESDEN 68 als Basismodul ein Formelement, das als dekoratives Muster an der Fassade eines Warenhauses verwendet wurde. Die Umwandlung der Skulptur in einen Beleuchtungskörper erinnert an die Verwendung von Kunstobjekten als dekorative Derivate für architektonische Zwecke. Im Fall von BASTEI ist es ein ornamentaler Stein, der zum Bau einer Mauer in einem Dresdener Einkaufsboulevard benutzt wurde, den Nicolai wieder verwendet. Der glatte Finish der Fiberglas-Gussformen und der modulare Körper verleihen ihm einen minimalistischen Look, der – verstärkt durch die variable Präsentation dieser «angewandten» plastischen Form – eine Bedeutungsverschiebung auslöst.

Da wir dazu verurteilt sind, hier und jetzt in dieser Welt zu leben, müssen wir einen Umgang mit den Formen finden, die sie bevölkern. Das kommt implizit in den Varianten der Serie DIE FLAMME DER REVOLUTION zum Ausdruck. DIE FLAMME DER REVOLUTION, LIEGEND (IN WOLFSBURG) (2002) ist eine Skulptur, die durch ein Denkmal Siegbert Fliegels zum 50. Jahrestag der Russischen Revolution angeregt wurde. Statt wie das Original aufrecht zu stehen, liegt die Skulptur. Man kann darin eine Anspielung auf das klassische Schicksal der Denkmäler sehen, die oft so enden, dass sie symbolhaft vom Sockel gestürzt werden. DIE FLAMME ... ist tatsächlich ein paradoxes Monument im Quadrat: Es gedenkt des Endes eines Gedenkens und als mögliches Denkmal am Ende der Revolution wird es, liegend, zu einer abstrakten formalen Geste. Derart seines «Gehalts» entleert und vom Aussenraum des öffentlichen Platzes ins Innere des Museums verfrachtet, wird es zur kulturellen Ware, ähnlich einem etwas barock geratenen Werk der Minimal Art. FLAMME DER REVOLUTION, FLIEGEND (2004) besteht aus einer Serie von technischen Zeichnungen, die neun Ansichten einer simulierten Rotation derselben Form im Raum zeigen, wie dreidimensionale Computerzeichnungen eines abstrakten Architekturmodells.

Während unsere Zeit besessen scheint von «Inhalten» verschiedener Medien und ihrem korrekten Gebrauch, interessiert sich Nicolai für die Form und ihre Verwendungsmöglichkeiten. Das ist nicht dasselbe wie Formalismus. Nicolai entwickelte die Idee, dass die künstlerische Arbeit, weit davon entfernt, unschuldige formale Spielerei zu sein, eine Methode sein könnte, um sich auf Formen einzulassen, womit er eine mögliche Definition für die aktuelle zeitgenössische Kunst liefert: Wenn Begriffe Werkzeuge sind und Philosophie die Kiste, in der sie aufbewahrt werden (wie Deleuze oder Foucault behaupten), kann man die Kunst als eine Praxis der Auseinandersetzung mit dem Leben in Formen verstehen und die Werke als spezifische Übungen.

(Übersetzung: Suzanne Schmidt)

1) Olaf Nicolai, «Even Better ... WYSIWYG», in: *Kritisches Lexikon der Gegenwartskunst*, Ausgabe 75, Heft 20, 3. Quartal 2006, München, 2006.
Glamorama, Roman von Bret Easton Ellis (engl. 1998, dt. 1999).
2) Gilles Deleuze, *Logik des Sinns*, Suhrkamp, Frankfurt am Main 1993, 2. Kapitel: «2. Serie der Paradoxa. Von den Oberflächeneffekten», S. 19–28, hier: S. 20.
3) Olaf Nicolai (siehe Anm. 1).
4) Christian Rattemeyer, *Model Modelisms* (Artist Space exhibition publication, 2005).

RE-PERCEPTIONS

CHARLES ESCHE

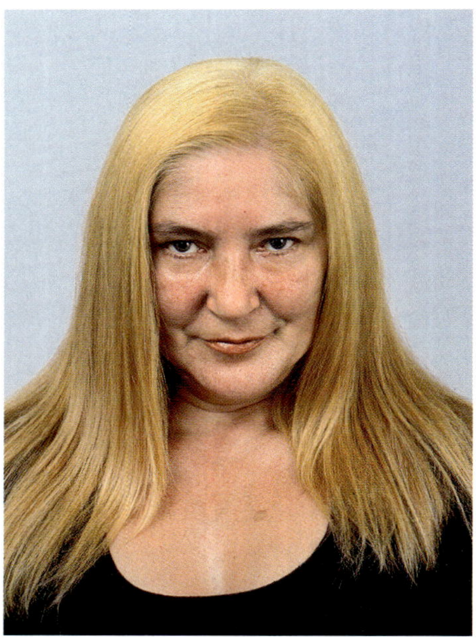

OLAF NICOLAI, THE BLONDES, 2003/2005, C-print, series of 42, each 13 3/8 x 9 7/8" / C-Print, 42-teilige Serie, je 34 x 25 cm.

Art isn't something most people think about on a daily basis. It is not bound into our social schedules the way political, economic, and entertainment news is thrust down our throats twenty-four hours a day. It doesn't have that kind of status in the media. It's not merely the representation of our society but more the actual experience of our globalized world. Most manifestations of art are therefore relatively easy to ignore, for the majority, and at a time when the need for intellectual-information filters is at a premium, it doesn't take much encouragement to ignore something. This is why populism arises in art institutions that want to command attention; much art is simply not very good at generating attention for itself, so other strategies are needed.

What art can do, however, is quietly create the necessary conditions that will cause us to stop and think differently about the things we encounter every day. It is this possibility to think again about what we already know that art affords. No matter how legitimate its source, art can still claim to be worth something over and above its exchange value as a specialized consumer product. This is, of course, similar to many other kinds of academic knowledge—from philosophy to physics—except these, by and large, all rely on the written word to communicate their revelations. Art isn't so constrained; it shakes us at other levels, releases other triggers in our brains.

CHARLES ESCHE is director of the Van Abbemuseum, Eindhoven, and co-editor of *Afterall* Journal and *Afterall* Books.

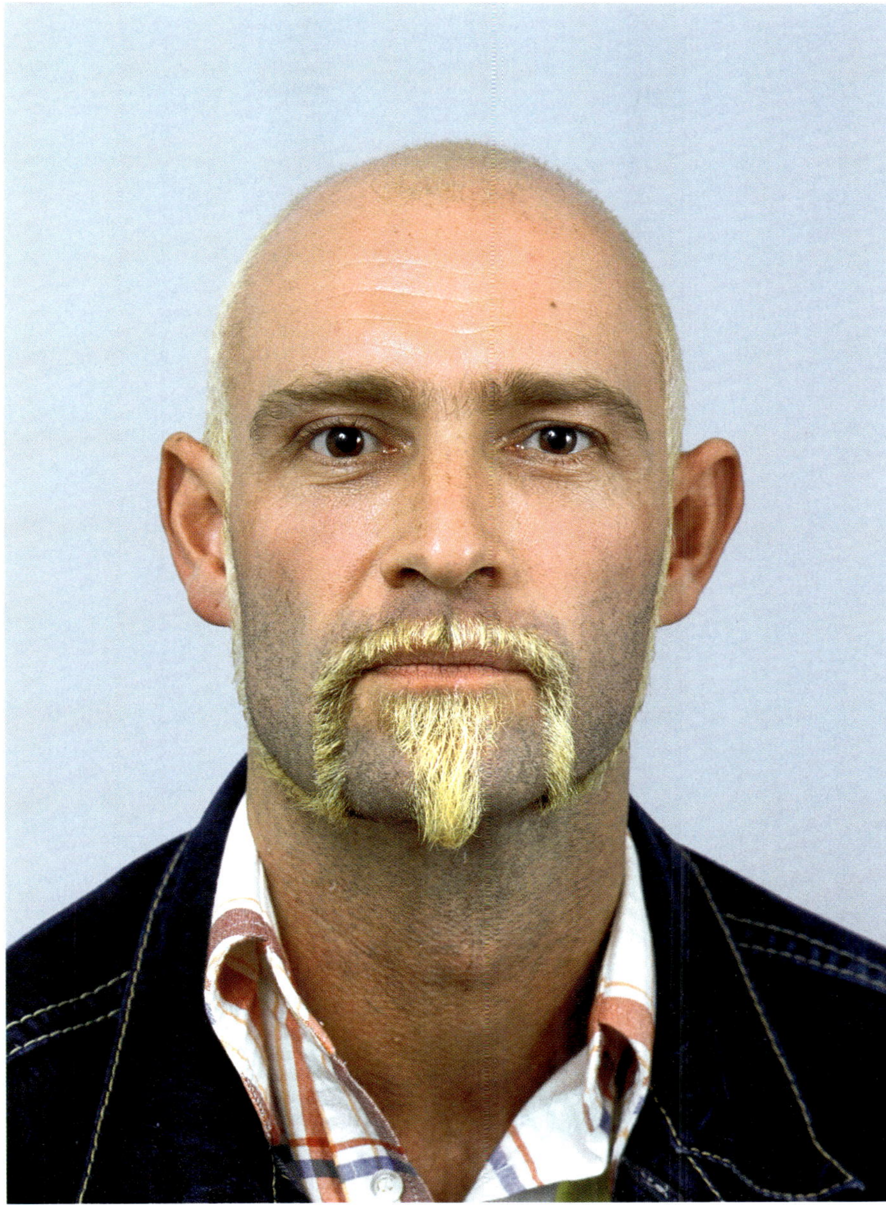

OLAF NICOLAI, THE BLONDES, 2003/2005, C-print, series of 42, each 13 3/8 x 9 7/8" / C-Print, 42-teilige Serie, je 34 x 25 cm.

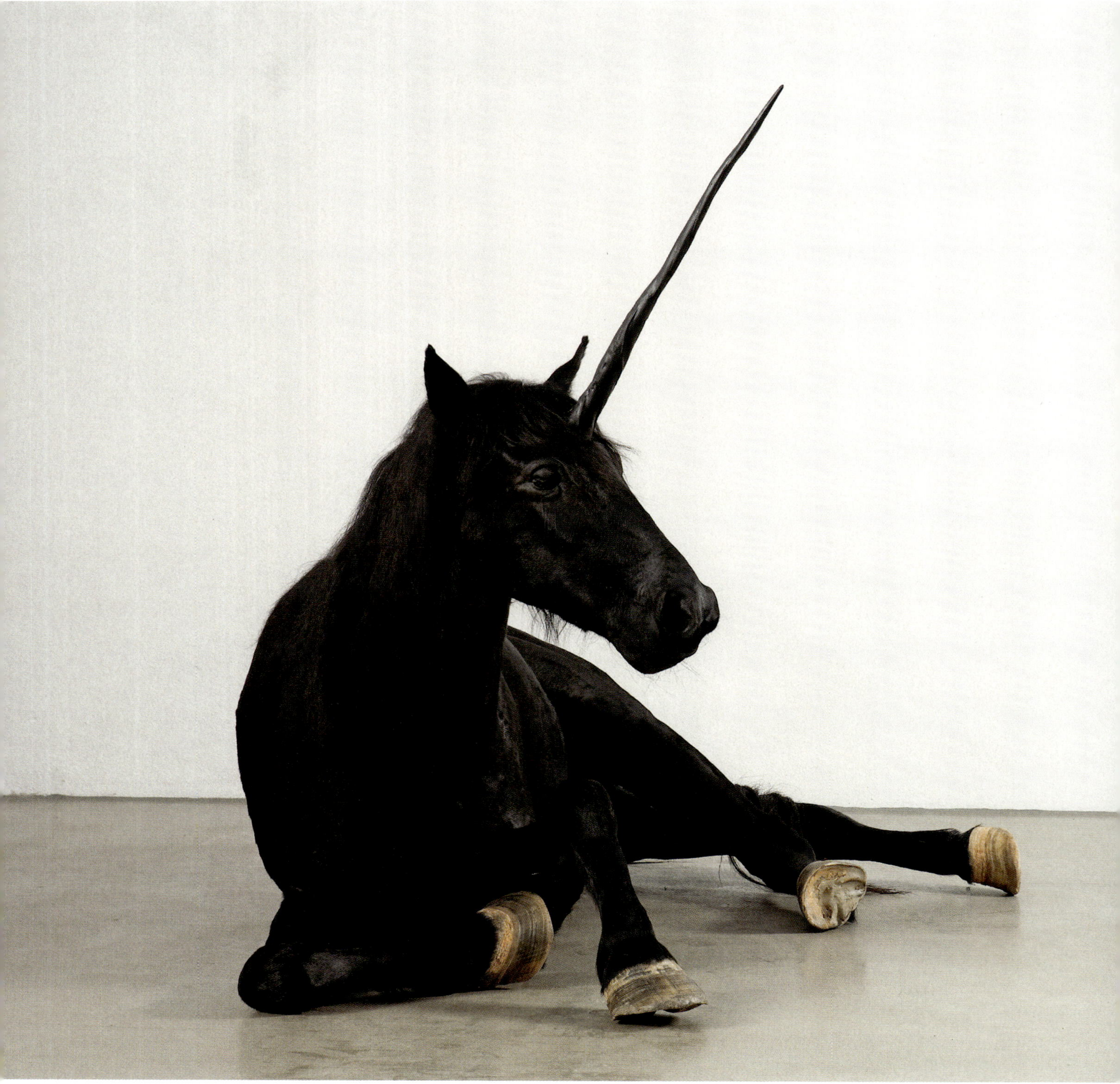

What's more, the best art does this simply for the sake of making us think differently, without the commercial or political agendas that underlie propaganda, advertising, and much science research. This is (contemporary) art's USP (Unique Selling Proposition) and its continuing raison d'être.

Having run a museum with a classical modern collection for the past two years, a question I ask myself in relation to this understanding of art's role in society is: does the art of the past (modernist art, for instance) still have this potential to make us see and think differently? Or, has it become normalized and incorporated into our aesthetic understanding to such a degree that it simply confirms the quality of the status quo? One of the few guides in thinking through this question is, for me, the artist Olaf Nicolai. Nicolai uses the license that his status as an artist gives him to be free of academia—free to abuse sources and reconfigure images and objects of entirely different statuses. Thus, while remaining securely within the identity of an artist, Nicolai performs a role as a researcher and combiner—a turner-upside-down-of-things to see what they look like from another angle, and ultimately create new modes of visibility. His strategy, it would seem, is a fine one at this point in our cultural development, given the current moment's political exhaustion and the universalizing of "creativity" for bland economic ends. It's a strategy I can endorse, share, and learn from, as I hope others can.

Take, for example, the modest publication *Show Case* (1999), "a text-image essay on the performativity of perception."[1] A photograph of Japan's Ocean Dome is followed by a reference to Huysmans in the text that runs parallel to the image. Then, via an image drawn from *Purple* magazine, it joins with a moment of text that reflects on the accuracy of Marx's analysis of alienation—and the fact that we are living through it in ways that are apparently quite tolerable. In this way, the whole book is a reframing or reanimation of its various parts: Dan Graham's Pavilions are reinvigorated with the original critique of the architecture they now seem simply to mimic; Neal Stephenson's 1990s futuristic science fiction juxtaposed with details of *Escape from LA* becomes a means to get a grip on the present; and Jeff Wall puts

OLAF NICOLAI, LA LOTTA, 2006, taxidermized hide, horn, polyester, electric heating, temperature control, 60 1/4 x 84 3/4 x 61" / Präpariertes Fell, Horn, Polyester, elektrische Heizung, Temperatursteuerung, 153 x 215 x 155 cm.

both of these iconographic genres back into circulation as images rather than as brand names.

This is something of an achievement in a culture that feels it knows too much already. It is also an appropriate move as a mild but crucial resistance to the cult of innovation and newness. At times, in Nicolai's work, there seems to be a plaintive cry to simply look around at what is already there and give it a little more consideration. Like Georges Perec, Nicolai wants to say that there is enough potential in the extraordinariness of the everyday to give us insight and intelligence. We don't need another new thing, another yet-more-perfect image to enlighten ourselves. Together with the literary movement to which he belonged, OuLiPo (Ouvroir de Littérature Potentielle), Perec is to literature as Nicolai is to art, for both use limited means and deliberate limitations to speak about the "truth of contradictions and exceptions," as the pataphysicist (another influence on Perec) would say.[2)] A work like LA LOTTA (2006), in which a black unicorn sits, apparently asleep, in a corner, is a fine example of the link—the animal feels alive to the touch, warmed to a temperature of 43.3 degrees, which is the point at which the human body ceases to function. This use of fable, familiarity, and absurdity dovetails perfectly with OuLiPo's own belief in changing the parameters of a given system in order to undermine the status quo—not revolution but "re-perception," which is precisely what Nicolai is concerned with.

The everydayness of Nicolai's work extends to an extremely perceptive take on the fashion and design industries, purveyors of good taste, and acceptable aesthetics. When he excerpts an article from *The Face* and posts the entire very long text on the connecting gallery walls around an inflated Nike shoe that is large enough to enter and sit on (BIG SNEAKER, THE NINETIES, 2001), he is pointing out the obvious—that such elements of our surroundings are as ubiquitous as nature, and perform a function similar to that of any background that provides a perspective on our individual human aspirations. Seeing it installed in Korea during the 2002 Gwangju Biennale, I remember being surprised by the text-piece circling around the walls, entitled A SHORT CATALOGUE OF THINGS THAT YOU THINK YOU WANT: A TEXT BY ZADIE SMITH FOR THE ANNIVERSARY ISSUE OF THE FACE, 05/2000 (2001), which talks about art and commerce and how each has fed into the other. Another work, RITORNELLO (2005), exhibits a similarly ambiguous criticality by importing Italian clothes lines from Naples to the United Arab Emirates, where their use is normally deemed uncivilized. The positioning of the lines mimics their original condition in Italy and even, shockingly, looks quite congruous in a city that reproduces the acceptable face of western globalized culture at every turn. (Even the lighting on the pavement was modeled after the Champs-Élysées.) Whether this is a firm critique or a thoughtful observation fortunately remains unclear—it is crucial in both these works that Nicolai avoids didacticism or the simple politics of the sneer. By retaining the ambiguity inherent in a smart, populist text or a barely-out-of-place reconstruction, he not only permits the necessary space to react but, furthermore, sidesteps the censoriousness of enlightenment thinking to allow pop culture, or western "copying," a respectable place in his discourse.

A similar kind of reaction—at least one that is related to the (dis)placement of one form onto another so as to create a different set of viewing protocols—is seen in Nicolai's recent work in Salzburg. In this rich city full of Mozart tourists, the artist asked a number of pavement painters to abandon their usual subjects and paint from a series of images he had selected from the daily newspapers. These photographs ranged from a Russian beauty queen with AIDS, to Peter Handke (the pro-Serbian writer who has offended German sensibilities by defending Milosevic), to a trial-evidence typewriter that had been used by a Mafia boss to both write love letters to his wife and issue assassination notices. The transfer from daily newsprint to the equally fugitive, but much more personal medium of chalk street drawing seems to have done little to the "message" of the image. If anything, it undermined the political narrative for which it originally stood when it functioned as an illustration. Instead, it conjured notions of recognition and remembrance (the expectation being that this image will be repeatedly drawn and has already existed many times before) since most

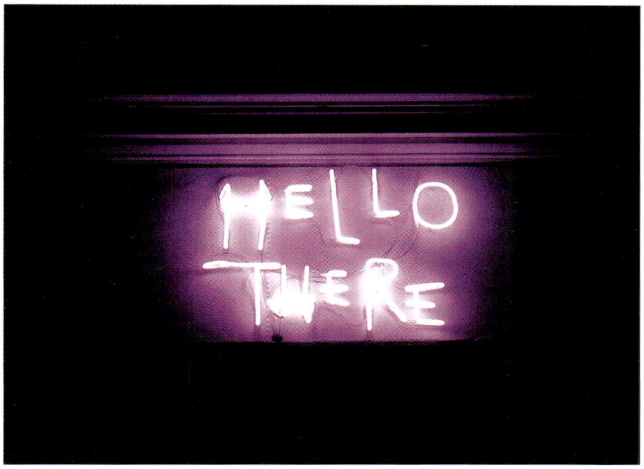

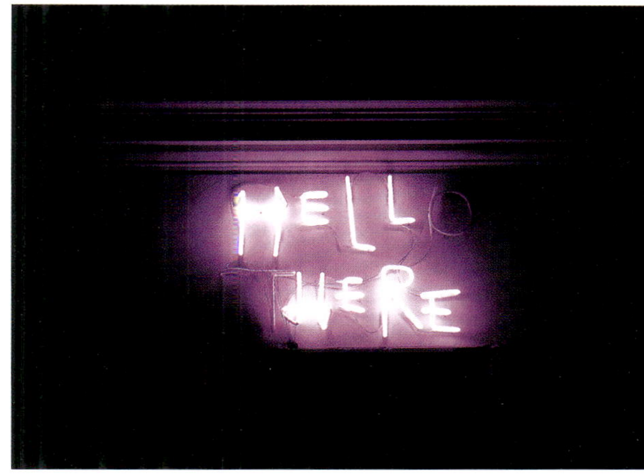

OLAF NICOLAI, HELLO THERE / HELL HERE, 2002, colored neon tubes, 31 1/2 x 27 1/2 x 5 1/2" /
HALLO DORT / HÖLLE HIER, farbige Leuchtstoffröhren, 80 x 70 x 14 cm.

news stories are simply slight variations on previous versions—new names and new faces diverting us from the repetitive manner of the narrative: for Blair read Thatcher, for Bush read Nixon, for Merkel read Brandt, for terrorism read anti-Semitism, for immigration read eugenics, for Chavez read Allende, for globalization read colonial expansion, and so on.

These stories reoccur because we reoccur as social animals, and the newness that we see is precisely in their aesthetic and technological framing. We have to see what we have at hand in order to understand the mediations that define our relationship to the world rather than retreat to a false sense of reality or to things as they really are. We don't need to go chasing after a vision of the future that will then restore what once was lost.

Instead, "the knowledge of 'how things are' is also the knowledge of how things might be," as Nicolai says in describing the internalized experience of pondering the glass-enveloped objects in *Show Case*.3) Representations and models are one and the same thing. At this point, the attempt to model our environment or our desires is no longer useful. It may be done, but why not go out and represent it anyway, and with the things that are already represented rather than by making new, pointless additions. Art, Nicolai seems to be saying here, is a way of looking at the world through aesthetic senses, rather than a discrete methodology for the production of high value objects. The possible artwork thus is subject rather than object; the aesthetic moment is something that is investigated and given consciousness rather than being enacted.

Nicolai turns the innovative drive of art on its head. In a world where everything is represented, it's the processing of the representations that offer something new. By "de-appropriating" their media, re-combining their clusters, un-folding their rhizomes, we arrive at a fresh understanding of the same old things. This is materialist but not Marxist, which, given Nicolai's background, is crucial. His work gives us the chance to be with ourselves right here and right now, surrounded by our Present rather than a wished-for future. This makes his work quite different from much art that is produced today or under the avant-garde legacy. Ultimately, his is an anti-utopian gesture, one meant to help us imagine things that otherwise exist in the dirty compromise of the here and now.

1) Olaf Nicolai, *Rewind Forward* (Ostfildern-Ruit: Hatje Cantz, 2003), p. 145.
2) http://en.wikipedia.org/wiki/'Pataphysics
3) Olaf Nicolai, *Show Case* (Nuremberg: Verlag für Moderne Kunst, 1999).

REPERZEPTION

CHARLES ESCHE

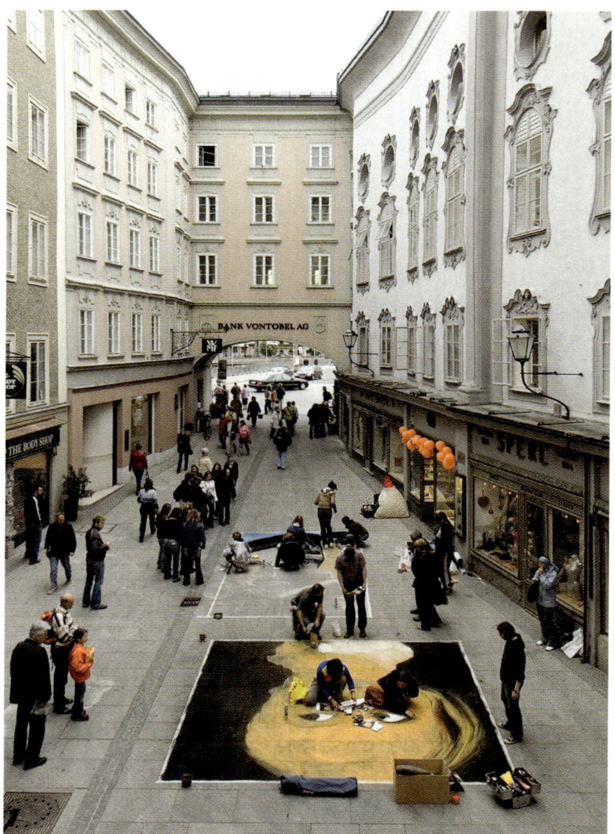

CHARLES ESCHE ist Direktor des Van Abbemuseums, Eindhoven, und Mitherausgeber der Zeitschrift *Afterall* sowie der Buchreihe *Afterall Books* (beide MIT Press).

Für die meisten Leute gehört Kunst nicht zu den Dingen, über die sie sich täglich den Kopf zerbrechen müssen. Sie ist nicht fester Bestandteil unseres sozialen Tagesprogramms wie die Nachrichten aus Politik, Wirtschaft und Unterhaltung, mit denen wir vierundzwanzig Stunden täglich berieselt werden. Sie geniesst nicht denselben Stellenwert in den Medien. Darin spiegelt sich nicht nur der Zustand unserer Gesellschaft, sondern mehr noch die aktuelle Erfahrung einer globalisierten Welt. Die meisten künstlerischen Manifestationen laufen daher leicht Gefahr, von der Mehrheit ignoriert zu werden, denn gerade in einer Zeit, in der die Notwendigkeit, intellektuelle Informationen zu filtern, oberstes Gebot ist, bedarf es keiner speziellen Ermutigung, etwas zu ignorieren. Das ist auch der Grund, warum der Populismus in Kunstinstitutionen, die Aufsehen erregen wollen, Einzug hält; viele Kunstwerke sind schlicht nicht geeignet, aus eigener Kraft Aufmerksamkeit zu erregen, also greift man zu anderen Mitteln.

Was Kunst jedoch erreichen kann, ist in aller Stille die notwendigen Bedingungen zu schaffen, die uns dazu bringen, innezuhalten und die Dinge, mit denen wir jeden Tag zu tun haben, einmal anders zu betrachten. Kunst bietet uns die Chance, erneut über bereits Bekanntes nachzudenken. Wie seriösen Ursprungs sie auch immer sein mag, Kunst kann für sich jederzeit einen Mehrwert gegenüber ihrem eigentlichen Marktwert – als hoch spezialisiertes Konsumgut – in Anspruch nehmen. Das ist natürlich bei vielen anderen akademischen Wissenszweigen, von der Philosophie bis zur Physik, ähnlich – bis auf die Tatsache, dass diese hauptsächlich auf das geschriebene Wort angewiesen sind, um ihre Ent-

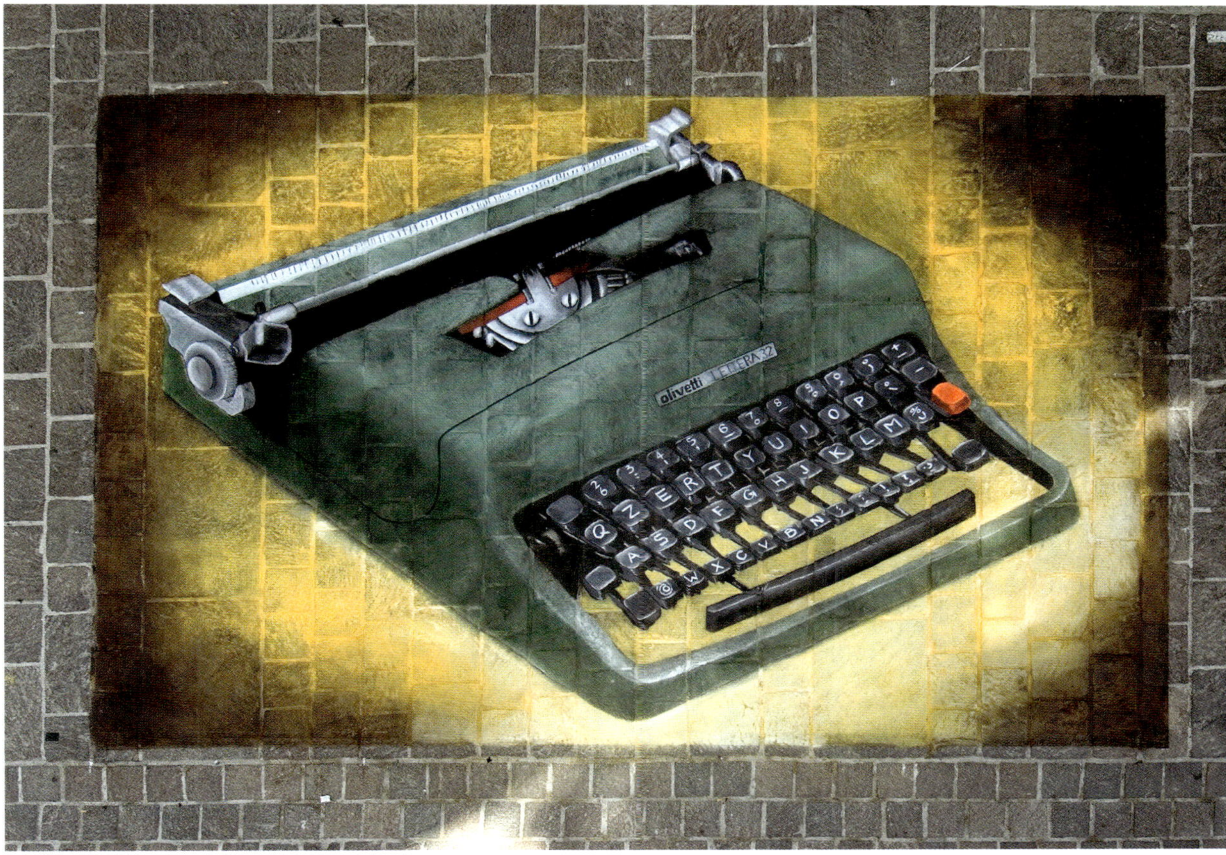

OLAF NICOLAI, UNTITLED, Salzburg, May-July 2006, 32 newspaper photographs as source material for pavement painters / OHNE TITEL, Salzburg, Mai-Juli 2006, 32 Photos aus Tageszeitungen als Vorlagen für Strassenmaler.

deckungen zu vermitteln. Die Kunst ist da unabhängiger, sie erschüttert und berührt uns auf andere Weise, zapft andere Gehirnwindungen an. Mehr noch, die beste Kunst tut dies einfach nur, damit wir anders zu denken beginnen, ohne kommerzielle oder politische Absichten, die wiederum der Propaganda, der Werbung und oft wissenschaftlicher Forschung zu Grunde liegen. Das ist die USP (Unique Selling Proposition), das «einzigartige Verkaufsargument» der Kunst – und ist und bleibt ihre *raison d'être.*

Da ich seit zwei Jahren ein Museum leite, das über eine Sammlung von Werken der Klassischen Moderne verfügt, beschäftigt mich im Hinblick auf die Rolle der Kunst in der Gesellschaft folgende Frage: Hat die Kunst der Vergangenheit, etwa der Moderne, überhaupt noch dieses Potenzial, uns dazu zu bringen, anders zu sehen und zu denken? Oder ist sie bereits zur Norm geworden und so sehr Bestandteil unserer ästhetischen Auffassungen, dass sie lediglich noch zur Bestätigung der Qualität des Status quo dient? Einer der wenigen, der uns bei der gründlichen Auseinandersetzung mit dieser Frage Hand bietet, ist für mich Olaf Nicolai. Nicolai macht Gebrauch von der Freiheit, die ihm sein Status als Künstler verschafft; er schert sich nicht um akademische Regeln, sondern treibt Schindluder mit seinen Quellen und rekonfiguriert Bilder und Objekte völlig unterschiedlicher Stellenwerte. So übernimmt Nicolai im Schutze seiner Künstleridentität die Rolle eines wissenschaftlichen Forschers und Kombinators – eines Verwandlers der Dinge, um sie aus einem anderen Blickwinkel zu beleuchten und schliesslich neue Arten der Sichtbarkeit zu schaffen. In Anbetracht der aktuellen politischen Ermüdungserscheinungen und der verallgemeinernden Rede von «Kreativität» im Zusammenhang mit rein wirtschaftlichen Zwecken, scheint mir, dass seine Strategie im Rahmen unserer kulturellen Entwicklung genau zum rechten Zeitpunkt kommt. Es ist eine Strategie, die ich unterstützen und mittragen kann und von der ich, wie hoffentlich auch andere, etwas lerne.

Man nehme etwa die unscheinbare Publikation *Show Case* (1999), «ein theoretischer Text-Bild-Essay zur Performativität von Wahrnehmung»[1]. Auf eine Photographie des *Ocean Dome* in Japan folgt im parallel zum Bild verlaufenden Text ein Verweis auf Joris-Karl Huysmans. Dann wird dies, über ein aus dem *Purple Magazine* stammendes Bild, mit einer Textstelle verbunden, die über die Exaktheit von Marx' Analyse der Entfremdung reflektiert, welche wir anscheinend gerade in ganz erträglicher Form durchleben. So ist das ganze Buch eine Uminszenierung oder unaufhörliche Neubelebung seiner einzelnen Teile: Dan Grahams Pavillons gewinnen neue Kraft durch die ihnen ursprünglich immanente Kritik jener Architektur, die sie mittlerweile nur noch zu imitieren scheinen; Neal Stephensons futuristische Science-Fiction der 90er Jahre wird – durchsetzt mit Details aus John Carpenters Film *Flucht aus LA* – zum Instrument, um die Gegenwart in den Griff zu bekommen; und Jeff Wall befreit die ikonographischen Genres von ihrem Labeldasein und bringt sie erneut in Form von Bildern in Umlauf.

Das ist eine beachtliche Leistung für eine Kultur, die wähnt, bereits zu viel zu wissen. Es ist auch ein guter Schachzug im Sinne eines sanften, aber entscheidenden Widerstandes gegen den herrschenden Innovations- und Neuheitskult. Manchmal vermeint man im Werk Nicolais die Aufforderung zu hören, sich doch einfach einmal umzuschauen – zu sehen, was bereits da ist, und diesem Etwas mehr Aufmerksamkeit zu schenken. Wie Georges Perec will Nicolai sagen, dass das Aussergewöhnliche des Alltags genügend Möglichkeiten zu Einsicht und besserem Verständnis bietet – wir brauchen nicht immer noch etwas Neues, ein noch perfekteres Bild. Zusammen mit der literarischen Bewegung OuLiPo (Ouvroir de Littérature Potentielle, der Perec angehörte) bildet er in der Literatur einen ähnlich wertvollen Kontrapunkt wie Nicolai in der Kunst, insofern er mit beschränkten Mitteln und bewussten Einschränkungen über die «Wahrheit der Widersprüche und Ausnahmen» spricht – wie die Pataphysik (ein weiterer wichtiger Einfluss bei Perec) sagen würde.[2] Eine Arbeit wie LA LOTTA (2006), in der ein schwarzes Einhorn scheinbar schlafend in einer Ecke sitzt, ist ein schönes Beispiel für diese Verbindung. Das Tier fühlt sich lebendig an, da es auf 43,3 Grad aufgeheizt ist (exakt die Temperatur, bei welcher der menschliche Körper den Geist aufgibt). Diese Verwendung von Fabelwelt, Vertrautheit und Absurdität verträgt sich perfekt mit OuLiPos Vertrauen auf die Veränderung der Parameter eines bestehenden Systems zur Untergrabung des Status quo – nicht Revolution, sondern Reperzeption, ein zweites Hinschauen, also genau das, worum es Nicolai geht.

Das Alltägliche in Nicolais Werk geht mit einem präzisen Gespür dafür einher, dass Mode- und Designindustrie längst bestimmen, was guter Geschmack und ästhetisch akzeptabel ist. Wenn er einen Artikel aus dem britischen Magazin *The Face* exzerpiert und in extremer Vergrösserung, wandfüllend, neben einem überdimensionierten Nike-Turnschuh anbringt (BIG SNEAKER, THE NINETIES, 2001), unterstreicht er das Offensichtliche: Solche Elemen-

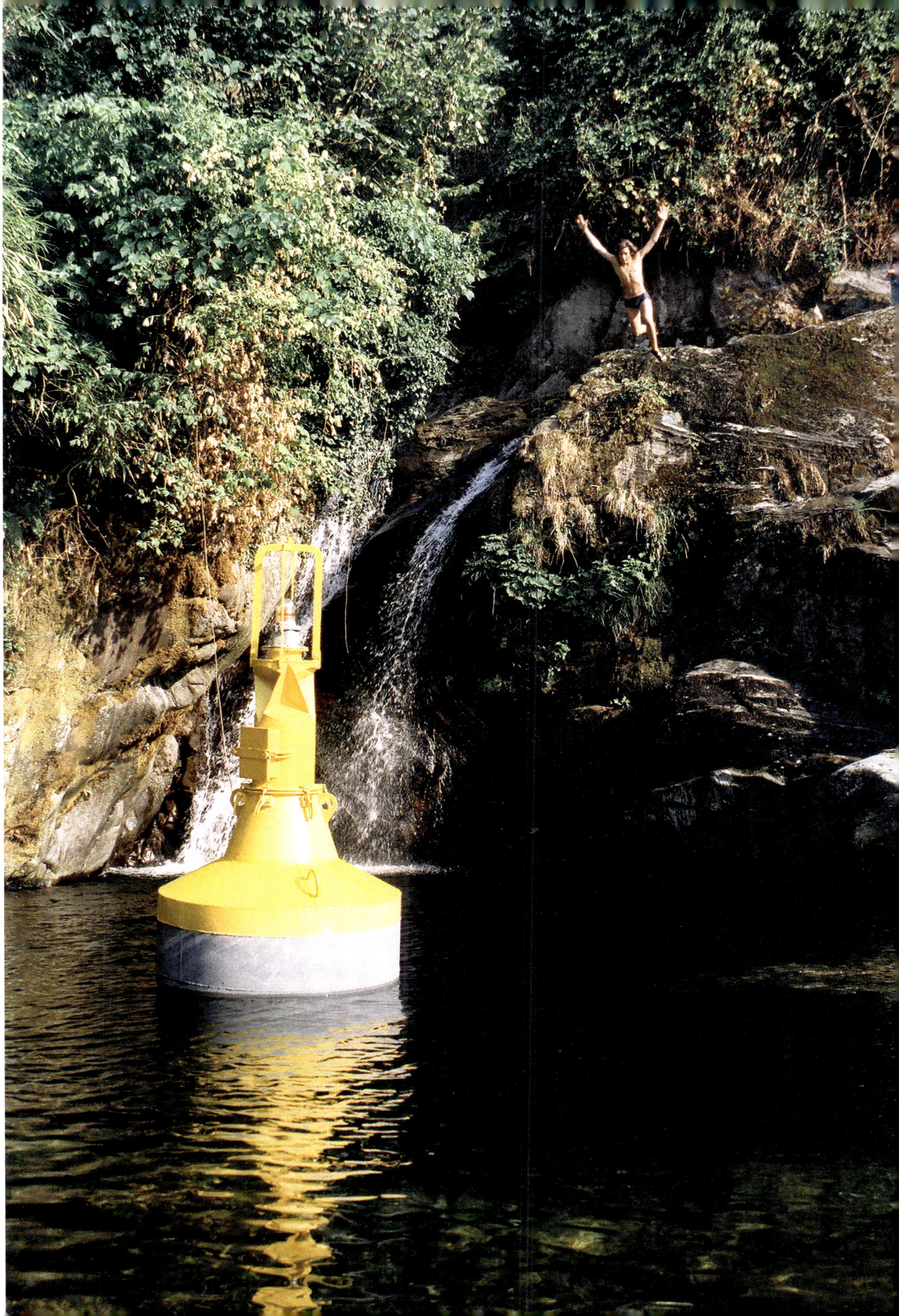

OLAF NICOLAI, BOA GIALLA, 2003, off-shore buoy with signal light, 163 3/8 x 55 1/8" diamter / Hochseeboje mit Signallicht, 415 x 140 cm Durchmesser.

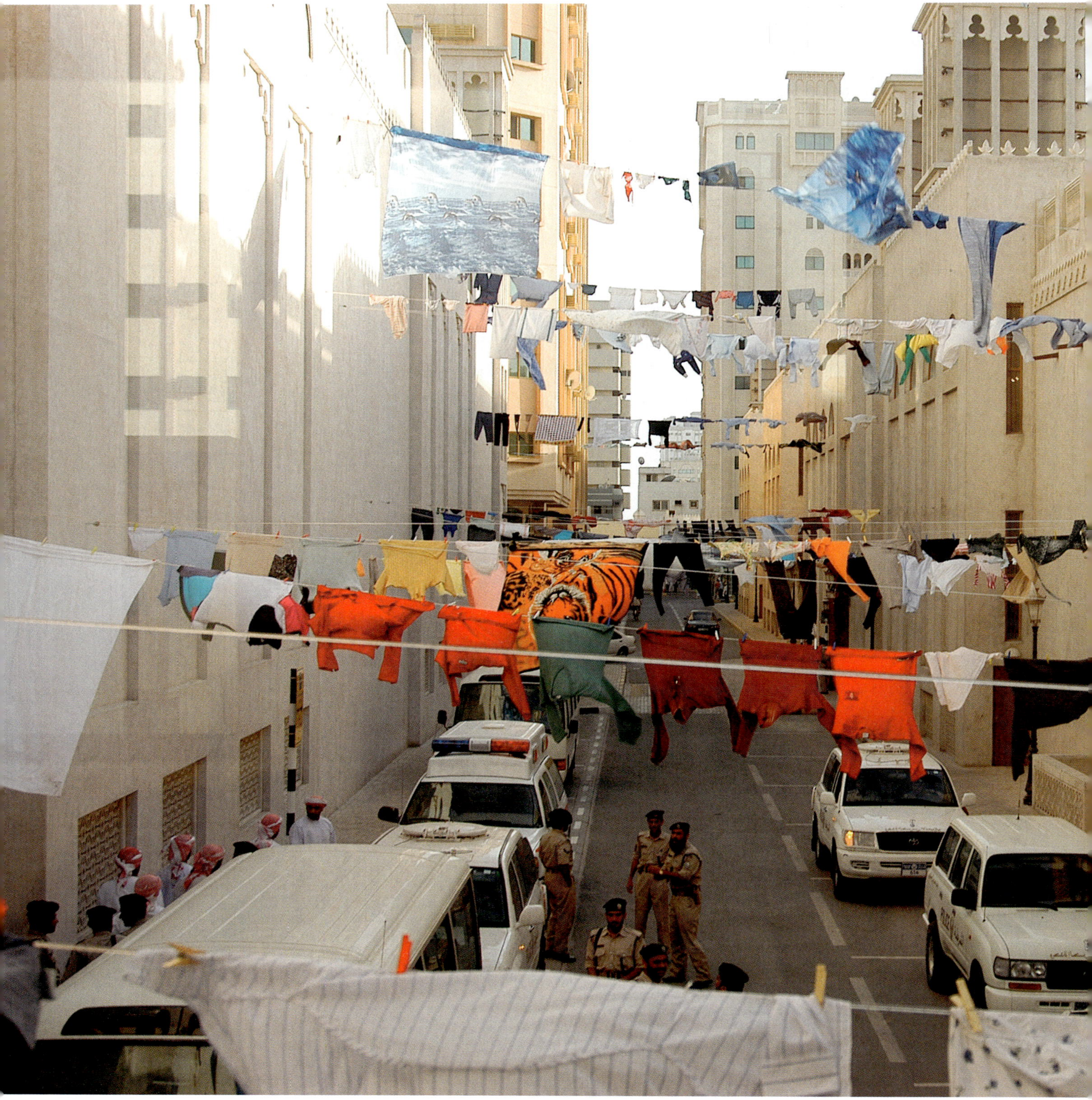

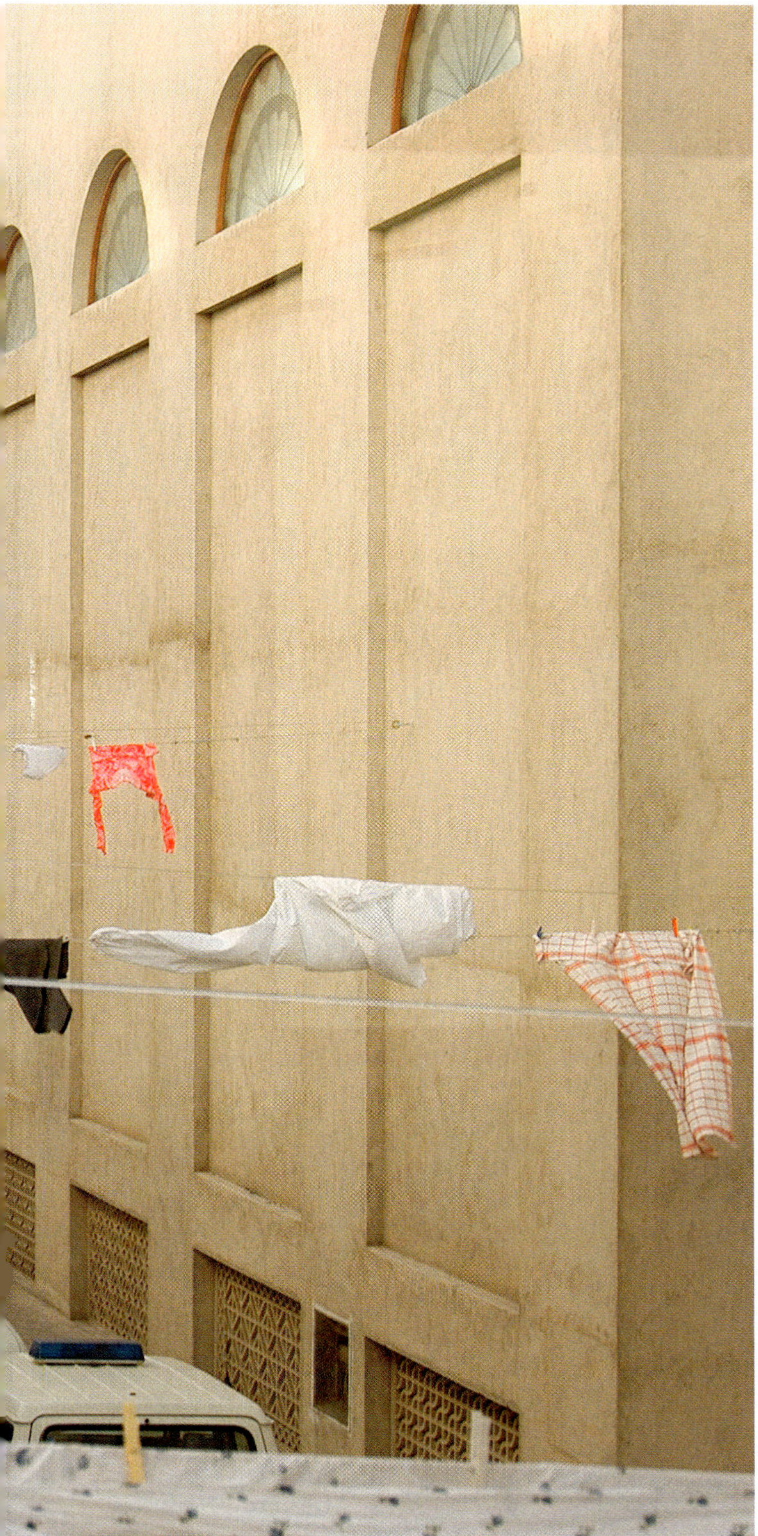

*OLAF NICOLAI, RITORNELLO, 2005,
clothing, clotheslines, variable dimensions,
installation view, center of Sharjah /
Kleidungsstücke, Wäscheleinen,
Masse variabel, Installationsansicht.*

te sind in unserer Umgebung so allgegenwärtig wie Natur und wirken als Hintergrund ähnlich bestimmend auf unsere individuellen menschlichen Zielsetzungen. Ich erinnere mich, wie sehr mich dieser sich rundum über die Wände hinziehende Text seinerzeit an der Gwangju Biennale 2002 in Korea überraschte. Der Titel der Arbeit lautete: A SHORT CATALOGUE OF THINGS THAT YOU THINK YOU WANT: A TEXT BY ZADIE SMITH FOR THE ANNIVERSARY ISSUE OF THE FACE, 05/2000 (2001), (Eine kurze Liste der Dinge, die Sie zu benötigen meinen – Ein Text von Zadie Smith für die Jubiläumsausgabe von *The Face* 05/2000); er handelte von Kunst und Kommerz und davon, wie das eine ins andere übergreift. Eine andere Arbeit, RITORNELLO (2005), zeigt eine ähnlich doppelsinnig kritische Haltung, indem sie voll behängte Wäscheleinen aus Italien in die Vereinigten Arabischen Emirate transferiert. Die Position der Wäscheleinen ist ihrer ursprünglichen Verwendung in Italien nachgestaltet und passt erstaunlich gut in eine Stadt, die sich an jeder Strassenecke den Anschein einer westlichen, globalisierten Kultur gibt. (Selbst in der Strasse, um die es hier ging, waren die Kandelaber auf den Gehsteigen jenen an der Champs-Élysées nachempfunden.) Ob es sich dabei um eine harsche Kritik oder eine nachdenkliche Beobachtung handelt, bleibt glücklicherweise unklar. Bei beiden Werken ist es von zentraler Bedeutung, dass Nicolai jegliche didaktische oder einfach nur hämische Haltung vermeidet. Indem er das Ambivalente eines raffinierten populistischen Textes oder einer kaum spürbar aus dem Rahmen fallenden Rekonstruktion beibehält, gibt er dem Betrachter nicht nur den nötigen Raum für seine persönliche Reaktion, sondern umgeht auch die zensorische Geste des aufklärerischen Denkens und räumt damit der Popkultur oder einer Nachahmung westlicher Kultur einen angemessenen Platz in der Diskussion ein.

Eine ähnliche Reaktion – zumindest eine, die mit der Verschiebung einer Form auf eine andere zur Erzeugung einer Reihe neuer Betrachtungsweisen zusammenhängt – lässt sich bei einer neueren Arbeit in Salzburg beobachten. In dieser von Mozart-Touristen wimmelnden Stadt bat der Künstler einige Strassenmaler, ihre üblichen Sujets vorübergehend aufzugeben und stattdessen eine Reihe von Bildern zu malen, die Nicolai aus Tageszeitungen ausgewählt hatte. Die Photos reichten von einer russischen Schönheitskönigin, die an AIDS erkrankt war, über Peter Handke, der mit seiner Verteidigung von Milosevic Gefühle der Deutschen gegen sich aufbrachte, bis zu einer Schreibmaschine, die als Beweismittel in einem Prozess diente und auf der ein Mafiaboss sowohl Liebesbriefe an seine Frau als auch seine Mordaufträge getippt hatte. Die Übertragung vom Bild aus der Tageszeitung zum nicht minder flüchtigen, aber sehr viel persönlicheren Medium der Kreidezeichnung auf der Strasse scheint an der ursprünglichen «Botschaft» des Pressebildes wenig geändert zu haben. Wenn überhaupt, untergräbt sie am ehesten noch den politischen Zusammenhang, der ursprünglich illustriert werden sollte. Plötzlich handelt ein Bild nun von Wiedererkennen und Erinnerung (weil sich die Erwartung damit verbindet, dass es immer wieder gezeichnet wird und schon viele Male zuvor gezeichnet worden ist) – die meisten Nachrichtenstories sind ja lediglich leichte Abwandlungen früherer Vorkommnisse, allein die neuen Namen und Gesichter lenken vom repetitiven Charakter der Handlung ab: Man braucht beim Lesen nur Blair durch Thatcher zu ersetzen, Bush durch Nixon, Merkel durch Brandt, Terrorismus durch Antisemitismus, Immigration durch Eugenik, Chavez durch Allende, Globalisierung durch Kolonialismus und so fort.

Die Geschichten wiederholen sich, weil wir uns wieder und wieder als gesellschaftliche Wesen aktualisieren, und das «Neue» liegt exakt in den ästhetischen und technologischen Rahmenbedingungen, unter denen wir es wahrnehmen. Wir müssen, was wir vor uns haben, begreifen als Instrument zum Verständnis unseres vermittelten medialen Verhältnisses zur Welt, statt auf ein «falsches» Verständnis von Realität oder von der Wirklichkeit der Dinge zurückzugreifen. Wir brauchen nicht einer Vision von der Zukunft nachzujagen, die eines Tages wiederherstellen soll, was wir verloren haben.

Stattdessen ist das Wissen darum, «wie die Dinge sind, auch das Wissen darum, wie die Dinge sein könnten», wie Nicolai selbst in *Show Case* über die internalisierte Erfahrung des «Vitrineneffekts» – sich selbst als Gesehenes zu sehen – sagt. Sujet und Darstellung sind ein und dasselbe. An diesem Punkt ist der Versuch, unsere Umwelt oder unsere Wünsche nach bestimmten Leitbildern zu gestalten, nicht mehr sinnvoll. Man kann es zwar trotzdem tun, aber warum nicht hingehen und sie einfach repräsentieren, und zwar mit den Dingen, die bereits da sind, statt sinnlos neue hinzuzufügen. Kunst, scheint Nicolai hier sagen zu wollen, ist eher eine Art Weltbetrachtung mittels ästhetisch gebildeter Sinne als eine bestimmte Methode zur Produktion hochwertiger Objekte. Das mögliche Kunstwerk ist damit eher Subjekt als Objekt; das ästhetische Moment besteht eher im Investigativen und einer Bewusstsein schaffenden Qualität denn in der Vorführung oder Darstellung.

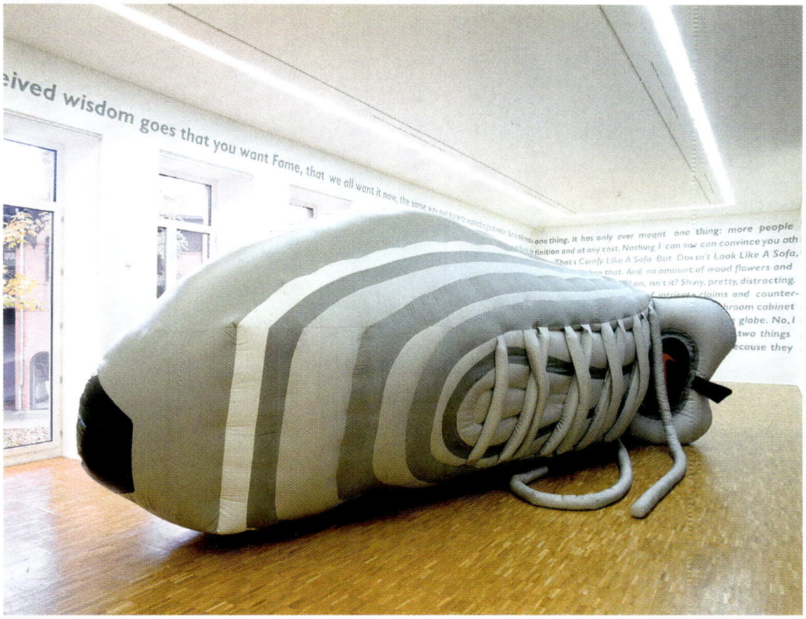

OLAF NICOLAI, BIG SNEAKER (THE NINETIES), 2001, fabric, film, inflatables, 157 1/2 x 354 1/2 x 118" / Verschiedene Stoffe, Folien, Gebläse, 400 x 900 x 300 cm.

Damit konterkariert Nicolai den Drang zur Innovation in der Kunst. In einer Welt, in der alles schon dargestellt ist, liegt das Neue in der Aufbereitung dieser Darstellungen. Indem man ihre Medien «de-appropriiert», ihre Gruppierung neu kombiniert, ihre Rhizome aufdröselt, gelangt man zu einem neuen, frischen Verständnis derselben alten Dinge. Das ist zwar materialistisch, aber nicht marxistisch, und das ist angesichts von Nicolais Hintergrund entscheidend. Seine Kunst gibt uns die Chance, hier und jetzt bei uns zu sein, inmitten unserer Gegenwart, statt in einer ersehnten fernen Zukunft. Das ist es, was sein Werk aus dem Grossteil der heute oder im Gefolge der Avantgardebewegung produzierten Kunst heraushebt. Letztlich ist seine Geste eine antiutopische und verhilft uns dazu, uns Dinge vorzustellen, die sonst nur im schmutzigen Kompromiss des Hier und Jetzt existieren.

(Übersetzung: Suzanne Schmidt)

1) Olaf Nicolai, *Rewind Forward*, (Ostfildern-Ruit, Hatje Cantz, 2003) S. 145.
2) http://de.wikipedia.org/wiki/'Pataphysik
3) Olaf Nicolai, *Show Case* (Nürnberg: Verlag für Moderne Kunst, 1999).

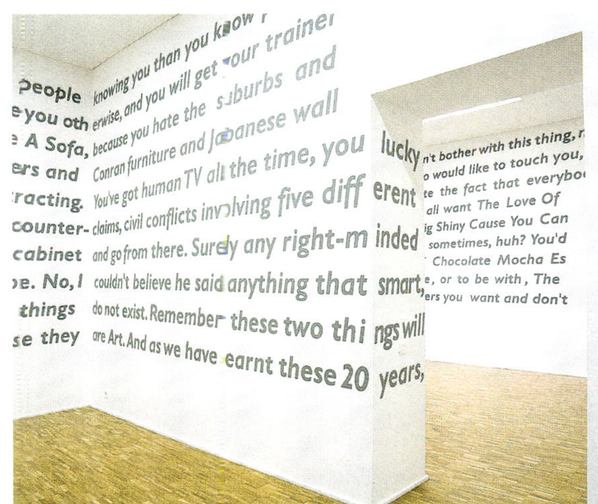

OLAF NICOLAI, A SHORT CATALOGUE OF THINGS THAT YOU THINK YOU WANT, (A TEXT BY ZADIE SMITH FOR THE ANNIVERSARY ISSUE OF THE FACE, 05/2000) 2001, wall lettering with Letraset, dimensions variable / EINE KURZE LISTE DER DINGE, DIE SIE ZU BENÖTIGEN MEINEN, Wandbeschriftung mit Letraset, Masse variabel.

In der Schwebe

Oder: Blicke und Sehstrahlen

ANNE VON DER HEIDEN

Niemand liest [...] die Meteore, weder die von Lukrez noch die von Descartes noch von irgendwem sonst. Warum diese Verdrängung? Weil die Philosophen, die Historiker, die Meister der Wissenschaft sich ausschliesslich um die antike Gesetzesidee kümmern. Um die exakte Determination oder rigorose Überdetermination, und um den Gott von Laplace. Um die absolute Kontrolle und daher um die Herrschaft ohne Freiräume und Unwägbarkeiten. Um die Macht und Ordnung.[1)]

Olaf Nicolai verteilte während der 51. Biennale in Venedig 2005 ein kleines Heft. *Welcome to the "Tears Of St. Lawrence". An Appointment to Watch Falling Stars* lautet sein Titel, der zugleich der Titel dieser Arbeit ist. Auf dem Cover, an dem aussen eine aufklappbare Karte befestigt ist, die sich in zwei Postkarten teilen lässt, ist die Zeichnung eines Sternbildes abgedruckt. Hell auf dunklem Grund – wie man es aus wissenschaftlichen Darstellungen der Himmelskörper kennt. Links unten sieht man neben den Sternbildern Triangulum und Aries das Sternbild Perseus, direkt unter der Linie des *Galactic Equator*. Ein

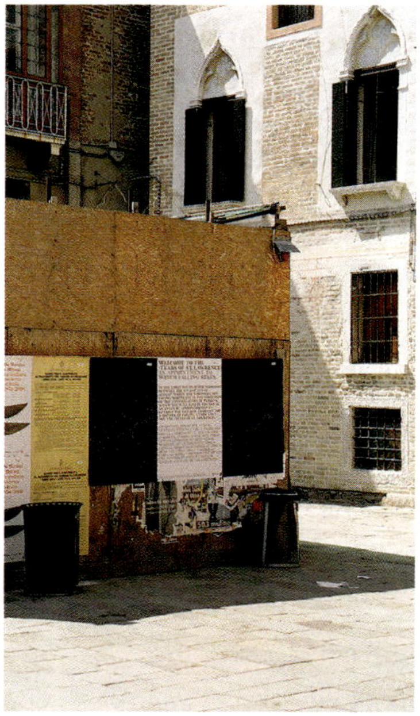

OLAF NICOLAI, WELCOME TO THE 'TEARS OF ST. LAWRENCE'. AN APPOINTMENT TO WATCH FALLING STARS, 2005, poster, installation view Campo Bandiera e Moro, Venice, / WILLKOMMEN ZU DEN TRÄNEN DES HL. LAURENTIUS. EINE VERABREDUNG ZUR BETRACHTUNG VON STERNSCHNUPPEN, Plakat, Installationsansicht, Venedig.

ANNE VON DER HEIDEN ist Kunst- und Medienwissenschaftlerin, Leiterin der Forschungsgruppe «Das Leben Schreiben. Medientechnologien und die Wissenschaften vom Leben 1800 – 1900» an der Fakultät Medien der Bauhaus-Universität Weimar. Sie publizierte verschiedene Studien zu Bildtheorie (Blickzähmung und Augentäuschung. Zu Jacques Lacans Bildtheorie, Diaphanes-Verlag), zu Bildlichkeit und Souveränität und zum Thema ideologische Mechanismen der Gewalt.

Index informiert auf der ersten Seite über den Inhalt des Bändchens und auf Seite zwei steht in grossen Buchstaben geschrieben: «Blicken Sie in den frühen Stunden nach Mitternacht, zwischen dem 8. und 13. August, zum nördlichen Himmel, Richtung Nordost, in einem Winkel von 45° vom Horizont werden Sie das Sternbild des Perseus finden. Halten Sie Ausschau nach Sternschnuppen – dies sind die Tränen des Heiligen Laurentius.» Die Zeilen fordern den Besucher der Biennale auf, ausgerüstet mit dem Heftchen, in dem auf Seite sechs und sieben detailliert darüber informiert wird, an welchem Ort der Erde man um welche lokale Uhrzeit das Sternenbild sehen kann, Beobachtungen zu machen. In der Erläuterung zu der Auflistung heisst es: «Für den Betrachter scheinen die Perseiden Sternschnuppen direkt aus dem Sternbild zu kommen. [...]. Der direkte Blick auf die Schweife ist nicht der beste, um die Sternschnuppen zu beobachten. Blicken Sie stattdessen rundherum oder darüber hinweg.» Das Heft enthält zudem ein Glossar, in dem wichtige Begriffe erläutert und photographische sowie zeichnerische Darstellungen aus der Astronomie vorgeführt werden, eine

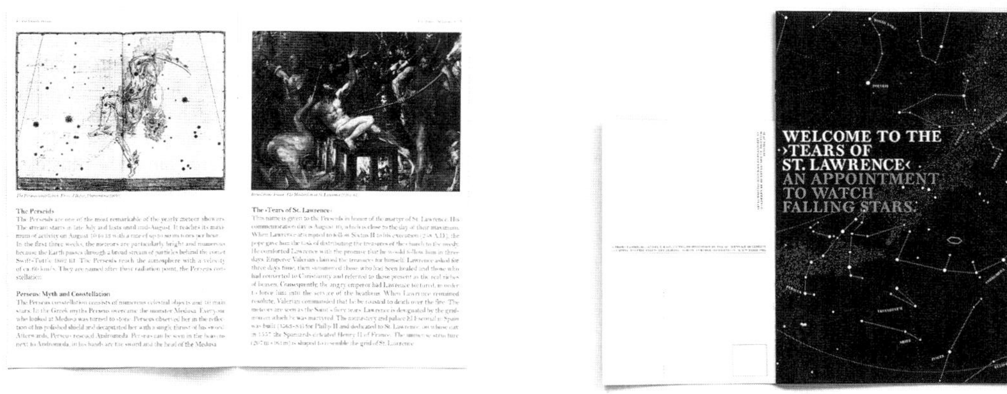

OLAF NICOLAI, WELCOME TO THE 'TEARS OF ST. LAWRENCE'. AN APPOINTMENT TO WATCH FALLING STARS, 2005, booklet, 8 1/3 x 5 4/5" / WILLKOMMEN ZU DEN TRÄNEN DES HL. LAURENTIUS. EINE VERABREDUNG ZUR BETRACHTUNG VON STERNSCHNUPPEN, Broschüre, 21 x 14,8 cm.

Tabelle der verschiedenen, im Jahr 2005 beobachteten *Meteor-Showers*, die Auflistung verschiedener Adressen von Internetseiten, die sich mit der Meteorologie und der Astronomie beschäftigen, Erläuterungen und Abbildungen zum Perseus-Mythos und der Legende vom heiligen Laurentius, die schon erwähnte Klapp-Postkarte, auf der man seine Beobachtungen anhand eines Fragenkatalogs notieren und an das Fireball Data Center / International Meteor Organisation zurücksenden kann, und verschiedene andere Materialien mehr.

Die Arbeit erscheint als wissenschaftliches Experiment und passt sich nicht nur deshalb kaum in die Reihe der üblichen Biennale-Kunstwerke ein. Sind es doch die Präsentationen der Länder, die in ihren Pavillons seit jeher versuchen, eine besondere Qualität ihrer Künstler und Kunstwerke in einem besonderen architektonischen Raum vorzuführen und damit Publikum und vor allem Rezensenten zu überzeugen. Die Besucher sollen sich durch die

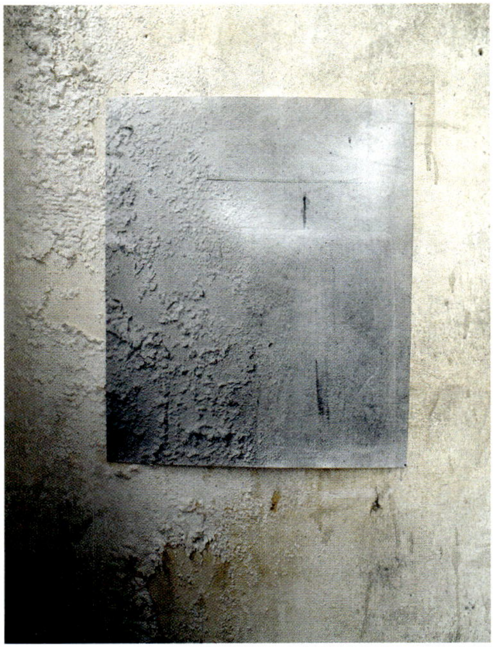

OLAF NICOLAI, DIFFERENZ (FÜR REINHARD PRIESSNITZ), 2006, wall, photographs, 9 1/2 x 14 1/8" / Wand, Photographien, 24 x 36 cm.

besondere Spezifik der Präsentation an den Beitrag des jeweiligen Landes erinnern und es wird zudem um die Auszeichnung des besten Pavillons gerungen. Nicolai verzichtet ganz auf diese Form der Präsentation und der mit ihr zusammenhängenden Werkästhetik. Radikaler sogar als bei seinem auf der Biennale 2001 gezeigten Werk MAZE. ODER: HELP THE DUKES IN GENERAL LEE TO FIND THE RODEO IN HAZZARD COUNTY (Labyrinth. Oder: Hilf den Dukes in General Lee bei der Suche nach dem Rodeo in Hazzard County) – das auch nicht im Inneren eines Ausstellungsraums, sondern an seiner Peripherie, am Übergang zum städtischen Raum, sogar in einer nicht zugänglichen militärischen Zone, angesiedelt war und das die Besucher durch sein Arrangement dazu aufzufordern schien, es erst in der sinnlichen Erfahrung, in der Begehung der vorgegebenen Felder und Linien, vollständig herzustellen – verzichtet WELCOME TO THE "TEARS OF ST. LAWRENCE" ganz auf die Bodenhaftung, den begrenzten Raum und die Form der Installation. Das Werk stellt sich erst in den Blicken der Betrachter her. Oder besser gesagt: Es antizipiert die Blicke der Betrachter und wird durch diese Annahme zu einer Art imaginärem Kunstwerk. Oder noch genauer: Der Betrachter stellt sich vor, dass tatsächlich die in ihre Heimatländer zurückgereisten Kunsttouristen dort jeweils zu einer bestimmten Zeit zum Himmel schauen. Durch ihre Blicke, die er imaginär vor sich zu sehen meint, erscheint ein riesiges, jeweils während der vom Künstler angegebenen Zeiträume realisiertes, imaginäres Arrangement von Sehstrahlen, die von den Betrachtern der verschiedenen Erdteile bis hin zu dem in weiter Ferne befindlichen Lichtphänomen reichen. Es entsteht also ein nicht sichtbares Werk, das nur durch die vergegenständlicht vorgestellten Blicklinien und durch die Übertragung des Gesehenen über das Medium der Schrift auf den Postkarten erscheint; Postkarten, von denen man sich vorstellt, dass sie im angegebenen Institut ausgewertet werden und so eine Art *kommunales* – wie Lacan sagen würde – Werk entstehen könnte.[2] Und es ist ein Werk, das neben dieser Blickkonstellation, die vielleicht am ehesten mit der Überkreuzung von Imaginärem und Realem zu beschreiben ist, eine symbolische Dimension aufruft. Die möglichen Verweise zu den Inhalten der alten Mythen, der Geschichte von Perseus, die eng an seinen Umgang mit der Macht des Blicks geknüpft ist, und der Erzählung von Laurentius, der vorausschauend echte Tränen vergiesst und bald später wegen der Verteilung von Kirchenschätzen an die Armen gemartert wird, erscheinen gleichfalls als Linien, als Blickrichtungen, denen das Denken der Betrachter nachgehen muss, um weitere sinnhafte Lichtpunkte sehen zu können. Im schillernden Glanz erscheint dann das so entstandene *tableau.*

Von der Überlagerung unterschiedlicher Blickregime lässt sich bei vielen Werken von Olaf Nicolai sprechen. Die Arbeit CHANT D'AMOUR (2003), in der nur das Loch eines kleinen Strohhalms zwei durch eine dicke Mauer getrennte Räume verbindet, ist beispielsweise ein solches Werk. Es erinnert an Pyramus und Tisbe. Auch seine Installation BARAQUE DE CHANTIER (2002/2003), ein Plexiglas-Nachbau der kleinen Fertigbau-Holzhütte von Le Corbusier, die der Architekt in der Nähe seines Wohnhauses in Südfrankreich als Atelier benutzte, antizipiert in besonderer Weise die Blicke der Betrachter. Sie sind gleichsam in dieses investiert gedacht. Alle Teile des Gebäudes sind vollkommen transparent. Raum und Nichtraum, Anspruch und Wirklichkeit, Plan und Konzept überlagern sich, gehen ineinander über, treten in ein komplexes Wechselspiel. Ein interessantes Werk in diesem Kontext ist auch DIFFERENZ (FÜR REINHARD PRIESSNITZ),

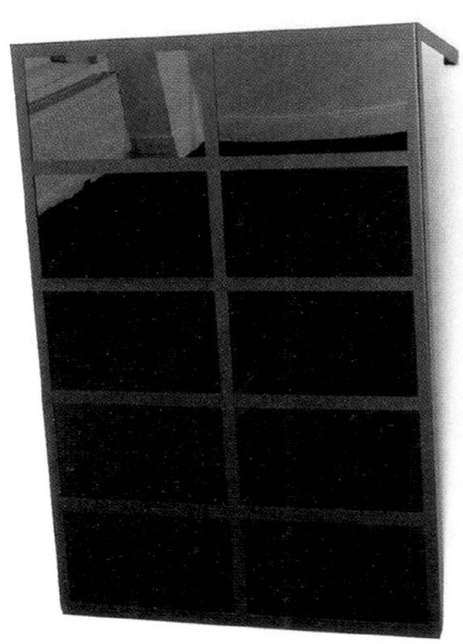

OLAF NICOLAI, CELIO, 2004, aluminum, acrylic glass, 51 1/8 x 35 1/2 x 11 3/4" / Aluminium, Acrylglas, 130 x 90 x 30cm.

da es die «Differenz» von technischem und menschlichem Blick vorführt und zugleich auf die Lyrik des österreichischen Dichters Reinhard Priessnitz verweist, die sich vor allem mit den Bedingungen des Sehens und der Darstellbarkeit auseinandersetzt. Nicolai fertigte Schwarz-Weiss-Photos von Wandabschnitten und heftete diese exakt an die Stellen der Wand, die er zuvor abgelichtet hatte. Dass die Photos nicht genau passen, beziehungsweise nie genau die Wandstelle ersetzen können, ist technisch nicht verwunderlich, widerspricht aber unseren Wahrnehmungsgewohnheiten.

René Descartes *Discours de la méthode* ist eine Schrift, die als eine der berühmtesten Texte der Neuzeit gilt. Sie wird als das Gründungsmanifest des frühneuzeitlichen Rationalismus verstanden. Der Sinnenerkenntnis misstrauend, die Vernunft als sichere Erkenntnisquelle annehmend, ist es eine Philosophie, die bekanntermassen das Verfahren der Deduktion als Methode für die Gewinnung von Aussagen entwickelt und damit den Grundstein für die naturwissenschaftliche und philosophische Theoriebildung gelegt hat. Doch dass Descartes auch eine Schrift über Meteore verfasst hat, die sogar einen der drei dem *Discours* angehängten Essays bildet, ist erstaunlicherweise fast unbekannt. Und tatsächlich ist seine Schrift über die Himmelserscheinungen ein ganz eigenständiges Werk, dessen Thesen sich nicht so leicht mit denen des *Discours* in eins setzen lassen. Die Erkenntnisse über die Himmelskörper entstehen nicht in einem mathematisch deduzieren Verfahren. Und auch dem aristotelischen Paradigma, das substantielle Eigenschaften der jeweiligen Körper annahm, um Entwicklungen erklären zu können, widersprach Descartes. Vielmehr geht er den entgegengesetzten Weg und verfolgt eine Theorie, derzufolge alle Phänomene auf der hypothetischen Grundlage der Gestalt und vor allem der Bewegung von Materieteilchen erklärt werden können. Doch wie lässt sich die enorme Vielfalt der Himmelsteilchen, die so chaotisch erscheint, erklären? Die Antwort auf diese Frage lässt einen Vergleich zu Nicolais Kunstwerk zu: Es müssen Erscheinungen beobachtet und an der Erfahrung geprüft und beschrieben, dokumentiert und abgeglichen werden; Abbildungen könnten nicht nur veranschaulichen, sondern auch dokumentieren helfen. Zu berechnen sind die Meteore nicht. Helfen könnten vielmehr Erfahrungsberichte von Seeleuten, denn – so Descartes – «die Augen [seien] die sichersten Richter».[3] Man brauche Geduld für Beobachtungen. «Die Beschäftigung mit Meteoren wird daher zwangsläufig zu einem Kollektiv-Unternehmen.»[4] Damit ist Descartes' Schrift über die Meteore in der Methode mit der Arbeit WELCOME TO THE "TEARS OF ST. LAWRENCE." AN APPOINTMENT TO WATCH FALLING STARS verwandt. Sind es doch die versammelten Blicke, die die Form und Gestalt des *tableaus* überhaupt erst ausmachen. Und nicht nur die Blicke selbst, sondern die Annahme dieser Blicke, die Annahme der *kommunalen* Dimension macht die Stabilität des Ganzen aus.

Doch warum sollte niemand wissen, dass René Descartes in den Jahren 1628 bis 1637 an einem Essay über Meteore arbeitet? Warum macht der Philosoph aus seiner Forschung ein Geheimnis? «Ich bitte Sie übrigens», schreibt er in einem Brief an Pater Mersenne, «zu niemandem in der Welt davon zu sprechen: Denn ich habe beschlossen, es als Probe meiner Philosophie öffentlich auszustellen und mich hinter dem Gemälde (*derrière le tableau*) zu verstecken, um zu hören, was man sagt.»[5] Descartes möchte, so hat es Hans-Hagen Hildebrandt formuliert, «seine Ich-Fiktionen mit den Fiktionen konfrontieren, die sie bei den ‹Betrachtern› seines Gemäldes hervorbringen».[6] Und das ist genau die These, die die Werke Descartes' und Nicolais – neben der Ähnlichkeit des Sujets – zu verbinden ermöglicht. Auch WELCOME TO THE TEARS von Olaf Nicolai scheint auf eine ähnliche Ich-Fiktion zurückzuführen zu sein. Der Künstler arbeitet zwar mit einer Zeige-Geste, bietet ausserordentlich

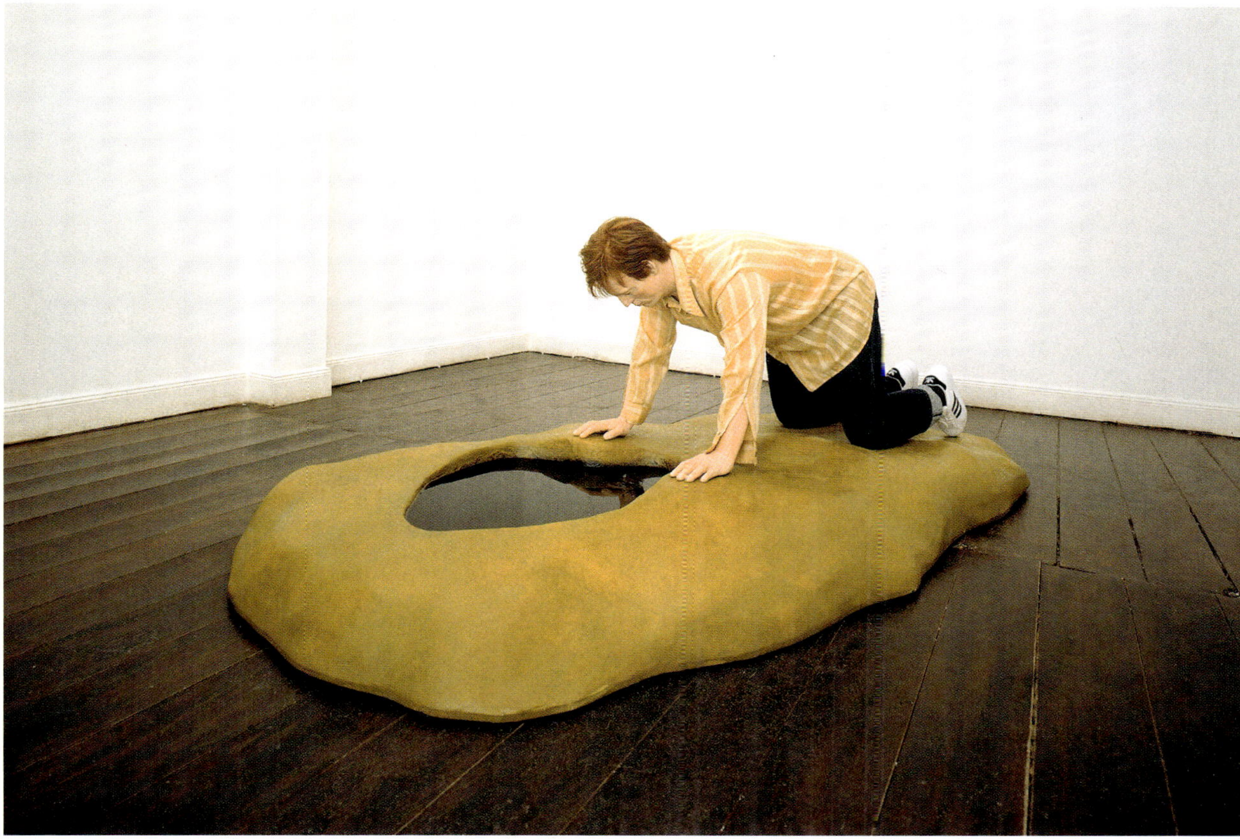

OLAF NICOLAI, A PORTRAIT OF THE ARTIST AS A WEEPING NARCISSUS, 2002, polyester, textiles, water, electronic pump, 35 1/2 x 105 1/2 x 61 1/2" / PORTRÄT DES KÜNSTLERS ALS WEINENDER NARZISS, Polyester, Textilien, Wasser, elektronische Pumpe, 90 x 268 x 156 cm.

sorgsam ausgearbeitetes Material, aber er nimmt sich selbst in der Hinsicht zurück, dass er keine These vertritt, die sein Werk erklären, seine Haltung zur Welt eindeutig fixieren könnte. Schon gar nicht will er seinen Blick ausstellen und in jedem seiner Werke erkenntlich machen, wie es in den 70er Jahren Jacques Lacan noch für die von ihm beobachtete, letzte Stufe der Gegenwartskunst in Vergleich zu früheren Kunstkonzepten konstatierte. Auch das Auftreten der Kunst im Gewand der Wissenschaft scheint in diese Richtung zu deuten.

Sein Werk A PORTRAIT OF THE ARTIST AS A WEEPING NARCISSUS (Porträt des Künstlers als weinender Narziss), in dem er sich selbst portraitiert, kann in diesem Sinne nur als Metapher für diese künstlerische Ich-Fiktion gesehen werden. Denn wenn das nachgegossene Double des Künstlers, das in die Pfütze schaut, die von seinen in einer Vertiefung angesammelten Tränen angefüllt ist, dann äussert sich hier gewiss nicht – wie einige Rezensenten meinten –die grosse Trauer oder der fürchterliche Katzenjammer des Künstlers über seine Situation oder Stellung im Kunstmarkt. Diese Tränen sind künstlich erzeugt und fliessen wie die des Papstes Clemens des III., der das exemplarische Weinen, also die Sichtbarkeit der Tränen vorführte, unaufhörlich und demonstrativ. Wichtig ist vielmehr, dass der Künstler sich mit seinen feuchten Augen in der bewegten Pfütze nicht mehr selbst sehen kann. Aber die Falschheit dieser Plastik-Geste zeigt eben einfach nur: Die Selbstbezüglichkeit des Künstlers ist keinesfalls der Schlüssel zur Kunst von Olaf Nicolai. Vielmehr ist es das Zurücktreten des Künstlers hinter die *kommunalen* Blicke.

1) Serres, Michel: *La naissance de la physique dans le texte de Lucrète. Fleurs et turbulences*, Editions de Minuit, Paris 1977, S. 85f.

2) Vgl. Anne von der Heiden, Claudia Blümle, «Einleitung», in: dies. (Hrsg.): *Blickzähmung und Augentäuschung. Zu Jacques Lacans Bildtheorie*, Diaphanes, Zürich/Berlin 2005, S. 30f.

3) René Descartes, *Les Météores/Die Meteoren*, hrsg. von Klaus Zittel, Klostermann, Frankfurt a. M. 2006, S. 277.

4) Klaus Zittel, «Einleitung», ebd., S. 11.

5) René Descartes, *Œuvres*. Bd. 1. *Correspondance, avril 1622–février 1638*, Paris 1956, S. 23.

6) Hans-Hagen Hildebrandt, *Ich-Fiktionen im Spiegel. Bruchstücke aus der Geschichte der Subjektfigurationen.* Habilitationsschrift, Essen 1985, S. 226.

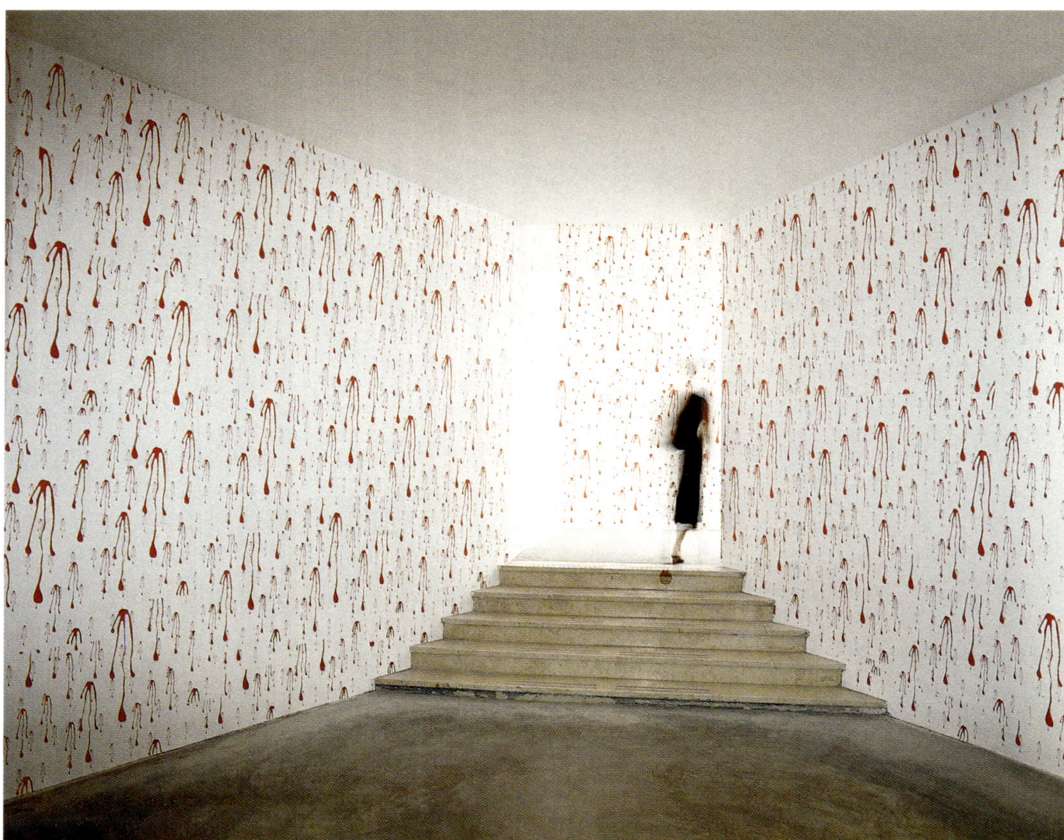

OLAF NICOLAI, UNTITLED (DROPS OF BLOOD), 2001, room with posters, each 39 1/2 x 27 1/2", dimension of installation variable / OHNE TITEL (BLUTSTROPFEN), plakatierter Raum, Plakate je 100 x 70 cm, Masse der Installation variabel.

In Abeyance, or: Views and Visual Rays

ANNE VON DER HEIDEN

Nobody reads ... the meteors, neither those of Lucretius, nor those of Descartes, nor those of anyone else. Why the repression? Because the philosophers, the historians, the masters of science devote themselves exclusively to the ancient idea of law. To determination or rigorous superdetermination, and to the God, Laplace. To absolute control and therefore dominion over free spaces and imponderabilities. To power and order.[1)]

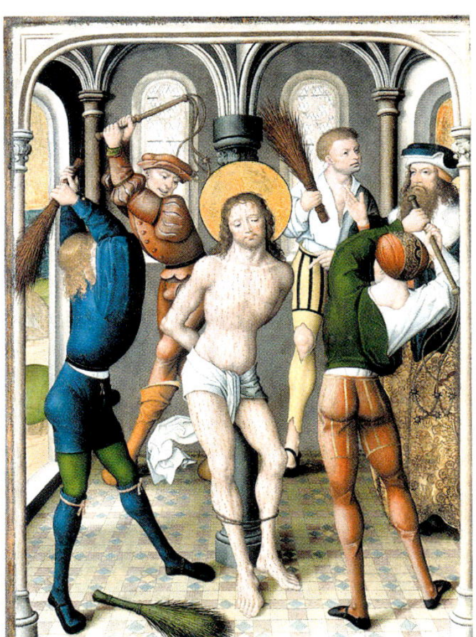

JAN BAEGERT, FLAGELLATION OF CHRIST / GEISSELUNG CHRISTI, 1507/13.

In 2005, during the 51st Biennale in Venice, Olaf Nicolai distributed a small brochure titled *Welcome to the 'Tears Of St. Lawrence'. An Appointment to Watch Falling Stars.* It was also the title of the corresponding work. A drawing of the constellation, reproduced on the front cover, folded out into two postcards showing a map—light on a dark background, like a typical scientific illustration of the constellations. On the lower left, the constellation of Perseus is seen next to Triangulum and Aries, directly under the line of the Galactic Equator. The contents of the brochure are listed in an index on the first page and on the second page we read in large print: "In the early hours after midnight, between the 8th and 13th of August, watch the Northern sky facing Northeast, in the direction of the constellation of Perseus, which you will find in the sky at an angle of approx. 45° up from the horizon. Look out for a shower of falling stars. They are the 'Tears of St. Lawrence.'" These lines invite visitors of the Biennale to watch the

ANNE VON DER HEIDEN is specialized in art history and media studies. She is the head of a research team on nineteenth century media technologies and the life sciences in the Department of Media Studies, Bauhaus University, Weimar. She has published several studies on visual theory and the ideological mechanisms of violence.

skies, equipped with the brochure, in which pages six and seven provide detailed information on the local times and places one can see the constellation all over the world. On the same page, Nicolai explains: "For the observer, tahe Perseid meteors seem to be flying out of this constellation. [...]. Looking directly at the radiant isn't necessarily the best way to observe the falling stars. Instead, look around and above it." The artist has also appended a glossary of important terms, astronomical drawings and photographs, a table of the meteor showers observed in the year 2005, a list of several websites on meteorology and astronomy, explanations and illustrations of the Perseus myth and the martyrdom of St. Lawrence, the above-mentioned postcard foldout on which we can note our observations on the basis of a number of questions and send them to the Fireballa Data Center/International Meteor Organization, and various other materials.

This work stands apart from the usual Biennale fare not only because it has the appearance of a scientific experiment but also because it disregards the default of a recognizable site. It is a Biennale hallmark that the countries each mount presentations in their own pavilions, that is, in a special architectural site, with the aim of persuading the public and, above all, the critics of the exceptional qualities of their artists and works of art. The presentations seek to make an impact, to be remembered, and, of course, to compete for the Best Pavilion award. Nicolai ignores this form of presentation and its intrinsic aesthetics, an approach already evident in the work he showed at the Biennale back in 2001: MAZE. ODER: HELP THE DUKES IN GENERAL LEE TO FIND THE RODEO IN HAZZARD COUNTY (2001). The MAZE was not placed inside the venue but rather on the periphery, on the border of urban space and, in fact, in an inaccessible military zone. The artist arranged the work in such fashion that it essentially found closure only through the sensual experience of the viewers walking around on the maze. But now, in WELCOME TO THE 'TEARS OF ST. LAWRENCE' (2005), Nicolai has become much more radical, having divested the work entirely of earthbound location, defined space, and the form of an installation. It emerges only in the act of gazing. Or rather: it anticipates the gaze of the viewer, thereby making an assumption that turns it into a kind of imaginary work of art. To put it more precisely: the viewer imagines art tourists, back home again, actually looking up at the skies at a specified moment. Through their gaze, which he sees in his mind's eye, there appears an immense imaginary arrangement of visual rays for the length of time defined by the artist, extending from viewers in specified locations all over the world to infinitely remote light phenomena. The outcome is an invisible work, consisting only of imagined sight lines and the events recorded through the medium of writing, which appears on the postcards. We imagine that the postcards have been evaluated in the indicated institute, producing something similar to what Lacan would call a "communal" work.[2] In addition to this constellation of gazes, which might best be described as the intersection of the imaginary and the real, Nicolai's work invokes symbolic content. Possible references to ancient myths, to the story of Perseus, so closely related to the power of the gaze, and to the story of St. Lawrence, auspiciously shedding genuine tears—as he is soon to be martyred for having distributed the treasures of the church among the poor—also appear as lines, lines of sight, which viewers must trace in their minds if they wish to see further meaningful points of light. The resulting tableau appears in all its iridescent glory.

Several gazes, as it were, are superimposed on many of Olaf Nicolai's works. In CHANT D'AMOUR (2003), for example, contact between two rooms separated by a thick wall is possible only through a hole the size of a straw. One is reminded of Pyramus and Thisbe. And the installation, BARAQUE DE CHANTIER (2002/2003)—a Plexiglas replica of the prefabricated

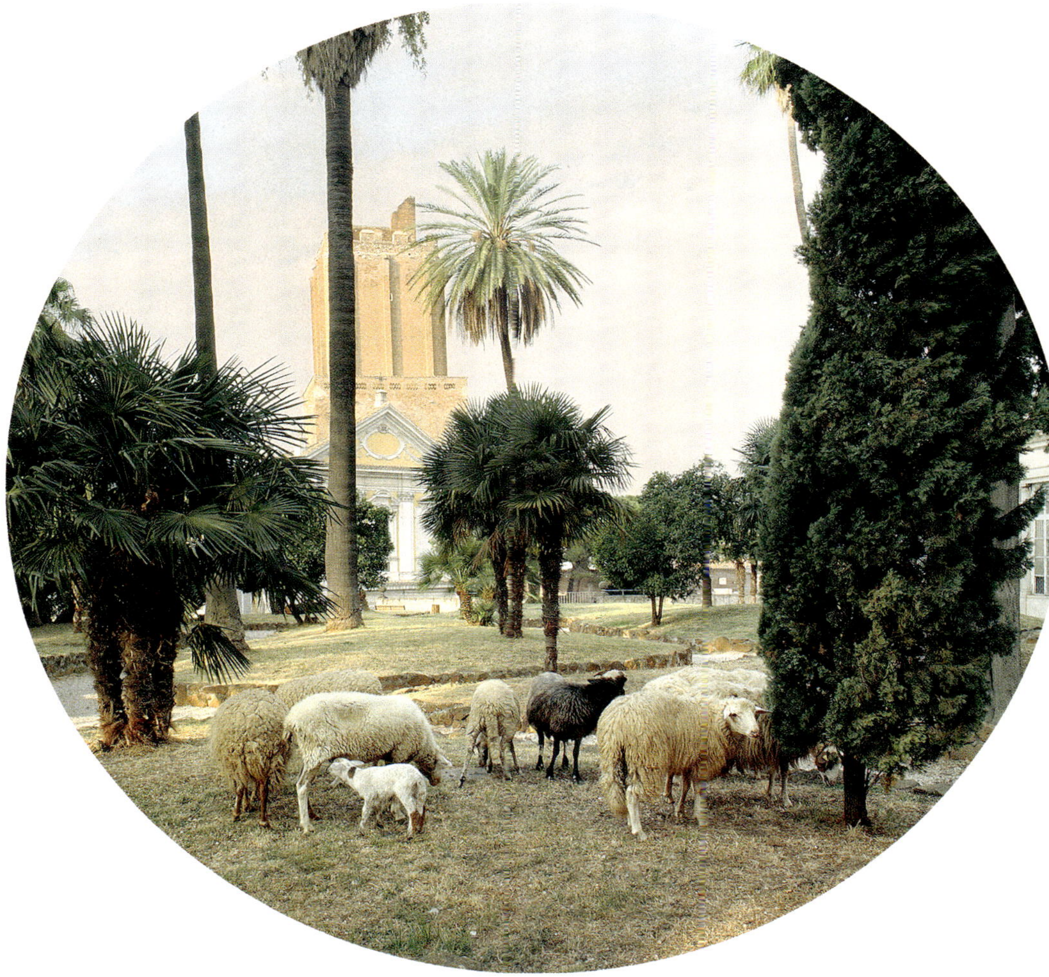

OLAF NICOLAI, ARCADIA. PAESAGGIO CON PECORE, ROMA, 16 SETTEMBRE, 2004, (landscape with sheep, September 16, 2004), park of the Villa Aldobrandini, Rome, C-print, 24 3/4 x 24 3/4" / Arcadia, Landschaft mit Schafen, Park der Villa Aldobrandini, Rom, C-Print, 63 x 63 cm.

wooden hut that Le Corbusier built near his home in southern France for use as a studio—, anticipates the gaze of viewers in a special way, as if that gaze were designed to be invested in it. Every part of the building is completely transparent. Space and nonspace, claim and reality, plan and concept are superimposed, overlap, and engage in a complex exchange. DIFFERENZ (FÜR REINHARD PRIESSNITZ), 2006, is another interesting work in this respect because it addresses the "difference" between the technical and the human gaze and also alludes to Austrian Reinhard Priessnitz's poetry, which primarily investigates the conditions of sensations and seeing as well as the limits of representation. Nicolai made black-and-white photographs of parts of the wall and then affixed them to exactly that part of the wall which he had photographed. The fact that the photographs are not an exact fit and can never replace a particular spot to perfection does not come as a surprise, technically, but it does contradict habitual perception. The experience also shows that "difference" necessarily embraces the potential for symbolic articulation to refer to something else.

As the founding manifesto of early modern rationalism, René Descartes' *Discours de la méthode* ranks among the most famous texts of the modern age. Suspicious of sensual knowledge and instead postulating reason as a certain source of knowledge, it is a philosophy that famously elaborated on the method of deduction as a means of arriving at conclusions, therefore laying the cornerstone for the development of scientific and philosophical theory. Astonishingly, however, Descartes' tract on meteors is barely acknowledged although it is one of the three essays appended to the *Discours*. It is, in fact, a completely self-contained work on celestial phenomena and advances theses that are not readily reconciled with those put forward in the *Discours*. Findings on the heavenly bodies do not stem from mathematical deduction, and the Aristotelian paradigm, which assumes that each of the bodies possesses substantial properties as an explanation for developments, contradicted Descartes' thinking. He pursued the opposite direction, a theory that proposes explaining all phenomena on the hypothetical basis of shape and, above all, the movement of particles. But how can the vast multiplicity of celestial particles, which seems to be so chaotic, be explained? The answer to this question invites comparison with Nicolai's TEARS OF ST. LAWRENCE: appearances must be observed, verified by experience, described, recorded, and evaluated; depictions not only illustrate, they also keep a record. Meteors cannot be calculated. More helpful, as Descartes remarks, is "the experience of our sailors" because "our eyes ... are the most certain judges."[3)] It takes patience to make observations. "The study of meteors is therefore inevitably a collective enterprise."[4)] It is here that Descartes' method, as described in his essay on meteors, shows an affinity with WELCOME TO THE 'TEARS OF ST. LAWRENCE'. AN APPOINTMENT TO WATCH FALLING STARS. For, without the accumulated gaze of viewers, there would be no form and shape to the tableau. And not only the gaze itself but even the assumption of this gaze, the assumption of a communal act, defines the stability of the whole.

But, then, why was the world not meant to know that René Descartes was working on an essay about meteors in the years between 1628 and 1637? Why did the philosopher make a secret of his research? In a letter to Father Mersenne, he asks him not to speak to anyone at all about his meteorological investigations, having decided to present them to the public as a test of his philosophy and to hide behind the painting (*derrière le tableau*) in order to learn how people react.[5)] As Hans-Hagen Hildebrandt observes, Descartes wanted "to confront the fictions of his own ego with those evoked in the minds of the 'viewers' of his painting."[6)] And that is exactly what allows us to link the oeuvres of Descartes and Nicolai, over and above the

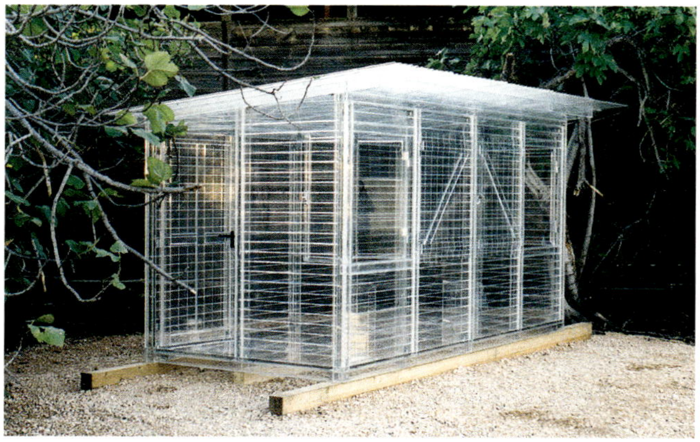

OLAF NICOLAI, BARAQUE DE CHANTIER, 2003, transparent acrylic glas, wood, 115 3/4 x 99 1/4 x 182 3/4" / Transparentes Acrylglas, Holz, 294 x 252 x 464 cm.

similarity of subject matter. TEARS OF ST. LAWRENCE can be traced back to a comparable ego fiction. In the extremely thoughtful and detailed presentation of his material, Olaf Nicolai does, of course, work with the gesture of pointing, but he holds back in the sense that he does not advance a thesis that would explain his work or unequivocally establish his attitude to the world. He certainly does not want to display his gaze and make it recognizable in each of his works, an approach that Jacques Lacan detected in the 1970s in his observations of the last stage of contemporary art in comparison to earlier artistic agendas. The fact that art now also appears in the guise of science seems to reinforce this change of direction.

A PORTRAIT OF THE ARTIST AS A WEEPING NARCISSUS (2000), in which Nicolai depicts himself, can be seen as a metaphor for this artistic ego fiction. For when the cast double of the artist gazes into the puddle of his own tears accumulating in a hollow, this is most certainly not an expression of the great anguish or woeful agony suffered by the artist about his situation or position in the art market, as some reviewers supposed. The tears are artificially generated and flow like those of Pope Clemens III, whose ceaseless and demonstrative display of weeping aimed to establish the visibility of tears. Far more important is the fact that the artist, blinded by his tears, can no longer see himself in the rippling puddle. However, the falsity of his sculptural gesture merely serves to show that artistic self-referentiality is certainly not the key to Olaf Nicolai's art. It is, rather, his retreat behind the communal gaze.

(Translation: Catherine Schelbert)

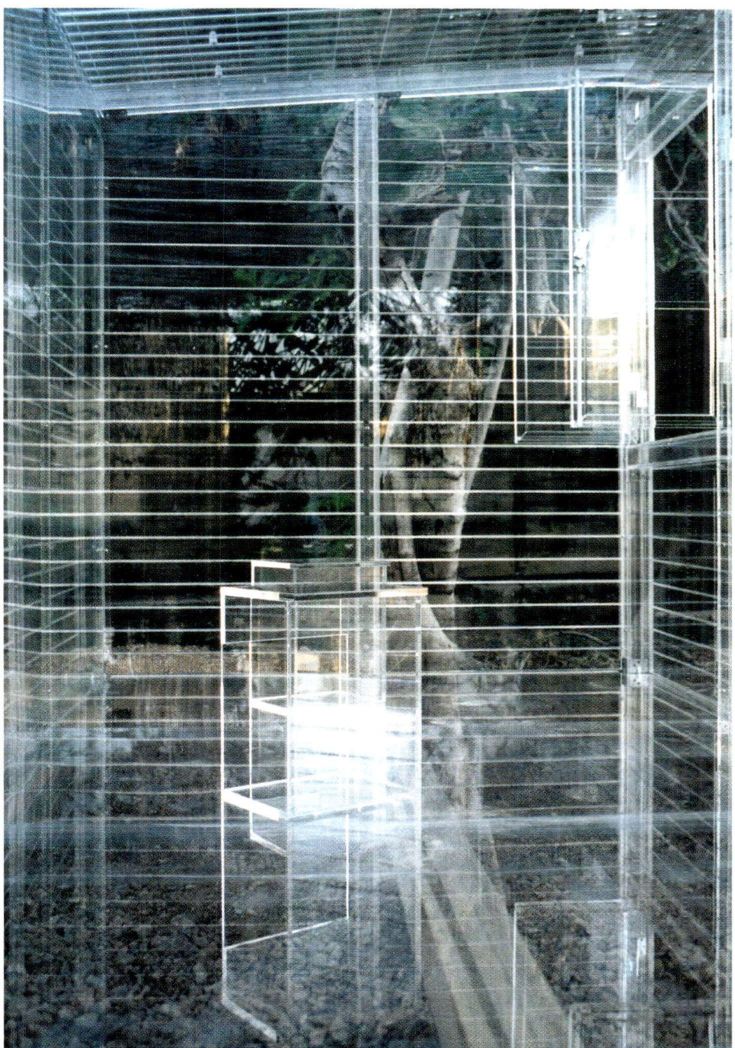

OLAF NICOLAI, BARAQUE DE CHANTIER, 2003, detail / Ausschnitt.

1) Michel Serres, *La naissance de la physique dans le texte de Lucrète. Fleurs et turbulences* (Paris: Editions de Minuit, 1977), pp. 85seq.
2) See Anne von der Heiden, Claudia Blümle, eds., "Einleitung," in *Blickzähmung und Augentäuschung. Zu Jacques Lacans Bildtheorie* (Zürich/Berlin: Diaphanes, 2005), pp. 30f.
3) René Descartes, *Discourse on Method, Optics, Geometry, and Meteorology*, trans. Paul J. Olscamp (Indianapolis: Hackett, 2001), pp. 296 and 295.
4) Klaus Zittel, ed., in his introduction to René Descartes, *Les Météores / Die Meteoren* (Klostermann, Frankfurt a. M. 2006), p. 11.
5) René Descartes, *Correspondance, avril 1622–février 1638, Œuvres*, vol. 1 (Paris, 1956), p. 23.
6) Hans-Hagen Hildebrandt, *Ich-Fiktionen im Spiegel. Bruchstücke aus der Geschichte der Subjektfigurationen,* Post-doctoral Dissertation (Essen, 1985), p. 226.

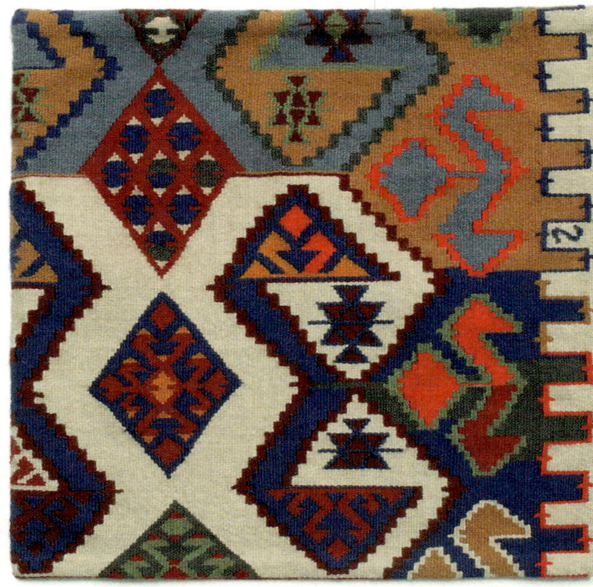

EDITION FOR PARKETT

OLAF NICOLAI

Georg's pillow, 2007
(Replica of a pillow from Georg Lukács' sofa in his study in Budapest)

Handwoven pillowcase, hand-dyed sheep's wool and red silk, 18 1/2 x 20".
Made by the Department of Textiles, Institute of Applied Arts, Schneeberg, Germany.
Edition of 35 / XX, signed and numbered certificate.

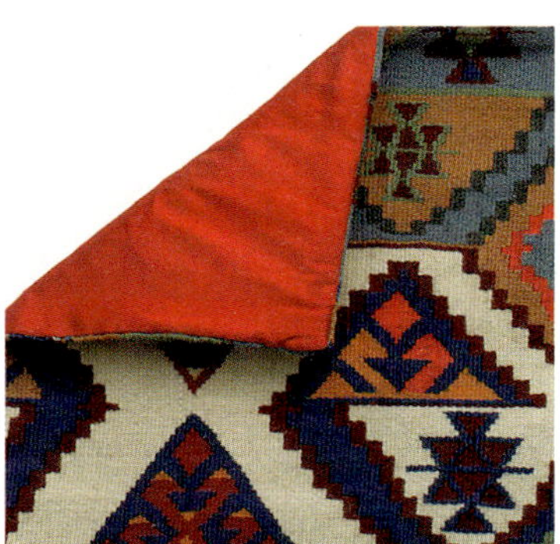

Georgs Kissen, 2007
(Replica eines Kopfkissens von Georg Lukács' Sofa aus seinem Budapester Arbeitszimmer)

Handgewebter Kissenbezug, handgefärbte Schurwolle und rote Seide, 47 x 51 cm.
Manufaktur: Werkstatt Textilkunst der Fachhochschule für Angewandte Kunst Schneeberg, Deutschland
Auflage 35 / XX, signiertes und nummeriertes Zertifikat.

(PHOTOS: UWE WALTER, BERLIN)

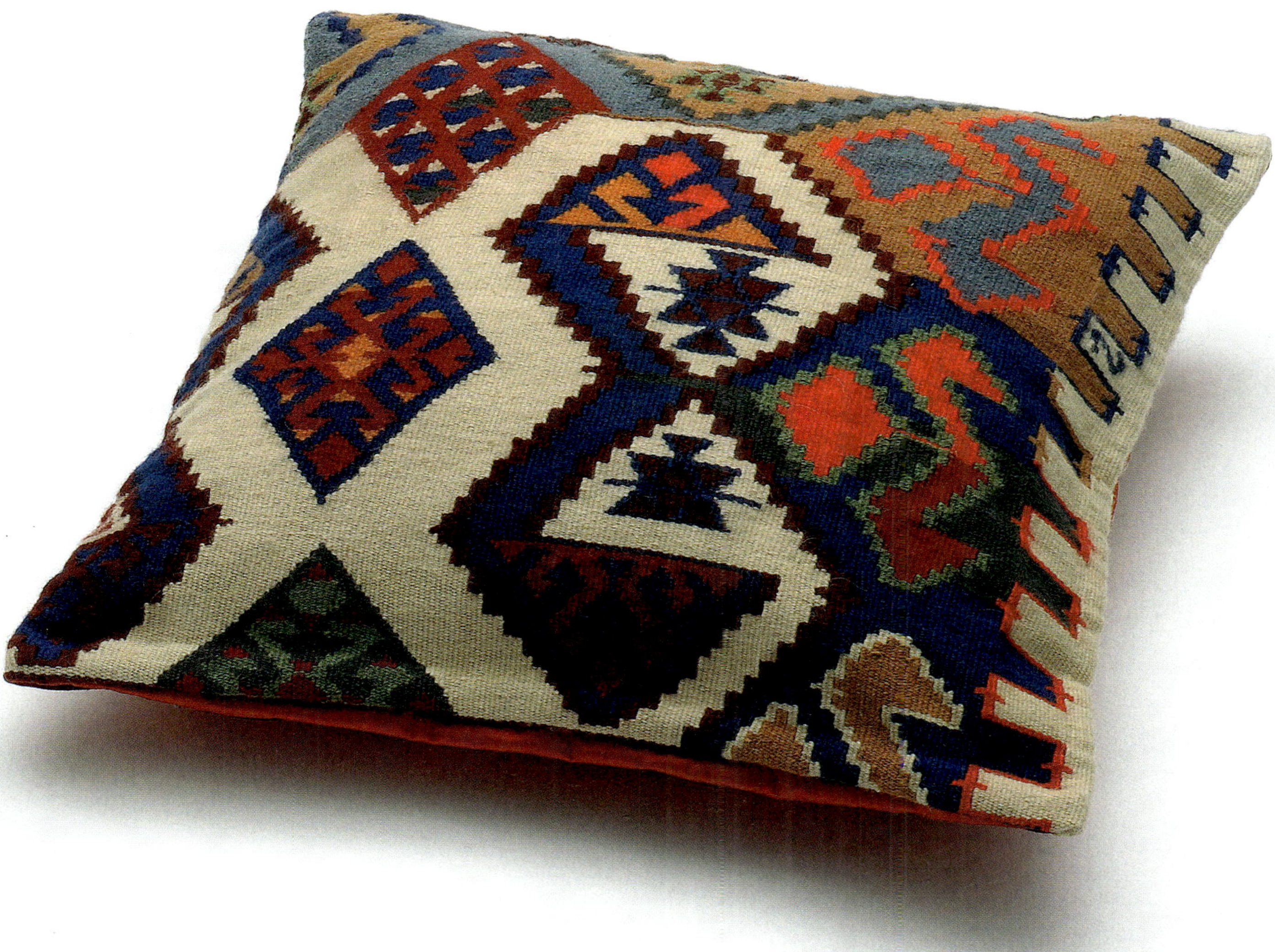

ERNESTO NETO

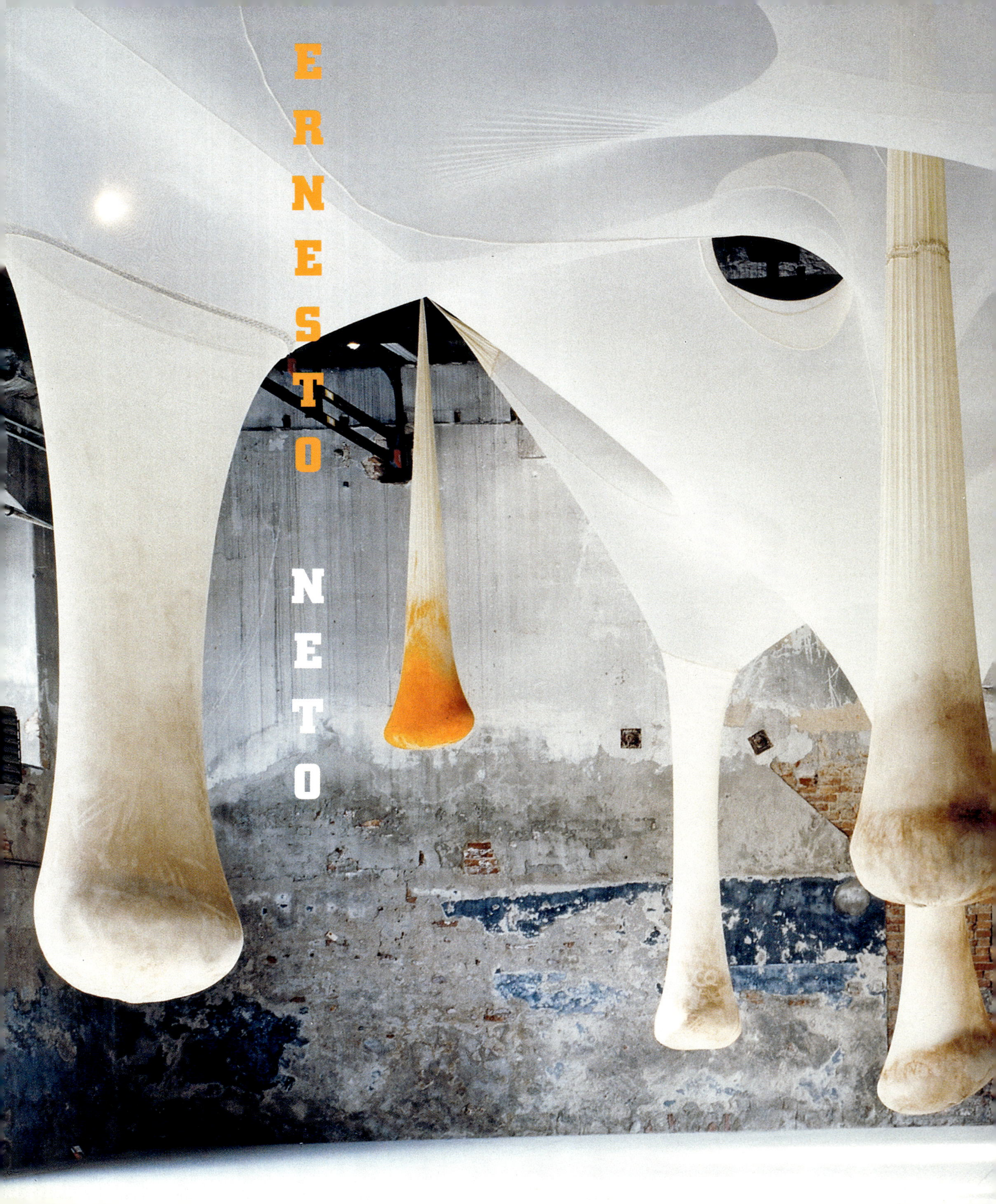

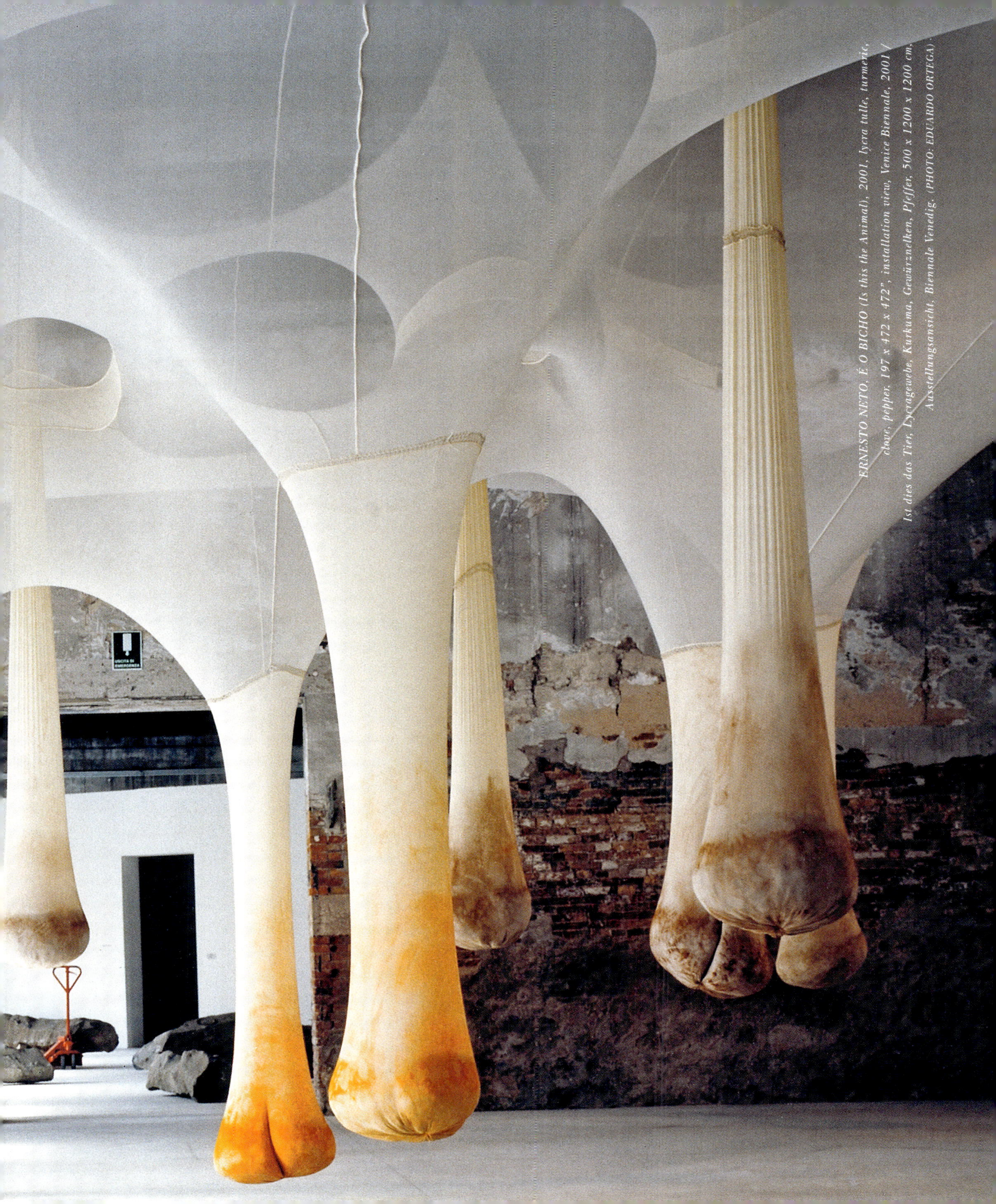

ERNESTO NETO, É O BICHO (Is this the Animal), 2001, lycra tulle, turmeric, clove, pepper, 197 x 472 x 472", installation view, Venice Biennale, 2001 / Ist dies das Tier, Lycragewebe, Kurkuma, Gewürznelken, Pfeffer, 500 x 1200 x 1200 cm, Ausstellungsansicht, Biennale Venedig. (PHOTO: EDUARDO ORTEGA)

Ein Tagtraum:

In Ernesto Netos Globiobabel Nudelioname Landmoonaia.

PHILIP URSPRUNG

Mit unseren beiden kleinen Kindern ist jeder Ausstellungsbesuch eine Zerreissprobe. Es ist ein Kampf an vielen Fronten. Wir möchten sie, die doch viel lieber auf dem Spielplatz wären, mit Kunstwerken vertraut machen und müssen sie zugleich daran hindern, diese zu berühren, durch die Säle zu rennen und laut zu jauchzen. Wir müssen die strafenden Blicke der anderen Besucher ignorieren und den besorgten Aufsehern die Illusion vermitteln, dass alles unter Kontrolle sei. Und schliesslich müssen wir selber jene Augenblicke der Musse finden, die Kunstwerke zu erfahren, zu geniessen, darüber zu reflektieren. Solche Besuche zeigen jeweils ganz handfest, was wir seit Pierre Bourdieus Buch *Die feinen Unterschiede* theoretisch wissen: Die Kunstwelt ist ein hochgradig exklusives, kontrolliertes, und segregierendes soziales Feld.

In die Ausstellung von Ernesto Netos Installation GLOBIOBABEL NUDELIONAME LANDMOONAIA (2000) in der Zürcher Daros Collection lockten wir sie mit dem Versprechen, dass sie die Kunstwerke ausnahmsweise würden anfassen dürfen. Wir zogen die Schuhe aus, zwängten uns durch die Eingangsöffnung und tapsten durch die weisse Stofflandschaft, die wie ein Zelt im Raum hing, aufgespannt an einigen Haken, am Boden fixiert durch kleine Beutel mit Ballast. Beim Gehen auf dem opaken Lycrastoff konnten wir den harten Boden fühlen und sehen. Und dennoch schienen unsere Tritte ein wenig abgefedert zu sein, etwas weicher, langsamer und leiser als sonst. Anfangs bewegten sich die Kinder ängstlich, aber bald fühlten sie sich wohl. Sie liessen sich mit Genuss in die weichen Kissen fallen, steckten die Hände in die mysteriöse Öffnung der Polster und entdeckten immer neue Wege durch

PHILIP URSPRUNG ist Professor für Moderne und zeitgenössische Kunst an der Universität Zürich.

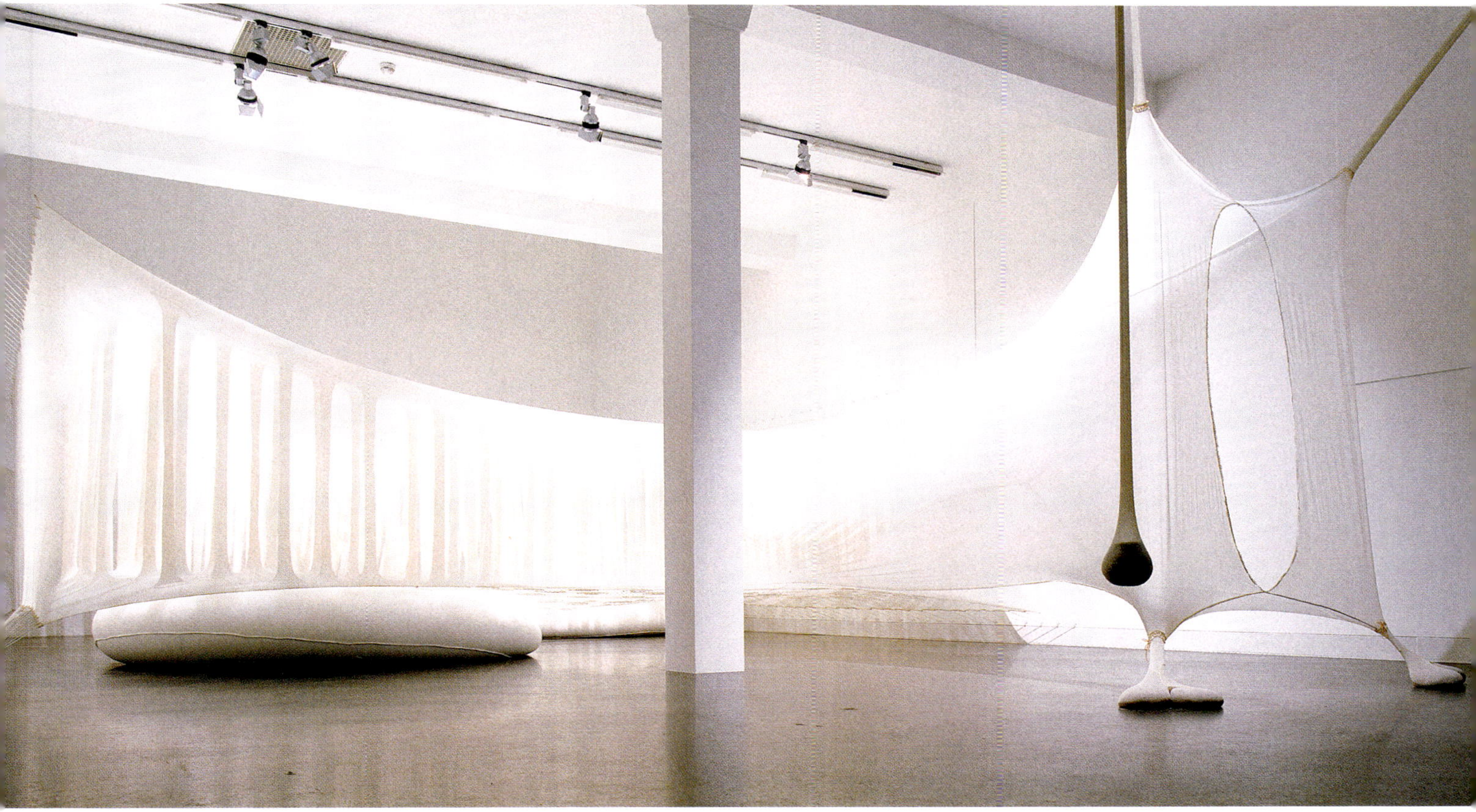

ERNESTO NETO, GLOBIOBABEL NUDELIONAME LANDMOONAIA, 2000, lycra tulle, styrofoam balls, sand, 118 x 325 x 968", installation view Daros-Latinamerica, Zurich / Lycra Tülle, Styropor-Kügelchen, Sand, 300 x 825 x 2460 cm.
(ALL PHOTOS OF GLOBIOBABEL NUDELIONAME LANDMOONAIA: ZOÉ TEMPEST, DAROS-LATINAMERICA, ZURICH)

das Labyrinth. Auch wir Eltern entspannten uns, als wir sahen, dass unsere fünfjährige Tochter nicht durch das Kunstwerk tobte und die Stoffbahnen in Fetzen riss, sondern sich ungewohnt sachte darin bewegte.

Ich hatte schon etliche Installationen von Ernesto Neto gesehen. Oder besser, ich hatte sie unter Zeitdruck in internationalen Grossausstellungen flüchtig zur Kenntnis genommen. Nun liess ich mich von der Begeisterung der Kinder anstecken. Wie sie nahm ich mir Zeit, die Stofflandschaft zu erkunden, sie mit den Fingern zu betasten, sie in Besitz zu nehmen. Anders als bei früheren Begegnungen erfuhr ich das Kunstwerk weniger als einen distanzierten Gegenstand der Betrachtung, sondern als Ambiente, als Atmosphäre, aus der herauszutreten ich es gar nicht mehr eilig hatte. Ich fühlte mich sogar ein wenig verantwortlich dafür. Ich gab mir Mühe, mich nicht in den Stoffschläuchen zu verheddern und hoffte, dass die Risse, die sich da und dort im Gewebe gebildet hatten, nicht grösser wurden. Nicht ich war dem Werk ausgeliefert, sondern es lag in meinen Händen. Ich empfand es als etwas Zerbrechliches, Vergängliches, Schützenswertes.

Ich versank in einem der Kissen, blickte zur milchig weissen Stoffdecke über mir. Die eierschalenweissen, cremefarbenen und leicht fleischfarbenen Textilien produzierten eine Atmosphäre von Ruhe und Abgeschiedenheit. Die anderen Besucher und die Wärter verschwammen hinter den Schleiern. Hier war es wieder, dieses entspannende Gefühl des Nichts, das erlaubt, sich gleichsam in einer wolkigen Umgebung aufzulösen und dennoch klar zu sehen. In meinen Gedanken flog ich zu anderen Orten, wo ich dieses Gefühl schon erlebt hatte. Ich stand im Wasserdampf von Diller + Scofidios Blur Building an der Schweizerischen Landesausstellung, der Expo.02 und blickte in den blauen Himmel. Dann lag ich auf dem Boden unter der riesigen verspiegelten Decke in Olafur Eliassons «The Weather Project» (2003–2004) in der Tate Modern. Und schliesslich befand ich mich vor Pierre Huyghes «L'expédition scintillante» (2002) und verfolgte, wie sich kleine Dampfsäulen wie Arabesken ineinander verschlangen, farbig beleuchtet, musikalisch untermalt.

Warum bereiten diese Effekte derzeit so vielen Menschen Genuss und warum empfinden sie es als zeitgemäss, fragte ich mich? Warum sprechen solche Werke nicht nur Kunstfreunde an, sondern auch kleine Kinder? In meinem Tagtraum tauchte plötzlich Fredric Jameson aus dem Nebel auf. Er flüsterte mir zu, dass er das Phänomen ja als Erster theoretisch zu

ERNESTO NETO, GLOBIOBABEL NUDELIONAME LANDMOONAIA, 2000, installation view / Installationsansicht.

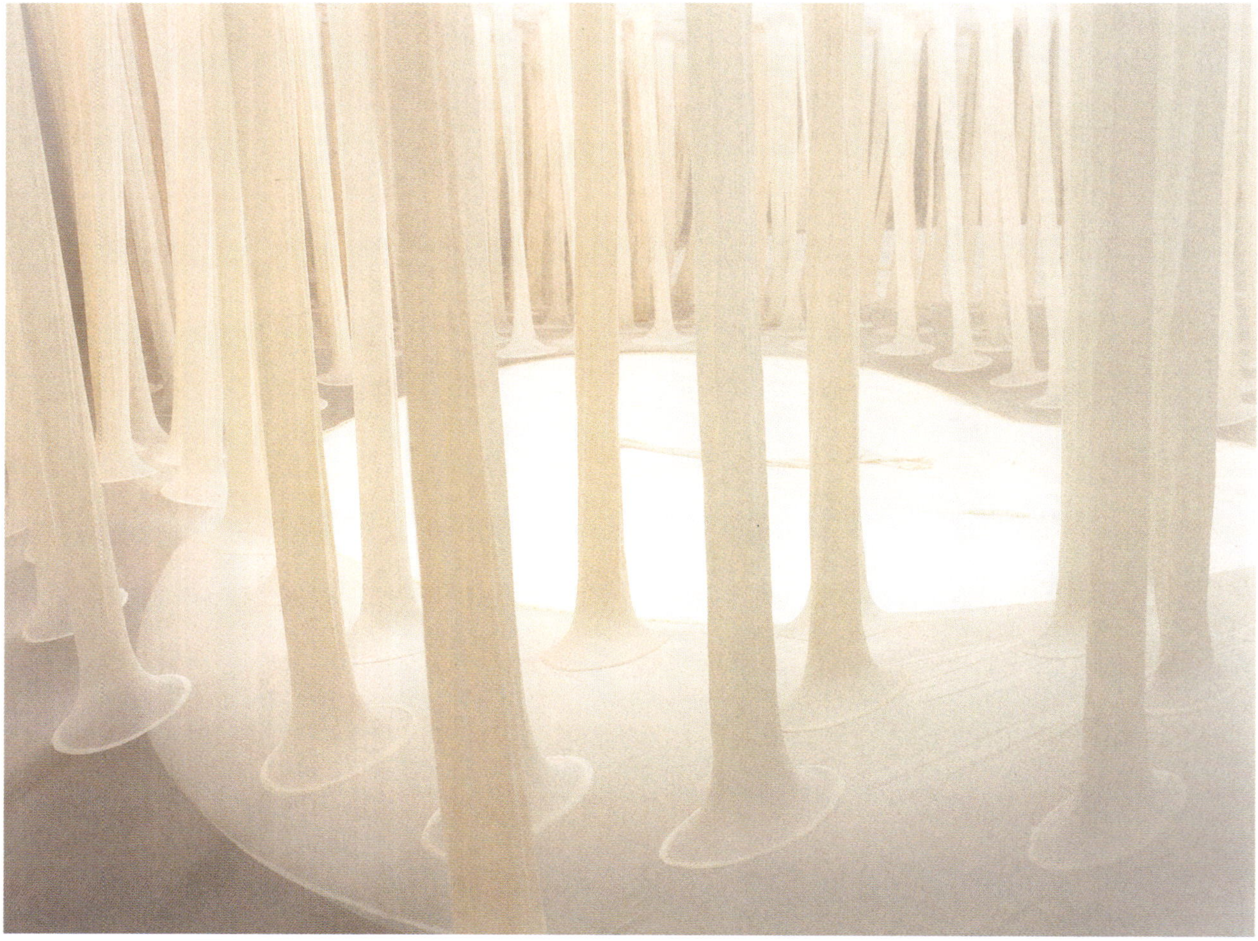

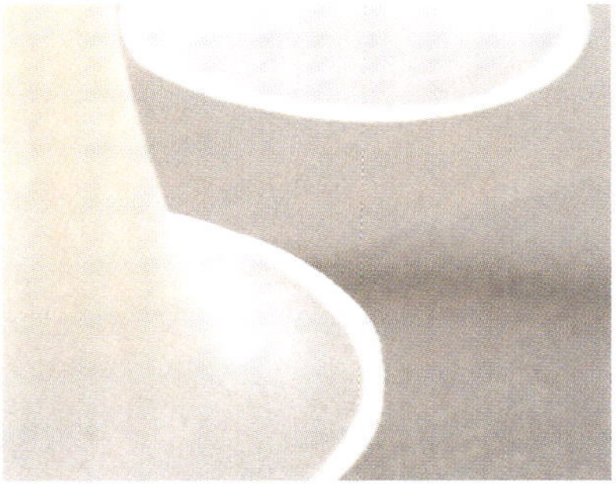

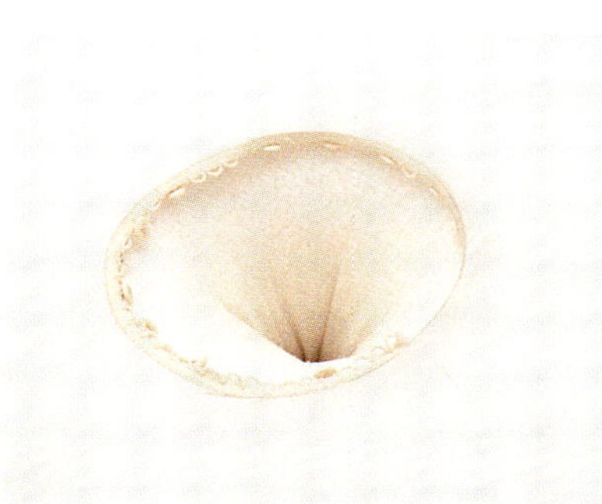

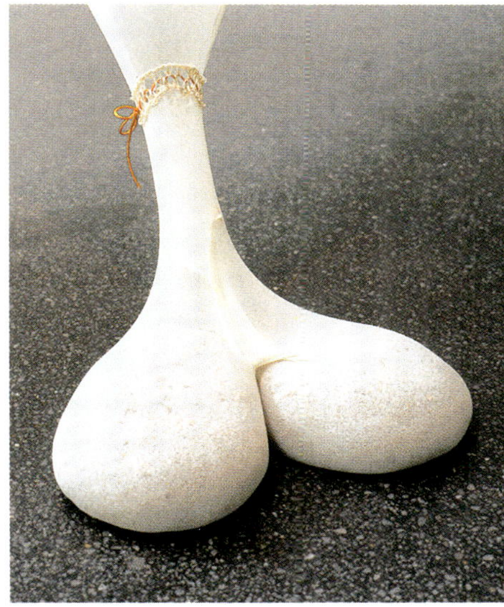

ERNESTO NETO, GLOBIOBABEL NUDELIONAME LANDMOONAIA, 2000, details / Detailansichten.

erfassen versucht habe. Vor bald zwanzig Jahren beschrieb er sein Erlebnis, im Atrium des Westin Bonaventure Hotels in Los Angeles in einen «Hyperspace» einzutauchen. Er erfuhr dieses, wie er in seinem Buch *Postmodernism, or, the Cultural Logic of Late Capitalism* (1991) schreibt, als einen «tiefenlosen» Raum, als etwas, das nur aus Oberfläche besteht. Er erklärte es damit, dass die Sphäre der Kultur sich in einer explosionsartigen Ausdehnung befand, dass sie gleichsam alle Bereiche der Wirklichkeit wie eine dünne Schicht überzog, aber zugleich ihre einstige Autonomie verlor. Wenn Kultur sich wie ein Sprühnebel überallhin ausdehnte, dann konnte sie kein Ort der Distanz mehr sein. Dies stellt alle Verfahren, die auf dem Konzept räumlicher Tiefe beruhen, von der Psychoanalyse bis zur Hermeneutik, radikal in Frage. Neben Jameson schwebte sein Schüler Michael Hardt herbei. Zusammen mit Antonio Negri beschreibt er im Buch *Empire* (2000) ein Szenario, in dem die Geschichte suspendiert und durch eine ewige Gegenwart ersetzt worden sei, in der alle räumliche und zeitliche Grenzen sich auflösen.

Solche Theorien der räumlichen Auflösung passen gut zu Netos ineinander gefalteten Oberflächen, «hinter» und «unter» denen nichts zu existieren scheint. Im Unterschied zu Eliasson oder Huyghes erzielt Neto solche Effekte allerdings nicht mittels technischen Apparaten, sondern mit preiswerten Medien wie Stoffen, Pigmenten und Gewürzen. Ihr Look ist nicht derjenige des Neuen, sondern des leicht Veralteten. Technisch wären sie in dieser Form bereits in den 50er oder 60er Jahren, spätestens seit es Kunstfasern gibt, herstellbar gewesen. Ihre Wirkung ist anthropomorph in dem Sinne, dass die Spuren des Lebens sich auf ihnen abzeichnen und sie uns an die Vergänglichkeit des Lebens erinnern. Es ist leicht, Netos Haltung als vormodernistisch zu kritisieren. Sein Essentialismus, also seine Skepsis gegenüber jeglicher Form von Repräsentation, etwa wenn er sagt, dass er «der Sprache misstraue», oder wenn er die Produktion einer Skulptur mit einem sexuellen Akt vergleicht, wirkt im Lichte des aktuellen Diskurses in der Tat etwas anachronistisch.[1)] Sein Œuvre bietet sich dem kritischen Diskurs tatsächlich weniger gut an als beispielsweise dasjenige von Olafur Eliasson, Pierre Huyghe oder Liam Gillick, die sich auf der Ebene der Theorie regelmässig einmischen. Aber was sein Werk mit demjenigen vieler seiner Zeitgenossen verbindet, ja, was es unverhohlener zeigt, ist, dass die «Bedeutung» oder der «Sinn» des Kunstwerks gleichsam in der Textur der Oberfläche absorbiert ist. Netos Werke sind geradezu ostentativ opportunistisch. Sie geben elastisch jedem Druck nach, passen sich an. Sie sind aus jedem Blickwinkel hinreissend schön. Sie sind so mühelos konsumierbar wie die Duftwolken, die manche von ihnen verstreuen – und lassen sich dennoch nicht festhalten.

Dies rückt sie nahe an ein Terrain, dessen Berührung die Kunst lange zu vermeiden suchte, nämlich das Design. Mein Tagtraum nahm eine neue Richtung. Plötzlich verwandelte sich die weiche, nachgiebige, passive Oberfläche, die mich eben noch sanft gestützt hatte, in ein gieriges, gefrässiges Wesen. Sie wurde zu einer aggressiven Kreuzung aus Organismus und Maschine, die sich nach allen Seiten hin ausdehnte. Sie stülpte fortwährend weitere Oberflächen aus sich heraus. Was sie herstellte, so schoss es mir durch den Kopf, war nichts anderes als Gegenwärtigkeit. Sie produzierte – Präsenz. Sie wucherte als topologisches Monstrum durch die Ausstellungshalle, verleibte sich die Kunstwerke ein und verwandelte sie in einem mysteriösen Stoffwechsel wiederum in elastische Oberflächen. Was, wenn das Design plötzlich die Macht an sich reisst und die Kunst absorbiert? Und dabei verstehe ich unter Design natürlich nicht Produktgestaltung, sondern den technischen, politischen, ökonomischen und sozialen Entwurf unseres Lebens, also etwas, was die Diskontinuität der Wirklichkeit zu einer Kette von Events verschmilzt. Was, wenn die Kunst einfach zu langsam geworden ist, zu wenig universell, zu schwer übersetzbar und konsumierbar, um mit der Realität noch Schritt zu halten? Je nach Standpunkt wäre Netos Kunst somit ein Vorbote der neuen Kunst oder eines der ersten Opfer eines allumfassenden Designs.

Als unsere Tochter sich kichernd auf mich fallen liess, erwachte ich aus dem Tagtraum und meinem imaginären Dialog mit anderen Männern. Ich hatte nicht auf die Uhr geschaut. Andere Besucher standen erwartungsvoll vor dem Eingang der Installation. Es war Zeit, den Platz freizugeben. Ich wälzte mich aus dem Kissen. Und zum ersten Mal wollten unsere Kinder eine Kunstausstellung nicht verlassen.

1) Diese Referenzen stammen aus dem Interview von Cecilia Pereira mit Ernesto Neto, «The fragility of the world», in: Ernesto Neto, *O corpo, nu tempo* (Centro Galego de Arte Contemporanea, Xunta di Galicia, 2001), S. 301–312.

ERNESTO NETO, GLOBIOBABEL NUDELIONAME LANDMOONAIA, 2000.

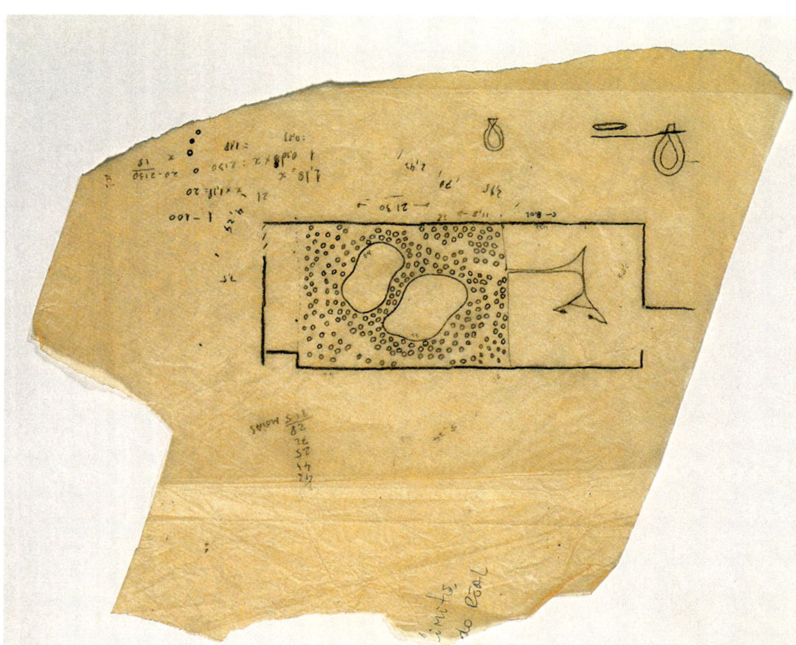

ERNESTO NETO, GLOBIOBABEL NUDELIONAME LANDMOONAIA, 2000, artist's sketch, pencil on parchment paper / Skizze des Künstlers, Bleistift auf Pergamentpapier.

A Daydream:

IN ERNESTO NETO'S GLOBIOBABEL NUDELIONAME LANDMOONAIA

PHILIP URSPRUNG

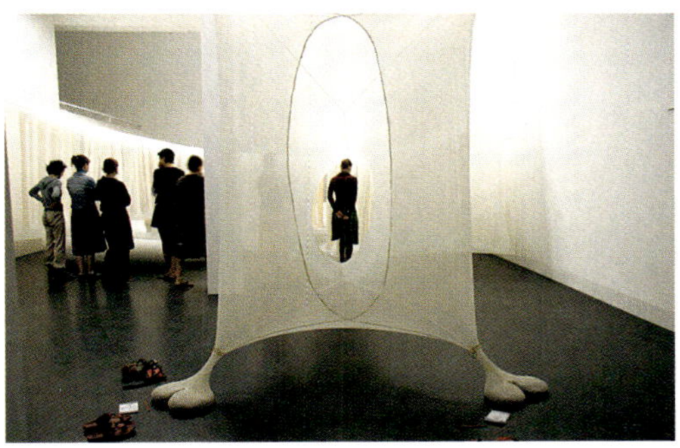

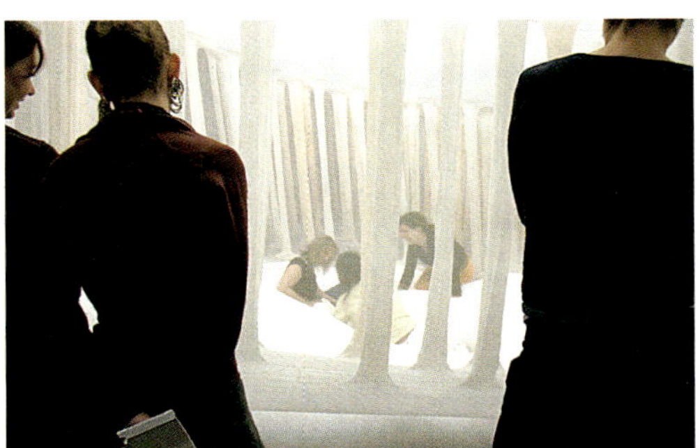

With our two small children in tow, any visit to an exhibition quickly becomes an endurance test. Battle is waged on a variety of fronts. We would like them to feel at home with works of art—they would much rather be out in the playground—but at the same time, we have to prevent them from touching the art or running from room to room yelping with glee. We have to ignore the baleful stares of other exhibition-goers and create the illusion, for the security staff, that everything is under control. And, in the end, we still have to find those moments of repose needed to take in the artworks, to enjoy them, to reflect on them. These visits confirm, in practice, what we already know to be true in theory—from Pierre Bourdieu's *Distinction: A Social Critique of the Judgement of Taste*—that the art world is a highly exclusive, controlled, segregating social field.

So we lured the children into the exhibition of Ernesto Neto's installation GLOBIOBABEL NUDELIONAME LANDMOONAIA (2000) at Zurich's Daros Collection with the promise that, for once, they would be allowed to touch the works of art. We removed our shoes, squeezed in through the entrance, and felt our way through the white fabric landscape hanging like a tent suspended from hooks and fixed to the floor by little sacks of ballast. Walking on the opaque lycra we could feel and see the hard floor, yet it was as though our steps had a different spring to them, as though they were softer, slower, and quieter than usual. At first the children moved with a certain hesitation, but soon they were completely at ease. They tumbled with rel-

PHILIP URSPRUNG is Professor of Modern and Contemporary Art at the University of Zurich.

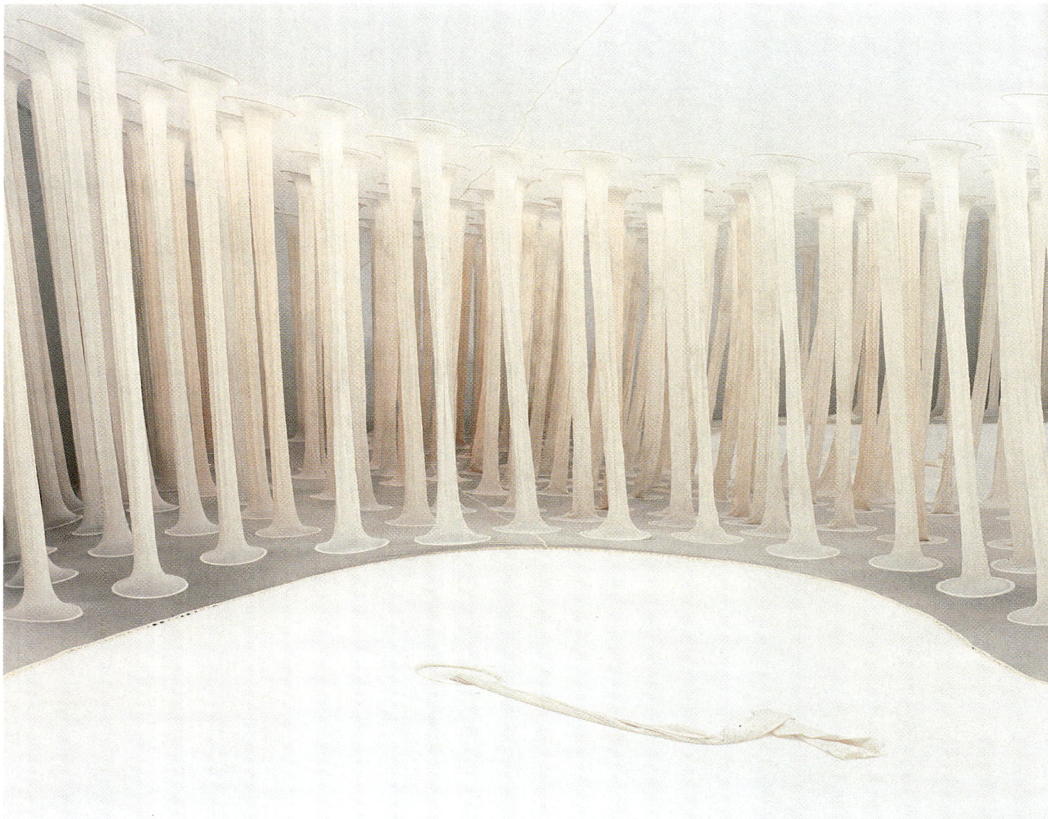

ERNESTO NETO, GLOBIOBABEL NUDELIONAME LANDMOONAIA, 2002.

ish into the soft cushions, pushed their hands into mysterious apertures in the padding, and discovered more and more ways through the labyrinth. And our own parental anxiety abated when we saw that our five-year-old daughter was not charging through the installation ripping the fabric to shreds, but making her way through it with unusual gentleness.

I had already seen a number of Ernesto Neto's installations. Or rather, I had fleetingly registered them under pressure of time in major international exhibitions. Now I allowed myself to be infected by the children's delight and took time to explore this lycra landscape, to touch it with my fingers, to take hold of it. Unlike those earlier encounters with Neto's work, rather than observing the work of art from a distance I now absorbed it as an ambience, an atmosphere that I was in no hurry to leave. I even began to feel a little responsible for it. I tried my best not to get tangled in the elastic tubes and hoped that the rips that had opened up here and there in the fabric wouldn't get any worse. It was not that I was exposed to the work; it was more that the work was in my hands. It seemed fragile, transient, worth protecting.

I sank into one of the cushions and gazed up at the milky-white fabric ceiling. The eggshell-white, creamy, almost skin-colored textiles created a sense of peace and seclusion. The other visitors and the security staff were little more than blurs behind the veils. Here it was again—the soothing feeling of nothingness that allowed me to merge into the misty scenario and yet still to see clearly. In my mind, I floated away to other places where I have enjoyed the same feeling: standing in the water vapor from Diller + Scofidio's Blur Building at the Swiss National Exhibition, Expo.02, and looking up into the blue sky; lying on the floor under the vast mirrored ceiling of Olafur Eliasson's "The Weather Project" (2003–2004) at Tate Modern; and, lastly, gazing at Pierre Huyghe's "L'Expédition Scintillante" (2002), watching little columns of steam intertwine like arabesques with colored lighting and a musical backdrop.

Why is it that these effects give so many people such pleasure these days? And what is it that makes them seem so contemporary? Why do these works appeal not only to art lovers but also to small children? Suddenly Fredric Jameson emerged from my misty daydream and, in a whisper, reminded me that he had been the first to attempt to grapple with the theory of this phenomenon. Almost twenty years ago, he described how it had felt to plunge into "hyperspace" in the atrium of the Westin Bonaventure Hotel in Los Angeles. As he describes it in his book *Postmodernism or, the Cultural Logic of Late Capitalism* (1991), he had a sense of "depthlessness," of a space that only consists of surface. His explanation for this was that the sphere of culture was expanding like an explosion, so that it now formed a thin covering over almost all areas of reality, but only at the expense of its former autonomy. If culture extends over everything like a fine mist, it can no longer have anything to do with distance. This, in turn, radically casts doubt on any processes that rely on the concept of spatial depth, from psychoanalysis to hermeneutics. And soon afterwards, Jameson's student, Michael Hardt,

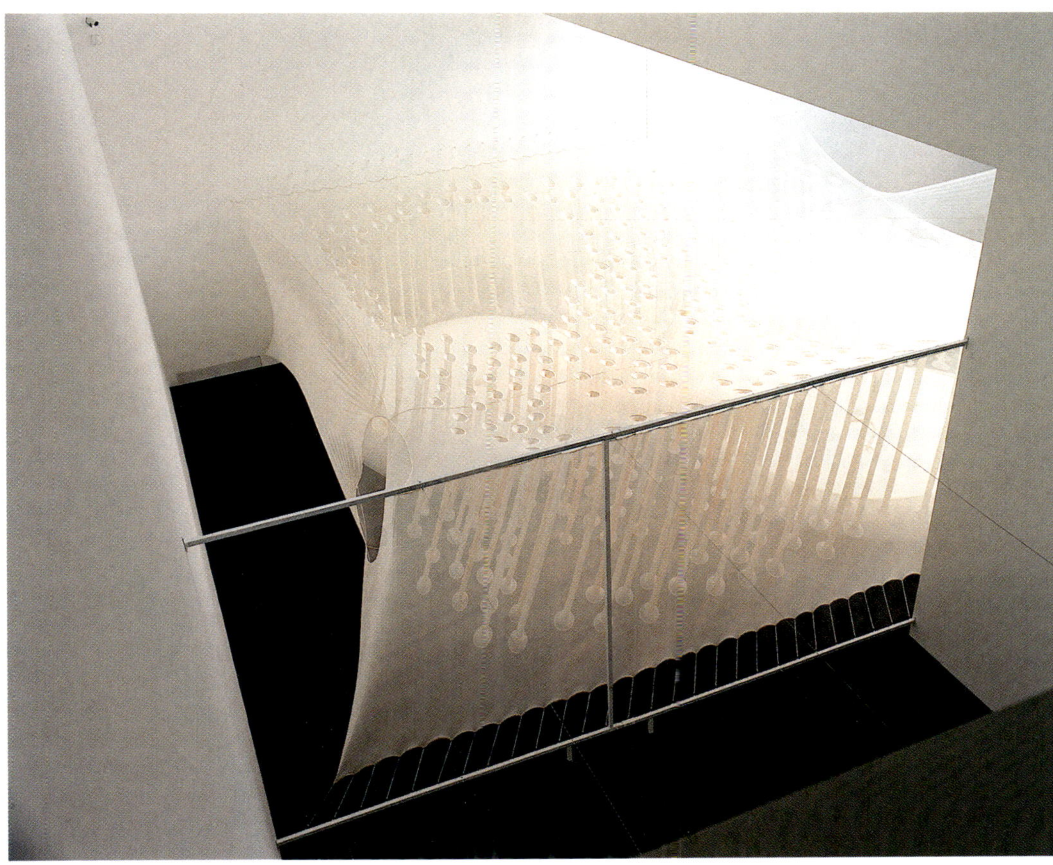

ERNESTO NETO, GLOBIOBABEL NUDELIONAME LANDMOONAIA, 2002.

also loomed into view. He and Antonio Negri, in their book *Empire* (2000), envisioned a scenario where history is suspended and replaced by an eternal present, in which all spatial and temporal distinctions are dissolved.

These theories of spatial dissolution chime perfectly with Neto's interfolded surfaces, behind and under which nothing seems to exist. However, unlike Eliasson or Huyghe, Neto doesn't achieve his effects with the aid of technical equipment but with inexpensive materials such as fabrics, pigments, and spices. And rather than appearing brand new, his work has a slightly worn air. In terms of the technology involved, his works could conceivably have been made, in the same form, as far back as the 1950s or 60s, ever since synthetic fibers have been on the market. Their effect is anthropomorphic in the sense that life leaves its mark on them and that they remind us of the transience of existence. It's easy to criticize Neto's approach as pre-modernist. His essentialism—that's to say his skepticism regarding any form of representation (evident, for instance, in his comment that he "mistrusts language a lot"), or when he compares the production of sculpture with a sexual act—actually seems somewhat anachronistic in the light of the present discourse.[1)] And it's true that Neto's oeuvre sits much less comfortably within the critical discourse of the day than that of, say, Olafur Eliasson, Pierre Huyghe, or Liam Gillick, who regularly join the fray on a theoretical level. But what does link his work with that of many of his contemporaries—what it blatantly reveals—is that the "meaning" or the "point" of the work is absorbed, so to speak, into its surface texture. Neto's works are nothing short of ostentatiously opportunistic. They readily yield to pressure; they adapt. They are ravishingly beautiful from every angle. They are as easy to consume as the clouds of scent that some of them emit—and yet, they staunchly refuse to be pinned down.

This all brings the work close to a terrain that art has long sought to avoid, namely design. My daydream suddenly took a new direction; the soft, malleable, passive surface that had up till now been gently supporting me turned into a voracious, ravenous being. It became an aggressive cross of organism and mechanism, extending in all directions. More surfaces kept tipping out of it. What it was producing, it suddenly hit me, was nothing other than "presentness." It was producing—presence. A topological monster, it was growing, spreading through the exhibition space, devouring works of art, and, in a mysterious metabolic process, transforming them into elastic surfaces. What happens when design seizes power and engulfs art? And by "design," I of course don't mean product design; I mean the technical, political, economic, and social design of our lives as a whole; something that melds the discontinuity of reality into a concatenation of events. What if art has simply become too slow, not universal enough, too hard to translate and consume, for it to keep up with reality? Depending on your point of view, that would make Neto's work either a herald of the new art or one of the first victims of all-embracing design.

When our daughter landed, giggling, on me, I woke from my daydream and my imaginary dialogue. I hadn't been keeping an eye on the time. Other visitors were standing expectantly at the entrance to the installation. It was time to vacate the piece. I rolled out of the cushion. And for the first time ever, our children didn't want to leave an exhibition.

(Translation: Fiona Elliott)

1) These comments come from Cecilia Pereira's interview with Ernesto Neto, "The fragility of the world," in Ernesto Neto, *O corpo, nu tempo*, Centro Galego de Arte Contemporanea, Xunta di Galicia, 2001, pp. 301–12.

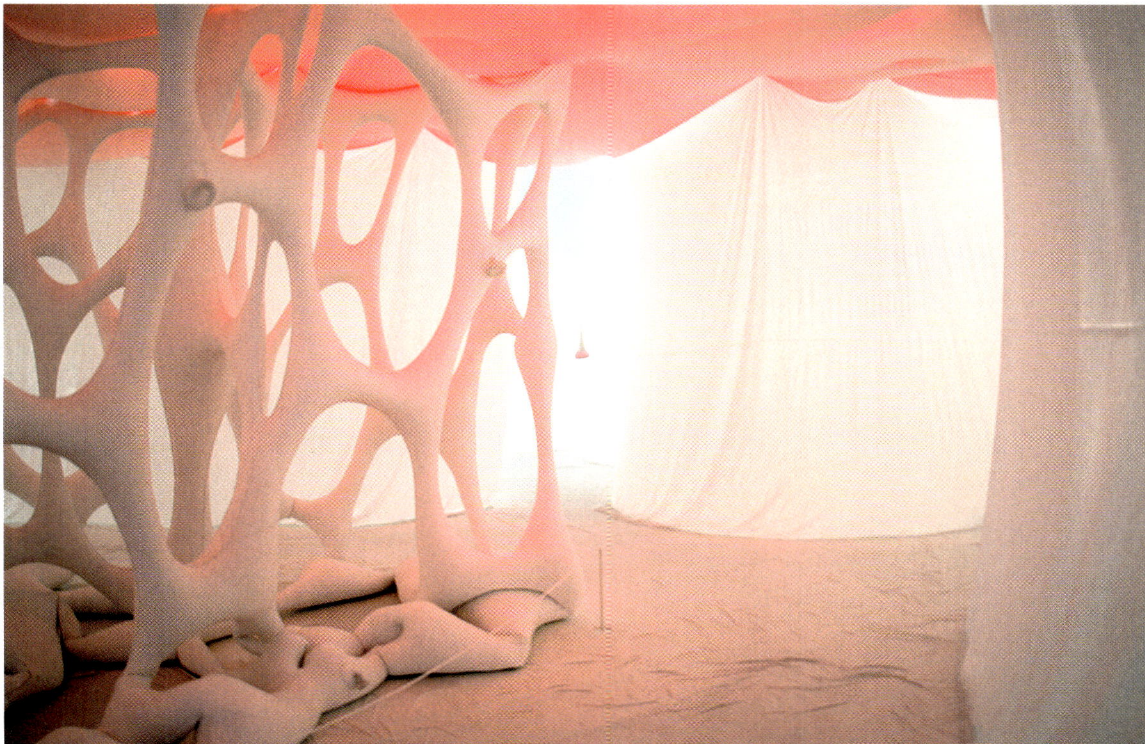

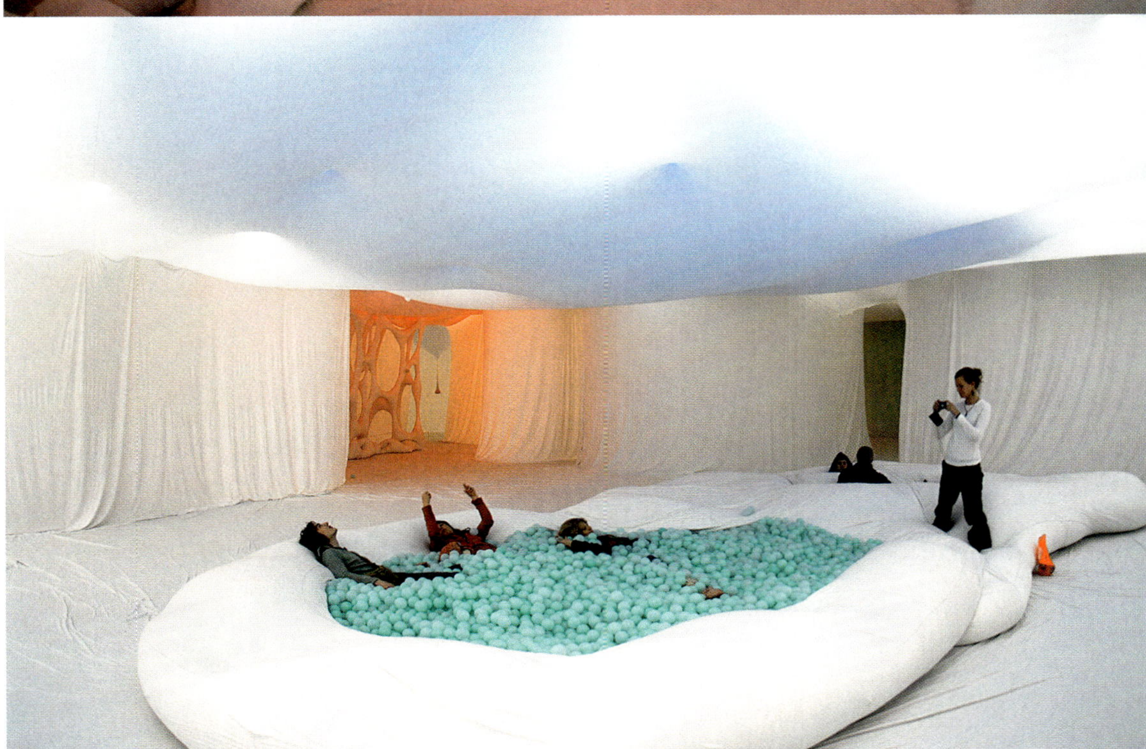

ERNESTO NETO, THE MALMÖ EXPERIENCE, 2006, *mixed media, dimensions variable, exhibition view, Malmö Konsthall /*
DIE MALMÖ-ERFAHRUNG, verschiedene Materialien, Format variabel, Ausstellungsansicht. (PHOTOS: KAJSA LINDSKOG)

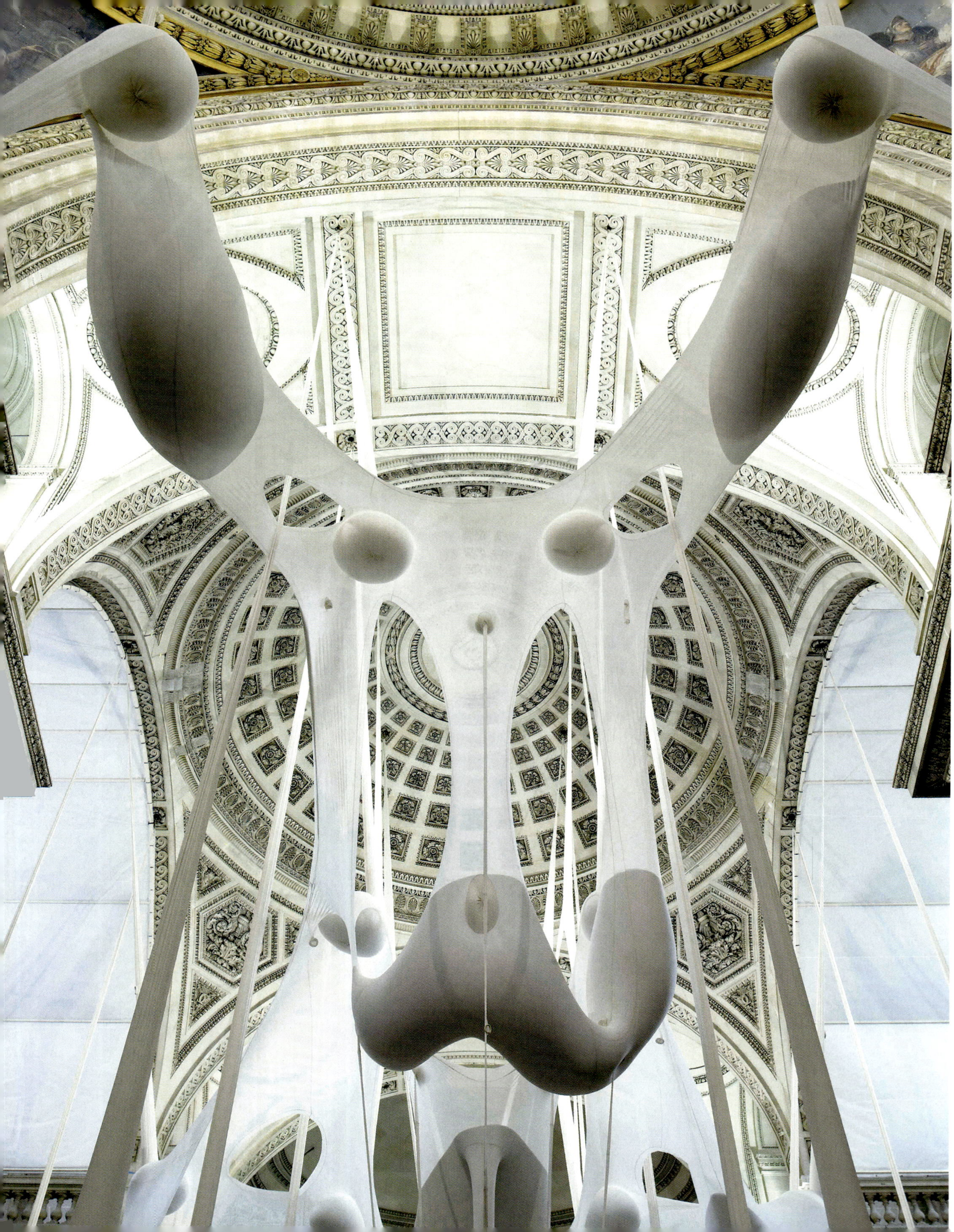

ERNESTO NETO, LEVIATHAN THOT, 2006, lycra tulle, polyamid fabric, styrofoam balls, installation views, Panthéon Paris /

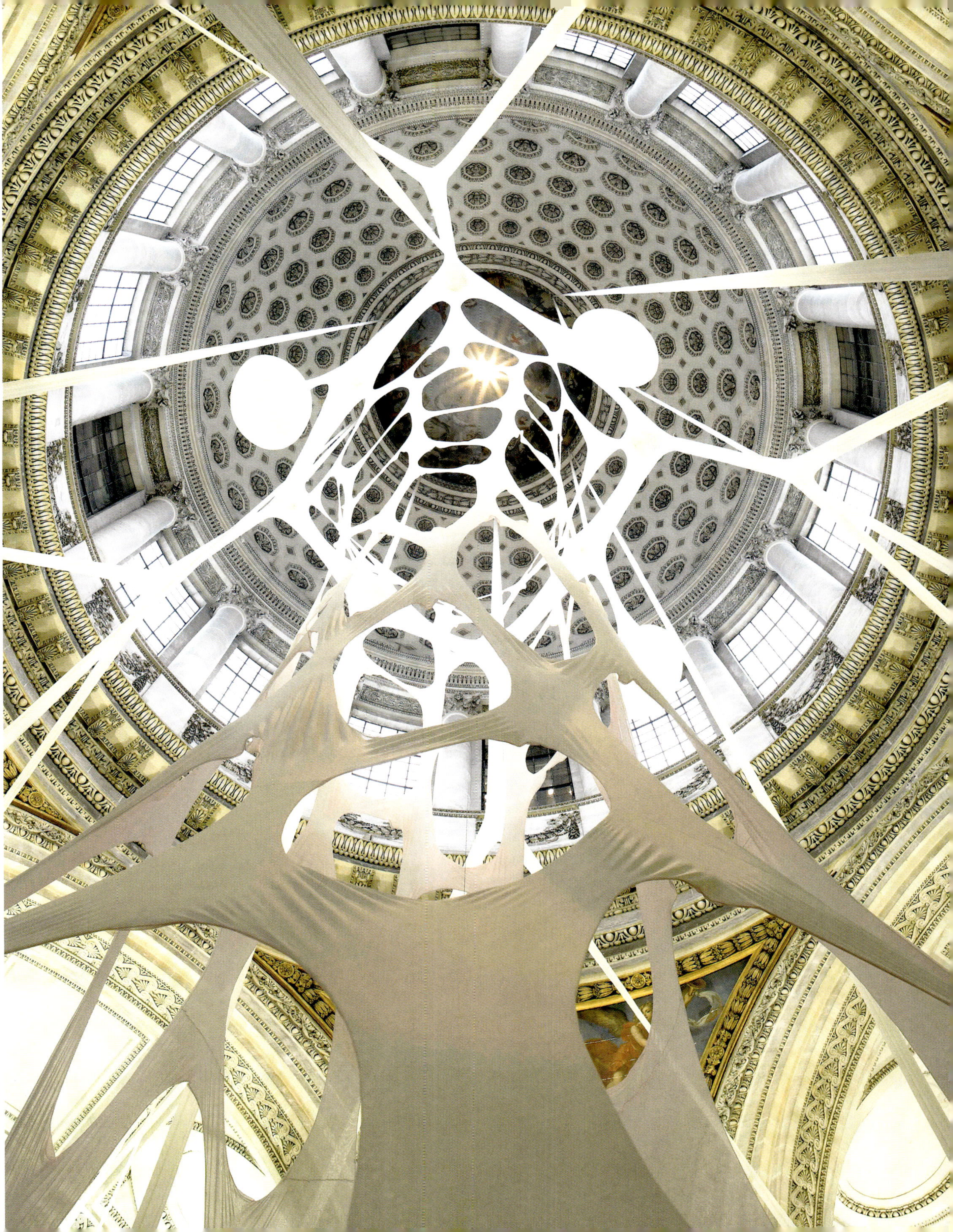

Lycragewebe, Polyamidgewebe, Styroporkugeln, Installationsansichten. (ALL PHOTOS OF LEVIATHAN THOT: MARC DOMAGE, PARIS)

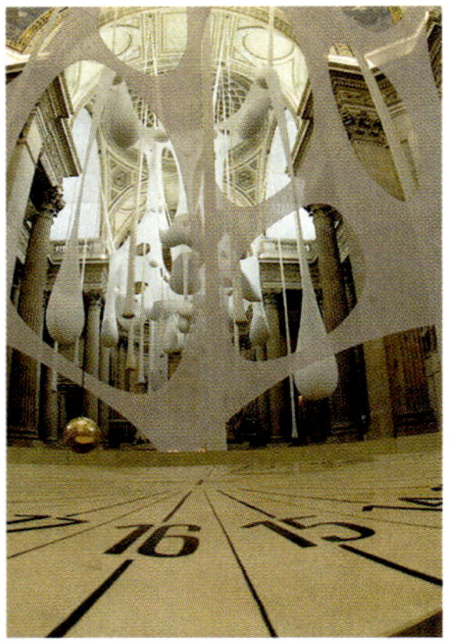

ERNESTO NETO, detail of LEVIATHAN THOT with Foucault's pendulum / Detailansicht mit Foucaults Pendel.

PAULO HERKENHOFF

LEVIATHAN THOT:

From 1985 to 1995 the Panthéon in Paris remained closed, following the collapse of stonework in its vaults. Some ten years later, the sculpture LEVIATHAN THOT (2006) that Ernesto Neto installed in the Panthéon in 2006 explores the political connotations of the building. The 273-foot-tall temple commissioned by King Louis XV to honor Sainte Geneviève, the patron saint of Paris, is a grandiose symbol of fine engineering. Designed in the neoclassical style by Jacques-Germain Soufflot, the church was secularized during the Revolution and converted into a mausoleum for the interment of great Frenchmen, providing eternal rest for the mortal remains of those who have not ascended to heaven—*Aux grands hommes, la patrie reconnaissante* (To great men, the grateful nation). Men of letters, of science, of the military, as well as numerous politicians are buried there, but artists there are none. Despite having decorated the building, artists do not rank among those who personify the moral substance of the French nation. The Panthéon's pediment, sculpted by David d'Angers, shows a group of distinguished Frenchmen receiving wreaths from the "hand" of France. In this frieze, which is emblematic of the Panthéon, "Nation" is situated between "Liberty" and "History." The pessimistic skepticism that informs Neto's LEVIATHAN THOT is the very antithesis of this frieze. In *Leviathan*—the book by Thomas Hobbes, inspired by Job's biblical monster—the original intent of the social contract was misrepresented by a "Confederacy of Deceivers that, to obtain dominion over men in this present world, endeavour, by dark and erroneous Doctrines, to extinguish in them the Light, both of Nature and of the Gospell."[1] One might ask, as in the Bible, who has opened the doors of LEVIATHAN THOT's face, for his teeth are terrible round about.[2]

In the year 1851 Léon Foucault suspended a pendulum on a long wire in the Panthéon—the lay temple of the French nation—in dynamic proof that the earth rotates. With Foucault, the Panthéon ceased to

PAULO HERKENHOFF is the director of the Museum of Fine Arts in Rio de Janeiro.

exist as "the place of connection between humans and the heavens," becoming instead a space for the scientific examination of the earth in the cosmos. Situated between Euclidean and Riemannian geometry, LEVIATHAN THOT perverts the logos and disembowels Charles Fourier's concept of utopian universal harmony. Thot, at once the tongue and heart of Ra (the ancient sun god in the Egyptian pantheon), was also a god of math, geometry, and the passage of time. For the Greeks, Thot invented astronomy and civilized government.[3] He made room for the sub-

A Politics of the Plumb

ject within the symbolic structure of the nation-state. The ordinary citizen, as he saw it, was the spectator. During the French Revolution the Panthéon was deconsecrated, but Neto's sculpture challenges the positivism of "official history" and awakens the dead. Outside the Panthéon the piece exists only as a corpse and a fetish, since its critical thrust is rendered hors de combat in the crossfire between the civilizing constructs of logos, science, state, and art. The wager on a new contract between human and nonhuman becomes more specific, also as regards political non-modernity.[4]

Anatomy

LEVIATHAN THOT brings to mind Jacques Callot's etching LA PENDAISON (The Hangman's Tree, 1633). In 1633, having received a commission from King Louis XIII to depict the sites of his hometown of Nancy, Callot refused to glorify the king and instead produced his edition of dramatically bleak etchings, *The Miseries of War.* LA PENDAISON bears similarities with depictions of hanged African-Americans swinging from poplar trees in the southern United States. But LEVIATHAN THOT does not relate to the lifeless bodies in the Panthéon or in Callot's etchings; it is rather a living anatomy that has taken up residence in the rigorous architectural perfection of this temple of enlightenment.

Ernesto Neto views himself as an illegal street vendor from Rio de Janeiro—a typical product of the underground economy exacerbated by the social marginalization attendant on inflated capitalist globalization. To evade state repression, street vendors display their merchandize on blankets that they pack up and swiftly take away the minute they spot trouble. Similarly, Neto works with the portability of large dimensions; his project, so he says, is carried around "inside small eggs, like culture in the time space of the social body."[5]

The "body" in LEVIATHAN THOT is organized into zones. Its development is rhizomatic. The head is the locus of fear, expression, the sharpening of human senses, thought, and confusion in the symmetry of space and spirit. The upper extremities (arms and hands) on the right and left sides of the body are the locus of action, affection, and sensory mechanisms. The artist views them as conveyors of endearment, a moral standing in the manichean dichotomy of good and evil, touch and blind gaze. Hands implement the mechanics of exchange, of social aggression, of the verdict and its political execution. In LEVIATHAN THOT, they represent the action of the state. Here, the values of equality and justice oppose the violence of the world.

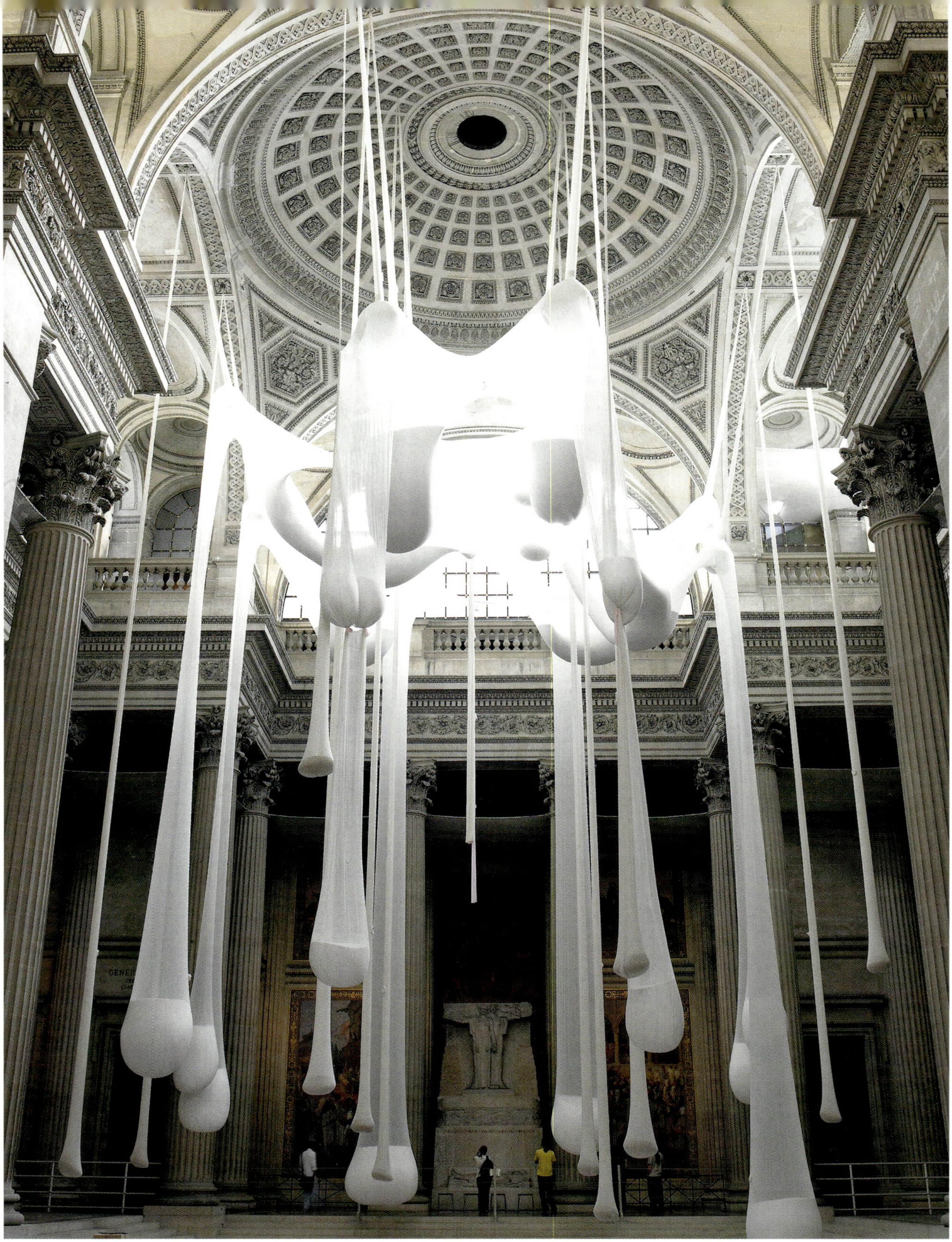

LEVIATHAN THOT is symbolically rooted in the tension between gravity and matter, reason and affectivity, or even nature and culture. Symmetry paradoxically undermines this bipolar condition. Neto is well aware of the impossibility of perfect symmetry in the human body, for it is inevitably approximate, at best. The invasion of the Panthéon's symmetry by the biological symmetry of LEVIATHAN THOT corrupts the Euclidean model, the balance of its bilateral symmetry demonstrating how its sagittal plane plays the role of an unfaithful imaginary mirror.

The area of the body from the lungs down, including the abdomen and legs, is the center of all movement, desire, will, and courage. The artist describes how in the preparation of his work "the outer skin was folded over and then cut." In Cartesian space, the baroque, Leibnizian fold is installed as "fleshless skin," its rarefied materiality heightening the sensual experience of matter. The interpretation of the world, and its explanation through science, is critically important for the composition of existence through pulsations, flows, *phantasmatics*, and the pleasures of an eroticized eye that seeks out the haptic body.

The sculpture's vital center (heart and brain) is situated in the dome. It incorporates Foucault's pendulum and articulates everything. According to Neto, this hybrid element is its body and backbone with, as he says, "swivel parts, the place of the existential essence [...] that ultimately connects the monster." Individual needs are linked to the central organ to ensure, in his own words, "survival, continuity, the blending of people and souls." It is the inflection point of the social contract.

FLUID MECHANICS

Understanding LEVIATHAN THOT requires investigation into fluid mechanics, geodesy, gravity, and verticality. Neto's works invariably engage the symbolization of physics, as opposed to dealing in the sterile reiteration of scientific concepts. For example, his work GLOBIOBABEL NUDELIONAME LANDMOONAIA (2000, Daros Foundation) is based on the porosity equation:

$$f = \frac{V_p}{V_m}$$

The solid mechanics consist of sand and minute polystyrene spheres; however, the symbolic function of these elements is altered the moment they enter the veins and organic vertebral columns of the sculpture, at which point they acquire the role of blood. "This white blood-cell matter is what nourishes the creature's body," the artist explains, introducing the concept of circulation. He adds that matter, despite being essentially solid, becomes "liquid in its spherical whole." Matter is perceived as fluid content that is reconfigured every time there is movement within the installation. It is, Neto says, like sand "trickling down from the top of an hourglass, defining the body of the work with its fluid mass." Materials shift from being non-Newtonian fluids to the imaginary behavior of a viscous Newtonian fluid. They circulate like blood. "Following the cutting and sewing," Neto explains, "the skin is nourished by the moving matter that constitutes its cellular mass." In Neto's sculptural bodies, viewers discover such attributes as plasticity, elasticity, viscosity, and porosity; the artist has created a form of sculpture that organizes matter in flux.

The great material stress—the *rheological* dimension of LEVIATHAN THOT—exists in the suspension of the sculptural body. The processes of lifting the work, of determining where to attach it and how to install it, required calculations involving fluid mechanics and changes in mass velocity dictated by external forces. During its installation, it was necessary to adjust the velocity of the small bodies so that they could circulate inside the large elastic tubes like a living and uniform fluid, so as to balance the hanging masses and keep them from becoming lopsided. This meant capturing the moment of passage from

ERNESTO NETO, LEVIATHAN THOT, 2006, installation view / Installationsansicht Panthéon, Paris.

inertia to the application of force, as defined in Newton's second law of motion. Force is equal to change in momentum per change in time:

$$F = \frac{dp.}{dt.}$$

In THOT's circulatory system, all interfering influences or accelerations of mass movement affect the stability of the momentum at its control point—at its "zero degree of relation with time." In the course of installing his work, Neto investigates sculpture as a dynamic conservation of momentum. His gestures seek the continual adjustment of the equation of momentum:

$$p = m_1v_1 + m_2v_2 + m_3v_3 - \ldots + m_nv_n$$ [6)]

This equation gives rise to other issues such as time and viscosity. Here, p is the momentum that ensures the balance of THOT as *homo erectus*—affected by the force of gravity, whenever there is movement in the course of the installation. As for *m,* it denotes the mass of materials and also the composition of THOT's blood. Finally, v is the random velocity of the blood's circulation every time the monster moves. The sculpture is rounded out with the fluids at rest, held in plumb position by gravity. In the course of his career, Neto has always designed sculptures in their relation to gravity, beginning with PRUMO INVERTIDO (1989).

The architecture of the Panthéon absorbs the monster's body in much the same way as the functioning of "mutualism in a tropical forest," claims Neto. The tensor—representing the effect of surface forces acting on fluids—is soon transformed into the torsion of muscle tissue. The plasticity of the materials tightens the whole thing up, like the energy of an active muscle. Since it has no spinal column, the body of LEVIATHAN THOT is a plumbed structure. Gravity puts a strain on the shape of the work and keeps the muscle power in check. Gravity is its invisible skeleton. It is not the physiognomy that makes the piece anthropomorphic and prepares it for its symbolic existence, but rather the equations of physics.

Pendulum

A centrifugal force connected with the rotation of the earth is installed in the core of the body. By incorporating Foucault's pendulum in that core, LEVIATHAN THOT establishes a *geodesic* relation, that is, a line perpendicular to the earth. Neto's oeuvre as a whole explores the relationship between desire and physics; here he has installed a work in one of the great landmarks of scientific history. As Foucault says, "the swing of the pendulum was fixed in absolute space."[7)]

In his proposition SOCLE DU MONDE (Base of the World, 1961), Piero Manzoni takes a look at geodesic perception. In this connection, LEVIATHAN THOT is positioned in such a way that its vertical axis is aligned with the gradients of the gravitational field. The verticality of the body, thus aligned with the direction of the gravitational pull, is visually represented as a plumb line. At this point, gravity is converted into affectivity. Neto speaks of a natural straight line "which is ubiquitous and yet invisible, except when revealed in physics experiments: 'the verticality of the fall'... gravity: the great Goddess, our prison and our life." The plumb line is thus viewed empirically as the absolute vertical. "Here we have two geometries (or perhaps two kinds of love): one that I view as Euclidean geometry, and the other, a Riemmanian geometry that addresses curves on minimal surfaces." The sculptor draws this conclusion, somewhat like the romantic mirage of Novalis. Upon examining the "beloved"—Novalis sees it as the microcosm of the universe, which is merely an extension of the loved one—Paul Virilio states that the force of attraction is in fact gravitation, universal weight, *axis mundi.*[8)]

After hoisting the piece, tensioned slings swing back, functioning as counterbalances to their destination at the center of the earth; this is Neto's "vertical truth, as the universal and yielding constant." The finger tips meet the horizontality of the hanging body, one that "somehow exposes its imprecision, organicity, subjectivity, and intimacy." The artist compares it to a pietà: "Between the revolution of life and the indifference of time, there rests the body of Jesus... Mary is eternal."

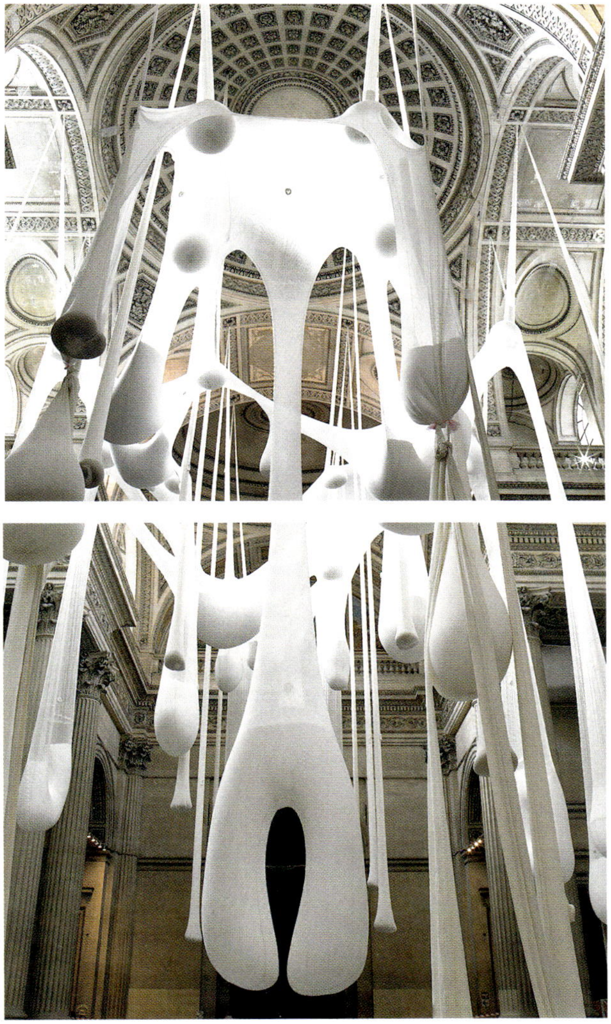

ERNESTO NETO, LEVIATHAN THOT, 2006,
installation view / Installationsansicht Panthéon, Paris.

The way in which LEVIATHAN THOT is suspended from the Panthéon's domed ceiling and spreads out in its interior has led Neto to describe it as a clash between verticality and horizontality of the kind "observed in a Mondrianesque painting." To Piet Mondrian, the expression of opposing forces in horizontal and vertical lines "is what constitutes life."[9] Mondrian's lines are invested with the visual function of expressing breadth, calm, and unity, starting from his observations of the sea, sky, and stars.

Francis Ponge analyzes Giacometti's work as "Man—and man alone—reduced to a thread—in the ruinous condition, the misery of the world—who looks for himself—starting from nothing. Thin, naked, emaciated, all skin and bone. Coming and going with no reason in the crowd." Rosalind Krauss discusses the economy of Giacometti's "nonbeing" in connection with Heidegger, who speaks of a fear of "the nothing."[10] In her *Carta a Mondrian* (Letter to Mondrian, 1959), Lygia Clark writes, "Man is not alone. He is form and void. He shifts from the void toward form (life) and from there to the full-void that would be a relative death."[11]

Giacometti and Neto would seem to be diametrically opposed in view of the former's elongated, emaciated human figures and the sensual exuberance of the latter's sculpture. Yet verticality is their shared borderline. In his search for continuity lost, i.e., our atrophied rationalism, Neto calls upon Foucault's pendulum to vibrate "in the heart of every individual." As a constant in Neto's output, the awareness of the gravitational field becomes a metaphor of the power of the state and the critical locus of the subject—the citizen—in contemporary social space.

Panthéon and Leviathan

"And here we arrive at the social body, the Leviathan, a monster we have created," Ernesto Neto announces, "... a strange creature that does not seem to be anywhere; it is invisible, untouchable, fleshless, lightless, lifeless ... yet it is everywhere." LEVIATHAN THOT refers to Hobbes's theory of a modern state, though informed with a Nietzschean bias of ironic skepticism—where Nietzsche's *Gay Science* makes light of the "spirit of gravity." The sculptor mentions the "organ-less body," the image of Deleuze and Guattari's "schizophrenic capitalism" in *Anti-Oedipus*. In his sculptural memorial, "vague words [are used] to speak the unspeakable": the "free" being, the "social body" and "rationalism." Leviathan is a *Moloch* that demands sacrifices. Neto deplores the pitiful crowd of anonymous people "overwhelmed by the abstract power that we have invented ourselves."

In Neto's words, the Panthéon—a monument of modernity lost—has become "a lightless, dark tomb." But LEVIATHAN THOT does not reconcile science and desire, subjectivity and politics, citizenship and the state. On the contrary, it is a political "anatomy lesson." The artist resists touching the outwardly impersonal and technical pendulum. The work is a space of separation. "Only there, where the state ceases—does the man who is not superfluous begin," Nietzsche writes in *Thus Spoke Zarathustra.*[12] Given that interment in the Panthéon is a prerogative of the president of the French Republic, LEVIATHAN THOT points to the theory of political representation by placing the spectator as a citizen at the center of this glory. Ernesto Neto's phenomenology turns the heart of each viewer into a Foucault pendulum.

(Translation: Izabel Murat Burbridge)

1) Thomas Hobbes. *Leviathan* XLIV "Of the Kingdome of Darkness" (Oxford: Claredon Press, 1909), p. 472.
2) The Bible, *Book of Job,* 41:14–15.
3) E. A. Wallis Budge, *Gods of the Egyptians* (New York: Dover Publications, 1969), vol. 1, pp. 410–414.
4) According to Ernesto Neto, the reading of *Nous n'avons jamais été modernes: Essai d'anthropologie symétrique* (1991) by Bruno Latour informed his conception of LEVIATHAN THOT.
5) Excerpt from the artist's e-mail to the author on September 22, 2006. Unless otherwise noted, all quotations by the artist reproduced in this essay come from this e-mail.
6) Here, p = momentum, m = mass and v = velocity. This is evidently the dynamic life of LEVIATHAN THOT.
7) Michael F. Conlin, "The Popular and Scientific Reception of the Foucault Pendulum in the United States," *Isis,* Vol. 90, No. 2, June, (Chicago: University of Chicago, 1999), p. 184.
8) Paul Virilio, *The Aesthetics of Disappearance,* transl. Philip Beitchma (New York: Semiotext(e), 1991), p. 77.
9) Octavio Morisani, "Verso la vera visione della realtá," in *L'Astrattismo di Piet Mondrian* (Venice: Neri Pozz Editore, 1956), p. 172.
10) Rosalind Krauss, "Alberto Giacometti: Museum of Modern Art, New York," *Artforum,* XL No. 4, December 2001, pp. 113–114. We further credit to Rosalind Krauss the quotations by Francis Ponge in this paragraph.
11) Lygia Clark *Lygia Clark* (Barcelona: Fundació Antoni Tàpies, 1998), p. 112.
12) Friedrich Nietzsche, *Thus Spoke Zarathustra* (1883–1892), transl. R. J. Hollingdale (England: Harmondsworth, 1961), pp. 77–78.

ERNESTO NETO, sketch of / Skizze von LEVIATHAN THOT, Panthéon, Paris.

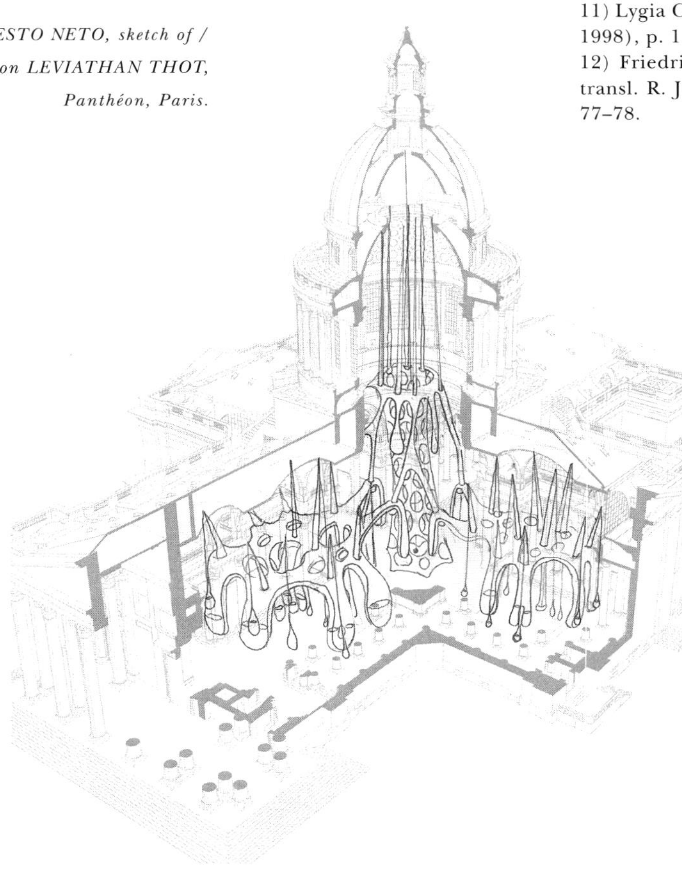

ERNESTO NETO, LEVIATHAN THOT, 2006, installation view / Installationsansicht, Panthéon, Paris.

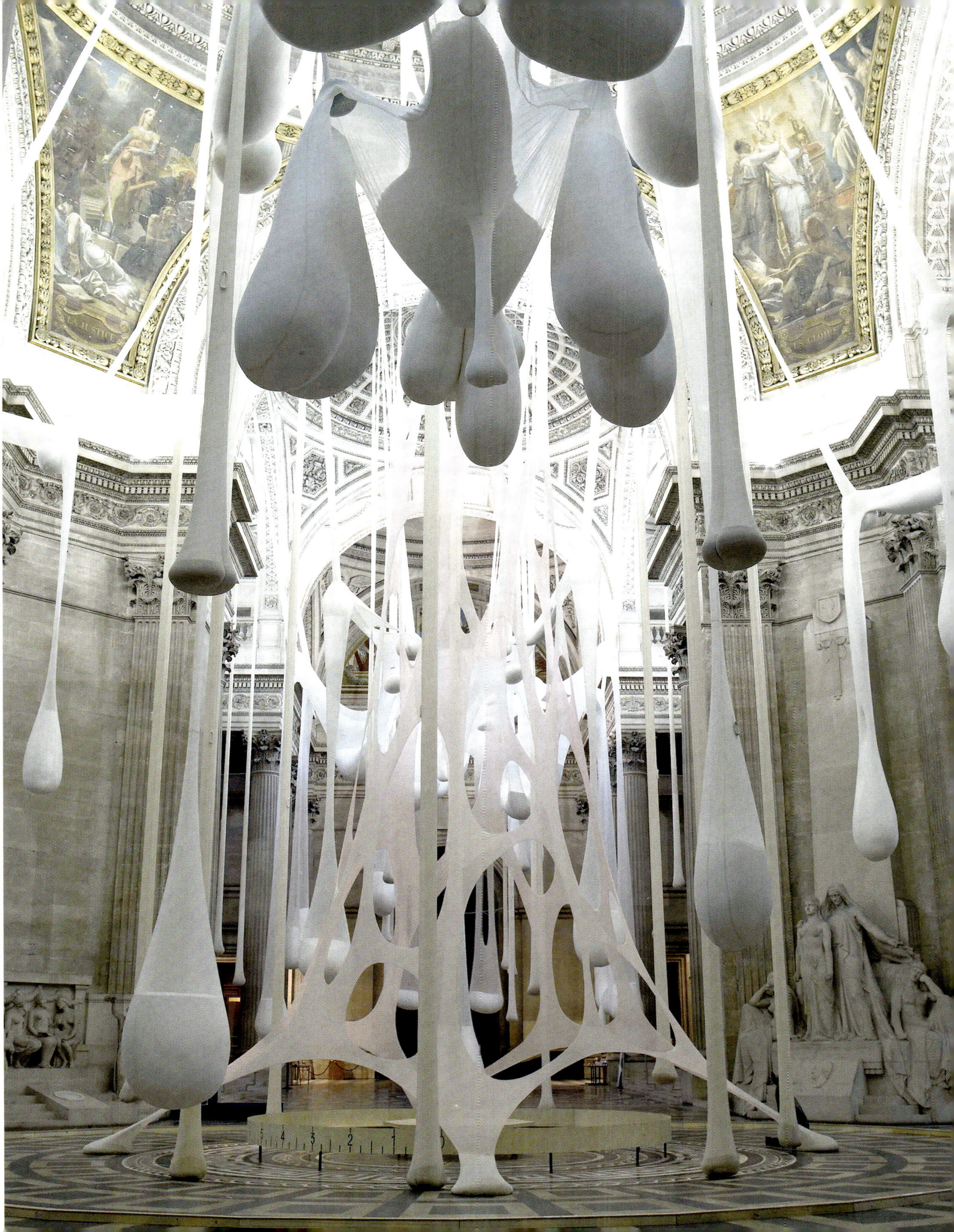

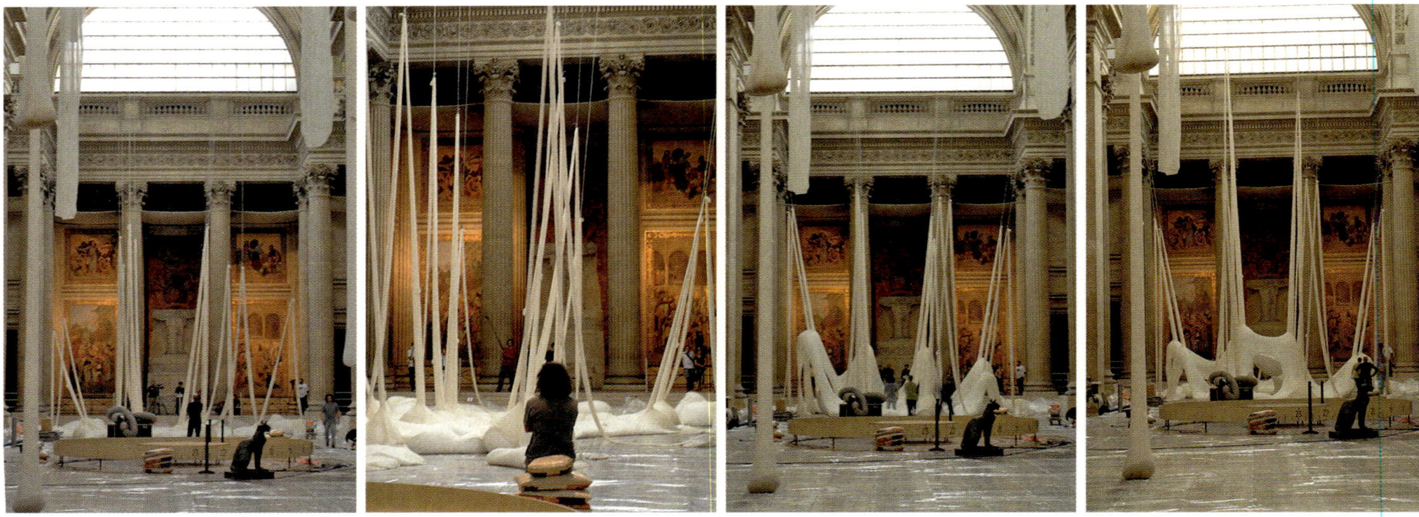

PAULO HERKENHOFF

LEVIATHAN THOT:

Zwischen 1985 und 1995 war das Panthéon geschlossen, weil Steine, die der Schwerkraft nachgaben, aus seinem Gewölbe herabfielen. Mit der im Panthéon errichteten Skulptur LEVIATHAN THOT (2006) erforscht Ernesto Neto die politischen Konnotationen des Gebäudes. Als Symbol der Ingenieurwissenschaft wurde dieser grandiose neoklassizistische Tempel (83 Meter Höhe) auf Geheiss Ludwig XV. von Soufflot entworfen, um Genoveva, die Schutzheilige von Paris, zu ehren. Die Revolution verweltlichte das Panthéon. Es wurde zum Mausoleum für die grossen Franzosen, deren sterbliche Überreste dort ihre ewige Ruhe finden, falls sie nicht ins Paradies aufsteigen: *Aux grands hommes, la patrie reconnaissante.* Es liegen dort Schriftsteller, Wissenschaftler und zahlreiche Politiker und Militärs. Künstler sind nicht darunter. Sie wurden lediglich eingeladen, das Gebäude auszuschmücken, doch keiner von ihnen trägt zur ethischen Substanz der Nation bei. Das Relief *La patrie couronnant les hommes célèbres* von David d'Angers ist Sinnbild des Panthéons. Die Heimat steht zwischen der Freiheit und der Geschichte. LEVIATHAN THOT ist wegen des pessimistischen Zweifels, den es enthält, seine Antithese. In Hobbes' Leviathan, der inspiriert war von dem biblischen Monster Hiobs, ist die Verkehrung des Gesellschaftsvertrags «eine Verschwörung von Betrügern, die zur Erlangung der Herrschaft über die Menschen in dieser gegenwärtigen Welt versuchen, durch dunkle

PAULO HERKENHOFF ist Direktor des Museum of Fine Arts in Rio de Janeiro.

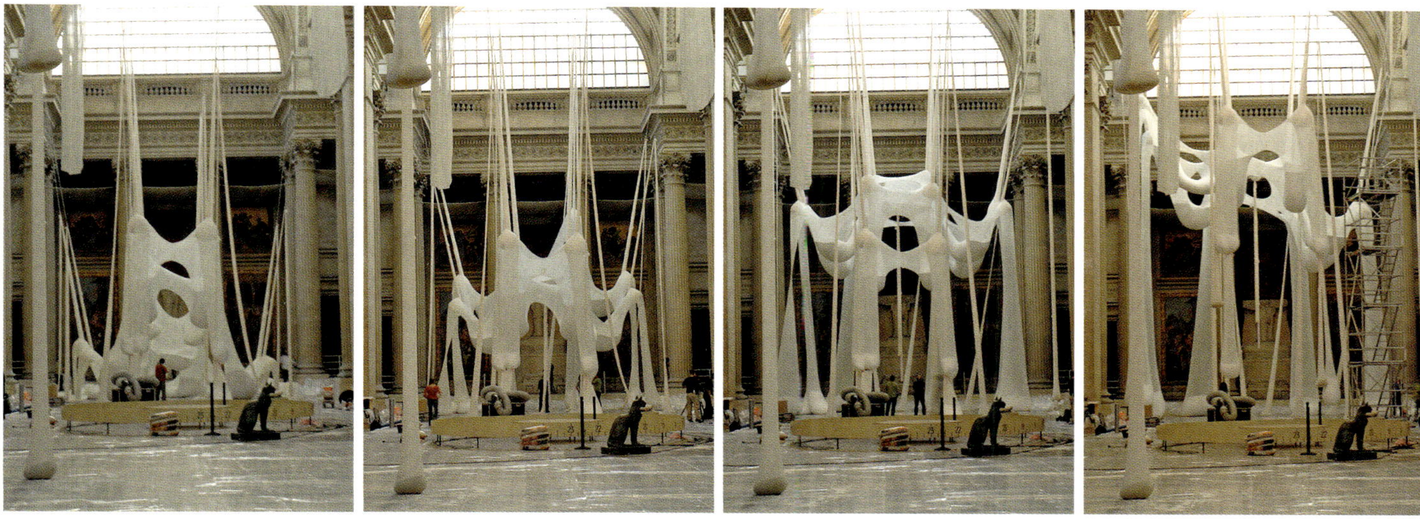

ERNESTO NETO, installing / Aufrichtung von LEVIATHAN THOT, 2006, Panthéon, Paris.

Politik des Lots

und irrige Lehren das Licht der Natur und des Evangeliums auszulöschen».[1] Wie in der Bibel beschrieben, hat LEVIATHAN THOT «die beiden Tore seines Rachens geöffnet, in dem um die Zähne des Monsters herum der Terror herrscht».[2]

Im Jahre 1851 hängte Léon Foucault im Panthéon, dem weltlichen Tempel der Nation, ein Pendel auf, um mittels eines empirischen Beweises die Erdrotation zu veranschaulichen. Durch Foucault wird das Panthéon, nicht nur Verbindungsort zwischen Mensch und Himmel, sondern zum Raum eines wissenschaftlichen Verständnisses der Erde im All. Zwischen Euklidischer und Riemannscher Geometrie stehend pervertiert LEVIATHAN THOT die menschliche Vernunft und weidet die Utopie der universellen Harmonie Charles Fouriers aus. Sprachrohr und Herz Ras (des Sonnengottes der ägyptischen Mythologie) ist Thot der Gott der Zeitmessung, der Mathematik und der Geometrie. Für die Griechen hat Thot die Astronomie und die zivilisierte Regierung erfunden.[3] Er schafft einen Platz für das Subjekt in der symbolischen Struktur von Staat und Nation. Der Zuschauer ist der gewöhnliche Mensch und Bürger.

Während die Revolution das Panthéon desakralisierte, rührt Netos Skulptur an der offiziellen positivistischen Geschichte und erweckt die Toten. Ausserhalb des Panthéons existiert LEVIATHAN THOT nicht, es sei denn als Kadaver und Fetisch, da er im Konflikt mit den zivilisatorischen Konstrukten des Logos, der Wissenschaft, des Staates und der Kunst seine kritische Kraft verliert. Das Streben nach einem neuen Vertrag zwischen dem Menschlichen und dem Nicht-Menschlichen wird klarer, auch in Bezug auf die politische Nicht-Modernität.[4)]

Anatomie

LEVIATHAN THOT verweist auf den Baum der Gehängten in Jacques Callots Radierung LA PENDAISON. 1633 von Ludwig XIII. aufgefordert, seinen Geburtsort Nancy zu repräsentieren, weigert Callot sich, den König zu verherrlichen und bringt die beklemmende Serie *Elend des Krieges* heraus. LA PENDAISON ähnelt Bildern von in Pappeln aufgehängten Schwarzen in den Südstaaten der USA. Die Installation LEVIATHAN THOT besteht jedoch nicht aus den leblosen Körpern des Panthéons oder denen Callots. Eine lebendige Anatomie hat sich in der strengen architektonischen Vollkommenheit dieses Tempels der Aufklärung bemächtigt.

Ernesto Neto sieht sich als illegalen Strassenverkäufer aus Rio de Janeiro, typisches Phänomen der Schattenwirtschaft, das sich durch die globalisierungsbedingte soziale Ausgrenzung immer stärker verbreitet hat. Um der Repression durch den Staat zu entgehen, ordnen sie ihre Waren auf einer Decke an, die sie blitzschnell zu einem Bündel zusammenraffen können. Neto arbeitet die Tragbarkeit grosser Dimensionen heraus. Sein Projekt bewegt sich «wie Kultur in der Raumzeit des sozialen Körpers, in kleinen Eiern», sagt er.[5)]

LEVIATHAN THOTs Körper ist in Zonen eingeteilt: Sein Wachstum geht von der Wurzel aus. Der Kopf ist der Sitz der Angst, des Ausdrucks, der Verfeinerung der Sinne, des Denkens, der Verwirrung – in der Symmetrie von Raum und Geist. Die oberen Gliedmassen zur Rechten und zur Linken (Arme und Hände) sind Mechanismen der Aktion, der Affektivität und der Sinneswahrnehmung. Laut Ernesto Neto lenken sie die Zärtlichkeit, den moralischen Standpunkt in der manichäistischen Zweiteilung in Gut und Böse, Berührung und blinden Blick. Die Hände treiben die Mechanik des Tausches voran, die soziale Aggressivität, das Urteil und seine politische Vollstreckung. Bei LEVIATHAN THOT stehen sie für die Handlungen des Staates. Die Werte Gleichheit und Gerechtigkeit stellen sich gegen die Gewalttätigkeit der Welt.

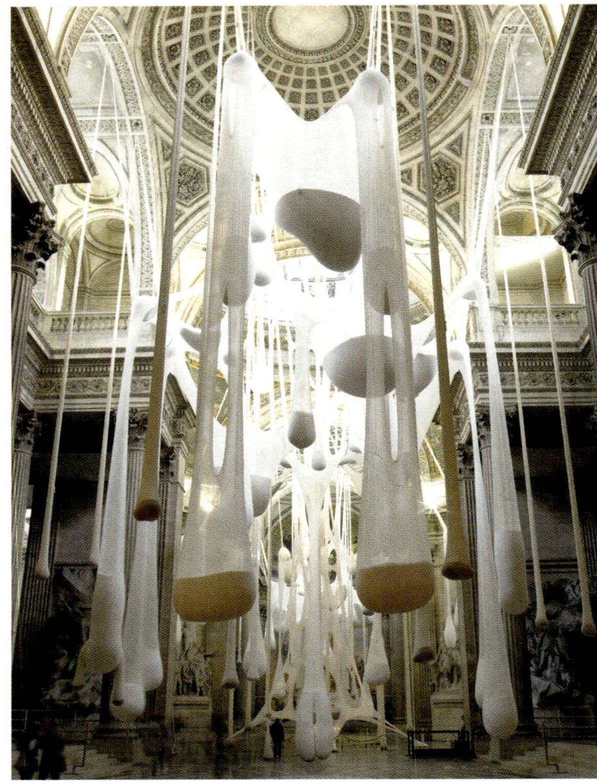

ERNESTO NETO, LEVIATHAN THOT, 2006, installation view / Installationsansicht, Panthéon, Paris.

Das symbolische Fundament LEVIATHAN THOTs ist die Spannung zwischen Schwerkraft und Materie, zwischen Vernunft und Affektivität oder Natur und Kultur. Diese Bipolarität bricht sich mit der Symmetrie. Ernesto Neto weiss um die Unmöglichkeit der Symmetrie im Körper, die höchstens eine annähernde Verdoppelung ist. Das Eindringen der Symmetrie ins Panthéon über die biologische Symmetrie LEVIATHAN THOTs korrumpiert sogar das euklidische Modell. Die Balance der Bilateralsymmetrie LEVIATHAN THOTs zeigt, dass seine Sagittalebene sich wie in einem imaginären falschen Spiegel verhält.

Unterhalb der Lungen, in Bauch und Beinen, befindet sich der Sitz der Bewegungen, der Lust, des Willens und des Herzens. Bei der Vorbereitung des Werks wurde die «äussere Haut», wie der Künstler es nennt, «umgestülpt und dann abgeschnitten». Im kartesianischen Raum installiert sich die barocke leibnizsche Falte wie Haut, «die kein Fleisch hat». Die lichte Stofflichkeit lässt sinnliche Erfahrungen der Materie zu. Die Deutung der Welt (und ihre Erklärung durch die Wissenschaft) ist entscheidend für den Aufbau der Existenz über das Pulsieren und Fliessen, über das Phantasmagorische und die Lust eines Auges in erotischem Zustand, das nach berührbaren Körpern verlangt.

Das vitale Zentrum (Herz und Gehirn) sitzt in der Kuppel, es bezieht das Foucaultsche Pendel mit ein und fügt alles zusammen. Laut Neto ist dieses hybride Element Körper und Rückgrat, «das die Teile dreht, der Ort des Wesens der Existenz, [...] es schafft die letzte Verbindung innerhalb des Monsters». Die Bedürfnisse einer jeden Individualität sind in diesem zentralen Organ angesiedelt, um «das Überleben, die Kontinuität, die Vermischung von Körpern und Seelen» zu gewährleisten. Es ist der Beugungspunkt des Gesellschaftsvertrags.

Mechanik der Flüssigkeiten

Um LEVIATHAN THOT zu verstehen, muss man die Mechanik der Flüssigkeiten, die Geodäsie, die Schwerkraft und die Vertikalität untersuchen. Jedes Werk Ernesto Netos läuft auf eine Symbolisierung der Physik hinaus und ist niemals nur der sterile Abklatsch wissenschaftlicher Konzepte. Der Bildhauer denkt mittels der Wissenschaft, um eine phänomenologische Existenz für seine Skulpturen zu

ERNESTO NETO, LEVIATHAN THOT, 2006, installation view / Installationsansicht, Panthéon, Paris.

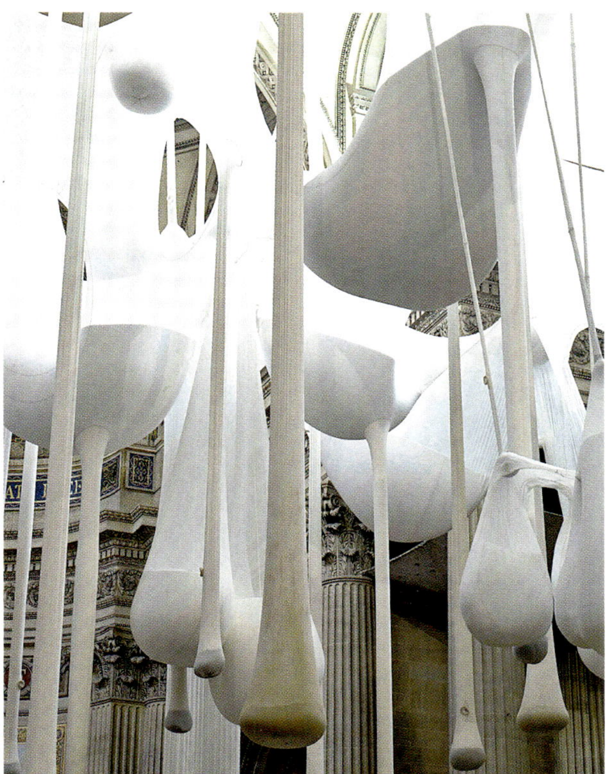

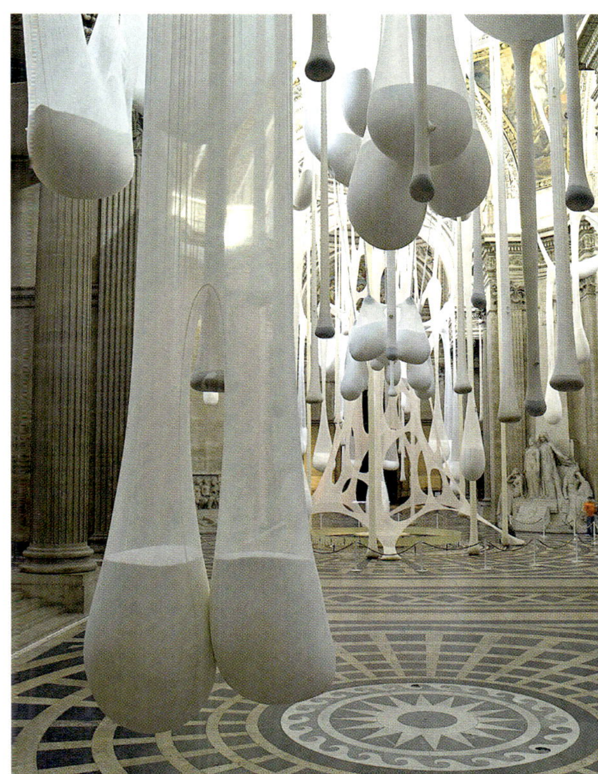

schaffen. Seine Arbeit GLOBIOBABEL NUDELIONAME LANDMOONAIA (2000, Daros Foundation) zum Beispiel wurde über die Porositätsgleichung verständlich:

$$f = \frac{V_p}{V_m}$$

Sand und winzige Polyesterkugeln sollen bei LEVIATHAN THOT wie eine Mechanik der Flüssigkeiten wirken. Doch verändert ihr Einfüllen in die organischen Adern und Wirbelsäulenschläuche der Skulptur ihre symbolische Funktion. Sie werden zu einer Art Blut. «Das Tier wird genährt», bemerkt Neto, und zwar über die «weissen Blutkörperchen», die den Begriff des Kreislaufs symbolisieren. Neto fügt hinzu, dass die Materie, die von ihrem Wesen her fest ist, dennoch «in ihrer kugeligen Gesamtheit flüssig ist». Sie wird als Flüssigkeit wahrgenommen und bettet sich bei jeder Bewegung innerhalb der Installation LEVIATHAN THOT um, «wie der strudelnde Sand einer Sanduhr, und definiert mit ihrer fliessenden Masse den Körper des Kunstwerks». Die Materialien wechseln von ihrem Zustand nicht-newtonscher Flüssigkeiten zu einem imaginären Verhalten zähflüssiger newtonscher Flüssigkeiten über. Sie zirkulieren wie Blut in LEVIATHAN THOT. «Nach dem Schnitt wird die vernähte Haut mit der beweglichen Materie genährt, die ihr Zellmasse gibt», begründet der Künstler. Die Erfahrung der Skulpturenkörper Netos wird beeinflusst durch Phänomene wie Plastizität, Elastizität, Viskosität und Porosität. Die Skulptur ordnet die fortlaufende Materie.

Die grosse Belastung des Materials – aufgrund der fliessenden Dimension von LEVIATHAN THOT – entsteht bei der Aufhängung des Skulpturenkörpers. Der Vorgang des Aufrichtens, des Befestigens der Enden und des Installierens des Objekts macht Berechnungen im Bereich der Mechanik der Flüssigkeiten und der Geschwindigkeitsveränderungen der Masse nötig, die von diesen äusseren Kräften bestimmt werden. Beim Montieren musste die Geschwindigkeit der kleinen, im Inneren der grossen elastischen Röhren fliessenden Körper unbedingt angepasst werden, damit das Ganze sich wie ein lebendiges, einheitliches Fluidum verhielt. Man suchte zu vermeiden, dass das Volumen aus dem Gleichgewicht geriet und auf eine Seite kippte. Dies ist laut dem zweiten newtonschen Gesetz die Stufe des Übergangs von der Trägheit zum Wirken der Kraft.

Die Kraft ist gleich der Änderung des Impulses, bezogen auf die Zeit:

$$F = \frac{dp.}{dt.}$$

Im Kreislaufsystem LEVIATHAN THOTs wirkt sich jede störende Einwirkung oder Beschleunigung der Bewegung der Masse auf die Stabilität des Impulses in seinem Kontrollpunkt aus, «seiner Stufe Null, bezogen auf die Zeit». Für Neto ist die Skulptur im Verlauf des Montageprozesses die dynamische Bewahrung des Impulses. Seine Gesten streben nach einer steten Angleichung der Hauptgleichung des Impulses:

$$p = m_1v_1 + m_2v_2 + m_3v_3 - \ldots + m_nv_n.$$ [6)]

Aus dieser Gleichung erwachsen weitere Fragen, wie die nach der Zeit und der Viskosität. Hier ist p der Impuls, aus dem das Gleichgewicht LEVIATHAN THOTs in seiner Eigenschaft als *homo erectus* resultiert, in seiner Beeinträchtigung durch die Schwerkraft, ausgehend von den Montagebewegungen der Skulptur. m ist zwar die Masse von Materialien, doch ebenso die Zusammensetzung des Blutes von LEVIATHAN THOT. v ist schliesslich die willkürliche Geschwindigkeit des Blutkreislaufs des Monsters, wenn es bewegt wird. Die Skulptur vervollständigt sich in der Ruhe der im Lot befindlichen Flüssigkeiten. Im Laufe seines Wirkens hat Neto seit PRUMO INVERTIDO (Verkehrtes Lot) (1989) stets Skulpturen entwickelt, die mit der Schwerkraft in Beziehung stehen.

Die Architektur des Panthéon saugt den Körper auf, wie ein «organischer Mutualismus in einem tropischen Regenwald». Der Tensor, Vertreter der auf Flüssigkeiten wirkenden Oberflächenkräfte, wandelt sich sogleich in die Torsion von Muskelgewebe. Die Plastizität der Materialien strafft das Ganze, als wirke die Energie eines arbeitenden Muskels. Da es kein

Rückgrat gibt, strukturiert LEVIATHAN THOTs Körper sich im Lot. Die Schwerkraft spannt die vom Künstler geschaffenen Formen und verleiht LEVIATHAN THOT einen Muskeltonus. Die Schwerkraft ist sein unsichtbares Knochengerüst. Es ist nicht der Gesichtsausdruck, der die Vermenschlichung bewirkt und LEVIATHAN THOT auf seine symbolische Existenz vorbereitet, sondern es sind die physikalischen Gleichungen.

Pendel

Eine Zentrifugalkraft, die in Beziehung zur Erdrotation steht, ist im Zentrum des Körpers installiert. An diesem Punkt schafft LEVIATHAN THOT, indem er das foucaultsche Pendel des Panthéons in seinen Kern einbezieht, eine geodätische Beziehung, sprich, eine senkrechte Linie zur Erde. Verweist Netos gesamtes Werk auf die Beziehung zwischen Lust und Physik, so baut er seine Installation diesmal an einem für die Wissenschaftsgeschichte denkwürdigen Ort auf. «Der Oszillationspunkt», sagt Léon Foucault, «gehört zum absoluten Raum.»[7)]

In seiner Skulptur SOCLE DU MONDE (1961) beschäftigt Piero Manzoni sich mit der geodätischen Wahrnehmung. In diesem Kontext gesehen, verläuft LEVIATHAN THOTs Ausrichtung über einen senkrechten Punkt, der auf dem Gradienten des Gravitationsfeldes liegt. Die Vertikalität des Körpers ist an der Richtung der an diesem Punkt herrschenden Schwerkraft ausgerichtet, sie materialisiert sich nach aussen als Lotfaden. Die Schwerkraft wird sich in Affektivität wandeln. Neto spricht von einer natürlichen geraden Linie «die an jedem Ort ist, die man jedoch nicht sehen kann, es sei denn, sie wird durch das physikalische Experiment sichtbar gemacht: die Vertikalität des Falls ... die Schwerkraft: die grosse Göttin, unser Gefängnis und unser Leben». Der Lotfaden wird empirisch als absolute Vertikale gesehen. «Wir haben zwei Geometrien (oder vielleicht auch zwei Arten von Liebe, wer weiss), eine sogenannte euklidische und eine, sagen wir mal, riemannsche, die der Kurve auf kleinsten Oberflächen», ergänzt der Bildhauer, ähnlich der romantischen Kurve bei Novalis. Im Hinblick auf «die Geliebte» – die Novalis als Mikrokosmos des Universums sieht, als dessen Erweiterung – hält Paul Virilio fest, dass die Kraft der Anziehung die Erdanziehung ist, das universelle Gewicht *axis mundi*.[8)]

Die Extensoren hielten das Kunstwerk und kehrten als Gegengewicht an ihren Bestimmungsort, das Zentrum der Erde, zurück. Das ist Netos «vertikale Wahrheit, eine Art universelle Konstante». LEVIATHAN THOTs Fingerspitzen finden die Horizontalität des hängenden Körpers, «die in gewisser Hinsicht seine Unbestimmtheit, sein Belebtsein, seine Subjektivität, seine Intimität zeigt» – der Künstler vergleicht LEVIATHAN THOT mit einer Pietà: «Zwischen der Umwälzung des Lebens und der Gleichgültigkeit der Zeit liegt der Körper Jesu'... ewig ist Maria.»

Die Art, wie LEVIATHAN THOT von der Decke herabhängt, und sich im Raum des Panthéons ausbreitet, ist für Neto Ausdruck des Zusammenpralls zwischen Vertikalität und Horizontalität, «wie in einem Gemälde Mondrians». Für Piet Mondrian schafft die Wechselwirkung zwischen horizontalen und vertikalen Linien das Leben.[9)] Die plastische Funktion der Linien drückt Weite aus, Ruhe und Einheit, erwachsend aus Beobachtungen des Meeres, des Himmels und der Sterne.

Francis Ponge analysierte den auf einen Strich reduzierten Menschen im Werk Giacomettis als jemanden in einem «ruinösen Zustand, das Elend der Welt – auf sich selbst gestellt – im Nirgendwo beginnend. Mager, nackt, ausgemergelt, nur Haut und Knochen. Ohne Grund in der Menge unterwegs». Rosalind Krauss stellt Giacomettis Ökonomie des «Nichtseins» Heidegger gegenüber, der von einer Angst vor «dem Nichts»[10)] zu sprechen pflegte. Lygia Clark schrieb in ihrem *Carta a Mondrian* (1959): «Der Mensch ist nicht allein. Er ist Form und Leere. Er kommt aus der Leere in die Form (Leben) und geht aus diesem in die volle Leere, was gleichbedeutend ist mit einem relativen Tod.»[11)]

Giacometti und Neto wirken wie Antipoden, betrachtet man die Magerkeit der Figuren des Schweizers und die sinnliche Fülle der Skulpturen des Zweiten. Bei beiden jedoch ist die Vertikalität die Grenzbedingung. Auf der Suche nach der verlorenen Kontinuität, nach unserer verkümmerten Rationalität, beschwört Neto das «im Herzen eines jeden Bürgers» vibrierende foucaultsche Pendel. Ein Faktor, der in Netos Produktion stets präsent ist, das Bewusstsein des Schwerkraftfeldes, dient bei LEVIATHAN THOT als Metapher für die Macht des Staates und den kritischen Platz des Individuums – des Bürgers – im gegenwärtigen sozialen Raum.

PANTHÉON UND LEVIATHAN

«Und wir kommen zum sozialen Körper, zu Leviathan, dem Monster, das wir geschaffen haben», verkündet Ernesto Neto, «ein fremdes Wesen, das an keinem Ort zu sein scheint, unsichtbar, unberührbar, ohne Fleisch, ohne Licht, ohne Leben ... das aber überall ist». LEVIATHAN THOT verweist auf die Theorie des modernen Staates von Hobbes, bewahrt sich jedoch seine ironische nietzschesche Skepsis. Stellt sich doch die Leichtigkeit des Geistes aus Nietzsches *Die Fröhliche Wissenschaft* wie eine Persiflage auf den «Geist der Schwere» dar. Der Bildhauer spricht von einem «organlosen Körper», Bild des schizophrenen Kapitalismus in Deleuzes und Guattaris Anti-Ödipus. Beim Memorial LEVIATHAN THOT sind alles «vage Worte, um das Unaussprechliche auszusprechen»: Das «freie» Wesen, der soziale Körper, die Rationalität. Leviathan ist ein Moloch, der nach Opfern verlangt. Neto beklagt die traurige Menge anonymer Menschen, die dominiert werden «von der abstrakten Macht, die wir selbst erfunden haben».

Für Neto ist das Panthéon, ein Monument verlorener Modernität, zu «einem Grab ohne Licht» geworden. Und LEVIATHAN THOT ist keineswegs der Versöhnungsraum zwischen Wissenschaft und Lust, Subjektivität und Politik, Bürgerrecht und Staat. Im Gegenteil, er ist eine politische «Anatomielehre». Dem Künstler widerstrebt es, das Pendel mit seinem äusserlich unpersönlichen, technischen Charakter zu berühren. LEVIATHAN THOT ist ein Raum der Spaltung. «Dort, wo der Staat aufhört, da beginnt erst der Mensch, der nicht überflüssig ist», schreibt Nietzsche in *Also sprach Zarathustra.*[12] Da die Bestattungen im Panthéon dem Präsidenten der französischen Republik unterstehen, verweist LEVIATHAN THOT auf die Theorie der politischen Repräsentation, indem er den Zuschauer als Bürger in das Zentrum des Ruhmes stellt. Nach Ernesto Netos Phänomenologie wird das foucaultsche Pendel zum Herzen eines jeden Einzelnen.

(Übersetzung: Marianne Gareis)

1) Thomas Hobbes, *Leviathan*, Suhrkamp-Verlag, Frankfurt am Main, S. 463.
2) *Die Bibel*, Buch Hiob, 41:5.
3) Ernest Wallis Budge, *Gods of the Egyptians*, New York, Dover Publications. Band 1, S. 410–414.
4) Ernesto Neto sagt, die Lektüre von Bruno Latours *Nous n'avons jamais été modernes: Essai d'anthropologie symétrique* (1991) sei wichtig für die Ausarbeitung von LEVIATHAN THOT gewesen.
5) Texte, die dem Autor per E-Mail am 22. September 2006 geschickt wurden. Alle Zitate des Künstlers ohne Quellenangabe stammen aus diesem Text.
6) Hier, p = Impuls, m = Masse und v = Geschwindigkeit. Diese Faktoren bestimmen das dynamische Leben von LEVIATHAN THOT.
7) Nach Stéphane Deligeorges. *Foucault et ses pendules*, Paris, Collections Vues des Sciences, 1995, S.47.
8) Paul Virilio, *Ästhetik des Verschwindens,* Merve-Verlag, Berlin, S. 86.
9) Octavio Morisani, «Verso la vera visione della realtá», in: *L'Astrattismo di Piet Mondrian*, Venedig, Neri Pozza Editore, 1956, S. 172.
10) Rosalid Krauss, «Alberto Giacometti: Museum of Modern Art, New York», *Artforum*, Dezember 2001. Wir schreiben Krauss auch das Zitat von Ponge in diesem Absatz zu.
11) Lygia Clark, *Lygia Clark*, Barcelona, Fondació Antoni Tàpies, 1997, S. 112.
12) Friedrich Nietzsche, *Also sprach Zarathustra*, Insel-Verlag, Frankfurt am Main, 1978, S. 54.

ERNESTO NETO, LEVIATHAN THOT, 2006,
installation view /
Installationsansicht, Panthéon, Paris.

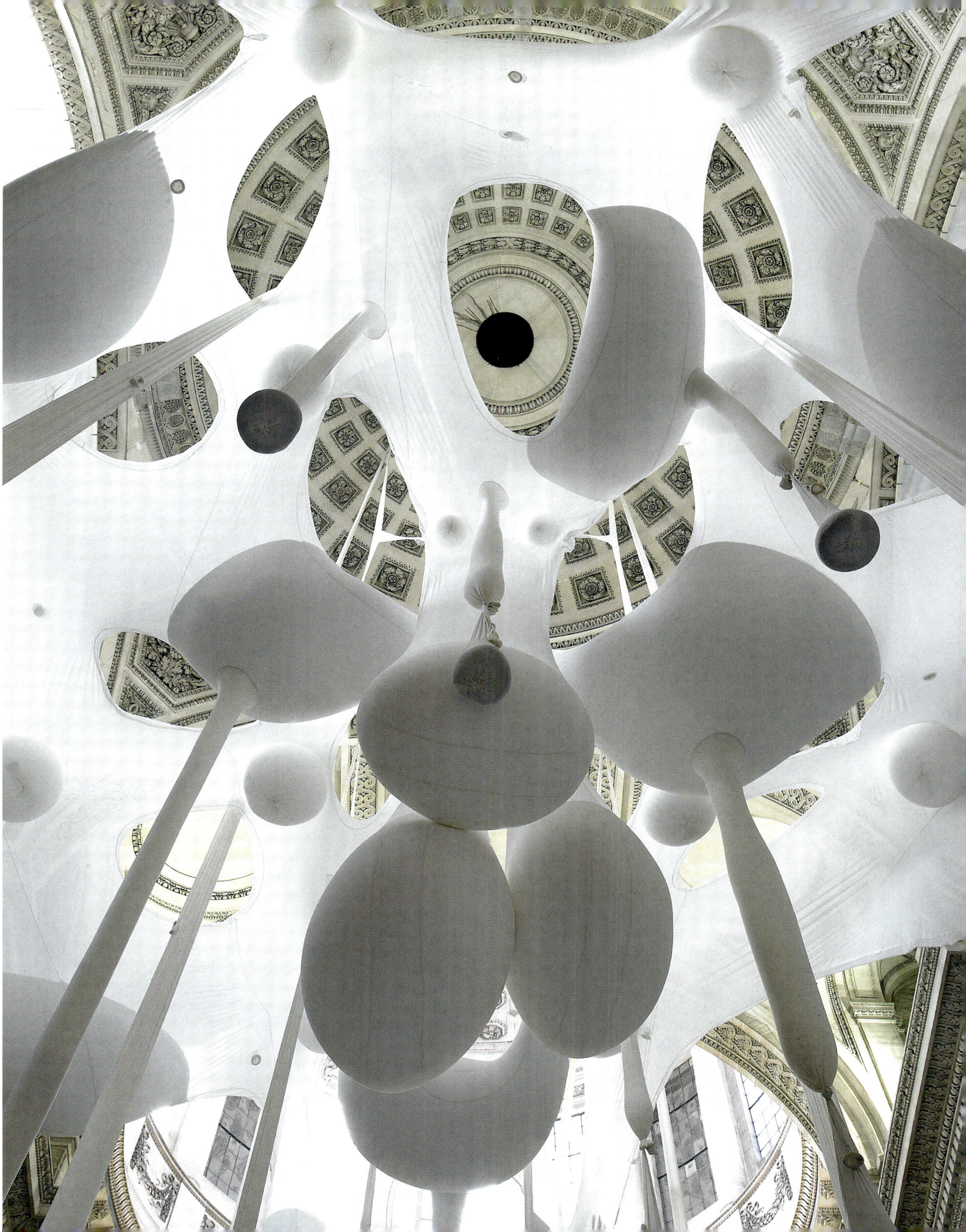

YUKO HASEGAWA

NEW PLACES OF CONTEMPLATION

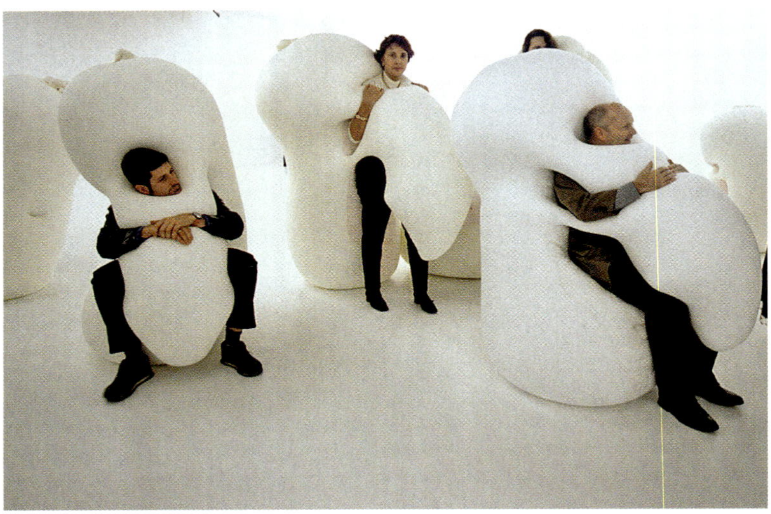

Hélio Oiticica discussed the body in terms of "a suspension of memory: the opposite pole of what race memory would be."[1] Encountering the works of Ernesto Neto gives us an opportunity to physically experience this philosophy through acts of confirmation that rely on the most basic physical sensations.

Metaphorically speaking, this process is similar to the cloning process one sees in science fiction movies whereby an entire human body is recreated simply by placing a single fragment of DNA in a culture solution. The thought of one's own DNA forming a lather and being reproduced brings home the reality that our bodies are made up of cells and quanta, that they are in fact being reproduced on a daily basis in a form as close as possible to that which they took the day before, although changes are necessary due to both external and internal factors. One day this body of ours appears, begins interacting with the world, moving around in space while changing its volume, and then one day it disappears.

In recounting the development of the monumental pieces that he calls *Naves*, Neto speaks about "places of contemplation," while he describes the human body as a temple of the soul, a sacred place. "Ultimately, if we ask ourselves what it is that humans possess, I think perhaps all we have is a body and time, and we simply live out our days until one day we are suddenly called, at which point we vanish off the face of the earth."[2] This is a very Buddhist-like

YUKO HASEGAWA is the Chief Curator at the Museum of Contemporary Art, Tokyo.

approach. However, while Buddhism teaches that there is a close relationship between death and the view of life as something transient and empty, stressing that for each day we live we are a day closer to

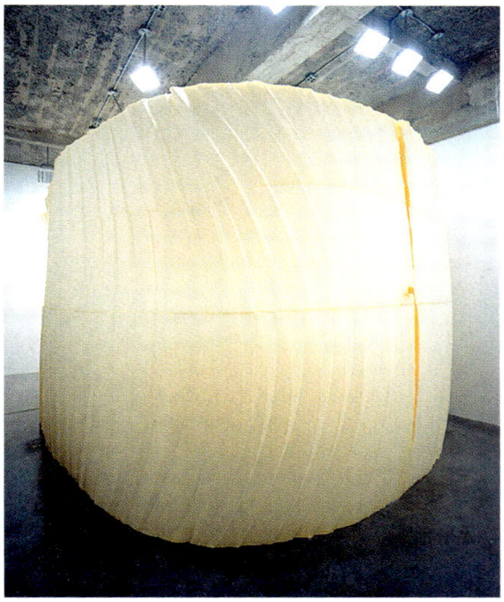

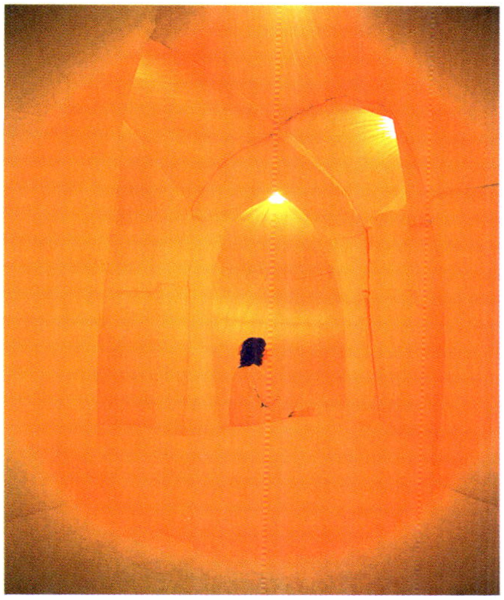

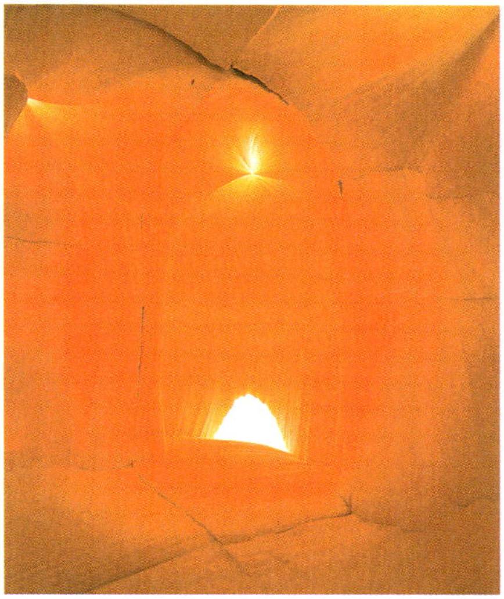

ERNESTO NETO, THE HOUSE, 2003, white polyurethane foam, 109 x 139 x 210", outside and inside views / weisser Polyurethan-Schaum, 277 x 353 x 553.4 cm, Aussen- und Innenansichten.
(PHOTO: TANYA BONAKDAR GALLERY, NEW YORK)

Left page / linke Seite:
ERNESTO NETO, HUMANOIDES 2001, lyra tulle, styrofoam balls, variable dimensions, installation view, Kölnischer Kunstverein, Cologne / Lycragewebe, Styroporkugeln, Format variabel, Installationsansicht.
(PHOTO: COURTESY ATELIER NETO)

death, Neto's approach is based on a visual model of the appearance and disappearance of the human body as a metaphor for internal space (in metaphorical terms, a spaceship).

From his early works, which involved hanging weights and using gravity and balance in an attempt to establish different gravitational fields and volumes in space, Neto gradually shifted to using organic, flexible forms, and in the process adopted a style in which the audience came to play a part in determining the form of the works by continually changing them. In the case of his "penetrable sculptures" (again a term borrowed from Oiticica), one could say that Neto is acutely conscious of the fact that at the moment of penetration, the body is on a borderline, and that this is political territory. While experimenting with various ways of exploring the boundary between the body and the outside world, Neto, in these early works, created a life-mask which he made by burying his face in plaster with a straw in his mouth to breath through. According to Neto, when he placed this life-mask on the gallery floor, the area underneath took on the appearance of a body of water on the surface of which floated his face. The steady accumulation of cases such as this, which verify the boundaries of the body and the imagination of space, serves as the foundation on which Neto has built his philosophy.

Inside the *Naves*, in the pliant "spaces" where the audience finds itself gently sinking under its own weight, one experiences a visual, physical sensation of being suspended in air and, at the same time, one is conscious of one's own body being different than normal, awkward yet elastic.

A number of translucent tubes traverses a space that has been shut off from the outside world by translucent curtains; the effect is reminiscent of blood vessels or nerve fibers, various kinds of tubes inside the body, tubes that are ceaselessly transporting something and, at the same time, stimulating some kind of metabolism. Transparency is one of the hallmarks of life, and in the sense that both parties are able to see each other, it is also a symbol of exchange.

Because it is a volume occupying a certain place in space, the human body is affected by gravity. This being the case, what kind of thought processes might an artist, who sets out to create an alternative body, go through?

Neto has developed his unique artistic world by following in order the scientific steps taken by humankind in studying the makeup of the world. First came physics. The study of gravity led to the study of quantum mechanics. Then came biology. Biology was the key to understanding the principles of life in the form of helical structures. There is a

Right page / rechte Seite:
ERNESTO NETO, A GENTE SE ENCONTRA AQUI HOJE, AMANHA EM OUTRO LUGAR. ENQUANTO ISSO DEUS É DEUSA. SANTA GRAVIDADE (People Meet here Today and Elsewhere Tomorrow, God as much as Goddess. Holy Earnest), 2003, textile, styrofoam, rice, installation view 2005, Thyssen-Bornemisza Art Contemporary, Vienna, / (Die Leute treffen sich heute hier und morgen dort, Gott wie Göttin. Heiliger Ernst), Textilien, Styropor, Reis, Installationsansicht.
(PHOTO: MICHAEL STRASSER / T-B A21, WIEN)

ERNESTO NETO, O TEMPO LENTO DO CORPO QUE É PELE (The Slow Pace of the Body that Is Skin), 2004, foam, lycra, rug, wood, polyamide, spices, 374 x 268 x 59" / Der langsame Gang des Körpers, der Haut ist. Schaum, Lycra, Decke, Holz, Polyamide, Gewürze, 950 x 680 x 150 cm.
(PHOTO: COURTESY GALERIE MAX HETZLER, BERLIN)

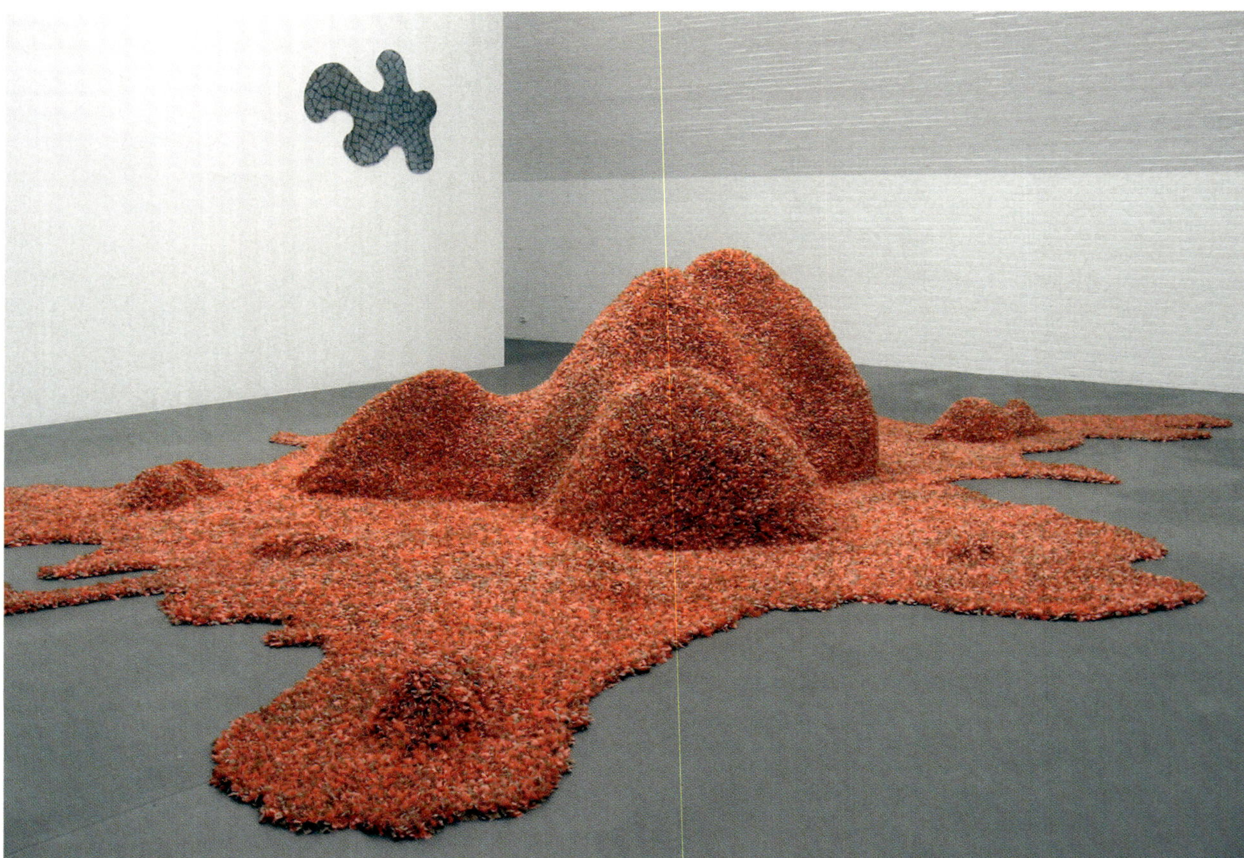

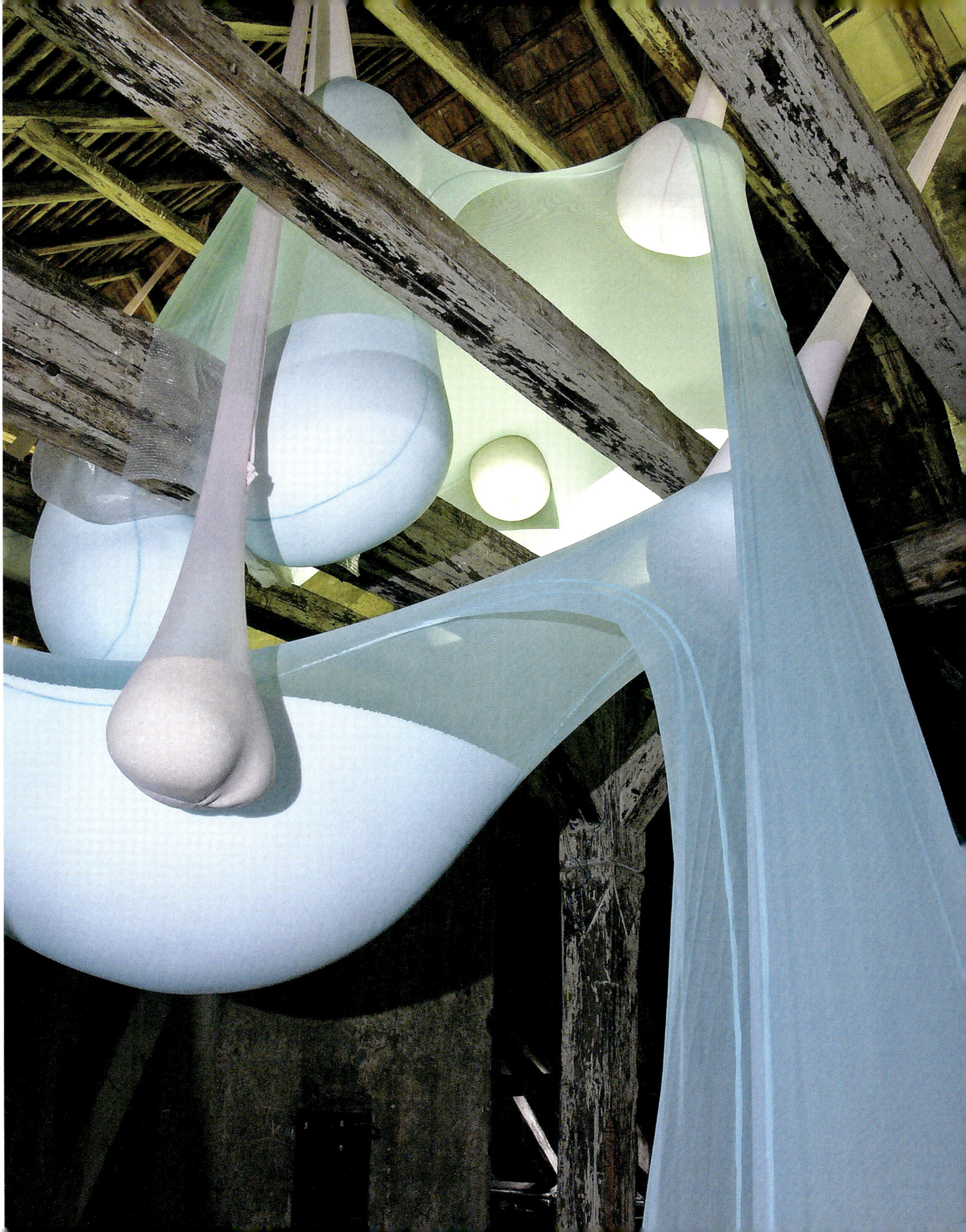

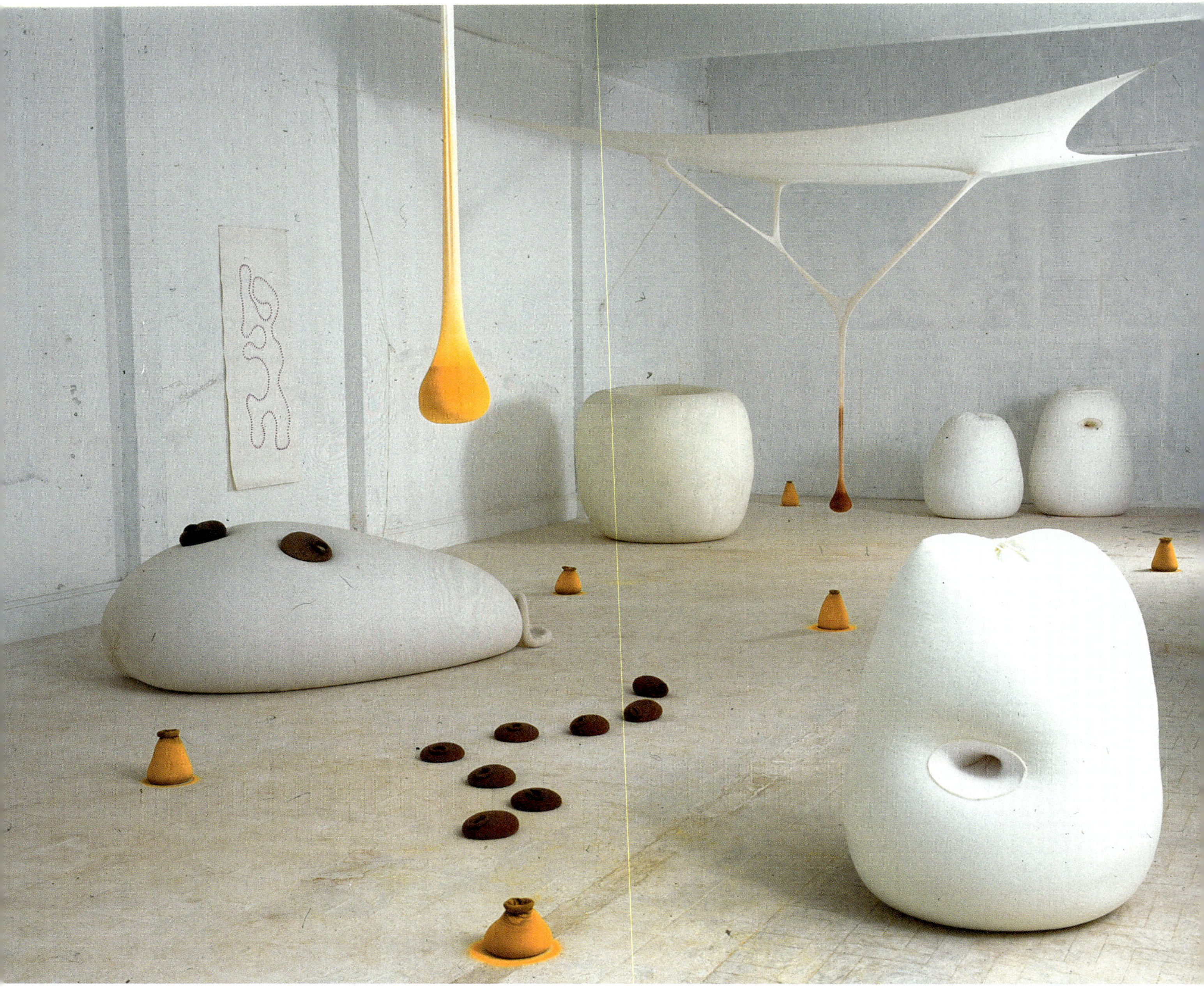

ERNESTO NETO, O HABITAT, 1999, lycra tulle, polyamid fabric and stockings, styrofoam balls, turmeric, annato / Lycragewebe, Polyamidgewebe und Strümpfe, Styropor-Kugeln, Kurkuma, Annato. *(PHOTO: GALERIA CAMARGO VILAÇA, SÃO PAULO)*

Right page / rechte Seite:
ERNESTO NETO, FROM WHAT WE ARE MADE, MADE OF OF, 2006, cotton, polypropylene, lycra, buchwheat shells, lavender, foam / WORAUS WIR GEMACHT SIND, GEMACHT AUS AUS, Baumwolle, Polypropyläen, Lycragewebe, Buchweizen-Hülsen, Lavendel, Schaum. *(PHOTO: TANYA BONAKDAR GALLERY, NEW YORK)*

correlation between this and Neto's biomorphic shapes.

Lastly, places of contemplation suggest a state of consciousness. This relates to the final mystery in science, to a question that preoccupies many neurologists: Where does our consciousness come from? If we can describe the *Naves* as one of the destination points on Neto's quest to find an answer to this question, then they can be thought of as embracing these three elements—physics, biology, and consciousness—while also tracing the steps of the scientific quest of humankind, and therefore representing the realization of another, ideal human body.

From the viewer's perspective, the sense of security and pleasure provided by these soft, delicate objects has a healing effect. At the same time, we must remain extremely conscious of the fact that behind the physiological and psychological relaxation afforded by Neto's works lies the simultaneous, all-pervasive violence of places like Rio and the realities of global terrorism. When Neto refers to his own works as political, he perhaps has in mind the strong sense of ambivalence suggested by placing tiny bullets inside a soft stocking and hanging it overhead, as he does in his work, PLUMO COLONIES (1989).

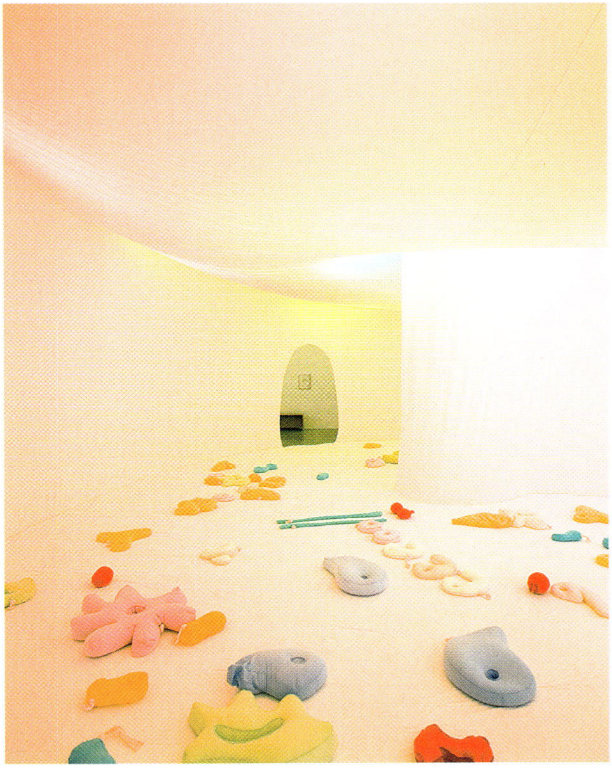

In the 1970s, "art in progress" works began to cast doubt on the permanence of art and materiality, including the change over time of matter itself. It's as if Neto has taken what Lygia Clark tried to achieve with her *Objetos Relacionais*, and Hélio Oiticica with his *Parangolé* tents (a concept he attempted to expand on with his *Bólide-cama*) and effortlessly transformed them into one comprehensive system. The Lycra fabric Neto uses for his works is repaired and replaced when it gets ripped or soiled, in much the same way that an injury heals. The existence of the works themselves is similar, in a way, to a system or program that generates space. Inasmuch as they resemble a program, they could be regarded as architectural, although it is difficult to apply the term 'architecture' in the sense of an external, self-supporting structure to something so closely resembling the human body that it could almost be called an extension of one's skin. This skin as a boundary, seeking to fuse with its surroundings, is created by blending structure (spatial experience) with the senses of touch and sight.

For his exhibition at the ICA London in 2000, Neto marked the walls of several gallery rooms with a succession of drawings resembling the puff marks made by gently pressing bags of powder, or perhaps the footprints left behind by someone taking a stroll. When we move, we leave signs of life in the places we visit. By basing his drawings on the individual chapters (cities) in Italo Calvino's *Invisible Cities*, Neto has created traces of travels that take place on a meta-level. Oiticica described his experiences in various cities around the world in terms of "psychogeography"; Neto would perhaps speak about the triad "body-mind-geography."

(Translation: Pamela Miki)

1) Lisette Lagnado, "Longing for the body: yesterday and today," in *Brazil: Body Nostalgia* (Tokyo: National Museum of Modern Art, 2004), p. 166.
2) From the Ernesto Neto Artist Talk held at Kanazawa Citizen's Art Center, November 16, 2002.

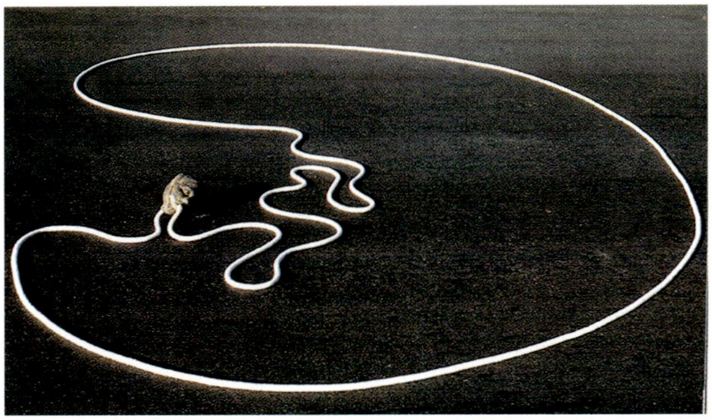

ERNESTO NETO, JANUS FETUS, 1995,
iron and cotton, 197 x 167 x 8" /
JANUS FETUS, Eisen und Baumwolle, 500 x 424 x 20 cm.
(PHOTO: TANYA BONAKDAR GALLERY, NEW YORK)

YUKO HASEGAWA

DER NEUE ORT DER KONTEMPLATION

Für Hélio Oiticica existiert der Körper «getrennt vom Gedächtnis, er steht konträr zum kollektiven Gedächtnis eines Volkes».[1] Die Werke Ernesto Netos geben uns die Gelegenheit, diese Philosophie am eigenen Leib zu erleben, denn ihre Wirkung zielt auf das Physische ab.

Diese Wirkung – so wie in Science-Fiction-Filmen in einem Nährboden aus einer einzigen Zelle ein ganzer menschlicher Körper geklont wird – ist ein Gefühl der pulsierenden Erneuerung. Es ist nichts anderes als das Erleben der Realität unseres eigenen Körpers, der aus Zellen und Quanten besteht, die sich selbst Tag für Tag auf der Basis ihrer Vorlage neu schaffen, aber – durch innere und äussere Faktoren beeinflusst – bei jeder Reproduktion notgedrungen verändern. Irgendwann einmal erscheint unser Körper, geht mit der Welt Beziehungen ein, treibt, sein Volumen ändernd, durch den Raum und verschwindet schliesslich.

Während Neto die *Naves* als «Ort der Kontemplation» schuf, betrachtete er den Körper als Tempel der Seele, als heiligen Ort. «Ich glaube, dass der Mensch letztendlich nichts als seinen eigenen Körper und seine Zeit besitzt. Er lebt sein Leben und irgendwann einmal läuft seine Zeit ab. Dann verschwindet er aus dieser Welt.»[2] Diese Ansicht scheint eine gewisse Affinität zur buddhistischen Philosophie zu haben, jedoch gibt es einen wichtigen Unterschied. Im Buddhismus herrscht die Ansicht, dass jeder gelebte Tag uns einen Schritt dem Tode näher bringt. Vergänglichkeit ist also sehr eng an den Tod gebunden. Neto setzt dagegen sein Konzept des inneren Raumes. Es ist der von ihm metaphorisch als Raumschiff begriffene Körper, der aus dem Nichts kommt und wieder ins Nichts verschwindet.

In seinen früheren Werken versuchte Ernesto Neto durch Gewichte, die er über den ganzen Raum

YUKO HASEGAWA ist die leitende Kuratorin des Museum für Gegenwartskunst des 21. Jahrhunderts in Kanazawa, Japan.

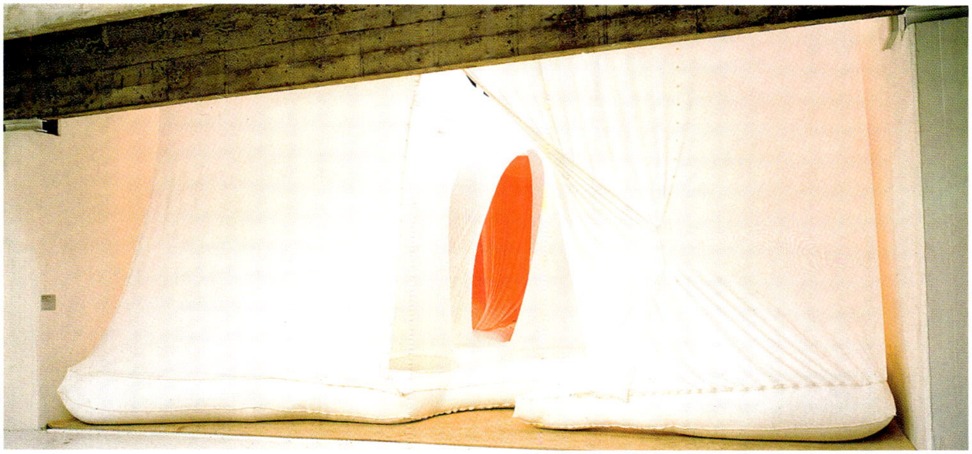

ERNESTO NETO, NASCIMENTO DA DEUSA, O EMBRIÃO (Birth of a Goddess, the Embryo), 2001, lycra tulle, styrofoam balls, 177 x 157 1/2 x 551", installation view, Venice Biennale, 2001 / (Geburt einer Göttin, der Embryo), Lycragewebe, Styropor-Kügelchen, 450 x 400 x 1400 cm, Installationsansicht, Biennale Venedig. (PHOTO: EDUARDO ORTEGA)

hinweg verteilt aufhängte, die Kraftfelder und die Volumen des Raums neu zu gestalten. Später nahmen seine Objekte oft geschmeidige und organisch anmutende Formen an, und er entwickelte einen Stil, der dem Betrachter eine wichtige Rolle zuweist, indem die Werke erst in der Auseinandersetzung mit ihm und durch ihre ständige Veränderung ihre eigentliche Form erhalten. Bei den «durchdringenden Skulpturen», ein von Oiticica entlehnter Begriff, setzte er sich mit dem Körper als Grenze gegen das Andere und somit politisches Territorium auseinander. Verschiedentlich versuchte er, die Grenze zwischen seinem eigenen Körper und dem Aussenraum zu erkunden. Für ein frühes Werk steckte er ein Rohr in seinen Mund und tauchte sein Gesicht in Gips, um eine Maske von sich selbst anzufertigen. Als er den Gipsabdruck auf den Boden einer Galerie legte, schien ihm der Boden wie eine Wasseroberfläche, auf der sein Gesicht schwebte. Mehrere Experimente dieser Art dienten dazu, die Grenzen seines eigenen Körpers und des Aussenraumes auszuloten – Themen, die zum Grundkonzept seiner Philosophie wurden.

Inmitten der *Naves*, dieser weichen Räume, in die man unter seinem eigenen Gewicht einzusinken scheint, hat man das Gefühl, in der Luft zu schweben. Gleichzeitig jedoch erscheint der eigene Körper auf eigentümliche Art und Weise sowohl schwerfällig als auch elastisch.

Mehrere aus halbtransparenten Materialien bestehende Röhren verlaufen quer durch einen Raum, der von der Aussenwelt durch halbdurchsichtige Vorhänge abgetrennt ist. Sie erinnern an Blutgefässe, Nervenfasern und andere den Körper durchlaufende Kanäle, in denen ständig Stoffe transportiert

ERNESTO NETO, RED, WHITE, PEOPLE; MATTER, MOTHER, LIGHT / HABITAT ... CONFLICT ..., 2005 / ROT, WEISS, LEUTE; MATERIE, MUTTER, LICHT / HABITAT ... KONFLIKT ... (PHOTO: TANYA BONAKDAR GALLERY, NEW YORK)

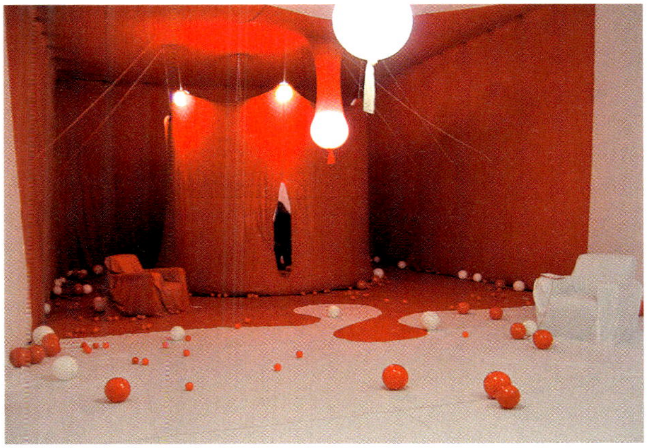

werden, um den Stoffwechsel in Gang zu halten. Durchlässigkeit ist das Element des Lebens und, da zwei voneinander getrennte Seiten in Sichtkontakt miteinander stehen, ein Symbol des Austausches.

Weil er ein gewisses Volumen im Raum einnimmt, ist der menschliche Körper zwangsläufig an die Schwerkraft gebunden. Vor diesem Hintergrund muss man sich fragen, welchen Prozess ein Künstler durchläuft, wenn er einen alternativen Körper schafft.

Die Entwicklung von Netos einzigartigem künstlerischem Universum kann parallel gesehen werden zur Entwicklung der wissenschaftlichen Erforschung der Welt. Zuerst versuchte die Physik die Welt mithilfe des Konzeptes der Schwerkraft zu erklären, dann trat die Quantenmechanik an ihre Stelle, gefolgt von der Biologie, die die Spiralstruktur als das Grundprinzip des Lebens erkannte. Netos biomorphische Formen korrelieren damit in gewisser Art und Weise.

Orte der Kontemplation setzen ein bestimmtes Bewusstsein voraus. Dies führt uns zu den letzten Fragen der Wissenschaft, also Fragen hirnphysiologischer Natur: Wie überhaupt entsteht unser Bewusstsein? Die *Naves* sind eine Etappe in Netos Versuch, eine Antwort auf diese Frage zu finden. Alle drei erwähnten Bereiche erfassend, folgen sie den Schritten der Wissenschaft bei ihrer Erforschung der Welt und vereinen sie in einem anderen, idealen Körper.

Das Wohlgefühl und die Gelöstheit, die durch diese weichen und fragilen Objekte vermittelt werden, wirken heilend auf den Betrachter. Man achte hier besonders auf die Tatsache, dass die psychisch-physische tröstende Wirkung, die von Netos Werken ausgeht, vor dem Hintergrund des gewalttätigen Alltags von Rio de Janeiro und der weltweiten Terrorwellen gesehen werden muss. Wenn Neto sagt, sein Werk sei politisch, bezieht er sich vielleicht auf die starke Ambivalenz der Arbeit PLUMO COLONIES (1989), wo Pistolenkugeln in einem weichen, aufgehängten Strumpf stecken.

In den 70er Jahren stellten die Werke der «art in progress» den Begriff der Ewigkeit von Kunst, die ja schliesslich auch nur aus Materialien besteht, die dem zeitlichen Verfall unterliegen, in Frage. In Netos Installationen wird der Stoff immer dann ersetzt oder ausgebessert, wenn er verschmutzt oder zerrissen ist, ganz so, als handele es sich um Wunden, die man zu pflegen hätte. Netos Werke sind ein System, fast ein Programm, das Räume konstruiert. In diesem Sinne könnte man sie «architektonisch» nennen, obwohl es schwierig ist, derartig körperliche Strukturen, die fast eine Erweiterung der menschlichen Haut darstellen, im Sinne eines selbständig existierenden Bauwerks zu beschreiben. Die Haut als Grenze, danach strebend, mit ihrer Umwelt zu verschmelzen, wird geschaffen, indem Strukturen (räumliche Erfahrungen) mit dem Haptischen und Visuellen verschmolzen werden. Das, was Lygia Clark mit *Objetos Relacionais* und Hélio Oiticica mit *Parangolé*-Zelten (ein Konzept, das er auf *Bólide-cama* ausweitete) anstrebten, brachte Neto mühelos in ein umfassendes integrales System.

Für seine Ausstellung im ICA (2000) in London versah er die Wände der Ausstellungsräume mit Zeichnungen, die Spuren ähnelten, die mit Puder gefüllte Säckchen hinterlassen würden, wenn man sie sanft auf den Boden drücken würde. Das Ganze sah aus wie Fussstapfen, die jemand auf einem Spaziergang hinterlassen hatte. Die Bewegung hinterlässt Lebensspuren an den Plätzen, die man besucht. Seine Zeichnungen, die er zu den einzelnen Kapiteln aus Italo Calvinos *Unsichtbare Städte* anfertigte, sind Spuren einer auf der Metaebene stattfindenden Reise. Oiticica nannte seine diesbezüglichen Erfahrungen in verschiedenen Städten dieser Welt «Psychogeographie», Neto würde wohl von «Körper-Geist-Geographie» sprechen.

(Übersetzung: Kimiko Nakayama-Ziegler und Heike Boudalfa)

1) Lisette Lagnado, «Longing for the body: yesterday and today», in: *Brazil: Body Nostalgia* (Tokyo: National Museum of Modern Art, 2004), S. 166.
2) Aus einem Gespräch mit Ernesto Neto im Kanazawa Citizen's Art Center, 16. November, 2002.

ERNESTO NETO, THE WEIGHT, THE TIME, THE BODY, THE MOON AND LOVE…WOW!, 2006, styrofoam, lycra tulle, polypropylene, glass seed beads, ca. 205 x 453 x 401", installation view, Gallery Bob van Orsouw, Zürich / DAS GEWICHT, DIE ZEIT, DER KÖRPER, DER MOND UND LIEBE… WOW!, Styropor, Lycragewebe, Polypropyläen, Glasperlen, ca. 520 x 1150 x 1020 cm. (PHOTO: COURTESY GALERIE BOB VAN ORSOUW, ZÜRICH)

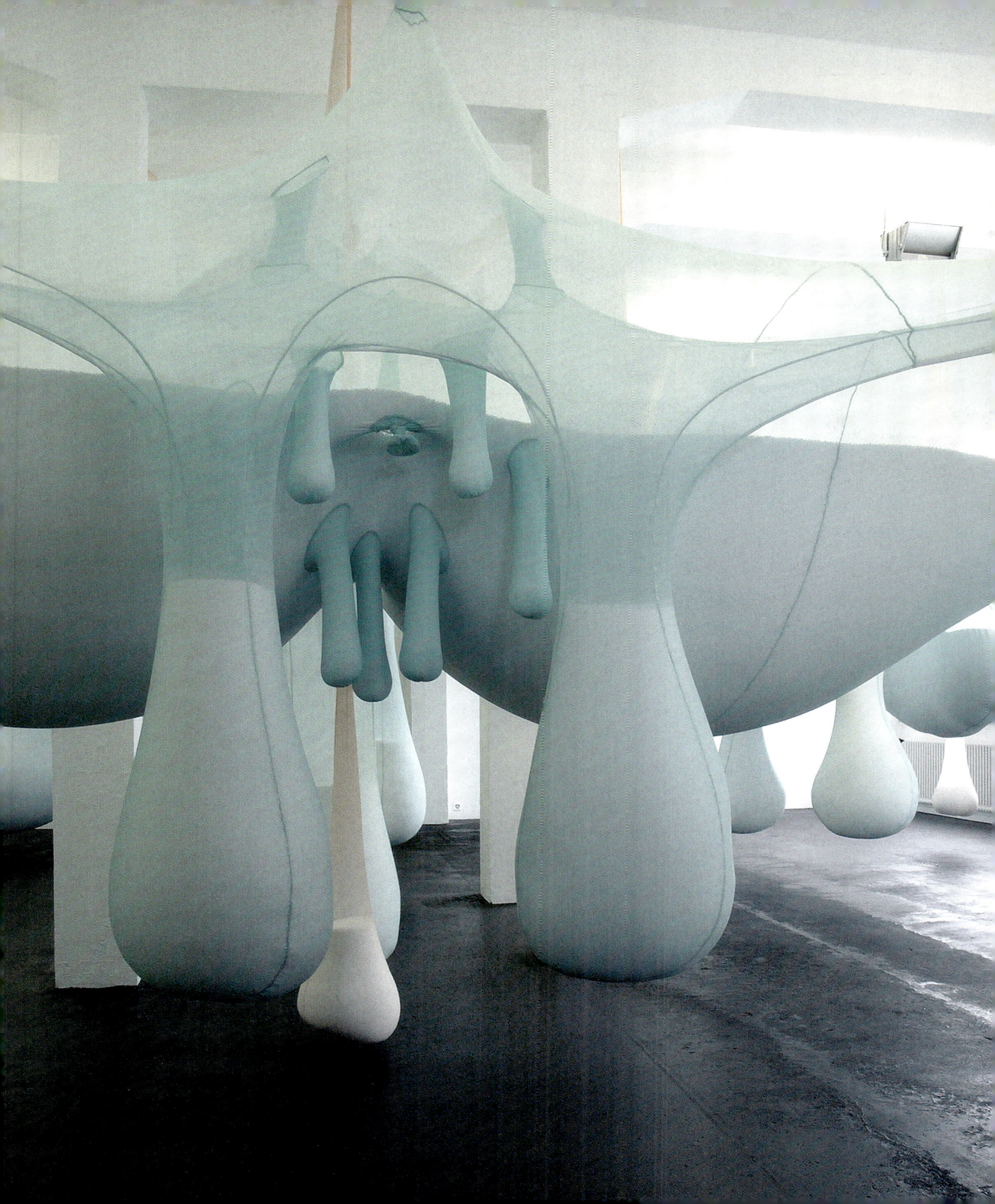

EDITION FOR PARKETT

ERNESTO NETO

Phytuziann, 2006

Green lycra tulle and polypropylene pellets,
$17\frac{3}{4}$ x $10\frac{3}{4}$ x 2"; weight, 4 lb.
Edition of 60 / XX, signed and numbered.

Grünes Lycragewebe und Polypropyläen-Kügelchen,
45 x 27 x 5 cm, Gewicht 1,8 kg.
Auflage: 60 / XX, signiert und nummeriert.

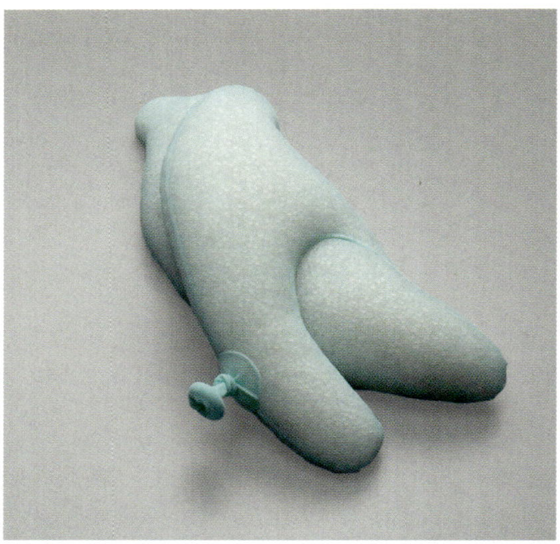

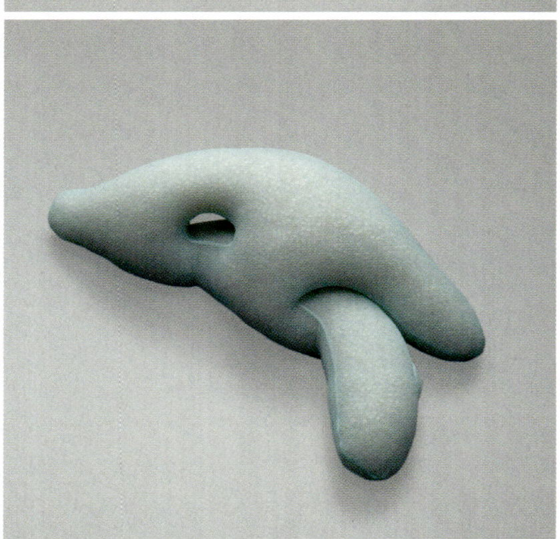

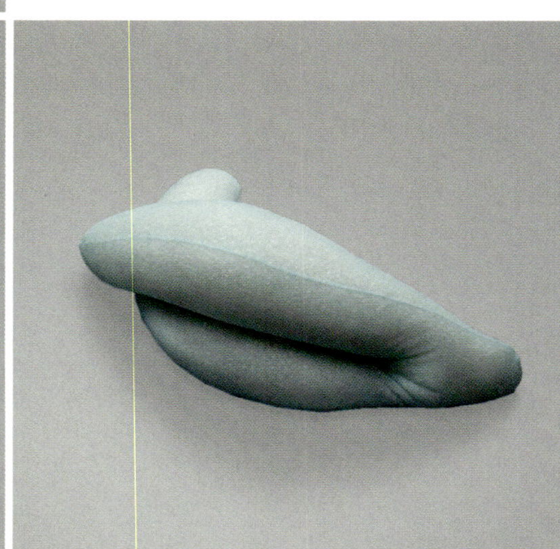

(PHOTOS: RETO RODOLFO PEDRINI, ZÜRICH)

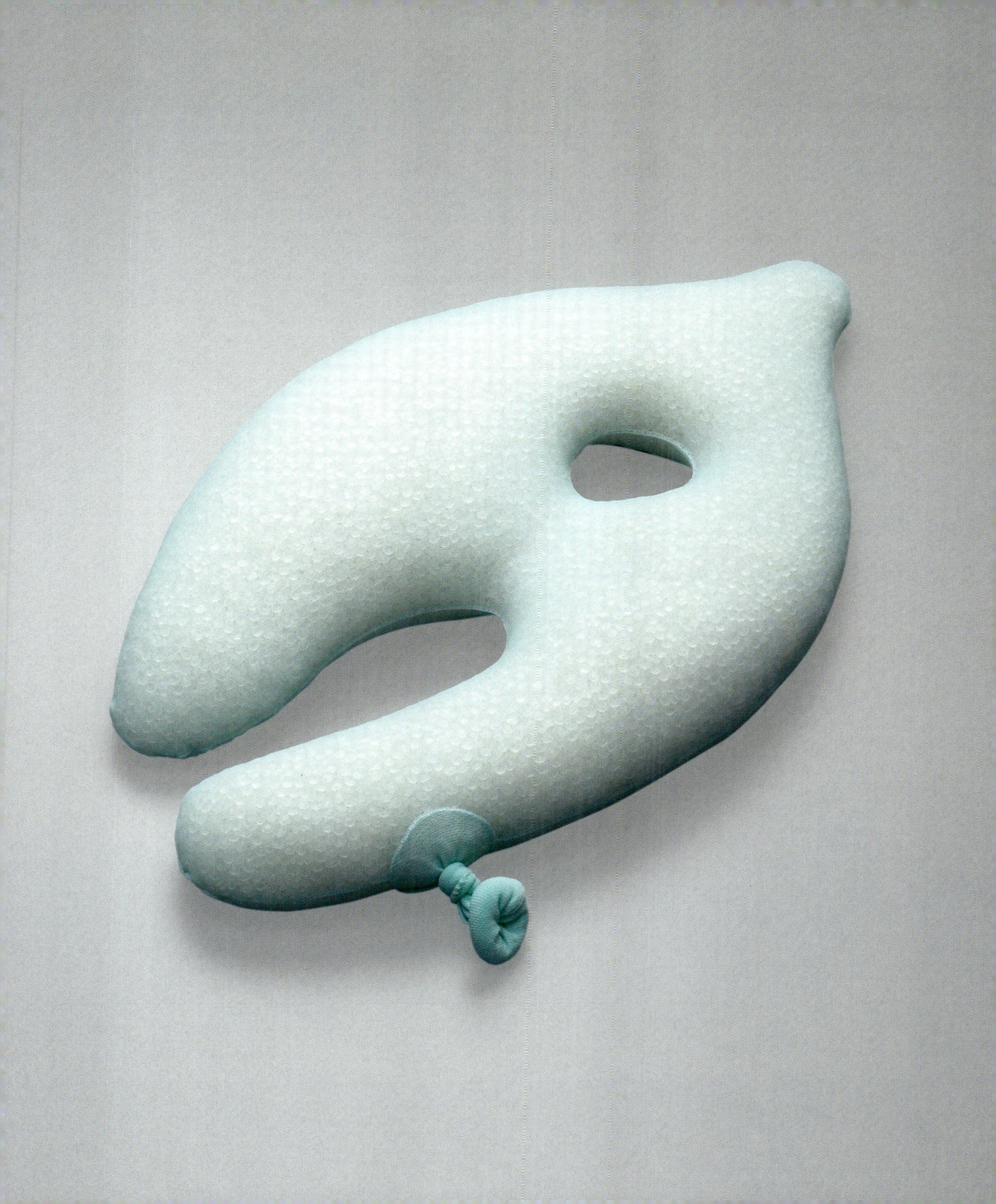

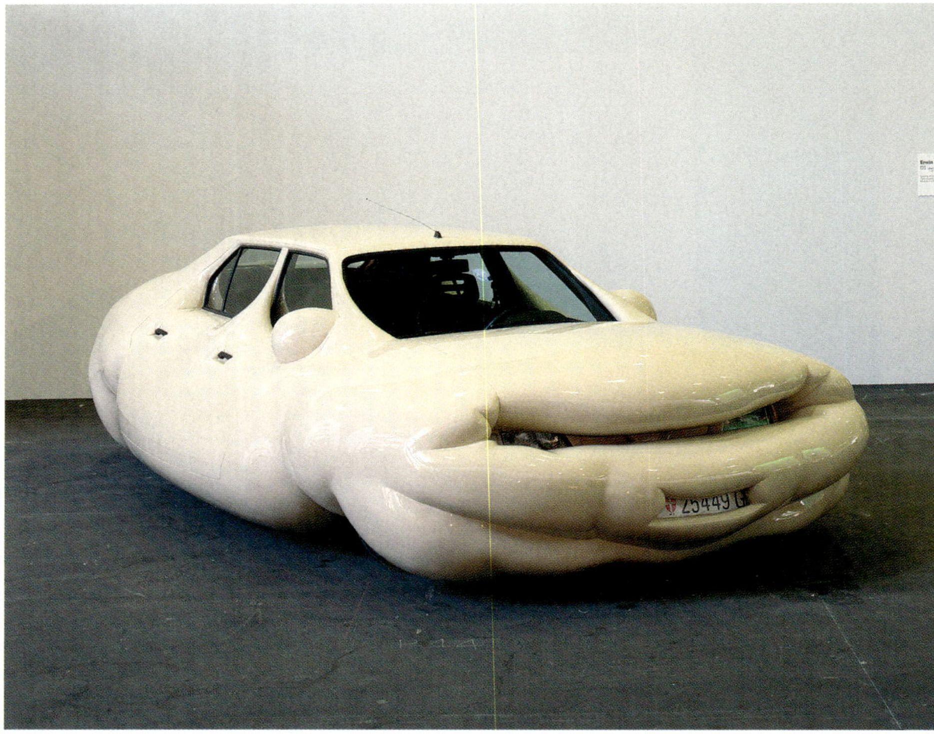

ERWIN WURM, FAT CAR, 2001, mixed media, 51 1/4 x 104 1/4 x 189" / FETTES AUTO, verschiedene Materialien, 130 x 265 x 480 cm.
(ALL PHOTOS: COURTESY STUDIO ERWIN WURM, VIENNA)

ERWIN WURM

ABRAHAM ORDEN

The Erwin Wurm many of us have become familiar with over the past ten years is changing rapidly before our eyes. Until recently, it has sufficed for critics, as a general rule, to begin their studies of his work with a distillation of the challenge he poses to existing sculptural norms. In his new essay on Wurm, Robert Pfaller characterizes the artist's oeuvre as a series of "pinpricks applied with devilish pleasure to a sedate, traditional concept of sculpture."[1] But when faced with Wurm's most recent work, this critical frame begins to flounder due to pieces like FAT HOUSE (2003), and the series of *Fat Cars,* which began in 2001. These life-size sculptures were produced at great expense, and through intensive labor they made a pronounced and immediate break from the artist's iconic *One Minute Sculptures* and *Instruc-*

ABRAHAM ORDEN is a writer based in Chicago.

tional Drawings. In their unexpected materiality—their plastic promise to exist forever—Wurm is seemingly producing the kind of sculpture that he has always protested, problematized, and undermined since his early "hanging sweater" sculptures of 1990.

These new works—the houses and the cars—were originally brought into the fold of the existing critical discourse by writers who have partially appealed to their fatness, a quality more directly contiguous with the artist's previous work (pieces like ME/ME FAT, 1993, and the *Curator/Imperator* series from the early 2000s.) In these photographs, the subjects—in the former case the artist himself, and in the latter a series of museum curators—are depicted first as themselves and then as themselves fattened. Weight gain is thus seen as yet another "sculptural moment," one just as sculptural as his "folded clothing hanging from a gallery wall" or "girl with a bouquet of flowers protruding from her trousers." This interpretation is enhanced by acknowledging a bit of cultural criticism: we know, for example, that Wurm associates the luxury of a fancy car with the wealth of the well fed. Nor will knowledge about the artist's politics help with WITTGENSTEINS RAUMKRÜMMUNG (Wittgenstein's Space Warp, 2005), a small statue of Wittgenstein lying on the floor and bent impossibly backwards, like a body possessed; nor with BUTTER BROT (Bread and Butter, 2006), an aluminum replica of a miniature house, sculpted in butter and smeared across a piece of rye bread. These works are clearly the product of a different mode of artistic practice, of an operation of thought unsounded by earlier critical distillations. The challenge is thus to relate Wurm's new work to the rest of what he has done.

It is most telling that in looking backward at Wurm's work one finds as great a disjunction as when looking forward. Before he began his *Dust* works in the early nineties, before his iconic *One Minute Sculptures* and his *Instructional Drawings*, Wurm was an obscure artist just out of school, making sculptures in a colloquial, somewhat exotic idiom totally out of keeping with the times (a quality that took great pains to cultivate). "This work was meant to be confrontational," he has said. "That was the era of Minimalism, of Conceptualism, of Land Art; you didn't see a single figure standing anywhere."[2] Reason enough, thought the young Wurm, to take up the figure in his own practice, for the idea was to "pose a challenge" to art's established hierarchy, and so adamant was his desire to do so that something needed only be considered "incorrect" by others for the young artist to take an interest in it.[3] Through his constant effort to position himself in exactly the wrong place, on the antipode of the zeitgeist, by the mid-eighties, Wurm had arrived at works like

BEGINNING WITH A SINGLE STEP

But this interpretation, though a good enough sort of patch-job, isn't robust enough to adhere these most recent works to older conceptions of his work. It cannot, for example, explain Wurm's thinking in making THE ARTIST WHO SWALLOWED THE WORLD (2006) and THE ARTIST WHO SWALLOWED THE WORLD WHEN IT WAS STILL A DISK (2006)—two life-size sculptures, human bodies that are radically distended like a cartoon snake that's just eaten something—the former possessing a giant bulging sphere, and the latter a similarly distorted disk.

UNTITLED (Lower Sepik, Newguinean sculpture, 1987) and UNTITLED (Colonie Française sculpture, 1987). In these totem-esque statues, human forms interact in uncanny ways with various containers, like an oil-can or a trash bin. The decidedly primitivist motif of these figurative pieces, which harkens back not to a primordial age so much as to a high modernist one, was, in this manner, defined negatively for the artist. This is not an anti-aesthetic exactly, but it is an aesthetic of the anti. "My work itself was conservative, a step backwards," Wurm has said, "but it was a provocative step."[4] Though this body of work gives no hint of the sculptural thresholds the artist's work would come to challenge, a concrete connection is made between the two through the reference to "stepping." Both the early figurative works and the later mature works begin with Wurm's disbelief—a thought given shape through the act of stepping away from the established norm. The young Wurm first took a relatively small step away from the aesthetic status quo of his milieu; in the more recent work he steps further out, putting himself at a skeptical distance from the history of sculpture.

If we replace our image of Wurm as an artist concerned with pushing sculpture to its ephemeral boundary with a picture of him as an artist concerned with this disbelieving step, we find the heterogeneous modes in which he has worked to be not only unified and historical but eminently contemporary. Wurm's early strategy of forcing himself into opposition as a means of searching out his place as an artist is itself the classic image of the avant-gardist, of the rebel, in other words, aspiring to overturn the existing order and replace it with his own. In this sense, Pfaller is right to identify Wurm as an artist of the high avant-garde.[5] But by the eighties, Wurm's deviation from that model revealed itself, causing the crucial change in his worldview to surface. For some time, these early primitivist works had done little, materially speaking, to advance Wurm's career, yet there did come a moment when he began to gain recognition for this body of work, when the tide of fashion turned and what the artist calls a "wave of nostalgia" produced a taste for the figurative in art once again.[6] For the classical avant-garde, such a moment would be considered a triumph, a coup by which the rebel-artist establishes him or her self at the top of the cultural order—the place, their faith had assured them, where they had always belonged. Not so for Wurm. It was at precisely this moment that he renounced the figurative, turning to the new problems he would generate with his *Dust* pieces. In so doing, he formalized his original gesture of stepping away from the consensus, and showed there to be no system to replace the existing order—only disbelief, which must be rigorously maintained even in the face of ostensible success.

With age, Wurm has evolved from provocateur into observant bystander; the most recent work represents the artist's turning of his questioning gaze away from art, and toward life itself. His pieces now exist as props he has planted in the world. This makes the sites of such ideological constructs not just apparent but pronouncedly strange, if not funny. The much-touted elements of mirth and mysticism in Wurm's work offer an important final point on his practice. The form of stepping away, of sustained disbelief, has proven itself to be thoroughly contemporary, but does this make it a thoroughly contemporary form of art? Is it not simply a form of critique? Wurm would perhaps not be so alone among his artist peers had he substituted the mode of the postmodern critic for the old revolutionary artist of the avant-garde, but when we look at a piece like TAKE YOUR MOST LOVED PHILOSOPHERS (2002) from the *Instructional Drawings* series, we can mark the distance he has put between himself and yet another trend. Here, the work's participants wedge classic philosophic treatises into the space between their arms and legs and simply hold them there. Wurm thus rebukes the encroachment of contemporary theory onto the field of artistic practice, an invasion he feels too many artists comply with: "Everybody [has been] throwing the names of these philosophers around, sounding so important and esoteric and intellectual. But that kind of art has a stronger connection to philosophy than to life itself, which strikes me as strange. So in my works with philosophy I have tried to rethink that connection, between texts and artwork, for instance. I would say [I am] making a little fun of it."[7] What is germane in this work to the question of critique is not only that Wurm takes

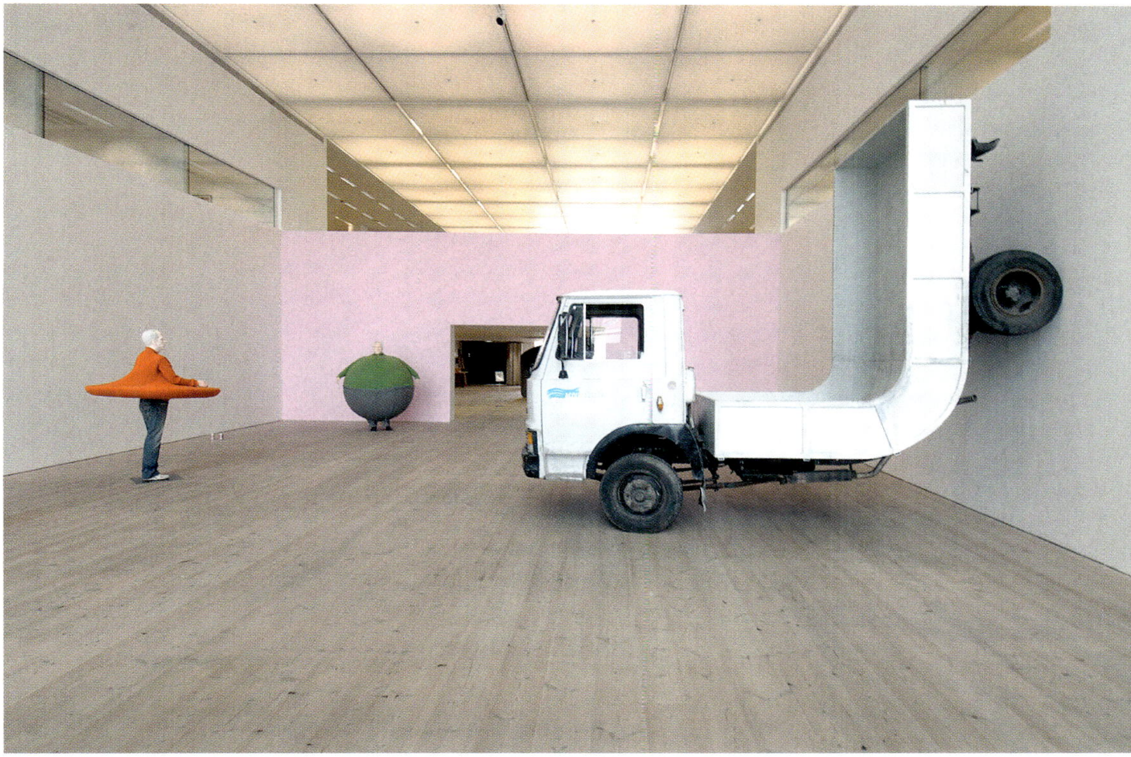

ERWIN WURM, from left to right: THE ARTIST WHO SWALLOWED THE WORLD WHEN IT WAS STILL A DISK, 2006 / THE ARTIST WHO SWALLOWED THE WORLD, 2006 / TRUCK, 2005 / von links nach rechts: DER KÜNSTLER, DER DIE WELT VERSCHLUCKTE ALS SIE NOCH EINE SCHEIBE WAR / DER KÜNSTLER, DER DIE WELT VERSCHLUCKTE / LASTWAGEN.

critical discourse—in the form of philosophy—as an object, thus declaring it other than art itself, but that the resulting work of art is so wholly un-rhetorical, so un-dialectical. Critique is mere rhetorical practice, bound to reason, ensnared by language. The work of art, by contrast—as this elegantly dumb piece shows us—cannot speak, but can only be. Art, then, may go where language may not; it may access life as discourse may not. A work like the pair of ARTISTS WHO SWALLOWED THE WORLD, seen in such a way, becomes Wurm's lyrical step away from the discourse of science. Again, these works do not amount to a constructed argument with science, which we are to "read" (for if it were, how bad it would be!); it is simply a distancing from that field, that kind of knowledge. The work's crucial, humorous spirit is the vehicle by which Wurm brings us in step with himself. Its whimsy ensures that we see the world—when looking at it through the lens of this piece—as he has seen it, as something for a moment totally alien, fundamentally other.

1) Robert Pfaller, "Splendor and Secrets of the Evident," *Erwin Wurm: The Artist Who Swallowed the World* (London: Hatje Cantz, 2006), p. 284.
2) "Twist and Shout: Erwin Wurm interviewed by Abraham Orden," *Erwin Wurm: The Artist Who Swallowed the World*, Addendum (Vienna: Museum Moderner Kunst Stiftung Ludwig, 2006), p. 25.
3) Ibid.
4) Ibid.
5) Pfaller (see note 1), p. 285.
6) Private correspondence with the artist.
7) "Twist and Shout" (see note 2), p. 29.

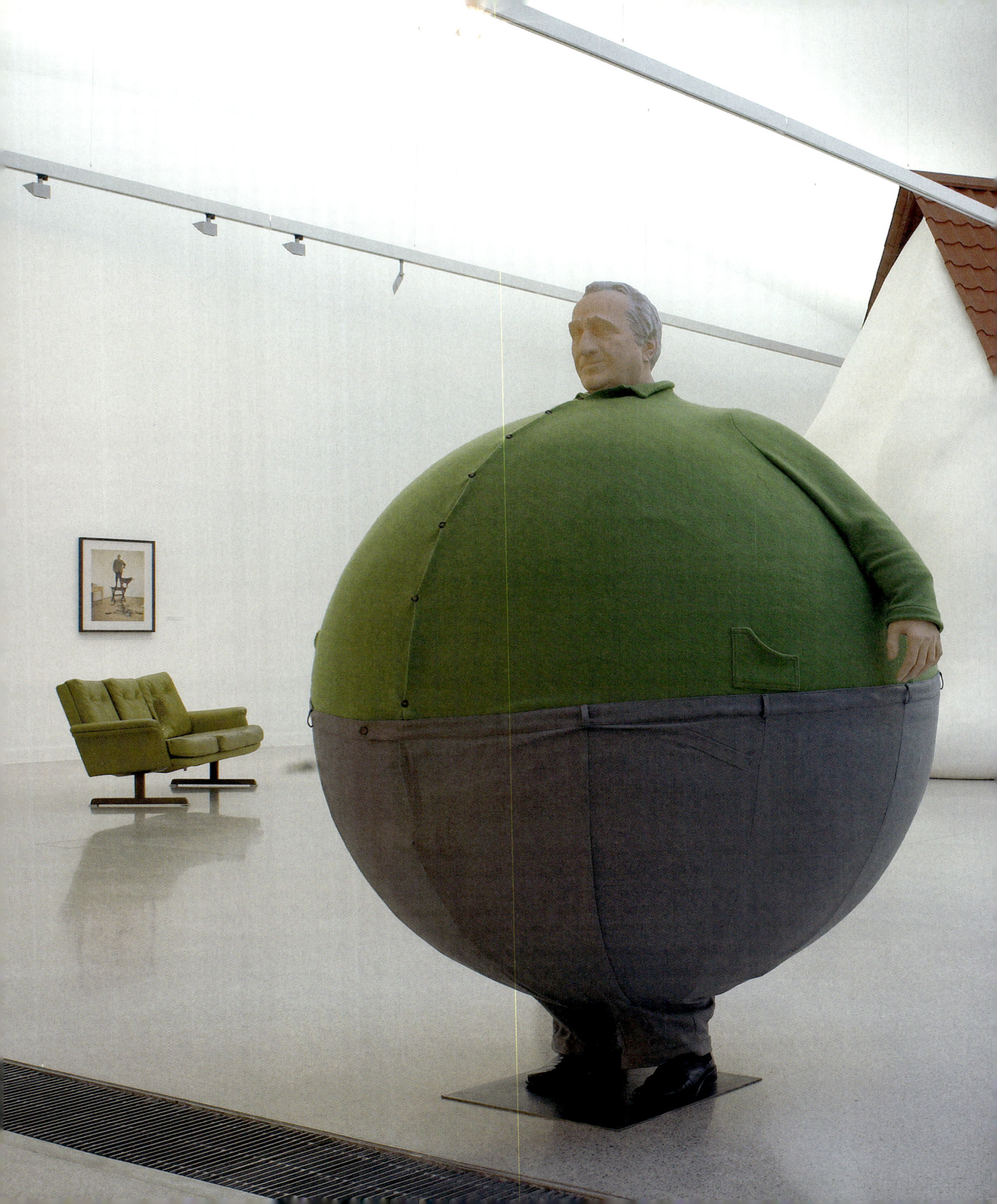

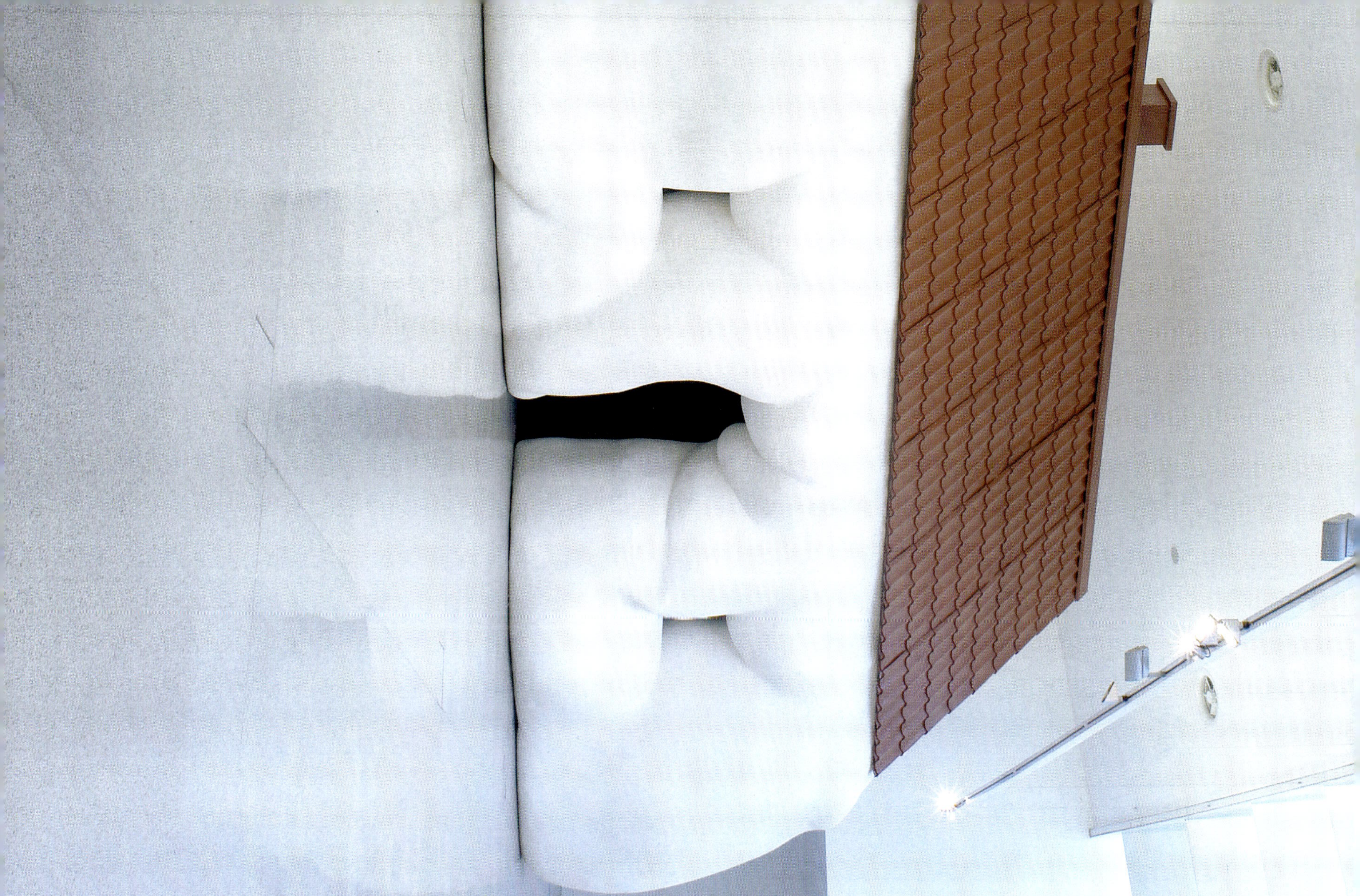

ERWIN WURM, THE ARTIST WHO SWALLOWED THE WORLD, 2006, mixed media, 74 $^{3}/_{4}$ x 55 x 55", FAT HOUSE, 2003, mixed media, 212 $^{1}/_{2}$ x 393 $^{3}/_{4}$ x 275 $^{1}/_{2}$" / DER KÜNSTLER, DER DIE WELT VERSCHLUCKTE, verschiedene Materialien, 190 x 140 x 140 cm, FETTES HAUS, verschiedene Materialien, 540 x 1000 x 700 cm. (PHOTO: BEATRIX FIALA)

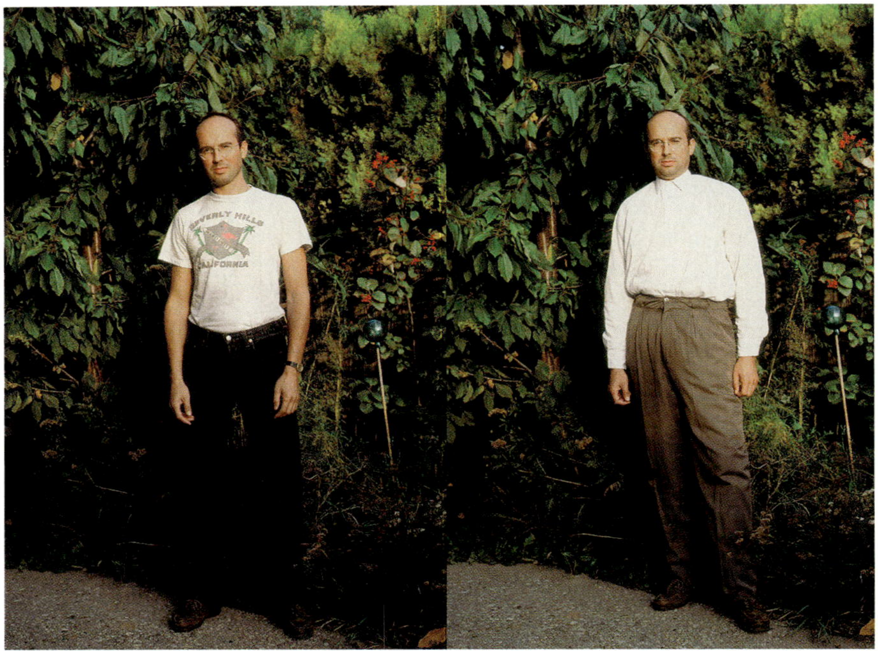

ERWIN WURM, ME / ME FAT, 1993, C-prints, each 70 3/4 x 45 1/4" / ICH / ICH FETT, C-Prints, je 180 x 115 cm.

ERWIN WURM

ABRAHAM ORDEN

Der Erwin Wurm, der in den vergangenen zehn Jahren bekannt geworden ist, wandelt sich rapide vor unseren Augen. Bis vor Kurzem reichte es für Kritiker in aller Regel, wenn sie Texte über seine Werke mit Wurms Infragestellung bestehender Normen der Skulptur begannen. In seinem neuen Aufsatz bezeichnet Robert Pfaller dessen Arbeiten als «Nadelstiche, die mit diebischer Freude gegen einen behäbigen, traditionellen Begriff von Skulptur geführt werden».[1] Angesichts der jüngsten Werke, Arbeiten wie FAT HOUSE (2003) und der 2001 begonnenen Serie *Fat Cars,* versagt dieses kritische Modell jedoch. Diese Plastiken in Originalgrösse, deren Produktion mit hohem Kosten- und Arbeitsaufwand verbunden war, markieren in ihrer unerwarteten Materialität das Versprechen dauerhafter Existenz, eine offenkundige und unmittelbare Abkehr von Wurms klassischen *One Minute Sculptures* und den *Instructional Drawings.* Hatte der Künstler seit seinen frühen hängenden Pulloverskulpturen der 90er Jahre nicht gerade gegen diese materielle Seite der Plastik polemisiert, sie problematisiert und untergraben?

ABRAHAM ORDEN ist Autor und lebt in Chicago.

Diese neuen Arbeiten, die Häuser und die Autos, wurden zunächst in den Rahmen des bestehenden Diskurses zurückgeholt, indem sich die Kritiker nicht zuletzt auf deren «Fettheit» beriefen, eine Eigenschaft, die an das frühere Schaffen des Künstlers anknüpft: Arbeiten wie ME/ME FAT (1993) und die *Curator/Imperator*-Serie der ersten Hälfte der 2000er Jahre. In diesen Photoarbeiten sind die dargestellten Personen – Erwin Wurm und verschiedene Museumskuratoren – als sie selbst und als ihr dickliches Double festgehalten; die «Gewichtszunahme» wird so zu einem weiteren «plastischen Moment» deklariert, ganz so wie seine gefalteten, an die Wand gehängten Kleidungsstücke oder das Mädchen mit dem aus den Hosen hervorragenden Blumenstrauss. Diese Interpretation gewinnt an Schlüssigkeit durch ein gewisses Mass an Kulturkritik, so verknüpft Wurm den Luxus eines schicken Wagens durchaus mit dem Reichtum der Wohlgenährten. Eine solche Lesart bietet, auch wenn sie die Sache halbwegs zusammen-

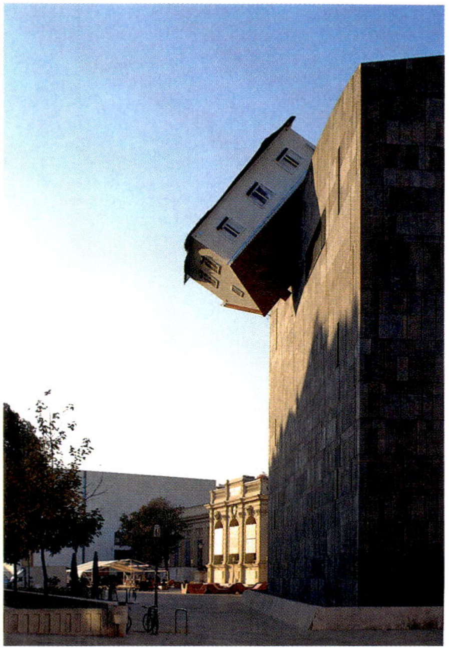

ERWIN WURM, HOUSE ATTACK, 2006, installation view at the Museum of Modern Art, Vienna / HAUS-ANGRIFF, Installationsansicht Museum Moderner Kunst, Wien. (PHOTO: LISA RASTL)

SCHRITT FÜR SCHRITT

hält, keinen hinreichenden Bogen, um die jüngsten Arbeiten mit dem Konzept der älteren Arbeiten zu verbinden. Sie kann zum Beispiel nicht das Denken erklären, das Arbeiten wie THE ARTIST WHO SWALLOWED THE WORLD (Der Künstler, der die Welt verschluckte, 2006) und THE ARTIST WHO SWALLOWED THE WORLD WHEN IT WAS STILL A DISK (Der Künstler, der die Welt verschluckte, als sie noch eine Scheibe war, 2006) zugrunde liegt – zwei lebensgrosse Menschenfiguren mit starken Ausbuchtungen, einer riesigen kugelförmigen Schwellung und einer überzeichneten scheibenförmigen Ausdehnung, wie man sie aus Karikaturen von Schlangen kennt, die gerade etwas verschlungen haben. Ebenso wenig hilfreich ist sie bei WITTGENSTEINS RAUMKRÜMMUNG (2005), einer kleinen Statue Wittgensteins, der in einer unnatürlich – wie besessen wirkenden – nach hinten gekrümmten Haltung auf dem Boden liegt. Das Gleiche gilt für BUTTERBROT (2006), eine Nachbildung in Aluminium eines in Butter modellierten und über eine Scheibe Schwarzbrot gestrichenen Miniaturhauses. Diese Arbeiten sind offensichtlich Produkte einer veränderten künstlerischen Praxis, einer bisher nicht erfassten Denkweise. Es gilt also, die neueren Arbeiten mit dem bisherigen Werk in Verbindung zu bringen.

Vielsagend ist, dass wir beim Blick auf Wurms zurückliegendes Schaffen eine ebenso grosse Verschiebung feststellen wie beim Blick nach vorne. Bevor er in der ersten Hälfte der 90er Jahre – vor

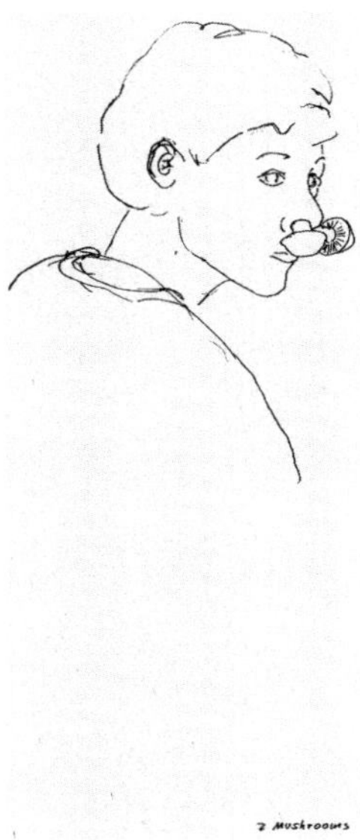

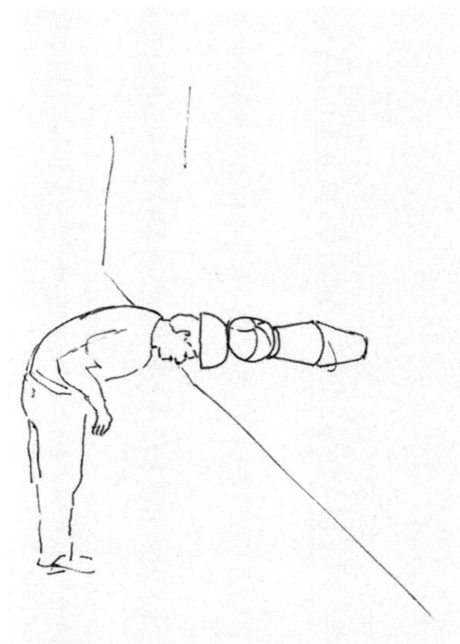

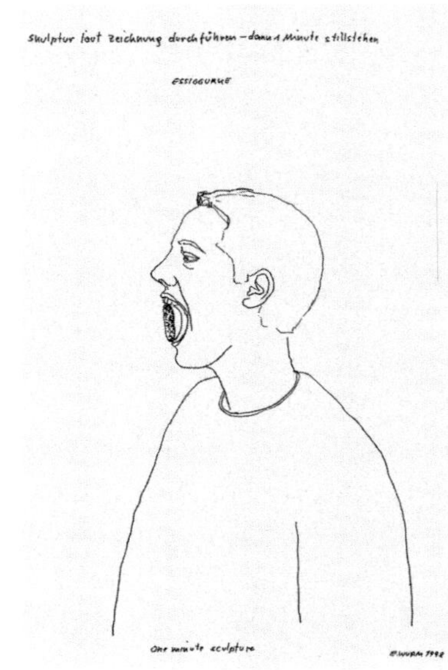

ERWIN WURM, 2 MUSHROOMS, One Minute Sculpture, 1998, felt pen, 11 3/4 x 8 1/4" / 2 PILZE, Filzstift, 29,7 x 21 cm.

ERWIN WURM, 2 BUCKETS, BALL, BOWL, One Minute Sculpture, 1997, felt pen, 12 3/8 x 8 1/2" / 2 KÜBEL, BALL, SCHÜSSEL, Filzstift, 31,4 x 21,5 cm.

ERWIN WURM, PICKLE, One Minute Sculpture, 1998, felt pen, 11 3/4 x 8 1/4" / ESSIGGURKE, Filzstift, 29,7 x 21 cm.

seinen klassischen *One Minute Sculptures* und den *Instructional Drawings* – seine *Staub*-Arbeiten begann, war Wurm ein unbekannter Künstler, der gerade sein Studium abgeschlossen hatte und Plastiken schuf, deren informelle, leicht exotisch angehauchte Formensprache ganz und gar unzeitgemäss war, eine Eigenschaft, die zu kultivieren einer besonderen Anstrengung bedurfte. Diese Werke sollten «eine Gegenposition markieren. Es war die Zeit von Minimalismus, Konzeptkunst, Land Art; man sah keine Plastik irgendwo herumstehen».[2] Grund genug, dachte der junge Wurm, um die Figur in seine eigene künstlerische Arbeit einzubeziehen. Es ging ihm darum, zu «provozieren», die bestehende Werteordnung in Frage zu stellen, dieses Anliegen war ihm so wichtig, dass etwas als «nicht korrekt» Empfundenes reichte, um das Interesse des jungen Künstlers auf sich zu ziehen.[3] Dieses Bemühen, genau die falsche Position – in Opposition zum Zeitgeist – zu beziehen, führte Wurm Mitte der 80er Jahre zu Arbeiten wie UNTITLED (1987, mit einer Skulptur aus Neuguinea) und UNTITLED (1987, mit einer Figur aus den ehemaligen französischen Kolonien). Bei diesen Arbeiten stehen Werke primitiver Kunst in einem nicht nachvollziehbaren Zusammenhang mit Behältern wie einem Ölkanister oder einem Abfalleimer. Das entschieden Primitivistische verweist weniger auf die Uranfänge der Kunst als auf die Epoche der Klassischen Moderne und war in diesem Zusammenhang negativ konnotiert: Es geht nicht so sehr um eine Antiästhetik als vielmehr um eine Ästhetik des «Gegen». «Mein Werk war als solches», so Wurm, «natürlich konservativ, ein Rückschritt, aber ein provokanter Rückschritt.»[4] Obwohl diese Werkgruppe noch nicht erkennen lässt, welche Grenzen der Skulptur sein späteres Schaffen in Fra-

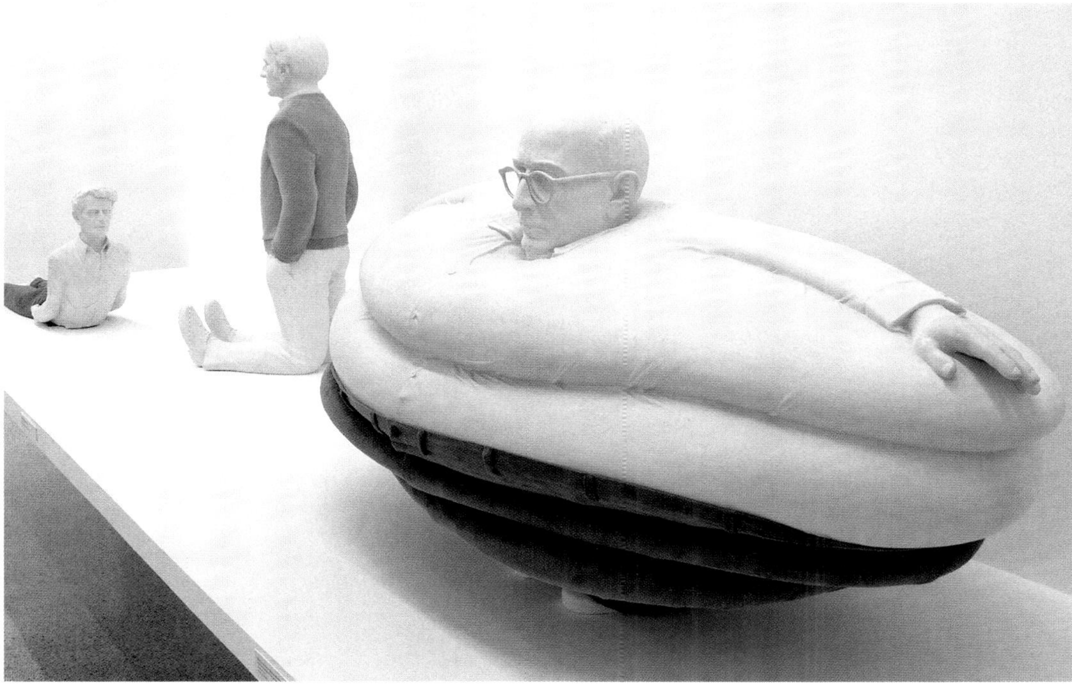

ERWIN WURM, from left to right: WITTGENSTEIN'S SPACE WARP, 2005 / DELEUZE KNEELING DOWN, 2006 / ADORNO AS OLIVER HARDY IN THE BOHEMIAN GIRL (1936), AND THE BURDEN OF DESPERATION, 2006 / von links nach rechts: WITTGENSTEINS RAUMKRÜMMUNG / DELEUZE NIEDERKNIEND / ADORNO ALS OLIVER HARDY IN THE BOHEMIAN GIRL (1936) UND DIE LAST DER VERZWEIFLUNG. (PHOTO: BEATRIX FIALA)

ge stellen sollte, ergibt dieses Bild des «Schritts» ein konkretes Bindeglied zwischen beiden. Die frühen figurativen Arbeiten und das spätere Schaffen haben beide ihren Ausgangspunkt in Wurms Skepsis, einer Denkweise, die im Akt des Zurücktretens, der Distanzierung von der etablierten Norm ihren konkreten Ausdruck findet. Der junge Wurm distanzierte sich zunächst in einem vergleichsweise kleinen Schritt vom ästhetischen Status quo seines Milieus; bei seinen jüngeren Arbeiten geht er auf skeptische Distanz zur Geschichte der Plastik schlechthin.

Wenn wir unser Bild von Wurm – einer, der an die flüchtigen Grenzen der Plastik rührt – ersetzen durch das Bild eines Künstlers, der an dieser skeptischen Distanz arbeitet, so erkennen wir nicht nur das Einheitliche und Historische, sondern auch das überaus Zeitgemässe der heterogenen Prinzipien seiner künstlerischen Arbeit. Wurms frühe Strategie, seinen Platz als Künstler aus einer Opposition heraus zu finden, entspricht dem klassischen Bild des Avantgardisten, des Rebellen, der die bestehende Ordnung umzustürzen und durch seine eigene zu ersetzen sucht. In diesem Sinn bezeichnet Robert Pfaller Wurm mit Recht als einen Künstler der klassischen Avantgarde.[5] Aber in den 80er Jahren wurde klar, dass er diesem Modell nicht mehr entsprach, und das entscheidend Andere seiner Weltauffassung trat zu Tage. Die frühen primitivistischen Arbeiten hatten, in einem materiellen Sinn, eine Zeit lang so gut wie keine Auswirkung auf Wurms Künstlerlaufbahn, irgendwann jedoch kam der Punkt, wo ihm diese Werkgruppe Anerkennung einbrachte, da im Zuge

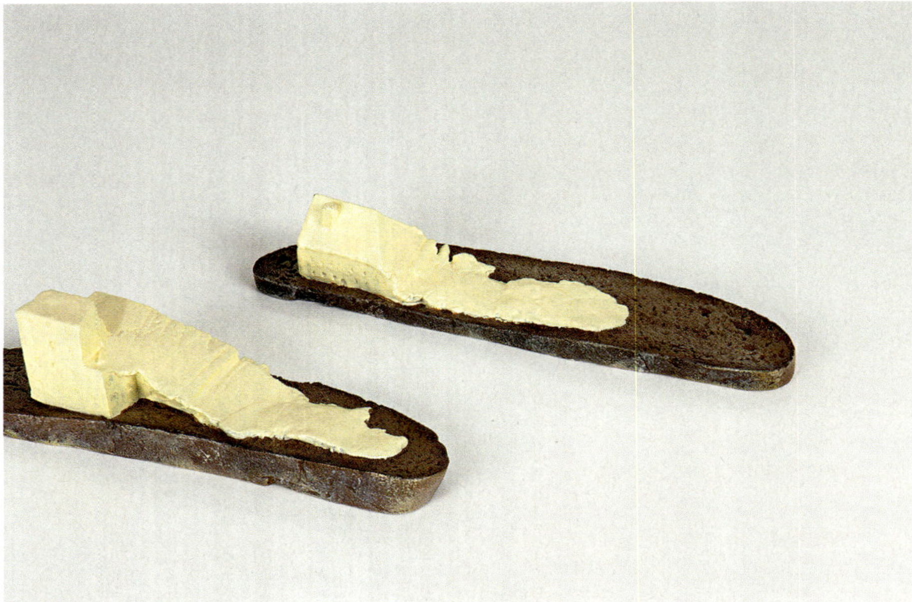

ERWIN WURM, BUTTERBROT I (Bread and Butter), 2006, aluminum, paint, 3 x 12 1/2 x 3" / bemaltes Aluminium, 7,5 x 32 x 7,5 cm / BUTTERBROT II , 2006, aluminum, paint, 2 1/2 x 12 1/2 x 3" / bemaltes Aluminium, 6,5 x 32 x 7,5 cm.

einer Trendwende und einer, wie der Künstler es nennt, «Welle der Nostalgie» das Figurative in der Kunst wieder an Wertschätzung gewann.[6)] Im Fall der klassischen Avantgarde gälte ein solcher Moment als Triumph, als ein Coup, im Zuge dessen der Künstlerrebell sich ganz oben in der kulturellen Rangordnung etabliert, dort, wo er seiner Überzeugung nach hingehörte. Nicht so bei Wurm. Zu diesem Zeitpunkt vollzog er eine Abkehr vom Figurativen und wandte sich neuen Fragen zu, die er mit seinen *Staub* Arbeiten aufwerfen sollte. Er formalisierte seine ursprüngliche Geste des Zurücktretens vom Konsens und machte klar, dass es für ihn kein System gibt, welches er an die Stelle der bestehenden Ordnung setzen wollte: Es gibt nur Skepsis, die es, selbst angesichts scheinbaren Erfolges, rigoros beizubehalten gilt.

Mit zunehmendem Alter hat sich Wurm vom Provokateur zu einem aufmerksamen Beoachter entwickelt; mt seinen jüngsten Werken wendet er seinen forschenden Blick von der Kunst ab und dem Leben als solches zu. Diese Arbeiten haben die Form von Requisiten, die Wurm in die Welt setzt, um Orte, an denen ideologische Konstrukte zu Tage getreten sind, zu markieren, sodass sie etwas ausgesprochen Sonderbares, wenn nicht gar Komisches erhalten. Die viel zitierten Elemente der Heiterkeit und des Mystizismus in Wurms Werk markieren einen wichtigen Punkt im Hinblick auf seine künstlerische Praxis. Das Prinzip des Zurücktretens, der anhaltenden Skepsis hat sich als zutiefst zeitgemäss erwiesen, doch ergibt es auch eine zutiefst zeitgenössische Kunst? Ist dies nicht einfach nur ein Art der Kritik? Hätte Wurm die Haltung des postmodernen Kritikers gegen die des «traditionellen» revolutionären Künstlers der Avantgarde ausgetauscht, so stünde er im Kreise seiner Künstlerkollegen vielleicht nicht alleine da. Jedoch eine Arbeit wie TAKE YOUR MOST LOVED PHILOSOPHERS (Nimm deinen liebsten Philosophen, 2002) aus der Serie der *Instructional Drawings* erlaubt es uns zu ermessen, welche Distanz er zwischen sich und allfällige Trends gelegt hat. Bei diesen Arbeiten klemmen die Mitwirkenden philosophische Standardwerke zwischen Arme und Beine und halten sie dort fest. Wurm prangert damit das Übergreifen zeitgenössischer Theorie in den Bereich der Kunst an, einen Übergriff, dem sich seiner Ansicht nach allzu viele Künstler fügen: «Die meisten dieser Philosophen werden von Kunstkritikern und Künstlern dauernd verwendet, als wäre dies die einzige Art über Kunst zu sprechen. Die meisten dieser Autoren hatten oder haben aber gar kein Interesse an der Kunst an sich. In meinen Arbeiten mit der Philosophie habe ich also versucht, dieses Verhältnis neu zu fassen, das Verhältnis von Texten und Kunst zum Beispiel.»[7] Das Wichtige an diesen Arbeiten in Bezug auf die Frage der Kritik ist nicht nur, dass Wurm den kritischen Diskurs – in Form der Philosophie – zum Gegenstand macht und ihn damit als etwas Anderes denn Kunst per se hinstellt, sondern dass das Kunstwerk, das sich daraus ergibt, ganz auf Rhetorik verzichtet, ja, wenn man so will, undialektisch ist. Kritik ist eine rein rhetorische Praxis, in der Sprache gefangen und an die Vernunft gebunden. Das Kunstwerk dagegen ist, wie uns diese sprachlose Arbeit auf elegante Weise vorführt, stumm: Es sagt nichts, sondern ist einfach nur. Die Kunst hat also Möglichkeiten, die der Sprache nicht offenstehen, sie hat einen Zugang zum Leben, der dem Diskurs verwehrt ist. In Arbeiten wie den beiden ARTISTS WHO SWALLOWED THE WORLD kristallisiert sich, so gesehen, Wurms lyrischer Schritt zurück vom Diskurs der Wissenschaft. Sie laufen, um es noch einmal zu betonen, nicht auf eine strukturierte Auseinandersetzung mit der Wissenschaft hinaus, die wir «lesen» sollten (es wäre wirklich schlimm, wenn dem so wäre), sondern sie sind schlicht und einfach eine Distanzierung von diesem Bereich, von dieser Art von Wissen. Die Komik der Arbeit, ein entscheidender Aspekt, ist das Vehikel, durch das Wurm uns auf seine Sicht einschwört. Ihr Humor sorgt dafür, dass wir die Welt durch die Brille dieser Arbeit so sehen, wie er sie gesehen hat, nämlich als etwas einen Augenblick lang völlig Fremdes und ganz und gar Anderes.

(Übersetzung: Bram Opstelten)

1) Robert Pfaller, «Glanz und Geheimnis der Evidenzen», in: Addendum zu *Erwin Wurm: The Artist Who Swallowed the World*, Hatje Cantz, Ostfildern 2006, S. 32.
2) «Twist and Shout: Ein Gespräch zwischen Erwin Wurm und Abraham Orden», in: Addendum zu *Erwin Wurm: The Artist Who Swallowed the World* (Wien: Museum Moderner Kunst Stiftung Ludwig, Wien 2006), S. 23.
3) Ebenda.
4) Ebenda.
5) Robert Pfaller, op. cit. (Anm. 1), S. 32.
6) Korrespondenz mit dem Autor.
7) «Twist and Shout» (Anm. 2), S. 28.

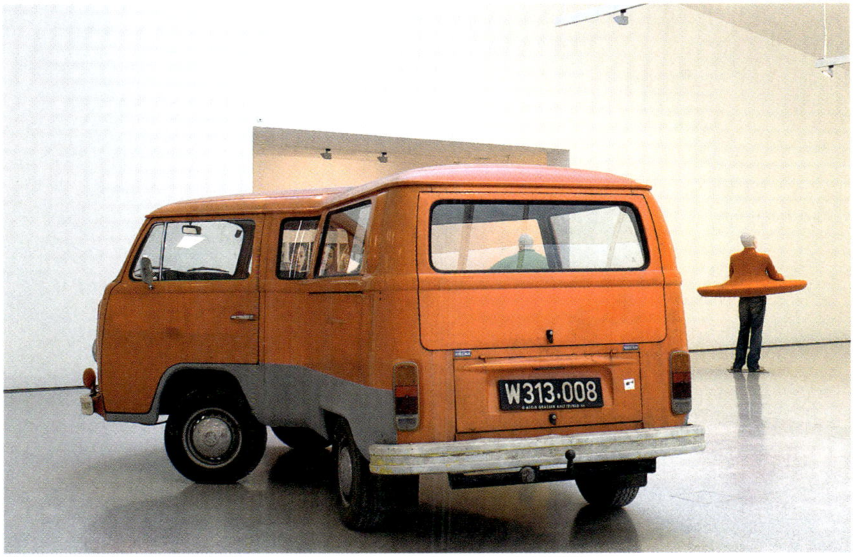

ERWIN WURM, TELEKINETICALLY BENT VW-VAN, 2006, 82 3/4 x 90 1/2 x 173 1/4" / TELEKINETISCH GEBOGENER VW-BUS, 130 x 230 x 440 cm.

Vito Acconci

MARJORIE PERLOFF

CONCEPTUAL POETRY: OLD AND NEW

Before conceptual art became prominent in the late 1960s, there was already, so Craig Dworkin has suggested in his "Anthology of Conceptual Writing,"[1] a form of writing identifiable as conceptual poetry, although that term was not normally used to discuss the chance-generated texts of John Cage and Jackson Mac Low or the "word events" of George Brecht and La Monte Young. In his Introduction to the anthology, Dworkin makes an interesting case for a "non-expressive poetry," "a poetry of intellect rather than emotion," in which "the substitutions at the heart of metaphor and image were replaced by the direct presentation of language itself, with [Wordsworth's] 'spontaneous overflow [of powerful feelings]' supplanted by meticulous procedure and exhaustively logical process."

The first poet in Dworkin's alphabetically arranged anthology is Vito Acconci, whose early "poetry," most of it previously unpublished, has now been edited and assembled, again by Dworkin, for a hefty, 411-page volume called *Language to Cover a Page*.[2] I place poetry in quotes here because, strictly speaking, Acconci's word texts—constraint-based lists, dictionary games, performance scores, or parodic translations—are not so much poems as they are, in the Wittgensteinian sense, complex language games, in which the page has not yet been replaced by the video screen, the tape length, or the gallery space. Indeed, as Dworkin argues in an earlier piece on Acconci for *October*, there was no sharp break between Acconci the poet and Acconci the video artist, performer, and recently architect and designer.[3] On the contrary, the later work is best understood as the continuation of the earlier by other means. And if this point is granted, then the writing of the sixties takes on added importance: it consti-

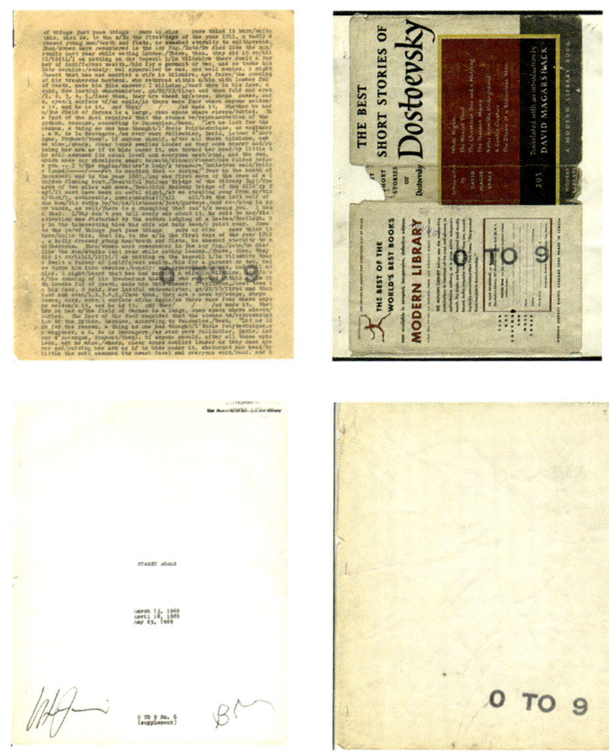

(clockwise, from top left / im Uhrzeigersinn, links oben beginnend) 0 TO 9, issue No. 3, January 1969 / No. 4, June 1968 / No. 5, January 1969 / No. 6, 1969, edited by Vito Acconci & Bernadette Mayer, 8 1/2 x 11" each / 0 BIS 9, Ausgaben 3, 4, 5 6, herausgegeben von Vito Acconci & Bernadette Mayer, je 21,6 x 28 cm. (PHOTO: JAMES HOFF)

MARJORIE PERLOFF is Sadie D. Patek Professor of Humanities Emerita at Stanford University. She is the author of many books on poetry and visual arts, including *The Futurist Moment: Avant-Garde, Avant Guerre, and the Language of Rupture*; *Radical Artifice: Writing Poetry in the Age of Media*; and *Poetry On & Off the Page*.

tutes, so to speak, the first act of the artist's complex meditation on the ability of language, whether verbal, visual, aural, or kinetic, to represent emotion and intellect.

To some degree, this preoccupation allies Acconci to Fluxus, but his is a very different trajectory from George Brecht's or Yoko Ono's. Born to Italian immigrant parents in 1940, Acconci grew up in the Bronx, graduated from Holy Cross College in Wooster, Massachusetts in 1962 and the University of Iowa Writing Workshop in 1964. The latter was, in Acconci's day, the place to go for initiation into the poetry establishment: Acconci took a course on translation from Mark Strand, and an exact contemporary of his at Iowa was Charles Wright, whose lyric of the period included lines like the following:

The moon, like a dead heart, cold and unstartable, hangs by a thread
At the earth's edge,
Unfaithful at last, splotching the ferns and the pink shrubs.[4]

Nothing could be more unlike Wright's intense, concrete imagistic evocation of the moon over Stone Canyon than Acconci's "READ THIS WORD" (1969):

READ THIS WORD THEN READ THIS WORD READ THIS WORD NEXT READ THIS WORD
NOW SEE ONE WORD SEE ONE WORD NEXT SEE ONE WORD NOW AND THEN SEE ONE
WORD AGAIN LOOK AT THREE WORDS HERE LOOK AT THREE WORDS NOW LOOK AT
THREE WORDS NOW TOO TAKE IN FIVE WORDS AGAIN TAKE IN FIVE WORDS SO TAKE
IN FIVE WORDS DO IT NOWSEE THESE WORDS AT A GLANCE SEE THESE WORDS AT
THIS GLANCE AT THIS GLANCE HOLD THIS LINE IN VIEW HOLD THIS LINE IN
ANOTHER VIEW AND IN A THIRD VIEW SPOT SEVEN LINES AT ONCE THEN TWICE
THEN THRICE THEN A FOURTH TIME A FIFTH A SIXTH A SEVENTH AN EIGHTH[5]

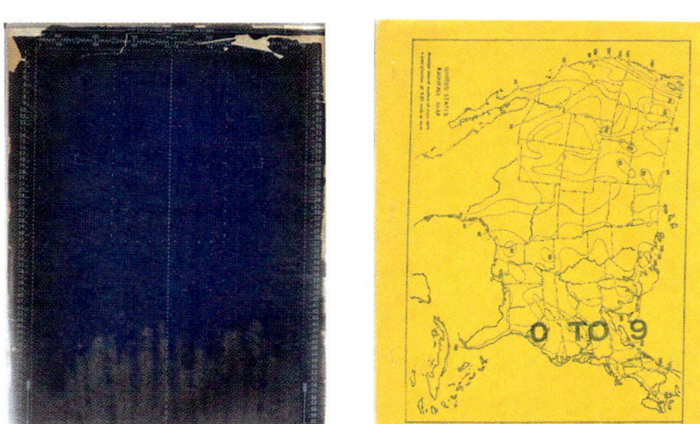

0 TO 9, issue No. 1, April, 1967 and No. 2, August, 1967, edited by Vito Acconci & Bernadette Mayer, 8 1/2 x 11" each / 0 BIS 9, Ausgabe 4, herausgegeben von Vito Acconci & Bernadette Mayer, je 21,6 x 28 cm. (PHOTO: JAMES HOFF)

Here the poet tracks the actual process of reading each word, one at a time, until they literally complete the eighth line. Arbitrary as these "instructions" seem, with their permutation of "next," "now," "then," and "again," and their morphing of "read" into "see," and then into "look at," "take in," and "hold this line in view," the fact is, as one learns when one tries to reproduce the poem, that Acconci had to work hard, adding spaces so as to produce a justified right margin and make eight, so to speak, equal eight.

Such early experiments paved the way for the publication of *0 TO 9*, the stapled mimeograph journal Acconci edited together with the poet Bernadette Mayer between 1967 and 1969. *0 TO 9*, which went through seven issues, featured poets like Clark Coolidge and Ted Berrigan, Fluxus performers like

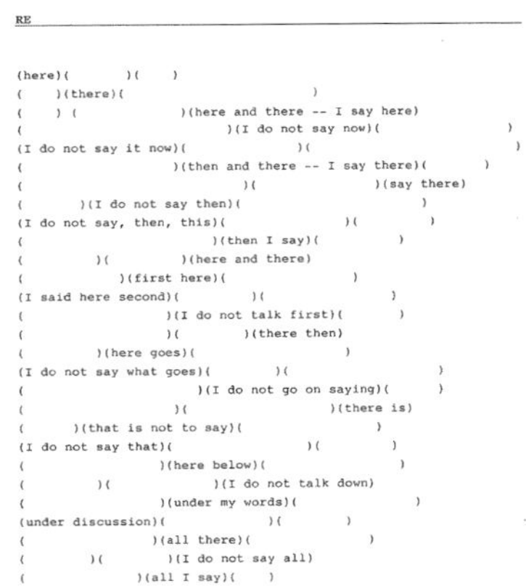
```
RE

(here)(          )(     )
(     )(there)(                              )
(     ) (                )(here and there -- I say here)
(                              )(I do not say now)(                )
(I do not say it now)(                  )(                              )
(                         )(then and there -- I say there)(         )
(                                 )(                  )(say there)
(         )(I do not say then)(                            )
(I do not say, then, this)(                    )(          )
(                               )(then I say)(            )
(          )(           )(here and there)
(              )(first here)(                  )
(I said here second)(           )(                  )
(                        )(I do not talk first)(        )
(                        )(          )(there then)
(          )(here goes)(                        )
(I do not say what goes)(         )(                  )
(                            )(I do not go on saying)(        )
(                         )(                    )(there is)
(       )(that is not to say)(                    )
(I do not say that)(                     )(         )
(                       )(here below)(                    )
(          )(             )(I do not talk down)
(                       )(under my words)(                 )
(under discussion)(                 )(          )
(                      )(all there)(                 )
(         )(          )(I do not say all)
(                    )(all I say)(     )
```

VITO ACCONCI, RE, 1969, type on paper / Schrift auf Papier. (PHOTO: VITO ACCONCI STUDIO)

Dick Higgins and Emmett Williams, and artists like Sol LeWitt, Adrian Piper, Dan Graham, and Robert Smithson. *0 TO 9* published Jackson Mac Low's first poem series governed by chance operations, the "Biblical Poems." Recognizing the journal's importance, the small but increasingly important Ugly Duckling Presse (Lost Literature Series, edited by James Hoff and Ryan Haley), based in Brooklyn, has just reprinted the entire run (736 pages) in one volume priced at $ 45.

Why the reprint of *0 TO 9* and the publication of Acconci's early writings at this particular moment? Why the new interest in the material word, in proceduralism, dictionary definition, and a dogged literalism that refuses the metaphoric mode of mainstream lyrics or the mimeticism of so much Establishment painting and photography? One reason, surely, is the current nostalgia for the Bohemia of the late sixties and early seventies, for the moment when poets and visual artists were still likely to live in Village walk-ups and Brooklyn tenements, defying not only the bourgeois world of business, but also the university. The tolerance and eclecticism of our own art world, which embraces abstraction as well as hyperrealism, neo-pop as well as austere conceptualism, was still unheard of: the *0 TO 9* poets were intentionally outrageous and confrontational, defying even the "advanced" aesthetic of Black Mountain and the Beats. Poetry, Acconci declared, contra Charles Olson's poetics of process, should "use language to cover a space rather than dis-cover a meaning."[6] And the lyric "I" was replaced by an "I" in dialogue with, and often shaped by, the "you" who confronts the words spoken or the action taken in a given performance, whether live or on video.

A second, more specific source of Acconci's current appeal is surely his anticipation of the new digital poetics. In recent years, we have witnessed electronically generated text that falls under the rubric of what Kenneth Goldsmith, its chief proponent, has dubbed "uncreative writing." In such writing—witness Goldsmith's own *Day*,[7] made by reproducing, word for word, and from first page to last, an entire issue of the *New York Times*—appropriation is all, or is it? In transforming newsprint into digital text and refusing to discriminate between headlines and snatches of advertising copy, between front-page article using oversized font and the tiny Dow Jones numbers, the *Times* becomes curiously unrecognizable. Goldsmith has argued that in the information age, the poetic function is not to produce new writing—we have too much already—but to force us to see what the language environment we live in looks and feels like, to make it strange.

According to Dworkin, Goldsmith produced *Day* and related texts without any familiarity of Acconci's early writings, most of them unpublished and hence quite unknown.[8] How uncanny, therefore, that thirty-five years before Goldsmith produced his book *The Weather*,[9] a transcription of a year's worth (December 21, 2002–December 20, 2003) of hourly weather bulletins on WINS (1010), New York's all-news radio station, Acconci should have produced a numbered text called "Act 3, Scene 4," that begins like this:

1. The sun rises today, Thursday, December 26, 1968.
2. At 7:18 A.M., sets at 4:34 P.M., and will rise
3. tomorrow at 7:18 A.M. The moon sets today at 11:49
4. rises at 12:10 P.M. tomorrow, and will set tomorrow
5. at 12:38 A.M. Warmer weather and clear to cloudy skies
6. will cover most of the eastern portion of the nation
7. today while snow is expected to fall on the western
8. lake region, the Northern Plains States, and from
9. the upper Mississippi Valley to the plateau region. Showers[10]

And it goes on in this vein for another ten pages, the sober report cut up into 350 more or less equal line lengths in all. Related texts that follow are based on the New York City Report, as heard on the telephone recorded at a particular moment. And these experiments pave the way for such early video pieces as FILLING UP SPACE (1970, 3 min.), in which, against the backdrop of a brick wall, the artist enters and walks from one side to the other, back and forth, row after row.

What interests me here, however, is less the similarity between "Act 3, Scene 4" and Goldsmith's *The Weather* than the difference. By taking his language not from the straightforward facts in the newspaper but from radio, where the announcer must jazz up the weather report so as to attract listeners, Goldsmith gives weather reporting an entirely different spin. For example:

Uh, it's that old Christmas song, "Let it Snow, let it Snow," not so this afternoon. A lot of cloud cover, twenty-six degrees but see, this is just one piece of our latest storm system. It's actually going to move farther away tonight, so the clouds part company, low fifteen to twenty, then clouds quick to return tomorrow.[11]

Goldsmith further thickens the plot by giving each one-minute broadcast one paragraph, arranging the paragraphs in a seasonal cycle with four chapters, "Winter," "Spring," "Summer," "Autumn," and—in a curious clinamen—omitting certain days (when he was on holiday or out of town), so that the prediction made in one broadcast is not followed up by the next. Indeed, even when the days recorded are consecutive, the weather forecast is often wrong. And then, in the spring of 2002, the weather news reported suddenly emanates from Baghdad, for the Iraq War has broken out. So *The Weather* turns out to be an ironic narrative.

Found text, we discover, can mean many different things, and not all appropriations are equally interesting or amusing. Digital recording and scanning, not yet available to Acconci in 1968, has made a great difference. All the more reason why *Language to Cover a Page* is such a timely and intriguing book. It provides the missing link between the first forays into a non-representational, non-expressivist poetics and its current incarnations. By the time he was thirty, Acconci seems to have recognized that body language, this time covering the video screen rather than the page, created a more satisfactory relationship between himself and his audience than the straightforward author–reader relationship could accomplish. But the verbal stage, as presented here, was never abandoned; it was merely incorporated into the larger space of such masterpieces as THE RED TAPES (1976).

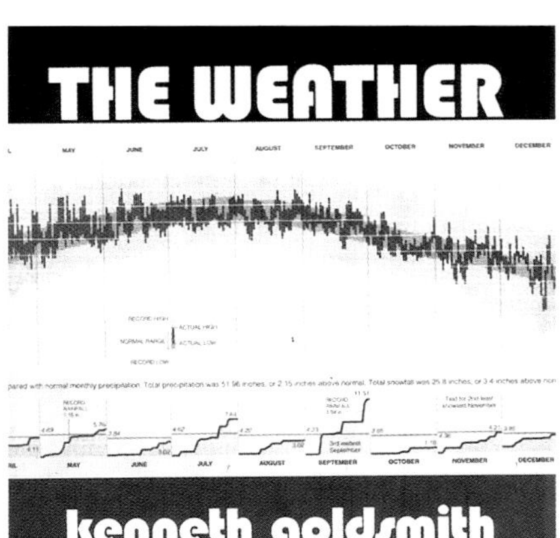

KENNETH GOLDSMITH, The Weather, 2004,
book cover, Make Now Press / DAS WETTER, Buchumschlag.

1) http://www.ubu.com/concept/index.html
2) Craig Dworkin, ed., *Language to Cover a Page: The Early Writings of Vito Acconci* (Cambridge: MIT Press, Writing Art Series, 2006).
3) Craig Dworkin, *October* 95, Winter (Cambridge: MIT, 2001), pp. 91–113.
4) Charles Wright, "Stone Canyon Nocturne," *Country Music: Selected Early Poems* (Middletown, CT: Wesleyan University Press, 1982), p. 139.
5) Craig Dworkin, ed., *Language to Cover a Page* (see note 2), p. 1[illegible]1.
6) Vito Acconci, "Early Work: Movement over a Page," *Avalanche* 6 (Fall 1972), p. 4.
7) Kenneth Goldsmith, *Day* (Barrington, VT, The Figures, 2003).
8) Craig Dworkin, ed., *Language to Cover a Page* (see note 2), p. xvi.
9) Kenneth Goldsmith, *The Wheater* (Los Angeles: Make Now Press, 2005).
10) Craig Dworkin, ed., *Language to Cover a Page* (see note 2), pp. 388–389.
11) Kenneth Goldsmith (see note 9), p. 26.

Vito Acconci

MARJORIE PERLOFF

ALTE UND NEUE KONZEPTUELLE POESIE

Schon bevor die Concept Art in den späten 60er Jahren in den Vordergrund trat, gab es, so Craig Dworkin in seiner «Anthology of Conceptual Writing» für Ubu Web, eine als konzeptuelle Lyrik identifizierbare literarische Ausdrucksform, auch wenn dieser Begriff auf die zufallsgenerierten Texte von John Cage und Jackson Mac Low oder die «word events» von George Brecht und La Monte Young normalerweise nicht angewandt wurde.[1] In seiner Einführung zur Ubu-Web-Anthologie gibt Dworkin eine interessante Darstellung einer nicht expressiven Dichtung, «einer Dichtung des Intellekts statt der Emotion», in der «die Metaphern und Bildern zugrunde liegenden Substitutionen durch die unmittelbare Präsentation der Sprache selbst ersetzt wurden; an die Stelle des ‹spontanen Überlaufens [starker Gefühle]› (William Wordsworth, 1770–1850) trat das akribische Verfahren und der detaillierte logische Prozess.»

Der erste Dichter in Dworkins alphabetisch angeordneter Anthologie konzeptuellen Schreibens ist Vito Acconci, dessen bislang grösstenteils unveröffentlichte frühe «Dichtung» jetzt ebenfalls von Dworkin unter dem Titel *Language to Cover a Page* in einem wuchtigen, 411 Seiten starken Band in der Writing

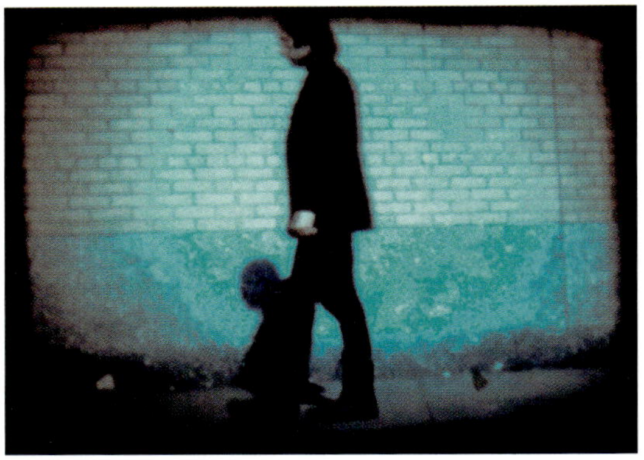

VITO ACCONCI, FILLING UP SPACE / DEN RAUM AUSFÜLLEND, 1970, *Super-8 film*. (PHOTO: VITO ACCONCI STUDIO)

Art Series der MIT Press zusammengestellt und ediert worden ist.[2] Ich setze das Wort Dichtung hier in Anführungszeichen, weil Acconcis Worttexte – constraint-basierte Listen, Wörterbuchspiele, Performance-Anweisungen oder parodistische Übersetzungen – weniger Gedichte als vielmehr komplexe Sprachspiele im wittgensteinschen Sinne sind, in denen das Blatt Papier noch nicht durch den Bildschirm, das Aufnahmeband oder den Galerieraum ersetzt worden sind. Tatsächlich gab es, wie Dworkin in einem früheren, in *October* veröffentlichten Text

MARJORIE PERLOFF ist Sadie D. Patek Professor of Humanities Emerita an der Stanford University. Sie hat zahlreiche Bücher über Dichtung und bildende Kunst verfasst, darunter *The Futurist Moment: Avant-Garde, Avant Guerre, and the Language of Rupture* (1986), *Radical Artifice: Writing Poetry in the Age of Media* (1992), und *Poetry On & Off the Page* (1998).

über Acconci ausführt, keinen scharfen Bruch zwischen Acconci, dem Dichter, und Acconci, dem Videokünstler, Performer und in jüngerer Zeit dem Architekten und Designer.[3] Im Gegenteil: Das spätere Werk lässt sich am besten als die Fortsetzung des früheren mit anderen Mitteln verstehen. Und wenn dem so ist, dann erhält das schriftliche Werk der 60er Jahre eine zusätzliche Bedeutung: Es bildet sozusagen den ersten Akt der vielschichtigen Betrachtungen des Künstlers über das Potenzial der Sprache, Emotionen und Gedanken darzustellen, verbal, visuell, akustisch oder kinetisch.

In gewissem Masse verbinden diese Betrachtungen Acconci mit Fluxus, auch wenn er eine ganz andere Richtung nahm als etwa George Brecht oder Yoko Ono. Acconci wuchs in der Bronx auf, wo er 1940 als Sohn italienischer Einwanderer geboren wurde. 1962 graduierte er am Holy Cross College in Wooster, Massachusetts, und 1964 an der University of Iowa. Der dortige Writing Workshop war damals d e r Ort, um in das Lyrik-Establishment eingeführt zu werden: Acconci belegte einen Übersetzungskurs bei Mark Strand, und zu seinen Studienkollegen gehörte Charles Wright, in dessen Gedichten aus dieser Zeit Zeilen wie die folgenden zu finden sind:

Wie ein totes Herz, kalt und unzündbar, hängt der Mond an einem Faden
Am Rand der Erde,
Endlich treulos geworden, bekleckst er die Farne und blassroten Sträucher.[4]

Welten liegen zwischen Wrights intensiver, konkreter imagistischer Beschwörung des Mondes über dem Stone Canyon und Acconcis «LIES DIESES WORT» (1969):

LIES DIESES WORT DANN LIES DIESES WORT LIES DARAUF DIESES WORT JETZT LIES DIESES WORT SIEH EIN WORT SIEH DARAUF EIN WORT SIEH JETZT EIN WORT UND DANN SIEH WIEDER EIN WORT SCHAU DIR DREI WÖRTER AN HIER SCHAU DIR DREI WÖRTER AN JETZT SCHAU DIR DREI WÖRTER AN JETZT NIMM GLEICH FÜNF WÖRTER AUF NIMM WIEDER FÜNF WÖRTER AUF NIMM ALSO FÜNF WÖRTER AUF TU ES JETZT SIEH DIESE WÖRTER AUF EINEN BLICK SIEH DIESE WÖRTER MIT DIESEM BLICK MIT DIESEM BLICK HALTE DIR DIESE ZEILE VOR AUGEN HALTE DIR DIESE ZEILE MIT NOCH EINEM BLICK VOR AUGEN UND MIT EINEM DRITTEN BLICK ERFASSE SIEBEN ZEILEN AUF EINMAL DANN ZWEIMAL DANN DREIMAL DANN EIN VIERTES MAL EIN FÜNFTES EIN SECHSTES EIN SIEBENTES EIN ACHTES[5]

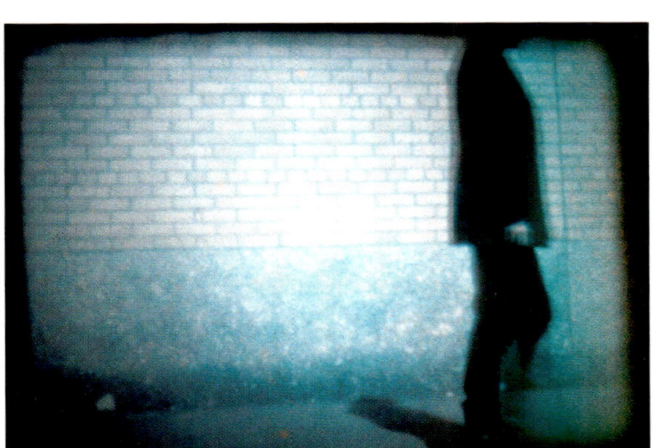

Hier protokolliert der Dichter den realen Prozess, jedes einzelne Wort nacheinander zu lesen, bis die achte Zeile buchstäblich vollendet ist. So beliebig diese «Anweisungen» mit ihren Vertauschungen von «darauf», «jetzt», «dann» und «wieder» und ihren Verwandlungen von «lesen» in «sehen» und dann in «anschauen», «aufnehmen» und «vor Augen halten» auch zu sein scheinen: Versucht man, das Gedicht zu reproduzieren, so zeigt sich, dass Acconci einiges zu tun hatte – er musste Leerzeichen einfügen, um einen am rechten Rand ausgerichteten Text zu erreichen und acht sozusagen acht gleichzumachen.

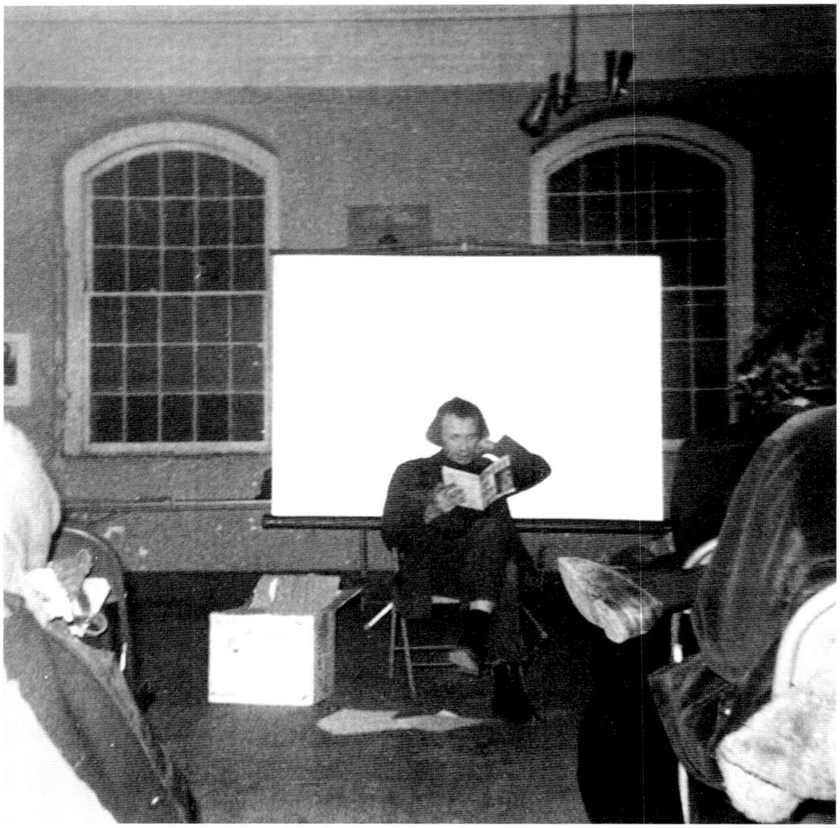

VITO ACCONCI, BUYING TIME, 1969, activity / ZEIT KAUFEND, Handlung.
(PHOTO: VITO ACCONCI STUDIO)

Frühe Experimente wie dieses ebneten der Zeitschrift *0 TO 9* den Weg, die zwischen 1967 und 1969 von Acconci und der Dichterin Bernadette Mayer herausgegeben und von ihnen selbst vervielfältigt wurde. Mit ihren insgesamt sieben Ausgaben war die Zeitschrift ein Forum für Dichter wie Clark Coolidge und Ted Berrigan, Fluxus-Performer wie Dick Higgins und Emmett Williams und Künstler wie Sol Le Witt, Adrian Piper, Dan Graham und Robert Smithson. Jackson Mac Low veröffentlichte in *0 TO 9* die «Biblical Poems», seine ersten auf Zufallsoperationen basierenden Gedichte. Die kleine, aber zunehmend an Gewicht gewinnende Ugly Duckling Presse in Brooklyn hat die Bedeutung dieser Zeitschrift erkannt und eben erst einen Nachdruck sämtlicher Ausgaben in einem Band herausgebracht (736 Seiten; $ 45).

Warum gerade jetzt der Nachdruck von *0 TO 9* und die Veröffentlichung der frühen Schriften Acconcis? Warum das neue Interesse am Material Wort, am Prozeduralismus, an Wörterbuchdefinitionen und an einem hartnäckigen Literalismus, der sich der Metaphorik der Mainstream-Lyrik oder dem Mimetismus eines so grossen Teils der etablierten Malerei und Photographie widersetzt? Ein Grund ist sicherlich die derzeitige Nostalgie nach der Bohemekultur der späten 60er und frühen 70er Jahre, als Dichter und bildende Künstler noch in fahrstuhllosen Häusern im Village und in Wohnblocks in Brooklyn lebten und sich nicht nur der bürgerlichen, sondern auch der akademischen Welt verweigerten. Die Toleranz und der Eklektizismus der Kunstwelt unserer Zeit, in der Abstraktion und Hyperrealismus, Neo-Pop und strenger Konzeptualismus nebeneinander existieren, war damals noch unbekannt: Die *0 TO 9*-Dichter wollten provozieren und waren auf Konfrontation aus; selbst die «fortschrittliche» Ästhetik der Black Mountain School und der Beat Poets lehnten sie ab. Gegen Charles Olsons Poetik des Prozesses erklärte Acconci, die Sprache der Dichtung müsse «einen Raum decken, nicht eine Bedeutung aufdecken».[6)] Und das lyrische «Ich» wurde durch ein «Ich» ersetzt, das sich mit dem «Du», das dem gesprochenen Wort oder der Handlung in einer bestimmten, live oder auf Video aufgeführten Performance gegenübertritt, in einem Dialog befindet und oft von ihm geformt wird.

Ein zweiter, konkreterer Grund für die Aufmerksamkeit, die Acconcis frühe Schriften heute auf sich ziehen, ist die Tatsache, dass die neue digitale Poetik darin vorweggenommen ist. In den letzten Jahren haben wir die Entstehung einer elektronisch generierten Literatur miterlebt, die unter die Rubrik fällt, die Kenneth Goldsmith, ihr wichtigster Fürsprecher, als «unkreatives Schreiben» bezeichnet. In seinem *Day*[7)] hat Goldsmith beispielsweise eine vollständige Ausgabe der *New York Times* reproduziert, Wort für Wort, von der ersten bis zur letzten Seite. «Appropriation» ist hier alles, oder? Indem sie in einen durchlaufenden, gleichförmigen digitalen Text transformiert wird, ohne Unterscheidungen zwischen Schlagzeilen und Werbeinseraten, zwischen Leitartikeln in übergrosser Schrift und winzigen Dow-Jones-Zahlen, ist die *New York Times* nicht mehr wiederzuerkennen! Im Informationszeitalter ist es Goldsmith zufolge nicht mehr die Aufgabe der Literatur, neue Texte hervorzubringen – davon gibt es schon zu viele –; vielmehr muss sie die sprachliche Umgebung, in der wir leben, verfremden, um uns die Augen zu öffnen.

Wie Dworkin schreibt, produzierte Goldsmith *Day* und verwandte Texte ohne Acconcis frühe Schriften zu kennen – die meisten dieser Texte waren unveröffentlicht und deshalb weithin unbekannt.[8)] Es hat schon etwas Unheimliches, dass fünfunddreissig Jahre bevor Goldsmith in seinem Buch *The Weather*[9)] für den Zeitraum eines Jahres (21. Dezember 2002–20. Dezember 2003) die stündlichen Wetterberichte des New Yorker Nachrichtenradiosenders WINS (1010) transkribierte, Acconci einen durchnummerierten Text mit dem Titel «Act 3, Scene 4» schrieb, der so beginnt:

1. Die Sonne geht heute, am Donnerstag, dem 26. Dezember 1968,
2. um 7:18 auf, um 16:34 geht sie unter und wird
3. morgen um 7:18 aufgehen. Der Mond geht heute um 11:49 unter,
4. geht morgen um 12:10 auf und wird morgen
5. um 12:38 untergehen. Klare bis wolkige Himmel werden bei
6. wärmerem Wetter den grössten Teil der östlichen Hälfte des Landes
7. bedecken, während heute für die westliche
8. Seenregion, die nördlichen Präriestaaten und vom
9. Upper Mississippi Valley bis zur Plateauregion Schneefall erwartet wird[10)]

Und so zieht es sich über zehn weitere Seiten hin; der nüchterne Bericht ist in insgesamt 350 mehr oder weniger gleich lange Zeilen aufgeteilt. Verwandte Texte, die darauf folgten, basieren auf dem Wetterbericht für New York City, wie er sich ihn zu bestimmten Zeiten am Telefon anhörte und aufzeichnete. Und diese Experimente ebneten frühen Videoarbeiten wie FILLING UP SPACE (Raumausfüllung, 1970, 3 Min.) den Weg, worin der Künstler vor dem Hintergrund einer Backsteinmauer ins Bild tritt und von einer Seite zur anderen läuft, hin und her, Reihe für Reihe.

Was mich hier interessiert, sind jedoch weniger die Gemeinsamkeiten zwischen «Act 3, Scene 4» und Goldsmiths *The Weather* als vielmehr die Unterschiede. Indem er die Sprache seines Textes nicht den nüchternen Fakten in der Zeitung entnahm, sondern dem Radio, wo der Sprecher den Wetterbericht «aufmotzen» muss, um die Hörer bei der Stange zu halten, gibt Goldsmith der Wetterberichterstattung einen völlig anderen Dreh. Ein Beispiel:

Hm, dieses alte Weihnachtslied, «Lass es schnein, lass es schnein» – heute Nachmittag jedoch nicht. Ein stark bewölkter Himmel, drei Grad minus, aber das ist nur ein Ausläufer des letzten Sturmsystems, mit dem wir es zu tun hatten. In der Nacht wird es sich weiter verziehen, und damit verschwinden auch die Wolken, zwischen neun und sieben Grad minus, und morgen kehren die Wolken dann schnell zurück.[11)]

Die «Handlung» wird noch zusätzlich verdichtet, indem Goldsmith jeder einminütigen Wettervorhersage einen jeweils eigenen Absatz zuweist, die Absätze zu einem Jahreszeitenzyklus mit den Kapiteln

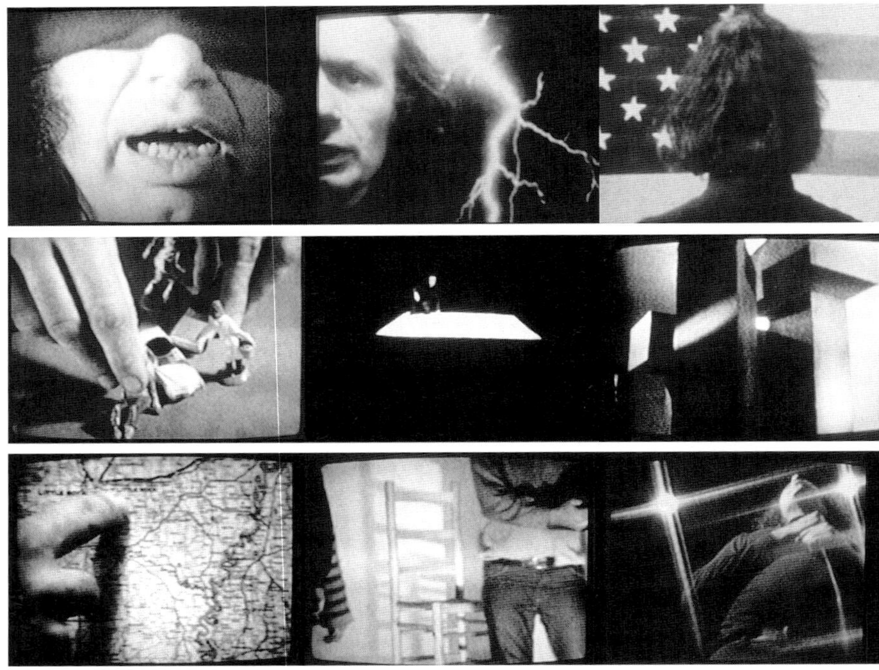

VITO ACCONCI, THE RED TAPES, 1976/1977, black-and-white video tape, sound / DIE ROTEN TONBÄNDER, schwarz-weisses Videoband, Klang.
(PHOTO: VITO ACCONCI STUDIO)

«Winter», «Frühling», «Sommer», «Herbst» zusammenstellt und – ein merkwürdiges Clinamen – bestimmte Tage (an denen er nicht zu Hause war) auslässt, sodass auf die eine Vorhersage nicht die nächste folgt. Doch selbst wenn sie zeitlich aufeinanderfolgen, sind die Wettervorhersagen oft falsch. Und dann, im Frühling 2002, wird der Wetterbericht plötzlich aus Bagdad gesendet: Der Irakkrieg ist ausgebrochen. *The Weather* erweist sich somit als eine ironische Erzählung.

Vorgefundener Text kann also Verschiedenes bedeuten, und nicht alle Appropriationen sind gleichermassen interessant oder amüsant. Digitale Aufzeichnungsgeräte und Scanner, die Acconci 1968 noch nicht zur Verfügung standen, haben ganz neue Möglichkeiten eröffnet. Gerade deshalb ist *Language to Cover a Page* ein so aktuelles und faszinierendes Buch. Es stellt das fehlende Glied zwischen den ersten Streifzügen in eine nichtrepräsentationale, nichtexpressivistische Poetik und ihren heutigen Verkörperungen dar. Als er dreissig Jahre alt war, scheint Acconci erkannt zu haben, dass er mit Hilfe der auf dem Video-Bildschirm vermittelten Körpersprache eine befriedigendere Beziehung zwischen sich und seinem Publikum erreichen konnte als mit der schriftlich fixierten Sprache auf Papier. Aufgegeben wurde diese Form der Vermittlung jedoch nie; sie wurde nur in den grösseren Raum solcher Meisterwerke wie THE RED TAPES (Die roten Tonbänder, 1976) integriert.

(Übersetzung: Wolfgang Himmelberg)

1) Siehe http://www.ubu.com/concept/
2) Craig Dworkin, Hrsg., *Language to Cover a Page: The Early Writings of Vito Acconci* (Cambridge: MIT Press, 2006).
3) Craig Dworkin, *October* 95, Winter (Cambridge: MIT, 2001), S. 91–113.
4) Charles Wright, «Stone Canyon Nocturne», in: *Country Music: Selected Early Poems* (Middletown, CT: Wesleyan University Press, 1982), S. 139.
5) Craig Dworkin, *Language to Cover a Page* (Anm. 2), S. 111.
6) Vito Acconci, «Early Work: Movement over a Page», in: *Avalanche* 6 (Herbst 1972), S. 4.
7) Kenneth Goldsmith, *Day* (Barrington, VT: The Figures, 2003).
8) Craig Dworkin, *Language to Cover a Page* (Anm. 2), S. XVI.
9) Kenneth Goldsmith, *The Weather* (Los Angeles: Make Now Press), 2005.
10) Craig Dworkin (siehe Anm. 2.), S. 388–389.
11) Kenneth Goldsmith (siehe Anm. 9), S. 26.

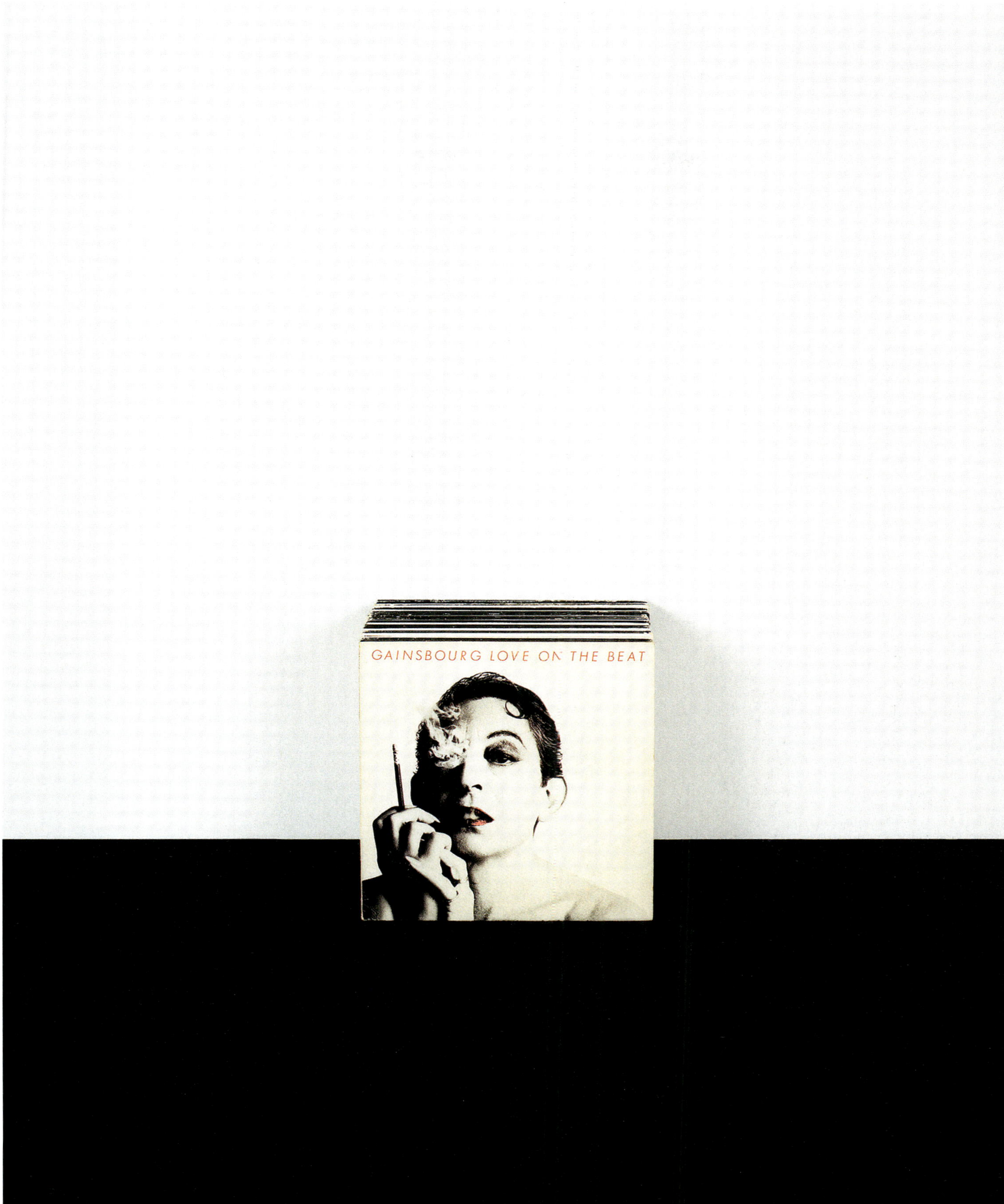
GAINSBOURG LOVE ON THE BEAT

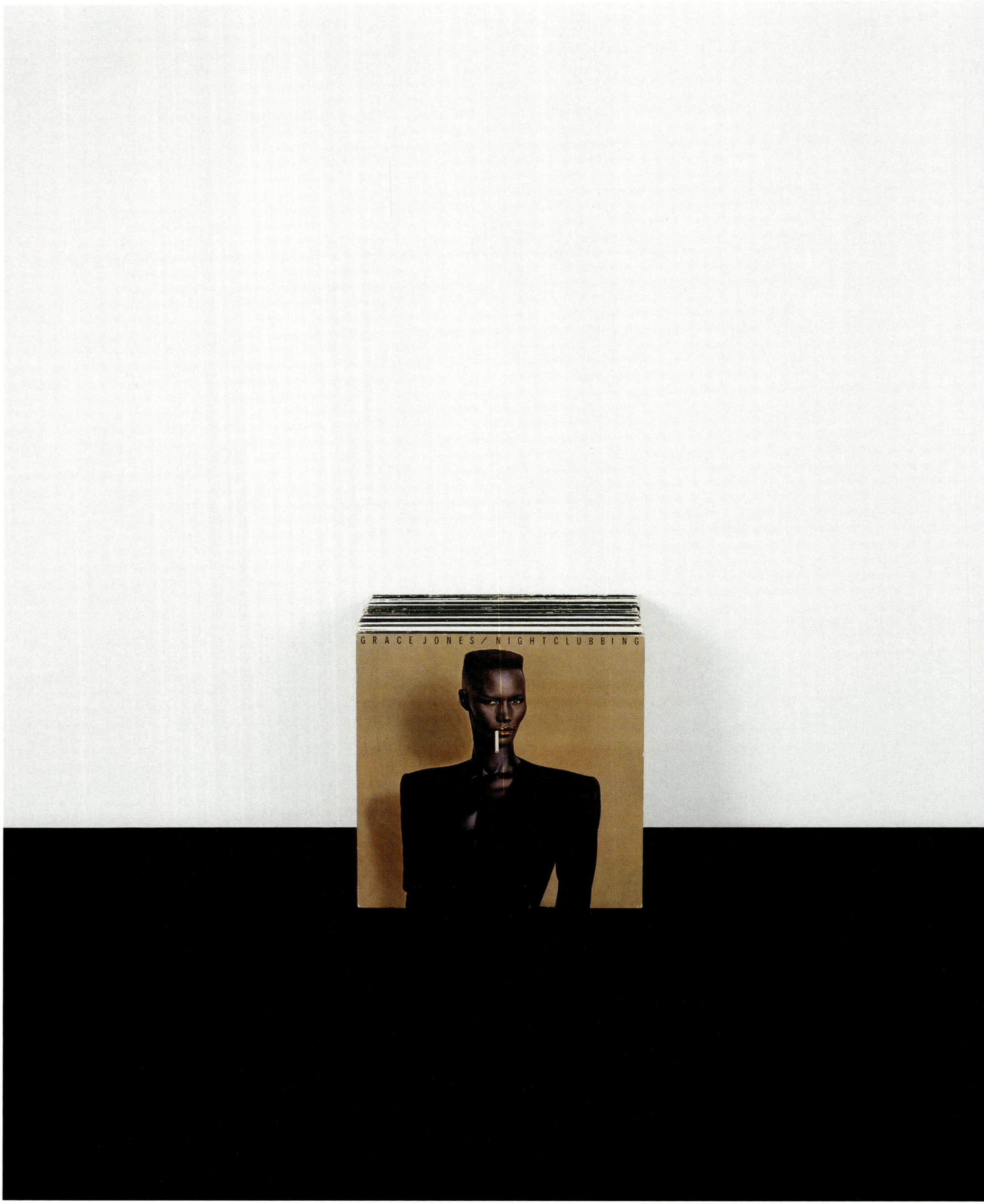
GRACE JONES / NIGHTCLUBBING

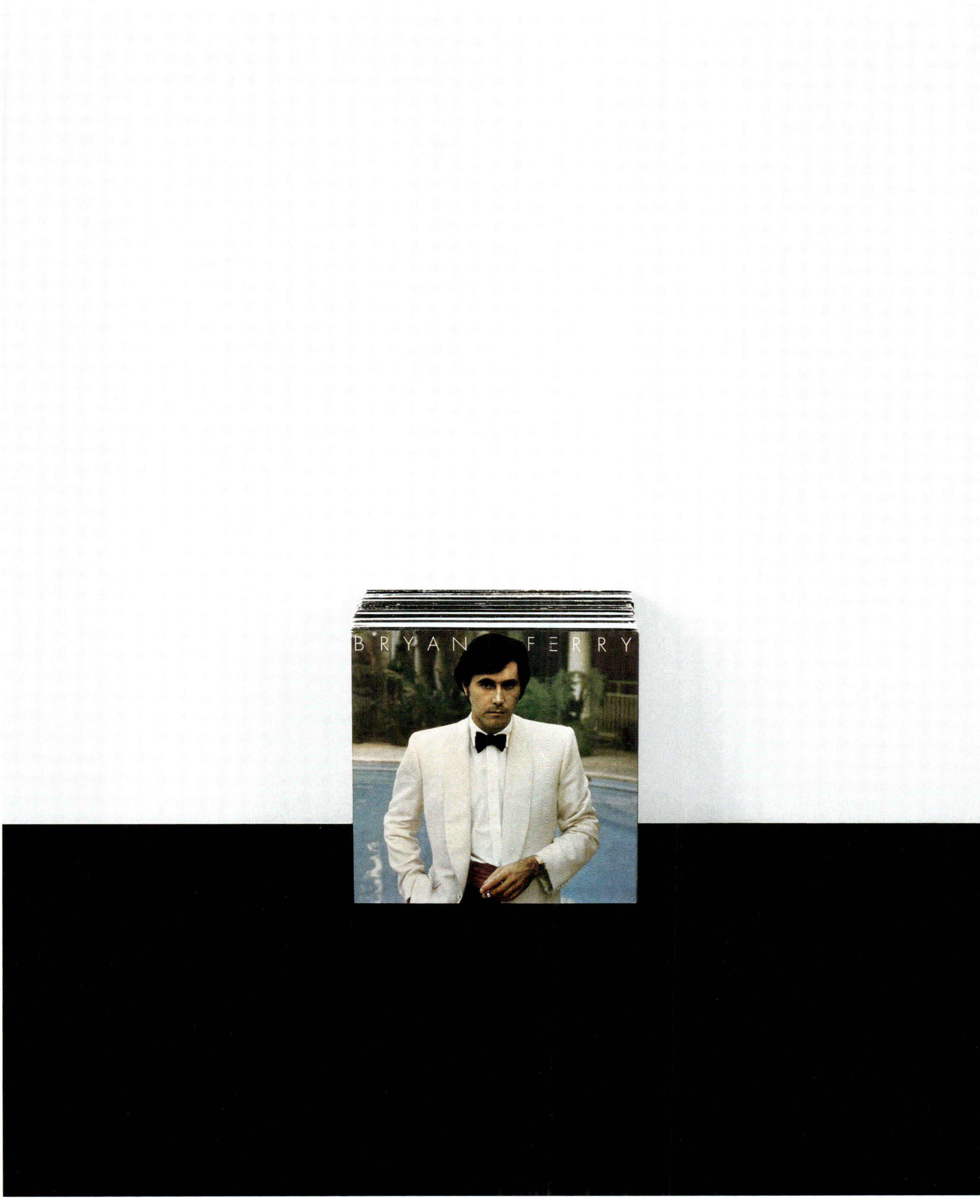
BRYAN FERRY

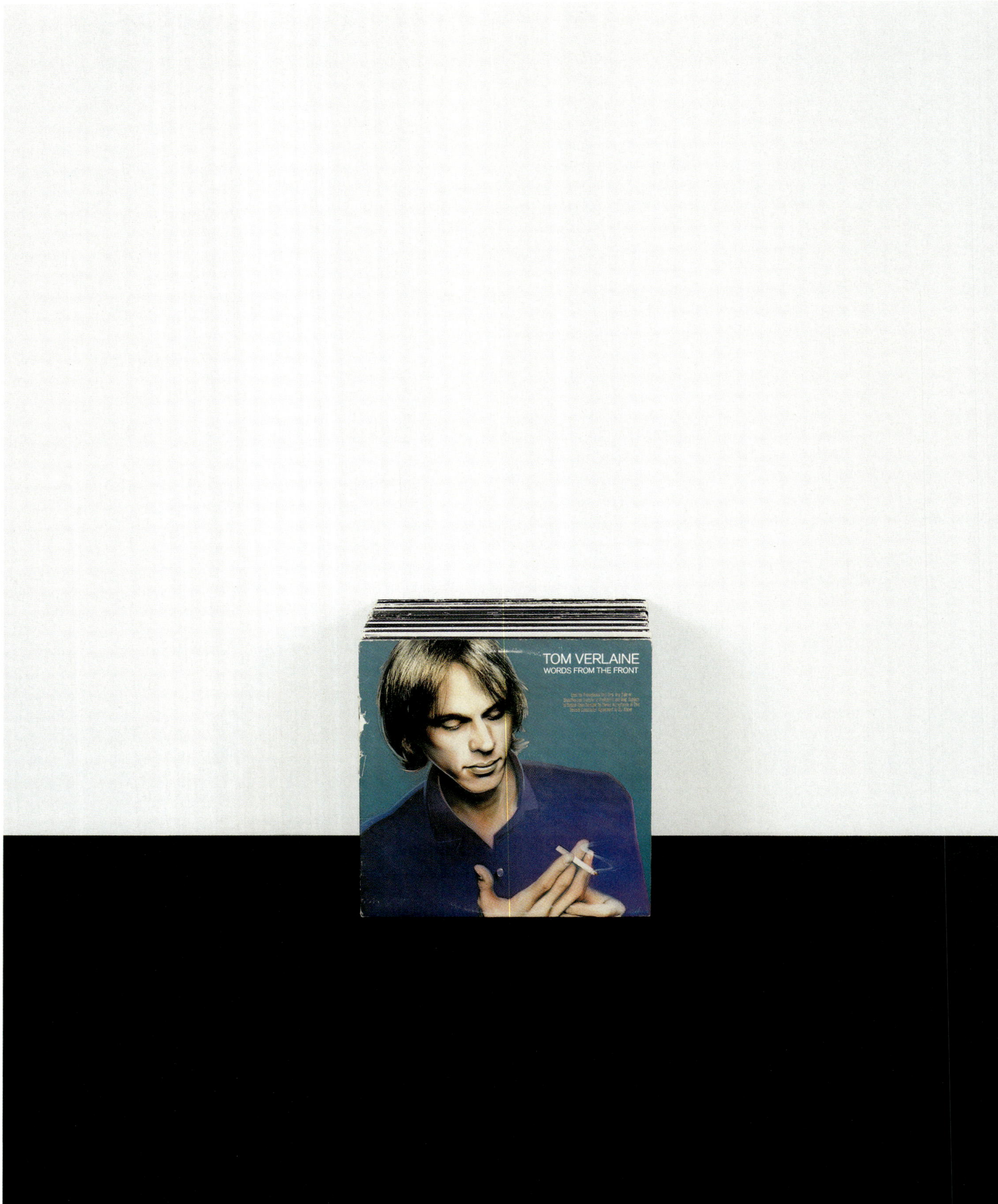
TOM VERLAINE
WORDS FROM THE FRONT

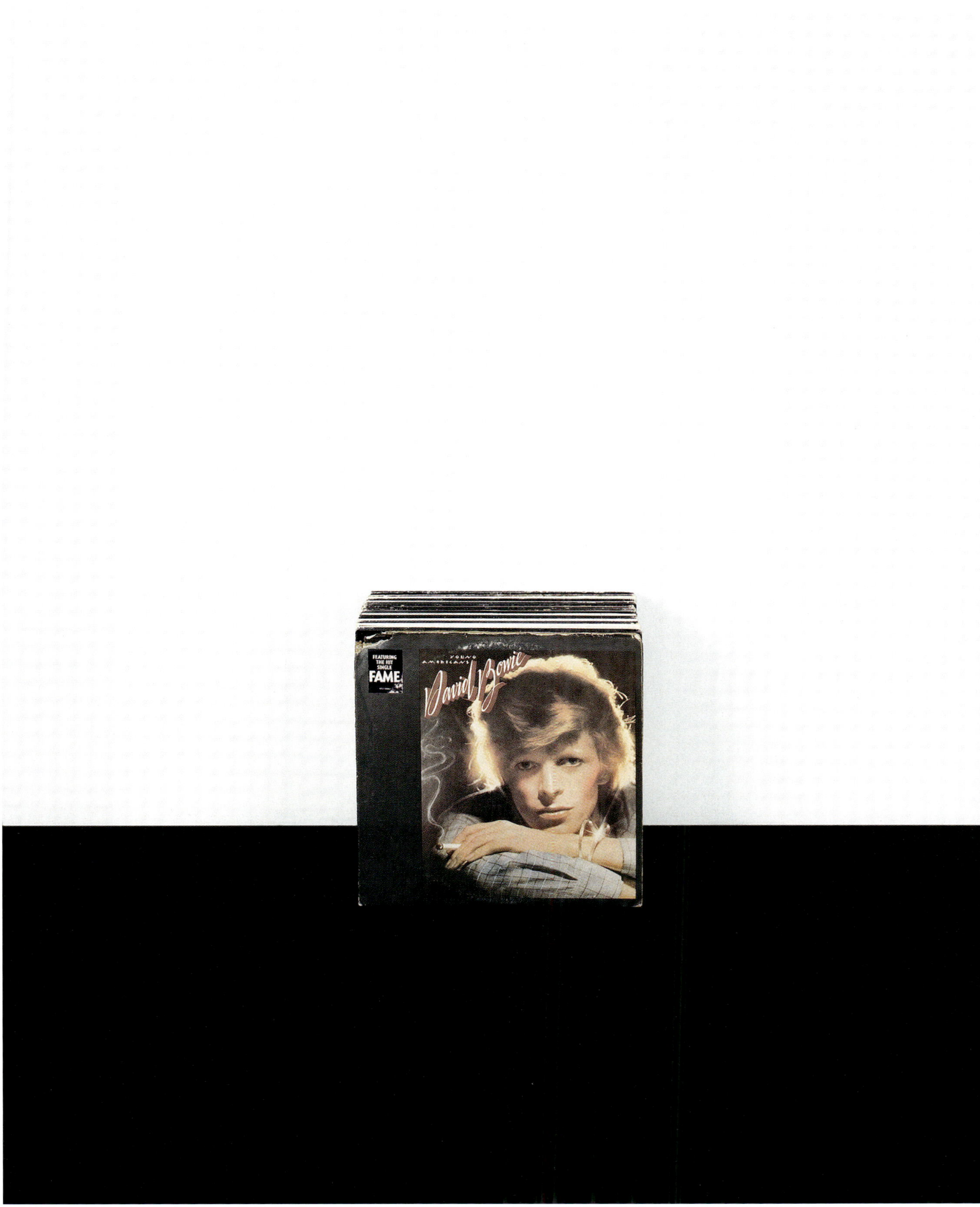
FEATURING THE HIT SINGLE FAME
YOUNG AMERICANS
David Bowie

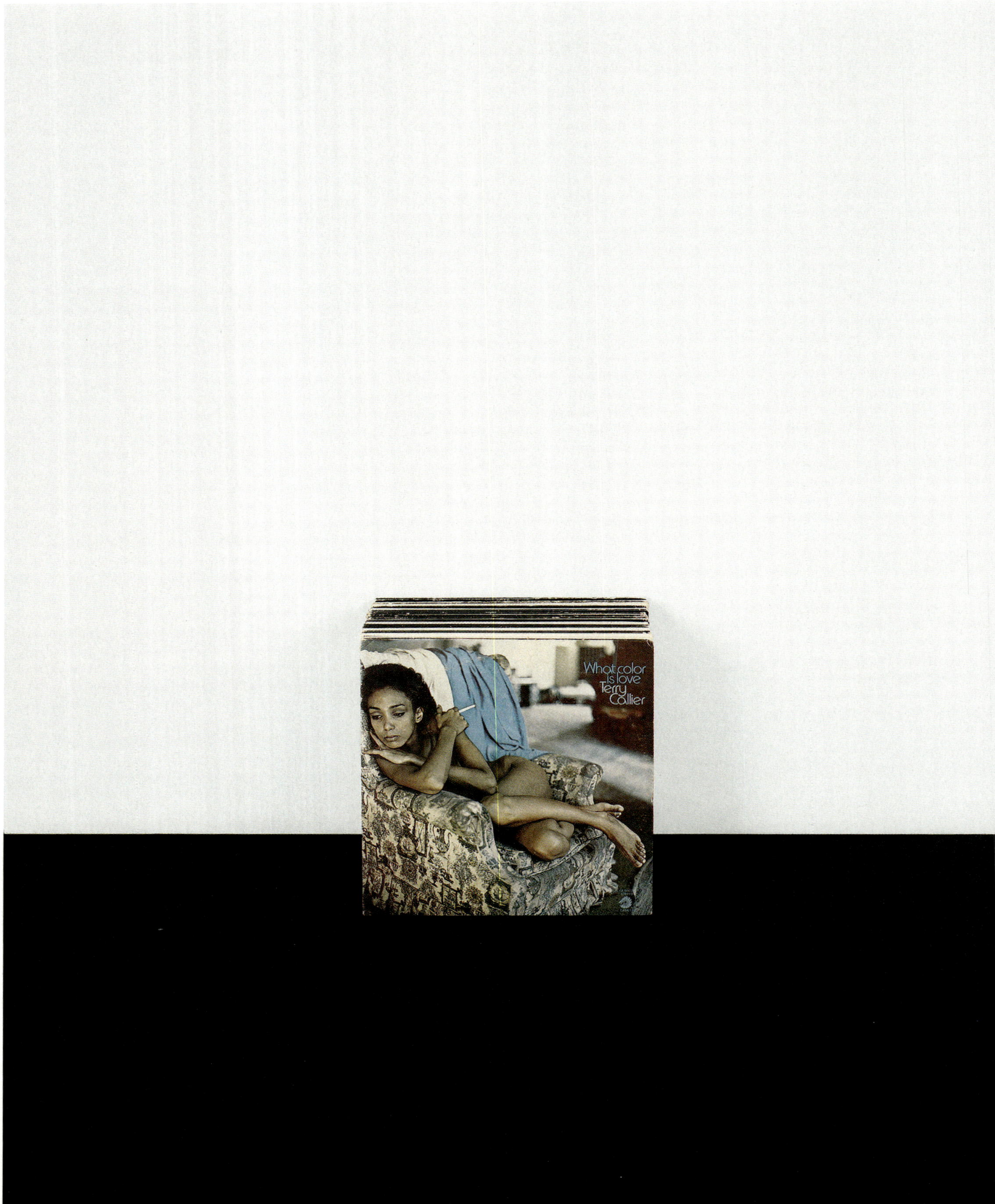
What color
is love
Terry
Callier

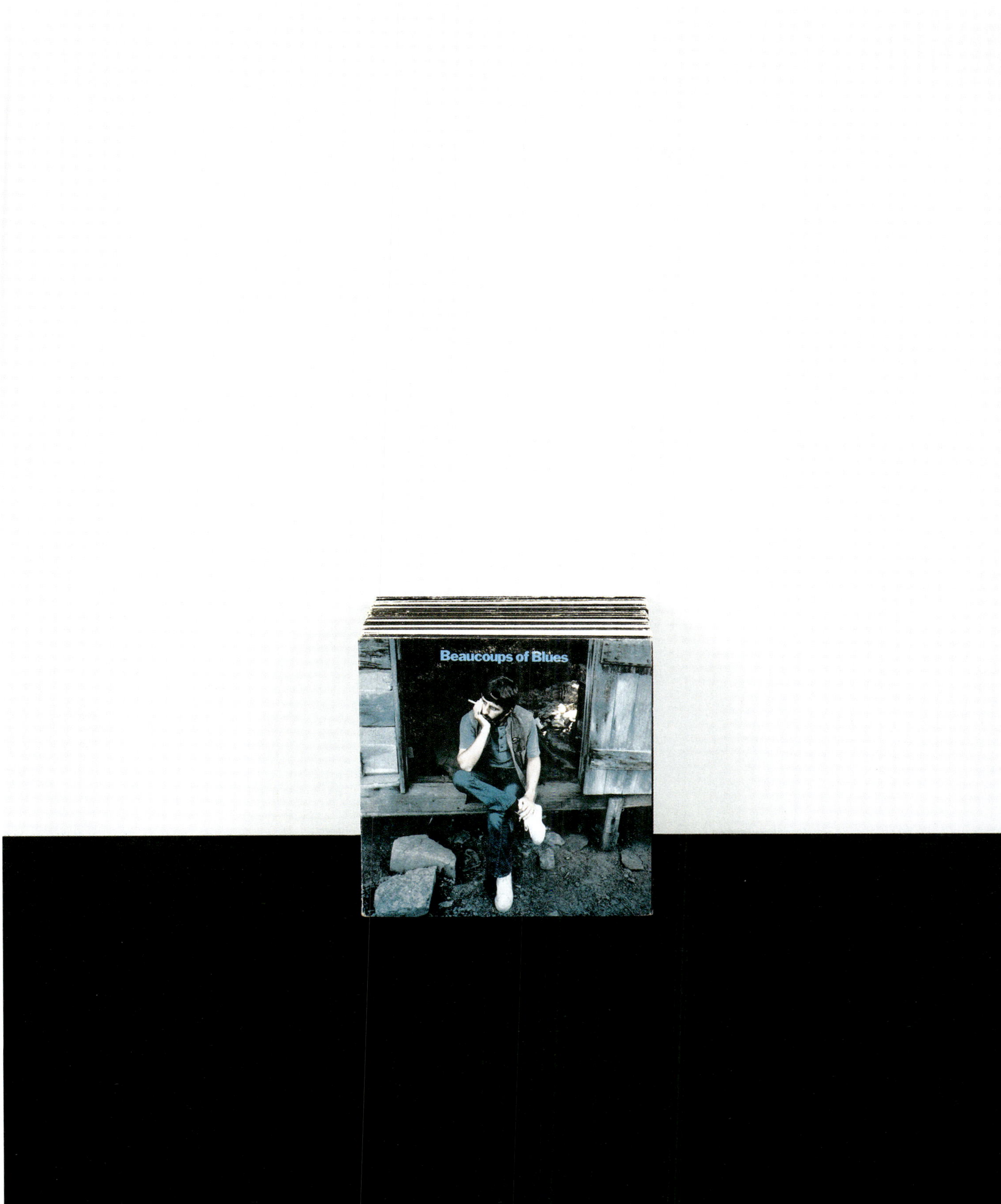
Beaucoups of Blues

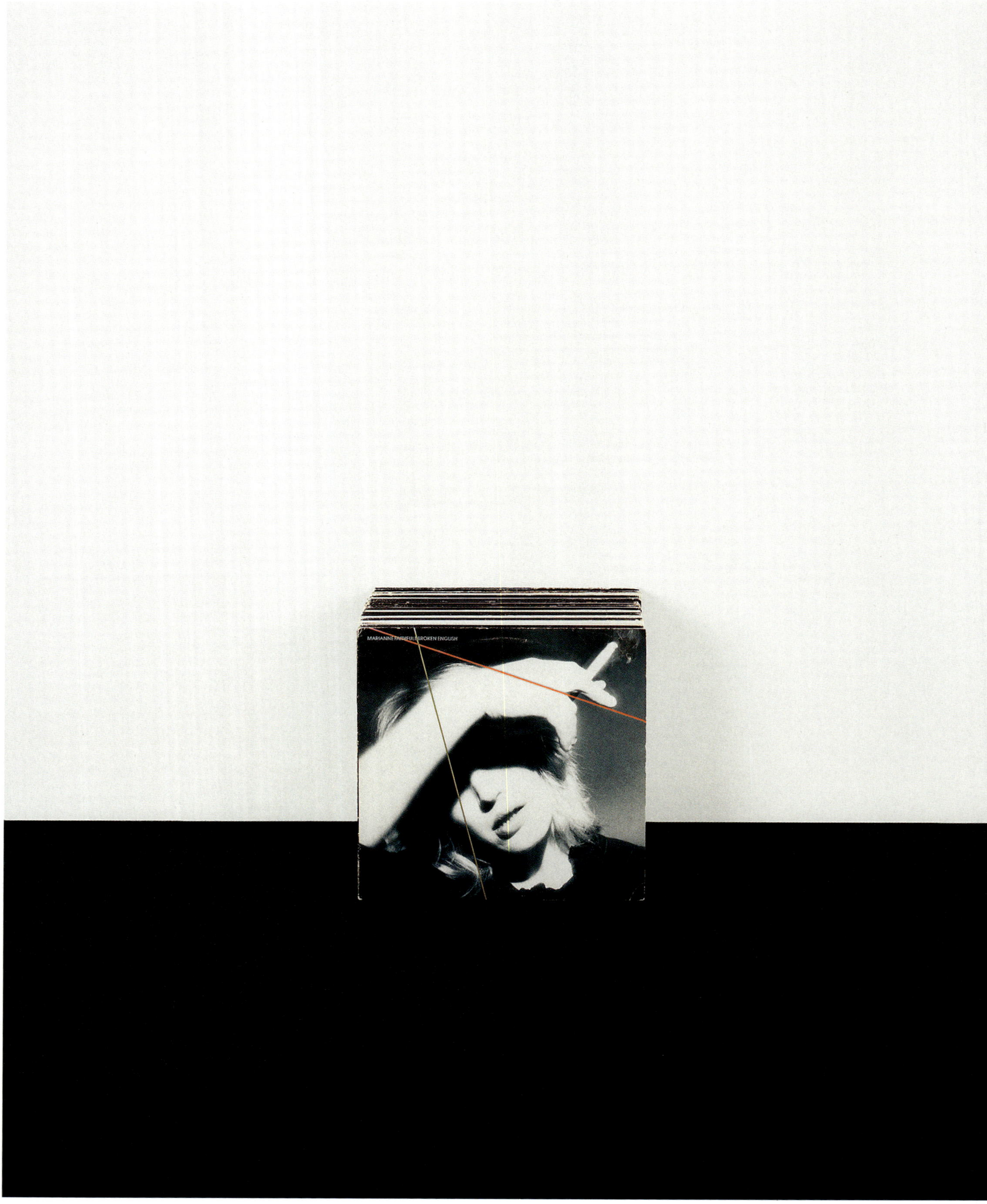
MARIANNE FAITHFULL BROKEN ENGLISH

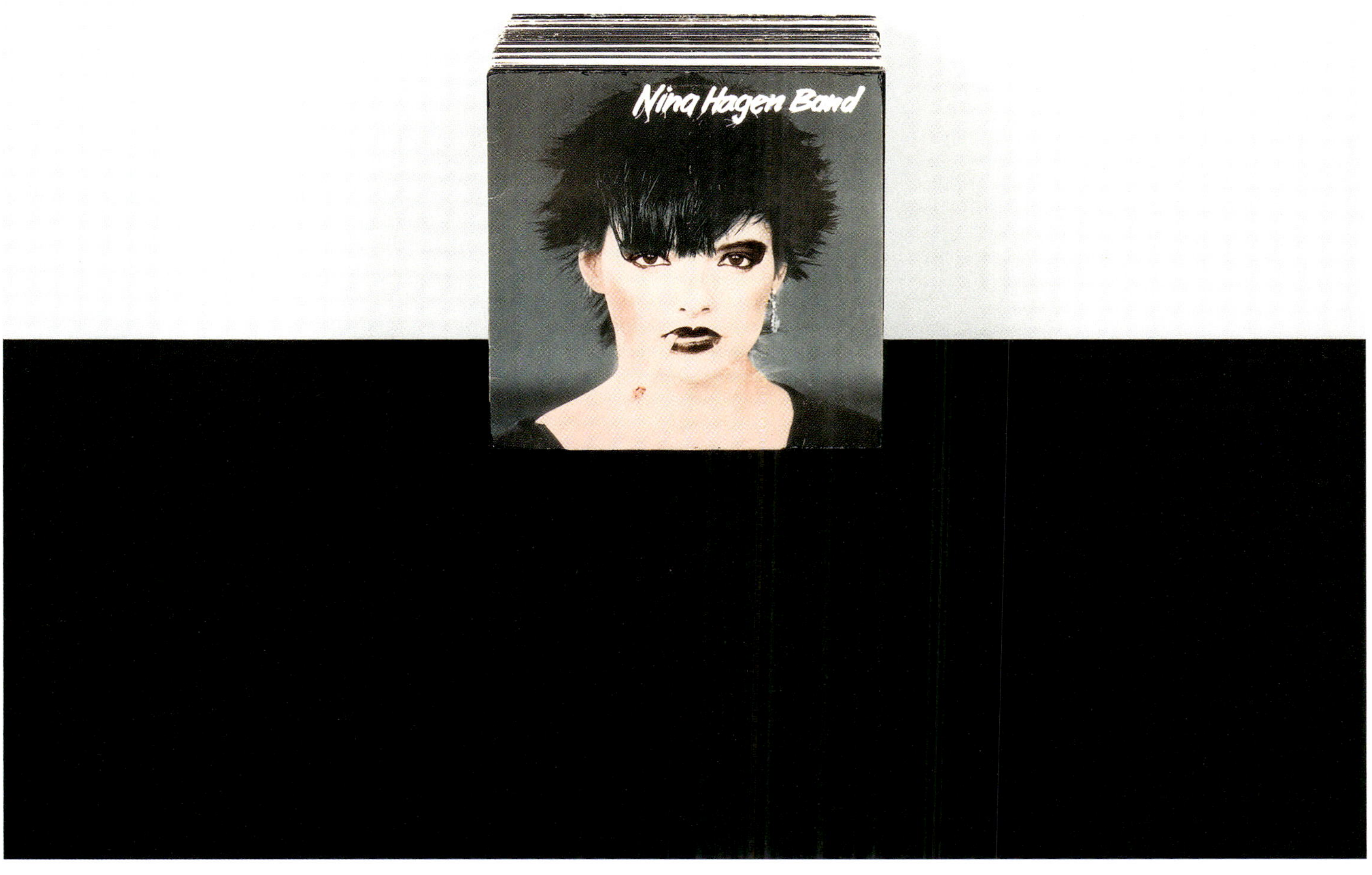
Nina Hagen Band

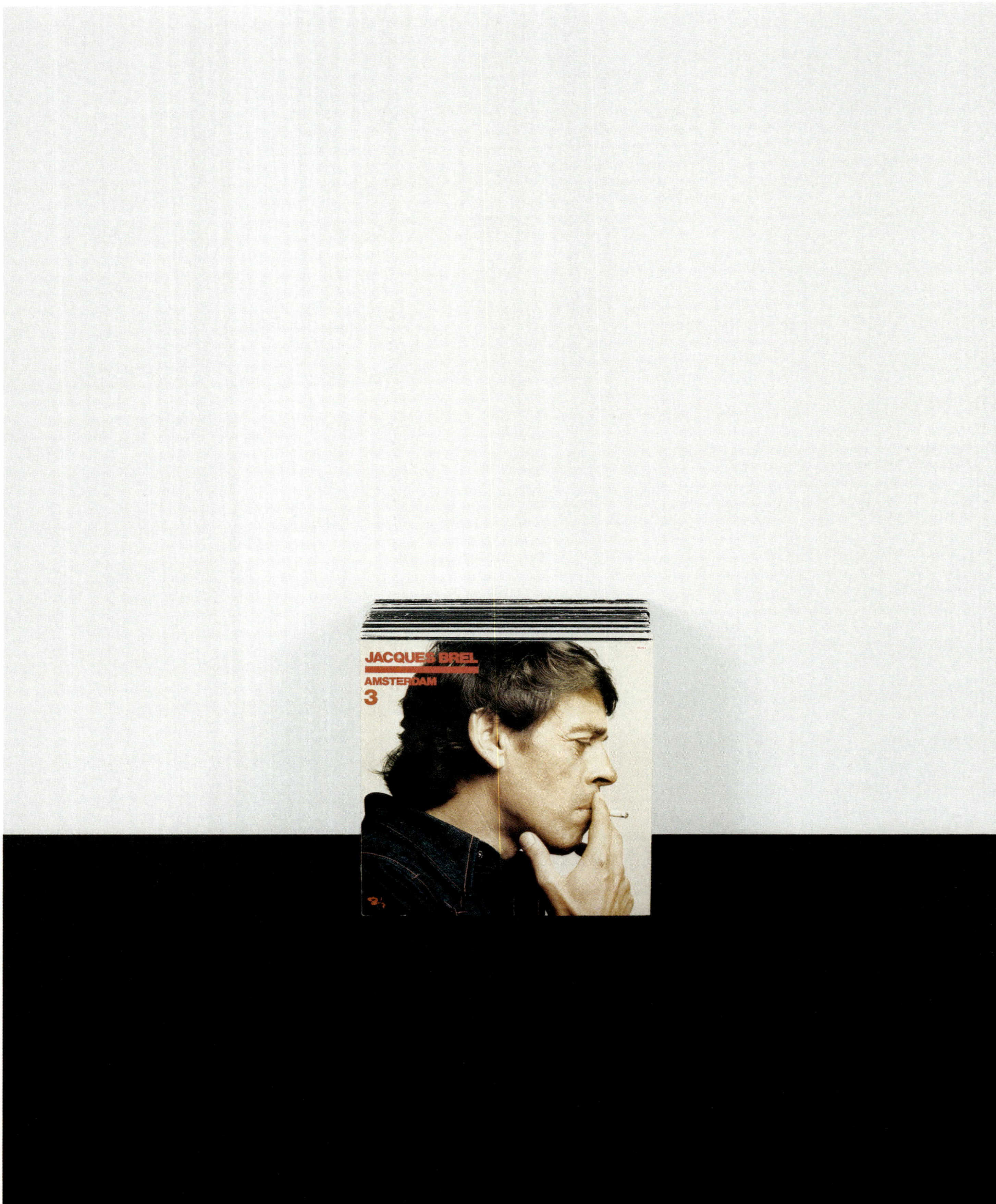
JACQUES BREL
AMSTERDAM
3

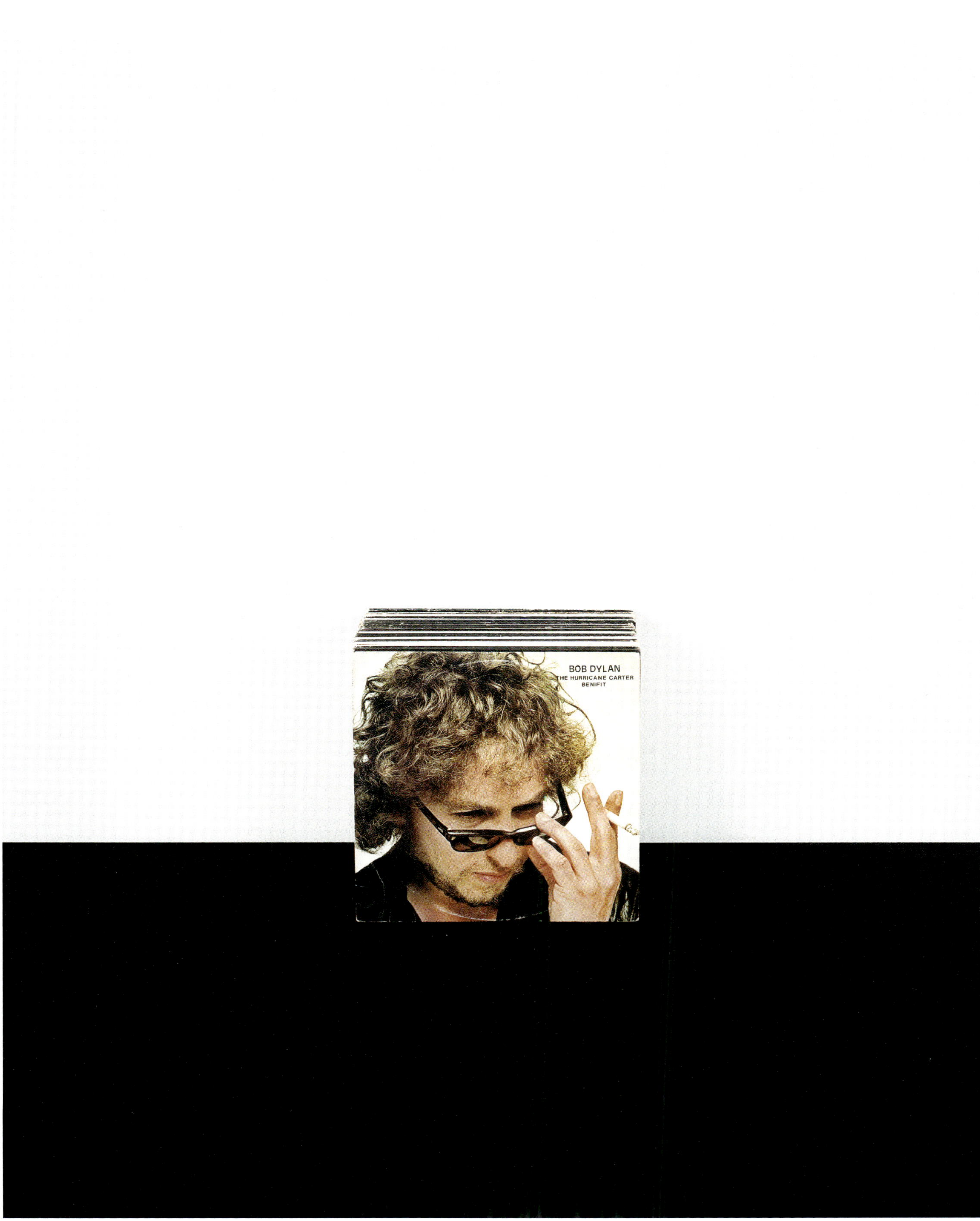
BOB DYLAN
THE HURRICANE CARTER
BENIFIT

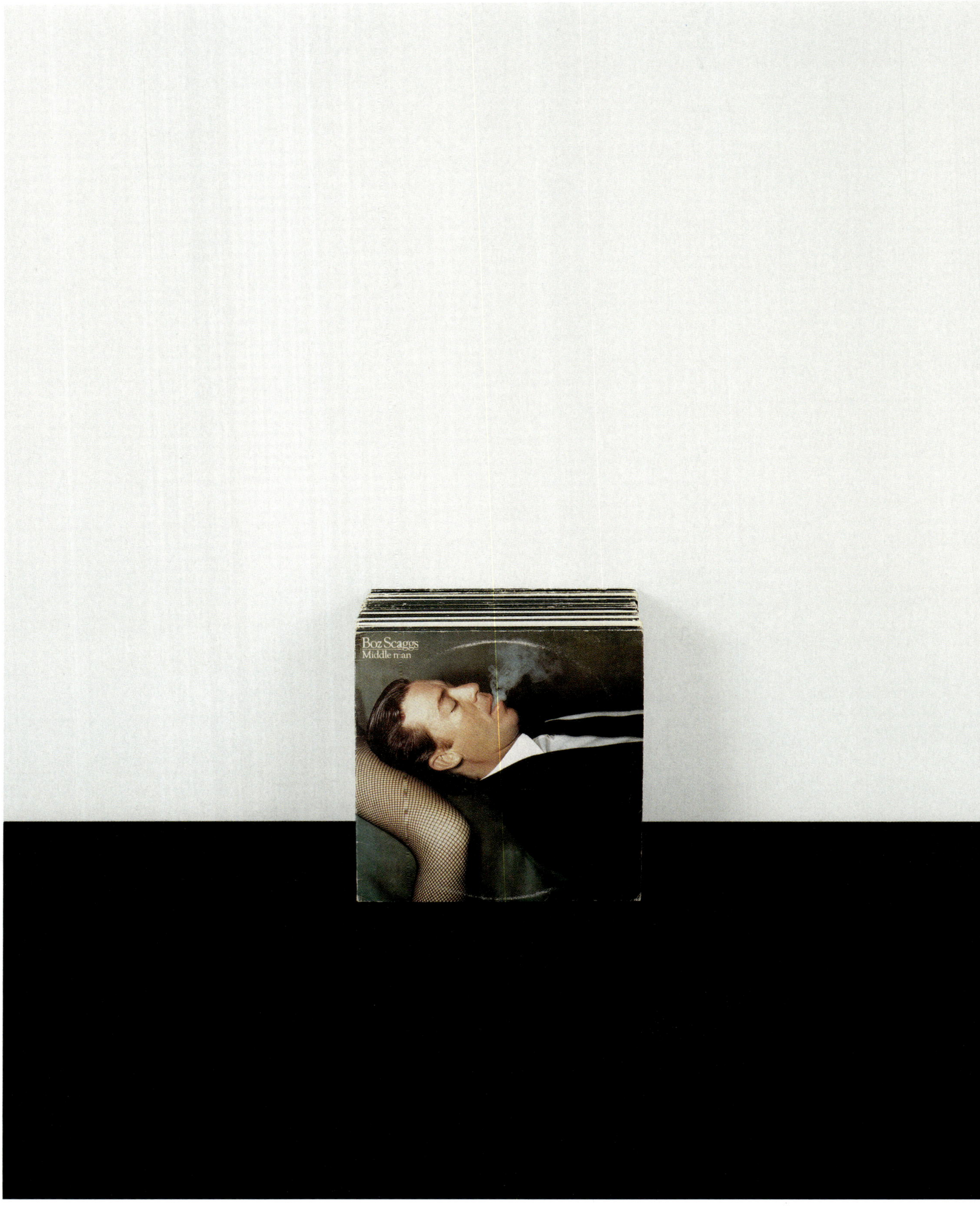

ANNE COLLIER **SMOKING**, INSERT FOR PARKETT 78, 2006

CUMULUS

From America

IN EVERY EDITION OF PARKETT, TWO CUMULUS CLOUDS, ONE FROM AMERICA, THE OTHER FROM EUROPE, FLOAT OUT TO AN INTERESTED PUBLIC. THEY CONVEY INDIVIDUAL OPINIONS, ASSESSMENTS, AND MEMORABLE ENCOUNTERS—AS ENTIRELY PERSONAL PRESENTATIONS OF PROFESSIONAL ISSUES.

KATE FOWLE

GROWING *PAINS*

If the nineties can be said to be synonymous with relational aesthetics, then this current decade will go down as the era that the curator came of age.

While there are ongoing arguments as to whether curating should be regarded as a profession or a passion, it could generally be said that the role of the curator has shifted from arbiter of taste to connector of art, space, and audience. Increasingly compared to an artist's practice, the position is less engaged in upholding an institutional mandate than in trying to transform it through experimentation with processes and materials. Key factors by which curating is measured today include the extent to which activities address and confront artistic, social, or political issues; the responsiveness of projects to the situations in which they occur; and the viability of exhibitions and events as platforms for both the curators' and artists' philosophies and interests.

Though I currently work in the U.S., I have recently spent time in both Asia and Europe, where I have conducted much research on this topic. Through conversations with artists and curators, together with articles I have recently read in the art press, I have been led to reflect on the current emphasis of the curatorial role and the different ways in which curators are positioned in relation to an evolving art world that is increasingly locating itself within larger sociopolitical arenas.

Harald Szeemann was regarded as the first "independent curator"; his career spanned nearly five decades and established precedents in terms of exhibition making and building relationships with artists, which are now regarded as integral to the current understanding of the curator's role. His passing in 2005 may have spurred more obituaries and articles in the non-art press than any curator has ever received, which reflects the way in which curators are being recognized in the media as celebrities newsworthy beyond their field, and quite apart from the conversations going on within it.

The onslaught of "viral" publishing, through blogs and websites, has also proliferated. The internet, once the domain of governments, activist organizing, gaming, and commercial sales, is now also the site for the proliferation of discussion over recent events in art—from fair openings and auctions

KATE FOWLE is Chair of the MA program in Curatorial Practice at California College of the Arts in San Francisco.

to resignations and protests. Through this mass availability of information, the curator has, in recent months more than ever, begun to be heralded in the news and even seen as a radical figure, with opposition to museums and other art institutions discussed in the same framework as other activist gestures. This was made evident when Chris Gilbert abruptly resigned from the Matrix position at the Berkeley Art Museum in California as a stand against what he calls the "imperialist capitalist values" of the art institution. The case attracted international attention through the viral dissemination of his essay-cum-resignation letter, which in turn provoked numerous blog discussions and therefore late-night bar conversations. The art press followed the frenzy most recently in the pages of *Artforum* in September 2006, where, inspired by Gilbert's resignation and the ongoing media attention, Liam Gillick questioned the potential for curatorial rhetoric to instill change. Similarly, the cancellation of Manifesta 6 in Nicosia, Cyprus and the ensuing legal battles attracted much attention via the Manifesta website and various independent writers on line as well as in the mainstream art press. In this case, the curators of the Manifesta Foundation chose to take on a contested region as its subject. Where Gilbert reportedly resigned over the museum administration's clamp-down on his solidarity with the Bolivarian struggle in Venezuela, shown by his choice of language on the labels for his exhibition program, the Manifesta team chose to use the positioning of exhibition-making and events to transcend political borders, which in the end proved to be beyond the current power and ability of the curatorial role. While all of this makes for good reading and conversation, the question is to what extent the curator, working in mainstream politics or even established art institutions, has succeeded in implementing meaningful statements or actions and laying groundwork toward future practices for artists, curators, and audiences.

An article in the September 2006 issue of *Frieze* suggests that curators have been able to radicalize centers for contemporary art in Europe.[1] This phenomenon, currently being termed "New Institutionalism" or "Experimental Institutionalism," involves previously independent curators taking on the directorship of public spaces and transforming their programs by placing equal emphasis on publishing, research, residency, and lecture series, as much as exhibitions. In the U.S., a comparison could be made with the hires being made at universities—from Robert Storr as Dean of Yale School of Art to Lawrence Rinder as Dean of California College of the Arts. Most recently, the San Francisco Art Institute has taken this current "faith in the curator" a step further by hiring Okwui Enwezor and Hou Hanru to transform not only the academic programs but

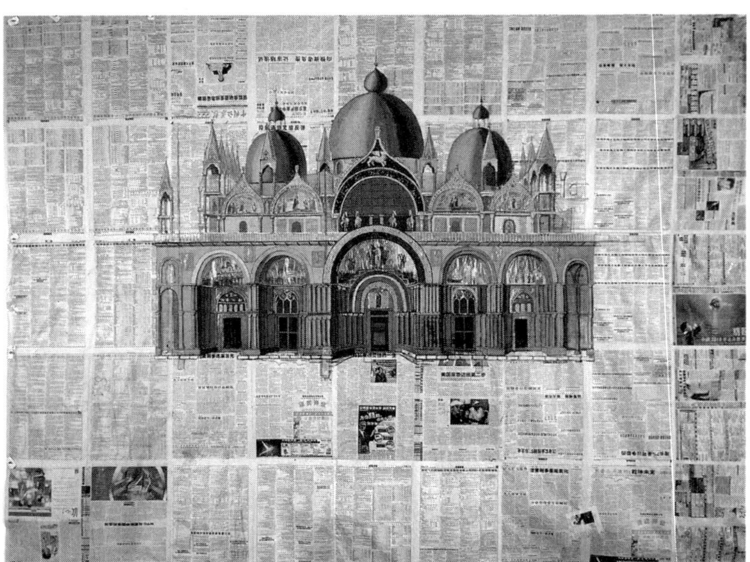

ZHOU TIEHAI, VENICE - ST. MARCO SQUARE, 2005, mixed media on paper, 102 1/4 x 131 3/4" / VENEDIG MARKUSPLATZ, verschiedene Materialien auf Papier, 260 x 335 cm.
(PHOTOS OF ZHOU TIEHAI'S WORK: SHANGHART GALLERY, SHANGHAI)

also the exhibitions and lecture series, with a similar "New Institutional" impetus. In effect, this is a transferal of roles: institutional critique, which has been the domain of the artist from the seventies on, is now in the hands of curators and directors, who are taking direct responsibility for questioning the mechanisms and activities of the institution in which they work.

While an increasingly large percentage of column inches in art magazines, journals, and the Internet are taken up with the processes and politics of curating, additionally, since 2000, there has been a proliferation of books specifically focused on the topic. Generated by people working within the field and emerging out of symposia, on-line discussions, diaristic accounts, and interviews, the commentaries and publications are indicative of the inherent self-reflexivity that comes from simultaneously initiating, producing, disseminating, and evaluating multiple projects. This accumulation of texts and articles is creating the beginnings of a critical framework, as well as establishing a rationale through which curatorial practices acquire a kind of autonomy from their social and cultural contexts and from the funding and bureaucratic structures that give them shape. But, while this can be regarded as important groundwork in identifying particularities of practice without due consideration of the bigger picture, it has the potential to inflate the value and importance of certain exhibitions, projects, or people, as in the case of the above-mentioned Manifesta project or Chris Gilbert's resignation.

For example, while attention is paid to artistic practices and the burgeoning art market in Asia, there are few articles in the Western press (and even fewer books) that discuss or compare parallel developments and changes in curating. The concept of "New Institutionalism," for instance, takes on a different meaning in view of developments in China. On one level, the climate is similar to that of Europe and the U.S., with institutions now being headed up by internationally recognized independent curators, such as Fan Dian at the National Museum in Beijing, Pi Li at a space called Universal Studios-Beijing in the East End Art District, and Gu Zhenqing at the Zhu Qizhan Art Museum in Shanghai. But this is only a subtext to the larger narrative of China's building boom. Since the turn of the century, the country has entered what curator Gao Minglu calls "the art museum age."[2] Depending on which report you read, between three hundred and one thousand new venues, financed by both corporate and government funds, will be opening across the country by 2010, making China the world's fastest growing market for museums. And the entrepreneurial interest is not only local—it is now confirmed that the Pompidou will build a new museum in Shanghai, and both the Guggenheim and MoMA are currently considering sites for their China branches.

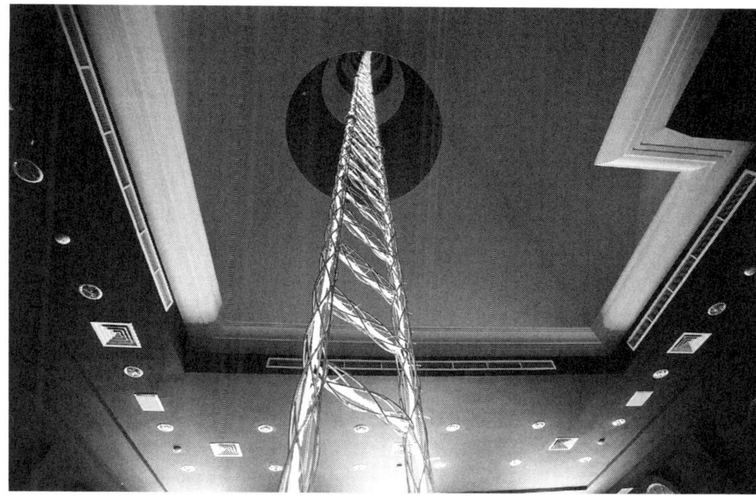

YAYOI KUSAMA, LADDER TO HEAVEN, 2006, installation view Singapore Biennale / HIMMELSLEITER, Installationsansicht.
(ALL PHOTOS OF THE SINGAPORE BIENNALE: NATIONAL ARTS COUNCIL, SINGAPORE)

Such frenetic activity is also fanning interest in the question of who will run these spaces, quite apart from the issue of where the funds will come from in order to maintain programming. Academies are now setting up arts management and curating courses, of which the first was established at the Central Academy in Beijing. Now with over one hundred students enrolled and pilot programs running in Shanghai, the curriculum has the task of providing both management and curatorial training that is not only relevant to needs in the national context, but that also reflects the burgeoning international exchange. In talking with curators and artists in Shanghai, I came to the conclusion that it is predominantly artists who have the greatest knowledge of contemporary strategies and a vision for the future of institutions. Shanghai-based artist Zhou Tiehai, for example, has been traveling, selling, and exhibiting internationally for the last ten years. As a result he has more first-hand experience of a variety of curatorial, art market, and management practices than many curators based in China. Although Zhou isn't about to become a curator, he is currently working with a consortium to organize the Shanghai Art Fair next year, and his position highlights the unique situation the country is in, whereby the prominent artists of the last decade are potentially the untapped advisors to the curatorial field today.

Radicalism also takes on different guises in the Asian context. It is common knowledge that curators and artists have experienced censorship from the Chinese government for years, the most well-known example of which is the infamous closing of the 1989 "China/Avant-Garde" exhibition at the National Gallery in Beijing only hours into the opening. The situation is improving, but censorship is still a concern, albeit one that is largely unreported in the U.S. and European art press. In the last year, the authorities in Shanghai closed two exhibitions for including what was deemed pornographic material—the first at the newly opened Zendai Museum and, more recently, a project organized by the alternative art space BizArt. Resigning from curatorial positions to protest such censorship is not a common strategy, not least because it would have little effect in terms of causing change or fueling a larger debate in the long term. This is due, in part, to the absence of broadly read reporting both on-line and in the print media. Instead people find ways to negotiate with the authorities and navigate the political system in order to advance the cause of contemporary art and build a viable art scene.

Another recent case in point is the first Singapore Biennale (2006), for which the artistic director Fumio Nanjo and his curatorial team spent hours meeting with government officials to negotiate permission for the presentation of works in non-art sites, or to have the content of works approved. Largely unaware of this behind-the-scenes activity, the international art world used a predominantly western-centric lens to review the project, commenting more on the originality of the concept, the roster of artists, and the location of works, than considering the project in relation to the political climate that artists and curators in Singapore confront on a daily basis. From the curators' perspective, the fact that the biennale opened with all selected artworks on display was an achievement that continues to pave the way for more public freedom of expression in the country, a point that was made all the more pertinent with the censorship of freedom of speech that took place during the IMF meeting in the city in September. In contrast, there was an unusual display of bi-national curatorial solidarity recently when David Ross and Charles Esche both retracted their participation in curating projects for the Korean "guest country" program at the forthcoming ARCO 2007 in Madrid. They made this move in support of Sunjung Kim's resignation as the country's appointed Commissioner of Artistic Programs, following the Korean Cultural Ministry's intrusive involvement in determining what cultural activities should be presented in Spain. This has, however, gone largely unreported in the Western press.

As 2006 draws to a close it could be said that the process of the curator coming of age is one of transforming the legacy of nineteenth- and twentieth-century art institutions and finding a voice within broader social, cultural, and political arenas. It is also a time when political awareness, on all levels, is heightened through increasing viral activity and the media, which at least provide rhetorical support. But, regardless of the chat, as opportunities open up internationally and curators take on increasingly politicized exhibition topics and roles, the growing pains are centered on the development of skills that enable face-to-face communication with a widening array of professionals, arts supporters, and collectors, as well as an ability to multitask between creative and bureaucratic activities. If the curatorial role is to create space for art to have a truly political and cultural impact, then the reality for the curator is that of sustaining a practice on the frontline.

1) Alex Farquharson, "Bureaux de change," *Frieze* 101, Sept. 2006, pp. 156–59.

2) Gao Minglu is currently a faculty member in the Art and Architecture department of the University of Pittsburgh. He was editor of China's leading art journal *Meishu* in the 1980s, and a key figure in reporting on the "85 Movement" in China. In 1989 he curated the "China/Avant-Garde" Exhibition at the National Art Gallery in Beijing. He left China for the U.S. in 1991 where he is now a leading researcher, writer, and authority of twentieth century East Asian art. Gao curated "Inside Out: New Chinese Art" in 1998, which was the first major show of Chinese art to tour the United States.

KATE FOWLE

PROBLEME DES *ERWACHSENWERDENS*

Falls man sagen kann, dass die 90er Jahre für relationale Ästhetik standen, wird dieses Jahrzehnt als die Zeit in die Geschichte eingehen, in der der Kurator erwachsen wurde.

Ohne die alte Streitfrage aufzubringen, ob das Kuratieren als ein Beruf oder eine Leidenschaft zu betrachten ist – generell könnte man sagen, dass die Rolle des Kurators sich gewandelt hat: Aus einem «Geschmacksrichter» ist ein Vermittler geworden, der Kunst, Raum und Publikum miteinander verbindet. Mehr und mehr wird die Tätigkeit des Kurators mit der des Künstlers verglichen; war es in früherer Zeit seine Aufgabe, im Sinne einer institutionellen Kontinuität zu arbeiten, so wird heute von ihm erwartet, die Institution fortlaufend zu transformieren und mit Prozessen und Materialien zu experimentieren. Zu den Schlüsselfaktoren, an denen die Tätigkeit des Kurators heute gemessen wird, zählen Fragestellungen wie diese: In welchem Ausmass werden künstlerische, gesellschaftliche und politische Fragen angesprochen? Wie reagieren die Projekte auf die Situationen, in denen sie realisiert werden? Inwieweit erfüllen die Ausstellungen und Events eine Plattformfunktion für die Philosophien und Interessen der Kuratoren wie der Künstler?

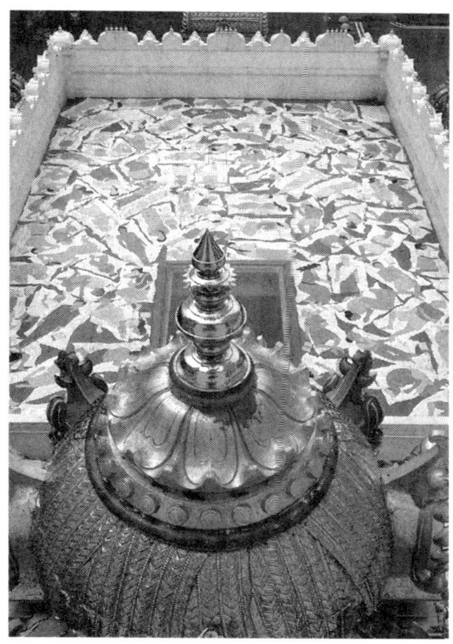

N.S. HARSHA, COSMIC ORPHANS, 2006, installation view Singapore Biennale / KOSMISCHE WAISENKINDER, Installationsansicht.

Meiner jetzigen Tätigkeit in den USA gingen längere Forschungsaufenthalte in Asien und Europa voran. Meine Gespräche mit Künstlern und Kuratoren und meine Lektüre der Kunstzeitschriften der letzten Jahre waren der Ausgangspunkt für meine Überlegungen zur heutigen stark hervorgehobenen Rolle des Kurators mit ihren verschiedenen Positionierungen in Bezug auf eine sich fortentwickelnde Kunstwelt, die sich in zunehmendem Masse in grössere gesellschaftspolitische Zusammenhänge integriert.

Harald Szeemann gilt als der erste «unabhängige Kurator»; in seiner sich über fast fünf Jahrzehnte erstreckenden Laufbahn organisierte er Ausstellungen und baute Beziehungen zu Künstlern auf, die heute als beispielhaft betrachtet werden und die Erwartungen, die die Öffentlichkeit an den

---

KATE FOWLE leitet das MA-Studienprogramm «Curatorial Practice» am California College of the Arts in San Francisco.

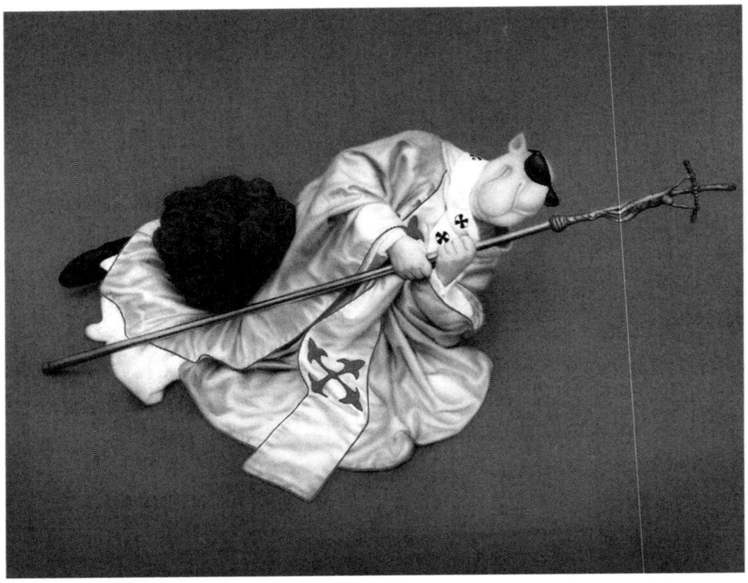

ZHOU TIEHAI, MAURIZIO CATTELAN, 2006, airbrush on canvas, 78 3/4 x 59" / Airbrush auf Leinwand, 200 x 150 cm.

Kurator stellt, entscheidend mitbestimmt haben. Szeemann starb 2005. Wie keinem Kurator zuvor wurden ihm in zahlreichen Zeitungen und Zeitschriften Nachrufe gewidmet – ein Zeichen dafür, dass die Medien in Kuratoren inzwischen «Celebrities» sehen, die für ein breites Publikum ausserhalb der Kunstwelt interessant geworden sind.

Auch das «Viral Publishing» über Blogs und Websites hat epidemische Ausmasse angenommen. Das Internet – einst die Domäne von Regierungen und politischen Aktivisten, von Glücksspielveranstaltern und kommerziellen Anbietern – ist heute auch ein Diskussionsforum für neueste Ereignisse in der Welt der Kunst, von Messeeröffnungen und Auktionen bis hin zu Rücktritten und Protestaktionen. Dieser freie Informationszugang hat in den letzten Monaten dazu geführt, dass der Kurator mehr denn je zuvor als eine für die breite Öffentlichkeit relevante Figur betrachtet wird, ja als eine radikale aktivistische Figur, die den Museen und anderen Kunstinstitutionen gegenübergestellt wird. Das wurde deutlich, als der Fall des abrupten Rücktritts Chris Gilberts als Matrix-Kurator am Berkeley Art Museum in Kalifornien – ein Zeichen des Protests gegen die in seinen Worten «imperialistischen kapitalistischen Werte» der Kunstinstitutionen – durch die virale Verbreitung seines Essays in Form eines Rücktrittschreibens zahlreiche Blog-Diskussionen auslöste und zum Gesprächsthema der Nachtschwärmer in den Bars wurde. Die etablierten Kunstzeitschriften wollten nicht zurückstehen; erst im September 2006 liess Liam Gillick sich in *Artforum* von Gilberts Rücktritt und dem anhaltenden Wirbel in den viralen Medien dazu inspirieren, die Möglichkeiten des Kurators, Änderungen herbeizuführen, in Frage zu stellen.

Aus ähnlichen Gründen haben auch die Absage der Manifesta 6 in Nikosia, der Hauptstadt Zyperns, und die folgenden juristischen Aussetzungen eine grosse Aufmerksamkeit auf sich gezogen, über die Manifesta-Website und verschiedene unabhängige Online-Autoren ebenso wie über die etablierte Kunstpresse. Auch hier ging es um eine umkämpfte Region, die jedoch in diesem Fall für die Kuratoren und die Manifesta Foundation nicht so sehr Thema als vielmehr Austragungsort war. Während Gilbert seinen Rücktritt mit der Torpedierung seiner ausdrücklichen Solidaritätsbekundung mit der «Bolivarischen Revolution» in Venezuela begründete – die Museumsdirektion hatte entsprechende Formulierungen im Wandtext zu der Ausstellung «Now-Time Venezuela: Media along the Path of the Bolivarian Process» abgelehnt –, wollte das Manifesta-Team mit seinem Ausstellungsprojekt politische Grenzen überwinden – ein Ziel, das, wie sich herausstellen sollte, ausserhalb der derzeitigen Möglichkeiten der Kuratoren lag. Das alles stellt sicherlich einen interessanten Lese- und Gesprächsstoff dar, die Frage ist jedoch, wie weit die Kuratoren sich ihrem Ziel angenähert haben, politische Aufklärungsarbeit zu leisten, in etablierten Kunstinstitutionen mit sinnstiftenden Statements oder Aktionen der Zukunft – für Künstler, Kuratoren und für das Publikum.

Ein Artikel in der *Frieze*-Ausgabe vom September 2006 lässt darauf schliessen, dass es einigen Kuratoren gelungen ist, Zentren für zeitgenössische Kunst in Europa zu radikalisieren.[1] Dieses Phänomen wird zurzeit als «New Institutionalism» oder «Experimental Institutionalism» bezeichnet: Zuvor unabhängige Kuratoren übernehmen die Leitung öffentlicher Kunstinstitutionen und geben ihnen eine neue Programmausrichtung, die sich nicht nur auf die Ausstellungspolitik auswirkt, sondern auch auf die Veröffentlichungen, die Forschungstätigkeit, Stipendien und Vortragsprogramme. Eine Parallele in den USA könnte in der Berufungspolitik einiger Universitäten gesehen werden – von der Verpflichtung Robert Storrs als Dekan der Yale School of Art bis hin zu der Lawrence Rinders als Dekan des California College of the Arts. Erst in jüngster Zeit ist das San Francisco Art Institute noch einen Schritt weiter gegangen und hat Okwui Enwezor und Hou Hanru engagiert, um nicht nur das akademische, sondern auch das Ausstellungs- und Vortragsprogramm unter vergleichbaren «New Institutional»-Vorzeichen umgestalten zu lassen. Letzten Endes findet hier nichts weniger als ein Rollentausch statt: Die Institutionskritik, seit den 70er Jahren die Domäne der Künstler, ist heute die der Kuratoren/Direktoren, die die unmittelbare Verantwortung für die Hinterfragung der Mechanismen und Aktivitäten ihrer Institutionen übernehmen.

Nicht nur in Kunstzeitschriften, in der Presse und im Internet wird den Kuratoren, ihrer Tätigkeit und dem Kontext, in dem sie arbeiten, eine immer grössere Aufmerksamkeit gewidmet, seit 2000 ist eine Fülle von Publikationen erschienen, die der Thematik gewidmet sind. Diese gehen aus Symposien, Online-Diskussionen, Tagebuchaufzeichnungen und Interviews hervor, verfasst werden sie von Menschen, die in diesem Bereich tätig sind. Aus solchen Texten spricht die inhärente Selbstreflexivität, die aus der gleichzeitigen Initiierung, Produzierung, Verbreitung und Bewertung mehrerer verschiedener Projekte herrührt. Diese sich anhäufenden Bücher und Artikel stehen für einen im Entstehen begriffenen kritischen Rahmen und etablieren darüber hinaus ein rationales Erklärungsmuster, das der Tätigkeit der Kuratoren eine Art Autonomie von den gesellschaftlichen und kulturellen Kontexten, aus denen sie hervorgeht, und von den Finanzierungs- und Bürokratiestrukturen, die diese Tätigkeit gestalten, verleiht. Mit diesen Veröffentlichungen sind zwar wichtige Vorarbeiten für die Identifizierung bestimmter Tätigkeitsbereiche geleistet worden, doch ohne eine gebührende Betrachtung des Gesamtbildes bergen sie die Gefahr, dass bestimmte Ausstellungen, Projekte oder Personen überbewertet werden, wie es in jüngster Zeit im Falle Chris Gilberts oder des Manifesta-Projekts geschehen ist.

Während sich zum Beispiel die Kunstproduktion und der florierende Kunstmarkt in Asien über mangelnde Aufmerksamkeit nicht beklagen können, gibt es in der westlichen Presse nur wenige Artikel, in denen auch parallele Entwicklungen und Änderungen im Bereich des Kuratierens zur Sprache kommen (von Büchern ganz zu schweigen). Das Konzept des «New Institutionalism» nimmt beispielsweise eine andere Bedeutung an, wenn man China in den Blick fasst. Auf einer Ebene herrscht dort ein ähnliches Klima wie in Europa und den Vereinigten Staaten: Kunstinstitutionen werden

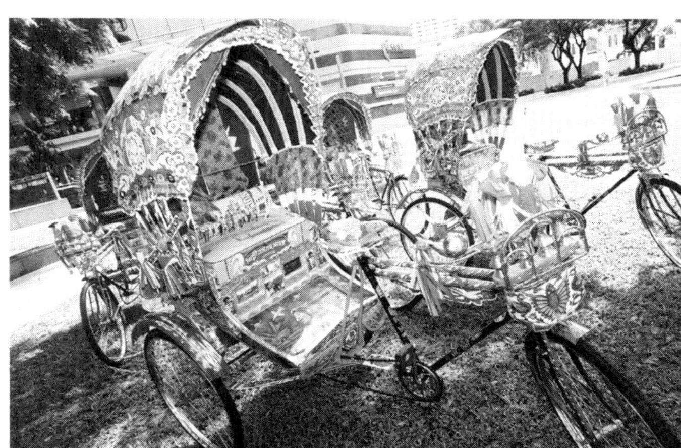

SHAHIDUL ALAM, BELIEF, AND PRACTICES, 2006, installation view Singapore Biennale / GLAUBE, UND BRÄUCHE, Installationsansicht.

heute von international anerkannten unabhängigen Kuratoren geleitet – Fan Dian steht dem National Museum in Beijing vor, Pi Li hat dort in der Nähe eines zum «Kunstpark» umfunktionierten Industrieareals die «Universal Studios» als «unabhängigen» Kunstraum gegründet, und Gu Zhenqing leitet das Zhu Qizhan Art Museum in Shanghai. Doch das ist nur ein Subtext zur grösseren Erzählung des chinesischen Baubooms. Mit der Wende zum 21. Jahrhundert hat in China das, wie der Kurator Gao Minglu sagt,[2)] «Zeitalter des Kunstmuseums» begonnen. Bis 2010 werden nach unterschiedlichen Angaben über das ganze Land verteilt zwischen 300 und 1000 neue Kunstinstitutionen entstehen, sowohl mit öffentlichen Mitteln als auch auf Initiative einzelner Unternehmen, und damit ist China der am schnellsten wachsende Museumsmarkt der Welt. Auch das Ausland ist beteiligt – inzwischen steht fest, dass das Centre Pompidou ein neues Museum in Shanghai bauen wird, und sowohl das Guggenheim als auch das MoMA sind zurzeit auf der Suche nach geeigneten Standorten in China.

Mit dieser rasanten Entwicklung gewinnt neben der Frage, woher die Mittel für die laufenden Kosten und die Finanzierung der Ausstellungen kommen sollen, auch die, wer diese Institutionen leiten soll, eine immer grössere Bedeutung. Aus diesem Grund richten die chinesischen Akademien jetzt Lehrgänge für angehende Kuratoren und Kunstmanagement ein, die nicht nur auf den nationalen Kontext zugeschnitten sind, sondern auch den zunehmenden internationalen Austausch berücksichtigen. Den Anfang machte die Zentralakademie in Beijing, wo jetzt mehr als 100 Studenten für diesen Studiengang eingeschrieben sind, auch in Shanghai ist inzwischen ein Pilotprogramm angelaufen. Nach meinen Gesprächen mit Kuratoren und Künstlern in Shanghai bin ich zu dem Schluss gekommen, dass eingehende Kenntnisse über moderne Kunstmanagementstrategien und Visionen für die Zukunft der Kunstinstitutionen hauptsächlich unter Künstlern zu finden sind. Der in Shanghai lebende Künstler Zhou Tiehai hat zum Beispiel in den letzten zehn Jahren die Welt bereist und seine Werke in westlichen Galerien und Ausstellungsinstituten gezeigt. Aus erster Hand hat er Erfahrungen mit verschiedenen Aspekten der Ausstellungspraxis, des Kunstmarkts und des Kunstmanagements sammeln können, die vielen chinesischen Kuratoren fehlen. Zhou wird zwar nicht die Position eines Kurators übernehmen, doch zurzeit arbeitet er mit einem Konsortium zusammen, das die für 2007 geplante Kunstmesse in Shanghai vorbereitet. In seiner Person verdeutlicht sich die singuläre Situation, in der China sich heute befindet: Die prominenten chinesischen Künstler des letzten Jahrzehnts sind heute die potenziellen Berater der Kuratoren ihres Landes.

Auch der Radikalismus nimmt im asiatischen Kontext eine andere Gestalt an. Es ist allgemein bekannt, dass Kuratoren und Künstler seit Jahren mit Zensurmassnahmen der chinesischen Regierung leben müssen; das berühmt-berüchtigtste Beispiel ereignete sich 1989, als die Ausstellung *China/Avant Garde* in der Nationalgalerie in Beijing nur wenige Stunden nach der Eröffnung geschlossen wurde. Diese Situation hält nach wie vor an, auch wenn sie sich verbessert hat. In amerikanischen und europäischen Kunstzeitschriften wird nur wenig darüber berichtet. Im letzten Jahr wurden in Shanghai zwei Ausstellungen von den Behörden geschlossen; zunächst war das neu eröffnete Zendai Museum betroffen und später das alternative BizArt Centre. In beiden Fällen wurde die Schliessung mit dem Vorwurf der Pornographie begründet. In China ist es nicht üblich, dass ein Kurator aus Protest gegen solche Zensurmassnahmen zurücktritt. Ein solcher Rücktritt

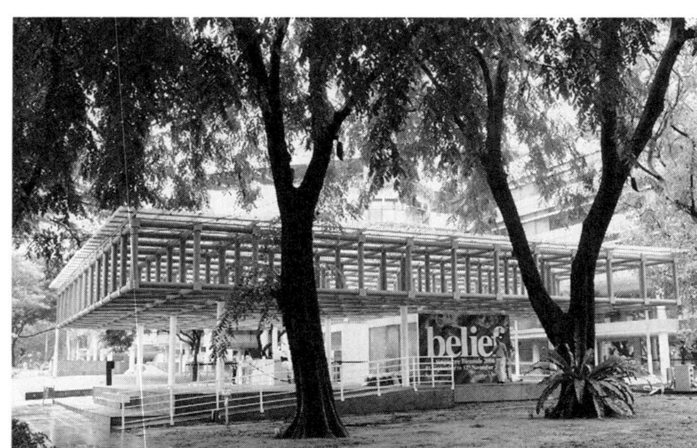

SHIGERU BAN, Paper House / Papierhaus, 2006, Singapore Biennale.

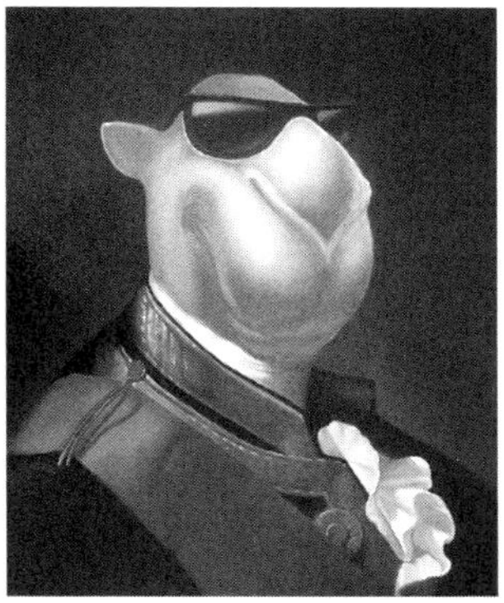

ZHOU TIEHAI, ADMIRAL LORD GEORGE BRYDGES RODNEY BRYDGES, 2006, airbrush on canvas, 23 3/4 x 20 1/2" / Airbrush auf Leinwand, 60 x 52 cm.

könnte weder kurzfristig etwas bewirken, noch nachhaltige Diskussionen in Gang setzen, zumal in den weit verbreiteten Online- und Print-Medien nicht darüber berichtet werden würde. Stattdessen suchen die Kuratoren nach Wegen, mit den Behörden zu verhandeln; sie lavieren sich durch das politische System, um die Sache der zeitgenössischen Kunst zu fördern und eine lebensfähige Kunstszene aufzubauen.

In diesem Zusammenhang muss auch die im September eröffnete erste Biennale in Singapur genannt werden. In stundenlangen Zusammenkünften mit Behördenvertretern mussten der künstlerische Direktor, Fumio Nanjo, und sein Kuratorenteam inhaltlich beanstandete Werke und die Präsentation bestimmter Werke ausserhalb des Ausstellungsgeländes genehmigen lassen. Was hinter den Kulissen vorging, blieb der internationalen Kunstwelt weitgehend verborgen. Das Projekt wurde hauptsächlich aus einem westlichen Blickwinkel heraus betrachtet; besprochen wurden die Originalität des Konzepts, die Auswahl der Künstler und der präsentierten Werke; das politische Klima, mit dem Künstler und Kuratoren in Singapur tagtäglich konfrontiert sind, blieb unbeachtet. Aus der Perspektive der Kuratoren war die Tatsache, dass sämtliche von ihnen ausgewählte Kunstwerke tatsächlich auch auf der Biennale präsentiert wurden, ein weiterer Schritt auf dem Weg, für sich und ihre Kollegen in Singapur eine grössere Ausdrucksfreiheit zu erreichen – ein Erfolg, der angesichts der Einschränkung der Redefreiheit anlässlich des Treffens des Internationalen Währungsfonds (IMF), das ebenfalls noch im September dort stattfand, von umso grösserer Bedeutung ist. Zu einer ungewöhnlichen nationenübergreifenden Solidaritätsaktion unter Kuratoren kam es dagegen erst kürzlich, als David Ross und Charles Esche ihre Mitarbeit an Projekten für das koreanische «Gastland»-Programm der in Planung befindlichen ARCO 2007 in Madrid aufkündigten, um Sunjung Kim zu unterstützen, die nach massiven Interventionen des koreanischen Kulturministeriums von ihrem Amt als Kommissarin für das künstlerische Programm zurückgetreten war. Auch das ist jedoch in der westlichen Presse kaum zur Kenntnis genommen worden.

Im Prozess des «Erwachsenwerdens» des Kurators transformiert sich, so lässt sich heute, gegen Ende des Jahres 2006, sagen, das Erbe der Kunstinstitutionen des 19. und 20. Jahrhunderts, und es findet jetzt eine Stimme in breiteren gesellschaftlichen, kulturellen und politischen Geltungsbereichen. Wir befinden uns heute in einer Zeit, in der das politische Bewusstsein durch wachsende virale Aktivitäten und die Medien auf allen Ebenen geschärft worden ist, und das bringt zumindest eine rhetorische Unterstützung mit sich. Entscheidend ist jedoch: Indem sich Möglichkeiten auf internationaler Ebene eröffnen und Kuratoren eine zunehmend politisierte Rolle übernehmen, konzentrieren sich die Probleme des Erwachsenwerdens auf die Entwicklung von Fähigkeiten, die eine unmittelbare Kommunikation mit einer sich erweiternden Vielfalt an Künstlern, Kunstförderern und Sammlern sowie den ständigen Wechsel zwischen kreativen und bürokratischen Aktivitäten ermöglichen. Falls es die Aufgabe des Kurators ist, Raum für eine Kunst zu schaffen, die einen wahrhaft politischen und kulturellen Einfluss ausüben kann, wird er auf unabsehbare Zeit an vorderster Front seine Stellung halten müssen.

(Übersetzung: Wolfgang Himmelberg)

1) Alex Farquharson, «Bureaux de change», *Frieze*, 101, September 2006, S. 156–159.
2) Gao Minglu lehrt zurzeit am Art and Architecture Department der University of Pittsburgh. In den 80er Jahren war er Herausgeber von *Meishu*, der führenden chinesischen Kunstzeitschrift, und eine Schlüsselfigur in der Berichterstattung über die «85 Movement» in China. 1989 kuratierte er die Ausstellung *China/Avant-Garde* in der National Art Gallery in Beijing. 1991 emigrierte er in die USA, wo er heute zu den führenden Autoritäten auf dem Gebiet der ostasiatischen Kunst des 20. Jahrhunderts zählt. 1998 kuratierte Gao *Inside Out: New Chinese Art*, die erste grosse Wanderausstellung moderner chinesischer Kunst in den USA.

CUMULUS

Aus Europa

IN JEDER AUSGABE VON PARKETT PEILT EINE CUMULUS-WOLKE AUS AMERIKA UND EINE AUS EUROPA DIE INTERESSIERTEN KUNSTFREUNDE AN. SIE TRÄGT PERSÖNLICHE RÜCKBLICKE, BEURTEILUNGEN UND DENKWÜRDIGE BEGEGNUNGEN MIT SICH – ALS JEWEILS GANZ EIGENE DARSTELLUNG EINER BERUFLICHEN AUSEINANDERSETZUNG.

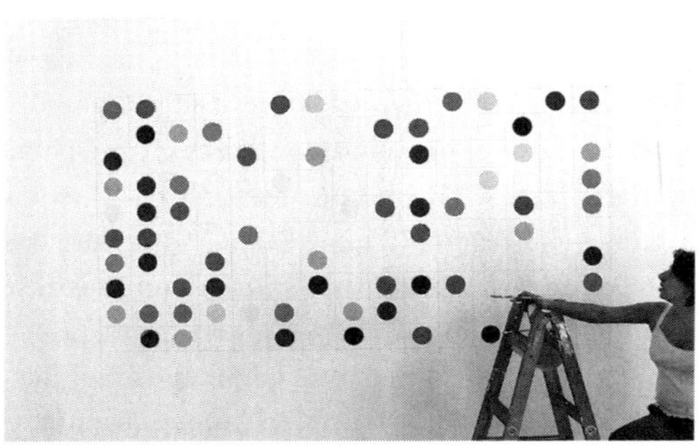

DAMIEN HIRST, FIVE BLACKS (PALESTINE VERSION, 1993/2006 / FÜNF SCHWARZE (PALÄSTINA VERSION). (ALL PHOTOS: ARTSCHOOL PALESTINE, LONDON)

NOTES FROM THE WALL

SIMON C. GRANT

"Where are you from? Why are you here? Where are you going?" asked the young Israeli security guard at Tel Aviv's Ben Gurion Airport. One would have liked to think she was making a wry reference to Gauguin's iconic painting, but this is Israel and she had far more serious thoughts on her mind. As I was en route to the Bethlehem Peace Center to observe the installation of a group show of international artists—the first of its kind in the occupied territories in the West Bank—I had been advised to say that my visit was "a cultural trip to Tel Aviv and Jerusalem" to avoid lengthy questioning. We were allowed to go on our way.

Along the route to Bethlehem it is usually enough to wave your British passport at the Israeli teenagers, doing their military service, who run the security checkpoints. Palestinians rarely get such a smooth ride. To pass through the eight-meter-high concrete *gader ha'hafrada*, or "separation fence" as the Israelis call it (the Palestinians prefer to call it *jidar al-fasl al-'unsun* or "racist segregation wall"), can sometimes entail up to three hours of strip-searching and questions. Barriers, walls, fences, gates, observation towers are increasingly becoming part of this landscape, slowly replacing the old olive and citrus trees.

The Bethlehem Peace Center is in the heart of Bethlehem, the main city in the West Bank under Palestinian authority (currently Hamas, many of whom are Christians). It sits on one

---

SIMON C. GRANT is editor of *TATE ETC.* magazine.

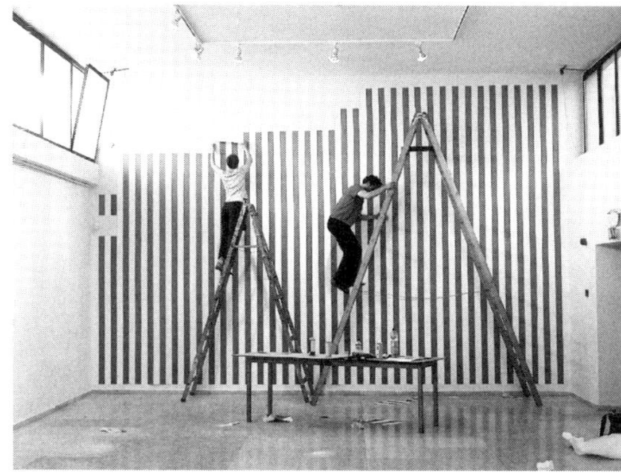

DANIEL BUREN, UNTITLED / OHNE TITEL, 2006.

side of Manger Square and diagonally opposite the Church of the Nativity, the supposed birthplace of Christ and more recently the place where twenty-six Palestinians spent five weeks barricaded inside during the Israeli army siege in 2002. The center was hit too. Nowadays the Swedish-funded building is the focus of more benign events. Here was the venue for "As If By Magic" that featured an impressive line up of international artists including Damien Hirst, Lawrence Weiner, Daniel Buren, Michael Craig-Martin, and Douglas Gordon. The curators, Charles Asprey (co-founder of ArtSchool Palestine) and Kay Pallister, invited the artists to deliver a set of instructions with a budget of no more than £ 50 per artist, so that their works could be made and installed by local technicians on site. The aim of the show, they said, was "to bring such art to the Palestinians, as they are often unable to travel." Of course there is more to it than that. And why, I wanted to know, did the artists agree to do it?

Art first, politics ... if you want them. Here you could see Daniel Buren's wall of green and white vertical stripes; a Damien Hirst spot painting; Martin Creed's lines of black brush-strokes painted up the wall next to each other in various thicknesses; Simon Periton's stencil of images of barbed wire, a hangman's noose, a wall, a skull; Andreas Slominski's two eggs thrown at the wall; Douglas Gordon's double-line text, "Open Your Mouth, Close Your Eyes, Close Your Mouth, Open Your Eyes"; Nathan Coley's sentence, "There Will Be No Miracles Here," drilled as half centimeter dots into the stonework of the building's exterior; and Ian Hamilton Finlay's little poem that read, "Revolution, Virtue, Eloquence, Transparency."

If you saw these works in the cozy confines of your workaday white cube or public space, some of them might even seem a little, well, one-liner-ish. Here, however, context is everything. One local described Buren's work as "a flag done in Hamas green." Was Buren's choice of color deliberate? Martin Creed's dark black lines looked like the beginnings of a more ominous kind of wall being built—like a black-out in progress. Gordon's work took on a less poetic, more descriptive meaning; this, in an area where the loudest voices you hear are those petitioning for a free Palestine, and where the most prominent vistas looking out from one of the balconies of the Center is onto the encroaching Israeli settler villages that lie, half empty, around Bethlehem. Even Slominski's smashed eggs had a suggestive edge—the yellow dripped and dried yolk with broken bits of eggshell stuck to the wall, a modest act of violence.

For those who live here, the experience of such an art exhibition is a world away from comparable events familiar to the country-hopping-biennale-traveler. As one local artist who traveled from Ramallah to come to the opening put it, "for us, art is a relief, not a luxury." His bus journey, which was only a distance of ten kilometers, had taken nearly two hours. An art opening is not something you can just "drop into" in these parts, and not everyone is guaranteed to get to their destination. And not everyone did this time. Suleiman Mansour, the respected Palestinian artist, was turned away at the Wall's security checkpoint for having "inappropriate papers."

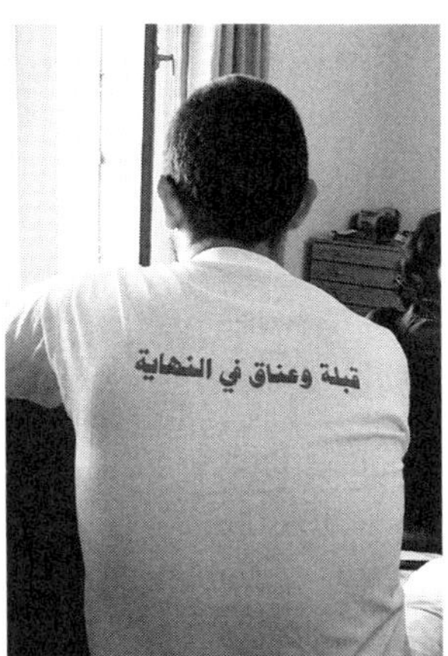

GARY ROUGH, ONE KISS ONE EMBRACE AT THE BEGINNING, ONE KISS ONE EMBRACE AT THE END / EIN KUSS EINE UMARMUNG AM ANFANG, EIN KUSS EINE UMARMUNG AM ENDE, 2006.

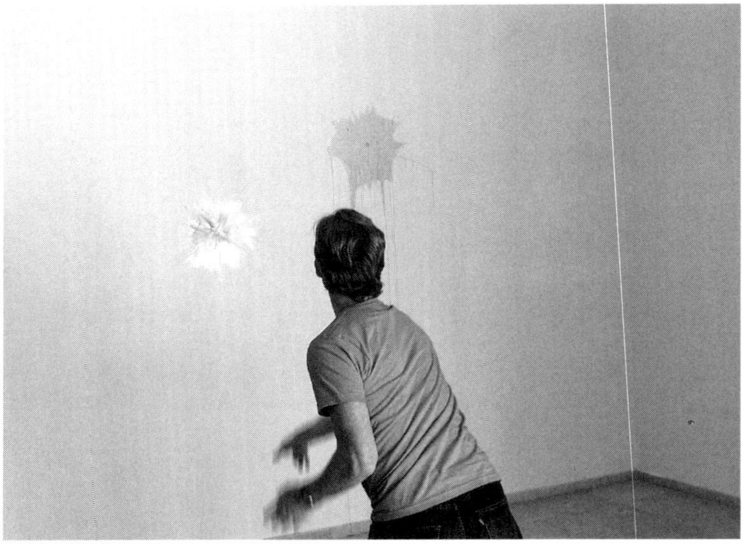

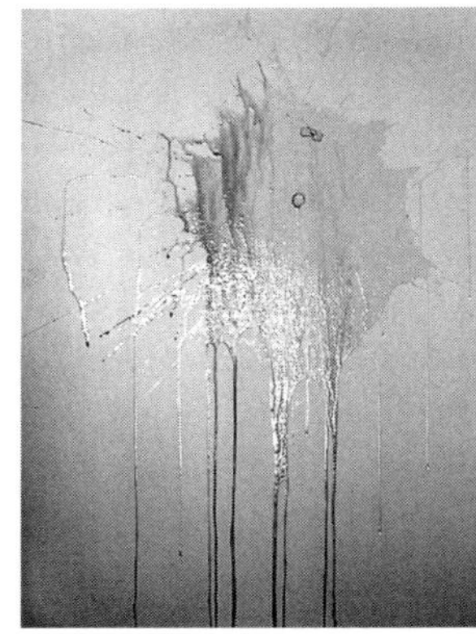

ANDREAS SLOMINSKI, UNTITLED / OHNE TITEL, 2006.

AUFZEICHNUNGEN

SIMON C. GRANT

«Woher kommen Sie? Was bringt Sie hierher? Wohin gehen Sie?», fragte die junge israelische Sicherheitsbeamtin am Ben-Gurion-Flughafen von Tel Aviv. Man hätte ihr gerne eine ironische Anspielung auf Gauguins berühmtes Gemälde unterstellt, wir waren jedoch in Israel, und sie hatte wesentlich ernsthaftere Dinge im Sinn. Ich war auf dem Weg zum Bethlehem Peace Center, wo ich bei der Einrichtung einer Gruppenausstellung internationaler Künstler, der ersten ihrer Art im israelisch besetzten Westjordanland, zugegen sein sollte, und bereits bei der Anreise hatte man mir geraten, anzugeben, mein Besuch diene «einer Kulturreise nach Tel Aviv und Jerusalem», um eingehendere Nachfragen zu vermeiden. Wir wurden durchgelassen.

Auf dem Weg nach Bethlehem genügt es für gewöhnlich, seinen britischen Reisepass den blutjungen israelischen Wehrdienstleistenden entgegenzuhalten, die die Sicherheitskontrollpunkte bewachen. Palästinensern wird die Sache selten so leicht gemacht. Um durch den acht Meter hohen «gader ha'hafrada» oder «Trennungszaun» zu gelangen, wie die Israelis die Betonmauer nennen (die Palästinenser bevorzugen die Bezeichnung «jidar al-fasl al-'unsun» oder «rassistische Ausgrenzungsmauer»), kommt es vor, dass man bis zu drei Stunden lang Durchsuchungen und Fragen über sich ergehen lassen muss. Absperrungen, Zäune, Gitter, Wachtürme gehören hier zunehmend zur Landschaft, wo sie die alten Oliven- und Zitrusbäume ersetzen.

Das Bethlehem Peace Center befindet sich im Herzen Bethlehems, der wichtigsten Stadt im Westjordanland unter palästinensischer Verwaltung (was zurzeit bedeutet unter der Verwaltung der Hamas, die zahlreiche Christen zu ihren Mitgliedern zählt). Es ist am Krippen-Platz schräg gegenüber der Geburtskirche gelegen, die die

SIMON C. GRANT ist Redaktor des Magazins *TATE ETC.*

Geburtsstätte Christi markieren soll und in der sich in jüngerer Zeit, während der Belagerung durch die israelische Armee im Jahr 2002, sechsundzwanzig Palästinenser fünf Wochen lang verbarrikadierten. Auch das Gebäude des Peace Center wurde getroffen. Heute gibt das von Schweden finanzierte Haus den Rahmen für friedlichere Veranstaltungen ab. Hier fand die Ausstellung «As If By Magic» statt, die mit einem eindrucksvollen Aufgebot internationaler Künstler wie Damien Hirst, Lawrence Weiner, Daniel Buren, Michael Craig-Martin und Douglas Gordon aufwarten konnte. Die Kuratoren Charles Asprey (Mitbegründer der ArtSchool Palestine) und Kay Pallister baten die Künstler, Anleitungen für Arbeiten einzusenden, deren Budget £ 50 nicht überschreiten sollte, sodass Techniker vor Ort diese Arbeiten realisieren und installieren konnten. Ziel der Ausstellung war es nach ihrer Aussage, «diese Art von Kunst zu den Palästinensern zu bringen, die in vielen Fällen keine Möglichkeit haben zu reisen». Natürlich geht es um mehr als das. Und warum, so wollte ich wissen, machen die Künstler mit?

Zuerst kommt die Kunst und bei Bedarf... die Politik. Zu sehen waren hier Daniel Burens Wand aus grünen und weissen vertikalen Streifen, ein Tupfenbild Damien Hirsts, Martin Creeds nebeneinander in verschiedener Dicke die Wand hoch gemalte schwarze Pinselstriche, Stencils (Schablonengrafitti) von Simon Periton, die Stacheldraht, eine Schlinge, eine Wand, einen Totenschädel darstellten, Andreas Slominskis zwei an die Wand geworfene Eier, Douglas Gordons Zweizeiler «Open Your Mouth, Close Your Eyes, Close Your Mouth, Open Your Eyes», Nathan Coleys mit einen halben Zentimeter tiefen Bohrlöchern in die Aussenmauer des Gebäudes gemeisselten Satz «There Will Be No Miracles Here» (Hier wird es keine

VON DER MAUER

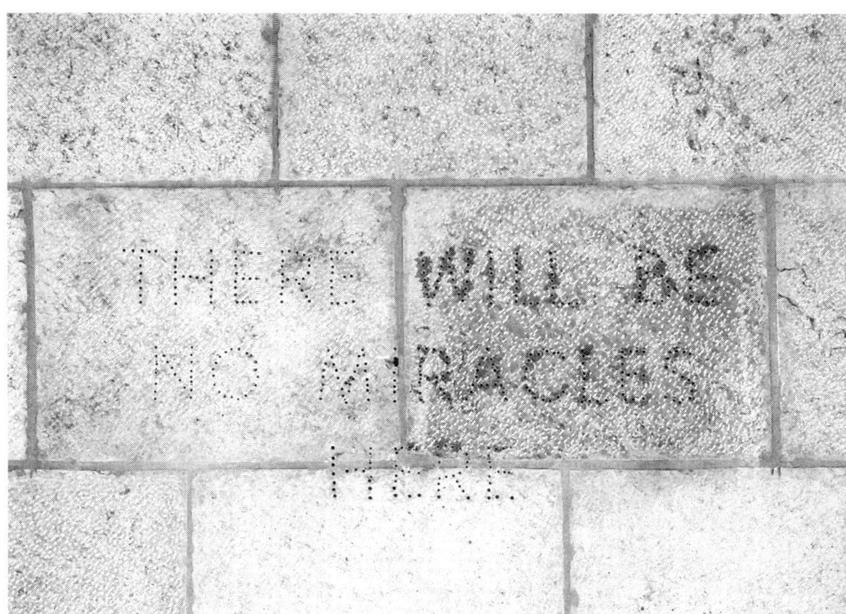

NATHAN COLEY, THERE WILL BE NO MIRACLES HERE / HIER WIRD ES KEINE WUNDER GEBEN, 2006.

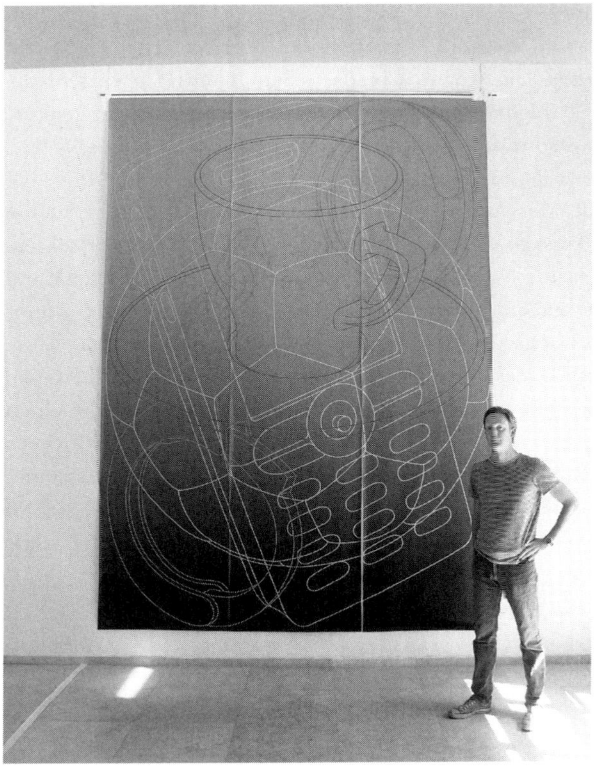

MICHAEL CRAIG-MARTIN, SIMPLE LIFE / EINFACHES LEBEN, 2006.

Wunder geben) und Ian Hamilton Finlays kleines Gedicht aus den Worten «Revolution, Virtue, Eloquence, Transparency» (Revolution, Tugendhaftigkeit, Beredtheit, Transparenz).

In der Behaglichkeit seines vertrauten *white cube* oder im öffentlichen Raum, würden manche dieser Arbeiten vielleicht ein wenig, nun ja, eindimensional anmuten. Kontext ist hier jedoch alles. Ein Einheimischer bezeichnete Burens Arbeit als eine in Hamas-Grün gehaltene Flagge. Hatte Buren die Farbe bewusst gewählt...? Martin Creeds dunkle schwarze Striche wirkten wie die Anfänge einer noch ominöseren Mauer, die hochgezogen wird – wie eine fortschreitende Verdunkelung. Gordons Arbeit nahm eine weniger poetische, mehr beschreibende Bedeutung an – in einem Gebiet, wo die lautesten Stimmen, die man hört, ein freies Palästina fordern und wo, wenn man von einem Balkon im Zentrum aus den Blick über die Umgebung schweifen lässt, die ringsum unübersehbar um Bethlehem gelegenen, halb leeren israelischen Siedlungen ins Auge fallen. Selbst Slominskis zerplatzte Eier wirkten irgendwie suggestiv – getrocknete Tropfen Eigelb mit Bruchstücken der Eierschale klebten an der Wand: bescheidene Akte der Gewalt.

Für die hier Lebenden ist das Erlebnis einer solchen Kunstausstellung Welten entfernt von dem des von Land zu Land reisende Biennalenbesuchers. «Für uns», so drückte es ein örtlicher Künstler aus, der von Ramallah zur Eröffnung der Ausstellung anreiste, «ist Kunst kein Luxus, sondern Linderung.» Für die Anreise mit dem Bus aus dem lediglich zehn Kilometer entfernten Ramallah hatte er fast zwei Stunden gebraucht. Eine Ausstellungseröffnung ist in diesen Regionen nicht etwas, wo man einfach mal kurz hereinschauen kann. Es ist nicht einmal sicher, dass man es schafft, hinzukommen. Und dieses Mal schaffte es tatsächlich nicht jeder: Suleiman Mansour, der angesehene palästinensische Künstler, wurde am Kontrollpunkt an der Mauer wegen «ungeeigneter Papiere» zurückgewiesen.

(Übersetzung: Bram Opstelten)

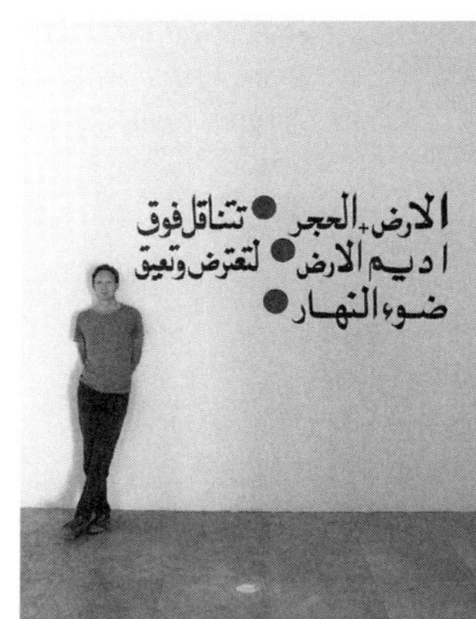

DOUGLAS GORDON, A FEW WORDS ON THE NATURE OF RELATIONSHIPS / EINIGE WORTE ÜBER DIE NATUR VON BEZIEHUNGEN, 2006.

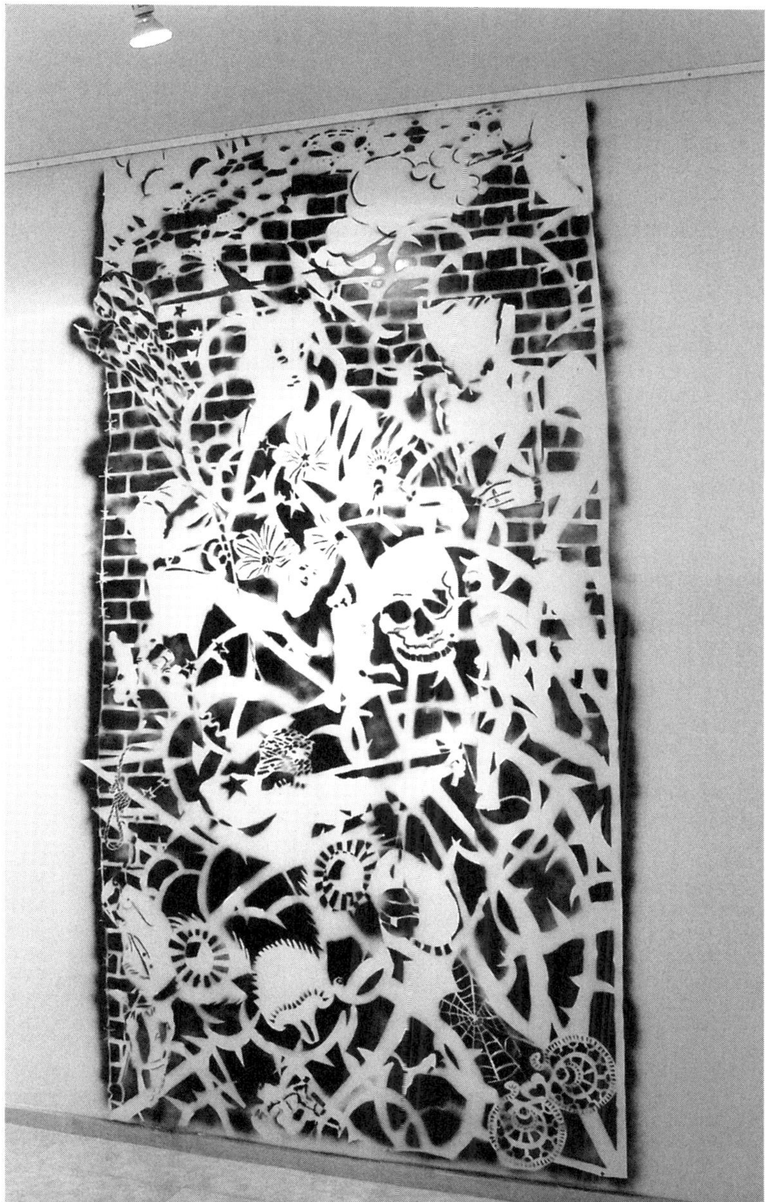

SIMON PERITON, YOUR LOVE, MY WAR / DEINE LIEBE, MEIN KRIEG, 1996 / 2006.

COMPLETE YOUR PARKETT LIBRARY
VERVOLLSTÄNDIGEN SIE IHRE PARKETT-BIBLIOTHEK

OUT OF PRINT / VERGRIFFEN: **NO. 1** ENZO CUCCHI, **2** SIGMAR POLKE, **3** MARTIN DISLER, **4** MERET OPPENHEIM, **5** ERIC FISCHL, **6** JANNIS KOUNELLIS, **7** BRICE MARDEN, **8** MARKUS RAETZ, **9** FRANCESCO CLEMENTE, **10** BRUCE NAUMAN, **12** ANDY WARHOL, **13** REBECCA HORN, **16** ROBERT WILSON, **17** FISCHLI/WEISS, **18** ED RUSCHA, **19** JEFF KOONS, MARTIN KIPPENBERGER, **20** TIM ROLLINS&K.O.S., **22** CHRISTIAN BOLTANSKI, JEFF WALL, **24** ALIGHIERO BOETTI, **25** KATHARINA FRITSCH, **26** GÜNTHER FÖRG, PHILIP TAAFFE, JAMES TURRELL, **27** LOUISE BOURGEOIS, ROBERT GOBER, **29** CINDY SHERMAN, JOHN BALDESSARI, **30** SIGMAR POLKE, **31** DAVID HAMMONS, MIKE KELLEY, **33** ROSEMARIE TROCKEL, CHRISTOPHER WOOL, **35** GERHARD RICHTER, **36** STEFAN BALKENHOL, SOPHIE CALLE, **37** CHARLES RAY, FRANZ WEST, **38** ROSS BLECKNER, MARLENE DUMAS, **39** FELIX GONZALEZ-TORRES, WOLFGANG LAIB, **45** MATTHEW BARNEY, SARAH LUCAS, ROMAN SIGNE

For out-of-print issues you can register your name and address with Parkett and you will be notified, if your issue(s) become(s) available on the secondary market / Für vergriffene Bände nimmt der Verlag gerne Ihren Suchauftrag entgegen und macht Ihnen bei allfälliger Verfügbarkeit im Handel ein Angebot.

COLLABORATIONS

PARKETT – 20 YEARS OF ARTISTS' COLLABORATIONS
MIRJAM VARADINIS, ED.
KUNSTHAUS ZÜRICH
"A RARE BEHIND-THE-SCENES LOOK AT ONE OF THE ART WOLRD'S MOST RESPECTED ART MAGAZINES"
(D.A.P., NEW YORK)
248 PAGES, 22 COLOR PAGES, 1 COLOR POSTER
248 SEITEN, DAVON 22 IN FARBE 1 FARBPOSTER
€ 32 / USA: **$ 39** / **CHF 45**
PLUS POSTAGE / ZZGL. VERSANDKOSTEN

ISBN 3-907582-24-1

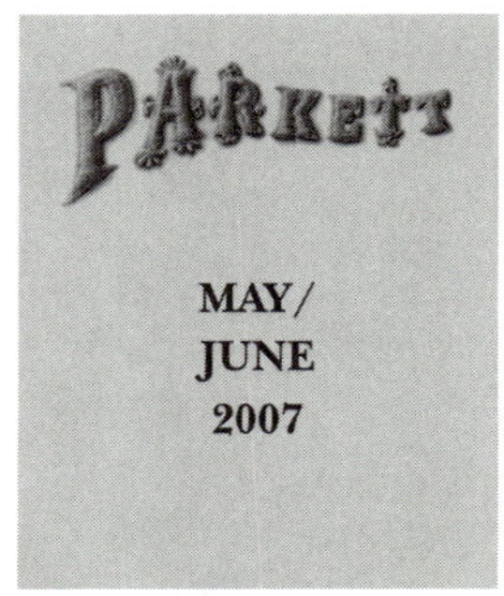

No. 79 - ISBN 978-3-907582-39-8

JON KESSLER
MARILYN MINTER
ALBERT OEHLEN

REBECCA WARREN
OLAF NICOLAI
ERNESTO NETO
BROWN, HERBERT, LAMPERT
PÉCOIL, ESCHE, VON DER HEIDEN
URSPRUNG, HERKENHOFF, HASEGAWA
INSERT: **ANNE COLLIER**
ZOLGHADR: **ANDRO WEKUA**
SCHOR: **CINDY SHERMAN**
ORDEN: **ERWIN WURM**
PERLOFF: **VITO ACCONCI**
CUMULUS AMERICA: KATE FOWLE
CUMULUS EUROPA: SIMON GRANT

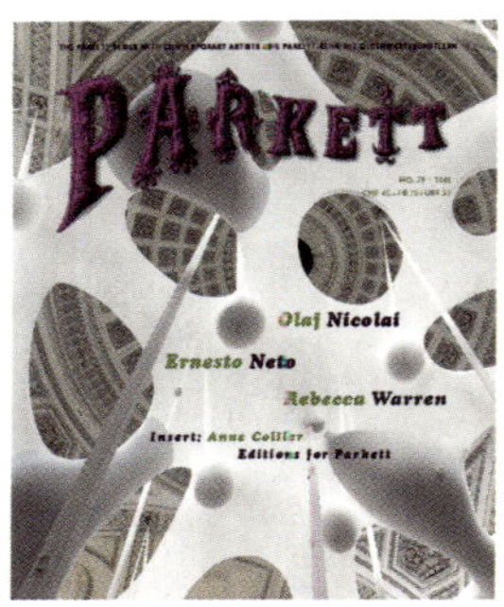

No. 78 - ISBN 978-3-907582-38-1

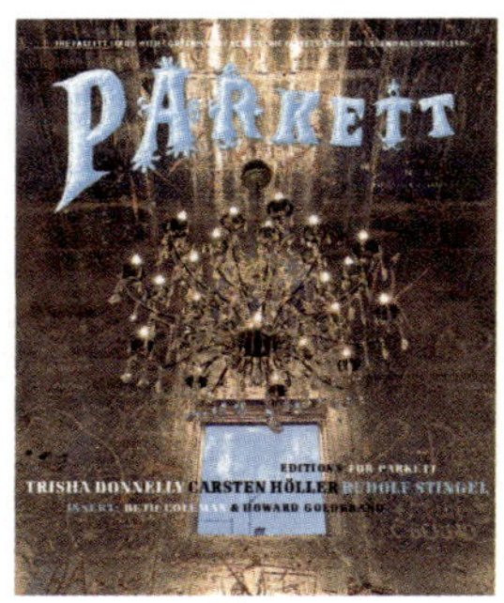

No. 77 - ISBN 3-907582-37-3

CARSTEN HÖLLER
TRISHA DONNELLY
RUDOLF STINGEL
MORGAN, ALLEN, MOUFFE
HOPTMAN, HAINLEY, RUF
RABINOWITZ, HEISER, BONAMI
INSERT: **BETH COLEMAN, HOWARD GOLDKRAND**
RISALITI: **GRAZIA TODERI**
MAC GIOLLA LÉITH: **GERARD BYRNE**
SPINELLI: **ERIK STEINBRECHER**
RATTEMEYER: **CHRISTOPHER WILLIA**
LES INFOS: CHRISTOPH BIGNENS
CUMULUS AMERICA: ALI SUBOTNICK
CUMULUS EUROPA: TIRDAD ZOLGHADR

JULIE MEHRETU
YANG FUDONG
LUCY MCKENZIE
ZUCKERMAN, ABANI, SCHUPPLI
BECCARIA, HASEGAWA, WEI
MULHOLLAND, GRAW, SIMPSON
INSERT: **STEVEN SHEARER**
SMITH: **ROBERT MACPHERSON**
KAISER: **JOHANNA BILLING**
BURTON: **RACHEL HARRISON**
PÉCOIL: **OLIVIER MOSSET**
LES INFOS: **HANS RUDOLF REUST**
CUMULUS EUROPA: MATTHIAS HALDEMANN
CUMULUS AMERICA: BILL ARNING
BALKON: MARK WELZEL

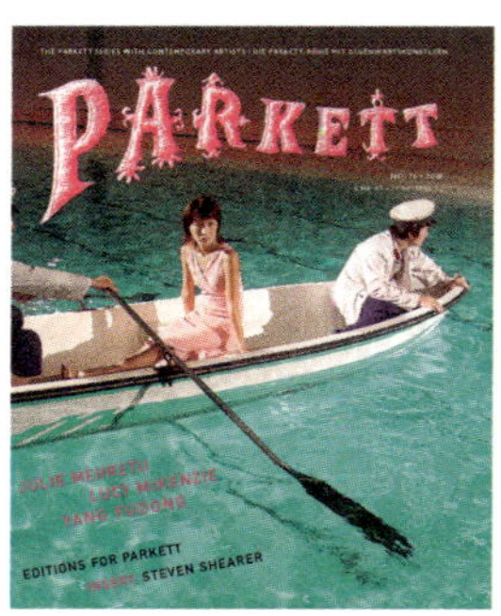

No. 76 - ISBN 3-907582-36-5

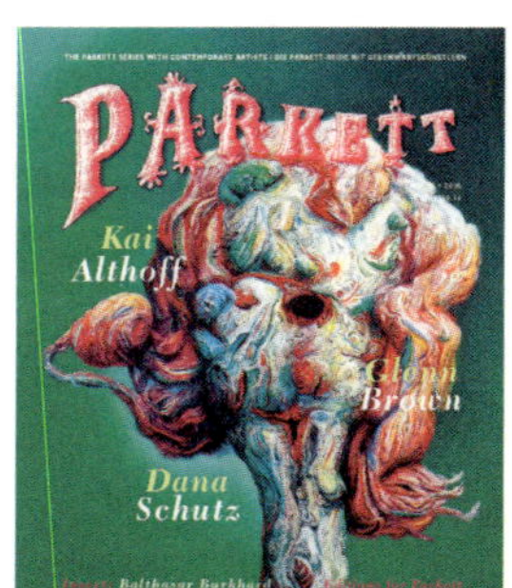

No. 75 - ISBN 3-907582-35-7

DANA SCHUTZ
KAI ALTHOFF
GLENN BROWN
WITTNEVEN, AVGIKOS, SHOLIS
KANTOR, LOERS, KOERNER VON GUSTORF
HIGGIE, SMITH, HEISER
INSERT: **BALTHASAR BURKHARD**
FALLOWELL: **GRAYSON PERRY**
AFFENTRANGER-KIRCHRATH: **RÉMY MARKOWITSCH**
LOBEL: **STURTEVANT**
BAUMANN: **SETH PRICE**
CUMULUS OVERSEAS: RACHEL KENT
CUMULUS EUROPA: GIANFRANCO MARANIELL

PARKETT

SUBSCRIBE, COMPLETE OR SEND A GIFT SUBSCRIPTION TO THE BEST BOOK SERIES ON CONTEMPORARY ARTISTS – WWW.PARKETTART.COM

☐ I wish to subscribe to the PARKETT Series, starting with issue no. ______
☐ I wish to send a gift subscription, starting with issue no. ______ (a gift card in my name will be sent to the recipient):

- ☐ for 1 year (3 issues) at US $ 88 (USA/Canada), € 85 (Europe), € 98 (Rest of the World)
- ☐ for 2 years (6 issues) at US $ 160 (USA/Canada), € 155 (Europe), € 188 (Rest of the World)
- ☐ for 3 years (9 issues) at US $ 225 (USA/Canada), € 220 (Europe), € 278 (Rest of the World)
- ☐ for 1 year (3 issues) at the special student discount (US $ 76 for USA/Canada, € 72 for Europe). A copy of my student ID is enclosed. Postage included. All prices subject to change.

☐ I wish to complete my PARKETT library and order the following issue(s):

No. ______

at € 30 each, postage not included.
Within the USA & Canada $ 32, add postage: $ 5 (USA), $ 10 (Canada).
Sold out: No. 1–10, 12, 13, 16–20, 22, 24–27, 29–31, 33, 35, 36, 38, 39, 45.

☐ I wish to order _____ copies of the PARKETT Postcard Set with Text Booklet on MoMA Show. 172 color postcards, booklet with 2 essays, color reproductions, 64 p., packed in a box, 6¼ x 4¾ x 2⅜", € 32 (USA $ 39) per set, plus postage.

☐ I wish to order _____ copies of "PARKETT – 20 Years of Artists' Collaborations," providing "a rare behind-the-scenes look at one of the art world's most respected art magazines." 248 p., 22 color pages, 1 color poster, € 32 (USA $ 39), plus postage.

NAME: ______
ADDRESS: ______
CITY: ______
STATE/ZIP/COUNTRY: ______
TEL.: ______ FAX: ______
E-MAIL: ______
GIFT RECIPIENT: ______
ADDRESS: ______
CITY: ______
STATE/ZIP: ______
COUNTRY: ______

☐ Charge my Visa Card ☐ Mastercard ☐ AMEX
Card No. ______ Expiration date ______
☐ Payment enclosed (US check or money order) ☐ Bill me
DATE ______
SIGNATURE ______

Send this form to the PARKETT office nearest you:
PARKETT PUBLISHERS 145 AV. OF THE AMERICAS NEW YORK, NY 10013 PHONE (212) 673-2660 FAX (212) 271-0704
PARKETT VERLAG QUELLENSTRASSE 27 CH-8031 ZÜRICH TELEFON +41-44-271 81 40 FAX +41-44-272 43 01
Visit our website: www.parkettart.com

PARKETT

ABONNIEREN, VERVOLLSTÄNDIGEN ODER VERSCHENKEN SIE DIE UMFASSENDSTE BUCHREIHE ÜBER GEGENWARTSKÜNSTLER – WWW.PARKETTART.COM

☐ Ich abonniere die PARKETT-Reihe ab Nr. ______
☐ Ich verschenke ein PARKETT-Abonnement ab Nr. ______ (Der/die Beschenkte erhält eine Geschenkkarte in meinem Namen)

- ☐ für 1 Jahr (3 Bände) zu: € 85 (Europa), CHF 120.– (Schweiz),
- ☐ für 2 Jahre (6 Bände) zu: € 155 (Europa), CHF 222.– (Schweiz),
- ☐ für 3 Jahre (9 Bände) zu: € 220 (Europa), CHF 324.– (Schweiz),
- ☐ für 1 Jahr (3 Bände) zum Studenten-Sonderpreis (Europa: € 72 /Schweiz: CHF 105.–). Eine Kopie meines gültigen Studentenausweises lege ich bei. Preise einschliesslich Versandkosten. Preisänderungen vorbehalten.

☐ Ich möchte meine PARKETT-Bibliothek vervollständigen und bestelle die folgenden noch erhältliche(n) Ausgabe(n):

Nr. ______

zu je € 30 / CHF 45.–, zzgl. Versandkosten (vergriffen: Nr. 1–10, 12, 13, 16–20, 22, 24–27, 29–31, 33, 35, 36, 38, 39, 45).

☐ Ich bestelle _____ Ex. des aktualisierten PARKETT-Postkarten-Sets mit Textbüchlein zur MoMA-Ausstellung. 172 Farbpostkarten, Büchlein mit zwei Texten, Farbabb., 64 S., in bunter Schachtel, 16 x 12 x 6 cm. € 32 / CHF 45.– pro Set, zzgl. Versandkosten.

☐ Ich bestelle _____ Ex. «Parkett – 20 Years of Artists' Collaborations», das neue Buch, das «Einblick hinter die Kulissen der weltweit hoch geschätzten Kunstzeitschrift gewährt». 248 S., dt./engl., 22 Farbseiten, 1 Farbposter, € 32 / CHF 45.–, zzgl. Versandkosten.

NAME: ______
STRASSE: ______
PLZ/STADT: ______
LAND: ______
TEL.: ______ FAX: ______
E-MAIL: ______
BESCHENKTE(R): ______
STRASSE: ______
PLZ/STADT: ______
LAND: ______

☐ Ich zahle mit Visa ☐ Eurocard/Mastercard ☐ AMEX
Karten Nr. ______ Gültig bis ______
☐ Mein Scheck über CHF/€ ______ liegt bei.
☐ Bitte senden Sie mir eine Rechnung.
DATUM ______
UNTERSCHRIFT ______

Senden Sie die Bestellkarte an das PARKETT-Büro in Ihrer Nähe:
PARKETT VERLAG QUELLENSTRASSE 27 CH-8031 ZÜRICH TELEFON +41-44-271 81 40 FAX +41-44-272 43 01
PARKETT PUBLISHERS 145 AV. OF THE AMERICAS NEW YORK, NY 10013 PHONE (212) 673-2660 FAX (212) 271-0704
Besuchen Sie unsere Website: www.parkettart.com

PARKETT

ARTISTS' EDITIONS FOR PARKETT SUBSCRIBERS
WWW.PARKETTART.COM

The PARKETT Series is created in collaboration with artists, who contribute an original work available exclusively to the subscribers in the form of a signed limited SPECIAL EDITION. The available works are also reproduced in each PARKETT issue.

Each SPECIAL EDITION is available by order from any one of our offices in New York or Zurich. Just fill in the details below and send this card to the office nearest you. Once your order has been processed, you will be issued with an invoice and your personal edition number. Upon receipt of payment, you will receive the SPECIAL EDITION. (Please note that supply is subject to availability. PARKETT does not assume responsibility for any delays in production of SPECIAL EDITIONS. Postage is not included.)

☐ **As a subscriber to PARKETT, I would like to order the following Special Edition(s), signed and numbered by the artist.**

PARKETT No.	ARTIST	NAME:
PARKETT No.	ARTIST	ADDRESS:
PARKETT No.	ARTIST	CITY:
PARKETT No.	ARTIST	STATE/ZIP:
PARKETT No.	ARTIST	COUNTRY:
PARKETT No.	ARTIST	PHONE:

☐ **I have indicated my way of payment on the reverse side of this form.**

Send this form to the PARKETT office nearest you:
PARKETT PUBLISHERS 145 AV. OF THE AMERICAS NEW YORK, NY 10013 PHONE (212) 673-2660 FAX (212) 271-0704
PARKETT VERLAG QUELLENSTRASSE 27 CH-8031 ZÜRICH TELEFON +41-44-271 81 40 FAX +41-44-272 43 01
Visit our website: www.parkettart.com

PARKETT

KÜNSTLEREDITIONEN FÜR PARKETT-ABONNENTEN
WWW.PARKETTART.COM

78

Die PARKETT-Buchreihe entsteht in Zusammenarbeit mit Künstlern, die eigens für die Abonnenten einen Originalbeitrag in Form einer limitierten und signierten EDITION gestalten. Diese Editionen sind auch in der Zeitschrift abgebildet und können mit dieser Bestellkarte in jedem unserer Büros in Zürich oder New York bestellt werden. Sie erhalten dann Ihre persönliche Editionsnummer und eine Rechnung. Sobald wir Ihre Zahlung erhalten haben, schicken wir Ihnen Ihre Edition(en). Lieferung solange Vorrat. PARKETT übernimmt keine Verantwortung für allfällige Verzögerungen bei der Herstellung der Vorzugsausgaben. Versandkosten und MwSt (Schweiz) nicht inbegriffen.

☐ **Ich bin PARKETT-Abonnent(in) und bestelle folgende EDITION(EN), nummeriert und vom Künstler signiert:**

PARKETT Nr.	KÜNSTLER/IN	NAME:
PARKETT Nr.	KÜNSTLER/IN	STRASSE:
PARKETT Nr.	KÜNSTLER/IN	PLZ/STADT:
PARKETT Nr.	KÜNSTLER/IN	LAND:
PARKETT Nr.	KÜNSTLER/IN	TEL.:

☐ **Meine Zahlungsweise habe ich auf der Rückseite angegeben.**

Senden Sie die Bestellkarte an das PARKETT-Büro in Ihrer Nähe:
PARKETT VERLAG QUELLENSTRASSE 27 CH-8031 ZÜRICH TELEFON +41-44-271 81 40 FAX +41-44-272 43 01
PARKETT PUBLISHERS 145 AV. OF THE AMERICAS NEW YORK, NY 10013 PHONE (212) 673-2660 FAX (212) 271-0704
Besuchen Sie unsere Website: www.parkettart.com

RICHARD SERRA
BERNARD FRIZE
KATHARINA GROSSE
FOSTER, NESIN, VISCHER, BAKER
SIEGEL & MATTICK, KANTOR, FALGUIERES
VOLK, OBRIST, KURZMEYER
BRIELMAIER: **WANGECHI MUTU**
SHAW: **JOCKUM NORDSTRÖM**
THOMPSON: **JEREMY DELLER**
BOOGERD: **LUCY MCKENZIE**
VEGH: **COREY MCCORKLE**
LES INFO: NERI ON TRISHA BROWN
CUMULUS AMERICA: LARRY RINDER
CUMULUS EUROPA: CHRISTY LANGE

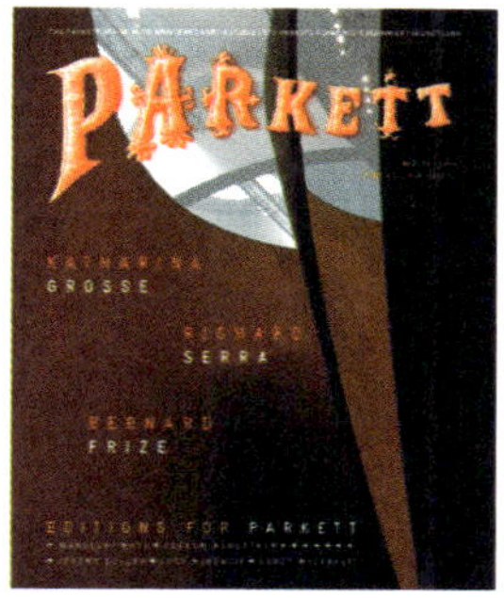

No. 74 - ISBN 3-907582-34-9

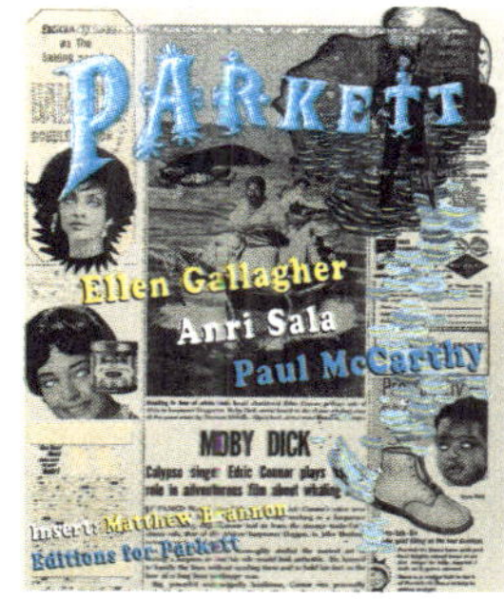

No. 73 - ISBN 3-907582-33-0

ELLEN GALLAGHER
ANRI SALA
PAUL McCARTHY
CLIFF, OKRI, NICHOLS GOODEVE
GODFREY, COOKE, VERWOERT
RELYEA, SIGLER & McCARTHY
INSERT: **MATTHEW BRANNON**
A. ROSENBERG: **JASON DODGE**
R. GOLDBERG: **TANIA BRUGUERA**
T. BEZZOLA: **HARALD SZEEMANN**
CUMULUS AMERICA: DEBRA SINGER
CUMULUS EUROPA: NATAŠA PETREŠIN
BALKON: F. STROUN ON **STEVEN PARRINO**

MONICA BONVICINI
URS FISCHER
RICHARD PRINCE
REBENTISCH, LERUP, HEISER
RICHARDSON, RUF, WEISSMAN
BLAIR, FOGLE, GINGERAS, PÉCOIL
INSERT: **LOREDANA SPERINI**
A. FRANKE: **MATTHEW BUCKINGHAM**
D. KURJAKOVIC: **SILVIE DEFRAOUI**
M. GLÖDE: **CHRISTIAN JANKOWSKI**
CUMULUS: S. SMITH, H. R. REUST
20 YEARS OF PARKETT: ESSAY BY BORIS GROYS
ARTISTS' PAGES, SPECIAL COLLABORATION:
ALEX KATZ IN CONVERSATION WITH
ENA SWANSEA & BRUCE HAINLEY

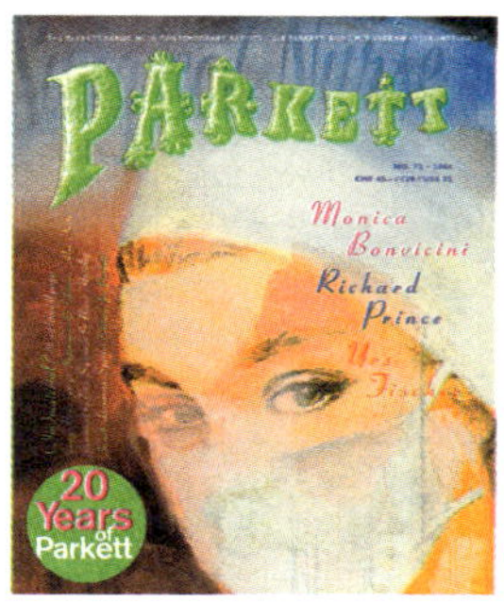

No. 72 - ISBN 3-907582-32-2

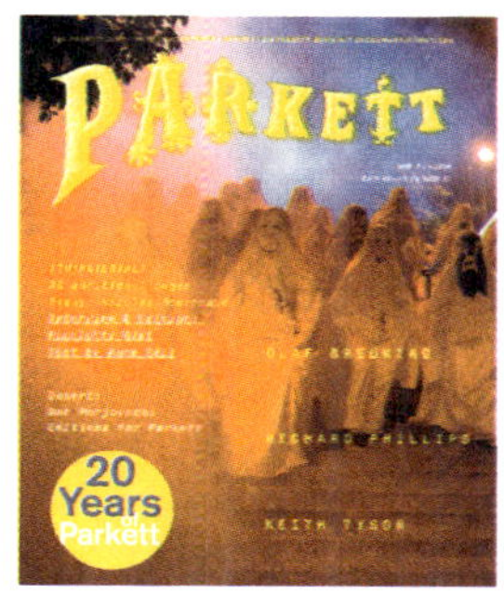

No. 71 - ISBN 3-907582-31-4

OLAF BREUNING
RICHARD PHILLIPS
KEITH TYSON
WAHLER, RODRIGUEZ, JETZER
DIEDERICHSEN, KOETHER, RATTEMEYER
ARCHER, WAGNER/TYSON, REUST
INSERT: **DAN PERJOVSCHI**
V. KATZ: **KIKI SMITH**, M. NICOL: **WALTER PFEIFFER**, F. McKEE: **FIONA BANNER**
CUMULUS: P. BIANCHI, W. BAERWALDT
BALKON: KLAUS THEWELEIT
20 YEARS OF PARKETT: ESSAY BY NICOLAS BOURRIAUD; ARTISTS' PAGES; SPECIAL COLLABORATION: **PIPILOTTI RIST**
ÄNNE SÖLL; CONVERSATION / GESPRÄCH

CHRISTIAN MARCLAY
WILHELM SASNAL
GILLIAN WEARING
SHERBURNE, SCHAFFNER, VERGNE
DAILEY, SZYMCZYK, JANSEN; CAMERON
BURN, WEARING/RABINOWITZ
INSERT: **NIC HESS**
GREG HILTY: **REBECCA WARREN**
D. VAN DEN BOOGERD: **AERNAUT MIK**
LES INFOS: C. WOOD ON **MARK LECKEY**
CUMULUS: C. THEA, G. SCHOR
BALKON: TINEKE REIJNDERS
20 YEARS OF PARKETT: ESSAY BY
JOHANNA BURTON, ARTISTS' PAGES
SPECIAL COLLABORATION: **FRANZ WEST**

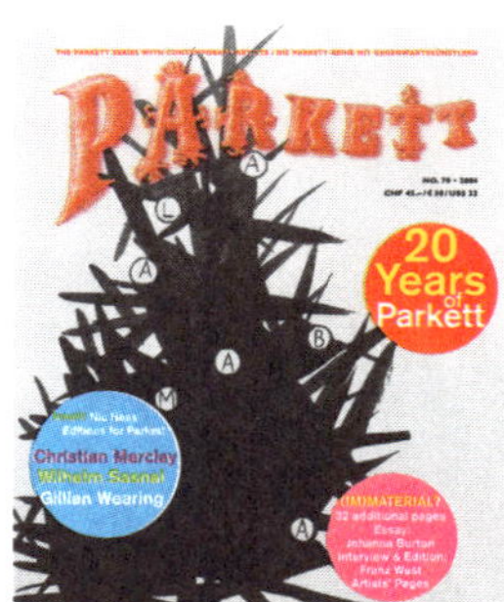

No. 70 - ISBN 3-907582-20-9

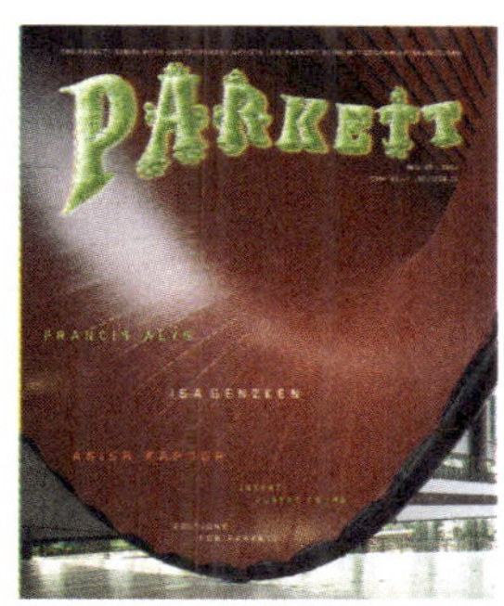

No. 69 - ISBN 3-907582-19-5

FRANCIS ALŸS
ISA GENZKEN
ANISH KAPOOR
SCOTT, ANTON, STORR, HEISER
LEE, KRAJEWSKI, BRYSON
FORSTER, WARNER
INSERT: **ROBERT CRUMB**
KAISER: **AMELIE VON WULFFEN**
COMER: **SWETLANA HEGER**
INQUIRY: CONSENSUS/KONSENS
CUMULUS AMERICA: J. PEARSON
CUMULUS EUROPE: E. TRONCY
BALKON: SERGIO RISALITI

FRANZ ACKERMANN
EIJA-LIISA AHTILA
DAN GRAHAM
FOGLE, DECTER, STANGE, ILES, ELFVING
KOCH, GUAGNINI/SCHNEIDER, MACDONALD
DI BARTOLOMEO, ROSENBERG MILLER
INSERT: **JONATHAN MONK**
D. KURJAKOVIC: **BOJAN SARCEVIC**
H. U. OBRIST: **BERNARD FRIZE**
G. JANSEN: **DIRK SKREBER**
LES INFOS: J. MURPHY
CUMULUS: C. RABINOWITZ, J. HOFFMANN
BALKON: HANS RUDOLF REUST

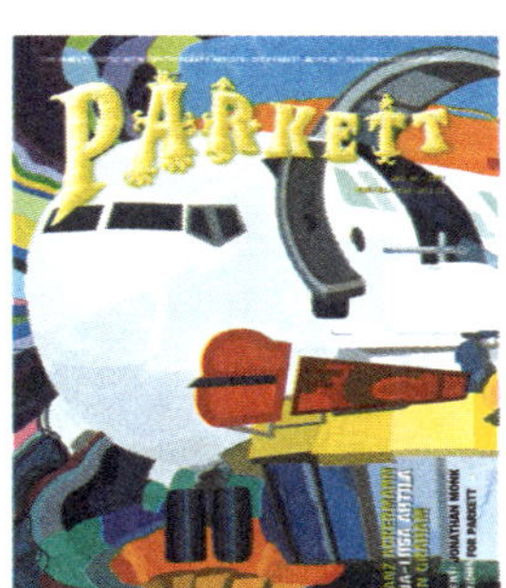

No. 68 - ISBN 3-907582-18-7

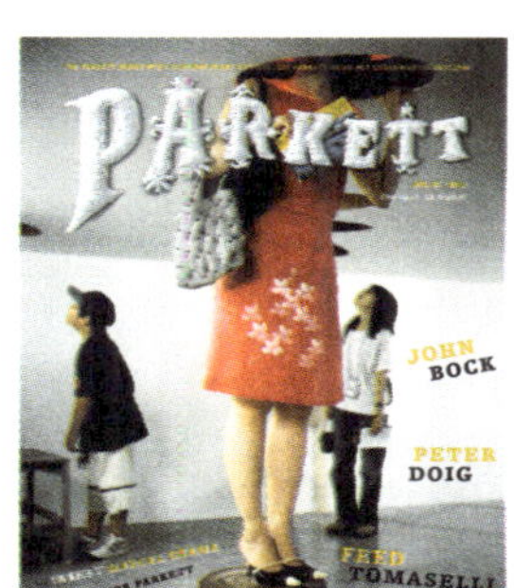

No. 67 - ISBN 3-907582-17-9

JOHN BOCK
PETER DOIG
FRED TOMASELLI
HOFFMANN, BIRNBAUM, AVGIKOS
BONAVENTURA, FUCHS, RUF
CAMERON, RONDEAU, PINCHBECK
INSERT: **MARCEL DZAMA**
T. SELVARATNAM: **SIMON STARLING**
S. OMLIN: **HANNE DARBOVEN**
VISCHER/HERZOG: SCHAULAGER BASEL
LES INFOS: H. BÖHME ON **WANG FU**
CUMULUS: FIRSTENBERG, KERSTING
BALKON: DANIELE MUSCIONICO

ANGELA BULLOCH
DANIEL BUREN
PIERRE HUYGHE
REBENTISCH, WILSON, PRINZHORN
RORIMER, GINGERAS, BUREN/HUYGHE
MILLAR, OBRIST, HOBBS
T. NICHOLS GOODEVE/G. BRUNO
E. DIMENDBERG: **ALLAN SEKULA**
LES INFOS: ROBERTO OHRT ON
MONICA BONVICINI
CUMULUS AMERICA: NATO THOMPSON
CUMULUS EUROPA: GREG HILTY

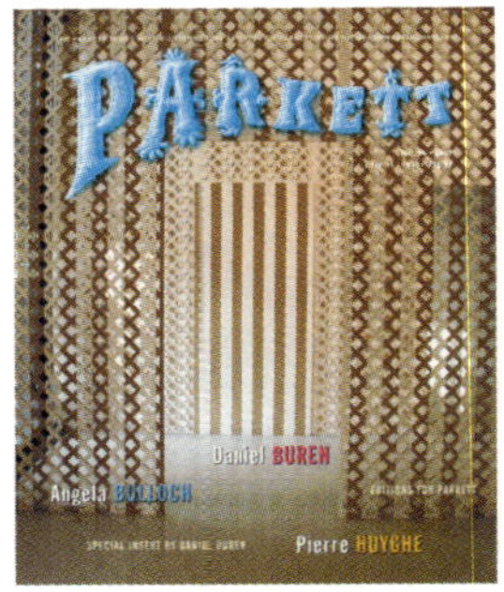

No. 66 - ISBN 3-907582-16-0

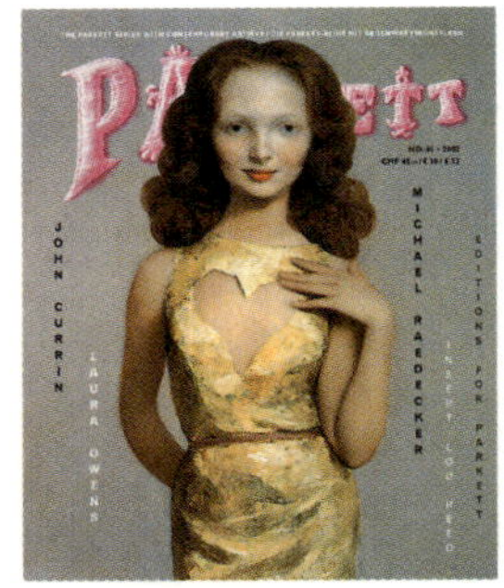

No. 65 - ISBN 3-907582-15-2

JOHN CURRIN
LAURA OWENS
MICHAEL RAEDECKER
SEWARD, VAN DE WALLE, BERG
FERGUSON, THOMSON, WEISSMAN
VERSCHAFFEL, MYERS, EGGERS
INSERT: **LOU REED**
KURT W. FORSTER: **JEFF WALL**
STORR: **DIETER ROTH & D. IANNONE**
K. BITTERLI: **HUBBARD/BIRCHLER**
LES INFOS: CHRISTINA VÉGH
CUMULUS: O. WESTPHALEN, T. HAHN
BALKON: SHEENA WAGSTAFF

OLAFUR ELIASSON
TOM FRIEDMAN
RODNEY GRAHAM
BLOM, MORGAN, CAMERON, MATSUI
WATERS/FRIEDMAN, COOKE, HALE
INSERT: **AMY SILLMAN**
VÉRONIQUE D'AUZAC:
XAVIER VEILHAN
INTERVIEW:
A.M. HOMES: **CHRIS VERENE**
HAKAN NILSSON: **ANNIKA LARSSON**
INQUIRY/UMFRAGE:
LEARNING FROM "DOCUMENTA"

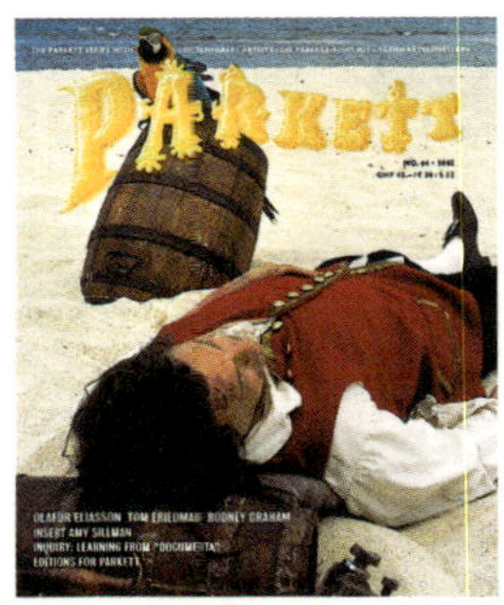

No. 64 - ISBN 3-907582-14-4

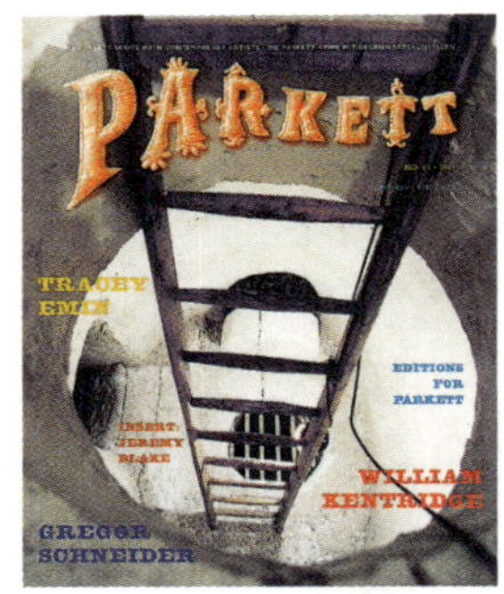

No. 63 - ISBN 3-907582-13-6

TRACEY EMIN
WILLIAM KENTRIDGE
GREGOR SCHNEIDER
BARBER, MUIR, PREECE
GUNNING, STEWART, GOLDBERG
PUVOGEL, LOOCK
INSERT: **JEREMY BLAKE**
CLAUDIA SPINELLI: **FABRICE GYGI**
RAINER FUCHS: **KATHARINA GROSSE**
ADRIAN DANNATT: **THE THREE**
CUMULUS: CHRISTIAN RATTEMEYER
DANIEL BIRNBAUM
BALKON: MICHAEL OPPITZ

JOHN WESLEY
TACITA DEAN
THOMAS DEMAND
MILLAR, CARABELL, SCHWARZ
NORDEN, KÖNIG/STOCKEBRAND
HAINLEY, SEARLE, RUBY, HEISER
INSERT: **G. STEINER & J. LENZLINGER**
PHILIP URSPRUNG: **ALLAN KAPROW**
RUSSELL FERGUSON: **GLEN WILSON**
EDWARD A. SCHEER: **MIKE PARR**
LES INFOS: DAVID GREENBERG
CUMULUS: G. CARMINE, S. DIETZ

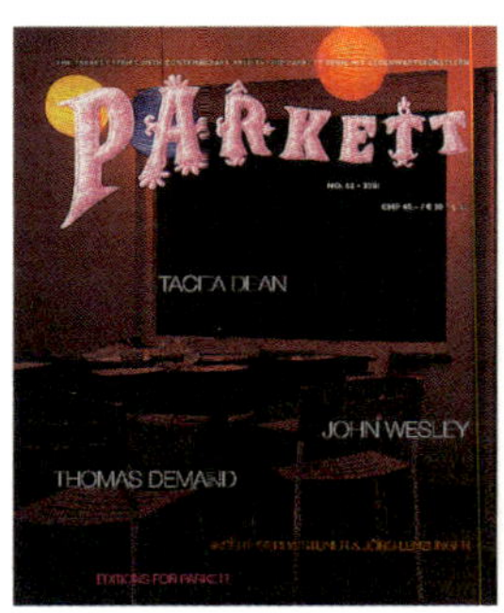

No. 62 - ISBN 3-907582-12-8

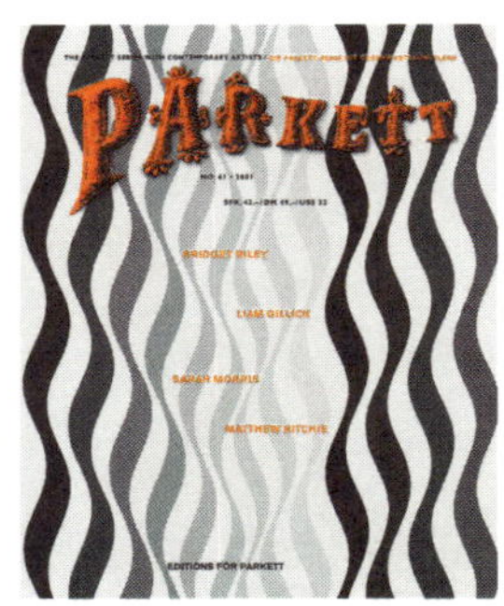

No. 61 - ISBN 3-907582-11-X

BRIDGET RILEY
LIAM GILLICK
SARAH MORRIS
MATTHEW RITCHIE
KUDIELKA, HICKEY
GILLICK, STEMMRICH, WOLLEN
NICHOLS GOODEVE, KLEIN
PRINZHORN, RABINOWITZ
GALISON/JONES, MARCUS
ELISABETH KLEY: **PAUL LINCOLN**
CUMULUS: O. ENWEZOR, M. WARNER
BALKON: STELLA ROLLIG

CHUCK CLOSE
DIANA THATER
LUC TUYMANS
PROSE, CLOSE/PEYTON, SHIFF
CLOSE/CURIGER, ARRHENIUS
HASLINGER, GILBERT-ROLFE
HOPTMAN, MOSQUERA, REUST
INSERT: **SHIRANA SHAHBAZI**
GREG HILTY: **JEREMY DELLER**
HOWARD SINGERMAN: **DAVID BUNN**
LES INFOS: T. DE DUVE—INTERVIEW
CUMULUS: F. WARD, H. U. RECK

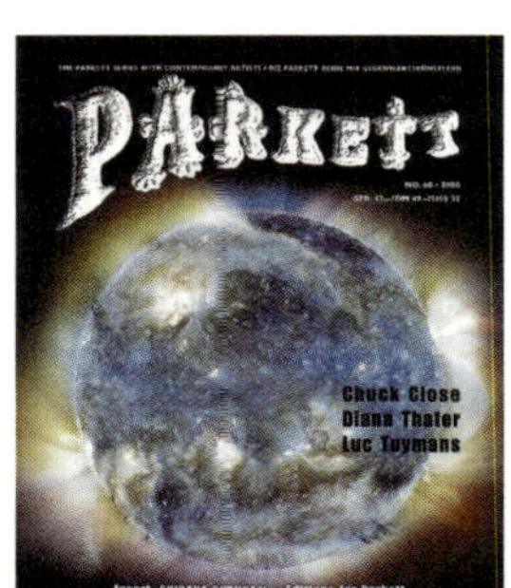

No. 60 - ISBN 3-907582-10-1

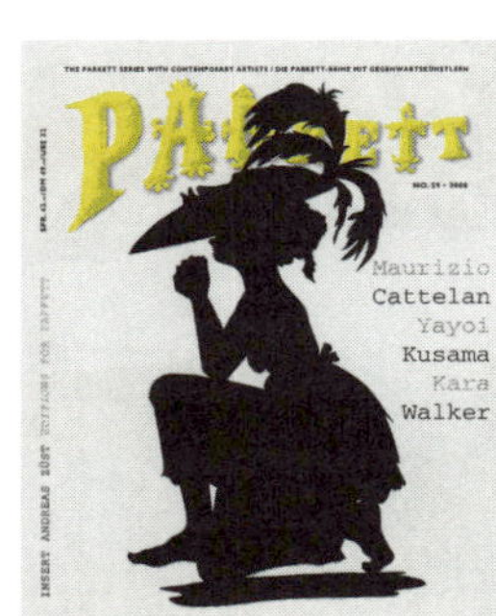

No. 59 - ISBN 3-907582-09-8

MAURIZIO CATTELAN
YAYOI KUSAMA
KARA WALKER
BOURRIAUD, GINGERAS, BONAMI
PANHANS-BÜHLER, MATSUI, POLLOCK
DUBOIS SHAW, JANUS, WALKER
INSERT: **ANDREAS ZÜST**
VINCENT KATZ
E. BRONFEN: **ANNETTE MESSAGER**
JAN AVGIKOS: **ANNA GASKELL**
LES INFOS: ALI SUBOTNICK
CUMULUS: M. ROWELL, L. FÖLDENYI
BALKON: MICHELLE NICOL

JAMES ROSENQUIST
SYLVIE FLEURY
JASON RHOADES
RUSSELL, KOONS/ROSENQUIST
HULTEN, FELIX, GLENN, LOBEL
DANNATT, RUF, KOETHER, FERGUSON
ORTH, SCHEIDEMANN/HERMANN
INSERT: **HENRY BOND**
G. WILLIAMS: **JANE & LOUISE WILSON**
S. ZIZEK, PAUL D. MILLER & CHRIS OFILI
LES INFOS: ANNA HELWING
CUMULUS: D. ROBBINS, H. TEERLINCK
BALKON: KNUT EBELING

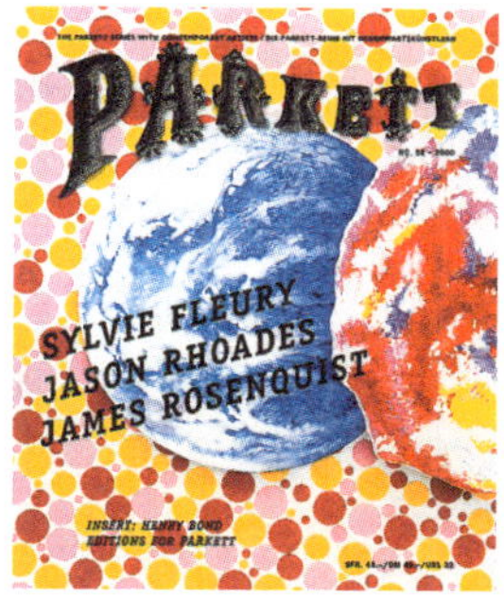

No. 58 - ISBN 3-907582-08-X

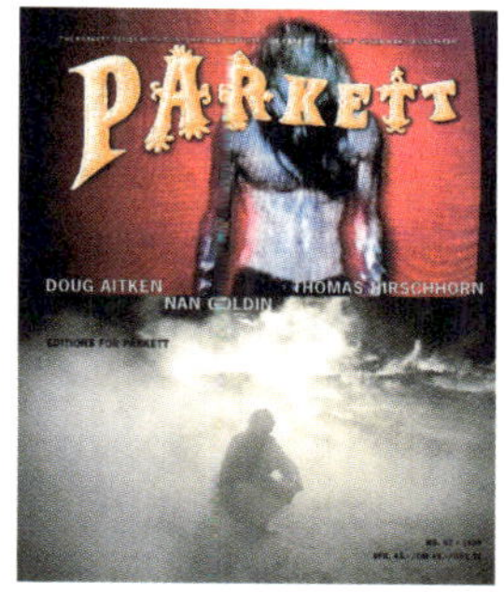

No. 57 - ISBN 3-907582-07-1

DOUG AITKEN
NAN GOLDIN
THOMAS HIRSCHHORN
ROBERTS, BONAMI, VAN ASSCHE
LEBOVICI, DANTO, LIEBMANN
FRIIS-HANSEN, HAKERT, EISENBERG
FLECK, GINGERAS, VERGNE, STEINWEG
D. GREENBERG: **DONALD BAECHLER**
ANDREA KROKSNES: **LOUISE LAWLER**
LIONEL BOVIER: **JOHN MILLER**
LES INFOS: RUDOLF SCHMITZ
CUMULUS: H.U. OBRIST, C. BUTLER
BALKON: J. STEINER/ANNELISE COSTE

ELLSWORTH KELLY
VANESSA BEECROFT
JORGE PARDO
KELLEIN, FER, MAURER, RIMANELLI
BRYSON, TAZZI, SEWARD, AVGIKOS
FERGUSON, VÉGH, VAN WINKEL
FRANGENBERG, BUSH
GREG HILTY: **CERITH WYN EVANS**
THOMAS Y. LEVIN: **CHRISTIAN MARCLAY**
LYNNE COOKE: **DIANA THATER**
LES INFOS: DIANE LEWIS
CUMULUS: A. DANNATT, P. NEDOMA

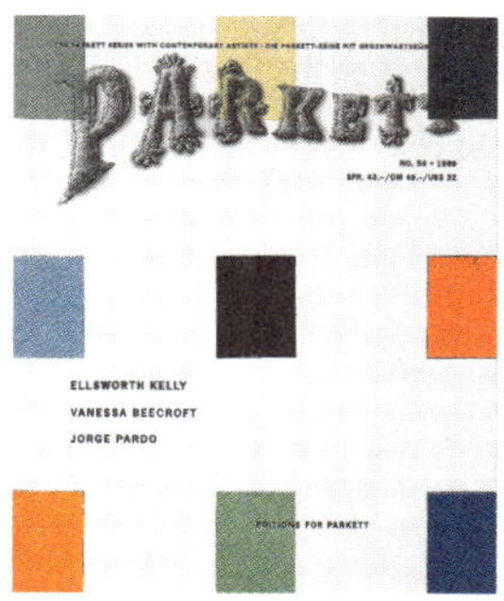

No. 56 - ISBN 3-907582-06-3

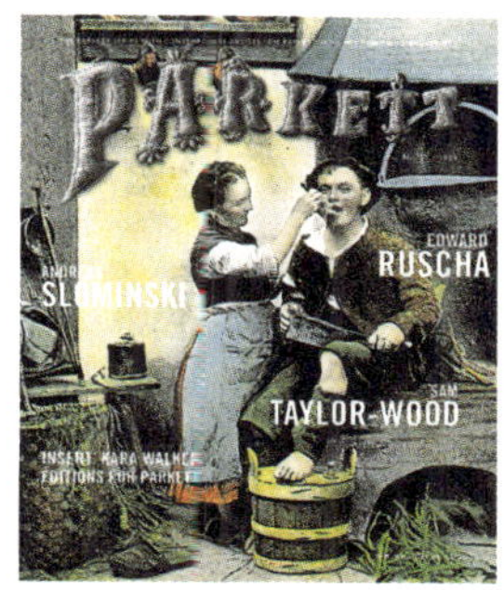

No. 55 - ISBN 3-907582-05-5

EDWARD RUSCHA
ANDREAS SLOMINSKI
SAM TAYLOR-WOOD
PERRONE, HIGGIE, SINGERMAN
SCHENKER, SCANLAN, SPECTOR, FREY
HEYNEN, GROYS/FUNCKE/HOFFMANN
BRONFEN, BONAMI, LAJER-BURCHARTH
INSERT: **KARA WALKER**
BORIS GROYS: **PAVEL PEPPERSTEIN**
RUDOLF SCHMITZ: **ALEXANDER KLUGE**
BEATRIX RUF: **EIJA-LIISA AHTILA**
CUMULUS: M. NICOL, S. ROLNIK

RONI HORN
MARIKO MORI
BEAT STREULI
SCHORR, GUNNARSSON, GOROVOY, LEWIS
SPECTOR, BRYSON, NAKAZAWA, NICHOLS
GOODEVE, STALS, DANTO, AMANO, SMITH
INSERT: **MATTHEW RITCHIE**
VINCENT KATZ: **ALEX KATZ**
H. BREDEKAMP: **STEPHAN VON HUENE**
PAUL D. MILLER: **SHIRIN NESHAT**
LES INFOS:
OKWUI ENWEZOR & WILLIAM KENTRIDGE
CUMULUS: VALÉRIA PICCOLI, MARIA LIND

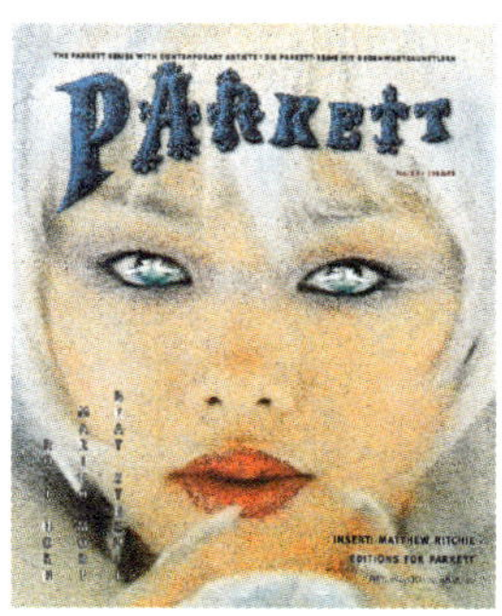

No. 54 - ISBN 3-907582-04-7

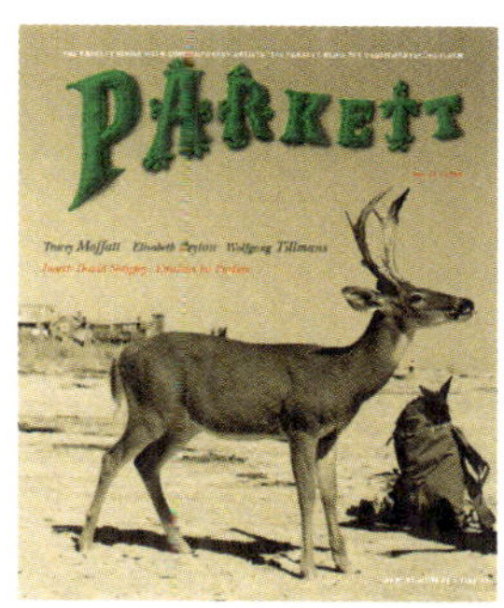

No. 53 - ISBN 3-907582-03-9

TRACEY MOFFATT
ELIZABETH PEYTON
WOLFGANG TILLMANS
MARTIN, LAJER-BURCHARTH, RIMANELLI
PILGRIM, URSPRUNG, LIEBMANN, MATSUI
WAKEFIELD, BUDNEY, NESBITT, ZIEGLER
INSERT: **DAVID SHRIGLEY**
C. BERNARD: **JOHAN GRIMONPREZ**
BERNARD MARCADÉ: **ROBERT GOBER**
LES INFOS DE L'ENFER: V. LIEBERMANN
CUMULUS: BLESSING, AUPETITALLOT
BALKON: STEINER/MAGNAGUAGNO

KAREN KILIMNIK
MALCOLM MORLEY
UGO RONDINONE
SCHORR, BÜRGI, JUNCOSA
MORLEY, LEBENSZTEJN, BONAMI
VERWOERT, HOPTMAN
INSERT: **THOMAS BAYRLE**
ED WHITE: **JEAN MICHEL OTHONIEL**
NEVILLE WAKEFIELD: **RICHARD SERRA**
GILDA WILLIAMS: **GILLIAN WEARING**
R. GRESKOVIC: **MERCE CUNNINGHAM**
CUMULUS: WALKER, KURZMEYER
BALKON: CECILIA VICUÑA

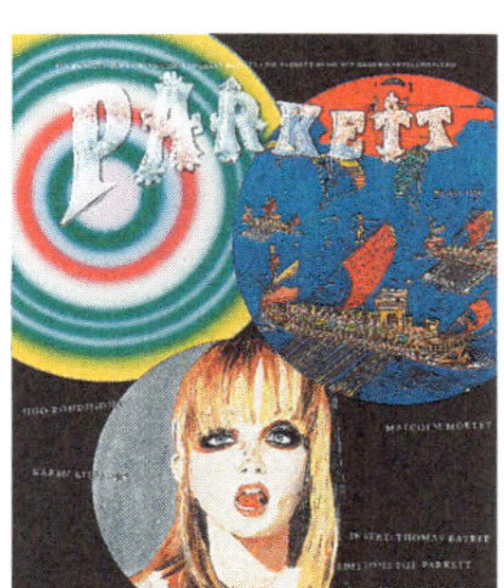

No. 52 - ISBN 3-907582-02-0

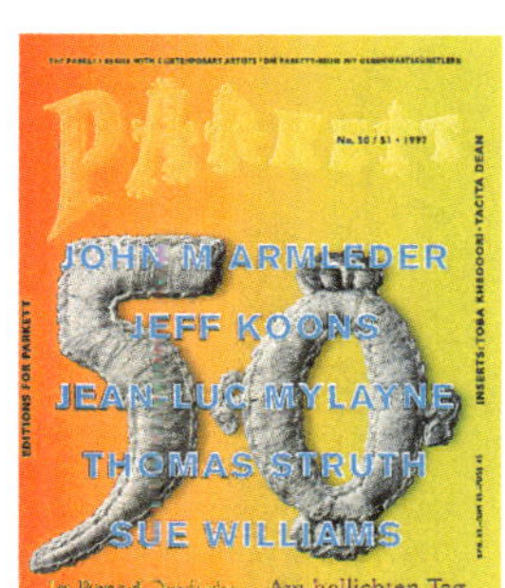

50/51 - ISBN 3-907582-00-4

JOHN M ARMLEDER, JEFF KOONS
JEAN-LUC MYLAYNE
THOMAS STRUTH, SUE WILLIAMS
DI PIETRANTONIO, BOVIER, MUNIZ
SEWARD, LOERS, NICHOLS GOODEVE
COOKE, DION, ARNAUDET, MYLAYNE
CURIGER, LINGWOOD,OKUTSU, BRYSON
SCHJELDAHL, NESBIT, DANNATT, CAMHI
INSERTS: **TOBA KHEDOORI, TACITA DEAN**
ONFRAY: **H. RIGAUD,** NICOL: **SAM SAMORE**
MURPHY, VAN DER WALLE, STEINER
KURT W. FORSTER: **FRANK GEHRY**
CUMULUS: COLEMAN, BIRNBAUM

LAURIE ANDERSON
DOUGLAS GORDON
JEFF WALL
FLOOD, BEZZOLA, FERGUSON
GILLICK/GORDON, BRYSON
PONTBRIAND, SCHORR, ANDERSON
BURCKHARDT, BUDNEY
INSERT: **SILVIA BÄCHLI**
COLIN DE LAND: **JOHN WATERS**
ROBERT STORR: **SEYDOU KEITA**
D. SALVIONI: **CLEGG & GUTTMANN**
CUMULUS: KITTELMANN, MEYER

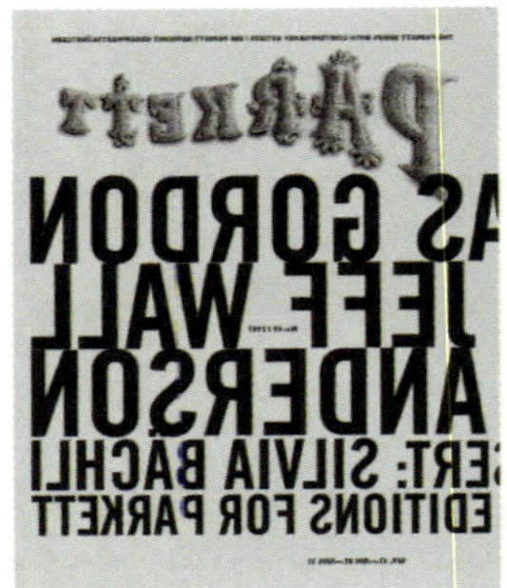

No. 49 - ISBN 3-907509-99-4

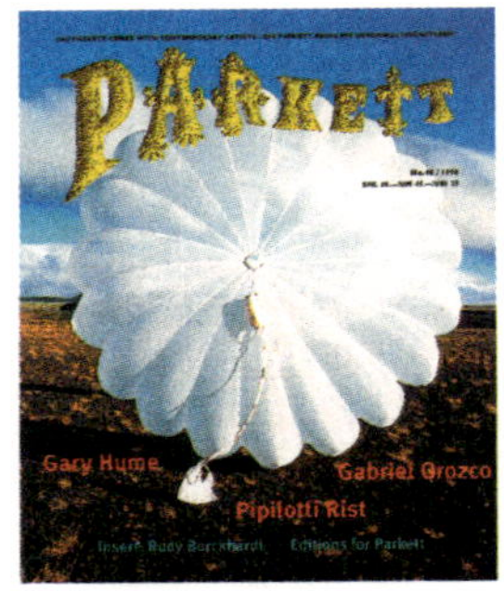

No. 48 - ISBN 3-907509-98-6

GARY HUME
GABRIEL OROZCO
PIPILOTTI RIST
BOVIER, MUIR, FOGLE, BONAMI
DE ZEGHER, SPECTOR, URSPRUNG
BABIAS, COLOMBO, ANDERSON
INSERT: **RUDY BURCKHARDT**
V. KATZ: **RUDY BURCKHARDT**
MARK VAN DER WALLE:
CHARLES LONG & STEREOLAB
FAYE HIRSCH: **BRUCE CONNER**
CH. DOSWALD: **IAN ANÜLL**
CUMULUS: LEGGAT, SCHNEIDER

TONY OURSLER
RAYMOND PETTIBON
THOMAS SCHÜTTE
COOKE, RICHARD, NERI
LEWIS, GROYS, ALS, RUGOFF
GOODEVE, SEARLE, MARI, REUST
WAKEFIELD, LOOCK, JANUS
INSERT: **ZOE LEONARD & CHERYL DUNYE**
JURI STEINER: **EMMA KUNZ**
M. WECHSLER: **CHRISTOPH RÜTIMANN**
SUSAN MORGAN: **DIANE ARBUS**
CUMULUS: PRINCENTHAL, BOVIER/CHERIX

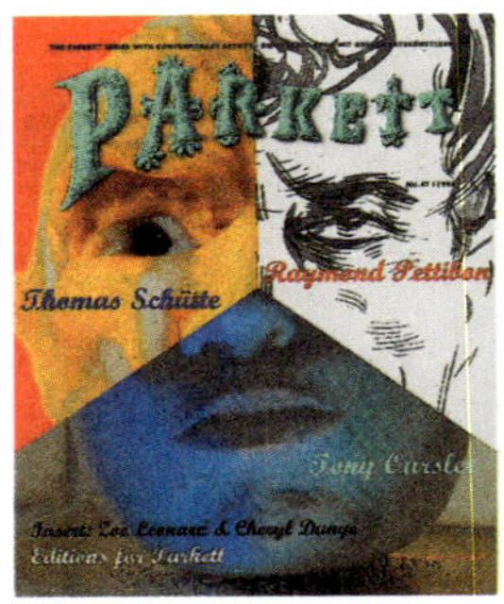

No. 47 - ISBN 3-907509-97-8

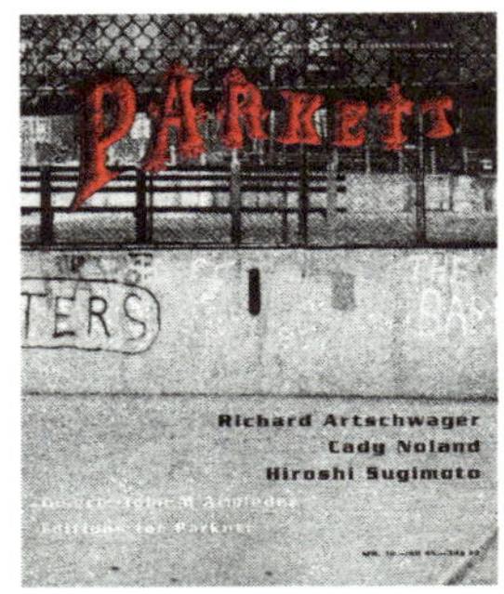

No. 46 - ISBN 3-907509-96-X

RICHARD ARTSCHWAGER
CADY NOLAND
HIROSHI SUGIMOTO
DEITCHER, SCHAFFNER, FORSTER
MUNIZ, ARMSTRONG, RELYEA
BOGDAN, GOODEVE, NICKAS
BRYSON, RUGOFF, DENSON
INSERT: **JOHN M ARMLEDER**
ROLAND WÄSPE: **ERWIN WURM**
D. BIRNBAUM: **ÖYVIND FAHLSTRÖM**
LES INFOS DU PARADIS: ROBERT FLECK
CUMULUS: MILLER, VETTESE
BALKON: MARTIN HELLER

VIJA CELMINS
ANDREAS GURSKY
RIRKRIT TIRAVANIJA
PRINCENTHAL, LEWIS, SILVERTHORNE
SHIFF, CRIQUI, BURCKHARDT, WAKEFIELD
SCHORR, MELO, GILLICK, FLOOD, STEINER
INSERT: **HANS DANUSER**
LES INFOS: LIAM GILLICK /DOUGLAS GORDON
LYNNE COOKE, DAVID DEITCHER
DANIEL KURJAKOVIC: **MARIE JOSÉ BURKI**
NAN GOLDIN: **PETER HUJAR**
NOEMI SMOLIK: **ANDREAS SLOMINSKI**
JASON SIMON: **MARK DION**
LUK LAMBRECHT: **MARK LUYTEN**

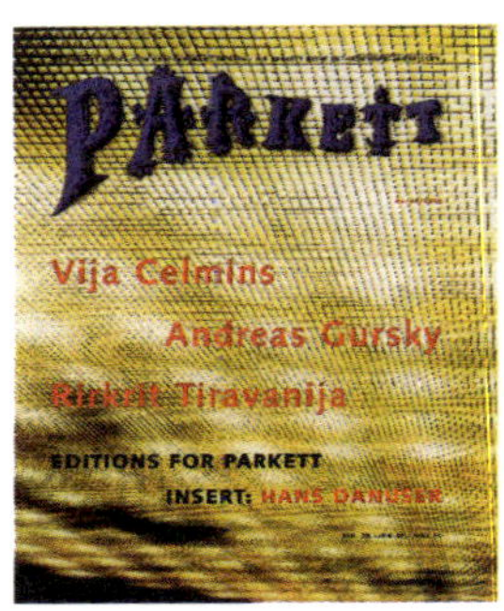

No. 44 - ISBN 3-907509-94-3

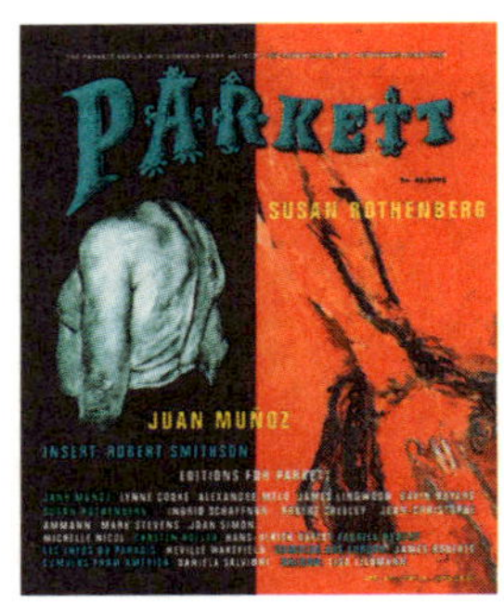

No. 43 - ISBN 3-907509-93-5

JUAN MUÑOZ
SUSAN ROTHENBERG
LYNNE COOKE, ALEXANDRE MELO
JAMES LINGWOOD, GAVIN BRYARS
ROBERT CREELEY, INGRID SCHAFFNER
JEAN-CHRISTOPHE AMMANN
MARK STEVENS, JOAN SIMON
INSERT: **ROBERT SMITHSON**
NEVILLE WAKEFIELD
MICHELLE NICOL: **CARSTEN HÖLLER**
H.U. OBRIST: **FABRICE HYBERT**

LAWRENCE WEINER
RACHEL WHITEREAD
B. ADAMS, F. RICHARD
D. SCHWARZ, D. SALVIONI
E. LEFFINGWELL, L. RELYEA
N. WAKEFIELD, R. SCHMITZ
T. FAIRBROTHER, S. WATNEY
INSERT: **NAN GOLDIN**
VINCE LEO: **ROBERT FRANK**
C. RITSCHARD: **MARKUS RAETZ**

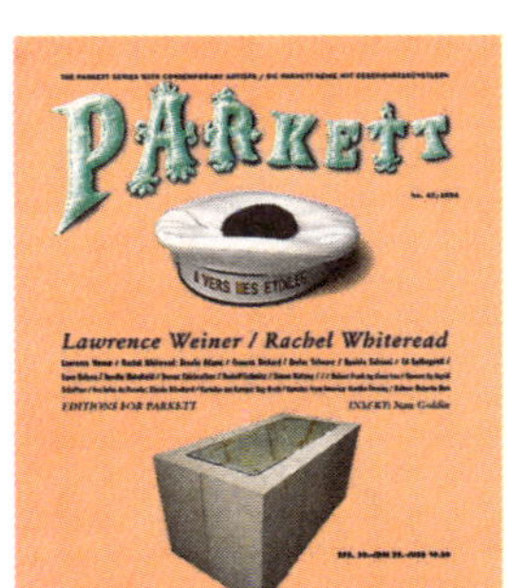

No. 42 - ISBN 3-907509-92-7

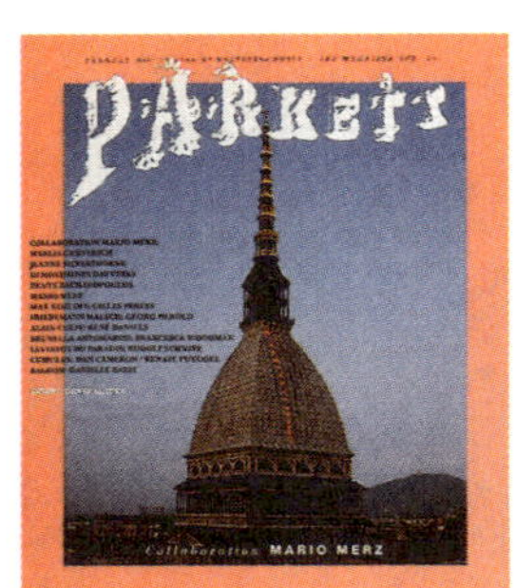

No. 15 - ISBN 3-907509-65-X

MARIO MERZ
MARLIS GRÜTERICH, JEANNE
SILVERTHORNE, DEMOSTHENES
DAVVETAS, HARALD SZEEMANN
DENYS ZACHAROPOULOS
INSERT: **GENERAL IDEA**
MAX KOZLOFF: **GILLES PERESS**
FRIEDEMANN MALSCH:
GEORG HEROLD
BRUNELLA ANTOMARINI:
FRANCESCA WOODMAN

Each volume of PARKETT is created in collaboration with artists, who contribute an original work specially made for the readers of PARKETT. The works are available in a signed and numbered Special Edition. Prices are subject to change. Postage is not included.

EDITIONS FOR PARKETT

Jeder PARKETT-Band entsteht in Collaboration mit Künstlern, die eigens für die Leser von PARKETT Originalbeiträge gestalten. Diese Vorzugsausgaben sind als nummerierte und signierte Editionen erhältlich. Preisänderungen vorbehalten. Versandkosten und MwSt. (Schweiz) nicht inbegriffen.

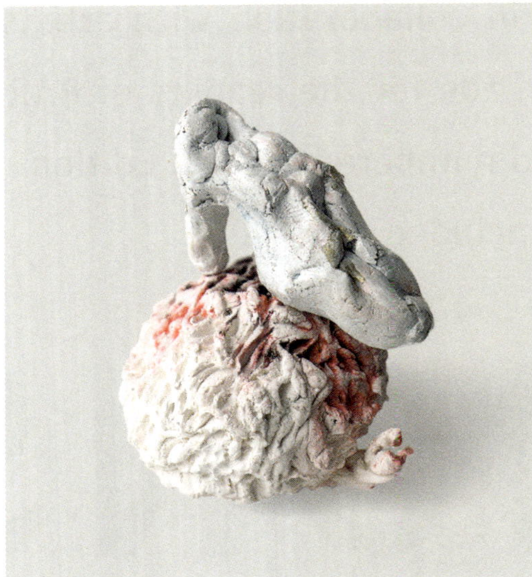

VOM VERSCHWINDEN ERGRIFFEN –
HINTERLASSENSCHAFT EINER SCHAUMGEBORENEN.

THE SLIPPER OVERLOOKED IN FOAM AS
APHRODITE EMERGES.

PARKETT 78
REBECCA WARREN
POINCARÉ, 2006
Pompom and shoe, hand painted, mixed media,
$2\,^3/_4$ x $2\,^3/_4$ x $2\,^3/_8$".
Edition of 35 / XX, signed and numbered certificate.
$ 2000 / € 1250

Pompom und Schuh, handbemalt, verschiedene Materialien.
7 x 7 x 6 cm.
Auflage 35 / XX, signiertes und nummeriertes Zertifikat.
CHF 2500 / € 1250

PROTOTYP FÜR EINEN FREIEN GEIST,
BEWEGLICHKEIT IN ALLEN LEBENSLAGEN.

DO TOUCH: THE METAMORPHOSIS
OF PERCEPTION IS IN THE HANDS
OF THE BEHOLDER.

PARKETT 78
ERNESTO NETO
PHYTUZIANN, 2006
Green lycra tulle and polypropylene pellets,
$17\,^3/_4$ x $10\,^3/_4$ x 2"; weight, 4 lb.
Edition of 60 / XX, signed and numbered.
$ 2400 / € 1900

Grünes Lycragewebe und
Polypropylen-Kügelchen,
45 x 27 x 5 cm, Gewicht 1,8 kg.
Auflage: 60 / XX, signiert und nummeriert.
CHF 2900 / € 1900

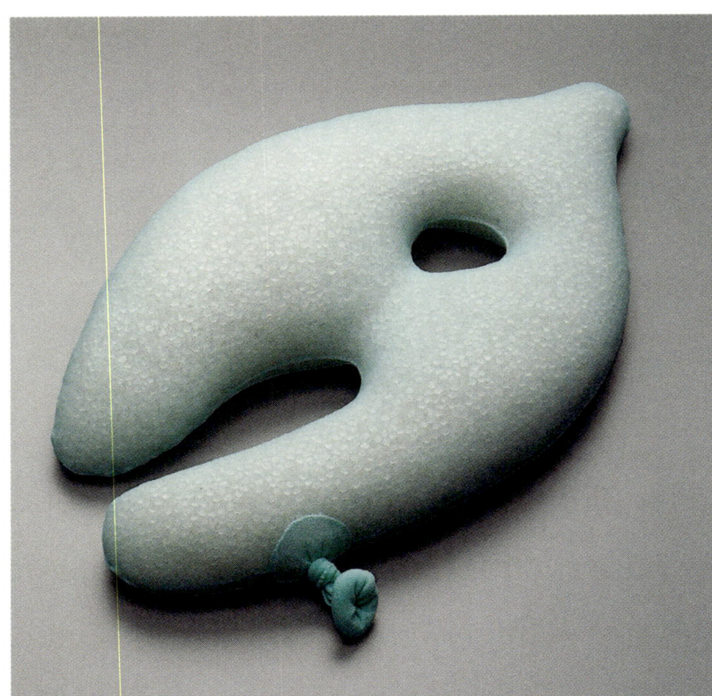

EIN MIMETISCH ANVERWANDELTES KISSEN ALS EINLADUNG, ÜBER LUKÁCS' LIEBLINGSTHEMA, DEN REALISMUS, NACHZUDENKEN?

A MIMETICALLY CHARGED PILLOW WHICH OFFERS AN INVITATION TO REFLECT ON GEORG LUKÁCS' FAVORITE THEME, REALISM.

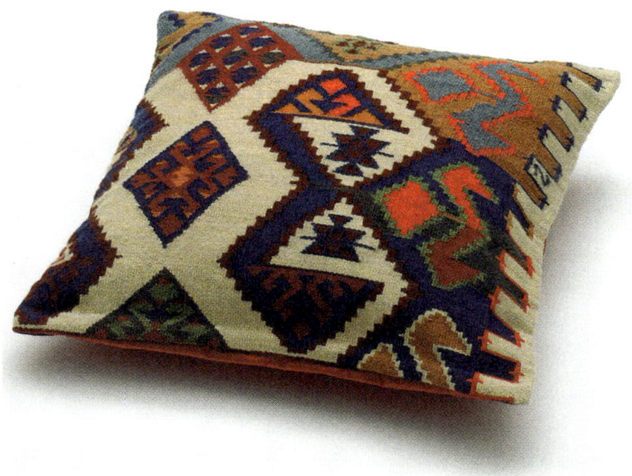

PARKETT 78

OLAF NICOLAI

GEORG'S PILLOW, 2007

(Replica of a pillow from Georg Lukács' sofa in his study in Budapest)

Handwoven pillowcase, hand-dyed sheep's wool and red silk,
18 1/2 x 20".
Made by the Department of Textiles,
Institute of Applied Arts, Schneeberg, Germany.
Edition of 35/ XX, signed and numbered certificate.
$ 2800 / € 2200

GEORGS KISSEN, 2007

(Replica eines Kopfkissens von Georg Lukács' Sofa aus seinem Budapester Arbeitszimmer)

Handgewebter Kissenbezug, handgefärbte Schurwolle und rote Seide,
47 x 51 cm.
Manufaktur: Werkstatt Textilkunst der Fachhochschule für
Angewandte Kunst Schneeberg, Deutschland.
Auflage 35/XX, signiertes und nummeriertes Zertifikat.
CHF 3500 / € 2200

ANNIVERSARY EDITION PARKETT 70

FRANZ WEST

2 x 20 JAHRE PARKETT, 2004

Büchergestell. Armierungsstahl, Plexiglas, vier Räder,
120 x 60 x 30 cm.
Auflage: 99 / XXX, signiertes und nummeriertes Zertifikat.
CHF 4400 / € 2900

2 x 20 YEARS OF PARKETT, 2004

Bookshelf. Reinforcing steel, Plexiglas, four wheels,
47 1/4 x 23 5/8 x 11 13/16".
Edition of 99 / XXX, signed and numbered certificate.
$ 3800 / € 2900

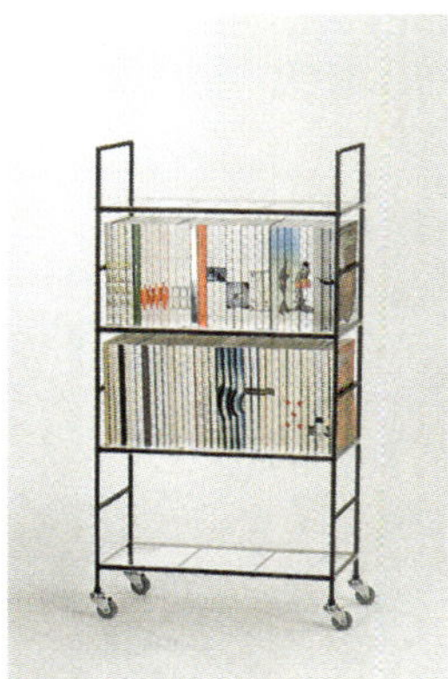

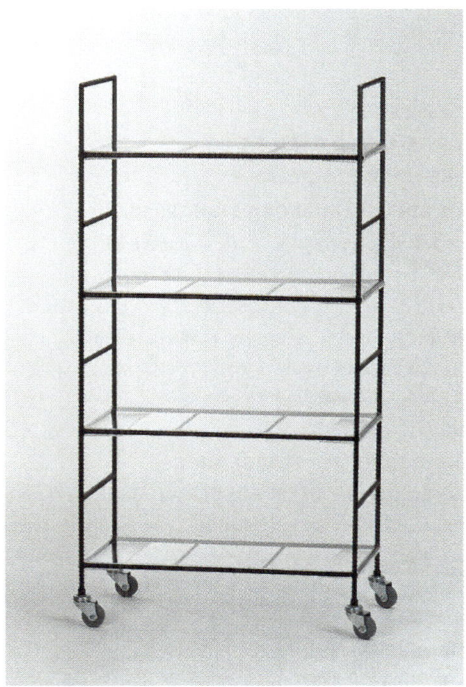

THIS WHEELED COMPANION TO THE GLOBETROTTER'S "POUCH FOR PARKETT" (1993) WILL HOUSE ALL THE VOLUMES OF PARKETT THROUGH 2024.

NACH DEM SACKERL FÜR UNTERWEGS FOLGT DIE BEWEGLICHE «LIBRAIRIE EN APPARTEMENT» MIT PLATZ FÜR ALLE PARKETT-BÄNDE BIS 2024.

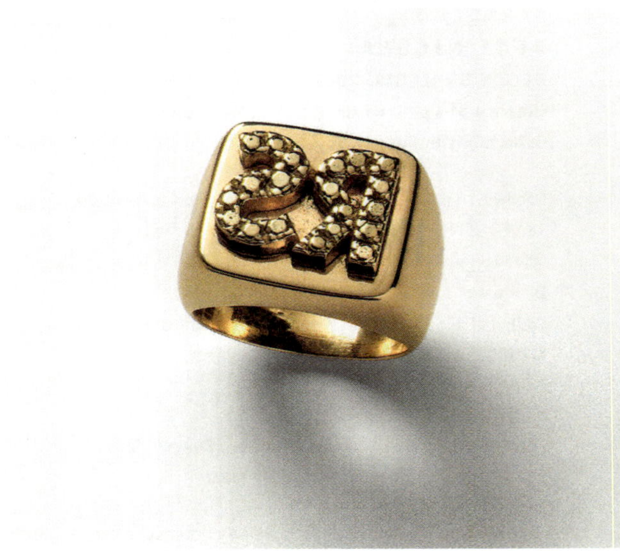

IN SPIEGEL SIEHST DU DEINER ANMUT SEGEN,
UND AUF DER UHR DIE GOLDNEN STUNDEN FLIEHN,
DOCH DIESER RING WIRD DEINE SINNE PRÄGEN
IN SEINEM GLANZ MAGST DU DURCH'S LEBEN ZIEHN.

WEAR IT RIGHT SIDE DOWN,
TO SEAL A FRIENDSHIP, AS KINGS ONCE DID.

PARKETT 77

RUDOLF STINGEL

RS, 2006

Signet Ring, 18 carat gold, approx. 1 x 3/4 x 1/2", jewelery box.
Production by Markus Frühauf, Jeweler, Meran, Italy.
Edition of 22 / XVI, initials engraved and numbered.
$ 3900 / € 3300

Siegelring, 18 Karat Gold, ca. 2,5 x 2 x 1,5 cm, Schmuckschachtel.
Produktion: Markus Frühauf, Juwelier, Meran, Italien.
Auflage 22 / XVI, Initialen eingraviert und nummeriert.
CHF 4900 / € 3300

TWELVE MONTHS OF MYSTERY: TEN UNPREDICTABLE MESSAGES THAT WILL (OR WILL NOT) BE DECODED IN THE RECORD LEFT BEHIND.

EINE FOLGE SCHÖNER ÜBERRASCHUNGEN, EIN ABZÄHLREIM: 10-9-8-7-6... TRÄGT DEN NAMEN «HAMMETT» IM KEIM.

PARKETT 77

TRISHA DONNELLY

**THE DASHIELL DELAY –
AN EDITION SUBSCRIPTION, 2006**

Edition in 10 installments made and delivered
every 1–2 months over a period of one year.
Varied media, each approx. 8 x 10".
Edition of 45 / XXV, signed and numbered certificate.
(selected edition installments)
$ 2200 / € 1800

**DIE DASHIELL VERZÖGERUNG –
EINE EDITION IN 10 FOLGEN, 2006**

Edition aus 10 Teilen, die innerhalb eines Jahres hergestellt
und alle 1–2 Monate einzeln versendet wird.
Unterschiedliche Materialien und Techniken, jeweils ca. 20 x 25 cm.
Auflage: 45 / XXV, signiertes und nummeriertes Zertifikat.
(Ausgewählte Einzelteile der Edition)
CHF 2700 / € 1800

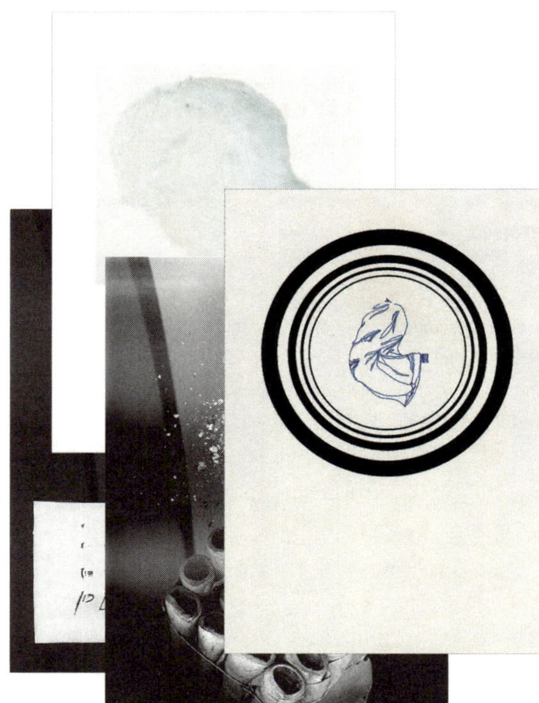

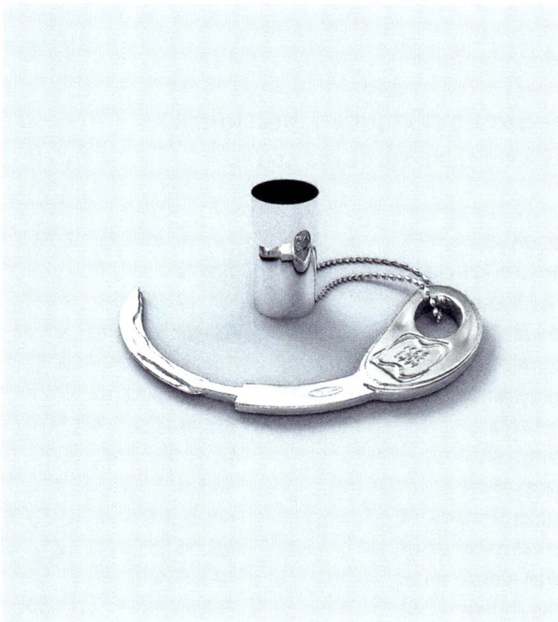

LIEBT SIE MICH, LIEBT ER DICH,
LIEBEN SIE SICH, LIEBT ER MICH,
ZWEIFELN SIE NOCH?

BEGIN WITH CERTAINTIES AND
YOU SHALL END IN DOUBTS.
BUT BEWARE: DOUBT IS NOT THE KEY TO CERTAINTY.

PARKETT 77

CARSTEN HÖLLER

KEY TO THE LABORATORY OF DOUBT, 2006

Anamorphic key, cast in sterling silver, approx. 3 $^1/_8$ x $^3/_4$ x $^1/_8$"
polished stainless steel cylinder, 1 $^1/_2$ x $^3/_4$"
silver necklace approx. 27 $^1/_2$".
Production and 3-D scanning by Factum Arte, Madrid.
Edition of 50 / XXV, initials engraved and numbered.
$ 2900 / € 2400

SCHLÜSSEL ZUM LABORATORIUM DES ZWEIFELS, 2006

Anamorphischer Schlüssel, gegossen in Sterling-Silber, ca. 8 x 2 x 0,5 cm
Zylinder aus poliertem Edelstahl, 4 x 2 cm
Halskette aus Silber, ca. 70 cm.
Produktion und 3-D-Scanning, Factum Arte, Madrid.
Auflage 50 / XXV, Initialen graviert und nummeriert.
CHF 3600 / € 2400

YOU'VE READ THE STORY OF MAO TSE TUNG
OF HOW HE LIVED AND DIED;
IF YOU'RE STILL IN NEED
OF SOMETHING TO READ
HERE'S THE STORY OF MS. HUANG ON A RIDE.

IHR FRAU KÖNIGIN SEID DIE SCHÖNSTE HIER,
DOCH MS. HUANG IN SHANGHAI
IST TAUSENDMAL SCHÖNER ALS IHR!

PARKETT 76

YANG FUDONG

MS. HUANG AT M. LAST NIGHT, 2006

Black-and-white photograph, Lambda print on Kodak
Endura paper. Paper size 19 $^1/_2$ x 29 $^1/_2$", image 18 $^7/_8$ x 28 $^3/_4$".
Edition of 60 / XX, signed and numbered certificate.
$ 1400 / € 1200

Schwarz-Weiss-Photographie, Lambda-Print auf Kodak
Endura Papier; Papierformat 50 x 75 cm, Bild 48 x 73 cm.
Auflage: 60 / XX, signiertes und nummeriertes Zertifikat.
CHF 1900 / € 1200

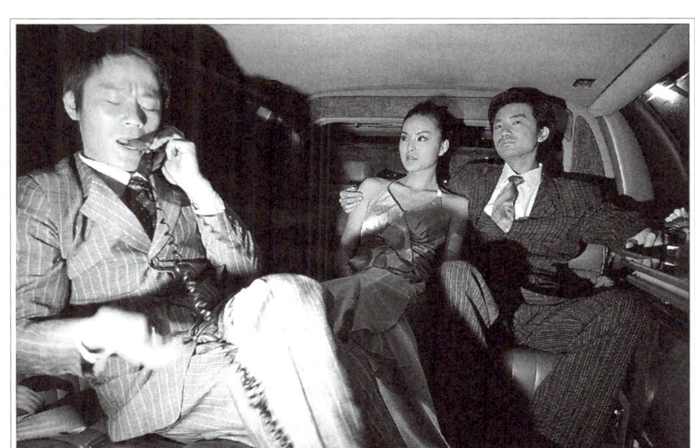

PARKETT

ARTISTS' MONOGRAPHS & EDITIONS / KÜNSTLERMONOGRAPHIEN & EDITIONEN

FOR AVAILABILITY SEE NEXT PAGE / LIEFERBARKEIT SIEHE FOLGENDE SEITE

Franz Ackermann, vol. 68
Eija-Liisa Ahtila, vol. 68
Doug Aitken, vol. 57
Kai Althoff, vol. 75
Francis Alÿs, vol. 69
Laurie Anderson, vol. 49
John Armleder, vol. 50/51
Richard Artschwager, vol. 23, vol. 46
John Baldessari, vol. 29
Stephan Balkenhol, vol. 36
Matthew Barney, vol. 45
Georg Baselitz, vol. 11
Vanessa Beecroft, vol. 56
Ross Bleckner, vol. 38
John Bock, vol. 67
Alighiero e Boetti, vol. 24
Christian Boltanski, vol. 22
Monica Bonvicini, vol. 72
Louise Bourgeois, vol. 27
Olaf Breuning, vol. 71
Glenn Brown, vol. 75
Angela Bulloch, vol. 66
Daniel Buren, vol. 66
Sophie Calle, vol. 36
Maurizio Cattelan, vol. 59
Vija Celmins, vol. 44
Francesco Clemente, vol. 9 & 40/41
Chuck Close, vol. 60
Enzo Cucchi, vol. 1
John Currin, vol. 65
Tacita Dean, vol. 62
Thomas Demand, vol. 62
Martin Disler, vol. 3
Peter Doig, vol. 67
Trisha Donnelly, vol. 77
Marlene Dumas, vol. 38
Olafur Eliasson, vol. 64
Tracey Emin, vol. 63
Urs Fischer, vol. 72
Eric Fischl, vol. 5
Peter Fischli / David Weiss, vol. 17, 40/41
Sylvie Fleury, vol. 58
Günther Förg, vol. 26 & 40/41
Tom Friedman, vol. 64
Katharina Fritsch, vol. 25
Bernard Frize, vol. 74
Ellen Gallagher, vol. 73
Isa Genzken, vol. 69
Franz Gertsch, vol. 28
Gilbert & George, vol. 14
Liam Gillick, vol. 61
Robert Gober, vol. 27
Nan Goldin, vol. 57
Felix Gonzalez-Torres, vol. 39
Douglas Gordon, vol. 49
Dan Graham, vol. 68
Rodney Graham, vol. 64
Katharina Grosse, vol. 74
Andreas Gursky, vol. 44
David Hammons, vol. 31
Thomas Hirschhorn, vol. 57
Damien Hirst, vol. 40/41
Carsten Höller, vol. 77
Jenny Holzer, vol. 40/41
Rebecca Horn, vol. 13 & 40/41
Roni Horn, vol. 54
Gary Hume, vol. 48
Pierre Huyghe, vol. 66
Ilya Kabakov, vol. 34
Anish Kapoor, vol. 69
Alex Katz, vol. 21, 72
Mike Kelley, vol. 31
Ellsworth Kelly, vol. 56
William Kentridge, vol. 63
Jon Kessler, vol. 79
Karen Kilimnik, vol. 52
Martin Kippenberger, vol. 19
Imi Knoebel, vol. 32
Jeff Koons, vol. 19, 50/51
Jannis Kounellis, vol. 6
Yayoi Kusama, vol. 59
Wolfgang Laib, vol. 39
Sherrie Levine, vol. 32
Sarah Lucas, vol. 45
Christian Marclay, vol. 70
Brice Marden, vol. 7
Paul McCarthy, vol. 73
Lucy McKenzie, vol. 76
Julie Mehretu, vol. 76
Mario Merz, vol. 15
Marilyn Minter, vol. 79
Tracey Moffatt, vol. 53
Mariko Mori, vol. 54
Malcolm Morley, vol. 52
Sarah Morris, vol. 61
Juan Muñoz, vol. 43
Jean-Luc Mylayne, vol. 50/51
Bruce Nauman, vol. 10
Ernesto Neto, vol. 78
Olaf Nicolai, vol. 78
Cady Noland, vol. 46
Albert Oehlen, vol. 79
Meret Oppenheim, vol. 4
Gabriel Orozco, vol. 48
Tony Oursler, vol. 47
Laura Owens, vol. 65
Jorge Pardo, vol. 56
Raymond Pettibon, vol. 47
Elizabeth Peyton, vol. 53
Richard Phillips, vol. 71
Sigmar Polke, vol. 2, 30 & 40/41
Richard Prince, vol. 34, 72
Michael Raedecker, vol. 65
Markus Raetz, vol. 8
Charles Ray, vol. 37
Jason Rhoades, vol. 58
Gerhard Richter, vol. 35
Bridget Riley, vol. 61
Pipilotti Rist, vol. 48, 71
Matthew Ritchie, vol. 61
Tim Rollins & K.O.S., vol. 20
Ugo Rondinone, vol. 52
James Rosenquist, vol. 58
Susan Rothenberg, vol. 43
Thomas Ruff, vol. 28
Edward Ruscha, vol. 18 & 55
Anri Sala, vol. 73
Wilhelm Sasnal, vol. 70
Gregor Schneider, vol. 63
Thomas Schütte, vol. 47
Dana Schutz, vol. 75
Richard Serra, vol. 74
Cindy Sherman, vol. 29
Roman Signer, vol. 45
Andreas Slominski, vol. 55
Rudolf Stingel, vol. 77
Beat Streuli, vol. 54
Thomas Struth, vol. 50/51
Hiroshi Sugimoto, vol. 46
Philip Taaffe, vol. 26
Sam Taylor-Wood, vol. 55
Diana Thater, vol. 60
Wolfgang Tillmans, vol. 53
Rirkrit Tiravanija, vol. 44
Fred Tomaselli, vol. 67
Rosemarie Trockel, vol. 33
James Turrell, vol. 25
Luc Tuymans, vol. 60
Keith Tyson, vol. 71
Kara Walker, vol. 59
Jeff Wall, vol. 22 & 49
Andy Warhol, vol. 12
Rebecca Warren, vol. 78
Gillian Wearing, vol. 70
Lawrence Weiner, vol. 42
John Wesley, vol. 62
Franz West, vol. 37, 70
Rachel Whiteread, vol. 42
Sue Williams, vol. 50/51
Robert Wilson, vol. 16
Christopher Wool, vol. 33
Yang Fudong, vol. 76

vol.	Collaboration		
79	Albert Oehlen		
	Jon Kessler		
	Marilyn Minter		
78	Ernesto Neto	m	e
	Olaf Nicolai	m	e
	Rebecca Warren	m	e
77	Trisha Donnelly	m	e
	Carsten Höller	m	e
	Rudolf Stingel	m	e
76	Lucy McKenzie	m	e
	Julie Mehretu	m	
	Yang Fudong	m	e
75	Kai Althoff	m	e
	Glenn Brown	m	
	Dana Schutz	m	
74	Bernard Frize	m	
	Katharina Grosse	m	e
	Richard Serra	m	
73	Ellen Gallagher	m	
	Paul McCarthy	m	
	Anri Sala	m	e
72	Monica Bonvicini	m	
	Urs Fischer	m	
	Richard Prince	m	
71	Olaf Breuning	m	e
	Richard Phillips	m	e
	Keith Tyson	m	e
70	Christian Marclay	m	e
	Wilhelm Sasnal	m	e
	Gillian Wearing	m	e
69	Francis Alÿs	m	
	Isa Genzken	m	
	Anish Kapoor	m	
68	Franz Ackermann	m	e
	Eija-Liisa Ahtila	m	e
	Dan Graham	m	e
67	John Bock	m	e
	Peter Doig	m	e
	Fred Tomaselli	m	
66	Angela Bulloch	m	e
	Daniel Buren	m	e
	Pierre Huyghe	m	e
65	John Currin	m	
	Laura Owens	m	e
	Michael Raedecker	m	e
64	Olafur Eliasson	m	
	Tom Friedman	m	
	Rodney Graham	m	
63	Tracey Emin	m	e
	William Kentridge	m	
	Gregor Schneider	m	
62	Tacita Dean	m	e
	Thomas Demand	m	
	John Wesley	m	
61	Liam Gillick	m	
	Sarah Morris	m	e
	Bridget Riley	m	
	Matthew Ritchie	m	e

vol.	Collaboration		
60	Chuck Close	m	
	Diana Thater	m	e
	Luc Tuymans	m	e
59	Maurizio Cattelan	m	
	Yayoi Kusama	m	
	Kara Walker	m	
58	Sylvie Fleury	m	
	Jason Rhoades	m	
	James Rosenquist	m	
57	Doug Aitken	m	e
57	Nan Goldin	m	
	Thomas Hirschhorn	m	
56	Vanessa Beecroft	m	
	Ellsworth Kelly	m	
	Jorge Pardo	m	e
55	Edward Ruscha	m	
	Andreas Slominski	m	
	Sam Taylor-Wood	m	
54	Roni Horn	m	
	Mariko Mori	m	
	Beat Streuli	m	
53	Tracey Moffatt	m	
	Elizabeth Peyton	m	
	Wolfgang Tillmans	m	
52	Karen Kilimnik	m	e
	Malcolm Morley	m	e
	Ugo Rondinone	m	e
50/51	John Armleder	m	
	Jeff Koons	m	e
	Jean-Luc Mylayne	m	
	Thomas Struth	m	
	Sue Williams	m	
49	Laurie Anderson	m	e
	Douglas Gordon	m	
	Jeff Wall	m	
48	Gary Hume	m	
	Gabriel Orozco	m	
	Pipilotti Rist	m	
47	Tony Oursler	m	
	Raymond Pettibon	m	
	Thomas Schütte	m	e
46	Richard Artschwager	m	
	Cady Noland	m	
	Hiroshi Sugimoto	m	
45	Matthew Barney		
	Sarah Lucas		
	Roman Signer		e
44	Vija Celmins	m	
	Andreas Gursky	m	
	Rirkrit Tiravanija	m	e
43	Juan Muñoz	m	
	Susan Rothenberg	m	
42	Lawrence Weiner	m	e
	Rachel Whiteread	m	
40/41	Francesco Clemente	m	
	Fischli/Weiss	m	
	Günther Förg	m	
	Damien Hirst	m	

vol.	Collaboration		
	Jenny Holzer	m	
	Rebecca Horn	m	
	Sigmar Polke	m	
39	Felix Gonzalez-Torres		
	Wolfgang Laib		
38	Ross Bleckner		
	Marlene Dumas		
37	Charles Ray	m	
	Franz West	m	e
36	Stephan Balkenhol		
	Sophie Calle		
35	Gerhard Richter		
34	Ilya Kabakov	m	
	Richard Prince	m	
33	Rosemarie Trockel	m	
	Christopher Wool	m	
32	Imi Knoebel	m	
	Sherrie Levine	m	
31	David Hammons		
	Mike Kelley		
30	Sigmar Polke		
29	John Baldessari		
	Cindy Sherman		
28	Franz Gertsch	m	
	Thomas Ruff	m	
27	Louise Bourgeois		
	Robert Gober		
26	Günther Förg		
	Philip Taaffe		
25	Katharina Fritsch		e
	James Turrell		
24	Alighiero e Boetti	m	
23	Richard Artschwager	m	
22	Christian Boltanski		
	Jeff Wall		
21	Alex Katz	m	
20	Tim Rollins + K.O.S.	m	
19	Martin Kippenberger		
	Jeff Koons		
18	Ed Ruscha		
17	Fischli/Weiss		
16	Robert Wilson		
15	Mario Merz	m	
14	Gilbert & George	m	
13	Rebecca Horn		
12	Andy Warhol		
11	Georg Baselitz	m	
10	Bruce Nauman		
9	Francesco Clemente		
8	Markus Raetz		
7	Brice Marden		
6	Jannis Kounellis		
5	Eric Fischl		
4	Meret Oppenheim		
3	Martin Disler		
2	Sigmar Polke		
1	Enzo Cucchi		

m = available monograph / erhältliche Monographie, e = available edition / erhältliche Edition
Delivery subject to availability at time of order / Lieferung solange Vorrat

PARKETT IN BOOKSHOPS (Selection)

PARKETT IS AVAILABLE IN 500 LEADING ART BOOKSHOPS AROUND THE WORLD. FOR FURTHER INFORMATION CONTACT:
PARKETT GIBT ES IN 500 FÜHRENDEN KUNSTBUCHHANDLUNGEN AUF DER GANZEN WELT. FÜR WEITERE INFORMATIONEN WENDEN SIE SICH BITTE AN:
PARKETT VERLAG, QUELLENSTRASSE 27, CH-8031 ZÜRICH, TEL. +41-1 271 81 40, FAX 272 43 01, WWW.PARKETTART.COM;
PARKETT, 145, AVENUE OF THE AMERICAS, NEW YORK, N.Y. 10013, PHONE +1 (212) 673-2660, FAX 271-0704, WWW.PARKETTART.COM

NORTH & SOUTH AMERICA, ASIA, AUSTRALIA

DISTRIBUTOR / VERTRIEB
D.A.P. (DISTRIBUTED ART PUBLISHERS)
155 AVENUE OF THE AMERICAS,
2ND FLOOR,
NEW YORK, NY 10013

USA

AUSTIN, TX
BOOK PEOPLE
603 N. LAMAR

BEACON, NY
DIA: BEACON
3 BEEKMAN STREET

BERKELEY, CA
BERKELEY ART MUSEUM
2625 DURANT AVENUE

CODY'S BOOKS
2454 TELEGRAPHE AVENUE

BEVERLY HILLS, CA
RIZZOLI
9501 WILSHIRE BOULEVARD

BOSTON, MA
INSTITUTE OF CONTEMPORARY ART
955 BOYLSTON STREET

TRIDENT BOOKSELLERS
338 NEWBURY STREET

BUFFALO, NY
TALKING LEAVES
3158 MAIN STREET

CAMBRIDGE, MA
MIT PRESS BOOKSTORE
292 MAIN STREET

CHICAGO, IL
ART INSTITUTE OF CHICAGO
104 S. MICHIGAN

MUSEUM OF CONTEMPORARY ART
220 EAST CHICAGO AVENUE

QUIMBY'S
1854 W. NORTH AVENUE

SMART MUSEUM OF ART
5550 S. GREENWOOD AVENUE

CINCINNATI, OH
CONTEMPORARY ARTS CENTER
115 E. 5TH STREET

COLUMBUS, OH
COLUMBUS MUSEUM OF ART
372 COMMONS MALL

WEXNER CENTER BOOKSTORE
30 W. 15TH STREET

CORAL GABLES, FL
BOOKS & BOOKS
296 ARAGON ROAD

HOUSTON, TX
BRAZOS BOOKSTORE
2421 BISSONNET

CONTEMPORARY ARTS MUSEUM
5216 MONTROSE BOULEVARD

MENIL COLLECTION
1520 SUL ROSS

HUNTINGTON, WV
HUNTINGTON MUSEUM OF ART
2033 MCCOY ROAD

LOS ANGELES, CA
BOOK SOUP
8818 SUNSET BOULEVARD/
3333 BRISTOL ST.

MUSEUM OF CONTEMPORARY ART
250, S. GRAND

LOS ANGELES, CA
UCLA / ARMAND HAMMER MUSEUM OF ART
10899 WILSHIRE BOULEVARD

MIAMI, FL
BOOKS & BOOKS
296 ARAGON AVENUE, CORAL GABLES

MUSEUM OF CONTEMPORARY ART
770 N.E. 125TH STREET NORTH MIAMI

MIAMI BEACH, FL
BASE, 939, LINCOLN ROAD

MINNEAPOLIS, MN
THE WALKER ART CENTER BOOKSTORE
VINELAND PLACE

NEW YORK, NY
MUSEUM OF MODERN ART
11 WEST 53RD STREET

NEW MUSEUM OF CONTEMPORARY
ART STORE
556 WEST 22ND STREET

RIZZOLI
454 WEST BROADWAY

SAINT MARK'S BOOKSTORE
31 3RD AVENUE

COLISEUM BOOKS INC.
11 WEST 42ND STREET

OAKLAND, CA
DIESEL, A BOOKSTORE
5433 COLLEGE AVENUE

OAK PARK, MI
BOOK BEAT LTD.
26010 GREENFIELD

OMAHA, NE
JOSLYN ART MUSEUM
2200 DODGE STREET

PHILADELPHIA, PA
AVRIL 50
3406 SANSOM STREET

WATERSTONE BOOKSELLERS
2191 HORNIG ROAD

PITTSBURGH, PA
CARNEGIE INSTITUTE
4400 FORBES AVENUE

PORTLAND, OR
POWELL'S BOOKS
7 NW 9TH STREET

PROVIDENCE, NY
ACCIDENT OR DESIGN
128 N. MAIN STREET

RHODE ISLAND SCHOOL OF DESIGN
2 COLLEGE STREET, 1765

SAN ANTONIO, TX
SLOAN / HALL SAN ANTONIO
5930 BROADWAY

SAN FRANCISCO, CA
A CLEAN WELL LIGHTED PLACE
601 VAN NESS AVENUE

CITY LIGHTS BOOKSHOP
261 COLUMBUS AVENUE

SF MUSEUM OF MODERN ART,
MUSEUMBOOKS
151 3RD STREET, 1ST FLOOR

ST. LOUIS, MO
LEFT BANK BOOKS
399 NORTH EUCLID

SANTA MONICA, CA
ARCANA
1229 3RD STREET PROMENADE

BERGAMOT BOOKSTORE
2525 MICHIGAN AVENUE, G-5B

HENNESSEY & INGALLS BOOKS
214 WILSHIRE BLVD

ST. PAUL, MN
HUNGRY MIND BOOKSTORE
1648 GRAND AVENUE

SEATTLE, WA
UNIVERSITY BOOKSTORE
4326 UNIVERSITY WAY

WASHINGTON D.C.
NATIONAL GALLERY OF ART
6TH STREET & CONSTITUTION
AVENUE, NW

CANADA / KANADA

MONTREAL
OLIVIERI LIBRAIRIE BOOKSTORE
185 STREET CATHERINE WEST

TORONTO
ART GALLERY OF ONTARIO
317 DUNDAS STREET WEST

ART METROPOLE
788 KING STREET WEST

DAVID MIRVISH BOOKS ON ART
596 MARKHAM STREET

VANCOUVER
VANCOUVER ART GALLERY
750 HORNBY STREET

AUSTRALIA / AUSTRALIEN

DARLINGHURST
EAST SYDNEY BOOKSTORE
THE DOME, THE ELAN BUILDING
1 KINGS CROSS ROAD

SYDNEY
MUSEUM OF CONTEMPORARY ART
140 GEORGE STREET,
CIRCULAR QUAY NORTH

GLEE BOOKS
191 GLEBE POINT ROAD, GLEBE

NEW ZEALAND / NEUSEELAND

AUCKLAND
MAGAZZINO SUBSCRIPTION
P.O. BOX 905909

ASIA / ASIEN

JAPAN

TOKYO
AOYAMA BOOK CENTRE, SHIBUYA-KU
COSMOS AOYAMA GARDEN FLOOR B2F
5-53-97, JINGUMAE

ART & BOOKS
2-1-13-307
TAKANAWA, MINATO-KU

EOS ART BOOKS
DOMILE KITA 108
1-10-21 KICHIJOJI-KITAMACHI

SINGAPORE / SINGAPUR

PAGE ONE BOOKSTORE
20 KAKI BUKIT VIEW TECHPARK

CHINA

TAIPEI
ARTLAND BOOKS CO., LTD.
B1 122 JEN AI RD., SEC3

GREAT BRITAIN / GROSSBRITANNIEN

DISTRIBUTOR / VERTRIEB
CENTRAL BOOKS
99, WALLIS ROAD
LONDON E9 5LN

BIRMINGHAM
IKON GALLERY
1 OOZELLS SQUARE

BRIGHTON
BORDERS BOOKSHOP
CHURCHILL SQUARE SHOPPING CENTRE

BRISTOL
ARNOLFINI BOOKSHOP
16 NARROW QUAY

CARDIFF
CHAPTER ARTS CENTRE
MARKET ROAD

CARLISLE
CASTLE THE STORE
LONDON ROAD

LONDON
ARTWORDS BOOKSHOP
RIVINGTON STREET

BORDERS BOOKSHOP
120 CHARING CROSS ROAD

BORDERS BOOKSHOP
203–207 OXFORD STREET

BORDERS BOOKSHOP
N1 CENTRE ISLINGTON

CAMDEN ARTS CENTRE
ARKWRIGHT ROAD
HAYWARD GALLERY
SOUTH BANK
IAN SHIPLEY BOOKSHOP
70 CHARING CROSS ROAD
INSTITUTE OF CONTEMPORARY ARTS
12 CARLTON HOUSE TERRACE
THE MALL
SERPENTINE GALLERY
KENSINGTON GARDENS
TATE MODERN
BANKSIDE
WHITECHAPEL ART GALLERY
80 WHITECHAPEL HIGH STREET

OXFORD
MODERN ART OXFORD
30 PEMBROKE STREET

SCOTLAND / SCHOTTLAND

EDINBURGH
SCOTTISH GALLERY OF MODERN ART
75 BELFORD ROAD

IRELAND / IRLAND

CORK
LEWIS GLUCKSMAN GALLERY
UNIVERSITY COLLEGE

DUBLIN
DOUGLAS HYDE GALLERY
TRINITY COLLEGE

GERMANY / DEUTSCHLAND

DISTRIBUTOR / VERTRIEB
GVA VERLAGSSERVICE GÖTTINGEN
PF 2021
D-37010 GÖTTINGEN

BERLIN
BÜCHERBOGEN AM SAVIGNYPLATZ
STADTBAHNBOGEN 593
GALERIE 2000 KUNSTBUCHHANDLUNG
KNESEBECKSTRASSE 56/58
WIENS LADEN & VERLAG
LINIENSTRASSE 158 (HOF)

BIELEFELD
THALIA UNIVERSITÄTSBUCHHANDLUNG
FILIALE PHÖNIX, OBERNTORWALL 23

BREMEN
BEIM STEINERNEN KREUZ GMBH
BEIM STEINERNEN KREUZ 1

DRESDEN
WEISSLACK
LUISENSTRASSE 52

DÜSSELDORF
LITERATUR BEI RUDOLF MÜLLER
NEUSTRASSE 38
WALTHER KÖNIG BUCHHANDLUNG
HEINRICH-HEINE-ALLEE 15

FRANKFURT
KUNST-BUCH, KUNSTHALLE SCHIRN
RÖMERBERG 7
WALTHER KÖNIG BUCHHANDLUNG
DOMSTRASSE 6

HAMBURG
HELMUT VON DER HÖH BUCHHANDLUNG
GROSSE BLEICHEN 21
SAUTTER + LACKMANN BUCHHANDLUNG
ADMIRALITÄTSTRASSE 71/72

HANNOVER
MERZ KUNSTBUCHHANDLUNG
KURT-SCHWITTERS-PLATZ

HERFORD
PROVINZBUCHLADEN GMBH
HAEMMELINGER STRASSE 22

KARLSRUHE
HANS MENDE BUCHHANDLUNG
KARLSTRASSE 76
ZENTRUM FÜR KUNST &
MEDIENTECHNOLOGIE
MUSEUMSSHOP, LORENZSTRASSE 19

KÖLN
WALTHER KÖNIG BUCHHANDLUNG
EHRENSTRASSE 4
KIOSK-BUCH-EVENT GMBH
IM MEDIAPARK 7

MÜNCHEN
HANS GOLTZ BUCHHANDLUNG
FÜR BILDENDE KUNST
TÜRKENSTRASSE 54
ILKA KÖNIG BUCHHANDLUNG
MAXIMILIANSTRASSE 35
L. WERNER BUCHHANDLUNG
RESIDENZSTRASSE 18

NÜRNBERG
WALTHER KÖNIG BUCHHANDLUNG
LUITPOLDSTRASSE 5

STUTTGART
LIMACHER BUCHHANDLUNG
KÖNIGSTRASSE 28 / KÖNIGSBAU

SPAIN / SPANIEN

BARCELONA
LAIE – CAIXAFÒRUM
MARQUES DE COMILLAS 6–8
LAIE – CCCB (CENTRE DE CULTURA
CONTEMPORÀNIA DE BARCELONA)
MONTALEGRE 5

BILBAO
GUGGENHEIM MUSEUM
ABANDOIBARRA ET. 2

MADRID
MUSEO NACIONAL REINA SOFIA
C/ SANTA ISABEL, 52

FRANCE / FRANKREICH

PARIS
CENTRE POMPIDOU, FLAMMARION 4
26, RUE JACOB
GALERIE NATIONALE DU JEU DE PAUME
1, PLACE DE LA CONCORDE
LIBRAIRIE DU MUSÉE D'ART MODERNE
9, RUE GASTON DE SAINT-PAUL
CHRISTOPH DAVIET-THERY,
LIVRES & EDITIONS D'ARTISTES
10, RUE DUCHEFDELAVILLE
COLETTE
213, RUE SAINT-HONORÉ

ITALY / ITALIEN

MILANO
A&M BOOKSTORE
30, VIA TADINO

ROMA
GALLERIA NAZIONALE D'ARTE MODERNA
131, VIA DELLE BELLE ARTI
GALLERIA PRIMO PIANO
203, VIA PANISPERNA

NORWAY / NORWEGEN

OSLO
THE NATIONAL MUSEUM OF
CONTEMPORARY ART
BANKPLASSEN 4 / SKATTEFOG

PORTUGAL

LISBOA
MODULO CENTRO DIFUSOR DE ARTE
CALÇADA DOS MESTRES 34 A–B

PORTO
MODULO CENTRO DIFUSOR DE ARTE
AV. BOAVISTA 854

DENMARK /DÄNEMARK

COPENHAGEN
CHARLOTTENBORG EXHIBITION HALL
NYHAVN 2

SWEDEN / SCHWEDEN

STOCKHOLM
KULTURHUSET KONSTIG
MEDIA & KONSTBOKHANDEL
SERGELS TORG 3
MODERNA MUSEET
SKEPPSHOLMEN

GÖTEBORG
GÖTEBORGS KONSTMUSEUM
GÖTAPLATSEN / AVENYN

TURKEY / TÜRKEI

ISTANBUL
ROBINSON CRUSOE BOOKS PUSULA
PRODUCTIONS
389 ISTIKAL CADDESI BEYOGLU

NETHERLANDS, BELGIUM AND LUXEMBURG

DISTRIBUTOR / VERTRIEB
IDEA BOOKS
NIEUWE HERENGRACHT 11
NL-1011 RK AMSTERDAM

NETHERLANDS / NIEDERLANDE

AMSTERDAM
ART BOOK
VAN BAERLESTRAAT 126
ATHENAEUM NIEUWSCENTRUM
SPUI 14–16

EINDHOVEN
MOTTA
BERGSTRAAT 35

GRONINGEN
SCHOLTENS / WRISTERS BOOKSHOP
FULDENSTRAAT 20

HAARLEM
ATHENAEUM
GED. OUDE GRACHT 70

HENGELO
BROEKHUIS
WEMENSTRAAT 45

MAASTRICHT
DE TRIBUNE
KAPCENSTRAAT 8

BELGIUM / BELGIEN

ANTWERPEN
COPYRIGHT BOOKSHOP
NATIONALSTRAAT 28A

BRUXELLES
PEINTURE FRAICHE
10, RUE DU TABELLON
TROPISMES LIBRAIRIES
GALERIE DES PRINCES 11

GENT
COPYRIGHT BOOKSHOP
JACOBIJNENSTRAAT 8

LUXEMBOURG / LUXEMBURG

LUXEMBOURG
CASINO LUXEMBOURG
41, RUE NOTRE-DAME

SWITZERLAND / SCHWEIZ

DISTRIBUTOR / VERTRIEB
SCHEIDEGGER & CO. c/o AVA
CENTRALWEG 16
CH-8910 AFFOLTERN A. A.

BASEL
FONDATION BEYELER
BASELSTRASSE 77, RIEHEN
GALERIE STAMPA
SPALENBERG 2
JÄGGI BUCHHANDLUNG
FREIE STRASSE 32
KUNSTHALLE BASEL
KLOSTERGASSE 5

BERN
BUCHHANDLUNG FÜR ARCHITEKTUR UND
DESIGN, BRUNNGASSE 60
STAUFFACHER BUCHHANDLUNG
NEUENGASSE 25-37

GENÈVE
LIBRAIRIE PAYOT
5, RUE DE CHANTEPOULET

LUZERN
KUNSTMUSEUM LUZERN
EUROPLATZ 1

MENDRISIO
GABRIELE CAPELLI LIBRERIA
ARCHITETTURA
4, VIA NOBILI BOSIA

ST. GALLEN
RÖSSLITOR BÜCHER
WEBERGASSE 5

ZÜRICH
CALLIGRAMME BUCHHANDLUNG
HÄRINGSTRASSE 4
HOWEG BUCHHANDLUNG
WAFFENPLATZ 1
KUNSTGRIFF BUCHHANDLUNG
LIMMATSTRASSE 270
KUNSTHAUS ZÜRICH
HEIMPLATZ 1
ORELL FÜSSLI BUCHHANDLUNG
FÜSSLISTRASSE 4
SPHÈRES
HARDTURMSTRASSE 66

E X H I B I T I O N S

ZÜRICH

GALERIE ANDREA CARATSCH	Limmatstrasse 291 8005 Zürich Tel. 044 272 50 00 info@galeriecaratsch.com	PIERRE & GILLES	**Januar–März 2007**
		PABLO PICASSO	**April–Mai 2007**
ELISABETH KAUFMANN	Müllerstrasse 57 8004 Zürich Tel./Fax 043 322 01 15 www.elisabethkaufmann.com info@elisabethkaufmann.com	HANNE DARBOVEN. CLAUDIA WIESER	**12.1.–10.3.2007**
		PAVEL PEPPERSTEIN – HADASSAH EMMERICH – YESIM AKDENIZ GRAF	**17.3.–12.5.2007**
		A very modest exhibition by KEREN CYTTER	**19.5.–Mitte Juli 2007**
GALERIE LELONG	Predigerplatz 10–12 8001 Zürich Tel. 044 251 11 20 www.galerie-lelong.com galerie.lelong@dplanet.ch	URS LÜTHI Registered Trademark	**3.2.–14.4.2007**
		ARNULF RAINER	**21.4.–2.6.2007**
LUTZ & THALMANN	Wettingerwies 2B 8001 Zürich Tel. 044 262 76 00 www.lutz-thalmann.com galerie@lutz-thalmann.com	HUGO WEBER New York 1960–1971 Bilder und Arbeiten auf Papier	**2.2.–24.3.2007**
		BARBARA HEÉ	**30.3.–19.5.2007**
MAI 36 GALERIE	Rämistrasse 37 8001 Zürich Tel. 044 261 68 80 www.mai36.com mail@mai36.com	EARLY RETIREMENT curated by Glen Rubsamen	**Januar–Februar 2007**
		MANFRED PERNICE	**März–April 2007**
		Arco'07, Madrid	**15.–19.2.2007**
		The Armory Show, New York	**22.2.–26.2.2007**
MARK MÜLLER	Gessnerallee 36 8001 Zürich Tel. 044 211 81 55 www.markmueller.ch mail@markmueller.ch	STEFAN GRITSCH Guestroom: MARCIA HAFIF	**13.1.–24.2.2007**
		Arco'07, Madrid – Artists of the gallery	**15.–19.2.2007**
		MONIKA BRANDMEIER, KNUT ECKSTEIN, MAMIKO OTSUBO	**17.3.–21.4.2007**
BOB VAN ORSOUW	Limmatstrasse 270 8005 Zürich Tel. 044 273 11 00 www.bobvanorsouw.ch mail@bobvanorsouw.ch	WAWRZYNIEC TOKARSKI Cannot be seen from within	**20.1.–24.2.2007**
		Arco'07, Madrid	**15.–19.2.2007**

E X H I B I T I O N S

ANNEMARIE VERNA	Neptunstrasse 45 8032 Zürich Tel. 044 262 38 20 www.annemarie-verna.ch office@annemarie-verna.ch	RITA McBRIDE hex.pro.jig	**3.11.–20.1.2007**
		DAN FLAVIN	**27.1.–17.5.2007**
		DAVID RABINOWITCH Phantom Group	**23.3.–12.5.2007**
NICOLA VON SENGER	Bleicherweg 45 8002 Zürich Tel. 044 201 88 10 www.nicolavonsenger.com info@nicolavonsenger.com	MADELEINE BERKHEMER	**13.1.–17.3.2007**
		Arco'07, Madrid, Projects, Black Box	**15.–19.2.2007**
		GELITIN	**30.3.–7.6.2007**
JAMILEH WEBER	Waldmannstrasse 6 8001 Zürich Tel. 044 252 10 66 www.jamilehweber.com info@jamilehweber.com	JOEL SHAPIRO Sculptures	**bis 27.1.2007**
		ROBERT RAUSCHENBERG	**Februar–April 2007**
		SEAN SCULLY	**Mai–Juni 2007**
BRIGITTE WEISS	Müllerstrasse 67 8004 Zürich Tel. 044 241 83 35 www.likeyou.com/brigitteweiss brigitteweiss@bluewin.ch	EL FRAUENFELDER	**12.1.–10.3.2007**

BASEL

NICOLAS KRUPP	Erlenstrasse 15 4058 Basel Tel. 061 683 32 65 www.nicolaskrupp.com nic@nicolaskrupp.com	JÜRG STÄUBLE	**12.1.–24.2.2007**
		THOMAS BAUMANN	**2.3.–28.4.2007**
		Düsseldorf Contemporary	**19.4.–22.4.2007**

BERN

GALERIE GRANERO	Nydegggasse 15 3011 Bern Tel. 031 311 71 41 www.granero.ch info@granero.ch	ASIEN, AFRIKA Skulpturen, Masken & Schmuck	**16.12.2006–31.3.2007**
		MEIST SCHWARZ WEISS. HUNDERT JAHRE PHOTOGRAPHIE Verkaufsausstellung einer Basler Sammlung	**7.4.–31.5.2007**

ST. GALLEN

WILMA LOCK	Schmiedgasse 15 9000 St. Gallen Tel. 071 222 62 52 wilmalock@freesurf.ch	XAVIER NOIRET-THOMÉ «tout arrive…» Nouvelles Paintures/New Paintings	**6.11.2006–27.1.2007**

DONALD YOUNG GALLERY

933 W Washington Blvd
Chicago Illinois 60607
Telephone 312.455.0100
www.donaldyoung.com

REBECCA WARREN

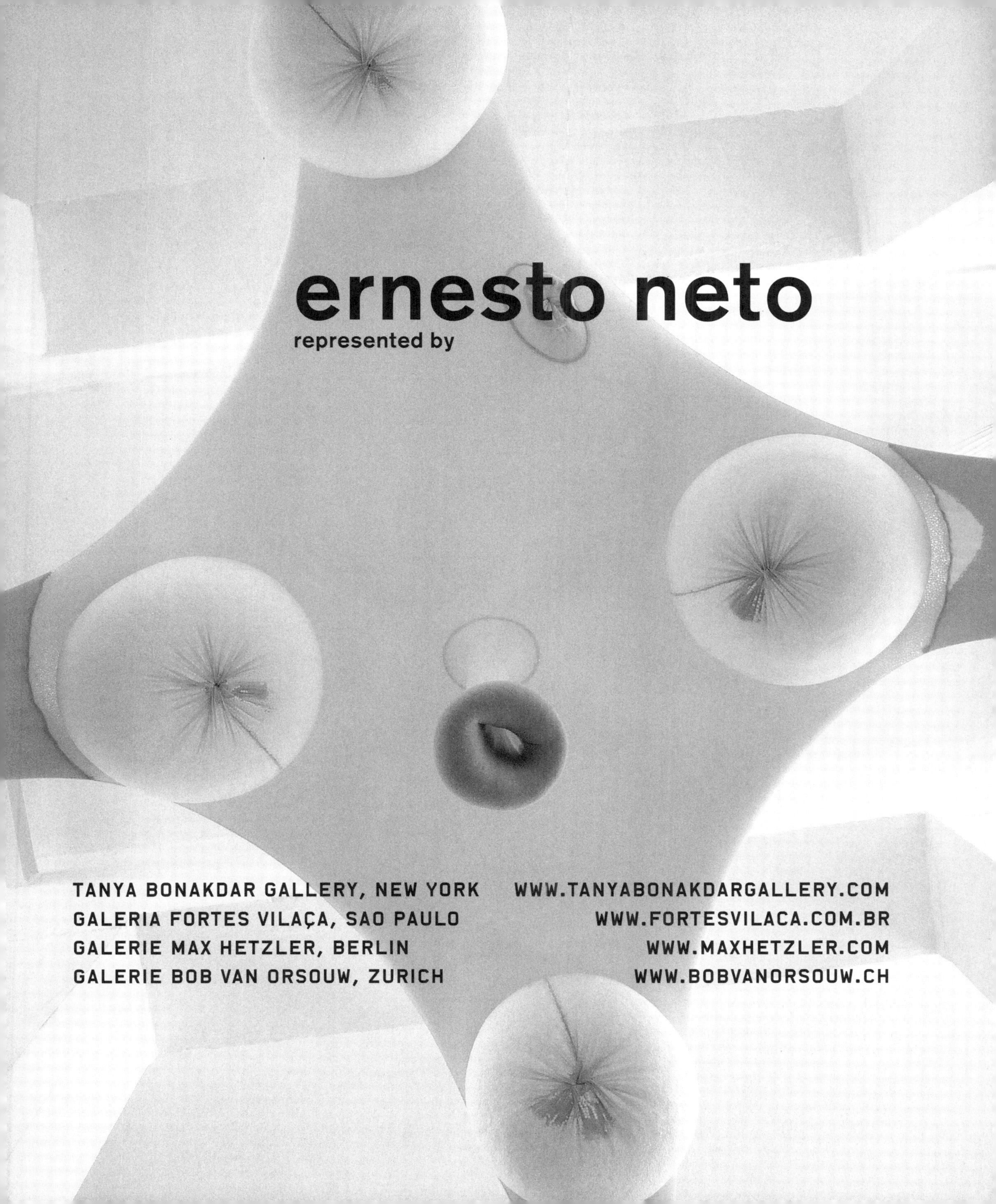
ernesto neto
represented by
TANYA BONAKDAR GALLERY, NEW YORK
WWW.TANYABONAKDARGALLERY.COM
GALERIA FORTES VILAÇA, SAO PAULO
WWW.FORTESVILACA.COM.BR
GALERIE MAX HETZLER, BERLIN
WWW.MAXHETZLER.COM
GALERIE BOB VAN ORSOUW, ZURICH
WWW.BOBVANORSOUW.CH

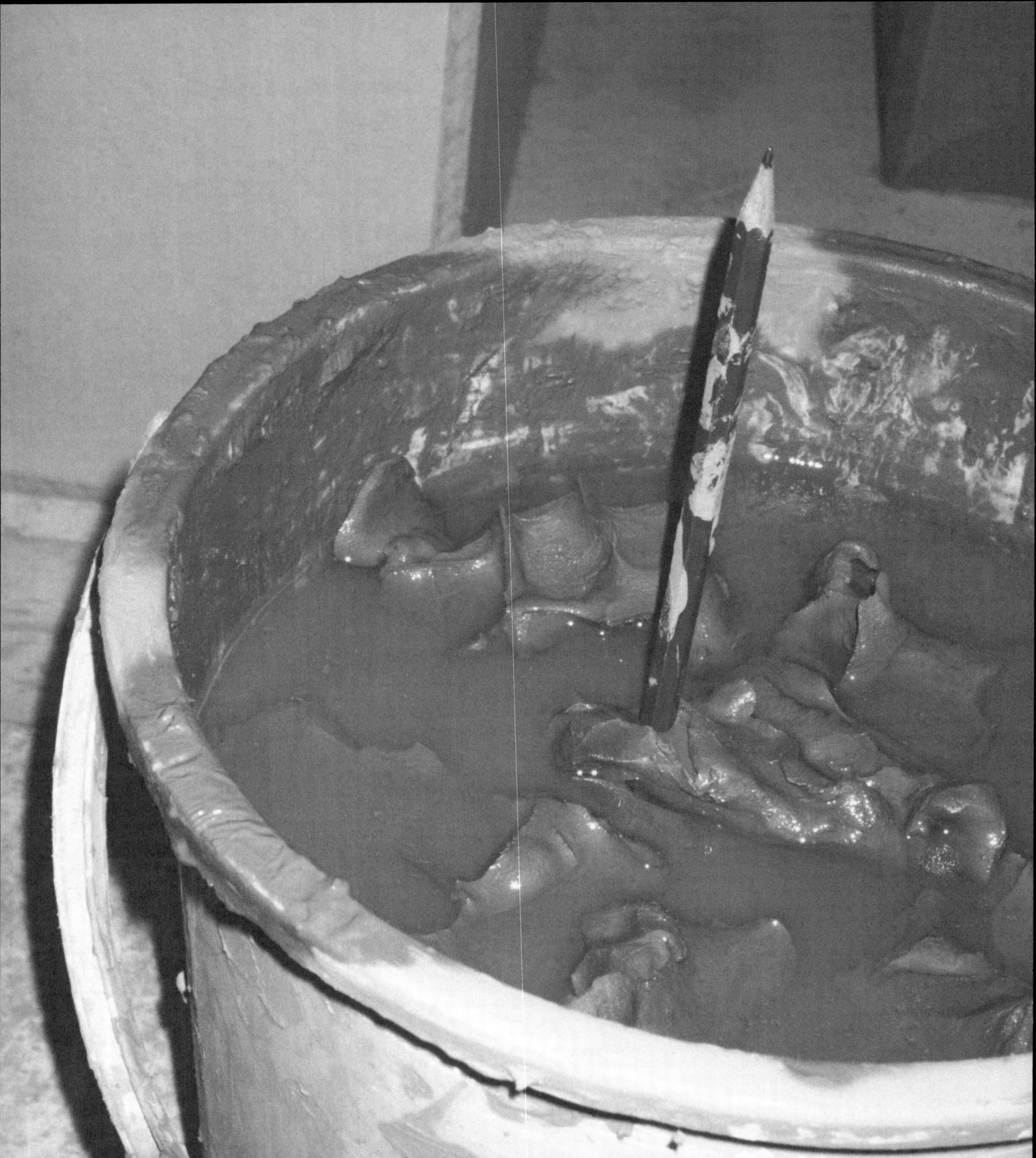

OLAF NICOLAI

courtesy Galerie EIGEN + ART Leipzig/Berlin

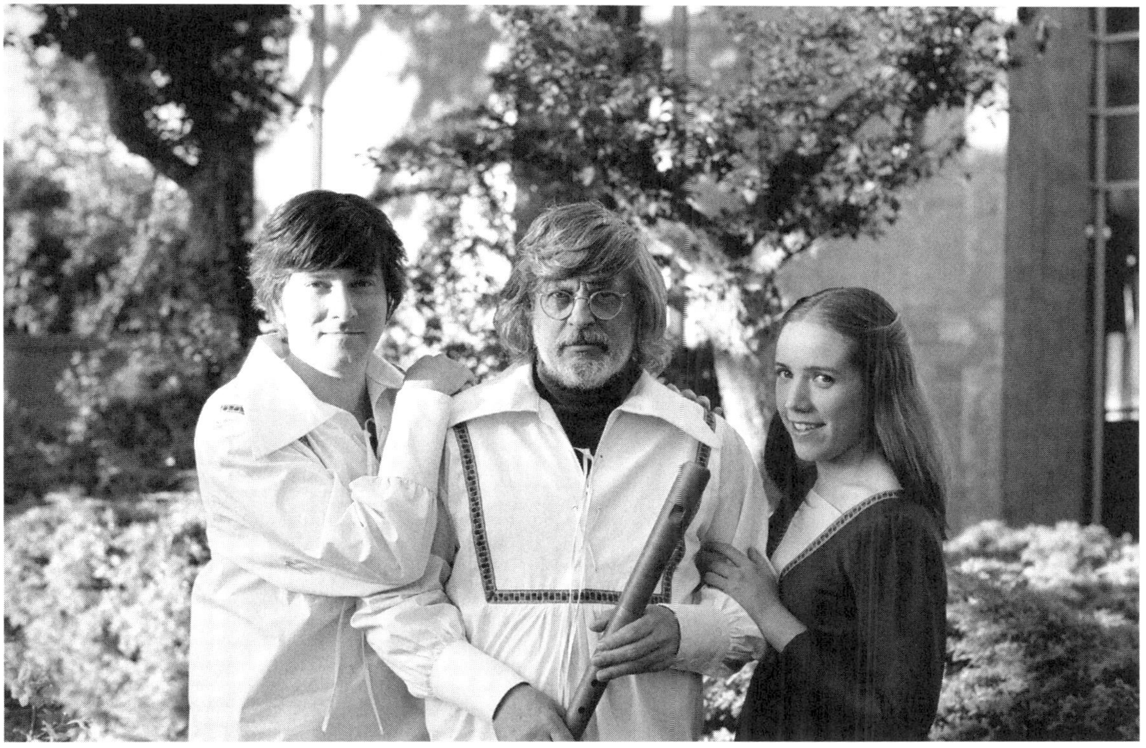

RENAISSANCE FARE
♡
HAUSER + WIRTH

ROBERT WILSON

13 JANUARY – 3 FEBRUARY 2007

534 West 21st Street

WALID RAAD

10 FEBRUARY – 10 MARCH 2007

521 West 21st Street

ROBERT GROSVENOR

17 FEBRUARY – 17 MARCH 2007

534 West 21st Street

JULIAN LETHBRIDGE

24 MARCH – 21 APRIL 2007

534 West 21st Street

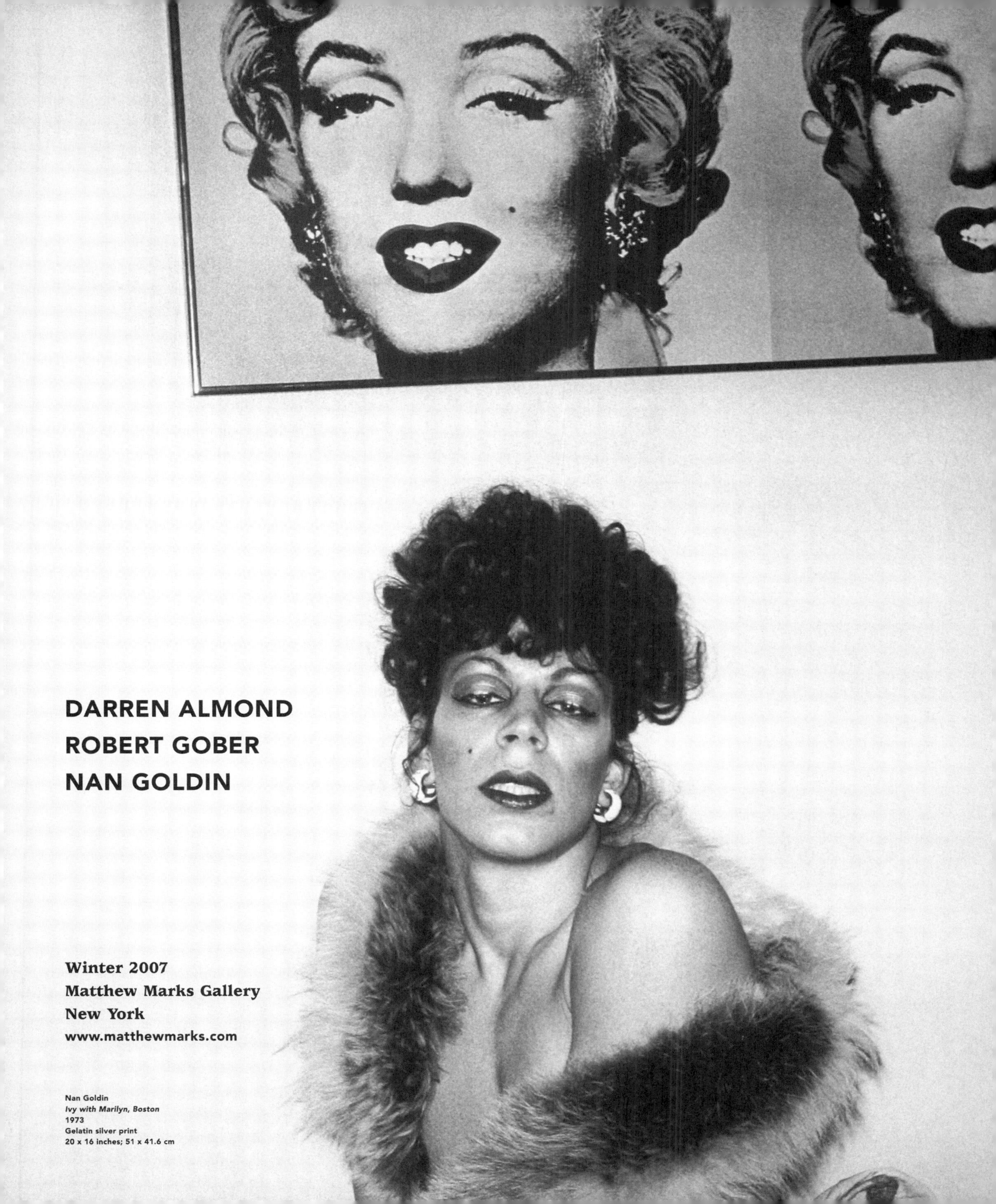

Nan Goldin
Ivy with Marilyn, Boston
1973
Gelatin silver print
20 x 16 inches; 51 x 41.6 cm

GALERIE NÄCHST ST. STEPHAN
ROSEMARIE SCHWARZWÄLDER

November 24, 2006 – January 13, 2007

RISS/LÜCKE/ SCHARNIER A

IDEA | HEINRICH DUNST

WITH WORKS BY

JOHN BALDESSARI
KONRAD BAYER
MARCEL BROODTHAERS
RAFAL BUJNOWSKI
ERNST CARAMELLE
CLEGG & GUTTMANN
HEINRICH DUNST
RAINER GANAHL
NIKOLAUS GANSTERER
LOUISE LAWLER
ACHIM LENGERER
JÁN MANČUŠKA
CHRISTIAN MARCLAY
MICHAEL S. RIEDEL
FERDINAND SCHMATZ
PETER TSCHERKASSKY
JOËLLE TUERLINCKX
RÉMY ZAUGG

February 22 – April 21, 2007

LEE UFAN

Grünangergasse 1/2, A-1010 Wien, Tel +43 1 512 12 66, Fax +43 1 513 43 07
galerie@schwarzwaelder.at, www.schwarzwaelder.at

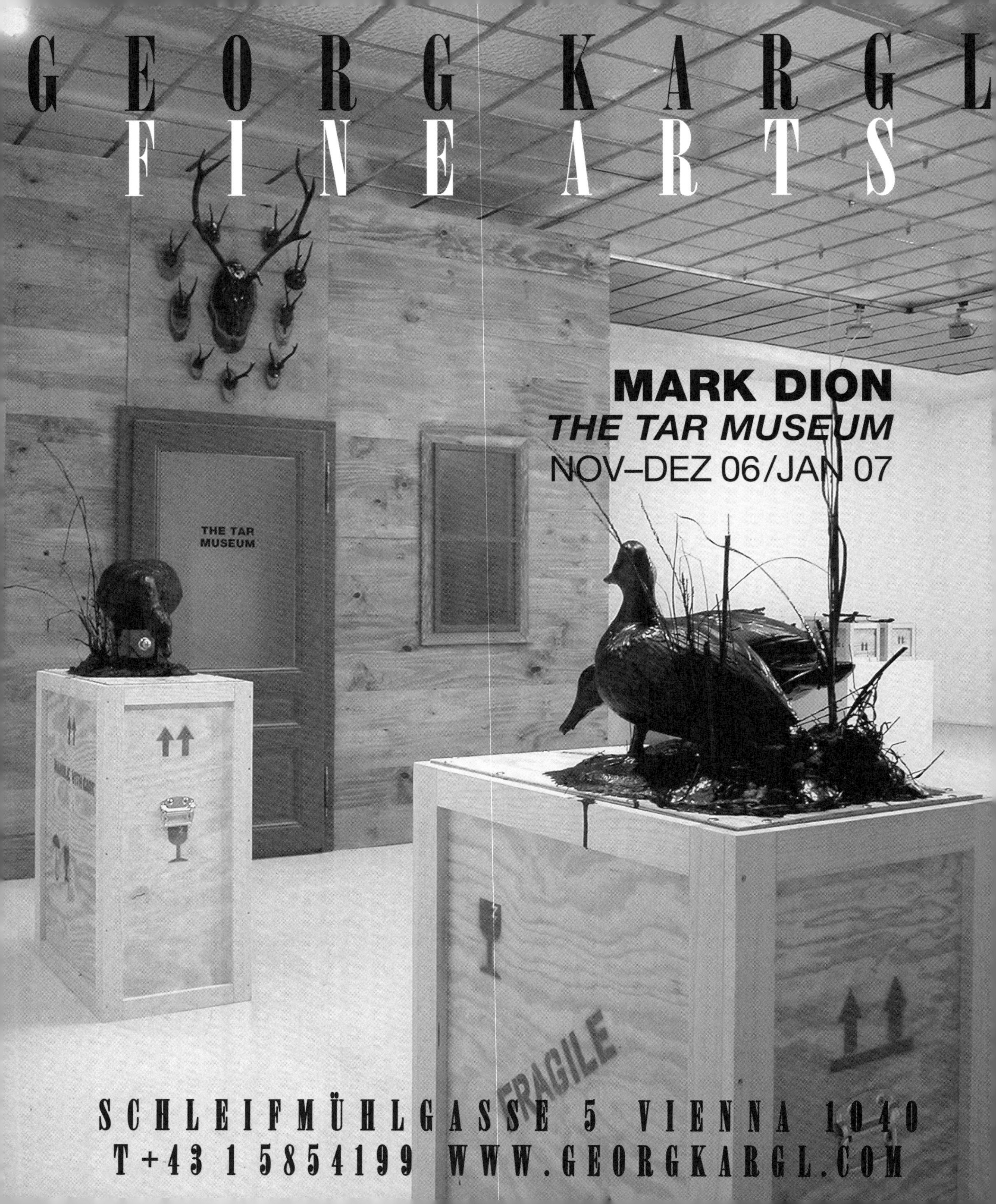
GEORG KARGL
FINE ARTS
THE TAR MUSEUM
MARK DION
THE TAR MUSEUM
NOV–DEZ 06/JAN 07
FRAGILE
SCHLEIFMÜHLGASSE 5 VIENNA 1040
T+43 1 5854199 WWW.GEORGKARGL.COM

ELINA BROTHERUS

New Works

November 2006–January 2007

GALERIE WILMA TOLKSDORF BERLIN

ZIMMERSTRASSE 88-89, 10117 BERLIN
TELEFON +49 30 2005 8812
www.wilmatolksdorf.de
office@wilmatolksdorf.de

FRANK AHLGRIMM

Le Parkour

December 2006–February 2007

GALERIE WILMA TOLKSDORF

HANAUER LANDSTRASSE 136
60314 FRANKFURT AM MAIN
TELEFON +49 69 4305 9427
www.wilmatolksdorf.de
fra@wilmatolksdorf.de

Urs Lüthi

Registered Trademark

Opening 3 February 11–13 p.m.

3 February until 14 April 2007

Arnulf Rainer

ARNULF RAINER

Opening

21 April 11–13 p.m.

21 April until 2 June 2007

GALERIE LELONG ZÜRICH

Predigerplatz 10–12 * CH-8001 Zürich

Öffnungszeiten * Opening Hours:

Di (Tue) – Fr 11–18 h * Sa 10–16 h

T +41(0)44 251 11 20 * F +41(0)44 262 52 85

www.galerie-lelong.com * galerie.lelong@dplanet.ch

JOSÉ MANUEL BALLESTER
SERGIO BELINCHÓN
DANIELE BUETTI
MERLIN CARPENTER
NAIA DEL CASTILLO
FILIPA CÉSAR
JOSÉ DAMASCENO
RICHARD DEACON
PIA FRIES
IÑAKI GRACENEA
ALEX HARTLEY
GUILLERMO KUITCA
ABIGAIL LAZKOZ
MAIDER LÓPEZ
JORGE MACCHI
MIQUEL MONT
FELICIDAD MORENO
MATTHIAS MÜLLER
JOAQUÍN PACHECO
FERNANDO RENES
JAMES RIELLY
LAURIE SIMMONS
RUI TOSCANO
ALBRETCH TÜBKE
TUNGA
DARÍO URZAY
PETER ZIMMERMANN

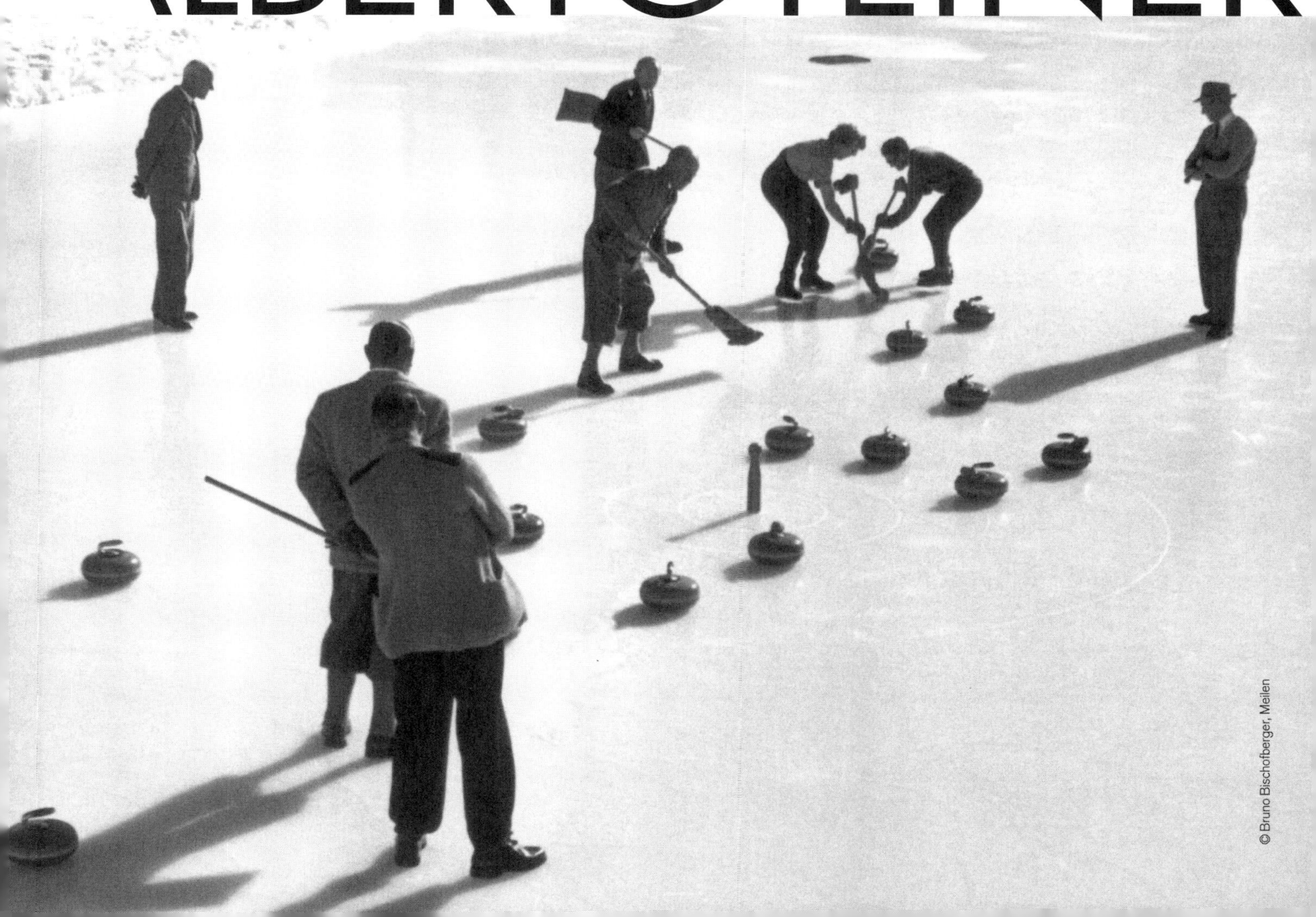

the best surprise is no surprise...

coming soon

e-flux: The Best Surprise Is No Surprise
Published by: JRP|Ringier
Full Color, 311 pgs,
ISBN 10: 3-905770-05-9
ISBN 13: 978-3-905770-05-6

QUALITY STREET®

fine art fair frankfurt
13.-15.04.2007

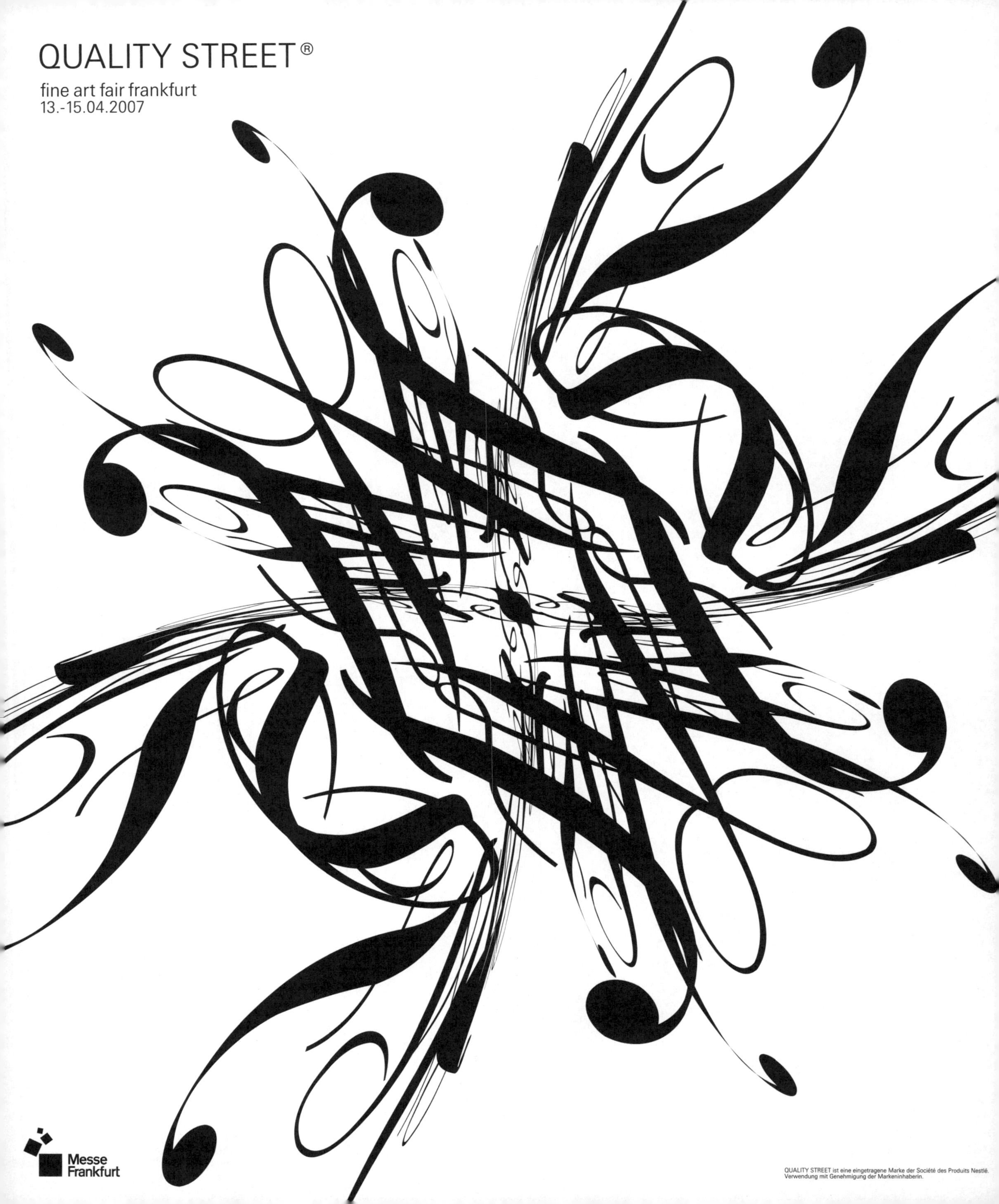

Messe
Frankfurt

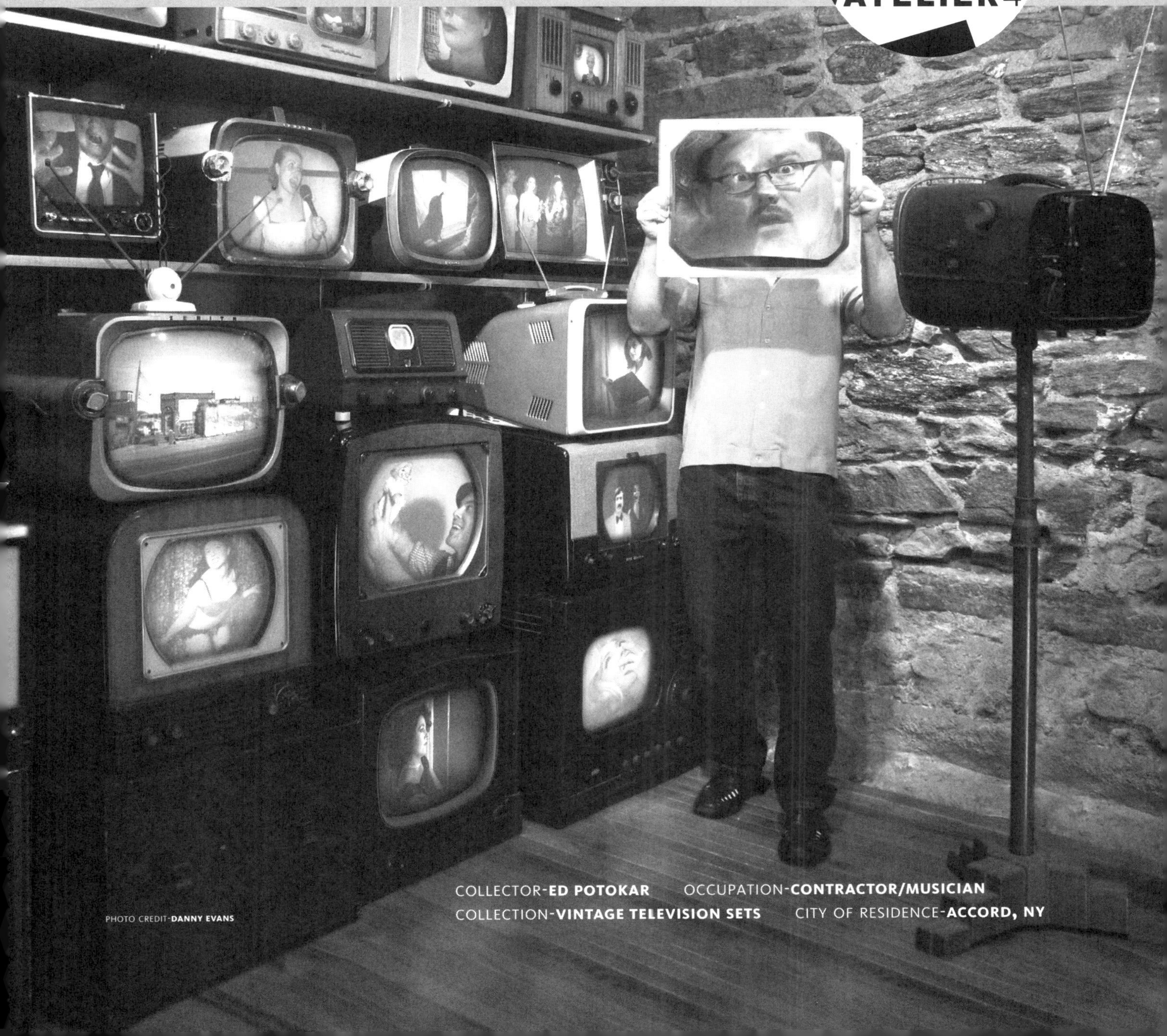

PHOTO CREDIT-**DANNY EVANS**
COLLECTOR-**ED POTOKAR** OCCUPATION-**CONTRACTOR/MUSICIAN**
COLLECTION-**VINTAGE TELEVISION SETS** CITY OF RESIDENCE-**ACCORD, NY**

EYEKON
intermedia lab

CHAMPIGNONS LEAGUE

Quellenstrasse 27
CH-8005 Zürich
+41 (0)43 444 77 77
F: 1995, www.eyekon.ch
T: Thomas Egloff, Marco Lardelli

C	IIIIIIIIIIIIIIIIIIIIIIIIIIIIIIIIII
IT	IIIIIIIIIIIIIIIIIIIIIIIIIIIIII
S	IIIIIIIIIIIIII
M	IIIIIIIIIIIIIIIIII

115

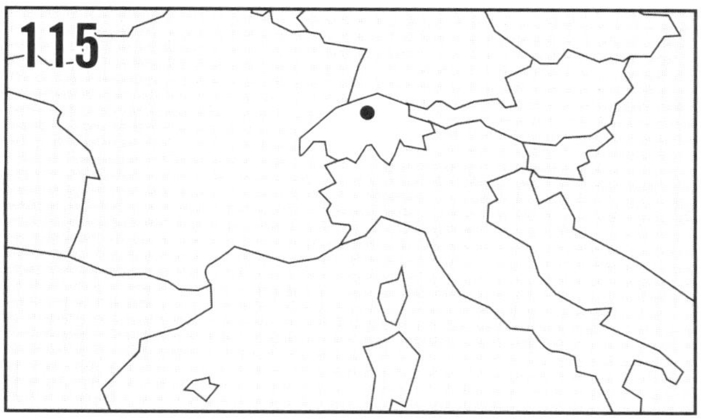

www.eyekon.ch/players

116
RONNY
BINDER
12.11.1982 Zürich (SUI)
1,85 m / E7 kg

117
THOMAS
EGLOFF
20.10.1963 Zürich (SUI)
1,86 m / 75 kg

118
FRANZISKA
ERIKSEN
10.08.1971 Seoul (KOR)
1,60 m / 52 kg

119
JONAS
FAHRNI
28.05.1974 Leutkirch (GER)
1,78 m / 78 kg

120
KARIN
GLEICHNER
03.02.1975 Zürich (SUI)
1,72 m / 54 kg

121
MARCO
LARDELLI
29.07.1969 Zürich (SUI)
1,86 m / 95 kg

122
SARAH
LOCHER
15.04.1982 Walenstadt (SUI)
1,68 m / 52 kg

123
KAORI MYIANISHI
REITINGER
20.04.1964 Awaji Island (JAP)
1,62 m / On Diet

124
IWAN
NEGRO
10.12.1979 Bern (SUI)
1,87 m / 70 kg

125
SARA
SCHORER
20.08.1978 Bern (SUI)
1,72 m / 59 kg

126
HANS-PETER
WOLLENMANN
02.10.1942 Wald (SUI)
1,74 m / 80 kg

127
URSULA
WILHELM
25.06.1963 Thusis (SUI)
1,65 m / 58 kg

SWISS INSTITUTE / CONTEMPORARY ART
495 BROADWAY / 3RD FLOOR
NEW YORK / NY 10012
TEL 212.925.2035
WWW.SWISSINSTITUTE.NET

SI

VIDYA GASTALDON
SOLO EXHIBITION: STOP BELIEVING, START KNOWING
JAN 17 – MAR 10 2007

GEORG GATSAS
THE PROCESS VII / EXHIBITION AND CONCERT SERIES
MAR 21 – MAY 6 2007

COMING SOON: DANIELE BUETTI, FISCHLI / WEISS, SHIRANA SHAHBAZI, TOM BURR, WALTER PFEIFFER

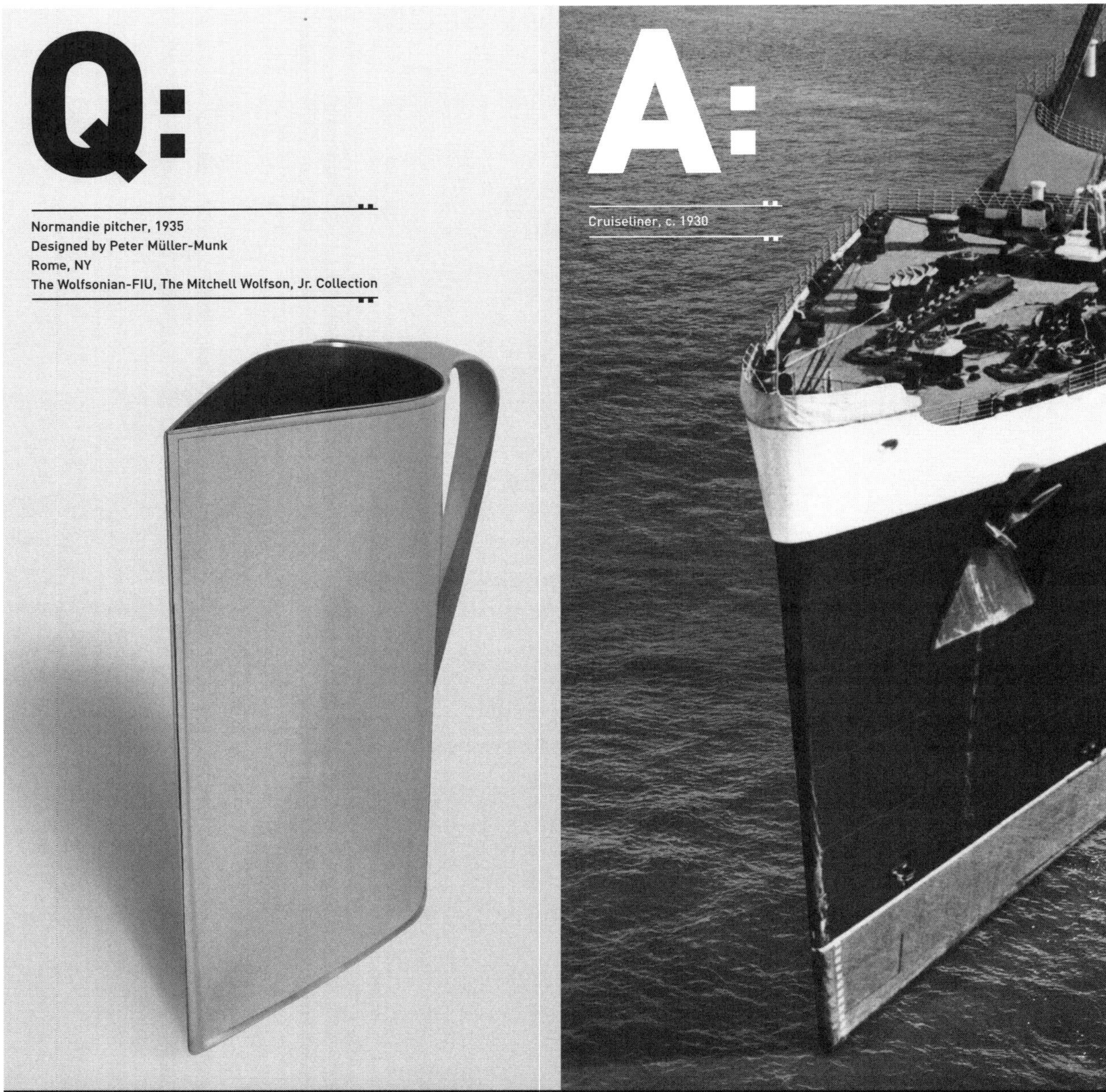
Q:
Normandie pitcher, 1935
Designed by Peter Müller-Munk
Rome, NY
The Wolfsonian-FIU, The Mitchell Wolfson, Jr. Collection
A:
Cruiseliner, c. 1930

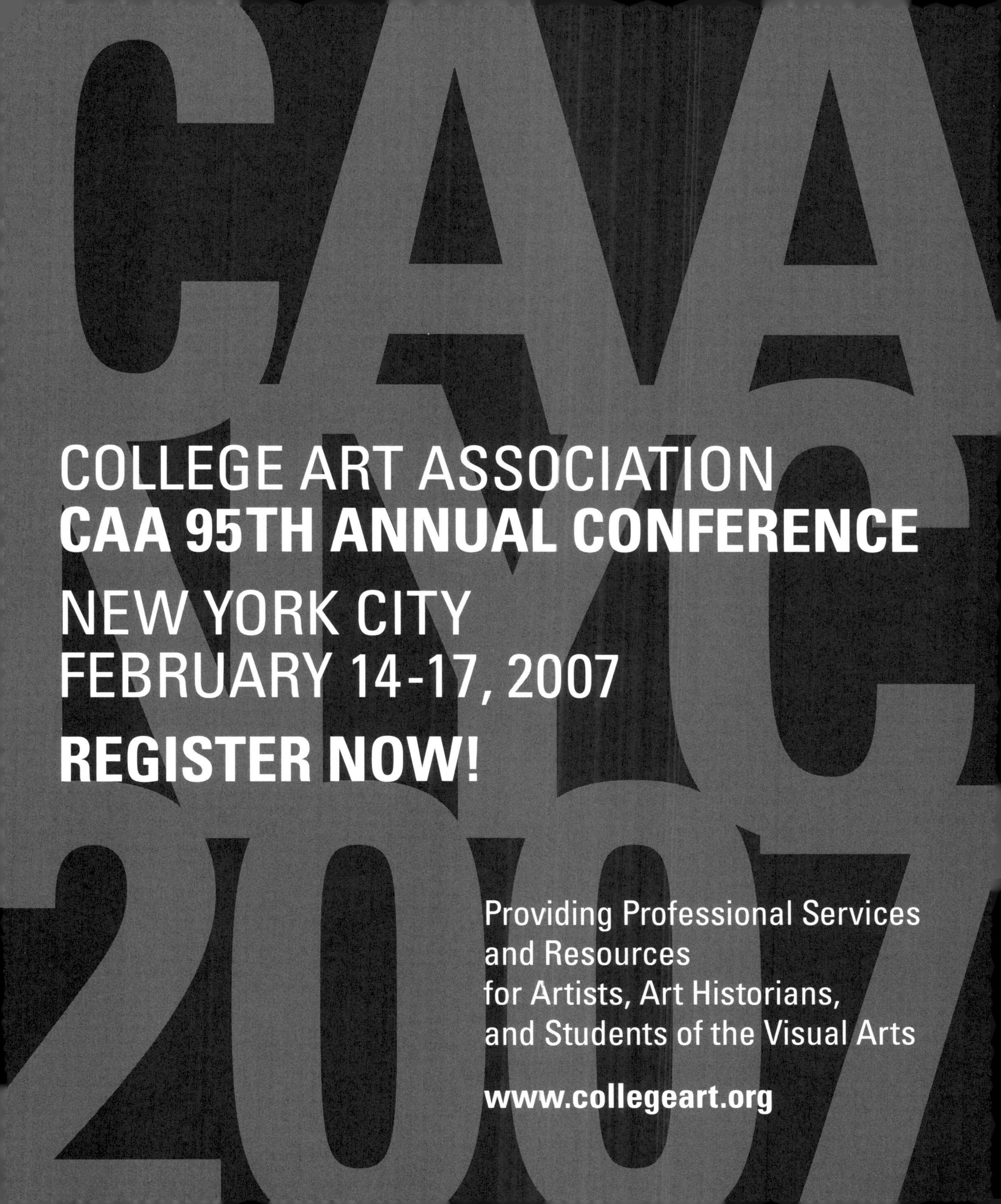
COLLEGE ART ASSOCIATION
CAA 95TH ANNUAL CONFERENCE
NEW YORK CITY
FEBRUARY 14-17, 2007
REGISTER NOW!
Providing Professional Services and Resources for Artists, Art Historians, and Students of the Visual Arts
www.collegeart.org

du – Zeitschrift für Kultur. Seit 65 Jahren widmet sich **du** zehnmal im Jahr dem denkbar breitesten Kulturbegriff. Die Hefte aus den Bereichen Kunst, Literatur, Architektur, Fotografie, Musik und Zeitgeschehen bilden in ihrer Gesamtheit eine «Enzyklopädie der Gegenwart», die Nummer um Nummer fortgeschrieben wird. Ein Heft für moderne Zeitgenossen und alle Kulturinteressierten. Erhältlich im Buchhandel und an ausgewählten Kiosken. Einzelheftbestellungen und Abonnemente unter Telefon +41 (0)71 644 91 12, Fax +41 (0)71 644 91 90 oder unter www.dumag.ch

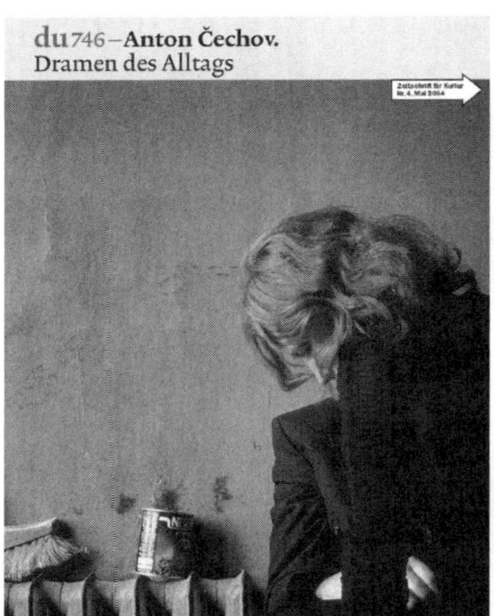

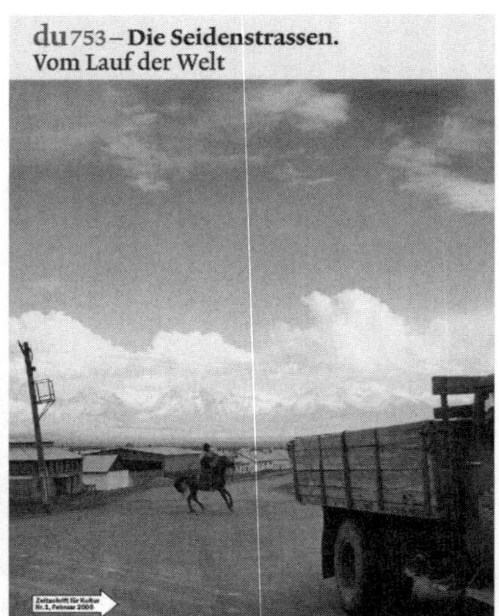

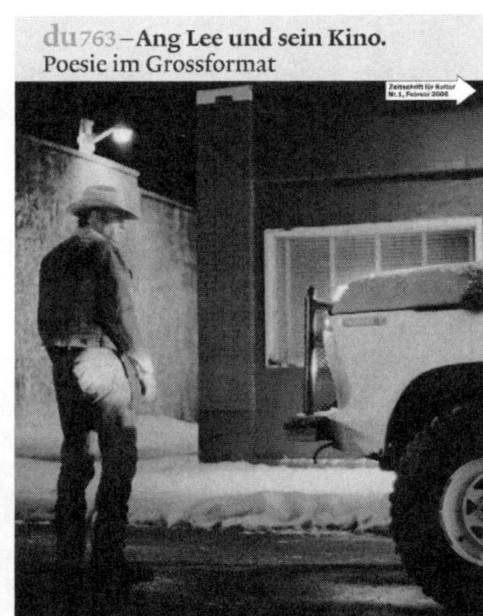

du – Zeitschrift für Kultur, ausgezeichnet mit dem Designpreis 2006 der Bundesrepublik Deutschland in Silber für die herausragende Gestaltung der Hefte.

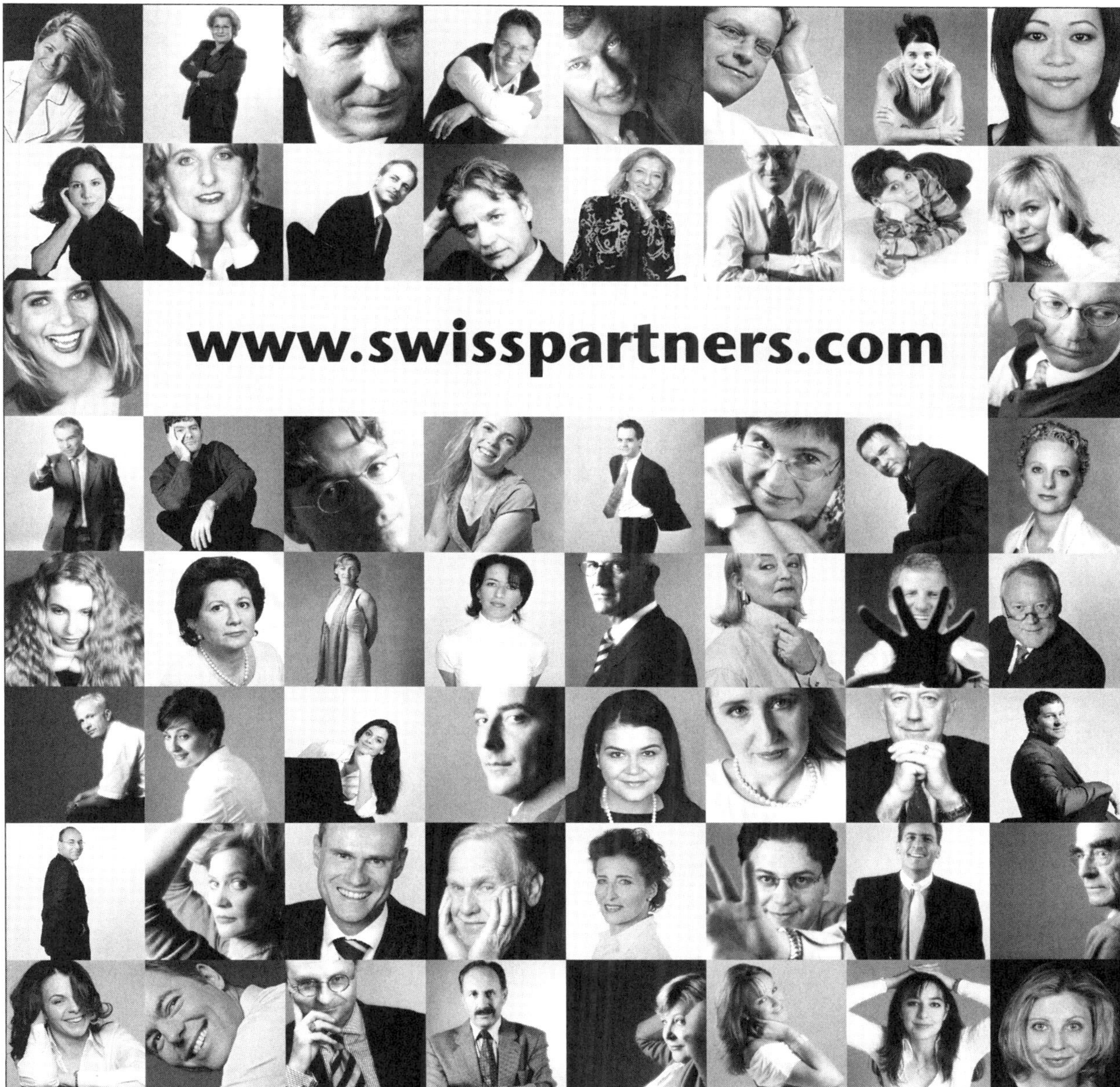
www.swisspartners.com

www.
bfasblondeau
.com

5 rue de la Muse

rhona
bitner
14_09_06-
21_10_06

FACES
18_05_06-
22_07_06

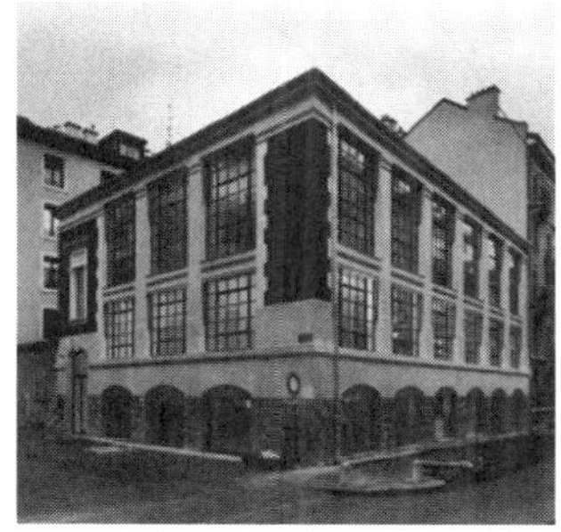

martin
bigum
16_03_06-
29_04_06

alex
brown
16_09_05-
22_10_05

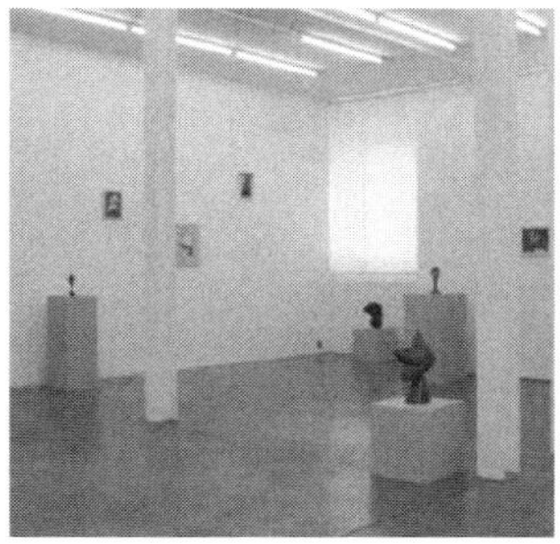

alessandro
twombly
20_01_05-
05_03_05

luc
andrié
06_11_04-
18_12_04

dan
McCarthy
16_09_04-
23_10_04

raymond
pettibon
18_03_04-
01_05_04

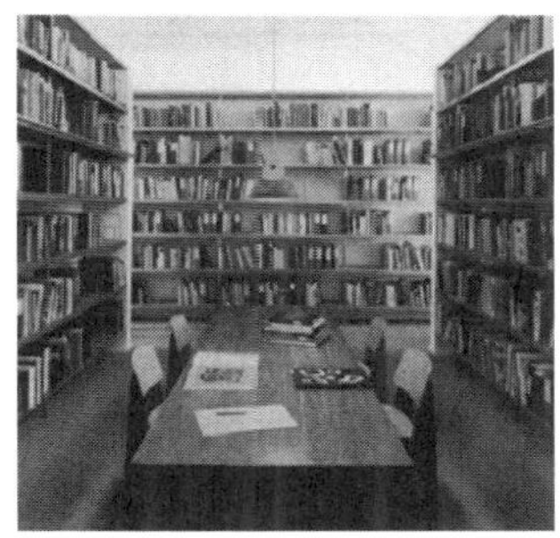

jean-luc
verna
18_03_04-
01_05_04

mamie
holst
18_09_03-
25_10_03

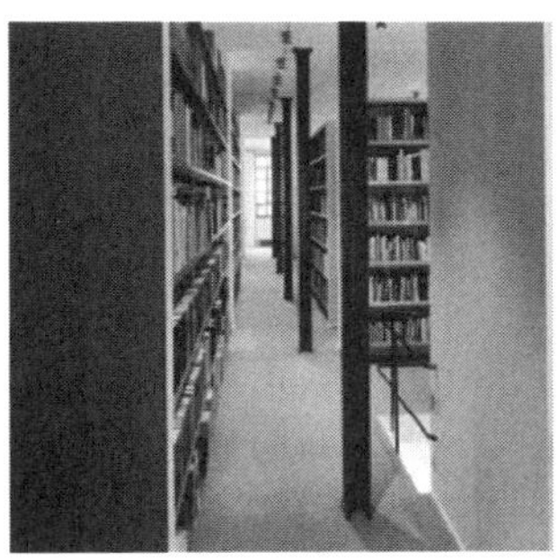

kiki
lamers
20_11_03-
20_12_03

louise
lawler
20_03_03-
03_05_03

BFAS
Blondeau Fine Art Services

5 rue de la Muse
1205 Geneva _ Switzerland
T +41 (0)22 544 95 95
F +41 (0)22 544 95 99
philippe@bfasblondeau.com

www.bfasblondeau.com

■ exhibition
THU-FRI 14h-18h30
SAT 11h-17h
■ office
MON-FRI 9h-12h30 / 14h-18h30

HAUNCH ØF VENISON

LONDON

6 Haunch of Venison Yard
off Brook Street
London W1K 5ES
United Kingdom

T +44 (0) 20 7495 5050
F +44 (0) 20 7495 4050
london@haunchofvenison.com
www.haunchofvenison.com

Simon Patterson
20 January—
24 February 2007

Ian Monroe
2 March—
31 March 2007

ZÜRICH

Lessingstrasse 5
8002 Zürich
Switzerland

T +41 (0) 43 422 8888
F +41 (0) 43 422 8889
zurich@haunchofvenison.com
www.haunchofvenison.com

Ergin Çavuşoğlu
Quintet Without Borders
2 February—
10 March 2007

Tony Cragg
16 March—
21 April 2007

galerie gmurzynska zurich

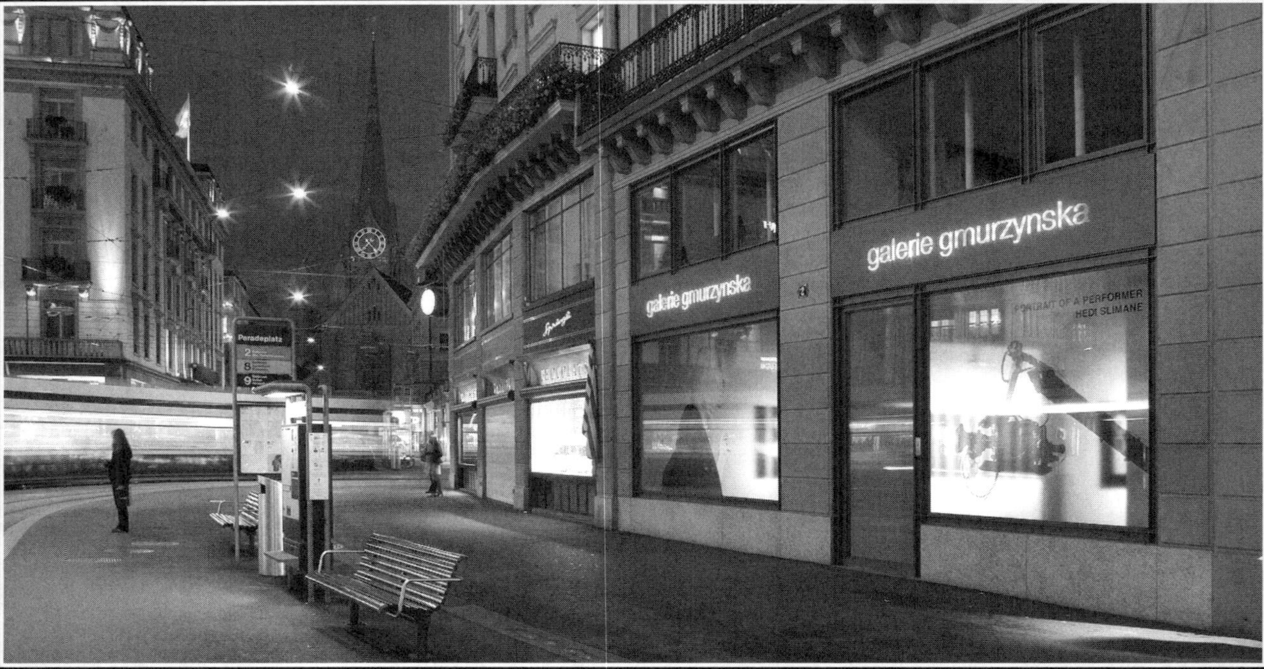

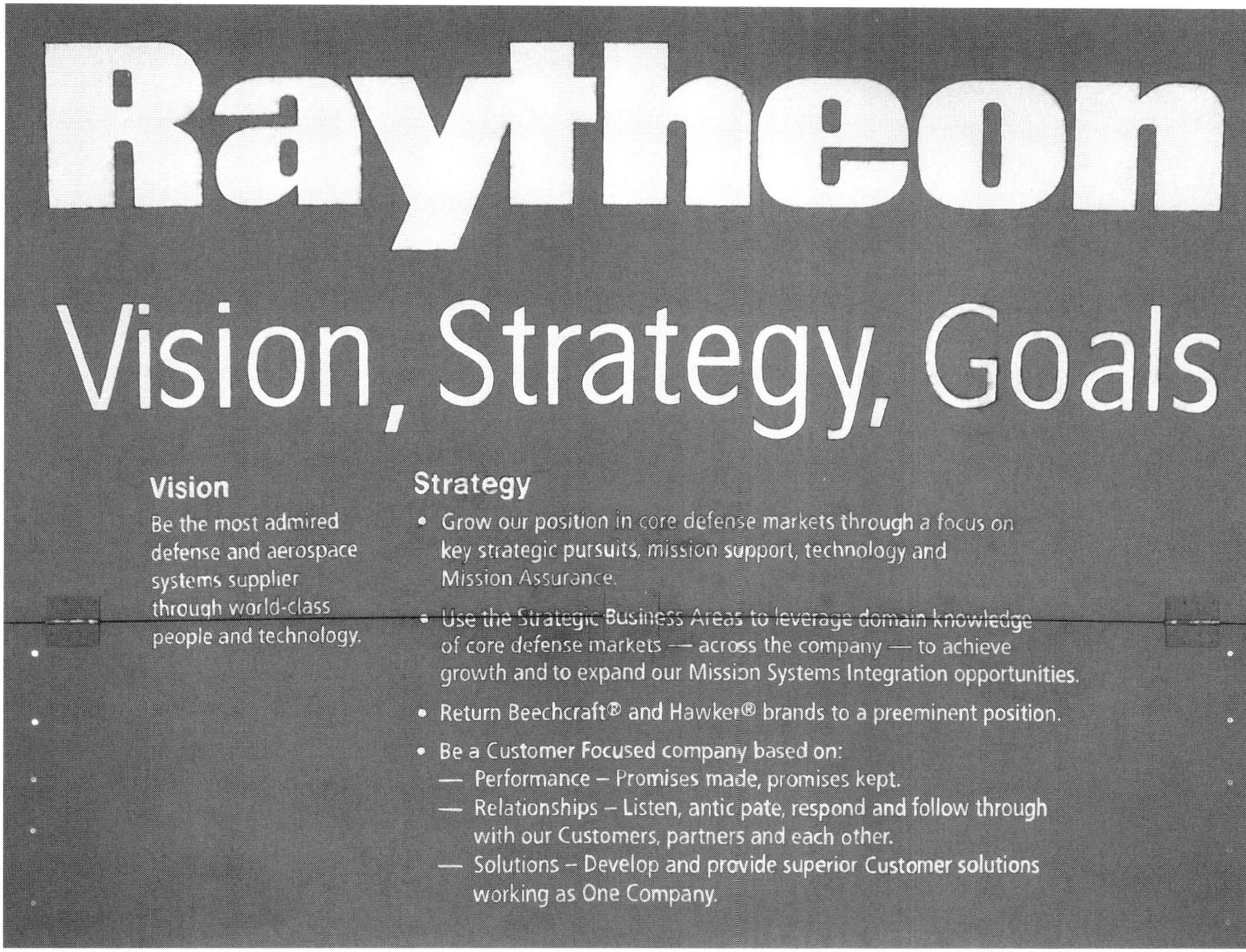
Raytheon
Vision, Strategy, Goals
Vision
Be the most admired defense and aerospace systems supplier through world-class people and technology.
Strategy
• Grow our position in core defense markets through a focus on key strategic pursuits, mission support, technology and Mission Assurance.
• Use the Strategic Business Areas to leverage domain knowledge of core defense markets — across the company — to achieve growth and to expand our Mission Systems Integration opportunities.
• Return Beechcraft® and Hawker® brands to a preeminent position.
• Be a Customer Focused company based on:
— Performance – Promises made, promises kept.
— Relationships – Listen, antic pate, respond and follow through with our Customers, partners and each other.
— Solutions – Develop and provide superior Customer solutions working as One Company.